The Rise of Inequality and the Fall of Social Mobility

Francesco Farina

The Rise of Inequality and the Fall of Social Mobility

Economic Policies for a Fairer Society

palgrave
macmillan

Francesco Farina
Faculty of Economics
Sapienza University of Rome
Rome, Italy

ISBN 978-3-031-92842-0 ISBN 978-3-031-92843-7 (eBook)
https://doi.org/10.1007/978-3-031-92843-7

This book is a translation of the original Italian edition „Il merito tradito: Perché la", published by Donzelli Editore in 2024. The translation was done with the help of artificial intelligence.
The original submitted manuscript has been translated into English. The translation was done using artificial intelligence. A subsequent revision was performed by the author(s) to further refine the work and to ensure that the translation is appropriate concerning content and scientific correctness. It may, however, read stylistically different from a conventional translation.
Translation from the Italian language edition: "Il merito tradito: Perché la mobilità sociale è scomparsa" by Francesco Farina, © Donzelli Editore 2024. Published by Donzelli Editore.

This Palgrave Macmillan imprint is published by the registered company Springer Nature Switzerland AG.
The registered company address is: Gewerbestrasse 11, 6330 Cham, Switzerland

La presenza delle opportunità di salire da umili origini al successo e alla prosperità è una condizione sia di felicità individuale sia di benessere sociale; quando il successo e la prosperità sono negati ad alcuni, mentre giungono copiosi ad altri, il danno è sia degli uni che degli altri.
[The presence of opportunities to rise from humble origins to success and prosperity is a condition of both individual happiness and social well-being; when success and prosperity are denied to some, while they come in abundance to others, the harm is to both.]
—*Richard H. Tawney,* Equality, *1931*

To Carlo and Francesco

Acknowledgment

I am grateful to Elisabetta Croci Angelini for having read the translation from Italian and revised the English.

Contents

1	**Introduction**	1
	Prologue	1
	The Talents of Everyone	6
	Methodological Individualism and "classical liberalism"	8
	"Systemic interdependence" and Social Conflict	10
	Status libertatis *and* status civitatis	22
	The Neoliberal Society: Interdependent Individuals but Free from Constraints	25
	Talents and Education	27
	The Sources of Inspiration for the Volume	29
	The "canvas"	32
	Bibliography	36
Part I	**The Theoretical Framework**	39
2	**Social Mobility in Political, Economic and Sociological Thought**	41
	The Social Class, Bridge Between Individual and Society	41
	The Asymmetry of Power in the Economy and Society	46
	At the Origin of Social Mobility: Economy and Culture	47
	The Liberal Thought of Friedrich Hayek and Milton Friedman	50
	Bibliography	57

3 Meritocracy 59
Merit and the "Work Ethic" 59
Earning Is Deserving? 64
Is Merit a "principle of justice"? 70
Merit or Power Relationship? 77
Are the Talents We Possess Deserved? 83
Bibliography 91

4 Social Mobility: From Birth to Decline 97
The Social Persistence in Medieval Communities 97
Social Classes and Collective Imagination 102
The Formation of the "Mass Society" in America and in Europe 106
The "Model of the Mind" and the Concept of Democracy 113
The Interplay Between Absolute and Relative Mobility 119
The Trente Glorieuses*: The Expansion of GDP and the Welfare State* 127
The Impact of Neoliberalism on Inequalities and Social Ascension 130
Bibliography 136

5 Social Dynamics: An Interpretative Scheme 141
Individual Freedom as Independence from Society 141
The Tension Between Freedom and Equality of "life chances" 143
The Crisis of Democracy in Advanced Societies 147
Freedom in Political Science and Economic Theory 150
From Group Membership to Multidimensional Well-Being 154
From the Social Function of Work to the Society of Interaction 158
From the "Open Society" to the "Liquid Society" 163
Populism and pensée unique*: Mirror Ideologies* 173
Bibliography 176

6 A Phenomenon Between Individual and Society 179
Competition in the Market and in Democracy: A False Equivalence 179
Capitalism and Solidaristic Democracy 182
Social Rights and Company Profits 186
The Market Is Not a *Morally-Free Zone* 192
Inherited Wealth and the Emergence of Talent 198
Bibliography 205

Part II The Crisis of Social Dynamics 209

7 Inequality of Opportunity and Intergenerational Mobility 211
Individual Aspirations and Socio-economic Context 211
The Driving Factors of Mobility: Sustained Growth and Low Inequality 217
Access to Opportunities and Well-Being of New Generations 222
The Great Gatsby Curve 225
The "social immobility" of Neet 232
Bibliography 236

8 Welfare Institutions and the Dynamics of Social Structure 239
The Multidimensionality of Inequality and Poverty 239
The Role of Welfare in Economic Resilience 244
Reduction of Poverty and Increase in Income Inequality 250
Bibliography 258

9 Global Social Mobility 261
The Expanding Global Middle Class 261
Trans-Continental Mobility: Migratory Flows 268
"Social capital" and Immigration 271
Bibliography 276

Part III Why It Happened 279

10 Technical Progress: Occupational and Wage Mobility 281
Power Asymmetry and New Technologies 281
Professional Skills and Job Mobility 290
Concentration of Companies and Wage Polarisation 296
Technological Change and the Dynamics of Social Classes 299
Bibliography 302

11 Mobility in Education: Economic Incentive or Family Resources? 307
"The School, Central Organ of Democracy" 307
The Market Incentive for Social Mobility: "The more you learn, the more you earn" 310

Intergenerational Mobility in Education and Income 319
Education and Social Mobility in Anglo-Saxon Countries 324
A World Apart: The Nordic Countries 342
Social Classes and Equality in Education: The Limits of "Universalism" 346
Unequal Opportunities for Education and the Emergence of Talents 354
Bibliography 361

12 The Education Market and the Talents of Young People 367
The "adaptation" of Education to the Market 367
Educational Opportunities and Economic Growth 371
Education and Human Capital 373
The "social cost" of Tracking 376
"Freedom of choice": The Formal Neutrality of the Voucher 379
For an *Affirmative Action* in Education 385
Bibliography 388

13 Conclusions 391
Bibliography 416

Bibliography 419

Index 457

About the Author

Francesco Farina has taught economics at various Italian universities (Perugia, L'Orientale di Napoli, Siena, Luiss) and foreign ones (University of Toronto). From 2014 to 2018 he was president of the Italian Association for the Study of Comparative Economic Systems (Aissec). He is currently a researcher at Cimeo, Sapienza-University of Rome. He is the author of numerous volumes and scientific contributions in international journals on topics of monetary macroeconomics, economic growth, inequality and Welfare institutions. In 2021 he published *The Social State. History, politics, economy* (Luiss University Press)

List of Figures

Fig. 6.1	University enrolment rate and parents' income percentile (United States, 2014). (Source: Piketty (2020). Translation: University enrolment rate (%), Parents' income percentile, Enrolment rate)	202
Fig. 7.1	Percentage of population in each geographical area belonging, in the income distribution, to the decile of top incomes. (Source: Milanović 2023. Translation: Africa, Asia, Latin America, Europe, Wenao, World)	212
Fig. 7.2	Number of generations needed for those born in low-income families to reach the average income of their own country. (Source: Oecd 2018. Translation: Denmark, Norway, Finland, Sweden, Spain, New Zealand, Canada, Greece, Belgium, Australia, Giappone, Netherland, Oecd, Portugal, Ireland, South Korea, United States, United Kingdom, Italy, Switzerland, Austria, France, Germany, Chile, Argentina, Hungary, India, China, Brazil, South Africa, Colombia)	213
Fig. 7.3	Percentage of children, respectively with a father with low income and with a father with high income, who as adults are placed in the richest 25% of the population. (Source: Oecd (2018). Translation: United States, Germany, Luxembourg, France, Austria, Oecd, Ireland, Netherland, United Kingdom, Italy, Spain, Hungary, Greece, Portugal, Denmark, Chile, Low-income father (black), High-income father (white))	215
Fig. 7.4	Conditions for high absolute mobility: sustained growth and low levels of inequality. (Source: Chetty et al. (2017). Translation: Son's probability of earning a higher-than-father's income (%), 1940, 1980, Income distribution 1940 and	

	income growth rate 1980, Income distribution 1940 and income growth rate 1980)	219
Fig. 7.5	United States: productivity growth and slower growth of average wage and median wage. (Source: Van Reenen (2020). Translation: Variation with respect to base year (1984), Falling labour share (dark grey area), Rising income inequality (light gray area), Productivity growth, Mean pay growth, Median pay growth)	223
Fig. 7.6	Inequality of opportunity and income inequality. (Source: Brunori et al. (2013). Translation: Inequality of opportunity, Income inequality, Europe, Central-South America, Africa, United States, India)	230
Fig. 7.7	Income inequality and "Disadvantage Transmission Index". (Source: Hufe and Peichl (2018). Translation: Income inequality, Disadvantage transmission index)	230
Fig. 7.8	Percentage of young people (25–34 years old) living with their parents. (Source: Eurostat, Office for National Statistics (United Kingdom))	234
Fig. 9.1	Global income distribution (1988, 2011, 2018). (Source: Milanović (2024). Translation: Frequency, Log of income in real terms (PPP))	262
Fig. 9.2	Position of Italy and China (urban population) by income deciles in the global income distribution. (Source: Milanović (2023). Translation: Percentile of the global income distribution, Italy, Decile of the income distribution, China, Decile of the income distribution)	267
Fig. 10.1	Wage share of income and wage inequality (% changes, 2000s). (Source: Oecd, income distribution database, Ocs Stan, Klms. Translation: Italy, Norway, Switzerland, United States, Canada, Germany, Denmark, Czech Republic, Luxembourg, UK, Belgium, France, Austria, Finland, Greece, Netherlands, Variation of the Gini Index (market income), Labour share (adjusted for autonomous labour))	289
Fig. 10.2	Change in employment by level of professional qualification (1995–2015). (Source: Oecd Employment Outlook, 2019. Translation: Low-skilled, middle-skilled, high-skilled, Austria, Switzerland, Ireland, Spain, Greece, Denmark, France, Sweden, Portugal, UK, Norway, Netherlands, Finland, Oecd, Italy, Germany, Belgium, United States, Slovenia, Canada, Slovakia, Japan, Hungary, Czech Republic)	291
Fig. 10.3	Percentage change in the share of employed by job (United States, 1982–2017). (Source: Elaboration in Jaimovich and	

Siu 2020, on Labor Force Statistics (Current Population Survey), United States. Translation: Non-routine cognitive, routine, non-routine manual) 294
Fig. 10.4 Share of income on total: poor, middle class, rich (2010). (Source: Pew Research Center, Washington DC. Translation: US, Spain, UK, Italy, Ireland, Germany, France, Luxembourg, Finland, Netherlands, Norway, Denmark, low-income, middle-income, high-income) 300
Fig. 10.5 Financialisation of the economic system. (Source: Bezemer et al. 2018. Translation: Share of bank credit to production, Total amount of bank credit / GDP ratio) 301
Fig. 11.1 Private return on education and social mobility. Translation: a) Intergenerational earnings mobility, private return on education, b) Multidimensional earnings mobility, private return on education. (Note: The values of the private return on education are calculated as the increase in earnings (difference between a job after obtaining a university degree compared to a job after high school graduation), net of taxes and individual private costs for university fees and for giving up paid activities. The values of multidimensional intergenerational mobility are derived from Table 1.1. Source: Author's own elaboration on Oecd data and Economic World Forum) 315
Fig. 11.2 Intergenerational income mobility in the United States by year of birth of children (1940–1985). (Source: Chetty et al. 2017a. Translation: Sons with income higher than their parents (%), Year of birth of sons) 317
Fig. 11.3 Expenditure of social groups (last and first quintile of income distribution) for children's education (in US dollars, 1972–2006). (Source: elaboration in Duncan - Mundane 2011, on data from the Bureau of Labor Statistics, United States. Translation: Rich quintile, Poor quintile) 318
Fig. 11.4 Quality of college and attendance of young people in the United States by parents' income level. (Source: Chetty et al. 2014a. Translation: Average quality of the college, Parents' income level) 318
Fig. 11.5 Intergenerational educational mobility and public spending/ GDP. (Source: Oecd 2018. Translation: Intergenerational mobility in education, Public expenditures in education as a percentage of 1995 GDP) 319
Fig. 11.6 Income mobility of young people without and with a university degree (% per quintile of parents' income: United

States 2021). (Note: Income adjustment based on family size. Source: Pew Research Center, Washington DC, 2021. Translation: Youngs sharing the same quintile of their household when adults, Breakdown by income quintile (left histogram: graduate parents; right histogram: ungraduated parents), Share of ungraduated youngs when adults, Share of graduate youngs when adults) 326

Fig. 12.1 Educational mobility of children, as a percentage of parents' education (Spain, 2019). (Source: elaboration in Salazar 2019 with data from the Survey on living conditions in Spain. Note: Low education: middle school diploma or lower. Medium education: high school diploma. High education: university degree. Translation: Sons' educational level (%), low, medium, high, Parents' educational level (%)) 387

Fig. 13.1 Institutions and the "worldview". (Source: Author's elaboration. Translation: Free Market, Market + Universalistic Welfare, Market + Solidaristic Welfare) 397

List of Boxes

Box 6.1	Should low-income people vote in favour of the welfare state?	190
Box 7.1	Intergenerational mobility and income and opportunity inequality	227
Box 8.1	Why do low-income people today vote against the Welfare State?	254
Box 9.1	Social mobility in an authoritarian regime: China	263
Box 11.1	The geography of social mobility opportunities in the United States	332
Box 11.2	The English middle class and low educational social mobility	335
Box 12.1	Vouchers and educational inequality in the United States	380
Box 12.2	Public schools and private schools in Sweden and Denmark	383

CHAPTER 1

Introduction

Prologue

The rise to success of Georges Duroy, the *Bel-Ami* of Guy de Maupassant's novel, benefitted from the charm he exerted on the protagonists of social life in late nineteenth-century Paris. The rise to success of Steve Jobs, from the computer made in his parents' garage to the reclaiming of the CEO position at Apple, is the result of great inventiveness, a talent for the development of new technologies. Different the context, different the means, equal the determination to climb to the top of the social ladder. Said like this, it would seem that a lively and versatile intelligence is the key—not only necessary, but also sufficient—for a young person to have a bright future. However, things are not like this.

Let's start with Table 1.1, in which appear the indices of the 2020 World Economic Forum Report on social mobility in 82 countries. The data processing took into consideration the main factors contributing to people's well-being: health, education, technology, work, social protection institutions and inclusion. The Report is an excellent fresco. However, what is upstream of social mobility is left out of the picture: people's talents. It is a completely justifiable omission, usually practised by economic theory. Talent is a very elusive aspect of the human being. Yet it cannot be denied that in life it plays a fundamental role. We are thus caught between Scylla and Charybdis: on the one hand, to ignore it completely is a bit like

F. Farina, *The Rise of Inequality and the Fall of Social Mobility*, https://doi.org/10.1007/978-3-031-92843-7_1

Table 1.1 Global Social Mobility Index 2020

1	*Denmark*	85.2
2	*Norway*	83.6
3	*Finland*	83.6
4	*Sweden*	83.5
5	*Iceland*	82.7
6	Netherlands	82.4
7	Switzerland	82.1
8	Belgium	80.1
9	Austria	80.1
10	Luxembourg	79.8
11	Germany	78.8
12	France	76.7
13	Slovenia	76.4
14	Canada	76.1
15	Japan	76.1
16	Australia	75.1
17	Malta	75.0
18	Ireland	75.0
19	Czech Republic	74.7
20	Singapore	74.6
21	United Kingdom	74.4
22	New Zealand	74.3
23	Estonia	73.5
24	Portugal	72.0
25	South Korea	71.4
26	Lithuania	70.5
27	United States	70.4
28	Spain	70.0
29	Cyprus	69.4
30	Poland	69.1
31	Latvia	69.0
32	Slovakia	68.5
33	Israel	68.1
34	Italy	67.4
35	Uruguay	67.1
36	Croatia	66.7
37	Hungary	65.8
38	Kazakhstan	64.0
39	Russian Federation	64.7
40	Bulgaria	63.8
41	Serbia	63.8
42	Romania	63.1
43	Malaysia	62.0

(*continued*)

Table 1.1 (continued)

44	Costa Rica	61.6
45	China	61.5
46	Ukraine	61.2
47	Chile	60.3
48	Greece	59.8
49	Moldova	59.6
50	Vietnam	57.8
51	Argentina	57.3
52	Saudi Arabia	57.1
53	Georgia	55.6
54	Albania	55.6
55	Thailand	55.4
56	Ecuador	53.9
57	Armenia	53.9
58	Mexico	52.6
59	Sri Lanka	52.3
60	Brazil	52.1
61	Philippines	51.7
62	Tunisia	51.7
63	Panama	51.4
64	Turkey	51.3
65	Colombia	50.3
66	Peru	49.9
67	Indonesia	49.3
68	El Salvador	47.4
69	Paraguay	46.8
70	Ghana	45.5
71	Egypt	44.8
72	Laos	43.8
73	Honduras	43.5
74	Morocco	43.7
75	Guatemala	43.5
76	India	42.7
77	South Africa	41.4
78	Bangladesh	40.2
79	Pakistan	36.7
80	Senegal	36.0
81	Cameroon	36.0
82	Ivory Coast	34.5

Source: World Economic Forum (2020)

assuming that the indices of the 82 countries refer to individuals who have received from mother nature the same, equal, endowment of talents; on the other hand, to tackle the issue head on, and establish how talent counts in the "mobility" of each individual is an impossible task.

The route traced in this book keeps away from the two rocks, but at the same time incorporates talents into the analysis of social mobility. As mentioned, the standard theory of economic science instead considers them outside its scope. The heterogeneity between the well-being outcomes would be essentially attributable to the free choice between work and leisure of individuals, and, above all, to the different commitment they put into education and work. In the fifties of the last century, merit began to be associated with effort as a decisive factor for success in life. With the Bell curve, an attempt was made to attribute the charisma of scientific truth to the measurement of the intelligence quotient, accrediting it as proof of the rooting of merit in biology. At this point, the step was short. From the foundation of merit in the transmission of genetic traits, the conclusion was reached that "those who commit themselves deserve". It is not only effort that counts, but above all being good at committing oneself to make use of one's talents. It's done: individualism is the right interpretative key to recognise merit.

The approach and narration of the issue proposed by economic theory are not convincing. As everyone knows, Aristotle wisely stated in the *Nicomachean Ethics*, that man is a *zoon politikon*, he is destined by nature to live in community. It follows that each one "deserves" in different measure also by virtue of the position he occupies in the world. Neoclassical economic theory avoids taking into consideration society. In an attempt to arrive at rigorous conclusions, it tries to focus on the essential; it therefore prunes the individual of all personal characteristics, it deals with a single "representative" individual, called to represent everyone. In the standard economic model, social well-being is calculated by aggregating the economic result of all individuals, under the simplifying assumption that they are identical. The operation, however, has a serious flaw. To put individualism on the pedestal of merit it is not enough to forget that society exists. If one believes that talents count, one should be able to say that everyone has an equal talent. A conclusion that no economist would subscribe to. We are thus back to the starting square, navigating between Scylla (the talents they play an important role in the well-being of each individual) and Charybdis (talents are different from individual to individual, but it is impossible for the tools of the economy to account for them).

How to get out of the goose game? Talents are not recognisable at birth. The individual becomes aware of them little by little. They express themselves in a complete form only once adulthood is reached. In aggregating the well-being result of identical individuals, economic theory gives up, in one fell swoop, taking into account two heterogeneities: that of individual talents, by their nature heterogeneous, and that of the many different contexts in which they manifest, contributing to the social mobility of each individual. It is the ambition of this book to try to use the tools of the economy to tie the two ends of the skein together, intertwining the two heterogeneities. In other words, we will try to move away from the "double escape" practised by the economy: from individual talents and from the different contexts in which the individual's performance takes place. We will therefore ask ourselves: how do personal talents connect to the social context in which they are expressed? If it is true that individuals are *zoon politikon*, the interaction between them is particularly complex. Social mobility depends on heterogeneous talents that are not tested by the individual in splendid isolation, but must find the route to come (or stay) afloat in contexts that are also strongly heterogeneous, because they are made by the socio-family environment, by markets and by political and economic institutions. To the point of realising, considering the two heterogeneities in the chapters of the book, that it is not at all easy to determine whether the performance of each one is more merit of talent or of context. So, page after page, we will have to broaden our view well beyond the troubled waters that surround talents, merit and social context, to ask ourselves the question: if, overall, things are not going well for social mobility, what needs to be fixed?

Table 1.1 therefore hides more than one problem. The values of social mobility of each nation are an aggregate data, processed based on the position that each of its members, at the end of the economic process, comes to occupy in well-being, considered in its various dimensions. Social mobility concerns however individuals whose life performance is peculiar: talents follow a slow path of emergence in their own socio-economic environment, to find realisation as adults in the form of "capabilities" (*capabilities*) that each individual has acquired. This book, in bringing talents into the analysis of social mobility, wants to draw attention to the strong diversity that characterises the living conditions of people. The socio-family context in which they form, and enter the labour market, individuals with different characteristics often decisively condition the emergence of talents. The issue does not bother standard economic theory. Being difficult to investigate, talents are set aside, and considered—perhaps too easily—a responsibility that concerns sociologists. However, one should not do as the fox that cannot reach the grapes, and then says they are sour.

Talents are here treated tangentially. At the centre of many chapters are the various dimensions of well-being. In the most important among them, inequalities of opportunity, wealth and income are in the foreground in posing obstacles to the effort that "disadvantaged" people put into bringing out their own talents. After having introduced from various angles the theme of social mobility, the chapters investigate the deep crisis that social dynamics is going through. The way in which the social context accompanies the emergence of individual talents during the years of training and then conditions in the markets the well-being performance of people will be critically examined. The main object of the research is the strategies implemented by companies and families to tilt the "playing field"—the market—towards the side that increases their economic result. For young people with a modest family condition, who do not have access to university education, or who live in historical phases in which progress rows against employment and economic growth is insufficient, expressing their own talents can be a very complicated task. Both the freedom to choose one's own life project and the achievement of the capabilities necessary to realise it using one's own talents are objectives studded with difficulties. For these young people, the road of life is an uphill journey, along which their social mobility upwards often gets blocked.

The Talents of Everyone

In recent centuries, the world has made great strides, economic availability and opportunities for social ascent have enormously increased. According to the statistical reconstruction of GDP from the Maddison Project Database of the University of Groningen, a gain of 6 dollars from 1800 became in 2018 in the United States a gain of 130 dollars, and in the United Kingdom, in Japan and in the Netherlands a gain of 100 dollars. But the degree of mobility of a population photographs the overall result of a country. It says nothing about the weight had by the multiple factors that determine the mobility upwards or downwards—or the social persistence—of each person or each group. At the time of entry as adults into the world of work, the unequal levels of income and culture of families, which cause the inequality of "circumstances"[1] among the young, and the unequal access to opportunities, produced by "market imperfections", have already had their effect. The possibility that the talents of young people from "disadvantaged" families can emerge is at this point, at least in part, already compromised. This book argues a strong thesis. That is, that today we are witnessing a substantial *impasse* of social mobility. To a large extent, this is due to the loss of efficiency and equity that the economic system suffers due to the failure to bring out the *talents of all*. This is "the" problem of the society in which we live.

There is a specific reason that makes social mobility "the" problem. In the world in which we live, a mixture of individualism and uncertainty, society increasingly needs a "cement" that holds it together. But it is increasingly difficult to find it. There are no absolute ideals, only "values", not always "golden", but flaunted in the media as such, even if with ever less conviction. Social classes are no longer defined based on production relations: the entrepreneurs-owners of resources on one side and salaried workers on the other. We are witnessing a lexical shift towards the definition of social groups no longer in ideological terms but generational. The list of social groups is compiled based on a classification by birth cohort: the *baby boomers* (1946–1964); the *generation X* (1965–1980); the *millennials* (1981–1996); the *generation Z* (those born in the mid-late nineties of the twentieth and the early years of the two thousand). In today's advanced societies, extremely fragmented in opinions and interests, to gain legitimacy the political and economic system must resort to very concrete signals of governance and progress. The most important is being able to boast a good ability to promote social mobility. It is mainly from the scarcity, if not the absence, of such a signal that the "crisis of democracy" arises. A sociologist, whose notoriety descends from having placed the welfare state at the centre of the question of mobility, wrote: "Class differences in school preparation are already evident when pupils enter the educational system, without schools being well equipped to remedy the problem" (Esping-Andersen 2015, p. 127). Advanced nations should

[1] This term synthesises the set of living conditions that contribute to individual formation before entering the labour market: parental care after birth, health and education conditions received in childhood, the socio-environmental context in which one grows up, the political and economic institutions of one's country.

therefore tackle the public policies necessary to start solving the problem of giving everyone adequate training. A daunting task, because it is a problem that has to do both with the education system and, more generally, with the distribution of power among social groups. Having said that, we are ready to start this journey into the myths and realities of social mobility. First, however, it is good to familiarise ourselves with some concepts, which will be useful for thinking about it.

Methodological Individualism and "classical liberalism"

The distinctive trait, the ***imprinting***, of the majority of interpretations of social mobility is today methodological individualism. The model of "general economic equilibrium" (Gee) developed by orthodox economic theory manages to present a harmonious vision of the functioning of markets because it is based on the ***autonomy*** and ***separation*** between subjects. In summary, it considers individuals as "atoms" that operate in the market independently of each other. By virtue of the ***reductio ad unum*** through the "representative" individual, orthodox (or neoclassical) economic theory focuses on differences such as the choice of work time versus free time, or productive or financial investment decisions, or consumption preferences. It never dwells on the socio-economic characteristics of individuals. How—and to what extent—they affect well-being and social mobility is considered a question alien to the first principles of economic theory.

Reality, however, says otherwise. In the real world, everyone is different from everyone else. Each individual is a ***unicum*** for the genetic heritage that distinguishes him. What allows him, or not, to express his own talents—regardless of how many they are—is the context in which he grows up as a young person and then realises himself, that is, the socio-cultural contents with which his being "unique" is enriched in the family environment, in the market and in society. That to construct a theoretical model one is content with the category of the "representative" individual reveals the limits of the "constellation of ideas" of orthodox thought. Orthodox theory effectively cuts off at the root the link that ties individual behaviour to the collective dimension. It is not surprising that in the history of economic science of the twentieth century—if we exclude the analytical advancements, not very systematic but ingenious, introduced by John

M. Keynes[2]—no significant methodological contribution has emerged to reconcile analytical rigour with the reality of the class structure of society.

The reductionism inherent in the indistinguishability between individuals, of which the specific position in society is erased, is shared from the main trunk of liberal political thought. This approach to political science—which I will call "classical liberalism"—theorises a society made up of "free and equal" subjects. As will be seen in the course of this, from this trunk, over the course of its history, liberalism has ended up cutting some of its most fruitful branches. These are particularly useful for understanding the world in which we live. In the idea of freedom of the "heretical liberals"—political scientists and economists like John Stuart Mill, Ralf Dahrendorf, Amartya Sen, Ronald Dworkin—the belonging of individuals to different social groups, bearers of values and interests often in conflict with each other, is highlighted.

Liberals are a much more varied family than is often made out. Alexis de Tocqueville was a liberal thinker whose main interest was understanding the history of peoples. This allowed him to escape the "straitjacket" of methodological individualism. The *incipit* with which he opens his *Democracy in America* is well known: "Among the new things that attracted my attention during my stay in the United States, one in particular struck me very deeply, and that is the equality of conditions". The liberal historian and political scientist, in the two volumes of his main book, goes very deep in explaining this belief. Tocqueville is today presented as the enthusiastic supporter of the "unfettered" individual (according to the current conception of *unfettered liberalism*). However, he had an ambivalent judgement on the "free and equal" individuals of the American nation born a few decades earlier. When his mind is turned to grasping the distance of the New World society from the stagnant staticity of the social structure of France's *Ancien Regime*, the pages of *Democracy in America* reveal in Tocqueville the singer of the virtues of individual freedom as the engine of social mobility. When he reflects on individualism, however, he

[2] The analytical schemes of the major works of Keynes are distinguished by the attempt to set up the treatment of economic facts based on socio-economic categories rather than on "pure" economic categories. In the *Treatise on Money*, the distinction between monetary circulation in credit and financial markets and monetary circulation in the goods market sheds light on the instability inherent in the functioning of the capitalist system. The model of the *General Theory*, dedicated to the interpretation of unemployment as a phenomenon endemic to capitalism, is based on the separation between the economic behaviours of capitalist-entrepreneurs and those of workers.

grasps the fragility of a society characterised by autonomy and separation between individuals.[3] Although Tocqueville wrote at the beginning of the nineteenth century, his words send a surprising echo of relevance. He fears the birth of a new despotism: "I see a crowd of countless similar and equal men who do nothing but [...] procure small and vulgar pleasures with which they satiate their soul. Each of these men lives for himself and is like a stranger to the fate of all the others" (Tocqueville 1995, p. 732). Of the French thinker, it is often emphasised his foresight in seeing the risks, inherent in democracy, of a "dictatorship of the majority". It would also be necessary to grasp his intuition that the capitalist economic system, which was expanding in his time, had within it the germs of the erosion of collective well-being.

"Systemic interdependence" and Social Conflict

Orthodox economic theory, it is worth reiterating, has its weak point in two false assumptions: 1) that a rigorous analysis of the economic system requires the assumption of substantial *homogeneity* among individuals; 2) that to demonstrate the efficiency of the market equilibrium position it is necessary to consider individuals *strangers to each other*. The first assumption, homogeneity, has very little rigour, since it eliminates the inequalities that distinguish one subject from another. The second assumption, aimed at conferring on economic analysis the chrism of the "impartiality" of the general equilibrium of the system, refers to a social contract between "free and equal" individuals; an assumption, as we will see, implausible. In reality, the consideration of free individuals and strangers to each other, in order to make the determination of the system equilibrium "neutral"—immune from value judgements—fulfils a specific function in orthodox economic theory: it is the conceptual shield aimed at neutralising the analysis of social conflict—instead of the social contract—as the distinctive trait of society. It is well known that orthodox economists and liberal thinkers have little regard for the idea that humanity's path has consisted of a succession of conflicts. Their distancing from this idea is almost instinctive. It probably has to do with the concern not to give space to the Marxist analysis of historical materialism. Economists passionate about long-term socio-economic analysis, however, argue—with arguments

[3] Also surprising for their foresight are the pages dedicated to the alienation of factory work and to the massification linked to consumerism.

based on serious empirical tools—that it is historical development that proves that social conflict is the constitutive factor of living in community. The exodus from Africa of the first hominids, which took place 10,000 years ago, would have initiated a very long process of cultural differentiation. Within populations, as they became sedentary, diversity in attitudes towards trust in others, preferences for solidaristic social norms and so on would have grown (Arbatlı et al. 2020).

The reality of advanced societies exposes the false premises on which the orthodox vision is based. First, in Latin *persona* means "mask": people are different because each has a different "mask". The behaviours of people are characterised for the *heterogeneity*, both for the genetic reasons mentioned, and because the actions of the individual are influenced by the specific social context in which they were formed. Secondly, the behaviours that each individual puts into play in market participation, and in the various areas of life that contribute to the formation of well-being, are not characterised by *separation* and *autonomy* but by *interdependence* with other subjects. In the system of equations of the Gee model, interactions between people are not contemplated. Suffice it to say: as grotesque as it may appear, in the Gee model the equilibrium price at which the exchange of each good is established a priori with respect to the demand and supply made by the subjects in the market. The first limit of the model is that the agents operating in the market are not attributed an "active" behaviour.[4]

Closely connected to the extreme distance from reality of the conceptual and analytical scheme of the Gee is the cancellation of the emotional sphere of people, as if in analysing individual behaviour this motivational area were incompatible with—and not complementary to—the sphere of rationality. Orthodox economic theory has long removed motivations from its "toolbox", based on the consideration that to understand the preferences expressed by people in the market it is sufficient to observe their choices.

This *absurdum* logic deserves a brief deepening. It is indeed appropriate to explain why the incongruity in which the epistemological approach of economic theory has become stuck has tended to procrastinate over time. In the second half of the twentieth century, game theory tried to "fill the gaps" of the standard model. By virtue of this new theoretical

[4] The equilibrium position should reflect the actions of the subjects, but "what the theory of general equilibrium does is to ensure that *market prices exist provided they are independent of such actions* "(italic in the text) (Hahn 1980, p. 130).

paradigm, the indistinguishability between subjects and the "atomistic" character of their behaviours have left the scene. Playing in a strategic context, subjects actively live their rationality, but also express psychological intentions and motivations: everyone's behaviour depends on the expectation of others' behaviour. However, it cannot be said that the step forward was sufficient to pull economic theory out of the suffocating analysis of behaviour offered by orthodox thought. In the new paradigm, the behaviour of the players is indeed studied with reference to their gains which are fixed—in what in technical language is called the "pay-off matrix"—once and for all. In other words, the numbers that appear in the matrix of a game are not subject to change in the process of determining the equilibrium of the game. Can we judge it satisfactory that the consideration of the interaction between subjects does not go beyond the moment when each player—taking into account their own beliefs on strategies and the beliefs of others—sets up their own strategy? It is not satisfactory.

A satisfactory presentation of the dynamics of interaction between subjects has not yet been achieved even in the most recent theoretical strand of *Psychological Game Theory* (Pgt), in which players proceed to revise their beliefs at various stages of the development of an "extended form game". Although it opens up to the consideration of emotions as a source of motivation for behaviours, the analytical framework of the Pgt is not yet suitable for accommodating the emotional reactions triggered by the formation of new beliefs. Yet, in real life the process of revising beliefs deeply influences the intentions that drive the behaviours of subjects.

To really focus on a social context made up of a very sophisticated network of individual behaviours, something else is needed. A theoretical model that really intends to capture the essence of social interaction cannot ignore the fact that the norm of living in a community consists in the fact that, in pursuing their own interest, the actions of people or social groups give rise to *consequences* on the well-being of other individuals, other groups or the entire community.

Let's delve into the issue by introducing the category of "externality". This economic category has to do with the interdependence that develops between individuals operating in the market. An externality (also defined through its *spillovers*) arises when one subject influences the well-being of another subject, without the latter receiving compensation (in the case of a negative externality) or paying a price (in the case of a positive externality). In short, an externality puts the market mechanism described by the orthodox model "out of play". Since externalities do not "pass through" the market, the compensation due to those who suffer a negative externality cannot be established with its own instrument, namely with a negotiation that concludes with the fixing of a price. Negative externalities are therefore produced by individual or group behaviours that penalise other subjects, without these latter having the possibility to avoid the loss of well-being they suffer.

In support of actions that produce negative externalities, markets often implement strategies based on "asymmetric information". Joe Stiglitz won the Nobel Prize for economics in 2001 because his models demonstrate how the functioning of markets is distorted when "some individuals know something that others do not know". The link between the concept of externality and the concept of freedom is indisputable: a person is indeed free to act unless the behaviours of others infringe upon their freedom. Clearly, the Gee model, the standard-bearer of freedom and equality among subjects in the market, is not predisposed to accommodate a central characteristic in the interaction between people. In social interaction, "imperfections in information and asymmetries are pervasive and help to explain the difference between what is observed and what theory predicts" (Stiglitz 2013, p. X).

Game theory does not predict the phenomenon of externality because—in analysing a predetermined earnings matrix—*it admits* that the *game behaviour* is influenced by the expectation of the behaviour of others, but *does not admit* that the *final level of earnings* of a player is affected by the behaviour of others. The explanation is simple. Since each person's earnings are set from the start in the *payoff* matrix, the strategic context is confined to the study of how each player positions themselves in relation to the equilibrium position predicted by the game.[5] As observed above, however, the equilibrium position that the economic system actually reaches should reflect the entire process leading to the final earnings, not simply the reasoning that the strategic context initially induces subjects to develop. In a summary: "psychologists tend to discover individuals' beliefs *after* they have made their decisions in various strategic contexts, economists *before*" (Attanasi and Nagel 2008, p. 222). Therefore, externalities

[5] A "Nash equilibrium" arises from the set of beliefs and strategies of each individual. In this equilibrium, each player's strategy is the best response (because it gives the maximum *payoff*) given the expectation on the strategy of the other player. No player would be able to increase their own gain (*payoff*) by adopting an alternative strategy.

are not taken into account not only by the Gee, but also by game theory, because the beliefs that are formed during the game are not fully accounted for even by the Pgt.

What is reflected in an externality can be defined as a pure manifestation of power: it consists in the narrowing of the space of freedom and well-being that a person or a group suffers due to the behaviour of another person or group. Orthodox economic theory catalogues externalities among "market failures" and relegates them among "exceptional cases" because it is precisely in cases of externality—contrary to the centrality attributed to market coordination—that the price mechanism is unable to function. Externalities are, on the contrary, one of the main laws of operation of today's social reality.

By lowering the well-being performance of people, negative externalities bring to light the power asymmetry between social classes. Externalities are a very pervasive phenomenon. For example, a negative externality is generated whenever insurance companies in fact do not offer a health policy to poor people at risk of serious illnesses. For these people, the "price of health" is not even formed, so their well-being inevitably decreases. As written in the "Financial Times", "changing the funding of the NHS[6] from general taxation to health insurance is equivalent to causing a health crisis" (Wolf 2023b). More generally, the limited chances of a good life for "disadvantaged" people—*before* the market and *in* the market—constitute a huge iceberg. In the reality of the markets in which we operate, we only see the tip of the iceberg, because externalities are sunk in the sea of economic and social life, which is rarely illuminated by the theoretical elaboration of economists.

It is quite simple to understand the reason for the oblivion in which orthodox economic theory wraps the category of externality. The assumption on which it analyses exchanges is that markets are populated by "free and equal" individuals. However, as we will see better later, being citizens "free and equal" is a definition that acquires the chrism of truth only in a democracy that recognises and makes social rights effective. The Constitution of the Roman Republic of 1849 declared as a fundamental principle in art. 1: "Sovereignty is by eternal right in the people. The people of the Roman State are constituted in a democratic republic". Clearly, that Constitution was far ahead of its time. The first European Constitution in which the right of the people to have social rights

[6] The NHS (National Health System) is the public health system of the United Kingdom.

recognised—that is, in addition to a dignified remuneration for work, access to health, education, housing and so on—was the Constitution of the Weimar Republic of 1919. We know how it ended. One aspect that puts the Italian constitutional charter at the forefront among the constitutions of the world is what art. 3 states. It affirms that rights must not remain, precisely, on paper. Legislation must continually operate in order to make rights effective. Society and market remain distinct areas. In the current neoliberal era, it happens that the latter tends to engulf the former. Individual action should be placed in an analytical scheme equipped—much more than those of the Gee and game theory—to deal with the many externalities present in every capitalist system. A social interaction context in which a social group enjoys the privilege of establishing the "optimal" strategy, with such autonomy that it does not need to form expectations about the strategy of another group, imposes a negative externality on the latter. In fact, the members of such a group are not "free and equal". Among social scientists, economists should be the first to construct the theoretical categories and analytical tools necessary to open the doors to the analysis of the different power of individuals and social groups in the economy and society. A fundamental fact of reality is that the context in which social interaction takes place has a systemic character. We will define it as the context of "systemic interdependence" (Farina 2021).[7]

Power asymmetry shapes social and political interdependence among people. Our era provides many examples, and of great importance, of the command of large corporations and finance. Consider the decisions to introduce innovations that are made in the sectors of advanced production, or the decisions to invest in public securities made by investment banks. These autonomous choices can result in significant losses of collective well-being. Millions of people, belonging to classes that do not control economic resources, must bear the cost—in the form of layoffs, low wages, stock market crashes and austerity policies required of countries with high public debt to avoid bankruptcy—of crises caused by groups of people motivated only by personal profit. Once negative externalities

[7] A context of "systemic interdependence" should be conceived as a game of "non-coordination with conflict of interests", in which there typically exists an asymmetry of power between the players. In other words, only one of the two—the player with power in the market—enjoys the privilege of establishing their own strategy in full autonomy, without needing to anticipate the other's strategy and take it into account in establishing their own.

reduce their well-being, people belonging to the weaker classes see their social mobility severely penalised.

The theoretical scheme known as the *The tragedy of the commons* fully falls within the concept of "systemic interdependence". We are all exposed to decisions that individual *corporations* and individual states make under the impulse of selfish interest, without taking into account the impact on everyone else. The most typical example is the environment, where property rights are not defined at the international level, so it is quite rare for the case where causing pollution (of air, water etc.) is a fault that can be precisely attributed to individuals or states. Even less realistic is the hypothesis of appointing an international court for the purpose of sanctioning the violation of the right to health.

The social group of workers is not normally in a position to protect their well-being from the behaviour of ownership and management aimed at maximising profit. Considering the company and the worker as two players, the decisions made in full autonomy by the company are able to determine the balance it desires without having to resort to forms of coordination with the workers. The reality of today's capitalist system is that of an economic power that—having the responsibility to generate economic growth—produces negative externalities at the expense of "disadvantaged" people, often preventing them from enjoying the increase in income and well-being. The concept of externality and the political theory of power converge in this definition: "A exercises power over B when A generates effects on B that are contrary to B's interests" (Lukes 1974, p. 25). It follows that the interaction between individuals in a democratic society must be analysed using the conceptual apparatus of social conflict, alternative to that of the "social contract".

Let's reflect for a moment on the democracy of the vote. Going to vote is irrelevant from the point of view of purposeful behaviour. Since it is very difficult for a voter to be decisive in transforming a party's defeat at the polls into a victory, voting is responsible citizen behaviour but is not the typical example of rational decision theory. The right to vote instead establishes a link between externality and democracy. "If by democracy we mean that the members of a society decide jointly, on an equal basis, their future" (Herzog 2024, p. 1), going to vote configures a link between the externality determined by the individual voter on everyone else (by depositing their ballot in the ballot box) and the conception of democracy as an expression of the common pursuit of collective well-being. This is a concept that lies between the individual and the collective, and is therefore very problematic. It reveals that between the free vote of the individual voter and collective well-being there is an aporia that is difficult to solve. A collective choice like voting does not overcome the conflict of opinions and interests that divides voters but exposes it. Normally, in fact, the majority vote of the community—in line with the context of social conflict typically present in a democracy—generates a balance between costs and benefits that is negative for some social groups and positive for others. Let's now reflect on the connection between individual and collective that is determined in the economy. Among the many definitions of social conflict, political science has proposed this: "There is social conflict when a person or group advances negative claims against other people or groups; claims that, if satisfied, would damage the interest of others, i.e. the other's probability of achieving a desirable situation" (Tilly 1992). The reality of today's capitalist system is that of an economic power that—when it generates economic growth—often produces negative externalities, at the expense of "disadvantaged" people, opposing their desire to improve their own well-being. The excessive concentration of wealth and income is the expression of the command over resources exercised by large corporations and finance. "Wealth is also a source of power. Shareholder control gives them direct power over companies" (Wolf 2023a, p. 91).

The externalities that arise in the outcome of democratic voting as in the functioning of the economy are the expression of "systemic interdependence". This is a fundamental concept for understanding the welfare opportunities that people have. Individual destinies—far from separating in the autonomy of the individual "free from constraints" imagined by orthodox theory—are very intertwined. Particularly in phases of macroeconomic instability, many people suffer an externality in the fundamental dimension of income; the complementarity between the dimensions means that this negative externality transmits its effects to other important dimensions such as health, education, housing and so on. One can think of the formation of a social class as a certain number of people who come to share a common condition of overall well-being. The origin of a social class lies in the accumulation over time, for these people, of equal externalities originating from social conflict, or of "results" favourable or unfavourable in all the main dimensions of well-being.

It is interesting to note how the systemic character of interdependence between people is closely in tune with the concept of freedom elaborated by John Stuart Mill. The liberal political philosopher clearly saw a constraint to which the actions of each individual should be subject: "the freedom of each ends where the freedom of others begins". In *Utilitarianism* (1861), Mill links the protection from others' behaviours that violate a rule of conduct with our natural sympathy for the other members of the community to which we belong. In this way, he seems to tell us that the condemnation of negative externalities to our detriment or that of others finds legitimacy in the protection, not only of individual people, but of social coexistence itself as a collective good. On the freedom guaranteed by the unrealistic assumptions of *autonomy* and *separation* of the Gee, the interdependence between people, which creates a link between one's own individual freedom and that of others, therefore prevails. A society in which it happens that the freedom of other individuals is limited by my actions—or that admits an inequality between people in front of rights—is not a society in which the freedom of all is respected. If it happens, as the society is characterised by a strong asymmetry of power, social mobility is severely impeded.

This is a fundamental issue when judging the link between democracy and capitalism. The distance between a "strong" idea of freedom—a conception of freedom as "freedom for all"— and the subjugation of society to the command of large companies and finance—in the pursuit of short-term profit—is rapidly widening. Neoliberalism has given a strong push to the increase of externalities that compress the "freedom of all". Progressive economists are becoming aware of this: "the social alienation and loss of power, associated with increasing levels of wealth and income inequality, should be interpreted as social externalities" (Kelly and Snower 2021, p. 34).

In the economy and society of advanced countries, there have recently been structural changes whose common characteristic is that of having significantly increased the degree of interdependence between people. Due to the asymmetry of power between social groups, this greater interdependence produces negative externality effects primarily on those who depend on the productive choices of those who decide on the use of economic resources. Let's see some examples.

First, the companies of advanced countries form a global network of transnational corporations linked in the *global supply chains* (Gsc), with the aim of making the organisation productive more efficient by minimising costs. What were decisions on semi-finished products, on intermediate goods, on the marketing of the final product, taken within companies, have become market transactions between companies that expose workers to the effects of *spillover* of productive choices on their jobs and their wages. As well as on workers who are laid off by the "mother" company, in moving production stages abroad, companies in the North of the world generate negative externalities also in low-cost labour countries where they make their "direct investments", through a hierarchy of subordination relationships with workers, suppliers and politicians of local institutions. Similarly, energy prices, being typically subject to the turbulence created by wars and international politics alliances, undergo sudden fluctuations. The increase in prices that energy supply difficulties determine in *futures* contracts negatively reflects on the budgets of families and companies. There are also consequences on economic integration processes. In the European Union, national subsidies aimed at cushioning losses, being of different amounts from country to country, generate distortions within the common market.

Second, technological progress is today a multiplier of externalities that are positive for some groups of workers and negative for others. The phase of technological evolution in which we find ourselves, in fact, does not select workers and does not assign them a "wage premium" directly based on the level of education and professional qualification, as it allows "a wider range of possibilities of substitution between groups of workers with equal *skills* [...]; the allocation of the *skill* is endogenised in tasks". Technological changes do not increase the wages of all workers, with the significant consequence that "a change favourable to one type of worker can reduce the wage of another group of workers [...]. A new machine can directly replace job tasks that were performed by workers at different levels of *skill*. [...]. This type of technological change [...] makes it more likely that negative effects on the real wages of the group that is directly replaced by the machine will occur" (Acemoglu and Autor 2011, p. 1158).

Third, the prices of financial assets are determined on financial markets that are closely interconnected. Financial transactions however take place under the sign of information asymmetries, as the most relevant information is held by the most powerful market operators. The exposure of financial institutions to the risk of losses depends on their size and the degree of interconnection of the operators (private agents and States). Before the financial crisis of 2008 many banks were saved because *too big to fail*. The subsequent decision to let Lehman Brothers fail, taken in order to restore the credibility of the incentive system, led to the explosion of systemic risk (Stiglitz 2019).

Fourth, we have entered the "post-industrial society". This has resulted in a profound socio-anthropological change. With the transition from industry to services as the majority share of GDP, consumer services have been parcelled out by innovations in information and communication technologies (Id. 1975). The current explosion of interaction has been greatly contributed to by telematics, with which interconnection transcends the spatial dimension. The time people spend interacting with each other—close up or remotely—would have reached, according to social psychologists, 80% of the total time lived during the day. A push in the direction of making social interaction "systemic" also came from the acceleration of the urbanisation process that has occurred in both rich and poor countries: the world population, which has grown by a good 2 billion and 300 million in the last 35 years, will live 86% in urban centres by 2050. The spread of digital technologies, in stimulating the birth of new interpersonal relationships, has increased the intermediation performed by the market, thus increasing the degree of interdependence between individuals. In the company, repetitive individual work on the assembly line of mass productions has been replaced by interaction between workers organised in teams. The processes of "marketisation", in society as within companies, only formally produce relationships between equals; the externalities that result from this have a negative impact on subjects with fewer opportunities.

Fifth, the increase in the average size of large companies increases their market power, both in terms of determining the mark-up on costs, and in markets where monopsony conditions exist, the market form in which there is only one entrepreneur as a buyer of the labour services of the workforce. The more the workforce is concentrated in a territory, the more workers looking for a job compete with each other and wages tend to go down. This form of externality that develops within the workforce also occurs when in a territory the conditions of monopsony are not present. The asymmetry of power in favour of the company is in fact strengthened by collusive behaviours between companies that reproduce its effects. Companies resort to collusion (in setting selling prices and in setting wage levels) in order to prevent the asymmetry of power towards workers from being weakened by the entry of new entrepreneurs. "The increase in market concentration raises concerns about the presence of monopsony in the labour market, the condition of dominance of a company in the market, or a lack (or absence) of competition for workers that keeps wages low" (Oecd 2019, p. 68).

Sixth, a process of integration is in fact a driver of externalities that in principle should occur on a plane of cooperation between equals. The asymmetry of power existing between States instead results in the predominant influence that the strongest country exerts on the others. The place of interdependence between nations is increasingly that of supranational political and economic institutions. The asymmetry of power—in tending to extend from the economy to politics—interferes with integration processes. The typical case is the heterogeneous impact on the countries of the continent of the policies of the European Monetary Union. Germany has imposed its own interests in the political negotiation on common rules between countries formally on an equal footing on the legal plane. Since its approval in 1998, the Stability Pact on fiscal matters between States linked by an integration of currency and markets has represented the Trojan horse of the hegemonic power, long committed to prioritising its own interests in the Union. Lacking in Europe the recognition of the principle of solidarity (starting from "mutuality": the "common guarantee" on debts contracted on the market to finance the Ngeu was an exception), the governments of the Union have encountered increasing difficulties in reacting to crises. The "noose" of strict rules on deficit and public debt has given way to the "austerity policy", which after the suspension for the pandemic is about to come back into force in a, if possible, worsened version. The negative impact of austerity on GDP growth means that the public debt/GDP ratio grows, accentuating the problem of market confidence in the sustainability of debt.[8] Due to the obtuse neoliberal ideology, according to which a complex and fragile society must be put in the market's trousers, Europe continues to ignore the bright (and lucid, because counterintuitive) teaching of Keynes. In 1937, the Cambridge economist warned: "the boom, not the recession, is the right time for austerity". The problem is not only that, due to the constraints on the deficit, public resources cannot support the recovery. Debt constraints have also exposed Union governments to the consequences of financial turmoil in very different ways. For countries burdened with a large stock of public debt to repay, the *spillover* of a huge increase in interest expenditure has materialised, due to the increase in the spread on rates. The integration process thus fails in the task of achieving real economic

[8] The purpose of the public budget restrictions to which the governments of the European Union are obliged by the Stability Pact is to prevent the increase in the public debt/GDP ratio, which would compromise the sustainability of the debt. However, due to their procyclicality, restrictive policies are inevitably followed by further falls in GDP, with the result that the ratio, instead of decreasing, increases and sustainability is reduced.

and social convergence between countries with economic systems at different levels of productivity (Croci Angelini and Farina 2016). One of the causes of the blockage of social mobility that afflicts many European Union countries is that the path of integration through the sole operation of the market has become increasingly narrow. Austerity policies have negative external effects that weigh mainly on the weakest social groups. Interdependence in Europe between countries linked by a process of integration on asymmetric bases thus intertwines with the internal context of the countries of asymmetry of power between social groups. On the one hand, the European Commission, due to its economic policies, is undermining the confidence of the Union's low-income classes in the prospects for social mobility. On the other hand, the problems of lack of convergence and of "disunion" economic and social between the member countries has been poured the "tsunami" of migratory flows. Governments, already in difficulty due to a national electorate whose well-being was put to the test by the pandemic, continue to ignore the need for mutuality and turn their heads the other way in the face of the search for transcontinental mobility of migrants landing on the European coasts in search of salvation. To the two main causes of the wind in favour of the sovereignist parties blowing in Europe—austerity and immigrants—is added the interest of multinationals in preventing a true European Union, made up of strong supranational institutions, from imposing itself on the international scene and redeeming politics from subjugation to the economy. The reflection on domestic politics is the progressive loss of credibility of European institutions and the concrete danger of a rejection of the very idea of a united Europe.

Status libertatis and *Status civitatis*

In the second century AD, Gaius, one of the fathers of Roman law, conceived the identity of the individual as the sum of personal freedom (*status libertatis*) and participation in the community (*status civitatis*).[9] Every individual is involved in social interaction with both *status*, as a single operator in the market and as a participant in society in economic-social interaction. This dual identity opens a gap between the individual and

[9] By *status* we mean the legal, political or social condition of a person within the structure of society.

society. Personal interest is a source of ambivalence in behaviours, such as to compromise social relations.

In the constitutional charters, the first articles are carved in stone. The reason is that it is primarily in these articles that the urgency, felt by the founding fathers, to bridge the gap between individual and society is manifested. To demonstrate the plurality of liberal conceptions of society, we will limit ourselves to two examples of the different ways in which this distance is eliminated. In the United States Declaration of Independence, Thomas Jefferson wrote that each man should be recognised the full individual right "to life, liberty and the pursuit of happiness". The founding fathers of the United States reaffirmed the centrality of the individual by inserting in art. 1 of the 1787 Constitution the individual's right to happiness. Differently, from the millennial history of the German peoples descends the centrality, in the Constitution of the Federal Republic of Germany born in 1949, of the concept of community. The Charter, which bears the imprint of the ordoliberal doctrine,[10] at art. 1 reads as follows: "The dignity of man is inviolable. It is the duty of every state power to respect and protect it". In the German Constitution the word *man* is to be understood as a collective noun. The United States Constitution begins with these words: "We, the people of the United States...". The English term *people* defines the exercise of sovereignty as a simple sum of the ends pursued by individuals. The German term *man* instead evokes the people, the *Volk* as an organic totality, as the holder of political power.

Although in all advanced countries it enjoys great respect, a Constitution represents only a compass to establish the rules that must preside over the functioning of society. To define the institutional structure of Western countries, the noun *democracy* is often added to the adjective *liberal*. The concept of freedom underlying the term *liberal democracy* is that proposed by "classical liberalism". On the political stage, "free and equal" individuals are described *as if* they had committed to observing the terms of a "social contract", and they compete on an equal footing in the democratic election of their representatives in political institutions. However, Gaius reminds us that the context of democratic coexistence is that of individuals whose identity is defined not only by the *status libertatis* but also by the

[10] Ordoliberalism differs from American neoliberalism in that it conceives the economic order not as natural but as an institutional construct. In ordoliberalism, the functioning of the market depends on individual behaviours that develop within a system of rules.

status civitatis, the place of people's interactive identity. The dual foundation of personal identity—in the individual and collective sphere—in itself paves the way for the centrality of social conflict as a constitutive fact of the interaction of individuals in the market and in society. Unlike what is assumed by classical liberal thought, the various classes have a different degree of power in society, which is inevitably a source of tension between the two components of identity. The affirmation of social norms, through beliefs about cooperation that self-fulfil in society, should favour the reduction of social costs linked to self-interested behaviours. The less the institutional structure of a community is of a vertical type, as has happened in the last three centuries through the replacement of the command of a sovereign with self-government by its members, the less intense is the social conflict and the more widespread is cooperative behaviour (Rustagi 2022).

The progress of civil coexistence has not, however, occurred in a harmonious way. It has often been the result of pressure for more freedom and more well-being that groups that have found themselves on the "wrong" side of the power asymmetry—in the guise of the "disadvantaged"—have exerted on the powerful in order to improve their position in society. As a prominent liberal political scientist wrote, "The subject of class conflict is life chances. More precisely, the unequal distribution of life chances" (Dahrendorf 1989, p. 36). This book argues that "the unequal distribution of life chances" is nothing more than the outcome of a game of "non-coordination with conflict of interests", centred on the power asymmetry to their own advantage enjoyed by the social groups that are leading the capitalist system. Many freedoms—making decisions about production and the introduction of technical progress without having to find a coordination with other social groups, moving large amounts of capital from one place to another, from the public debt of one country to another and so on—are in fact at the origin of the many externalities that affect the "disadvantaged" groups. On the other hand, as will be argued, in relating to the economy, politics is increasingly blunted. It is not far from the truth this drastic judgement: "The majority does not rule, at least not in the causal sense of actually determining the political outcomes. When a majority of citizens disagrees with the economic elites or organised interests, it usually loses" (Gilens and Page 2014, p. 566).

Several decades have passed since Dahrendorf developed his thought. In that span of time, instead of following a trend of decrease dictated by progress towards greater social mobility, the gap in life chances between classes has been increasing. There is today a contrast, as deep as it is latent, between the few who can aspire to social ascent and the many to whom such aspiration is precluded; or at least the conditions are not unlocked for them to be able to cultivate it. Individuals endowed with intangible capital[11] and financial and real estate wealth exercise power and enjoy great opportunities for profit and well-being. Individuals with few skills and few resources usable in the market are exposed to the risk of paying for their disadvantaged condition with precarious employment and an income sometimes just above the poverty line.

The Neoliberal Society: Interdependent Individuals but Free from Constraints

Interdependence today is in tension with a vision—like that of neoliberalism—of an individual without limits and constraints. The real world is far different from the autonomous and separate individual-monads of the Gee model. However, we are faced with a paradox: the increase in interpersonal relations produces the effect of increasing individualism. Despite the growing interdependence that develops between people in the economic and social sphere, the collective interconnection in the ether fuels the tendency of the individual to develop a distance from the society of which he is part and therefore also from the idea that one's own well-being is interrelated with that of others. During the pandemic, it was important to follow John Stuart Mill's warning to find a limit to our freedom in the right of others to have their own freedom respected. Although we have had the ability to keep our distance to avoid individualistic behaviours of underestimating the common danger of contagion, in many advanced societies of the West, the idea that the pursuit of individual well-being cannot be detached from collective well-being is not deeply ingrained. The mix of increasing interconnection and individualism that characterises the world in which we live often ends up weakening the collective component of personal identity. Consider the tendency of the rich in many countries to abandon the System. national health service (NHS) and turn to private healthcare, as their contribution to the NHS is higher—in probabilistic

[11] The form of capital that does not consist in machinery or financial assets, but in the knowledge that workers with advanced skills use in the production process.

terms, they enjoy better health than others—relative to the services they use. As a theorist of "complexity" has argued, in people's perception the simple truth that "we are part of the society that is part of us" (Morin 2017, p. 28) fades.

Parallel to the integration of markets at an international level, for several years we have been witnessing the continuous decay of the powers of national political institutions. With globalisation, governments have seen their ability to counter the growing economic power of multinationals weaken. This sets in motion a vicious circle: as uncritical adherence to the will of multinationals and finance increases, the political sovereignty of nations decays. Moreover, the ruling classes do not pay much attention to the fact that "at the root of the current crisis of capitalism is its malfunction, caused by social and environmental externalities" (Kelly and Snower 2021, p. 852). The two youth movements born a few years ago were Fridays for Future, for the defence of the environment, where Greta Thunberg raised the sign "Skolstrejk för klimatet", and Occupy Wall Street for the fight against inequalities, which raised the sign "We are the 99%". To prevent the combination of individualism and negative externalities fuelled by "systemic interdependence" from exacerbating the two main global problems—inequalities and environmental degradation—a process of cultural regeneration within advanced countries should be set in motion.

The "shape of the game" of capitalism needs to be changed, because the negative externalities caused by the decisions of business and finance are not controllable by parties other than the owners of capital—the workers and future generations—on whose well-being such externalities nevertheless fall. In the homogenisation created by the media and in the decline of that critical thinking that only the educational process—from primary school to university—is capable of giving, advanced societies have moved away from that ability to awaken the forces of change that in the past, with the exercise of democracy, they had. Movements for sustainable development and against inequalities have a hard life. To individual costs is thus added the collective cost, namely the declining degree of cohesion observed in contemporary societies. To give strength to these movements there is only education. It gives knowledge of things, and therefore also the awareness that it is necessary to join forces for change.

Talents and Education

This book focuses on the individual and social factors that are at the basis of social mobility. The method of analysis is however centred on the individual. The aim is to show the limits of an economic system that is not aimed at promoting individual talents. This analysis, however, distances itself from the approach of methodological individualism. It wants to show how in the behaviour and well-being of each individual is also variously implicated the behaviour and well-being of others (Sen 1985a). As has been observed, orthodox economic theory associates social mobility with the incentive of gain that drives individuals to make the most of their own talents in the competition for success. "Human capital", in the broadest sense of the term, consists of the set of knowledge, skills and relational abilities of individuals that guarantee the efficiency of the economic system. This concept has a dual nature, as it has a value not only individual but also collective. In individualistic and free market societies, the "capabilities" potentially possessed by young people with a disadvantaged socio-family background risk remaining unexpressed. Talents are indeed a resource that belongs to the individual, but they need a welcoming social environment to thrive (*flourish*).[12] It is rarely observed that, when the human capital of the population remains below the level that the natural talents of the individual members would have allowed to achieve, a country's economic growth is slow and well-being stagnates (Roemer and Trannoy 2016). The opposite also holds true. In turn, indeed, unsatisfactory economic growth negatively affects the aspirations and opportunities for social ascent of individuals, primarily the most "disadvantaged".

This book seeks to answer the following question: beyond individual commitment to work, why do the talents inherent in the genetic heritage find the way to emerge in some subjects, and are they valued by them, while they risk remaining unexpressed in other subjects? Amartya Sen makes us understand it in the simplest and clearest way.[13] The freedom of

[12] "From the socialist experience, liberalism has been able to ascertain that the problem of freedom was not summed up in an abstract declaration of rights, leaving in fact to the strongest the opportunity to assert their own to the detriment of those of the weakest; but that it was necessary to integrate the declaration with the practical sanction and with the means to assert those rights for all" (De Ruggiero 1925, p. 152).

[13] In writing that "the most urgent issue remains […] the need to re-examine the problems of social efficiency and equity by shifting attention to individual freedoms" (Sen 1990, p. 5),

the individual is not synonymous with autonomy. The 1998 Nobel laureate in economics has made a great contribution to getting economic theory out of the shoals of economic reductionism, without losing sight of the individual and without adhering to a holistic conception of society. For the Indian economist, freedom consists in acquiring the *capabilities* to realise one's life project.[14] When one questions the Social mobility, one must ask: is the distribution really fair among individuals of the essential opportunities to acquire the *skills* necessary to make the most of their talents (Id. 1985b)? In answering this question negatively, Amartya Sen associates his "idea of justice" with the need to counteract the negative impact that the unequal distribution of opportunities has on the *skills* that disadvantaged people manage to acquire (Id. 2009).[15] The term *empowerment* he used is particularly effective: "conferring of powers". In the social reality they are part of, young people obtain "conferring of powers"—their "emancipation"—through the acquisition of the *skills* necessary for self-realisation (Deneulin and Shahani 2009).

At this point, it should be clear that the existential and social space in which the phenomenon of social mobility is inscribed has an extension that goes far beyond the aspiration to individual success. It is not only as a result of the individual choice to commit to social ascent that an individual "transits" within social stratification.[16] The transition from one level of education to another, from one job to another, from one income and *status* position to another, depends on many things. The opportunities to express one's talents are heterogeneous, primarily due to the very different context in which people are immersed. Each person's life project develops

the Nobel laureate has in mind public policies that allow the individual to be effectively free "to be and to do". As Tony Atkinson (1997) observed, neoclassical economic theory has "put on ice" welfare economics, to the point of not seeing the progressive increase in inequalities.

[14] With the term "functionings", Sen's *Theory of Capabilities* refers to the *capabilities* that are actually realised. Ideally, each individual should find themselves in the conditions to choose the set of "functionings" most appropriate for their own personal life project.

[15] The *capabilities* represent, "unlike what happens to rights and merely formal freedoms, the real and substantive freedoms, as freedoms defined once all potential obstacles to their unfolding have been eliminated" (Robeyns 2011).

[16] With the term *class* we refer to the disparities between individuals and groups both in economic condition and in personal (gender, age, ethnicity etc.) and cultural (religion etc.) origin. Social stratification depends on the different methods of organising society that have succeeded each other throughout history, even overlapping one another: slavery, caste, status, class (Giddens 2001).

along paths that are traced by belonging to the family of origin, by the social context in which one becomes an adult and by the political and economic institutions of the country in which one lives (Oreopoulos 2003; Durlauf 2004). All these "belongings" make the paths that people find themselves on very different from each other: for some the width of the path is comfortable, for many the path is instead quite narrow.

The Sources of Inspiration for the Volume

The stilts on which the volume is built are three interpretative categories. The first is *capitalism*, defined by its two foundational elements: private property and decentralised market coordination. There would also be a third element, the public sector, but its role and relevance have been diminishing in recent decades on the scene of advanced economies. It is the result of the crusade launched by neoliberalism throughout the Western world against the supporting role that the State has always had in the economy. To complete the definition of capitalism, an element peculiar to itself must also be added, because it is not a constitutive characteristic, but derives from its history: the ability to be the mode of production that has distinguished itself for its recognised gift of knowing how to generate growth. During the Middle Ages, the social structure was very static: the substantial stagnation of economies consolidated the rigid organisation of society based on the hierarchical command of the powerful—from sovereigns to nobles, to religious authorities. The conflict between social groups smouldered under the heel of the sword, money and faith. In the most dynamic sectors of commerce, coercion replaced conflict with the obligation to participate (or submit) to corporations (Gurevič 1983). The slow emergence of the capitalist mode of production has been the midwife to the expansion of well-being that humanity has known in the last two centuries.

The socio-economic system of the West is "liberal capitalism" based on private property, the market and democratic institutions. In this system, the exercise of individual freedom is subordinate to respect for the law, a bulwark that opposes any attempt by the elite to abuse their power by distorting the functioning of democracy with the use of "majority dictatorship".[17] The importance of the law, as a means to keep latent social

[17] "The greatest danger for the American republics comes from the omnipotence of the majority" (Tocqueville 1995, p. 264).

conflict at bay, was well known to the "brigands", the bands of peasants who in France, a few days after the storming of the Bastille, assaulted the castles owned by the nobles to burn the acts containing the ancient feudal privileges, to which they rightly attributed the formal legality of the exploitation they suffered. However, legislation is always a step behind the guidance of the economy by businesses and finance. On closer inspection, the law can only set *ex post* limits to the autonomy of market forces. The law indeed represents for the economy a formal framework. The legal system is an institution without any prerogative to base on the basis of "impartiality" the relations between social classes. In simple terms, in assigning "to those who hold the resources the right to exclusive use and to the rents that will result from it, it allows capital to rule not by force, but according to the law" (Pistor 2021, p. 213).

The role of law in the capitalist system leads us to the second category, the *asymmetry of power* between individuals belonging to different social groups.[18] This conception of society is based on the belief that the strong concentration of wealth—or private property—generates in the capitalist system a tendency towards the centralisation of power. In other words, the *rule of law* is not enough to celebrate the marriage between capitalism and democracy. Law cannot contest the primacy of the socio-economic structure of the community; it is often used to sanction the asymmetry of power within society. The third category, closely connected to the first two, is the *social conflict*. In the cities of antiquity (Athens, Sparta, Rome), the identity and material condition of the poor classes were deeply marked by hierarchical command. Earnings and *status* depended on the fortunes—rising or falling—of the social aggregation (the tribes and the *gens*) to which the individual belonged (Siedentop 2016). With the recent, rapid, evolution towards individualism in society, social conflict seems to have entered a shadow cone. Nonetheless, the tension with the second category remains: the constitutive figure of social coexistence is the "inequality of power and authority that inevitably accompanies social organisations" (Dahrendorf 1963, p. 64).

It remains to explore the movement of the pawns on the chessboard. Or, how these three categories influence the dynamics of the social structure. What does social mobility consist of, beyond the intuitive meaning of the expression? This book tries to escape the trap in which even the most

[18] Social class is defined by the "awareness of each individual of being part of the common interests that bind him to his own social class" (Dahrendorf 1963, p. 17).

accurate analysis of social mobility risks being crushed. The traditional points of view are two, one the opposite of the other. On the one hand, individualism considers the social structure as a simple collateral consequence of individual action. On the other hand, holism considers the action of the subject in the world as a simple product of the social structure. To overcome this *impasse* epistemological it is not enough to push hard to keep the two extremes of the trap apart. It is necessary to find the thread of the skein. The methodological suggestion that is sought to develop here is this: we are individuals, distinct from each other, who once born grow in a new amniotic fluid that takes the name of society. The dynamics of the individual's life merges with that of the society, while the individual remains himself. This book brings many theoretical arguments, and many empirical proofs, in support of this conviction.

Let's go back to Table 1.1. The sense of that classification is much more difficult to grasp than it appears at first sight. The people who move along the income and *status* scale are distant from both the supermen splendidly described in the pages of Jack London's novels, and from the sulphurous Elon Musk, who in 2022 conquered the sceptre of the richest man in the world. Social mobility is a rather complex phenomenon, because it has to do with the whole of people, not just the individual. It indeed passes through the crossroads between the individual and society, which is rather busy.

The following chapters develop a theoretical scheme according to which it is the ideas that move the class interests at the origin of the widening recorded in inequalities. The setting of the book is in tune with the interpretation of the capitalist mode of production adopted by the economist Thomas Piketty: "Inequality is never economic or technological: it is ideological and political".

The book has several sources of inspiration. It shares with the political scientist Ralf Dahrendorf the belief that the presence of social conflict sets the goal of economic democracy in opposition to the liberal conception of the social contract: "What does 'free and equal' mean if one party needs to work to survive, while the other can select and choose, hire or fire?" (Dahrendorf 1989, p. 48); with the labour sociologist Alain Touraine (2005, p. 29), the analysis of stratification within society as "the result of class relations on social organisation"; with the sociologist of institutions T. H. Marshall (1950, p. 100) the persuasion that "having the right to" (*entitlement*)—a concept contiguous to that of "freedom of"—draws a dividing line between the competitive market, where the equivalence between labour productivity and wage prevails, and economic democracy, where instead the *entitlement* is "the universal right to a real income, not proportionate to the market value of the one who claims it"; finally, with the moral philosopher C. B. Macpherson (1985, p. 52) the idea "of economic democracy, which can be reasonably defined [...] as a type of society in which all people have an equal, effective, right to a fully human life".

In the following, to better characterise the foundation of the concept of "economic democracy" in the equal ability to participate in society, we will replace this expression with that of "solidaristic democracy".

The "canvas"

The canvas that this *pièce* stages is a dialogue on mobility—which often becomes persistence, or even decline—of individuals' income and *status* positions. At the centre of the stage will be the four "masks" of a person's life course, which I will list in order of appearance. The *talents* enclosed in the genetic heritage, which everyone receives at the moment of conception.[19] This is a very problematic actor: people belonging to groups with less power in society encounter many more difficulties than others in bringing out their own talents. Only *culture*—an educational path that helps *nature*—can ensure that young people—once they have become adults—are able to express them. It must indeed be taken into account first and foremost the *circumstances* of life in which everyone is catapulted at birth. Circumstances are very different: they depend on the country in which one is born, the family context and the social environment.[20] Together with "market imperfections", unequal circumstances translate into unequal access to *opportunities*.[21] Inequality of opportunity hinders

[19] The Treccani Encyclopedia defines talent as: "Ingenuity, predisposition, capacity and significant intellectual gifts [...] as natural and intended for particular activities".

[20] "The main institution that causes the reproduction of inequality is in fact the family, simply because everyone wants to provide their children with the best opportunities. However, families with more resources of all kinds succeed much more than those with few resources" (Ferreira 2023, p. 14).

[21] In a study conducted on data from the United States, Marrero and Rodríguez (2013) tried to separate work commitment attributable to the individual's responsibility from the "residual inequality", or the influence of the social context in determining class placement. The results suggest that income inequality and opportunity inequality "advantage" the income growth of the rich and "disadvantage" the income growth of the poor.

the acquisition by disadvantaged young people of the *skills* necessary to make talents flourish and realise their own life project.

Thomas Hobbes is credited with a definition of power that is very dense in its simplicity: "power simply is no more, but the excess of power of one above that of another" (*The Elements of Law, Natural and Politic*, Part 1, chap. 8, paras. 3 and 4). The definitions of power subsequently enunciated by political scientists, quite similar to each other,[22] all fit into the motivation formulated by Hobbes in chap. XI of the *Leviathan*: "a general inclination of all mankind, a perpetual and restless desire for power, which ceases only with death". From this premise descends a precise consequence. If it is true that in society coexist groups with opposing interests and with a different degree of power, it is social conflict—and not the harmonious action of "free and equal" individuals described by the theories of the "social contract"—the constitutive figure of society.[23] The same people meet from time to time in the market and in other areas of life. When things do not go well in the market sphere, they do not go well in society either. As the epigraph of the volume reminds us, when mobility is low, the loss of well-being affects both individuals and the community.

Social mobility is therefore a sort of litmus test of both individual and collective well-being. As in the incipit that started these pages, literature guides us. A particularly penetrating look at self-knowledge and one's life course, through the historical evolution of social groups, is that of the 2022 Nobel laureate for literature. Annie Ernaux has the rare gift of making the personal human story and the epochal scenario in which it is set inseparable. In *The Place* (1983), the family imprint perceived in childhood by the writer—the genetic one, the relationship with the father's food, and the cultural one, the small economies of the mother—evolves into the painful awareness of the material and cultural conditions of the

[22] "Dominance is a special case of authority [...], people's obedience to a command that has a specific content", "A has power over B to the extent that he can get B to do something he would not otherwise do" (Dahl 1957, pp. 202-3). "While power is essentially linked to the personality of individuals, authority is always associated with social positions and roles" (Dahrendorf 1963, p. 166). "Power should be understood as a structural characteristic, which pervades completely a relationship" (Elias 1978, p. 93). "Power reaches its highest effectiveness the less it is observable" (Lukes 1974, p. 20).

[23] David Hume (1739) believed that the concept of "social contract" was a mere "fiction". By definition, consent to the social contract must be voluntary. Anyone who disagreed should leave the community: but "can we seriously argue that a poor farmer or a craftsman have the free choice to leave their own country [...]?" (Hume 1985, p. 328).

social environment from which she comes. In *The Years* (2008), a polyphonic narrative texture makes the writer's *self* inseparable from the *we* of her own country. In discovering herself deeply involved in collective life, Ernaux experiences social mobility as the passage from the working class, the class of the dominated from which she comes, to the dominant one. But the shadow of her parents continues to cast itself on her life, makes her uncomfortable, constantly brings her back to her original dimension.

Ernaux, who has defined herself as an *ethnologist of herself*, testifies how the conquest of well-being and the growth of *status* generate an ambivalent feeling, situated on the ridge between the pleasure of individual success and the awareness of the collective dimension of one's own identity. Her writing is imbued with the existential figure of having lived her own social mobility as guilt. Every process of social ascent indeed represents an existential tear, which breaks the bonds of community belonging and tears interpersonal relationships. Moreover, the unhappiness that often associates with mobility is a feeling that is not only of the person who is involved, but is also found in the social sphere, when mobility is accompanied by a change that affects the community. The concept of social mobility must therefore be handled with care: the noun is firmly anchored to the individual, the adjective refers to the life of relationship.

The scenery of the *play* is now set. The performance begins. Here is a *vademecum* for reading of this book. In the first part, the theme of social mobility is illustrated in its various theoretical facets. The second part analyses the phenomenon from its slow emergence in history; presents the overall interpretive framework within which it must be placed; and describes the role that the market and the welfare state must play to counter the two problems of inequality and poverty. The third part discusses the two main issues at the origin of the current *impasse* of social mobility: the orientation of companies, in the introduction of technical progress, to profit more than to job creation; and the substantial abandonment by the ruling classes of the conception of education as a fundamental common good (or "merit good").[24] In an unequal society, tying the education of

[24] "Merit goods" (Musgrave 1959), not to be confused with "common goods", are produced by the public sector with the aim of satisfying important needs for the community (health, education, consumption necessary for the minimum vital etc.). According to the cultural values or social norms of some societies, in fact, these goods must be available to individuals regardless of their purchasing power in the market. The public budget has the task of ensuring production aimed at meeting needs. The reason is twofold: the particular value that society attributes to the merit good (the idea is that the benefit to society is greater

young people to the motive of profit, as is happening with the expansion of private education, risks colliding with the right of all to bring out their own talents. The conclusions underline how the crisis that social mobility is going through shows the urgency of a change of course in the "rules of the game" of the capitalist mode of production.

In order not to sacrifice rigour to completeness, it has been chosen to drastically limit the heterogeneity among the countries considered. The analysis will indeed concern the set of advanced nations, the OECD countries. It is however worth mentioning the fact that—according to a very representative database—social mobility, at a global level, turns out to be lower than that of countries whose average income is close to the average income of all the countries in the world. This empirical evidence contains a message of great relevance. Among the countries with income below the average level of the planet—whose population is therefore more projected towards the rise of well-being—there are the developing countries, in which a good part of the world's population resides. In these countries, in which income mobility is growing, intergenerational educational mobility is the lowest in the world: children have a very low probability of achieving a level of education higher than that of their parents. In the South of the world, the great difficulty of children to surpass in education their fathers, despite the educational level of these latter is usually very low, is a fact whose implications go beyond the borders of underdeveloped nations. It indeed draws attention to the fundamental role that—whatever the degree of development of a country—education plays. In all nations, even advanced ones, in which parents' education is scarce, their income, however much they participate in the growth of the country's GDP, is still too low to guarantee their children a suitable period of education. Everywhere in the world, income opportunities and education opportunities are strongly interconnected. Today, in the world, are in motion, fleeing from wars, persecutions and poverty, 80 million men and women. Many of them are children. The many walls that are being erected obstruct their mobility towards a more dignified life; they are the denial of the values of compassion and solidarity to which the Western civilisation claims to be inspired in the construction of well-being.

than the private benefit) and the possibility that the individual has "bounded rationality" and underestimates the importance of the merit good for his own well-being (not wearing a helmet on a motorcycle is for example a "short-sighted" behaviour) and others' (wearing a mask during a pandemic helps to contain the spread of the infection).

Bibliography

Acemoglu, D. & Autor, D. 2011 Skills, Tasks and Technologies: Implications for Employment and Earnings, *in Ashenfelter - Card 2011, pp. 1043–171.*

Arbatlı, C. E., Ashraf, Q. H., Galor, O., Klemp, M. 2020 *Diversity and Conflict*, in «Econometrica», LXXXVIII, 2, pp. 727–97.

Atkinson, A. B. 1997 Bringing Income Distribution in From the Cold, *in «Economic Journal», CVII, 441, pp. 297–321.*

Attanasi, G. & Nagel, R. 2008 A Survey of Psychological Games: Theoretical Findings and Experimental Evidence, *in Innocenti - Sbriglia 2008.*

Croci Angelini, E. & Farina, F. 2016 Integration without Convergence in the European Currency Area, *in Bosco - Guederzo 2016.*

Dahl, R. A. 1957 *The Concept of Power*, in «Behavioral Science», II, 3, pp. 201–15.

Dahrendorf, R. 1963 Soziale Klassen und Klassenkonflikt in der industriellen Gesellschaft, *Enke, Stuttgart 1957; (ed. am.* Class and Class Conflict in Industrial Society, *Stanford University Press, Stanford 1959).*

Dahrendorf, R. 1989 The Modern Social Conflict: An Essay on the Politics of Liberty, *Weidenfeld and Nicolson, London 1988.*

Deneulin, S. & Shahani, L. 2009 An Introduction to the Human Development and Capability Approach, Freedom and Agency, *Earthscan, London.*

De Ruggiero, G. 1925 Storia del liberalismo europeo, *Laterza, Bari.*

Durlauf, S. N. 2004 *Neighbourhood Effects*, in J. V. Henderson & J.-F. Thisse (a cura di), *Handbook of Urban and Regional Economics*, Elsevier Science, Amsterdam, IV, pp. 2173–242.

Elias, N. 1978 *What Is Sociology?*, Hutchinson & Co., London.

Esping-Andersen, G. 2015 *Welfare Regimes and Social Stratification*, in «Journal of European Social Policy», XXV, 1, pp. 124–34.

Farina, F. 2021 Lo Stato sociale. Storia, politica, economia, *Luiss University Press, Roma.*

Ferreira, F. H. G. 2023 *Is There a «New Consensus» on Inequality?*, Lse International Inequalities Institute, Working Paper n. 101.

Giddens, A. 2001 Sociology: Introductory Readings, *Polity Press, Cambridge.*

Gilens, M. & Page, B. J. 2014 Testing Theories of American Politics: Elites, Interest Groups, and Average Citizens, *in «Perspectives on Politics», 18 settembre, pp. 564–8.*

Gurevič, A. J. 1983 Le categorie della cultura medievale, *Einaudi, Torino.*

Hahn, F. 1980 *General Equilibrium Theory*, in «The Public Interest», Special Issue, *The Crisis in Economic Theory*, pp. 123–38.

Herzog, L. 2024 Citizen Knowledge, Markets, Experts, and the Infrastructure of Democracy, *Oxford University Press, Oxford.*

Hume, D. 1985 *Essays. Moral, Political, and Literary*, (ed) E. F. Miller, Liberty Fund, Indianapolis.

Kelly, C. & Snower, D. J. 2021 *Capitalism Recoupled*, in «Oxford Review of Economic Policy», XXXVII, 4, pp. 851–63.

Lukes, S. 1974 Power: A Radical View, *Macmillan, London.*

Marrero, G. A. & Rodríguez, J. G. 2013 *Inequality of Opportunity and Growth*, in «Journal of Development Economics», CIV, C, pp. 107–22.

Marshall, T. H. 1950 Citizenship and Social Class, and Other Essays, *Cambridge University Press, Cambridge.*

Morin, E. 2017 La sfida della complessità, *Le Lettere, Firenze.*

Musgrave, R. A. 1959 The Theory of Public Finance, *McGraw Hill, New York.*

Oecd 2019 Employment Outlook 2019: The Future of Work, *Paris.*

Oreopoulos, P. 2003 The Long Run Consequences of Growing up in a Poor Neighbourhood, *in «Quarterly Journal of Economics», CXVIII, 4, pp. 1533–75.*

Pistor, K. 2021 The Code of Capital: How the Law Creates Wealth and Inequality, *Princeton University Press, Princeton 2019.*

Robeyns, I. 2011 *The Capability Approach*, Stanford Encyclopedia of Philosophy, Stanford.

Roemer, J. E. & Trannoy, A. 2016 *Equality of Opportunity: Theory and Measurement*, in «Journal of Economic Literature», LIV, 4, pp. 1288–332.

Rustagi, D. 2022 *Historical Self Governance and Norms of Cooperation*, Working Paper, University of Nottingham, Nottingham.

Sen, A. K. 1985a *Goals, Commitment, and Identity*, in «Journal of Law, Economics, and Organization», I, 2, pp. 341–63.

Sen, A. K. 1985b Commodities and Capabilities, *North-Holland, Amsterdam.*

Sen, A. K. 1990 La libertà individuale come impegno sociale, *in Berlin - Sen 1990.*

Sen, A. K. 2009 *The Idea of Justice*, Allen Lane-Harvard University Press, Cambridge.

Siedentop, L. 2016 Inventing the Individual: The Origins of Western Liberalism, *Allen Lane, London 2014.*

Stiglitz, J. E. 2013 Selected Works of Joseph E. Stiglitz, *II*, Information and Capital Markets, *Oxford University Press, Oxford.*

Stiglitz, J. E. 2019 The End of Neoliberalism and the Rebirth of History, *Project Syndacate, 4 novembre.*

Tilly, C. 1992 Conflitto sociale, *in* Enciclopedia delle scienze sociali, *Treccani, Roma*, ad vocem.

Tocqueville, A. 1995 (1835–1840) La democrazia in America, *Rizzoli, Milano.*

Wolf, M. 2023a The Crisis of Democratic Capitalism, *Penguin Press, New York.*

Wolf, M. 2023b The Dangers of Magical Thinking on Health Policy, *in «Financial Times», 23 gennaio.*

World Economic Forum 2020 The Global Social Mobility Report 2020: Equality, Opportunity and a New Economic Imperative.

PART I

The Theoretical Framework

CHAPTER 2

Social Mobility in Political, Economic and Sociological Thought

The Social Class, Bridge Between Individual and Society

The events of history are produced by men and women whose actions are full of the theoretical elaboration sedimented in the culture of their peoples. Let's start, therefore, from the history of ideas.

Is there an "ideal bridge" capable of uniting society by reconciling the realisation of the individual with the tensions generated by personal interest? Immanuel Kant thought there was. He named this bridge "sociable unsociability".[1]

He trusted in man's ability to overcome the opposition between the tendency to aggregate to survive and prosper and the tendency to assert one's personality "overtaking" others in income and *status* social. The philosopher of Königsberg warned to take into account the fact that competition for social ascent—that which is called relative social mobility *relative* (see *infra*, chap. III, par. 5)—is inherent in a conflict that carries within it the germ of the disintegration of society. In Kant's Enlightenment vision, the natural propensity of the individual to excel should be tempered by reason, to be put at service of the "moral law that is in us".

[1] This expression is contained in the fourth thesis of the 1784 essay entitled *Idea for a universal history from a cosmopolitan point of view.*

F. Farina, *The Rise of Inequality and the Fall of Social Mobility*,
https://doi.org/10.1007/978-3-031-92843-7_2

Georg Wilhelm Friedrich Hegel and Karl Marx saw it differently. Starting the analysis of society by focusing on the individual seemed to them a way to start off on the wrong foot. There is the risk that the analysis, once anchored to the "vital spirits" of the subject, will be completely entangled in it. These two protagonists of the philosophical thought of the nineteenth century therefore centred their philosophical systems on the collective rather than the individual. Hegel posed as a barrier to the affirmation of the philosophy of history of liberal orientation, or that current of thought faithful to the dual primacy of reason and the individual, sanctioned by the Enlightenment thinkers and the thought system of Immanuel Kant. The philosopher from Jena believed that the condition of freedom was not rooted in the natural rights of the individual but was inscribed within his participation in the community. In the second part of the *Elements of the Philosophy of Right*, he juxtaposes *Moralität*, or the sphere of personal morality, with *Sittlichkeit*, social morality, which in the Greek world was the trait of "ethicality", and which was swept away by the advent of the Roman world and then of modernity.

It is a widely held opinion that Hegel's thought, in inserting the individual within the "manifold connection" (Hegel 1999, par. 116, p. 101) of institutions such as the family, civil society and the State, annihilates the freedom of the subject in an organicistic conception of society. However, it must be recognised that Hegel did not forget the individual. He observed that the individual finds in work both the source of his own identity and the recognition of his contribution to the well-being of the community. Unlike what functionalist sociology will do, which risks nullifying the one in the All,[2] he conceived the subject as a complete unity between personal identity on the one hand and civil society and the State on the other. Hegel, on the other hand, aligned himself with the cultural tradition of his own country, where the stability over time of social stratification has been elevated since the Middle Ages to a value that it is the responsibility of rulers to preserve. His thought indeed reflects the German *Weltanschauung*, as it had come to be formed over the many centuries

[2] According to the functional-structuralism of Luhmann (1973), the social structure has the function of reducing the complexity of the world. Society is interpreted in an organicist way, as composed of interconnected structures, each with its own function. The functionalist vision has been the subject of critique: "A class cannot be identified either with the source of income or with the function that an individual performs within the division of labour" (Giddens 1998, p. 80).

from the First Reich to his time: a unitary conception of politics and economics, aimed at seeking balance between the different classes in the life of society.

For quite different reasons, the concept of social mobility did not appeal to Karl Marx either. The economist and philosopher from Trier argued that Hegel's analysis of the social dimension of individual behaviour was flawed by legal formalism. It was his opinion that the result was to represent reality upside down. The subject of history is not the Idea that would find its moment of synthesis in the State—Marx objects in *For the Critique of Hegel's Philosophy of Right*—but man in his concrete existence in civil society. His criticism is without appeal. Contrary to what Hegel claimed, the State is not at all the apex of Ethicality, as it is based on the "religion of private property" (Marx 1943, p. 129). The failure to recognise the power structure on which capitalist society rests would prevent Hegel from understanding social mobility as a tool of class domination. Marx believes that capitalists use the dynamics of the social structure to disarticulate the compactness of the working class, undermining its internal solidarity through co-optation: "the more a ruling class is able to assimilate the most eminent men of the dominated classes, the more solid and dangerous is its domination" (Id. 1968, III, t. 2, p. 311). Therefore, the elites would promote social mobility only when it is necessary to prevent the explosion of the contradiction between the development of productive forces, which is driven by technical progress, and the social relations of production, centred on the conflict between capitalists and workers. In his materialistic conception of history, within the capitalist framework there is no room for any prospect of redemption for the proletariat. Marx was not interested in the convergence of the subordinate classes with those higher up in the social scale. The only social mobility in which the philosopher from Trier believed was the overthrow of the relations of production and property based on capital. He supported workers' struggles for wage increases and the reduction of inequality as an intermediate stage on the path to a classless society.

Understanding the complexity of the social structure is an endeavour that cannot do without a "Weltanschaung". Karl Marx built his own around the economic analysis of the subsumption of the working class to the owners of capital. The conflict between classes in capitalism is explained by the theory of surplus value: the wage worker is exploited because he receives a remuneration lower than the surplus he has helped to create (the excess of work delivered by the worker compared to the amount of work contained in the goods he buys with the wage he receives). Marx believed that the development of productive forces would have made the condition of exploitation of workers incompatible with the objective economic laws of capitalism, until the inevitable outcome in the proletarian revolution. In the emerging positivistic climate in which he lived, Marx thought that his conception of the economy could not do without receiving the chrism of scientific truth.[3] What has happened instead is that the development of productive forces has not come into conflict with the relations of production. On the contrary, the imbalance of power in favour of entrepreneurs has ended up reinforcing the stability of the relations of production, albeit at the cost of a split between the pursuit of profit and economic progress for the benefit of all society.

Like Marx, Max Weber conceives of capitalism as the system in which private property is prevalent and where the coordination between the choices of individuals is entrusted to the decentralised transactions of the market. From here on, their paths diverge. According to Marx, a social class is the relationship that social groups, such as capitalists and workers, have with tha ownership of the means of production: being capitalists-entrepreneurs or salaried workers. Weber (1905) instead affirmed the centrality in history of the ideological superstructure rather than the economic structure. In analysing social conflict, he clearly distanced himself from Marx's materialistic conception of history and from the idea of production as the place of exploitation.[4] He defined the concept of class not in relation to production and ownership of capital, but to the more general set of the many dimensions of life in which people are placed. The place of conflict, which for Marx is the company as an expression of private property, for Weber is the market. He believed that people's unequal chances depend

[3] The Marxian theory of exploitation consists of the excess of labour provided by the worker compared to the amount of labour contained in the goods he purchases with the salary he receives. To demonstrate the existence of exploitation in capitalist production, Marx developed the so-called transformation of values into prices. This mathematical method aimed to trace back the actual, but hidden, value that the exploitation of workers confers on goods, to the external reality of prices, visible in the market, which regulate the exchange of goods. However, his demonstration has been refuted.

[4] In tracing the emergence of capitalism to the affirmation of Protestant values, particularly the Calvinist spirit, he conceived the capitalist spirit in close harmony with religious transcendence. Based on the lexical equivalence between "profession" (*Beruf*) and "vocation" (*Beruf*), "the only way to live in a manner pleasing to God [lies] in the fulfilment of worldly duties, as they result from each person's position in life, which thus becomes his 'profession'".

on the different opportunities they find in the market. The concept of class, which in Marx is based on the distinction between owners and non-owners of capital, finds definition in Weber in the distinction between possessors and non-possessors. To the many divisions that run through society—from ethnicity, to gender, to age—are added the inequalities that mature in market relations, where the "privileged owning classes in a positive sense mainly constituted by rentiers [and the]" acquisitive classes "(entrepreneurs with an essentially positive privilege, and proletarians with an essentially negative privilege)" (Id. 1970, p. 300) operate.

In his opinion, a stable sharing of income, *status* and power gives rise to aggregation among people. A social class is formed "when a plurality of men have a specific causal component of their life chances in common, insofar as this component is simply represented by economic interests of possession and gain - in the conditions of the goods or labour market" (Id. 1974, p. 229). He is convinced that dominant groups tend to direct the economy and society towards the "closure" to their own advantage of opportunities for well-being. The "steel cage" of capitalism, however, proves fully capable of containing and metabolising social conflict. Weber's analysis of the social structure thus fits into an interpretative scheme tuned to the acceptance of the existing, far from the palingenetic twist of Marx's analysis. As Weber wrote in *Science as a Profession*, the "rationalisation" of existence achieved by capitalism invites man to accept his fate in a "manly" (*männlich*) way.[5]

The two key words, respectively coined by Marx and Weber to define the fracture that runs through society, are therefore exploitation in capitalist production and "closure" in the market. In both systems of thought, individuals who find themselves in similar conditions—of "advantage" or "disadvantage"—end up sharing the same worldview, assuming group or class behaviour.[6] For those with scarce economic resources, the obstacles to social ascent become difficult to overcome, so that mobility within

[5] Weber seems to believe that state power and its administrative apparatus are more the work of intellect than of the sword, because they have gradually formed based on the initiative and influence of princes, officials, public administrators. Once the work was completed, these figures managed to impose the authority of the State as the legitimate use of the monopoly of physical force.

[6] The term *class* was also adopted, in the last part of the last century, by liberal-democratic thought: "In general, the greater the degree of 'closure' of mobility opportunities - both within different generations and in the career of each individual - the easier it is to form identifiable classes as such" (Giddens 1975, p. 154).

social stratification is blocked. On closer inspection, therefore, if attention is focused not on the *causes* of value production but on its *consequences* within society, Marx and Weber are less distant than philosophical and political thought tends to present them.

The Asymmetry of Power in the Economy and Society

In the eyes of orthodox economists, the constantly evolving social structure resembles a "classic" cycling race: their attention is captured by the *bagarre* that breaks out after the start. Like sports journalists, they appear primarily interested in the events of the protagonists: first the group of champions, who break away and compete for the final victory; only much later to the second-tier riders, those who struggle and are inexorably dropped. It is therefore no surprise that in investigating social mobility the economist's balance tilts towards the individual who moves unfettered in the world.

Sociologists, on the other hand, are far from convinced that to deepen the dynamics of the socio-economic structure the unit of analysis to start from should be the individual, rather than society as a whole. Sociological theory, which began to develop in the second half of the nineteenth century in the cultural atmosphere of positivism, faced society like biology in front of a living organism. The sociologists of the time actually wanted to resemble entomologists, who study the internal organisation of colonies of "social insects", where the individual is completely integrated into the group to which he belongs. The methodological foundation of the discipline affirmed the idea that social action is more than the sum of the actions of individuals. The overall result is not equivalent to the simple sum of individual performances. One of the founders of the discipline, Émile Durkheim, argued that the impact of individuals on society "is found in their mixture". Like bronze—a metallic alloy whose "hardness" does not correspond to the characteristics of copper, tin and of the lead from which it is composed—the whole is of a different nature from the sum of the actions of individuals. The analysis of the French sociologist follows a fully organicistic perspective: social facts "are in a sense the moulds into which we are forced to pour our actions" (Durkheim 1963, p. 33).

Durkheim did not like the individualistic logic of the market. He emphasised instead the division of labour, as a factor at the origin of interdependence between individuals, in turn generating social cohesion.

However, he interpreted social cohesion in a conservative key: social stratification would be substantially impermeable to mobility, as "the antagonism of labour and capital" (Id. 2016, p. 340) would have turned into "organic solidarity" that holds society together. In his view, the social structure must remain stable over time. In *Le Socialisme*, the French sociologist argued that poverty "trains to accept docilely the collective discipline […]. What is required for social order to reign is that the majority of men are content with their lot" (Id. 1969, p. 309). The idea of sociality that each individual must interpret does not consist in the demands of their own group of belonging, but in the task of identifying their own place in the social division of labour.[7] From this perspective, social mobility appears almost as an evil to avoid.

During the twentieth century, faced with the "cultural imperialism" of the economy, self-proclaimed the "queen of the social sciences", sociology has been very committed to distancing itself from the "reductionism" of the neoclassical economic model. According to Mark Granovetter, the founder of the new economic sociology, "the idea that people are able to make all their own decisions and act in a fundamentally detached way from interactions in a network of social relations is […] an extreme form of methodological individualism". On the same vein was already the German sociologist Norbert Elias: "what is often held separate in thought as if it were two different substances or layers of man, his 'individuality' and his 'social determination' are nothing but two different functions of which men have at their disposal in their reciprocal relations: independently from each other they have no consistency […]. What we observe are people in their dynamic interdependence".

At the Origin of Social Mobility: Economy and Culture

In order not to remain suspended between individual and collective, the analysis of the dynamics of society needs precise interpretative coordinates. Epochs succeed each other, but the fundamental question is always the

[7] If such awareness is lacking, the dissonance between aspirations and one's own life reality plunges the individual into anomie. The most extreme form of the crisis that affects the man who feels excluded from society is suicide. This is also the title of one of Durkheim's most famous books.

same: as a driving force of social mobility, does the economic structure or the cultural superstructure matter more? Vilfredo Pareto and John H. Goldthorpe are two scholars who have the credentials to give a well-argued answer to this question. They indeed have a rare gift in the intellectual panorama: having practised with distinction both the study of sociology and the study of economics. This dual interest has led them to pay great attention to the phenomenon of social mobility. Comparing their ideas is particularly illuminating. Both see in the social hierarchy a very important key to understanding the internal functioning of the social structure of a market capitalist economy. At the same time, however, in reflecting on what is the force that moves the world, the primacy is assigned by Pareto to ideas, and by Goldthorpe to the economic structure.

Vilfredo Pareto (1919) developed an elegant analysis of the welfare of a community with a marked individualistic character: he indeed indicated as "optimal" equilibrium of the economic system the point where the welfare of any subject could be increased only if the welfare of another subject is decreased. This mathematical formulation of the efficiency point of general economic equilibrium incorporates a rather peculiar ethical conception of income distribution. Considering two subjects (A and B), a position of "optimal" equilibrium can be perfectly egalitarian (the division of the product into equal parts) or even not fair at all, even close to slavery. The ethical tolerability of the distribution is outside his field of vision: it is equally "optimal", in fact, the equilibrium corresponding to the distribution of a quantity equal to 100 in the measure 50/50, or in the measure of 99 that goes to subject A and of 1 that goes to subject B. As the economics texts recite, the Italian economist and sociologist expressed a judgement of "indifference" for the distributive outcome. The indifference for poverty probably finds explanation precisely in his particular conception of social mobility. Pareto thought of society as a natural entity based on the aristocracy of excellence. He conceived a high *status* social as the reflection of a particular ability in a certain field. He believed that the preservation of the hierarchy was functional to the fundamental role that elites play in society for the superior abilities of the people they are composed of. He found in the statistical evidence collected in some Italian areas a confirmation of his "rule" of a stable division of wealth between elites (80%) and mass (20%). And he drew the attention of the liberal ruling class to the need for social mobility not to modify the class stratification of society.

The shuffling within social stratification should be in his opinion, carefully evaluated. Vertical mobility—the climbing of the social ladder—could indeed represent a "powerful cause of disturbance of the balance" (Pareto 1964, p. 538). His idea was that instead the mobility of people from one job to another should be encouraged. Occupational mobility of the horizontal type would be a sign of the health of society, because it is the tool available to the elites to select and possibly co-opt into the governance of society the individuals of the lower classes most capable and prepared. It immediately follows that the function of governing the nation should not be the responsibility of the people but of the elite at the top of society. Pareto was a prominent exponent along with Gaetano Mosca (1896), of the elitist school of thought. According to Mosca, there is always an elite in power, but it is necessary that the masses are not aware of it. In 1922, Mussolini's march on Rome was greeted by Pareto with approval. In 1924, the assassination of Matteotti helped to soften Mosca's aversion to representative democracy.

From the standpoint of the primacy of the economic structure, Goldthorpe is following in the footsteps of Marx's historical materialism in believing that the material dimension of living takes precedence over the value system (Erikson et al. 1979; Goldthorpe 2007). The English sociologist has examined with great accuracy the impact of the evolution of the productive structure on social change. The centrality of the hierarchy is manifested in his empirical studies in two ways. First, through the type of occupation, from which usually descends a stable class placement within social stratification. The level of remuneration of work is transmitted to all the dimensions of the individual's well-being: "To the extent that individuals belonging to different social classes inhabit different economic worlds, regarding security, stability and future prospects, not only does class position compress their mobility [...], but this represents a constraint on their life choices, such as for example decisions related to education and work" (Goldthorpe and McKnight 2006, p. 130).

Second, in the context that has been defined here as "asymmetry of power". Mobility—rather than a tool of emancipation—can in his view turn into a support for the hierarchical organisation of society: "the meritocratic incorporation into the ruling classes or elites, initiates a process that, while on the one hand infuses efficiency and dynamism into the operation of economic and political institutions, on the other hand is essentially conservative in its implications for the overall class structure" (Goldthorpe et al. 1987, p. 10). In conclusion, the social hierarchy pleases

Pareto (perhaps because of the "excellence" he attributes to his own nature, as his writings reveal) and displeases Goldthorpe (perhaps because of the intolerance towards the "excellence" that is attributed to the "queen of social sciences", as his writings reveal).

The Liberal Thought of Friedrich Hayek and Milton Friedman

It has been said that the interpretation of society according to Karl Marx should be focused on its economic bases and according to Max Weber should be traced back to the evolution of cultural factors. Also the two opposing visions of social mobility of Pareto and Goldthorpe refer to this fundamental watershed. As we will see now, during the twentieth century the liberal thought has conquered the centre of the stage because it has found the way to express an effective synthesis between the two methodological approaches. The theoretical elaborations, autonomous but converging, of two among its "champions"—Friedrich Hayek and Milton Friedman, respectively Nobel laureates for economics in 1974 and 1976—are a pillar of the interpretative model of the socio-economic dynamics of capitalism that today is called neoliberalism.

Convinced champions of the market, they were inspirers and members of the Mont Pelerin Society, founded in 1947 to counter the growing political influence of Bolshevism in Europe and support the free market against the invasiveness of the State in the public and private sphere. Hayek has stated: "attempts to" correct "the results of the market in the direction of" social justice "have probably produced more injustice in the form of new privileges, obstacles to mobility and frustration of efforts, than they have contributed to alleviate the lot of the poor" (Hayek 1989, pp. 349–50). A similar thesis is supported by Friedman: "social immobility", the persistence of young people at the same income level as their parents, does not originate in the economy, but rather in politics that blocks social mobility: "In non-capitalist societies [...] inequality tends to be permanent, while capitalism eradicates the *status* and introduces social mobility" (Friedman 1967, p. 141). Friedman meant to say that the State offers legislative protection—through the regulation of markets—to rentier positions that shield subjects from the risk of putting themselves to the test, particularly in the labour market. As will be explored further on, Friedman also directed a criticism, similar to that of Hayek, to the welfare state: it would put the market in the impossibility of maximising social welfare, as it would put the worker in the position of assuming the *status* of being assisted. The works of Hayek and Friedman are a clear example of the tendency of liberal thought to conceive the freedom of the individual by negation with respect to the State and its role in realising welfare. Once the State is removed, the freedom of individuals will unfold without encountering limits.

Based on these common premises, social mobility is framed differently by the two liberal thinkers.

The Austrian economist applied to the order of the market the same logical process he followed in the interpretation of the order of the mind as the result of the connection between sensory perceptions (Hayek 1990). The liberal order would rest on the efficient "decentralised" coordination operated by the market of the actions of the *homo oeconomicus*. The aggregate of individuals, in using prices as signals for economic choices in a mutually independent way, reaches efficient equilibrium. By becoming mutually aware of each other's choices, subjects acquire that "diffuse knowledge" that allows them to modify their own plans, in order to ensure the "optimality" of the economic system. By virtue of the centrality of prices as "signals" that inform economic agents about excesses, or shortages, of demand and supply, markets would exercise a valuable and continuous action of adjustment of individual choices (Id. 2002). In extolling the virtue of prices as vehicles of information, Hayek is undoubtedly the chorus of the market, in which "we all benefit from knowledge we do not possess" and where the maximisation of individual well-being is achieved through "a spontaneous order, [which is] a product of the action of agents but not of their design" (Id. 1989, p. 15). The Austrian economist did not agree with Adam Smith at all.

The "invisible hand", evoked in the *Wealth of Nations* as the guide that leads subjects to the "optimal" equilibrium of the system, is in his view a completely redundant and certainly misleading metaphor. In Adam Smith's teleological vision, social welfare is the goal to be maximised to which subjects tend with their decentralised choices in the market. Hayek, on the other hand, considered the idea that the "optimal" result of collective well-being is generated by the behaviours adopted by individuals in pursuit of their own ends to be incongruous. Adam Smith's conception of the market would contain a "Trojan horse": the idea of superimposing a collective objective on individual objectives would effectively open the doors to state manipulation of the functioning of the market. In short, it would be the spontaneous order of the market that makes the individual free, rather than the individual determining efficient coordination in the free market.

The market naturally occupies a central place in Hayek's conception of individual freedom precisely because it allows them to become aware of the value of goods on the basis of supply and demand. However, "the argument in favour of competition does not rest on the condition that it is perfect" (Id. 1948, p. 104). Competition should be understood as the most effective mechanism—whatever the form of market, perfect or imperfect competition—capable of producing the continuous discovery and continuous use of knowledge. However, it is precisely this characteristic of knowledge, being fragmented among a huge number of subjects, that prevents the gain—as a reward for the "merit" of the worker—from being considered as a source of legitimisation of the market. In *The Constitution of Liberty* (1960) he warned against equating a large gain with great merit: "merit" cannot express the value of the "labour" good because it depends on the state of technology and the contingencies of demand and supply.

Hayek also refrained from asserting that in the capitalist system the distribution of income is "fair". Prices are primarily an expression of the virtues of the functioning of the market, rather than of the virtues of the individual. According to the liberal economist and philosopher, ethics should not find a place in economic reasoning. The fundamental problem would be the impossibility of ensuring that everyone has "an equal starting point and the same *chances*" (Id. 2011, p. 92). Only an authoritarian state organisation could achieve equality of opportunity. Public intervention would, however, inevitably lead to socialist economic planning, and therefore to the suppression of freedom. This led him to affirm the superiority of a state organisation that does not go beyond the "minimal state". As the title of one of his famous books states, the state is *The Road to Serfdom*: "the only alternative to submission to the impersonal and seemingly irrational forces of the market is submission to the power of other men, equally uncontrollable and therefore arbitrary" (Id. 1995, p. 263). However, this did not prevent Hayek from justifying the coup d'etat carried out in Chile in 1973 by General Pinochet, on the grounds of the need to "defend private property".

The palm of champion of the individual undoubtedly goes to Milton Friedman. He defended the concept of social welfare, as he interpreted it, unlike Hayek, as the expression of the ability of individuals to intentionally use the free market in order to maximise their own gain. In line with this vision, he associated the concept of gain with the concept of individual merit, before even the coordinating role played by the market. The 1976 Nobel laureate therefore attributed to the market an ancillary function, as a place where economic freedom is expressed, primarily that of the entrepreneur who takes on the risk of the enterprise. Having to remunerate the capital owned by shareholders, the company cannot in any way deviate from profit maximisation and serve what Friedman generically defined as "social objectives". For him, the market economy was the best, and also the only, tool for promoting social mobility. The market not only allows efficiency in production, but is able to guarantee anyone the opportunity to become rich, provided they are willing to take risks (Friedman and Savage 1948). The liberal imprint of his thought lies precisely in this conception of social mobility. The market would be configured as a sort of gigantic "lottery for success": the greater the entrepreneur's risk-taking attitude and the worker's investment in their own human capital, the greater the reward to which both are entitled.

One of the most original features of his thought is the relationship he establishes between social mobility and income inequality. It is true, Friedman argues, that by evaluating a person's income, relative to the income of other people in a certain year, one can perceive even very large inequality. And it is precisely this perception that puts the social phenomenon of inequality in a bad light, making it seem morally questionable. In his view, however, income inequality represents a false problem. The Gini index of interpersonal income inequality would not at all be the indicator that allows capitalism to be evaluated on an ethical level. Friedman's idea can be illustrated with this simple example: from one generation to the next, it could happen that the families that are initially the poorest (P) replace the richest (R) in the top positions of society. Between time t = 0 and time t = 1 (the succession of one generation to another), the interpersonal distribution of income does not change. With income set at 100, in the transition from $P_{t=0}$: 10; $R_{t=0} = 90$ to $P_{t=1}$: 90; $R_{t=1} = 10$, nothing changes from an aggregate perspective. There is only a substitution of people in the income scale: in the positions previously occupied by the old subjects, new poor subjects and new rich subjects will emerge. The Gini index does not change. The example highlights the virtue of social mobility in enhancing the individual's freedom of initiative in aspiring to achieve success. In the transition from one generation to another, inequality plays no role. The Gini index is in fact calculated on the *aggregate of individuals* at each unit of time. On the contrary, the inequality that should be focused on is that relating to the economic outcome of *each individual's* working career in the long term.

One could object that income inequality between people is the most socially relevant phenomenon in every society and therefore represents a real problem. However, Friedman does not bother to delve into the links between income distribution, social mobility and economic growth. As is typical of the liberal tradition of thought, the individual is primarily important; society, perhaps, comes after. And the pleasure, purely intellectual, of the theoretical excellence of one's own effort of elaboration counts. Friedman was firmly convinced of the robustness of his interpretive perspective on income inequality. If the protagonist is always and only the single individual, what is important to evaluate is not the *inter-personal* income inequality, but the *intra-personal* one, that is, measured for each subject by the distance between his initial income (the first salary) and the final one (the last before retirement). What Friedman wants to emphasise is that the Gini index of inequality—a value referring to the distribution of income between an *aggregate* of subjects—should be preferred to the measurement of the Gini index referring to the evolution over time of the economic result of the single subject—which represents an indicator readable only with the lenses of methodological individualism.

"Consider two societies that have the same distribution of annual income. In one there is a considerable degree of mobility and change, so that the position of individual families in the income scale varies considerably from one year to the next. In the other there is instead a great rigidity, so that each family remains in the same position for many years. Undoubtedly, the second of the two societies is the one that presents a greater degree of inequality. The first kind of inequality is a symptom of dynamic change, of social mobility, of levelling of opportunities; the second is a symptom of a static society" (Friedman 1967, pp. 229–30). He therefore invited to compare over time the dispersion of earnings within the personal life path of each subject. On careful examination, in his opinion, the *intra-personal* income flows most often present a present value (the term that in financial economics designates the value regardless of when the income was received)[8] very similar between people.[9] If, on the other hand, the present values of the flows *intra-personal* income of two people were different, his judgement is clear: the subject whose present value of income is higher is the one who has better faced the risk of investment in training and participation in the labour market. In other words, those who commit the most are also those whose income position progresses faster over time.

Friedman's reasoning isolates the individual dimension of social mobility, stripping any relevance from the dimension of society. The way in which individual earnings are distributed over time at an *interpersonal* level would be solely attributable to a personal choice, it would have nothing to do with the ethics of capitalism. His vision of equality is rooted in the individual incentive for social ascent. This aspiration will indeed push subjects with a lower initial income to commit to achieving a greater progression of their own earnings; until achieving, over time, convergence towards higher incomes. According to Friedman, a strong reshuffling of income positions in a certain period thus gives us the image of a dynamic society, in which social mobility is the purest expression of individual freedom.

The natural scope of the individual's commitment to the ascent towards success is that of a competitive market, free from the burden represented by both family dynasties accustomed to exploiting positions of rent, and excessive subsidies connected to public intervention. So here we are back to the point from which we started: it is not the market that makes individuals unequal to each other, but the intervention of the State. In attributing social ascent to the trend over time of the inequality *intra-personal* of income—or to the ability to climb positions in the ranking, to social mobility *relative*—the liberal economist points the finger against the "static society". The immobility of subjects in their respective places of the

[8] In financial mathematics, present value refers to the anticipated availability at the current date of the value of a capital that will be due at a future time.

[9] As we will see later, analyses of "economic vulnerability" however refute the idea that the functioning of the market guarantees a rising path of income convergence in the long term towards higher income levels. The impact of cyclical fluctuations on individual incomes—due to the diversity between people's "circumstances" and market imperfections—are usually of different magnitude for different subjects, so their incomes diverge from the equal present value they show at the beginning of the life path. Although it is likely that a severe crisis will negatively affect the "individual income growth" of all members of the community, the impact is much greater for the "disadvantaged".

income order signals that it is precisely the static society generated by public intervention, "in every plausible sense, to be the most unequal society" (ibid., p. 141). In short, Friedman says: you earn what you deserve.

The liberal economist strongly opposed any normative approach to inequality. As we have seen, he rejected the idea that even very wide income gaps can be considered a "collective evil". Combating inequality with public policies would mean fighting the disease with the virus that spreads it. Ultimately, Friedman conceived inequality as an "individual evil", which is however possible to overcome. A condition of "disadvantage" indeed harbours a positive value: it would serve as a necessary stimulus for a young person to commit and climb the rungs of the social ladder. In reinterpreting inequality as a purely individual issue, the libertarian Friedman cuts out from the analysis characteristic traits of every advanced society, such as the role that in social ascent is played by inequalities of opportunity, wealth and income. His conception reveals a misunderstanding inherent in his vision of social mobility. He establishes an infallible causal link—which in recent decades has proven fallacious—between the free functioning of the market and the success of the aspiration to a higher level of well-being.

Despite following different methodologies, Hayek and Friedman were critical about the traditional consideration of the concept of income inequality. When the functioning of the markets is perfect, the issue of inequality of circumstances and opportunities—or being a young person formed in a rich and educated family or a poor and uneducated one, and the social environment in which he grew up—being out of the subject's control, should not be taken into consideration. In the purest liberal vision, the idea is that the space of freedom is inscribed within the boundaries of civil rights and political rights. It is not recognised that outside of these boundaries there is social conflict, which has always characterised the relations between individuals.

In the Introduction, in the list of actors that appear on the scene of this book a leading actor is not mentioned: merit. It was not an oversight. We have indeed just focused on two economists who have precisely linked social mobility directly to merit. It was a choice due to the overexposure of this concept, which has long been catapulted to the honours of the media circuit. Merit has been enlisted by neoliberal thinkers as a key interpretative concept of social mobility. The constant reference to merit serves to give strength to a radically individualistic interpretation of the link between market and social ascent. This volume tries to approach the concept in a somewhat more thoughtful way than a public discourse sometimes pervaded by an unconditional adherence to merit as a concept above all suspicion.

Bibliography

Durkheim, E. 1963 (1895) Le regole del metodo sociologico. Sociologia e filosofia, *Edizioni di Comunità, Milano.*

Durkheim, E. 1969 (1928) Le Socialisme. Sa définition. Ses débuts. La doctrine saint-simonienne, *Les Retz, Paris.*

Durkheim, É. 2016 *Du la division du travail social*, Presses Universitaires de France, Paris 1893.

Erikson, R., Goldthorpe, J. H, Portocarero, L. 1979 Intergenerational Class Mobility in Three Western European Societies: England, France and Sweden, *in «British Journal of Sociology», XXX, 4, pp. 415–41.*

Friedman, M. 1967 *Efficienza economica e libertà*, Vallecchi, Firenze (ed. or. *Capitalism and Freedom*, Chicago University Press, Chicago 1962).

Friedman, M. & Savage, L. J. 1948 *The Utility Analysis of Choices Involving Risk*, in «Journal of Political Economy», LVI, 4, pp. 279–304.

Giddens, A. 1975 The Class Structure of the Advanced Societies, *Barnes & Noble, New York 1973.*

Giddens, A. 1998 The Third Way: The Renewal of Social Democracy, *Polity Press, Cambridge.*

Goldthorpe, J. H. 2007 On Sociology: Volume Two: Illustration and Retrospect, *Stanford University Press, Stanford.*

Goldthorpe, J. H. & McKnight, A. 2006 The Economic Basis of Social Class, *in Morgan, Grusky, Fields 2006.*

Goldthorpe J. H., Llewellin, C., Payne, C. 1987 Social Mobility and Class Structure in Modern Britain, *Clarendon Press, Oxford.*

Hayek, F. A. 1948 *Individualism and Economic Order*, Chicago University Press, Chicago.

Hayek, F. A. 1989 Law, Legislation and Liberty: A New Statement of the Liberal Principles of Justice and Political Economy, *University of Chicago Press, Chicago 1973.*

Hayek, F. A. 1990 The Sensory Order: An inquiry into the Foundations of Theoretical Psychology, *Routledge and Kegan Paul, London 1952.*

Hayek, F. A. 1995 *The Road to Serfdom*, Routledge, London 1944.

Hayek, F. A. 2002 (1968) *Competition as a Discovery Procedure*, in «The Quarterly Journal of Austrian Economics», V, 3, pp. 9–23.

Hayek, F. A. 2011 *The Constitution of Liberty*, Routledge & Kegan Paul, London 1960.

Hegel, G. W. F. 1999 Lineamenti di filosofia del diritto, *Laterza, Bari-Roma.*
Luhmann, N. 1973 Theorie der Gesellschaft oder Sozialtechnologie, *1971.*
Marx, K. 1968 *Il capitale*, I e III, Editori Riuniti, Roma (ed. or. 1867).
Marx, K. (1943), Zur Kritik der Hegelschen Rechtsphilosophie.
Mosca, G. 1896 Elementi di scienza politica, *Fratelli Bocca, Torino.*
Pareto, V. 1919 *Manuale di economia politica*, Società Editrice Libraria, Milano.
Pareto, V. 1964 *Trattato di sociologia generale*, Edizioni di Comunità, Milano (ed. or. Barbera, Firenze 1916).
Weber, M. 1970 Die Protestantische Ethik und der Geist des Kapitalismus, *1905.*
Weber, M. 1974 *Wirtschaft und Gesellschaft*, Mohr, Tübingen 1922.

CHAPTER 3

Meritocracy

Merit and the "Work Ethic"

Merere in Latin means "to distribute the reward". Merit comes from *meris*, "portion". We are therefore accustomed to thinking that the remuneration received reflects the merit acquired by a subject based on his level of skills (*skills*) and the effort expended at work. Merit is also attributed to those who give their lives for their country and are rewarded with the "medal of merit". Those who have particularly distinguished themselves in their field of activity receive the cross of the order of merit of the Republic. The word *merit* is therefore used when one wants to highlight an exceptional performance. Conversely, one has "demerited" when the performance was mediocre, less than expected. To give the concept greater consistency, it is then essential to do a bit of exegesis.

The United States has been given the nickname of *land of opportunities* because there would prevail—in the words of Tocqueville—the "equality of conditions" among people. In the nation American, which is "immune from birth" from the medieval hierarchical structure, individual initiative is not opposed and everyone can seize the opportunities present in the market. This judgement calls into question the historical genesis of wealth inequality. While for Europeans the concentration of wealth in the assets of the wealthier classes reflects, more than a greater propensity to invest and work, the persistent influence of the hierarchical division of feudal society, the United States is the country where the association of merit

F. Farina, *The Rise of Inequality and the Fall of Social Mobility*,
https://doi.org/10.1007/978-3-031-92843-7_3

with commitment to work constitutes a sort of conditioned reflex. Most Americans seem to believe that wealth has been accumulated by family dynasties by virtue of their own work commitment (Alesina and Glaeser 2004).[1]

The Puritan ethic has acted as a midwife to the people of the United States. In the perception of much of the population, the relationship between the two factors by which one judges one's life performance—merit (M) and luck (F)—has a rather high value. In American culture, the "belief" that "luck" counts little is deeply rooted.

Let's let the statistical data speak. Surveys reveal that a very high percentage of respondents believe that the poor do not deserve state support. If you are poor, you are probably lazy.[2] From this moral judgement stems the federal government's choice to support the poor by giving not monetary transfers but "food stamps", thus inflicting on those who receive them the stigma of "living on assistance". It is therefore the same government, whichever party is in power, that feeds the belief that "those who can't make it" deserve social protection that only saves them from extreme poverty. The negative judgement on the welfare state probably stems from the emotional repulsion of finding oneself in the condition of being "assisted". This outweighs any rational evaluation of the causes of socio-economic deprivation. The "food stamp" is the typical welfare tool expressing the religious roots of American culture. It aims to arouse a feeling of shame in those who receive the *stamps*. In the collective imagination of Americans, the association of the "food stamp" with the slogan *there is*

[1] Trust in the virtues of the market as a place of incentive to commitment and as a lever of social mobility does not get scratched beyond the Atlantic even in the darkest moments. The good reputation of the market has remained unchanged in public opinion even after the financial crisis of 2008. The courts of justice and the White House have avoided sanctioning the heads of banks and strengthening the regulation of the sector. The financial restructuring that followed the crisis allowed the country's companies to stay on the frontier of technology (Dallinger 2010).

[2] The findings of the World Value Survey indicated years ago that 70% of Americans—against 40% of Europeans—believe that the poor should work harder; similar percentages, in reverse order, were recorded regarding "luck" as a source of success in life more important than merit. Conversely, 60% of Europeans, against only 30% of Americans, would seem to believe that luck is the primary cause of success in life; 54% that the poor is not to blame for his condition and only 24% that he is lazy, against, respectively, the 29% and 60% of Americans.

no such thing as a free lunch coined by Milton Friedman, the idea of the "free lunch" as a disvalue.[3]

The principle of "individual responsibility" does not only apply to being poor; it is also encapsulated in the moral evaluation given to the concept of inequality. According to empirical research, if you believe that earnings are essentially attributable to "merit", understood as commitment to work, inequality is "justified"; if you think instead that the dominant factor is good luck, "fortune", inequality is "unjustified" (Alesina and Angeletos 2005). Giving Americans the near certainty that low income and poverty are the consequence not of "circumstances" but of a lack of commitment is the "work ethic", from which "merit" derives. This belief is reflected in social norms and economic legislation: the number of working days per year of an employee, the number of workers in the population (labour market participation rate) and even the retirement age are at higher levels than in European countries (Prescott 2004; Kuhn and Lozano 2006). Between 1980 and 2010, those recording the greatest increase in hours worked per week in the United States were the wealthy workers (*top incomes*) (Markovits 2019). A recent comparative check of experimental economics documents a robust negative correlation between self-confidence and "preference for redistribution" (Grimalda et al. 2022). The more you believe in individualism, the less you need public support, the less you appreciate it. The prevailing opinion in the population is therefore that inequality is "justified" because a low income can only be attributed to your "demerit". The idea that success is identified with merit sets the line of demarcation beyond which there is nothing but individual

[3] Despite the fact that income inequality in the country has greatly increased over the last 40 years, the *surveys* show that the demand for Welfare tends even to decrease. From the findings of a questionnaire recently administered to a very large number of respondents, it appears that the unfavourable opinion to the welfare state has increased precisely in layers of population with greater economic "fragility", such as the elderly and African-Americans (Ashok et al. 2015). It is interesting to note that the only explanatory variables of the preference of the elderly for redistribution that in the econometric analysis turn out to be significant are the degree of education (probable proxy of the income level) and the fear of a decrease in funds for healthcare. Regarding African-Americans, the decline in support for redistributive policies could depend on the need for homologation with the Wasps (*white, anglo-saxon, protestant*) and from corresponding decline in the desire to belong to their own area cultural. On the other hand, 45% of the fall of the "preference for the redistribution" seems to be explainable with the increase in the last decades of the income level of this social group.

responsibility. The *responsibility cut* makes the American citizen feel like the only architect of their own economic result (Roemer and Trannoy 2016).

The two major political parties are both very careful not to question the centrality of the "work ethic" in their electoral programmes. This is why the majority of voters vote against a broad welfare state and why government policies are marked by a strong tolerance for inequality. Europeans, on the other hand, declare in *surveys* that they believe the *merit/luck* ratio is low; they therefore tend to judge the presence of high-income inequality in the economic system as "unjustified". Even in Europe, beliefs tend to self-fulfil in the vote: Europeans express in elections a preference for a much higher level of income redistribution than overseas.

Inducing low-income voters to vote for a low taxation is the expectation that their offspring, if all resources are channelled into private investment, will benefit from a higher number of jobs and a greater reshuffling at various income levels within social stratification (Hassler et al. 2007). This was explained by the theoretical model based on the hypothesis of "expected social mobility" (Poum, *prospect of upward mobility*) (Benabou and Ok 2001). According to this hypothesis, the voter who has an income lower than the per capita income of his country at time t, but is convinced that GDP growth will bring him (and his family) earnings above the average value at time t + 1 (the threshold above which it is not convenient to vote in favour of Welfare), rationally chooses to vote against income redistribution. In fact, if he voted today in favour of the welfare state (see Box 6.1), he would suffer a loss tomorrow: the taxes he would pay would be higher than the Welfare transfers he would be entitled to. The reason for the optimistic expectation about his future income is trust in the market: "less state and more market" would be the reasoning that would lead the majority of voters to trust in a prosperous economic condition in the near future, so as not to have to be interested in Welfare support. The strong adherence to this belief in the population is in reflective equilibrium with the design of the economic system, which in the United States is based on low taxation (and therefore also few Welfare benefits) and on the central role of the free market. The impact of cultural and economic factors on the conception of social mobility is immediate. As will be explored in Chap. 4, *absolute* mobility means more income for everyone, *relative* mobility means that some incomes rise and others lose positions. Confidence in the growth of the country's GDP (the origin in the free market of absolute mobility) is combined with individual commitment (the origin in the commitment to work of the expectation of social climbing, or of one's relative mobility).

The judgement of Americans on redistributive policies and social mobility seems, however, to be the result of a perception that is far from the reality of the country. From the interviews of the *survey* it appears that the more ideologically opposed one is to public income redistribution policies, the more one believes that the opportunities to ascend to higher income positions are high. In the perception of Americans, the probability that a child born in the quintile[4] of the poor will reach the income level of the middle class (the third quintile of the distribution) as an adult is 24.1% according to Republican voters and 19.3% according to Democratic voters: in reality, it is 18.7% (Alesina et al. 2020). The *survey* also tells of the distrust of Americans for those who are strangers to their *demos*: voters overestimate the number of immigrants (36%, against an actual figure of 13.5%, including irregulars). The Welfare benefits that immigrants—in the opinion of Republican voters—would receive are proportionally double compared to the estimate of Democratic voters. The former also believe that 25.2% of immigrants are Muslim, compared to 20.7% in the estimate of Democratic voters. The actual figure is much lower: 10%.

The opinions expressed in the interviews on which surveys are built in the United States coincide very little with objective data also regarding social mobility. The decline that has occurred in recent decades is confirmed by many, rigorous, econometric analyses (Jäntti et al. 2007; Chetty et al. 2017, 2018). Alongside the fall in social mobility, the vote for the Democratic Party expressed by the middle classes has also fallen. A possible explanation refers to the role that ideology has in political preference. The unconditional favour enjoyed by the market would also be explained by the need—expressed by the middle class at the polls—not to antagonise the rich by voting for more taxes and more Welfare and to contain at the same time the pressure of low-income classes eager to rise with the help of the State in the social ladder (Acemoglu et al. 2018).

The neoliberal cultural climate has further shifted the pendulum in favour of the market and a small-sized state, the "minimal state". This has favoured a process of significant lowering of the progressivity of tax rates. Tax pressure has been reduced in recent decades to the benefit of the rich. Estimates show that the highest rate of profit taxation has fallen from

[4] A quintile groups a fifth of the subjects present in succession, for example, in the distribution of income.

about 50% in the middle of the last century to 35% in 1994, to 21% in 2018, and that billionaires have even ended up paying less taxes than the middle class in 2018. All this, "without any correlation being found in the last hundred years between capital taxes and capital accumulation" (Saez and Zucman 2019, p. 39).[5] The hypothesis that the annual number of working hours, much higher than in European countries, is also the flip side of their low "preference for redistribution", is completely alien to the way Americans think, the other side of the absence of a true and proper welfare state. For those, like the Americans, who must save and accumulate wealth to self-finance their health, education and pension expenses in old age, working a lot is often a necessity (Gylfason 2016). Ultimately, once the idea of the market as a regulatory mechanism of society is embraced, the "work ethic" is combined not only with work commitment but also with the need to balance the family budget.

Earning Is Deserving?

Through what mental process do we come to associate earnings with merit? To measure merit, economic theory uses the criterion of "individual equity". In the equilibrium position of the standard model, the worker's wage is equal to his productive contribution. The wage can therefore only represent his "just reward". Merit has also been linked to the "character traits that enhance the productivity" of the worker (Jencks and Tach 2006). The concept thus becomes a kind of predisposition of the rational individual to conform his behaviour to the "theory of incentives" developed by orthodox economic thought: the earnings that are expected must be matched by the corresponding work effort. Under the stimulus for the worker to be productive–his earnings—the economic system achieves efficiency with the profit by the company. In the wake of this "rewarding" conception, there is a tendency to give to the *merere* resulting from commitment the "exclusivity" of the explanation of productive efficiency. It is legitimate to dissent from this idea. That work commitment is linked to "deserving" earnings is beyond question. The dissent does not derive, as

[5] The federal marginal tax on income, which between 1936 and 1980 exceeded 70%, in 2018 is almost halved (37%). The average taxation of the 400 richest Americans, which in 1960 was close to 60% of income, is today just above 20%, a percentage much lower than that which weighs on the poorest 50% of the population. Likewise, the taxation of inherited real estate—due to deductions and exemptions, and the weaker *enforcement* compared to the laws relating to income taxation—today gives a meagre revenue.

has been argued (Santambrogio 2021), from a (presumed) tendency to propagate social models contrary to work incentives, with the aim of devaluing the concept of merit.[6] The question we are asking is not whether merit, understood as a reason for the reward of a *recognisable work contribution*, has value. It certainly does.[7]

Merit is undoubtedly a noble concept. The problem lies elsewhere. In focusing attention on this concept, there is a tendency to disregard everything that precedes work performance. How much of the economic result, of the earnings, is attributable to "merit", and how much instead to who generated you and where you were born, i.e. to the "lottery of life"? We all usually applaud those who have acquired great merits, for example researchers engaged in the fight against still incurable diseases. However, we often tend to forget that inequality of means and opportunities makes people unequal in their *ability* to make their talents flourish. A valuable economist, who has been very committed to the economic analysis of *fairness*, has argued: "if two people have put in the same work effort they must receive the same income, regardless of any difference in circumstances. [To deviate from this principle] because individuals should not be considered responsible only for what is under their control [...] leads the theories of justice into a metaphysical dead end" (Fleurbaey 2008, p. 247). It may well be metaphysical. For many, however, the problem of providing for their bread remains.

The political philosopher John Rawls has affirmed the primacy of "what is right" over "what is good": in other words, moral judgement should be directed *in primis* at the fairness of the "procedure", the way in which a goal is achieved (he indeed fought in all his works against the idea that the goal of a community is the maximisation of utility; we will see this later). On the opposite side, as early as 1874, the English philosopher Henry Sidgwick in his *The Methods of Ethics*, stated that "right" and "good"

[6] If this were the case, the first ones to be accused of inconsistency are the supporters of the free market based on incentives, who too often forget to punish demerit. For example, after the disastrous financial crisis of 2008 the orthodoxy of the rule to expel from the market who does not deserve because it is not efficient, forcing to bankruptcy the credit institutions on the brink of bankruptcy. As is known, the idea prevailed that first and foremost the political interest of protecting the operation of interbank transactions and saving the financial system should be put.

[7] The analysis of data relating to 11000 companies from 34 countries has shown that "countries where managers are recruited through competition have higher growth rates than countries that favour personal networks" (Wooldridge 2021, p. 368).

ultimately both fall into the speculative domain of utilitarianism. Simplifying greatly, "common sense" would suggest that "right" (the "right" conduct) and "good" are inseparable. The point that interests us here is that Sidgwick was well aware of the difficulty of demonstrating that a worker's performance should be attributed a precise merit. It was his belief that the factors involved are many and most often intertwined. Merit certainly needs to be rewarded, but in the result obtained by the worker, how to separate the influence of commitment from the influence of the socio-economic environment? I believe that the philosopher of "common sense" was absolutely right. But, exactly a century and a half later, few are interested in the question. Most of the time the concept of merit interests and fascinates because it has to do with success.

John Roemer (1998, 2008), who was the pioneer of studies on "inequality of opportunity", has made a step forward in understanding people's ethical preferences. Instead of the generic distinction between attributing success to merit or to "good luck" *in the market*, Roemer has thought that the evaluation of how fair a given society is should also take into account the "circumstances" of the subjects *before the* market. The American economist has given an analytical form to the distinction between "fair inequality" (that which depends on a different commitment between individuals) and "unfair inequality" (that for which the worker is not responsible, because it is caused by his disadvantaged circumstances and lack of access to opportunities).[8]

Take Sweden. It is going through a turbulent period politically, but it is a country where socio-economic relations are traditionally based on fairness and commitment to work is a national pride. Should we deduce that income inequality there is due to free choice, variable from person to person, between work and leisure? From a study conducted in the country, which considers different "types" of subjects with equal circumstances, it turns out that performance is only partly attributable to their commitment. The "commitment" variable, which is correlated with what the *surveys* define as "merit", in fact explains in Sweden 2/3 of the income inequality (Björklund et al. 2012). It follows that 1/3 of the diversity in remuneration corresponds to an "unfair inequality". It is true that in other

[8] Ronald Dworkin (1977) distinguished between bad luck (*brute luck*) and risky choice (*option luck*). Individuals are entitled to compensation only in the first case, when they have been victims of a negative event without their responsibility, not when they knowingly risk their own well-being.

countries, in explaining income gaps, commitment is attributed an even smaller role. In Latin America, for example, in public opinion "merit" and "life lottery" equally share the origin of inequality: they each explain about 50%. However, that in an advanced country with a large welfare state like Sweden, circumstances and "market imperfections" account for about 33% of people's economic outcome is certainly a fact to reflect on. It is indeed an indication of the considerable extent to which—even in a country with a strong welfare state and a solid tradition of solidarity—the social context can make unequal the *abilities* that people manage to express.

Another problem is that the "context", today's condition of work, distances merit from earnings. Today, the supply of low-skilled labour has no defence against the continuous fall in low skilled wages. Contrary to the ideology of the market as a "perfect" allocation mechanism, this loss of value has no connection either with productivity or with merit. Recognising in the simple work performance the *origin* of merit is a daring endeavour, because a characteristic of productive activity is the complexity typical of a *joint venture* that is production. Whoever ignores complexity runs a risk: the simple evidence of a pay slip ends up appearing to him as the incontrovertible proof that the remuneration earned in the labour market is "fair", i.e. totally attributable to the level of skill required and the effort expended. It is not easy to collect and evaluate all the factors that are at the basis of work performance. On closer inspection, one discovers how much today's change in the nature of capital counts. The most valuable is not what was once called "machinery", but rather "intangible" capital, the knowledge of excellent workers employed in new technologies.[9] It seems, however, that a job that gives the opportunity to "deserve" a high income depends not only on the level of qualification but also on the needs of companies. Although the content of innovation in digital and robotics with which work is combined is very heterogeneous, empirical evidence indicates that "artificial intelligence creates new tasks and new positions for workers who have the right skills" (Oecd 2023, p. 104). Workers who are *peer* in terms of professional qualification perform different tasks—and therefore have different levels of employment and salary—because of the type of organisation in which the relationship between their *skills* and new technologies

[9]The value of companies today tends to depend mainly on intangible capital. A typical example is Nike. Its intangible assets are the researchers responsible for design and brand care. Its market value was 11 billion dollars at the beginning of 2000. Today Nike is worth about 212 billion.

is embedded (we will see this, in this volume, in Chap. 10). The type of company in which one works also counts a lot, due to the greater propensity of the large *corporation* to introduce new technologies. Each worker achieves a different level of productivity—and therefore a different remuneration—depending on whether he is employed in a large or small company, equipped with innovative or traditional technologies. So how can one accurately measure how much of the *surplus* of the company is a worker's "merit"?

A further problem is the link between "deserving" and the incentive of earning. The "theory of incentives", one of the pillars of the orthodox view of economics, narrows the discussion on merit to the simple slogan "if you commit yourself you will succeed in the market". Empirical evidence does not authorise such certainty. Recently, for example, the link between merit and human relations within the company has begun to be investigated. When the worker is informed of his work performance relative to that of his colleagues, his "incentive system" is subject to disturbance: alongside the positive value that we are used to associating with the pursuit of merit, the "dark side" of the competitive spirit at work emerges. Experimental economics research has documented how competition acts as an incentive: it increases the likelihood that a worker will adopt an opportunistic behaviour, damaging his colleagues, in order to gain an advantage for himself (Charness et al. 2014).

But the discussion on the concept of profit cannot stop at the psychological impulse of the instinct for appropriation; it must be developed in all its breadth, starting from the place in the world of the income earner. The neoliberal economic logic is rooted in the vision of the individual as fully autonomous from society; according to some, even from the institutions of his country. The concept of merit is thus associated with the right to the exclusive enjoyment of one's own profit. However, a progressively higher tax as income increases is nothing more than the application to public finance of an ethical principle: allowing those who are not responsible for their own mediocre economic result, those who have not "demerited", to receive support from society through public policies financed by taxation. The relationship between public ethics and fiscal compliance is very complicated. By taking the idea of "individual responsibility" to the extreme, the most libertarian currents of individualism unequivocally reject the principle of redistributive taxation. Applying a higher tax rate as income increases would represent the denial of the individual's commitment and his right to the exclusive enjoyment of what he has "earned" through his own work commitment (Scheve and Stasavage 2016). The belief that profit reflects what the worker "has earned" not only impacts redistributive policies after the market. It also reflects on what happens in the market, on how the market is thought to work. The core of neoliberal thinking lies in the idea that the deregulated operation of the market is the only context in which a country's aspiration to grow, perhaps climbing positions in the G20 ranking, can succeed. The deceptive thesis of trickle-down is being proposed again, according to which the elite—in which many, starting from Pareto, have recognised the "aristocracy of merit"—should be put in a position to transform the low taxation of the flat tax regime into greater well-being for all. The lightening of the tax burden associated with the abolition of progressive taxation would allow the wealthier classes to invest more and earn more. This would result not only in an increase in aggregate GDP, but also an expansion of the income level along all percentiles of its distribution, or the "trickling down" of the income increase to the benefit of the middle class and the poor. The OECD has observed that the middle and poor classes do not see it this way. According to the main research institute of advanced countries, there is a lot of pessimism about the promise that putting more money in the hands of wealthy investors would make social stratification more dynamic: "In many countries there is a widespread perception that intergenerational social mobility is declining [...]. The decline in perceived mobility is also associated with the decline in the perception of meritocracy: a growing number of people think that the fortunes and advantages of parents represent a major factor in people's lives" (OECD 2018, p. 20). The fact remains that presuming a priori the coincidence of profit with merit arouses a certain consensus (Mijs 2019). An experimental economics study concluded that when they are given complete information about the performance carried out in the laboratory, experimental subjects agree in attributing importance to merit and therefore to differentiate, even greatly, the remuneration between more and less "deserving". However, if it is not possible to establish the origin of the performance difference between subjects, people tend to favour as egalitarian a distribution of income as possible (Cappelen et al. 2022). The "treatments" of the experimental protocol in which subjects are not involved in the distribution that follows their decision, when their choice is "impartial", are however quite indicative of the perception of what is the "fair" distribution of earnings. It is enough that the "good luck" that may have favoured their performance has also been accompanied by even a small "dose" of merit to induce them to a distributive decision strongly favourable to the remuneration of merit (Cappelen et al. 2017). The scepticism that the OECD survey has found, in people's perception, about the link between merit and reward has its good reasons. The vision of trickle-down is far from an approach to "deserving" that takes into account, in addition to the need for tax collection, the factors for which one is not responsible, from circumstances to opportunities offered by the market. Scandinavian populations, for example, are much less inclined than the American population to believe in the role of merit as a tool for social mobility and to show tolerance for inequalities (Almås et al. 2020). Today we are witnessing the return of the idea—a real "historical recurrence" in the Vichian sense—that social mobility consists in being co-opted by the powerful: "'equal opportunities', which are a utopia, do not count, but "good opportunities", which excellent and socially sensitive elites create for everyone" (Abravanel 2021, p. 51). This means "speaking clearly"! To find out how much social reality contradicts the theory of a harmonious diffusion of well-being, just scroll through a report from an institution that can be defined as "non-partisan", the International Monetary Fund (IMF). The empirical evidence goes in the opposite direction. to the idea that greater income inequality leads to greater wealth creation: "if the income share of the richest 20% increases by 1%, GDP growth decreases by 0.08% in the following five years, suggesting that the benefits will not trickle down" (Dabla-Norris et al. 2015, p. 6). Piketty's judgement on why meritocrats are not concerned about the increase in inequalities is *tranchant*: "The meritocratic discourse usually glorifies the winners of the economic system and stigmatises the losers for their alleged lack of merit, virtue and diligence. Meritocracy is naturally an old ideology, on which the *élite* of all times and places have always relied, in one way or another, to justify their own dominance" (Piketty 2020, p. 710).

Ultimately, it is very difficult to isolate merit in its "pure state" in remuneration. In the evaluation of earnings, merit is not a reliable key to interpretation.

Is Merit a "principle of justice"?

"People need to believe they live in a world where they get what they deserve" (Lerner 1980). Is this enough? Is personal commitment, for example, that exerted by an individual at work, enough to legitimise merit as a "principle of justice"? English sociologist Walter G. Runciman thought not. According to him, the race to deserve is intimately linked to "competition among equals". He suggested that competition is stimulated by sharing the same living conditions. "Relative income" is defined as the comparison of one's own income with that of the average individual in the group to which a subject feels they belong: "People often choose reference groups closest to their actual living conditions rather than those to which they would belong if their opportunities were better" (Runciman 1966, p. 29). On the other hand, as Aristotle observed in the *Rhetoric*, it is precisely among those who perceive themselves as equals that envy flourishes.[10]

However, it is a fact that in many advanced countries, individualistic logic fosters fierce competition for success within society. The phenomenon of social mobility thus ends up representing a degeneration of the individual's competitive spirit. Many, especially among the well-off, are not interested in social stratification as a whole, but focus exclusively on their own "playing field", the environment to which they belong. The obsession of these people is the anxiety they are pervaded by: the feeling of having the same chances of success as work colleagues or neighbours—"the Joneses", according to the cultural stereotype of the United States—indeed generates the fear of failing in the race to "earn more than others".

One can agree or disagree with individualism. The fact remains, however, that "competition among equals" is not what many young people face. Young people's aspirations only become substantial if the playing field is truly levelled. An institution with a good international reputation like the World Bank gives a very clear judgement on the *feasibility*, on how much young people are actually able to cultivate their aspirations, on the "freedom of choice" in education: "The time period for 'aspiring' for boys with a low *status* socio-economic is limited because it is likely that boys from such families grow up in a social environment that contributes to making it rather short [...]. What matters is not the lack of high aspirations, but the extinguishing of aspirations during the years of training" (Narayan et al. 2018, p. 29).

This condition is typical of young people with "disadvantaged" circumstances, due both to an unfavourable family environment (due to the economic and cultural background of the parents), and to a socio-economic

[10] It should be remembered that Aristotle, believing that by nature some men are free and others slaves, was not referring to all men.

environment that induces myopic choices, or "bounded rationality".[11] The evidence in this sense is overwhelming. Both sociological and economic research shows that the "disadvantaged" student tends to undervalue their own life chances and to underinvest in education (Bourdieu 1984; Durlauf 2002). Young people exposed to psychological discouragement end up developing a "taste" against education, which leads them to downsize their own ambitions, making it increasingly difficult to transform their talents into actual *capabilities* (Cohen 1989).[12] The principle of "individual responsibility" screens the recognition of this problem. But the problem exists.

Indicating how little "free" the desire of young people to realise their life project is, there is a very eloquent estimate. Based on a careful statistical elaboration, Branko Milanović (2017) concludes that a person's income depends approximately 60% on the nation of birth, 20% on the income of the parents and only the remaining 20% on effort and luck (in which are also included gender and ethnicity). The hypothesis of the "endogeneity of preferences", which only in recent times relatively recent is contemplated and subjected to verification by economic theory, it refers precisely to the tendency to adjust one's expectations to one's social context: "Preferences are 'imprinted' on people by their environment" (Roemer 1996, p. 271). The *Aspiration view* (Appadurai 2004; Ray 2006) argues that "aspirations are never individual. They are formed through interaction" (Appadurai 2004, p. 67). In a society characterised by unequal opportunities, Runciman's "competition among equals" is not therefore generalisable, unless it is intended to confine it to one's specific socio-economic environment. An experimental economics study shows how "meritocrats" "do not take into account the fact that the choices that subjects make are influenced by external circumstances, so they consider people responsible despite their choices being made in environmental conditions characterised by inequality" (Andre 2022, p. 5).

[11] This expression indicates the limits of information and cognitive abilities that make behaviour fallible.

[12] In the United States, the children of parents who at the beginning of the new millennium belonged to the highest quintile of the income distribution have a 36.5% chance of remaining there, against a probability of 10.9% of moving to the lowest one; those belonging to the lowest quintile have a probability of remaining there of 33.7%, and of moving to the higher quintile of 7.5%; while the children of middle-class parents have almost equal probability of ending up in any of the various quintiles (Chetty et al. 2014).

A logic very different from the individualistic logic that has been mentioned is the one that welcomes the suggestion of Narayan and van der Weide, the two World Bank economists, to take into account the context. We all find ourselves in the context of "systemic interdependence", where our well-being is influenced by the externalities—positive and negative—that are created in social interaction. In other words, being in continuous relationship with the world obliges—and also helps—us to build the social component of our identity. The question on which we are questioning ourselves in this paragraph is: what induces us to consider "fair", and therefore "deserved", a certain level of income? First of all, it is necessary to clear the fog that surrounds the link between "fair remuneration" and a very narrow conception of "merit", elevated by neoliberal culture to a totem, a simulacrum object of worship rather than understanding.

Let us then question the ways through which the individualistic vision of "deserving" has reached its full development. In the seventeenth century, the disturbing prospect of the *homo hominis lupus* led Thomas Hobbes not to consider man truly free to engage in self-realisation, not to see alternatives to the iron fist of the absolute sovereign. With John Locke the concept of the "deserving" individual began to re-emerge. His idea is that property is morally justified because the individual acquires through hard work his resources, and uses them to satisfy his vital needs. This idea will accompany the affirmation of "deserving" in the following centuries. In Enlightenment thought, the link between justice and merit then found recognition in the conception of the individual by Immanuel Kant, who identified moral behaviour with rational behaviour. No one could have disagreed more with Kant than David Hume.

The English moral philosopher thought that in every society the cooperation and solidarity are slow conquests that men owe to the custom of living together; certainly not to the Empyrean, the highest of the heavens where Kantian reason resides. At the same time, Hume believed that experience is nothing more than a "bundle of impressions". He was therefore quite sceptical about the possibility of founding a "principle of justice" on merit: among men "such is the uncertainty of merit, both for its natural obscurity and for the arrogance of each individual, that no rule of conduct can result from it" (Hume 1777, sec. III, Part II). The progressive expansion of the right to vote that took place in the nineteenth century, leading to the conquest in the twentieth century of political democracy in the West, served to sweep away any uncertainty around the idea of the "sovereignty of the individual". From then on, in ever wider strata of the population, the association of individual freedom with "merit", understood as a "principle of justice" that all men should make their own, has taken root.

What is wrong with establishing a close link between "merit" and "justice"? In the last century, a distancing from the foundation in "justice" of the concept of merit was expressed by John Rawls. In his vision, the economic system is not populated by many Robinson Crusoes. Although he was convinced that individual behaviour in the market is at the basis of the expansion of social well-being, he conceived of the economy as a collective enterprise, as a *joint venture*. And he added that a "just" society is one in which "the system of cooperation between free and equal people is fair". His approach to fairness is based on the "principle of difference", according to which only that income inequality is allowed which is accompanied by the pursuit of the maximisation of the well-being of the least advantaged (principle of the *maximin*). In other words, in a liberal society economic and social inequalities should be tolerated, but under the condition that the functioning of the market is embedded in a set of political and economic institutions such as to direct the distribution of the surplus generated by economic growth primarily to the improvement of the well-being of the *worst-off*, of "those who are worse off": "a just society should aim at maximising the lowest level opportunities within the social system" (Id. 1985, p. 240).

According to Rawls, by fictitiously placing oneself "behind a veil of ignorance" (a sort of state of nature, an "original position" in which one is unaware of one's own *status* economic and social), all individuals would choose the type of society in which they are most protected from the eventuality of finding themselves in their life in a condition of indigence and would therefore agree on the necessity of applying the criterion of the *maximin*.[13] For instance, between the two possible tax regimes of progressive taxation and the *flat tax*, the former should be chosen, because it is the one that allows those who are worse off to reach a higher level of well-being than they would enjoy in the other tax regime. Rawls, on the other hand, was opposed to the redistribution of incomes "after the market".

[13] Rawls, however, did not want to accept the interpretation of *maximin* according to which every rational individual behind the "veil of ignorance", can only assume an "infinite" risk aversion (Hörisch 2007). This refusal is not however in line with the Kantian rationalistic tradition in which his thought is framed. According to Kant, only if the individual is rational should they be recognised as a person; and probabilistic calculation is a cornerstone of the theory of individual rationality.

The level of taxation that the financing of a broad welfare system would require could prove excessive and compromise economic growth. A margin of inequality is, in his opinion, necessary so that the most efficient individuals receive adequate economic incentives, the necessary stimulus to the willingness to take business risks. In the absence of market incentives, investments would stagnate, causing enormous damage to everyone.

Rawls entrusted institutions, particularly legislation, with the goal of equality of opportunity (his first principle of justice calls for the need for "positions to be open to all"). However, he failed to see that it is not enough to contain the inequalities caused by the rentier positions that can arise in the market. The inequalities that occur before the market must also be addressed. Afterward, it might be too late.[14] In showing a large gap between the "revealed" preferences from individuals' choices and the actual preferences they would express in other life conditions, studies in social psychology and economics highlight the importance of "circumstances". The "poverty trap" is the phenomenon that sees the poor penalised by lack of access to opportunities, to the point of being stuck in low-productivity activities and therefore at very low-income levels (Bowles et al. 2006; Balboni et al. 2021).

The idea that society is made up of "free and equal" individuals thus seems a reckless abstraction. In the Nicomachean Ethics, Aristotle argued that "justice" consists in the existence of a proportionate relationship between an individual's inputs and their outputs. Today we would say: "justice" consists in the correspondence between the length of the educational journey and the scores obtained in learning tests on the one hand, and the remuneration achieved in the market, on the other. The concept of merit in vogue today has the limitation of having forgotten Aristotle's lesson. Merit is assessed without taking into account the role played by inputs, the circumstances of the family and social context, and different access to market opportunities.

Aristotle expressed a very nuanced judgement on "merit". In his proverbial clarity, he was well aware that the concept of merit is among those most lacking the requirement of "universality": "everyone agrees on the need for the concept of justice to accord with that of merit, but each gives a different definition to merit: for democrats, merit lies in being born a

[14] However, he must be recognised for having had a very clear position both on production as a *joint venture* and on the inherent injustice in the "random" distribution of individual talents (see *infra*, in this chapter, par. 5).

free person, for oligarchs in wealth or, for some of them, in noble lineage, for aristocrats in excellence". The class division of society, the "belonging" to a social group is a strong impediment to the attempt to give the concept of merit an objective definition, as "universal".

In the *Politics*, Aristotle pondered the solution to the dilemma of who—among different people—deserved to receive a flute. And he answered: "the one who extracts the best music from it"; but he added that the link between deserving and obtaining the flute is inseparable from the purpose with which the decision is motivated. He therefore deduced that "deserving" acquires its true value only when the choice of the "deserving" person is aimed at the common good. That is, it is only when everyone—and not just democrats, or oligarchs, or aristocrats—is given the opportunity to try to "play the flute well" that a community will be "virtuous". Placing a person's merit in the sphere of the community's good, rather than in the individual sphere, is exactly the thesis argued in this book: everyone has the right to test their own talents.

Aristotle was right: the opposing interests of individuals stand as an insurmountable obstacle that prevents the achievement of a universal judgement on merit. As suggested by Runciman's theory of "relative income", the rich compare themselves with those who are as rich as they are or just richer. The poor, on the other hand, avoid comparing and competing with people just less needy than them, so as not to risk becoming the target of stigma. They are often inclined to accept the condition of poverty of their own group of belonging. Separating the concept of "justice" and the concept of "merit" is the vast territory of the family and social environment in which inequalities develop. In the sequence the rationale that gives value to the concept of merit—the greater the worker's commitment to training and work, the greater their economic outcome—lacks the initial piece: for many young people, the transformation of talents into *abilities* often encounters an insurmountable obstacle in the disadvantageous conditions they suffer due to negative circumstances. The judgement on people's behaviour cannot therefore be issued based on the impartiality to which the concept of "merit" is associated. Even with equal commitment to training and work, there are obstacles—from unequal circumstances to unequal opportunities—such that the ability to bring out talents is limited and the aspiration to social mobility is frustrated. It is therefore futile to see merit as a "principle of justice". As Victor Hugo wrote in *Les Misérables*, "We live in a grey society; to succeed, that is the teaching instilled by the dominant corruption. Let it be said in passing, success is a rather sordid thing; its false resemblance to merit deceives men" (Hugo 1981, Part IV, l. III, chap. XII).

Merit or Power Relationship?

In the search for the correct interpretation of merit, we have already identified some tears in the fabric with which this concept is usually woven. Here's another: in determining the incomes of company executives, the "political factor" is often more important than merit (Stiglitz 2017). As much as executives in command positions are skilled in keeping the major *corporations* on the frontier of technical progress, it cannot be said that the stratospheric amount of their earnings has everything to do with "merit". "The top managers [...] are hired by the companies at the top of the sector [...]. The demand for *top managers* is mainly aimed at those with market power; they are increasingly rewarded as they manage to extract a greater rent through market power" (Bao et al. 2022, p. 11). In the United States, the increase in the profit margin on costs has been staggering; "mark-ups have been steadily growing since 1980, increasing from 21% to 61% on marginal cost [...]. Few large firms have the largest mark-ups, while they have not increased in the majority of firms, which have thus lost market share" (De Loecker et al. 2020, p. 562). The profits obtained by companies belonging to the 90th percentile, where large multinational companies are present, have become in the last decade six times greater than those of the median company, with an increase of about 300% compared to 1990 (Furman and Orszag 2018). The managerial ability of CEOs is also accompanied by increasing power in negotiating emoluments. Their remuneration increases as the company's performance improves, but does not decrease as much in "dark times", when a drop in sales reduces profits. The remuneration of company executives seems to contradict the principle of "fair remuneration".

The growing influence of the behaviours of private economic powers on the public regulation of the economy is expressed in the "capture of politicians" by companies, a phenomenon that has experienced a strong acceleration with the policies of privatisation and deregulation of recent decades. It is a widespread opinion that "managerial capitalism", i.e. the role of managers in leading the company with the aim of "maximising value for shareholders", has entered the phase of *crony capitalism*. This sharp definition denounces how the public regulation agencies of labour and capital markets are often prone to the interests of entrepreneurs and businessmen, to the detriment of fair market competition (Zingales 2012; Stiglitz 2019).

The factors that help the appropriation of the surplus by the rich at the top of companies, and distort the processes of social mobility, are many: a) the weakening of antitrust legislation, which should be aimed at preventing the erection of entry barriers, is one of the most used tools to protect the profits derived from new knowledge, and to enjoy them longer; b) the favourable legislation that in advanced countries benefits the rich in the process of optimising their substantial portfolios of financial activities (Chetty et al. 2020); c) the reduction of inheritance taxes, which is increasing the concentration of wealth passed down from generation to generation through inheritances (Alvaredo et al. 2017); d) the strategy pursued in various ways by large companies to detach themselves from the rules to which nation-states subject the functioning of markets, in order to evade the contribution necessary to finance the production of public goods. The case of the profits of multinational companies is emblematic: the large discrepancy that is found between macroeconomic data and the significantly lower levels of microeconomic data indicates that tax evasion increases with the growth of company size. It is estimated that large multinational companies manage to hide from the tax authorities an amount of taxes equal to as much as 40% of their profits (Wier and Erasmus 2023). In compromising the respect of "codes of conduct" and in manipulating the remuneration of productive factors, the top management of large companies end up inflicting a *wound* on the ethics of capitalism (Hart and Zingales 2017; Zingales 2017; Stiglitz 2017).

The role played in setting the remuneration of another "political" type relationship, that between managers and shareholders, should not be forgotten. When the owners of the company are bright and attentive in monitoring their company, it is a tough time for the appetites of CEOs. In fact, the alignment between CEO compensation and company performance increases especially when in *corporate governance* there is strong control by shareholders over the management of the company (Bell et al. 2021). The level of manager remuneration is therefore not immediately attributable to the work commitment provided, it depends a lot on a "political" factor. The most striking example concerns the banking sector after the financial crisis of 2008. In the United States as in Europe, the top managers of banks were not sanctioned for excessive risk-taking; nor was a serious reform of supervision over the banking system initiated. Establishing the "merits" and "demerits" of the heads of banks, financial intermediaries, and rating agencies that should evaluate their work, is a desperate task: it is in fact not possible to examine the management of a single bank without taking into account the complex interactions between banking institutions.[15]

To attribute solely to "merit" the dividends of shareholders and the remuneration of the top managers of *corporations* therefore seems a bit exaggerated. With the deregulation of the labour market, the anchoring of remuneration to actually having "earned" has "jumped" even in the lower section of the income distribution. One of the victims of labour market deregulation was the centralised wage bargaining. The sharp decline in the bargaining power of trade union organisations makes it less advantageous for workers to join a union. The consequence is immediate: the lowest wage level that the worker is willing to accept drops to converge with the highest wage level that a company is willing to offer him.

Another clue that leads to identifying earnings with power rather than with merit is provided by the various forms of discrimination—often very little "visible"—of a social, cultural and psychological nature. When a person is not recognised as having equal rights, when for example they are prevented from advancing in career in a work organisation, the metaphor of the *glass ceiling* is used, an invisible obstacle to social ascent. This expression was born to designate gender discrimination. According to the *Global Gender Gap Report* for 2023 of the UN's World Economic Forum, in no UN country does gender equality exist; 90% of the world's female population (3.1 billion women) live in countries where the level of *empowerment* of women is low or medium, and less than 1% live in countries where it is high. The "places" of disparity are well known. More than half of these women are not on the same level as men in finding work. A possible pregnancy puts women at a disadvantage compared to men in getting a job. Female social mobility, or access to a stable job with career progression, is penalised by the lack of public nurseries and the increasing cost of private ones. An experimental economics study has shown how in the

[15] "One of the lessons taught by the financial crisis was that a micro-prudential approach to supervision and regulation is in itself insufficient to avoid a financial crisis. A macro-prudential level is also needed, as from the point of view of financial sustainability the interactions between financial institutions are as important as the conditions of individual institutions" (De Smedt et al. 2019, p. 323).

United States women, despite often achieving levels of education on average higher than those of men, have a short-sighted behaviour with respect to the "cost" of becoming mothers: many women tend to underestimate the impact of motherhood on their work activity and end up suffering a heavy slowdown in the progress of their career shortly after the birth of their first child (Kuziemko et al. 2018).

However, a positive note should be mentioned. Social reality is in motion. If things change, if rights from formal become *de facto*, it is not due to the "magnificent destinies and progressive", of the harmonious race of humanity towards progress. It is social conflict that changes things. In the gender power relationship, social conflict manifests itself in the pressure that those who suffer injustice (a negative externality) exert in order to change balances. Furthermore, "if a right obtained *de jure* is devoid of robust *enforcement*, the legal position of women is much weaker" (Tertilt et al. 2022, p. 33). As shown by Claudia Goldin (1990), Nobel laureate in economics 2023, in the eighteenth century 60% of married women had a job, usually in agriculture; it is with the Industrial Revolution and factory work that the collapse of female participation in the labour market occurs; in the twentieth century, with the expansion of services, participation increases, but the wage gap with men also grows. The real factor capable of changing things—for women as for men—is the *empowerment* of the person, which only education can give.

With the increase in schooling, women's participation in the labour market has also increased: "Most of the jobs in the 'new economy' require a higher level of education; women are often more educated and therefore better equipped to occupy high-level jobs" (Eurofound 2017, p. 27). That in a phase of slow and discontinuous expansion of GDP, the most dynamic section of employment growth is that of female work is explainable with the political claim of the right to equality and with the most advanced training achieved by a good percentage of women seeking work. In the two most dynamic economies in the world—China and India—it has long been noted that young women from low-income families are more inclined than males (pushed by the conservative values of their fathers to remain tied to traditional family occupations) to take up the challenge of education and job opportunities in advanced sectors (Munshi and Rosenzweig 2006).

In European nations, the progressive increase in women's employment from the generation of *baby boomers* is reflected differently in various cohorts and countries. An important factor in increasing the fluidity of the labour market for young people of the *Generation X* was the pressure exerted by cultural change, such as the leading role played in some countries by women's emancipation movements:[16] "In Germany and Spain, relative mobility has increased for men [...], while social origin has been a hindrance for women; conversely, in the United Kingdom, relative mobility has increased for women, while social origin has led to a decrease in relative mobility for men of the *Generation X*" (ibid., p. 33). Scandinavia, as already mentioned, is a world unto itself. In most Nordic countries, relative mobility has increased for both men and women, demonstrating a probable complementarity between the scope and characteristics of the welfare state and the health of civil society.[17]

Another type of discrimination that penalises merit, also called "glass ceiling" because it is usually carefully hidden, is that created by "relationship power" (*influence*). Co-optation into a power group is a formidable tool of social control. One way to exercise one's *influence* is indeed to impose on people—in exchange for support, for example in finding a job—a sort of "non-monetary bribe". The *influence* is thus aimed at making people blackmailable in order to obtain behaviours prone to one's own interests. It is no coincidence that this distortion of the market is more frequent in less competitive sectors, in which "rent-seeking positions" lurk. In hindering the association of "finding a job" with merit, the "relationship power" of families with substantial economic means and a prominent social *status* plays an important role. In supporting each other, in the market and in society, by creating solid "social networks", wealthy families create a real "club good", i.e. those goods from whose consumption

[16] The following quotation considers relative social mobility. For the distinction with respect to the concept of absolute social mobility, see *infra*, par. 5.

[17] Two characteristics have distinguished the social state of the Nordic countries (despite significant differences in terms of percentages between the indicators of the various countries) compared to other Welfare systems: a) the services *in-kind*/cash transfers ratio has always been particularly high. The high production of common goods such as health and education is evidenced by the volume of social spending on public services compared to cash transfers in social spending; b) the income tax/social contributions ratio has always been particularly high. Social spending is in fact mainly financed on a "universalistic" basis through general taxation rather than through social contributions. These two ratios have a reducing impact on income inequality: the first, because there is considerable implicit redistribution in favour of low-income classes, due to the greater use of *in-kind* services by the middle-low classes and the poor, in the face of their lower tax contribution compared to that borne by higher incomes; the second, because a tax levy more skewed towards social contributions normally weighs on low and middle income subjects more than on the rich.

others are excluded except for the "comrades" with whom they exercise the *influence*. The children of the elite "inherit" the "relationship power" from their parents whenever the social environment of the family facilitates them in "finding a job", which among wealthy people often means embarking on a prestigious career.[18]

At the time of entering the labour market, the chances of a young person from a "disadvantaged" family—his or her chances of success in life—have usually already diverged from the chances of a young person from an "advantaged" family. One of the most important reasons is another "place" where "relationship power" ends up distorting "merit" to the advantage of a few: education. Particularly in countries with a predominantly private offer, education is far from representing the "great equaliser" of young people's life chances. In the United States, as we will see in Chap. 11, "highly placed" families support their children's performance in the university education process in a thousand ways. The activity of *influence* aimed at facilitating their path is explained by the signalling effect that an excellent diploma has in the search for a prestigious job position. In evaluating the hiring of graduates, the company benefits from the cost-free information represented by the diploma obtained (Arrow 1973; Spence 1973). This information is a means of estimating his or her professional abilities (*screening*), it signals his or her "quality" as a possible employee of the company (Stiglitz 1975).

The privilege enjoyed by young people whose parents have large economic resources is another "glass ceiling effect". We often doubt that access to the highest income positions occurs based not on merit but on privilege. Merit often has little to do with the job positions that children end up occupying. A study conducted on young people with equal levels of education in 14 advanced countries found that those from high-income families get better jobs than young people from low-income families (Ballarino and Bernardi 2016). Upon entering the labour market, elite families often manage to facilitate their children's access to successful

[18] In the aspiration to a good position in the world of work, the son of an entrepreneur is favoured. The father's membership of a "social network", often made up of people with a certain degree of social power, creates a kind of class bond between wealthy families. The hiring of the young person in a company led by an entrepreneur from the "social network" generates in the latter the expectation of reciprocal behaviour, the expectation that a member of his own "network" will provide a job for his own son (Franzini et al. 2020).

employments despite their scant abilities.[19] The reason certainly has to do with the "power of relationship", with the ability of families with *high status* to use for the benefit of their offspring the "social networks" in which they are inserted. The words of the World Bank are very clear: "a labour market that rewards a privileged background rather than the *skills* can represent a major obstacle to intergenerational mobility" (Narayan et al. 2018, p. 161).

The privilege enjoyed by young people whose parents have large economic resources generates a "glass ceiling" effect also within companies. The fact that a high worker productivity does not always result in a high salary is often due to his social origin. From the comparison between the subjects who occupy the most prestigious job positions, it turns out that those who come from a working-class family background receive a salary that is on average 17% lower than those who come from the middle class and the elite (Friedman and Laurison 2016). When the aspiration to social ascent of young people without a solid family background is mortified by the "glass ceiling" constituted by consolidated "social networks", it is difficult to attribute univocally to merit a good intergenerational social mobility.

Are the Talents We Possess Deserved?

In the search for a theoretical foundation of merit, it is necessary to investigate its relationship with talents. The problem is that at birth, as has been said, talents are not observable. They only become so *ex post*, when people have had the opportunity to express them through the *abilities* acquired. A vicious circle from which it is difficult to escape. Can we argue that we "deserve" our talents?

Let's go in order. We must start from biology, that is from the human being before he becomes an adult individual and becomes part of society. A measure, quite controversial, of natural talent is the "*intelligence quotient*" (IQ,), widely used in the statistical analysis of education, especially in the United States. Its detection through the form of the "Bell curve" unequivocally places nature *nature* as almost the only determinant of success.

[19] The term "parachute" (*parachute*) refers to the protection of the family network of relationships that prevents a fall down the social ladder for young people with *skill* that are not highly marketable (Raitano and Vona 2016).

But is it really so? Some are sure of it. In his book of unconditional defence of meritocracy, an editor of the "Economist" emphasises the "impartial" role that the "Bell curve" plays in the promotion of talents. The curious argument is that the use of IQ to judge merit should be considered an infallible method, as IQ is not affected by the socio-cultural factors that can affect the evaluation of young people's skills. An argument comparable to the idea that when you lose your house keys in the dark the best thing is to look for them under a lamppost. The conclusion of the reasoning is the ban on any idea of *affirmative action* in favour of the "disadvantaged". The author of the article shows a pleased sympathy for the "sanctuaries that the students of Singapore, world capital of meritocracy, erect to the 'God Bell Curve' [aware of the fact that] the tests will accompany them even after school and university [...], as companies use attitudinal and personality tests in 72% of hires in middle management positions" (Wooldridge 2021, p. 350).

Is it sensible to believe that a high IQ is a unique signal of the presence of a great intellectual potential, of the talents that the subject should develop, without the characteristics of the "environment" in which they must blossom mattering at all? Over the years, two positions have been compared. On the one hand, Herrnstein and Murray (1994) estimate that intelligence is inheritable in a percentage between 40% and 80%; it would manifest itself in talents that the social environment can only slightly shape and translate into effective *abilities*. On the other hand, Feldman et al. (2000) argue that the detection of a high correlation of IQ between successive generations of a "family dynasty" should be explained based on cultural transmission, before genetic transmission.

In the last decade, the first hypothesis seems to have gained consensus. Among neuroscientists, the conviction that the cognitive abilities of the subject are the expression of his innate talent, of his genetic characteristics, has been strengthening. If this is true, if the chances of success in realising one's life project are largely in the individual, the unequal circumstances that he encounters just after birth do not matter at all. Why then resort to public policies of "equalisation" of "starting conditions", in an attempt to increase the chances of success of the young "disadvantaged", if we know that they can have little impact?

The answer that will be sought to argue is of a probabilistic type. The "champions", in soccer as in physics, are a small minority. Even when they are born in a *favela*, or in a village of the steppe, a combative nature and the good health to express the excellence that nature has bestowed upon them. The vast majority of individuals, however, are made up of people endowed with a talent, often even great, but not "out of the ordinary". The problem, as has been said many times, lies in the obstacles that "circumstances" put in the way of ordinary people being able to express their own talent. It is therefore the law of large numbers that suggests that public policies would have a fundamental role to play, in preventing the talent of young people with "disadvantaged" circumstances from being lost. The goal is not to help Stakhanov become the "hero of socialist labour". Rather, the idea is that every young "talented" person, in realising themselves, has the right not to be conditioned by their own origins. Much to the chagrin of today's neoliberals, it was a staunch supporter of economic freedom like Luigi Einaudi who sided in favour of policies, such as limiting the transmission of inheritance, that promote "equality of starting points". From this perspective, the goal of equity in public policies naturally combines with the goal of efficiency: when an entire new generation—and not the *happy few*—is fully in command of their own qualities, economic growth and the well-being of the community receive a strong boost.

The sociologist Michael Young, in his *The Rise of Meritocracy* (1958), defined merit as the combination of talents (or intelligence) with commitment to work: "Iq + effort = merit". A definition, this one, consistent with microeconomic theory, which ties to the system of market incentives—the gain achievable with commitment to professional training and work[20]—the manifestation of a talent. The monetary compensation that the worker obtains would be proof both of the talents that one possesses and of the merit earned with the effort put into work. Today's champions of merit seem to ignore that behind the title of his book Young hid a very critical judgement on the soundness of such a link. The English sociologist was convinced that the "rising classes" of English society in his time cloaked with the claim of "merit" what was in reality an ascent favoured by class privilege. Young also ventured into a bizarre prophecy: he pointed to 2034 as the year in which the advent of the "perfect meritocracy" would coincide with enormous disasters.

[20] The role of institutions has long been ignored even in assessing developing countries. For many decades, in advising their governments on the most appropriate policies, the World Bank has focused entirely on the defence of property rights. For social mobility, as well as for the approach to the average income of the nations of the world and the levels of well-being of advanced countries, the quality of political and economic institutions is very important.

One of Young's insights—this one of surprising foresight—was the return to something similar to castes, precisely in advanced societies oriented to exalt merit. Let's look at the country that is today the world leader. In American society, the number of couples who—in addition to love—share a PhD, and perhaps even a top position in society, has been skyrocketing for several decades. From 1960 to today, the percentage of couples with a college degree has grown eightfold. A very significant fact about the complex and ambiguous relationship that is established among women in the United States between emancipation and career is the following data: the probability of divorcing within the first ten years of marriage for graduate women is only 50% of the probability of women who are not. Statistics indeed say that the alliance of brains is more common in married couples: the percentage of *top incomes* males married to *top incomes* females has gone from 10.6% in 1970 to 23.3% in 2018 (Yonzan 2020). To secure a position rent and outperform the competition, PhD couples combine their forces to climb the income ladder. It seems that the most educated couples have a stronger sense of competition. Just as Joseph Schumpeter theorised that the companies that obtain extra-profits are those that invest more in innovation and become more competitive, these couples succeed in work and earnings because they have been able to invest heavily in education. A hint, this one, that the link of earnings with merit gains greater significance when it is associated with having enjoyed "advantageous circumstances" during one's own formation.

In the English society that was the subject of Young's investigation, the elite still tries today to defend its own privileges. One would expect that within that society, and others where privilege is widespread, a subversive political movement would rise. The fuse of the *exit*, according to Albert Hirschman's terminology, tends however to extinguish prematurely, because it is less costly to resort to protest (*voice*). Hirschman, an economist who dedicated his research activity to "complicating the economy", highlighted how the *voice* is effectively countered: "It is increasingly obvious that in societies characterised by the mobility of those at the top the fracture between upper and lower classes tends to widen and become more rigid. But this is not an easy observation to advance; especially in a culture where it has long been taken for granted that equality of opportunity, combined with upward social mobility, is able to ensure both efficiency and social justice". In his opinion, the "disadvantaged", failing to achieve equality of opportunity, would end up suffering the privilege granted to a minority. He was a good prophet.

In recent decades, epigenetics has made significant progress. The subject of study is the role of cellular differentiation processes that are not directly due to the DNA sequence, but represent the result of the subject's interaction with the environment. This branch of biology warns us of how important the diversity of the social environment is in which people's talents flourish. In the varied script of the human species, the DNA of each individual is a role that is interpreted differently even by identical twins. According to the anthropological approach of Richerson and Boyd (2005), in fact, an intense collaboration develops between genes and culture. The human cognitive system could not have developed without the stimuli to knowledge that the living environment has already offered to the first hominids. Two evolutionary psychologists have said: "Once everything that is internal to human beings is removed from the human world, what mostly remains is the air between them" (Tooby and Cosmides 1992, p. 47). The fact is that the environment has penetrated genetics; for millennia, *culture* is no longer separated from nature. A study on brain structure shows that "biological and social factors both contribute to neurological disparities and that *policy* interventions can influence and interact with biological factors" (Kweon et al. 2022, p. 7).

If the cognitive architecture of human beings were a product attributable solely to natural selection, if only adaptation to the environment counted, the stimuli linked to social interaction that over the millennia led from mutual recognition of the face to the formation, and perhaps already to the sharing, of a *social mind* could not be explained. The current way of conceiving merit, as completely enclosed within the individual sphere, does not take into account the role of society. The biological data is not everything: the brain reflects the context to which it is exposed. The interconnection between neurons occurs in the brain "live", in continuous time. This means that the whole world—in imagining its Monads, Leibniz had intuited it—is reflected in each of us. As epigenetics argues, "the experience of the world modifies genes, determining which are silenced and which are amplified".

It is established, moreover, that "cognitive abilities", or the ability to learn and set up complex reasoning from available information, depend on the link between intelligence and environment (Cunha et al. 2010; Caucutt and Lochner 2020). Talents are potential and evolve into effective *abilities* also thanks to *nurture*, cultural nourishment, or the active role played by a series of factors, such as the care received in the family and the social environment in which one grows up. The social context increases—or reduces—the gaps between the "potentialities" that genetics assigns to people to realise their life project. Many scholars—biologists, psychologists, economists—place in early childhood the moment when the accumulation of the "advantage"—or "disadvantage"—connected to the quality of the environment in which one is inserted begins. Perhaps everything begins in the maternal womb, also considering the physiological and psychological health of the mother.

In the process of transforming talents into *abilities*, political and economic institutions play an important role. They should facilitate the existence of equal conditions for everyone in translating talents into effective *abilities* in order to realise their life project. As we know, today's *Zeitgeist* tends to orient economic and social reality in a completely different direction. The political class leading the institutions does not seem aware of the deposit of intellectual resources—not observable, therefore not knowable *a priori*—kept in each human being. Many of these resources could be usefully employed, and are instead wasted, because those who possess them lack the means to exploit them. The empirical verification of social analysis conducted in advanced countries tells us that young people from wealthy families have a much greater chance than others to get the most benefit from their genetic heritage. For people who have found themselves in "disadvantage" in interacting with the environment during adolescence, showing little talent often does not signal a "demerit", but testifies to a social discomfort destined to intensify in adult life.

The famous English paediatrician Donald Winnicott said that each child makes history for himself. "The child does not exist", there is only the relationship between the child and others. Good parental care from early childhood opens a life path for offspring marked by emotional balance (Cunha and Heckman 2007). Even if endowed with a certain talent, it has already been observed, a young person who in the context in which he grew up received insufficient care, a deficient "sentimental education" to life, is exposed to the risk of depression and the failure to commit to the formation of his own human capital and work. What then to think of the tendency to reduce merit to IQ? In fact, since cognitive development is influenced from early childhood by family background and the socio-economic environment, it seems logical to think that IQ should also be considered a "circumstance" of the person.

The American philosopher Michael Sandel (2020) has distanced himself from supporters of the origin of merit in talents, accusing them of often boasting non-existent merits: "Meritocratic arrogance reflects the tendency of winners to become too intoxicated with their own success, forgetting the luck and good fortune that helped them along the way [...]. This attitude is the moral side of technocratic politics" (ibid., p. 25). Emphasising privilege forces a return to the eternal question: "Is possessing (or not possessing) certain talents really our own doing?" (ibid., p. 24). The problem with highlighting merit is not in the rightful aim of promoting individual commitment, but in ignoring that market efficiency is the result not only of individual productivity but also of a socio-economic context that allows talents to emerge. It has been said that John Rawls was very lukewarm about associating merit with the concept of justice. His position on the link between fairness and talents is much clearer. As we will see, it is precisely on the unfair distribution of talents by Mother Nature that Rawls' opinion seems to be based, according to which his "A Theory of Justice" does not envisage a meritocratic society. Let's ask him a question about the talents "contained" in the genetic heritage: given the same commitment to work by two subjects, is the differential in earnings attributable to the greater talent of one of them because—obviously—he is "deserving" more? Or is that differential not "fair", because talents should be considered a gift from the "lottery of life"? In his "A Theory of Justice" (1971), the American political philosopher leans towards the second view. People do not "deserve", but only possess, their own talents. Considering equal access for all to opportunities, an income distribution can be defined as "fair" when these two conditions are jointly determined: a) inequality depends on a different level of commitment; b) an increase in inequality induced by growth is corrected by redistribution in favour of the worst-off, in order to allow the poor to improve their own well-being. Being convinced that the production process is a joint venture in which all social classes participate, he would have wanted to bring "the distribution of natural talents to be a common good". Although in "A Theory of Justice" he was inspired by his conception of rational behaviour, in his works Rawls progressively distanced himself from Immanuel Kant's idea that each person must be "aware that it is up to him" to show his own talent. The American philosopher argued that a public intervention before the market was needed, aimed at redistributing the fruits of talent. Those who as adults are manifestly more talented (for example, Nobel laureates, and stars of entertainment and sport) should agree to pay a monetary compensation to those who have less talent. So the question arises: if talent is a gift from the "lottery of life", once it becomes observable thanks to the fact that those who possess it have committed themselves fully to using it and the market rewards them with good earnings, can a high position in the income scale be said to be deserved? If earnings also depend on talents—which we have not "deserved" because they are a gift of nature—Rawls' answer is negative. At the very least, it should be recognised that commitment, and its reward according to the economic theory of incentives, rest on a fortunate pedestal called talent. Rawls entrusted the legitimisation of capitalism to its ability to "lift all boats" by promoting economic growth. As we have seen, in his view, in order for the inequality that may accompany growth to be legitimate, the most "disadvantaged" individual—or the social group of the poor—must be able to improve his position. Therefore, the high ethical value that the individualistic American culture attributes to social ascent is combined by Rawls with the idea that society must commit itself to correcting the indigence suffered by people at the bottom of the social scale. As we have already seen with Appadurai (2004), aspirations have a collective nature because the functioning of the economic system depends on social interaction. Certainly, Rawls did not believe in the meritocratic and neoliberal principle of "individual responsibility". Rawls was indeed opposed to the redistribution of incomes operated by the welfare state not because he feared that it would induce workers to laziness, distancing them from respect for the "theory of incentives", but because of the negative impact on economic growth of a contraction of market spaces in favour of the welfare system. The accounts of "deserving", moreover, do not always add up. The context in which social interactions take place often leads people to achieve an economic result higher than they deserve. And it also happens that, without having demerited, one obtains a poor income. Literature, a mirror of real life, is full of characters who attempt social climbing but succumb—not necessarily because of themselves—in the struggle between personal nature and the context in which they move. In Stendhal's "The Red and the Black", Jean Sorel's ambition is defeated not because of the protagonist's "demerit", but because the hypocrisies and intrigues of the social environment from which he is managed to be welcomed are stronger than his desire for assertion.

Michael Sandel (2020) thus describes the "dark side" of meritocracy: "if you don't have a degree and you struggle in the new economy, failure is only your fault [...]. The meritocratic ideal [...] is a justification of inequality" (ibid., p. 122). If production is a *joint venture*, a collective enterprise that sees at work a complex network of interdependencies, thinking of "gain" as a direct expression of an individual "merit" is a misleading simplification. It would seem that Amartya Sen hit the mark when he observed that "the concept of merit has great virtues, but among these there is not clarity" (Sen 2000, p. 16). Moreover, that not always merit is associated with reasoning with clarity was well understood by Miguel de Cervantes, when he makes Sancho Panza say: "That a wandering knight becomes mad without reason is something that does not make hot or cold; the merit is in losing the brain without reasons" (Miguel de Cervantes 1974, I, XXV, p. 244).

Bibliography

Abravanel, R. 2021 Aristocrazia 2.0. Una nuova élite per salvare l'Italia, *Solferino, Milano.*

Acemoglu, D., Egorov, G., Sonin, K. 2018 Social Mobility and Stability of Democracy: Reevaluating De Tocqueville, *in «Quarterly Journal of Economics», CXXXIII, 2, pp. 1041–105.*

Alesina, A. & Glaeser, E. R. 2004 Fighting Poverty in the US and Europe: A World of Differences, *Oxford University Press, New York.*

Alesina, A. & Angeletos, G.-M. 2005 *Fairness and Redistribution: Us versus Europe*, in eAmerican Economic Review», XCV, 4, pp. 960–98.

Alesina, A., Seror, M., Yang, D., You, Y., Zeng, W. 2020 *Persistence through Revolutions*, Bristol Economics Discussion Paper n. 20/722, University of Bristol.

Almås, I., Cappelen, A. W., Tungodden, B. 2020 Cutthroat Capitalism versus Cuddly Socialism: Are Americans More Meritocratic and Efficiency-Seeking than Scandinavians?, *in «Journal of Political Economy», CXXVIII, 5, pp. 1753–88.*

Alvaredo, F., Garbinti, B., Piketty, T. 2017 On the Share of Inheritance in Aggregate Wealth: Europe and the USA, 1900–2010, *in «Economica», LXXXIV, 334, pp. 239–60.*

Andre, P. 2022 *Shallow Meritocracy*, University of Bonn, Discussion Paper n. 318.

Appadurai, A. 2004 The Capacity to Aspire: Culture and the Terms of Recognition, *in V. Rao* & *M. Walton (eds.),* Culture and Public Action, *World Bank, pp. 59–84.*

Arrow, K. J. 1973 *Higher Education as a Filter*, in «Journal of Public Economics», II, 3, pp. 193–216.

Ashok, V., Kuziemko, I., Washington, E. 2015 Preferences for Redistribution in an Era of Rising Inequality: Some New Stylized Facts and Tentative Explanations, *in «Brookings Papers on Economic Activity», XXXIV, pp. 367–405.*

Balboni, C. A., Bandiera, O. R., Ghatak, M., Heil, A. 2021 *Why Do People Stay Poor?*, Nber Working Paper n. 29340.

Ballarino, G. & Bernardi, F. (a cura di) 2016 Education, Occupation and Social Origin: A Comparative Analysis of the Transmission of Socio-Economic Inequalities, *Edward Elgar, Cheltenham.*

Bao, R., De Loecker, J., Eeckhout, J. 2022 Are Managers Paid for Market Power?, *Cepr Discussion Paper 17182.*

Bell, B., Pedemonte, S., Van Reenen, J. 2021 Ceo Pay and the Rise of Relative Performance Contracts: A Question of Governance?, *in «Journal of the European Economic Association», XIX, 5, pp. 2513–42*

Benabou, R. & Ok, A. 2001 Social Mobility and the Demand for Redistribution: The Poum Hypothesis, *in «Quarterly Journal of Economics», CXVI, 2, pp. 447–87.*

Björklund, A., Jäntti, M., Roemer, J. 2012 Equality of Opportunity and the Distribution of Long-Run Income in Sweden, *in «Social Choice and Welfare», XXXIX, 2, pp. 675–96.*

Bourdieu, P. 1984 Distinction: A social critique of the judgement of taste, *Harvard University Press, Cambridge.*

Bowles, S., Durlauf, S. N., Hoff, K. (a cura di) 2006 *Poverty Traps*, Princeton University Press, Princeton.

Cappelen, A. W., Moene, K. O., Skjelbred, S. E., Tungodden, B. 2017 *The Merit Primacy Effect*, Working Papers 2017-047, Human Capital and Economic Opportunity Working Group.

Cappelen, A., Mollerstrom, J., Bjørn-Atle Reme, B.-A., Tungodden, B. 2022 A Meritocratic Origin of Egalitarian Behaviour («Income Inequality and Income Mobility in the Scandinavian Countries Compared to the United States»), *in «Economic Journal», CXXXII, 646, pp. 2101–17.*

Caucutt, E. M. & Lochner, L. 2020 Early and Late Human Capital Investments, Borrowing Constraints, and the Family, *in «Journal of Political Economy», CXXVIII, 3, pp. 1065–147.*

Charness, G., Masclet, D., Villeval, M. C. 2014 *The Dark Side of Competition for Status*, in «Management Science», LX, 1, pp. 38–55.

Chetty, R. et al. 2014 Is the United States still a Land of Opportunity? Recent Trends in Intergenerational Mobility, *in «American Economic Review», CIV, 5, pp. 141–7.*

Chetty, R. et al. 2017 The Fading American Dream: Trends in Absolute Income Mobility since 1940, *in «Science», CCCLVI, 6336, pp. 398–406.*

Chetty, R. et al. 2018 The Opportunity Atlas: Mapping the Childhood Roots of Social Mobility, *Nber Working Paper 25147.*

Chetty, R., Hendren, N., Jones, M. J., Porter, S. R. 2020 Race and Economic Opportunity in the United States: An Intergenerational Perspective, *in «Quarterly Journal of Economics», CXXXV, 2, pp. 711–83.*

Cohen, G. A. 1989 *Equality of What? On Welfare, Goods and Capabilities*, in «Recherches économiques de Louvain», LVI, 3/4, pp. 357–82.

Cunha, F. & J. J. Heckman 2007 *The Technology of Skill Formation*, in «American Economic Review», XCVII, 2, pp. 31–47.

Cunha, F., Heckman, J. J., Schennach, S. M. 2010 Estimating the Technology of Cognitive and Noncognitive Skill Formation, *in «Econometrica», LXXVIII, 3, pp. 883–931.*

Dabla-Norris, E. et al. 2015 Cause and Consequences of Income Inequality: A Global Perspective, *Imf, Staff Discussion Note 13.*

Dallinger, U. 2010 Support for Redistribution. What Explains Cross-National Differences?, *in «Journal of European Social Policy», XX, 4, pp. 333–49.*

de Cervantes, M. 1974 Don Chisciotte della Mancia, *Mondadori, Milano.*

De Loecker, J., Eeckhout, J., Unger, G. 2020 The Rise of Market Power and the Macroeconomic Implications, *in «Quarterly Journal of Economics», CXXXV, 2, pp. 561–644.*

De Smedt, M., Giovannini, E., Radermacher, W. J. 2019 *Measuring Sustainability*, in Stiglitz, Fitoussi, Durand 2019.

Durlauf, S. N. 2002 Groups Social Influences and Inequality: A Membership Theory Perspective on Poverty Traps, *Wisconsin Madison-Social Systems Working Paper n. 18.*

Dworkin, R. 1977 *Taking Rights Seriously*, Harvard University Press, Cambridge.

Eurofound 2017 *Social Mobility in the EU*, Research Report, Luxembourg.

Feldman, M. W., Otto, S. P., Christiansen, F. B. 2000 *Genes, Culture, and Inequality*, in Arrow, Bowles, Durlauf 2000.

Fleurbaey, M. 2008 Fairness, Responsibility, and Welfare, *Oxford University Press, Oxford.*

Franzini, M., Patriarca, F., Raitano, M. 2020 Market Competition and Parental Background Wage Premium: The Role of Human and Relational Capital, *in «Journal of Economic Inequality», XVIII, 3, pp. 291–397.*

Friedman, S. & Laurison, D. 2016 The Class Pay Gap in Higher Professional and Managerial Occupations, *in «American Sociological Review», LXXXI, 4, pp. 668–95.*

Furman, J. & Orszag, P. 2018 A Firm-Level Perspective on the Role of Rents in the Rise in Inequality, *in Guzman 2018.*

Goldin, C. 1990 Understanding the Gender Gap: An Economic History of American Women, *Oxford University Press, New York.*

Grimalda, G., Farina, F., Conte, A., Schmidt, U. 2022 Why Do Preferences for Redistribution Differ across Countries? An Experimental Analysis, Kiel Working Papers, 2230.

Gylfason, T. 2016 Efficiency, Fairness, and Social Cohesion in Europe and the United States: Incomes, Hours of Work, and Equality with an Afterthought on Iceland, *Cesifo Working Paper Series n. 6025.*

Hart, O. & Zingales, L. 2017 *Companies Should Maximize Shareholder Welfare Not Market Value*, in «Journal of Law, Finance, and Accounting», II, 2, pp. 247–75.

Hassler, J., Rodríguez Mora, J. V., Zeira, J. 2007 *Inequality and mobility*, in «Journal of Economic Growth», XII, 3, pp. 235–59.

Herrnstein, R. J. & Murray, C. 1994 The Bell Curve: Intelligence and Class Structure in American Life, *Free Press, New York.*

Hörisch, H. 2007 Is the Veil of Ignorance only a Concept about Risk? An Experiment, *Munich Discussion Paper n. 4.*

Hugo, V. 1981 *I miserabili*, Garzanti, Milano.

Hume, D. 1777 An Enquiry Concerning the Principles of Morals, *A. Millar, London.*

Jäntti, M. et al. 2007 American Exceptionalism in a New Light: A Comparison of Intergenerational Earnings Mobility in the Nordic Countries, the United Kingdom and the United States, *Warwick Economics Research Paper Series n. 781.*

Jencks, C. & Tach, L. 2006 Would Equal Opportunity Mean More Equality?, *in Morgan, Grusky, Fields 2006.*

Kuhn, P. & Lozano, F. 2006 Understanding Trends in Long Work Hours Among U.S. Men, 1979–2002, *in «Journal of Labor Economics», XXVI, 2, pp. 311–43.*

Kuziemko, I., J Shen, Pan, J., Washington, E. 2018 The Mommy Effect: Do Women Anticipate the Employment Effects of Motherhood?, *Nber Working Paper n. 24740.*

Kweon, H. et al. 2022 Human Brain Anatomy Reflects Separable Genetic and Environmental Components of Socioeconomic Status, *in «Science Advances», VIII, 18 maggio.*

Lerner, M. J. 1980 The Belief in a Just World: A Fundamental Delusion, *Plenum Press, New York.*

Markovits, D. 2019 The Meritocracy Trap: How America's Foundational Myth Feeds Inequality, Dismantles the Middle Class, and Devours the Elite, *Penguin Press, New York.*

Mijs, J. J. B. 2019 The Paradox of Inequality: Income Inequality and Belief in Meritocracy Go Hand in Hand, *in «Socio-Economic Review», XXXIX, pp. 1–39.*

Milanović, B. 2017 Global Inequality: A New Approach for the Age of Globalization, *Harvard University Press, Cambridge 2016.*

Munshi, K. & Rosenzweig, M. 2006 Traditional Institutions Meet the Modern World: Caste, Gender, and Schooling Choice in a Globalizing Economy, *in «American Economic Review», XCIV, 4, pp. 1225–52.*

Narayan, A. et al. 2018 Fair Progress? Economic Mobility across Generations around the World, *World Bank, Washington DC.*

Oecd 2018 A Broken Social Elevator? How to Promote Social Mobility, *Paris.*

Oecd 2023 Employment Outlook 2023: Artificial Intelligence and the Labour Market, *Paris.*

Piketty, T. 2020 *Capital et idéologie*, Éditions du Seuil, Paris 2019.

Prescott, E. C. 2004 Why Do Americans Work so Much More than Europeans, *in «Quarterly Review», XXVIII, pp. 2–13.*

Raitano, M. & Vona, F. 2016 Assessing Students' Equality of Opportunity in Oecd Countries: The Role of National- and School-Level Policies, *in «Applied Economics», XLVIII, 33, pp. 3148–63.*

Ray, D. 2006 *Aspirations, Poverty and Economic Change*, in A. Banerjee, R. Benabou, D. Mookherjee (eds), *Understanding Poverty*, Oxford University Press, New York.

Richerson, P. J. & Boyd, R. 2005 Not by Genes Alone: How Culture Transformed Human Evolution, *University of Chicago Press, Chicago.*

Roemer, J. E. 1996 *Theories of Distributive Justice*, Harvard University Press, Cambridge.

Roemer, J. E. 1998 *Equality of Opportunity*, Harvard University Press, Cambridge.

Roemer, J. E. 2008 Equality of Opportunity, *in S. N. Durlauf & L. E. Blume (eds)*, The New Palgrave Dictionary of Economics, *Basingstoke.*

Roemer, J. E. & Trannoy, A. 2016 *Equality of Opportunity: Theory and Measurement*, in «Journal of Economic Literature», LIV, 4, pp. 1288–332.

Runciman, W. G. 1966 Relative Deprivation and Social Justice, *Routledge and Kegan Paul, London.*

Saez, E. & Zucman, G. 2019 The Triumph of Injustice: How the Rich Dodge Taxes and How to Make them Pay, *W.W. Norton, New York.*

Sandel, M. J. 2020 The Tyranny of Merit. What's Become of the Common Good?, *Penguin Books, London.*

Santambrogio, M. 2021 Il complotto contro il merito, *Laterza, Roma-Bari.*

Scheve, K. & Stasavage, D. 2016 Taxing the Rich: A History of Fiscal Fairness in the United States and Europe, *Princeton University Press, Princeton.*

Sen, A. K. 2000 *Merit and Justice*, in Arrow, Bowles, Durlauf.

Spence, M. 1973 *Job Market Signalling*, in «Quarterly Journal of Economics», LXXXVII, 3, pp. 355–74.

Stiglitz, J. E. 1975 The Theory of «Screening» Education, and the Distribution of Income, *in «American Economic Review», LXV, 3, pp. 283–300.*

Stiglitz, J. E. 2017 *The Coming Great Transformation*, in «Journal of Policy Modeling», XXXIX, 4, pp. 1–14.

Stiglitz, J. E. 2019 The End of Neoliberalism and the Rebirth of History, *Project Syndacate, 4 novembre.*

Tertilt, M., Doepke, M., Hannusch, A., Montenbruck, L. 2022 *The Economics of Woman's Rights The Mary Paley and Alfred Marshall Lecture*, Discussion Paper Series N. 372, University of Bonn-University of Mannheim.

Tooby, J. & Cosmides, L. 1992 The Psychological Foundations of Culture, *in Barkow, Cosmides, Tooby 1992.*

Wier, L. & Erasmus, H. 2023 The Dominant Role of Large Firms in Profit Shifting, *in «Imf Economic Review», LXXI, 3, pp. 791–816.*

Wooldridge, A. 2021 The Aristocracy of Talent: How Meritocracy Made the Modern World, *Allan Lane, London.*

Yonzan, N. 2020 Assortative Mating and Labor Income Inequality: Evidence from Fifty Years of Coupling in the U.S., *Stone Center Working Paper n. 15.*

Zingales, L. 2012 A Capitalism for the People: Recapturing the Lost Genius of American Prosperity, *Basic Books, New York.*

Zingales, L. 2017 *Towards a Political Theory of the Firm*, in «Journal of Economic Perspectives», XXXI, 3, pp. 113–30.

CHAPTER 4

Social Mobility: From Birth to Decline

The Social Persistence in Medieval Communities

Paleo-anthropologists believe that what allowed the survival of the first hominids was membership of a group; they argue that vital needs made it essential to join forces. It is therefore likely that the hunter-gatherers who formed the small tribes of prehistory were cooperators, some perhaps reluctantly. The need to divide the tasks of procuring food and caring for offspring strengthened the blood ties between group members. The balance within those proto-communities and the stability of their composition probably depended on the principle of authority. The strongest imposed the fulfilment, even by force, of the assigned tasks. If a group member violated the rules of cohabitation, a punishment would come into play, up to expulsion from the group. A convincing threat, this, in times when being abandoned to oneself was equivalent to certain death. "Immobility" was also a characteristic of the collectivist societies of antiquity, as well as of the Sumerian city-states of Mesopotamia and the pre-Columbian civilisations of Latin America, regardless of the different forms in which power was exercised by the elders.

From this quick review, it is clear that at every historical moment society has a different internal dynamic. In ancient Greece and Rome, social mobility was little present, essentially concerning those who freed themselves from slavery. In the Middle Ages, the three dominant social

F. Farina, *The Rise of Inequality and the Fall of Social Mobility*, https://doi.org/10.1007/978-3-031-92843-7_4

groups—the sovereigns, the nobles and the clergy—organised communities according to a rigid hierarchical structure, based, respectively, on the sword, money and control of souls. Money, in particular, and the extreme concentration in a few hands of land and financial wealth allowed the nobles and landowners to occupy positions of economic and institutional power. The place of each individual in society—his prerogatives, his activities and his functions—were preordained by the powerful. Personal identity was forged by birth membership in a particular group; it coincided with the identity of the *nous*, or the family, the clan, the village. The rise in income and *status* was in various ways prevented or strongly discouraged. There was no certainty, moreover, that individual property rights would be recognised. Those who possessed wealth were always at risk of having it forcibly taken away; not only by bandits, but also by the sovereign or the local lord.

In the millennium from the fifth to the fifteenth century, those who did not belong to the elite of the powerful, or had not subjected themselves to them, were destined to live in precariousness: "Compared to the year 8000 BC, when agriculture was discovered and pastoralism developed, in 1500 the elite lived much better [...], but ordinary people - peasants or artisans - lived little better or no better than their ancestors" (DeLong 2022, p. 15). The beggars of the cities, without means of support, were destined for a very meagre life. The conditions of work often had the typical traits of slavery. To the peasants subjected to the *corvée*, to the servants and to the humble workers of the artisan shops, the mere thought of themselves as free people was prevented by hunger. The autonomy that was left to individuals was confined, if all went well, to the personal sphere.

The hierarchical structure of society did not, however, oppose culture. Around the year 1000, a factor began to appear on the scene in some European countries that promised to set social mobility in motion: education. From an idea of Charlemagne, who had founded the Palatine School in Aachen, and with the fundamental contribution of the Benedictine monks, a school-educational system was born and spread in Europe that guaranteed students the continuity of their educational journey and the uniformity of teaching programmes. In the *scriptorium* of the monasteries, books from the ancient Greek and Roman world were copied. In the following centuries, however, the impact on social dynamics was minimal. Although in Europe there were early signs of the link between knowledge of a trade and social mobility, in continental Europe, particularly in communities and peoples where slavery or serfdom was legal, the internal dynamics within the social body remained a marginal phenomenon. In the thirteenth century, however, the first "islands" of artisanal and industrial production were born. Some areas of continental Europe showed enterprise and industriousness: "in individual Italian cities, for example in Florence, it seems that trade took on forms with a more or less capitalistic imprint" (Sombart 1967, p. 316). In Florence, in fact, social ascent was not at all infrequent, and sometimes even too rapid: "the new people and the sudden gains", Dante comments scathingly in the *Inferno* (XVI, 73).

Judging by the results of a long-term historical statistical survey, on the Lungarni the economic power of the wealthiest families has been preserved over the centuries. The 2011 census data of the Florentines, compared on the basis of surname with those of their probable ancestors, highlighted a remarkable persistence of members of the families of today's Florence in the same income positions occupied by families in the late medieval city of 1427. The methods of statistical investigation applied to the data of family dynasties confirm a strong persistence of the level of earnings from one generation to the next. The high intergenerational elasticity coefficient clearly captures both the stability over time of the wealth endowment and the ability of its members to obtain a substantial income and to maintain their own privileged social *status* (Barone and Mocetti 2021). In the thirteenth century, the first universities in history were also born, which in the following centuries served to introduce young people to professions related to the administration of the Church and the State. The opportunity for social ascent, however, was very selective. Access to cultural education, which allowed entry into the liberal professions, was reserved for young people from noble or wealthy families. The dynamics of *status* within the social structure was therefore accelerated mainly by the free circulation of money in trade. There was, of course, also downward mobility. But for the nobles, bankers and wealthy merchants, this was a rare phenomenon.

Historical research today gives more weight than before to legal institutions and cultural values as factors capable of influencing social mobility. According to anthropologist and historian Alan Macfarlane, England in the Middle Ages was unique compared to continental Europe: already from the thirteenth century, society "showed considerable social mobility, based on wealth rather than blood, with few barriers between occupational groups, social strata, and city and countryside" (Macfarlane 1978, p. 165). Being the son of a landowner was not a guarantee of a comfortable life. The reason was legislation, which hindered the exercise of inheritance rights. Since the right to paternal inheritance was limited to the firstborn (but this transfer could be cancelled with a will; or the estate was alienated before death), the children of the rich who could not count on their parents' resources had to take responsibility for their own future and enter the labour market early. The regulation of property rights would therefore have favoured intergenerational social mobility, the "independence" of the level of children's earnings compared to those of their parents. The early development of the English economy, centuries before the Industrial Revolution, could therefore have been favoured by inheritance law.

Historical research has also begun to investigate the role played by social norms in the internal evolution of the social structure. A well-known biologist of human evolution, Joseph Heinrich, informs us of the testimony of a Franciscan missionary in Mexico, at the time of the *conquistadores* of Cortés. It seems that social acceptance of polygamy greatly increased competition for the conquest of the most attractive women. The aggregate data, however, is not a guarantee that the competition took place on an equal footing. The absence of monogamy seems rather to have had a significant impact in generating unequal opportunities for social mobility. In the Aztec empire of 1521 that preceded Spanish domination, there was indeed a strong divergence between men regarding the chances of finding an ever-increasing number of concubines. The equal attraction to female beauty became a factor of "inequality of opportunity" between wealthy males and males with scarce means. The gap in mating opportunities represented a factor of frustration that was added to poverty: "polygynous marriage has powerful social dynamics that create an excess of poor men with few hopes of mating and marrying, because most women marry 'up'" (Heinrich 2020, p. 274).

In late medieval Europe, things were different. The obligation of monogamous marriage acted as a natural presidium for the stability of the social organisation based on the nuclear family. However, the Church's prohibition of incest weakened the role of the kinship relationship, and therefore the power of the head of the family as a factor of social control (ibid.). More generally, the advancements of humanity—great inventions such as gunpowder, the printing press, galleons, and the expansion of trade—in modifying the professions, had a very varied impact within society. The succession of innovations undoubtedly had, at least indirectly, an impact on the life of communities, contributing to loosen the control of families over their children. The empire of the religious power of the popes and the secular power of the sovereigns, which blocked social dynamics, would not have held up for long. The economic enterprise of the individual would soon have unfolded. After the start of the Commercial Revolution, a term with which economic historians designate the leap forward of economic transactions between the fourteenth and fifteenth centuries, work and commercial activities were freed from the many constraints imposed, not only by the sovereign and the Church, but also by the aristocracy and the owners of large estates at the top of the local social hierarchy. With the progress of economic-social interaction, from the sixteenth century the transition to higher levels of income and *status* became the prerogative of representatives of well-defined groups: merchants and emerging urban classes, often gathered in the corporations of craftsmanship, professions and banking credit (Tanzini and Tognetti 2016). The market assumed the role of the most important institution for coordinating socio-economic interaction.

A new conception of the social structure emerged. From then on forward, the condition of the individual will be less and less determined by the position occupied in the social hierarchy (as was the case within the medieval hierarchy) and more and more by the economic position achieved in society with their own work activity. History began to turn in the direction indicated in 312 BC by the Roman censor Appius Claudius Caecus, towards the *homo faber fortunae suae*. The value that is recognised to the individual as master and architect of their own destiny is not only the result of secular thought that was undermining the religious conception of the world, or of humanism that was affirmed in the late Middle Ages. An important role in the advancement of society towards the emancipation of males was indeed played by technical progress. Progress in production techniques changed the economic convenience in favour of the substitution of slavery and servitude with the combination of wage labour with machinery owned by entrepreneurs and the tools of work of the wealthier craftsmen. With the progressive recognition of civil rights to the person, dependency relationships began to decline in the public sphere. The family, however, remained the place of society where interpersonal relationships were strongly marked by command. Rigid behaviour norms imposed submission to women.

Social Classes and Collective Imagination

In Rome of 494 BC, Menenius Agrippa, with his well-known fable, reminded the plebs that in a *res publica* social classes are closely linked, so that it is the collaboration between them that allows civil coexistence. The awareness that the existence of each social class is possible only thanks to the existence of the others has become over the centuries—albeit with difficulty and very slowly—common sense. Which is not surprising. The arbitrariness of the powerful, or even just the income and *status* distances too large often proved unbearable for the subordinate classes. In many local communities of European countries, the living conditions of workers were so miserable as to provoke protests, up to the resort to violence. The most well-known episodes are the popular rebellion that occurred in response to the economic crisis of 1381 in the English countryside; and between 1524 and 1526 the peasant revolt led by a Protestant pastor, Thomas Müntzer, whose "millenarianism" was not satisfied with the simple Lutheran religious reform. The repression of the insurrection he fomented led to the loss of more than one hundred thousand human lives.

In order to root collaboration between classes in society, and avert the danger of subversion threatened by the subordinate classes, a community needs symbols that preside over the rational decision of the various social groups to balance the opposing interests, of an idealisation that gives value and legitimacy to the search for a compromise. The birth of the iconography of the "social body" should be considered the announcement of the exit from the medieval hierarchical order. After William Harvey discovered the venous and arterial circulation of blood in 1616, anthropomorphic images of nations began to proliferate. The change in mentality towards the idea of the "social body" accelerated the evolution of the "collective imagination". As mentioned, the European peoples had acquired a new idea of living in community, that of a conscious coexistence, no longer imposed by hierarchies. The State, as we conceive it today, was born in the most politically evolved nation in Europe, England, to put a stop to violence. In Thomas Hobbes' vision, social conservation could only be based on the strength of the empire. The English political philosopher associated power with the positive figure of a giant, Leviathan, and the monster Behemoth, personification of the dystopian reality of the English civil war. Already in the course of the seventeenth century, however, in the major European countries the state administration evolved—with the birth of representative institutions—towards greater citizen control over the absolute power of the sovereigns. The nation-state was emerging. The image of the "social body" would soon take on more reassuring forms than those imagined by Hobbes.

Meanwhile, technological innovations were stimulating competition among nations. The expansion of transoceanic maritime trade and the birth of the first colonial possessions aroused in the great powers that confronted each other at sea the ambition to compare themselves with other countries. It was probably in the eighteenth century that the power of the nation-state began to find recognition and representation also within the countries that had experienced greater development. Iconography was put at the service of the dynamics that were emerging in society. The figurative reproduction of the "social body" had the task of inviting the people to a common commitment to the construction of the primacy and prosperity of the nation. This was a very heartfelt issue in the ruling classes. Interaction in society was no longer regulated by absolute rule, and in the "collective imagination" the nightmare of finding oneself in the "realm of fear" of Hobbesian memory was disappearing. In many nations, the possibility that social conflict would find an outlet in a rebellion against established authority was still latent. From being the object of political regulation within the medieval hierarchy of power, the conflict between groups in society was becoming an endemic characteristic of the economic and social processes of the nation-state.

The Industrial Revolution represented a cultural break destined to have great consequences in the following centuries. If shared ideas are the brain of the "social body", economic growth is the motor system that allows movement. As we will see, social mobility depends both on economic growth and on the distribution of the *surplus* that is created. The problem that the ruling classes faced was the danger that social conflict in general, or social turbulence generated by growth, would set in motion processes capable of triggering the disintegration of society. Moreover, it was the rooting of the presence of the State in collective consciousness that instilled in peoples the value of social cohesion. However, there was still a significant problem to be solved in order for the phenomenon of social mobility to gain consistency in Europe. To activate a dynamic within the social structure, the fuel of GDP was missing: "An Englishman of 1750, as far as material goods are concerned, was closer to a legionary of Caesar than to his own great-grandchildren". According to a convention based on data processed by the English economist and historian Angus Maddison (2001), in a period of time that goes from the end of the eighteenth century to the first decades of the nineteenth century, after centuries of economic stagnation, productive expansion began in the most advanced European nations.

The die was cast. Not only material production began to speed up. Society also began to evolve at a less slow pace than before. The growth of GDP immediately became the main factor accelerating social mobility. More income for everyone (absolute mobility), but also some incomes that rise and others that lose positions in the ranking (relative mobility). If on the one hand the process of economic growth highlighted the importance of "gross domestic product" as a tool for social cohesion, on the other hand social distances were accentuated. The first, natural, consequence of the manifestation of growth was that the distances between the rich and the poor widened. The Gini index of income inequality, calculated on the global population, was less than 0.5 in 1820, but in the following decades it rose with increasing progression. At the end of the nineties of the twentieth century it then reached almost 0.7, declining to 0.6 in 2020 thanks to the progress of poor countries (Milanović 2024).

In the Middle Ages, the rigid hierarchical system generated in the power groups a stubborn indifference to the economy and social fractures. The social change produced by the impetuous explosion of the Industrial Revolution, on the other hand, had the effect of increasing in the English ruling class the need to strengthen social control. Hence the need to ensure that the economic system continued to expand. If this happens, a ruling class can hope that the conflict over the division of the surplus does not put at risk the sustainability of the social order.

In increasing the responsibilities of the elite, the Industrial Revolution also gave impetus to the self-representation of the nation-state. The "social body" of the British nation had its ideal incarnation in the powerful symbols linked to the monarchy: its various realms find a synthesis in the *pattern* of the Union Jack and in the composite iconography of the Sovereign's Sceptre. In serving the collective imagination, artistic creation took on a direct educational intent, becoming a factor of social pedagogy. In the paintings of many English countryside painters, bucolic views gave way to a forest of smoking chimneys. The collective effort put into industrial production will soon also find a metaphorical explanation in the description of the pin factory in *The Wealth of Nations* (1776). Adam Smith's analysis identified the distinctive characteristic of emerging capitalism in the division of labour, where each phase is specialised for the purpose of efficiently producing the final product.[1] The idea began to take hold that the condition for the existence of the "social body" was the expansion of production as a *joint venture*.

Thirteen years after the publication of Adam Smith's most famous work, the French Revolution broke out. This striking historical event of social conflict explosion was generated by exceptional material contingencies. The Terror gave vent to the repressed violence that had been smouldering from the previous century, when the asymmetry of power between the aristocracy, which with political power defended the values of property conservation, and the peasants, reduced to conditions of extreme poverty, had become enormous in France. In 1792, two years before the arrest and execution of Robespierre, the National Convention abolished the monarchy. The *French Republic* was born. The symbolic representations of its advent helped to overcome the strong trauma of the social fabric caused by the Revolution. Even before the birth of the Empire—during which the glory of the nation was reflected by the decorative splendour of the Napoleonic style—the republican state had found exemplary iconography in the beauty of the forms of Marianne. Eugène Delacroix immortalised her—and elected her as a symbol, in the title of the painting, as "liberty leading the people"—while she waves the French Tricolour on the barricades. Also in the other great European nations anthropomorphic representations of the Nation proliferated in the nineteenth century. The Spanish Constitution promulgated by the Cortes of Cadiz in 1812, considered the manifesto of political liberalism, took the form of allegory in a celebrated painting in which the Charter magically assumed female features. In 1861, the "towered Italy" personified by a female face will become the representation of national unity. Not only that, the iconography changes with the evolution and the turbulences of national history. In 1835, Philipp Veit painted a Germany crowned with oak branches, in a romantic landscape with castle, imperial crown, sword and double-headed eagle. Thomas Mann, in his speech in Stockholm on the occasion of the

[1] When the production of a good, even not particularly elaborate like a pin, is organised by dividing it into many distinct operations each entrusted to a specific worker, the productivity of the individual worker increases enormously.

Nobel Prize (1929), will instead compare the Germany of the agitated years of the Weimar Republic to Andrea Mantegna's Saint Sebastian, "that young man at the stake, whom arrows and darts press on every side, and who smiles in suffering".

The Formation of the "Mass Society" in America and in Europe

The changing social landscape showed—as has been said—more income for everyone, but also, for some, rising incomes, and for others a loss of position in the earnings scale. What distinguished was the new social group of the middle class, whose members, for the most part, knew a continually expanding income. The contours of a plurality of social strata groupable under the category of the bourgeoisie were now becoming recognisable: the emerging classes, linked to progress in production techniques, such as entrepreneurs and company managers, bureaucrats, professionals, traders and so on. A step lower were employees and teachers, small traders and small professionals: in short, that area with not well-defined boundaries that was already then indicated as lower middle class or petite bourgeoisie. At the beginning of the nineteenth century, however, on a quantitative level, the middle class had not yet reached in Europe a size such as to affect the tendentially dichotomous image of the nascent industrial society: on the one hand, the capitalist-entrepreneurs committed to organising the productive factors for the achievement of profit; on the other hand the wage workers of manufactures and agricultural companies, plus small tenant farmers and peasants, lacking the resources necessary to own productive capital and also with scarce opportunities to acquire professional skills.

The class contours naturally appeared much more nuanced in the United States. When Alexis de Tocqueville in 1830 cast his gaze on the "new world", he noted that beyond the Atlantic a story was unfolding with very particular contours, if compared with the divisions that crossed the social fabric in Europe. In the United States he described, social tensions did not mount, because the right of people to social ascent—facilitated as it was by the wide range of opportunities present in the labour market—did not encounter great obstacles in realising. In praising "the ability of the inhabitants of the United States to almost always combine their own well-being with that of their fellow citizens" (Tocqueville 1995,

p. 357), Tocqueville appreciated the sense of collectivity—an embryonic *status civitatis*—that he found in their personal identity. It was the fortune of being the country of "equal conditions" that allowed the United States to be—from its constitution as a nation—a democracy, the first of the modern era. The French political scientist observed that in that country, where instead of the aristocracy of birth the aristocracy of money prevailed, "the privileges of the few are always very great, but the possibility of acquiring them is open to all. [...]. Since the social value of men is no longer visibly and permanently fixed, but varies infinitely according to wealth, classes always exist, but it is no longer possible to clearly and quickly distinguish those who compose them" (ibid., p. 585). As was mentioned in the Introduction, Tocqueville was however far from analysing social mobility based on an uncritical exaltation of the *status libertatis* of people. Indeed, he did not fail to perceive disturbing signals about the future of social cohesion: "I am not aware of any country [...] where the love for money is so deeply rooted among men's affections, and where a deeper contempt is directed at the theory that would want a permanent equality in property" (ibid., p. 481).

Tocqueville had understood that among the constitutive characters of a society there is not only the greater or lesser fluidity of the change of place of individuals in the various boxes of income distribution. In his description, very lucid and pertinent, stands out the main character of the phenomenon of social mobility: it is individual people who climb or descend the steps of the social ladder; but this dynamics, in modifying the set of members that each class is composed of, is at the same time also a phenomenon of collective regeneration.

In the economic sphere, social mobility progressed parallel to the development of the manufacturing industry also in Europe. The wealthiest and most enterprising young people began to have the opportunity to project themselves into a new socio-economic context, permeated by uncertainty about the profitability of the risk investment made by the entrepreneur. In the most advanced countries, the increase in GDP of the first decades of the nineteenth century brought the lives of young wealthy people, for the first time in history, out of the staticity of the condition of life of the family of origin, and from its always equal reproduction from generation to generation. With the birth of the novel of formation, of which Goethe's *Wilhelm Meister* was the archetype, being young began to be conjugated with modernity. The young person is indeed removed from the destiny of replicating the paternal path of work and life, to open up to the vast world and dedicate themselves “to the uncertain exploration of social space. Exploration necessary because the new imbalances and the new laws of the capitalist world make random the continuity between generations, and impose a mobility previously unknown”.

During the nineteenth century, in many nations the transition from absolute monarchy to constitutional sovereignty and to the liberal conception of the State took place. The life destinies of young people were however very divergent. Young people from subordinate classes were initiated into participation in the market as wage workers. The increase in what we now call the aggregate GDP of economies corresponded to an increasingly unequal distribution among classes. To make the population accept inequalities and the difficulties of social ascent, and to obtain their identification in a collective imaginary of cohesion, the construction of symbols that represented the ideals of the national community could not be enough. The century of the birth of liberal democracies is studded with episodes of social revolt with a revolutionary intent, from the insurrections of 1848 to the Paris Commune of 1871. Economic expansion, on the other hand, did not sufficiently mitigate the discomfort of the weak classes: it was subject to cyclical phases, also long, of interruption (like the 20-year period 1875–1895 of crisis of the world economy).

The way in which the European ruling classes faced the prospect of “social inclusion” was quite ambiguous. If the aristocracy and the high bourgeoisie of state administration at the head of the great European nations—not without hesitation and not giving up the control, also authoritarian, of workers’ organisations—set out on the path of building mass consensus for capitalist society, they did so to advance their own interests. At the end of the nineteenth century, in fact, the conflicts generated by colonial enterprises made it clear that Europe was entering the era of confrontation between imperialisms. In the owning classes and in governments both the turbulence created by the hegemonic aims of the great powers and the fear of revolutionary impulses aimed at overturning capitalist institutions mounted. Prefect Haussmann, the architect of the modernisation of Paris between 1850 and 1870, conceived the capital as a battleground of class struggle: he indeed widened the streets, with the aim of making the reaction with cannon fire more effective to the erection of barricades. After the Paris Commune of 1871, and after the failed Russian revolution of 1905, the persistent insurrectional danger was very much felt by the ruling classes, and would then reach its peak with the success of the Bolshevik Revolution of 1917. In many European countries conscription was introduced through compulsory military service, which allowed governments to recruit a large number of young people. For the purposes of social cohesion within and the defence of the homeland from the threats of other powers, the cultural elevation of the popular classes also had great importance.

The promotion of the country's progress thus became an ambiguous mixture, in which the strengthening of armies was married with the progressive strengthening of public education. Governments chose to produce more weapons. Economic growth and social mobility would have required more school desks. It was also chosen to combine a tight control of workers' trade union aggregations through legislation with the concession to increasing strata of the population on a census basis of the right to vote. The start of inclusive policies had the effect of attenuating social tensions. The need to keep one's own country ready for a war conflict also brought out the need to strengthen a shared ideology that united social classes under the national flag.

In the Europe that was undergoing a process of accelerated industrialisation and urbanisation, the advent of political democracy gave rise to a phenomenon hitherto unknown: the interclass mass society. In the *Belle Époque*, the years when European nations were reaching greater prosperity between the end of the nineteenth century and the First World War, a tragic misunderstanding was born, according to which the growing social strata were led to believe that the world was heading towards a path of harmonious development, along which economic progress and the advent of political democracy would transform the "entry of the masses into history" into an acceleration of upward social mobility. However, economic development was running much faster than the development of society. The change in the economic and social structure highlighted the deep imbalance between the demand for social ascent from the poorer classes and the narrow political bases on which power rested.

For social stratification to have evolved in the form of "social inclusion", a *governance* would have been needed in which political power had the strength to condition economic power. Neither in Great Britain, nor in the central empires, nor in France was this condition being realised. The major European economies were led by an elite whose culture was still deeply aristocratic. Political democracy was far from complete. More than half of those entitled—female citizens—were not admitted to vote, and in many countries the right to vote was still linked to the census.[2] The political parties of "social inclusion", the social-democratic and social-Christian inspired ones, were not strong enough either at the polls or in relation to economic power. If wages remained low, while the increase in productivity rapidly increased the number of goods produced, not enough demand was created internally. Advanced countries therefore had to compete for export markets by all means. A framing of the origins of the First World War from the dual perspective of increasing income inequality within nations and the succession of inter-imperialist conflicts was developed, at the beginning of the century, in the classic volume *Imperialism: A Study* John A. Hobson (1902) skilfully outlined the link between the search for outlets abroad, due to an accumulation of capital exceeding investment opportunities at home, and imperialist impulses. Colonialism, which began in conjunction with the global economic crisis of 1873–1895, turned into imperialism, because alongside the economic reasons identified by Hobson was the need for European governments to dampen social unrest by fuelling nationalist ideology. The symbols and allegories of the early century underwent a perverse evolution in the "race for colonies". European powers vented their urge for domination and domination on colonised peoples. The myth of the nation, based on cultural superiority and territorial expansion, merged with the myth of race, the pseudo-scientific mystification of biological superiority.

Hannah Arendt described totalitarianism as the combination of three main elements: imperialism, mass politics and anti-Semitism. The war between the empires of 1914–1918 had regimented citizens under the banner of the nation. Once the conflict was over, all the wounds inflicted by the war appeared on the "social body" of the belligerent countries. The crisis that followed the world conflict, by worsening the economic conditions of the population, only aggravated the "social question". Those who John M. Keynes would soon call the "animal spirits" of capitalism were not prepared for the birth of the modern "mass society". The owning classes of many European countries began to distrust the extension of the right to vote to wider strata of bourgeois and popular classes, fearing that

[2] The first country where the right to vote was extended to women was Finland (1906). In the United Kingdom, universal suffrage was introduced in 1918, in Germany in 1919, in the United States in 1920, in Sweden in 1921, in Spain in 1931, in France and Italy in 1946.

the formation of the "mass society" could threaten their profits. Workers' struggles in factories and squares triggered a strong political instability, which turned—in Germany and Italy, in particular—into a multiplier of social conflict.

With the disintegration of socio-economic relations prior to the world conflict, it became clear that the mix of granting political rights, compulsory education and compulsory conscription was not suitable, in the absence of deep economic reforms, to produce the amalgam of the "cement of society". The subordinate classes, who had paid the highest human price in the conflict and who in the following years saw their misery increase, fell into existential disorientation. The timid post-war economic recovery was followed, with the Wall Street crisis of 1929, by the Great Depression of the thirties. The process of "inclusion" of the masses in democratic life was interrupted by the sharp setback in well-being suffered by the popular classes.

Faced with the immense consequences of the war—the increase in the prices of basic necessities, the difficult reintegration of veterans into civilian life, the danger that street violence would trigger a Bolshevik-style subversive process—the ruling classes of some Western and Eastern European nations resorted to the authoritarian solution. In the interclass society, which had placed commercial law at the service of freedom in business and economic development, the need to strengthen social control, to keep the impoverished masses at bay, was entrusted to the issuance of codes full of laws aimed at repressing freedom of opinion and the Freedom of the press and to demonstrate in the square. The reactionary turn that Europe experienced between the two world wars made it clear that the birth of modern mass society had not been accompanied by institutions capable of safeguarding social cohesion with the tools of democracy. The thirties were a demonstration of the failure of the idea that with the "entry of the masses into history" social mobility would have been set in motion. Mass society, rather than representing the scenario in which democracy should have found expression and prospered, had become the manoeuvring mass of economic powers.

In the period between the two world wars, in some European countries, a sort of collective fanaticism was the most complete expression of the arrival at the "mass society". Economic prostration and the identity disorientation of young people, who saw their hope for social ascent frustrated, drove millions of people across Europe to seek refuge in the collective identity forged by the most retrograde political forces. The Nazi regime in power in Germany, which, along with expansionist ambitions throughout the European continent, fomented anti-Semitism and discriminatory policies against the "different", would plunge Europe into the tragedy of the Second World War.[3]

The thirties represented the moment of rupture between the generation of fathers, born in the years of nationalist delirium fermented between the end of the nineteenth century and the First World War, and that of the sons, who were about to suffer the consequences with the Second World War. In focusing attention on young people, the sociologist Karl Mannheim, a careful scholar of the "turns of history", observed: "in stable communities - in societies of status or 'traditional' – 'being young' takes shape only in biological differentiation". In the twentieth century, however, Mannheim continued, history has now entered the lives of young people: in generational placement, as well as in class condition, "one finds oneself, and it is also secondary whether one is aware of it or not, whether one wants to recognise this belonging or not" (ibid., p. 338). Mannheim means to say that in the twentieth century the individual condition of being young has come to be more closely linked to the collective condition. However, a distinction must be added. While the imprint of the socio-economic family placement is reproduced unchanged on the identity formation of young people, their cultural dimension tends to increasingly assume the distinctive traits of the historical moment in which young people find themselves living.

The cultural identity of the new generations will become in the post-war period the battleground—an ideological contest, perhaps more decisive than the distributive conflict—on which the power asymmetry between classes will manifest. It will be good to delve deeper.

[3] A complex interweaving of political, economic and social factors led to the affirmation of reactionary forces and the formation of authoritarian regimes in Italy, Portugal, Hungary, Spain, Bulgaria and Romania. Political democracy coexisted with the conquest of better living conditions for workers only for very short periods, in France with the governments of the Popular Front of Léon Blum between 1936 and 1938, and in Spain with left-wing coalitions in 1931 and 1936.

The "Model of the Mind" and the Concept of Democracy

The *social mind* is a discovery of the twentieth century. The "model of the mind" comes to be outlined—and to be shared—among people formed in a given cultural context primarily within their own generation. Karl Mannheim, following the analysis developed by Marx and Engels in *The German Ideology*, was clear that the way people think is conditioned by their position in society.[4] Hannah Arendt was on the same wavelength: "every living being depends on a world that appears as a place for its own appearance, from its peers to play its part with them, from the spectators so that its existence is admitted and recognised". People, from a young age, need to build a "model of the mind", in order to understand on the basis of which motivating factors others act, and to form expectations on how others will react to their own behaviours. This construction takes place both on the psychic and cultural level. Regarding the former, it is now recognised that brain circuits are stimulated by social interaction.[5] It is, for example, through the "system of 'reading the gaze', i.e. the set of mechanisms through which we observe the direction and movement of others' eyes, that we infer what they want, know and believe". The emotions and intentions that individuals in various ways communicate to other individuals are the subject of continuous processing. Self-awareness

[4] "Individuals who mature in the same period, live in the years of maximum assimilation capacity, but also later, experience the same determining influences both from the dominant intellectual culture and from political social situations. They represent a generation, a contemporaneity, since these influences are unitary".

[5] In the line of thought of the *social mind*, to which scholars from different disciplines contribute, very different positions are compared. In the vision of the model of the mind proposed by neuroscientist Michael S. Gazzaniga (1985, 2009; see also Reuter-Lorenz et al. 2010), the sensation of possessing a unified conscious awareness of reality is due to the functioning of the left hemisphere of the brain. However, this vision of the "social mind" is quite questionable. Gazzaniga starts from the premise that all mental processes depend exclusively on the brain, on whose functioning social phenomena would have no impact. On the opposite side, evolutionary psychologist Michael Tomasello, following the historical-cultural psychology of the 1930s, studies the "shared intentionality" linking the functioning of the mind to man's socio-cognitive abilities. This ability leads him to "identify with others […] and to understand them as intentional and mental beings like the Self. [This] has made possible […] cultural artefacts and behavioural traditions that change cumulatively in historical times […]. Children grow up […] profiting from the knowledge and skills accumulated by the social groups they belong to" (Tomasello 2005, p. 28).

and awareness of others' ways of being give rise, in social dynamics, to a common "way of being". The key moment is when the different elaborations converge in the birth of common sense among people. In the brain of each human being, his world is indeed represented: the context in which individuals live, its nature—the places where the community lives—and its history—the evolution of society and its conflicts. Without the external world, the community to which it belongs, the Self does not exist. "Our brain is so interested in social interaction that it has developed special dedicated programmes: primitive functions aimed at dealing with issues of rights and duties" (ibid., p. 97).

On a cultural level, civil coexistence does not originate in the individual, but is formed through the connections that the individual has with their socio-cultural environment (Wilson 2012). People are aware that they are not strangers to each other.

To understand the link between social mobility and the distribution of power in society, it is necessary to analyse how the "social mind" is shared among people, becoming the "model of the mind" of a community. The coexistence between classes suggests that in society—at every historical stage—a "model of the mind" is formed, shared by citizens (Denzau and North 1994; Roy and Denzau 2020). The balancing of values and interests is a socio-cultural process. Starting from the *Weltanschauung* of various social groups, different ideological elaborations—even in the presence of social conflict—are compared and harmonised. Often, this process takes place under the guidance of the most prominent social groups. "The images of social order, created by the efforts of society's elites to overcome their own contradictions, have been handed down in the institutions, laws and cultural forms of modern societies" (Greenfeld 1992, pp. 490–1). In the two greatest political cultures of antiquity, the sharing of a "model of the mind" took institutional form in a "common house" above the parties. The Greek and Roman peoples gave this political institution the name, respectively, of πολιτεία and *res publica*. In modern times, it is the articles of the Constitution of the democratic state that establish the rules that different ideologies must follow to make the sharing of a "model of the mind" sustainable over time. If this does not happen, and a "model of the mind" is not formed in a people, disagreement among the members of the community results—sometimes after a violent conflict—in the establishment of an authoritarian regime in which the government proclaims to represent "power in the name of the people". An authoritarian regime sometimes defines itself as "illiberal", as elections of representative assemblies take place with a vote for candidates of a "single party".

If the norm for most nations is civil, albeit often turbulent, coexistence between social groups, what is its *ratio*? In the vision of the democratic state proposed here, the real protagonist of a community's life is the "model of the mind", not directly the institutions of political democracy. The rules of civil coexistence written in the Constitution, which take institutional form in the democratic state, are meant to last. The "model of the mind" of a country, on the other hand, is "flexible", leading to a certain form of *res publica* at one time and another form of *res publica* at another time. Being part of the life of society—as it is continuously reworked by people in their interaction—the "model of the mind" must have the flexibility necessary to ensure the long-term sustainability of the compromise between social classes on which the state is based. What makes *res publicae* different from each other—despite the continuity of the state form reflected by the Constitution—is the degree of power asymmetry that characterises the balance that is achieved between social classes in the economic sphere. Each type of *res publica* is associated with a different—more or less unequal—distribution of economic surplus between social classes, which in turn is influenced by the distribution of wealth that characterises the country. We will define a *socio-economic equilibrium* as a "state of quiet" of the conflict.

Groups that find themselves in a situation of "disadvantage" in fact accept a certain degree of power asymmetry. The nineteenth century was the century in which the spread of constitutions coincided with the affirmation of liberalism. In summary, liberalism identifies democracy with the *res publica* and the *res publica* with the liberal state (or its equivalent, such as the constitutional monarchy). In the vision of social conflict, the tension between social groups is always latent. The less social mobility there is for the "disadvantaged" social classes, the less their tolerance for the existing degree of power asymmetry in principle. We can think of the logic behind the acceptance by low-income social groups of the compromise implicitly negotiated between classes—the "socio-economic equilibrium" in place—as a probabilistic rational calculation. Although they are often not aware of it, individuals belonging to "weak" social groups behave as if they were faced with the choice between two options: *participation* or *subversion*. The second option is normally excluded, because the cost of refusing to accept the "power asymmetry"—the cost of "subversion"—appears to them greater than the benefit—the share of surplus to "negotiate" within the political and economic institutions—that they expect to obtain from a revision of the compromise.

The first option, the ***participation*** in the shared "model of the mind", can therefore appear in the course of history in the form of a plurality of *res publica*, each corresponding to a different distribution of economic surplus among social groups. This is not a concept accepted by the mainstream school of thought in political science. Having theorised that its object of study is society conceived as a collection of "free and equal" subjects, whose differences in position in society are the result of autonomous individual choices, much of twentieth-century liberalism has rejected the ideas of social conflict and an asymmetry of power between classes. Instead of a shared "model of the mind", civil coexistence is interpreted based on the adherence of the members of the community to what psychology defines as the "social mind". The idea is that, being individuals "free and equal", public discourse within society is able to lead to agreement between them. In "classical" liberal thought, the "social mind" therefore does not cross the boundary of the person, it remains a prerogative of the individual, it remains within the realm of individual psychology. To deny that the form of democracy can change, when liberal thought refers to the State, as established by the articles of the Constitution, the noun democracy becomes an adjective. The reason is the need to distinguish between States that embody the idea of "free and equal" subjects—the States, precisely, defined as liberal-democratic—and those that are not—authoritarian States. The democracy favoured by "classical liberalism", not foreseeing the presence of social conflict, is that of "liberal democracy". In all countries immune from authoritarian temptations, there would be a single institutional form—the democratic state—in which subjects identify themselves as "free and equal". Not surprisingly, in commenting on the collapse in 1991 of the authoritarian regime of one of the two superpowers, the Soviet Union, the American political scientist Francis Fukuyama went so far as to declare the "end of history"; to be understood, precisely, as the affirmation of a single winning ideology. From the liberal analytical perspective, it is inconceivable that in historical development, within the various national communities, the *res publica* knows an evolution. The *res publica* can only express itself in political democracy, whose representative institutions are formed by voting.

The history of the institutions of advanced democratic countries, however, does not seem to be reflected in a single model of *res publica*. The flexibility of the "model of the mind" is substantiated in the possibility that the type of *res publica* changes. This is the guarantee of the sustainability over time of the State.[6] It is this flexibility that ensures that the values and interests of social groups overcome the tensions inherent in social conflict to reach a provisional composition from time to time. It consists of a new "socio-economic balance", corresponding to a different distribution of resources among social groups. The field of expression of consensus, which confers legitimacy on the State, is not the formal seats of representation that lead to the succession of one government to another through a parliamentary vote of confidence; it is the social context, in which the asymmetry of power between classes is reflected. Democracy is therefore a system based on competition between parties representing the opposing interests of social groups that finds its outlet in the electoral confrontation: "the vote derives value from the ex post correspondence between the laws to which everyone must obey and the will of a majority" (Przeworski 2009, pp. 19–20).

The path of approach to political democracy taken by European countries between the nineteenth and twentieth centuries was very tormented. It has been observed that a theorist of liberalism like Benedetto Croce, in his *History of European Liberalism in the Nineteenth Century*, expressed himself in rather sceptical terms about the adherence to democratic values of liberal governments: "a liberal elite imbued with 'liberal sentiment' can imprint a much freer character on the whole society than the abstract and merely arithmetic instrument of suffrage extended to all" (Canfora 2004, pp. 141–2). In the first half of the twentieth century, even in countries with consolidated democratic institutions, the ruling classes could not conceive of the "social inclusion" of the popular masses except in terms of the extension of the right to vote.

For the hope of an evolution from political democracy to economic democracy to mature, it was necessary that in 1945 the exceptional conditions of post-war reconstruction were determined. The enterprise system needed to involve the working masses in the cooperative enterprise aimed at achieving a process of sustained growth. In some countries, the involvement of the subordinate classes in the *joint venture* of reconstruction and

[6] In addition to the classic example of France, there are many countries that have changed the form of the *res publica* by implementing constitutional reforms aimed at modifying the socio-economic balance between social classes, so as to preserve social order. In Argentina, for example, the Constitution enacted in 1853, inspired by the liberal one of the United States, was modified in 1947 by Juan Domingo Perón, with the aim of realising his conception of democracy as a political system that attributes power to the masses.

economic expansion took on conflictual characteristics. It was mainly the workers of the manufacturing industry who exerted political pressure for the recognition of rights in the factory and higher wages. In the end, the opposition of interests between the groups of the "advantaged" and the "disadvantaged" came to a composition and a new "socio-economic balance" was established, characterised by less income inequality.

The *Trente Glorieuses* were the period of highest growth and most moderate inequalities known by Europe in the post-war period. Progressive political parties and trade unions managed to limit the power of companies in the economic system. The asymmetry of power, and the consequent latency in society of the conflict between classes, seemed to bend to the idea—inspired by the concept of "systemic interdependence"—that everyone's freedom is subject to the limit that a "privileged" social group does not create serious externalities that are detrimental to the well-being of other social groups. In post-war Europe, a less unequal distribution of surplus and well-being was emerging, and therefore, in Dahrendorf's words, a "less unequal distribution of life chances", the premise for the reshuffling of positions on the income scale (relative social mobility *relative*).

The *res publica* of the *Trente Glorieuses*, an embryo of solidary democracy, was a historical exception, a parenthesis limited to a certain period and certain countries. In the period from the eighties to today, in fact, the system of companies and finance has reacted to the reduction suffered from its advantageous position, using command over production decisions, or choices related to the introduction of technical progress and job creation, in order to decide autonomously what the distribution of surplus should be. It was said above that the "model of the mind" evolves both on the psychic and cultural plane. To favour the "backward flexibility", the return to the *res publica* "liberal", the media of the social groups in power have progressively monopolised public discourse. Although the institutions of political democracy, on a formal level, do not change, the battlefield for ideological contestation has been transferred from the tables of collective wage negotiation between companies and unions—surpassed, in the world of parcelled work—to information, strongly biased towards the "*pensée unique*"[7] and populist sovereignty, to the point of being polluted

[7]The expression is due to Ignacio Ramonet, director of "Le Monde Diplomatique", who in an issue of May 1995 wrote: "What is the *pensée unique*? It is the transposition in ideological terms, which are claimed to be universal, of the interests of a set of economic forces, and specifically those of international capital".

by *fake news*. This is what is happening today, in different ways and measures, in the United States and in Europe. That the United States is now described as a country torn apart, split in two, is precisely the consequence of the degeneration of public discourse and the "disease" that corrodes the sharing among citizens of a "model of the mind".

To recap. A tool for analysing the dynamics of society cannot be confined to the formal institutions of political representation. The flexibility of the "model of the mind" is different from the variability of the democratic majority expressed by the ballot box, as its elaboration is at the base not of the formation of a government but of the negotiation of a shortening of the power distance between the groups of society. In a "model of the mind" shared, the composition of interests gives life to a certain type of *res publica*. In the *Trente Glorieuses*, upward social mobility found support in two factors: (1) the sharing of a "model of the mind" in society, which makes in the "disadvantaged" classes the strategy of ***participation*** to prevail over that of ***subversion***, thus putting in "state of quiet" the social conflict; (2) a sustained rate of economic growth and with income inequality less skewed than the current one, conditions that made it easier to agree on the division of surplus, and facilitated the pursuit of social ascent by the "disadvantaged" groups.

From the eighties onwards, socio-economic development has led to the disappearance of both factors. The "model of the mind" has undergone an evolution on the psychic plane with the abandonment of class identity based on frontal confrontation in favour of ***participation***, and on the cultural plane with the triumph of individualism that has consecrated the primacy of neoliberalism.

The Interplay Between Absolute and Relative Mobility

It is time to delve into the two concepts of mobility ***absolute*** and mobility ***relative*** (Jenkins 2011; Jäntti and Jenkins 2015). The expansion of income level and social *status* in the 30-year period 1945–1974 saw the virtuous interplay of absolute mobility and relative mobility. Absolute social mobility depends on "individual income growth". The metaphor of the tide that "lifts all boats" is reflected in the simplifying assumption of GDP expressed in terms of *per capita income*. The growth of GDP per capita consists in the measurement of a hypothetical "individual income growth" of equal magnitude for all members of the population (Jenkins 2011).[8] When the GDP per capita does not grow or declines, the definitions of mobility are respectively replaced by those of persistence and downward trend.

The concept of relative mobility emphasises the fact that usually, it is different people who suffer the consequences of the change induced in absolute mobility by economic fluctuations. When establishing a link between GDP and social mobility, it is too often intended to closely associate robust growth with adequate job creation for all young people entering the labour market, whether they are "advantaged" or "disadvantaged". Of course, this is not the case. At the end of the last century, in many advanced countries, due to the slowdown in GDP expansion and the increase in income inequality, along with absolute mobility, relative mobility also began to decline (Berman 2022). As we will see now, the virtuous intertwining between the two mobilities is far from the rule.

With the concept of relative income mobility, we mean "positional income mobility", the reshuffling of people's positions in the various percentiles of income distribution.[9] "The rate of relative mobility compares the probability of subjects from different origin classes to different destination classes, which signals the degree of 'social fluidity'" (Goldthorpe 2013, p. 5). The heterogeneity of the income position occupied by people along the steps of the income scale depends, in addition to the individual disposition to engage in professional training and work, on the life circumstances to which they were exposed at birth, during their educational journey, and subsequently due to "market imperfections". All these factors are decisive in facilitating, or hindering, the emergence of personal talents.

In writing a great book that has as its theme an aggregate—"the wealth of nations"—Adam Smith seems to forget what he had written a few years earlier in his first great book, *The Theory of Moral Sentiments*. In that book, he had described how the individual psychology that shapes society, living in community, is imbued with the mutual feeling of "sympathy", or the ability to "penetrate" the feelings of others without giving up being oneself. Between the moral philosopher Adam Smith of the first book and the

[8] "Although not all individual incomes react in the same way to economic growth, one can still expect a certain common impact of growth on individual incomes" (Oecd 2018a, p. 96).

[9] The distribution of income (from the subject with the lowest income to the one with the highest income) can be represented by dividing a population made up for example of 1000 people into ten groups of equal size—the deciles—each formed by 100 individuals. The percentile instead represents 1% of any distribution.

economist Adam Smith of the second, however, there is a change of scene, not a continuity. In *The Theory of Moral Sentiments*, it is a representation of society, as introduced here with the concept of "systemic interdependence", that leads him to say that "it is common knowledge that being all self-interested is essential to understanding other-regarding social behaviour". If everyone indeed knows that at the origin of every action is personal interest, only behaviours that tend to benefit, to proceed from the right intentional motivations, because only these generate approval or arouse sympathetic gratitude (ibid., p. 78).

Social well-being, *The Wealth of Nations*, comes into being by virtue of the defence of property rights on which civil coexistence is based. In *The Wealth of Nations*, however, Smith does not refer to individuals whose behaviours lead to an "optimal" functioning of the market mechanism: the set of individuals find themselves enjoying benefits that they did not set as the end of their actions. If we do not see the "invisible hand" that in the vulgate is associated with the idea of a perfect functioning of the market, it is therefore not only—as Joe Stiglitz cleverly observed—because there is no such thing in the economic system, but primarily because in *The Wealth of Nations*, Smith is not dealing with the goodness of the functioning of the market. If the overall result that gives the title to the book is achieved unintentionally, it is not for him a merit of the market. The result rather descends from the close complementarity that binds the two main individual behaviours, the selfish and the "attention to the other" (other-regarding) described in *The Theory of Moral Sentiments.*

Therefore, the two books are inscribed in a common space, in which the selfish attitude and the other-regarding coexist. It is the space in which what we have here defined as the "model of the mind" is formed, where opinions converge until they reach a "socio-economic equilibrium". Similarly to David Hume, Smith believes that the key lies in the "collective" character of economic life, in the habit of repeating the "economic game". Vernon L. Smith, who won the Nobel Prize for economics in 2002 along with psychologist Daniel Kahneman, has written illuminating pages on this subject.[10]

[10] "In repeated games, people do not need to have *other-regarding* preferences to have *other-regarding* behaviour [...]. Both 'goodness' towards others and actions aimed at the well-being of others are sophisticated forms of action that individuals are inclined to find compatible with long-term self-satisfaction - their own reputation has value" (Smith 2008, p. 201).

In the common space created by the shared "model of the mind", civil coexistence does not develop harmoniously. Although Writing in the years preceding the full unfolding of the new productive techniques in the Industrial Revolution, Adam Smith clearly saw that *competition* does not coincide with *perfect competition*, to which "the private interest of many individuals [...] the masters of manufactures" (Smith 1776, l. IV, cap. II, p. 460) is opposed. What Smith did not see is that the pursuit of selfish interest—even if it is expressed in a relationship of complementarity with the *other-regarding* sentiment—does not automatically generate the "progress" of the community. Because of what we have here defined as the "power asymmetry" between social groups, the dynamics of society is marked by conflict, which manifests itself in the phenomenon of externalities, the costs that some impose on the entire community in pursuing their own exclusive interest.

This reality is far from what is described in the aseptic and stylised form of the standard model of economic theory. Social dynamics is not the offspring of the *individual-monad* of Gee's analysis adopted by orthodox economic theory, but of the *interdependence* between individuals. The macroeconomic factors that underlie a country's growth and the microeconomic factors that influence individual performance in the market, in their intertwining, produce significant consequences within social stratification. Changes such as globalisation, technological innovations, or phases of severe economic turbulence like the 2008 financial crisis and the recent pandemic, have an impact on the reshuffling of positions. In the perspective of social conflict analysis presented by Marx and Engels in *The German Ideology*, competition takes place between individual subjects or between the social groups they form due to the proximity of socio-economic condition and the opportunities they have access to.[11] Depending on the ideological orientation, *relative* mobility is then seen as typical of historical phases of greater effectiveness of the capitalist system in offering the opportunity to engage in work to climb higher on the income scale, or as typical of historical phases in which the distributive conflict between social classes is more intense. In its intergenerational sense, social *relative* mobility

[11] "Individuals form a class only insofar as they must wage a common struggle against another class, otherwise they are on hostile terms with each other as competitors".

indicates the percentage of children whose income level is "independent" from that of the family, i.e. is higher or lower than the parents' income.[12]

Economic growth and the aspiration to social ascent generate an intertwining between absolute and relative mobility. One question this volume seeks to answer is whether social mobility is more contributed to by income growth, the *absolute* mobility inherent in the dynamics of the *capitalist system*, or the conflict around income distribution, the *relative mobility* fuelled by the *power asymmetry* that develops within it. The answer is that both dimensions of growth and conflict weigh heavily. A capitalist economy, where accumulation cannot know stops, relies substantially on the expansion of GDP. At the same time, in addition to representing the fundamental determinant of *absolute* mobility, economic growth is one of the factors also involved in the other expression of mobility. It is intuitive to understand how *relative* mobility depends *also* on *absolute* mobility, as through the dynamics of GDP, due to the externalities generated by "systemic interdependence", the conflict around income distribution is also activated.

The study of the reshuffling of individual income positions requires particular attention. Indeed, to assess how much in a certain historical phase *relative* mobility counts in the evolution of social structure, the income distribution under examination must have been "purged" of the economic growth that triggered it. In other words, the change in position in the income ranking must be studied "at a standstill", or net of growth. *Absolute* mobility and *relative* mobility are therefore not fully separable concepts; on the contrary, they are complementary to each other. A clue comes from studies on intergenerational mobility, which link the educational, income and *status* success of children to the parents' income at different stages of life. These studies document not only how important the family context is for the dynamics of the children's condition, but also that in the increase in well-being of new generations, *absolute* mobility (economic growth) counts before even *relative* mobility (the overtaking of positions in the income ranking) (Eshaghnia et al. 2022).

[12] The *relative* mobility of income from one generation to the next is measured using a two-dimensional table called a transition matrix. Subjects are divided into groups (quintiles) of equal number. In the rows and columns, the distribution of the parents' income and that of the children as adults appear. It is estimated what percentage of children belonging to each quintile (defined by the level of income of the parents) appear as adults in each quintile of the income distribution.

Between the two forms of social mobility, what changes most is the perspective from which the dynamics of the social structure are examined. In the case of *absolute* mobility, the focus is on the extent to which each individual contributes—with their work time, and productivity determined by their knowledge and skills—to the growth of the country's GDP. In the case of *relative* mobility, the focus is on the degree to which an individual (or group) manages to improve their income position compared to other individuals (or groups) with whom they are in competition in the distributive conflict that develops in the economy and society.

The aspiration to social mobility takes on profoundly different characteristics in the different "worldviews" of individuals belonging to different social classes in terms of wealth and income. At the elite level, the aspiration to rise to top positions in the group of the super-rich lies in the desire to self-represent as individuals capable of achieving a *status* of excellence. Positional goods, symbols of successful social ascent, satisfy the need for "social distinction". In economic theory[13] this name is given to those goods—a Vermeer displayed on the living room wall, a villa located in a charming mountain corner—that perform the very special function of enhancing the identity of the individual who owns them. Social ascent is often accompanied by the rich distancing themselves from the rest of society, from the national community, of which they are still part. Those who, unable to display wealth, are not admitted into the *koiné* of the elite, are perceived as belonging to a separate world, as if they did not exist. The "exclusion" of others is indeed the other side of self-representation as a successful individual.

A characteristic feature of the era of individualism is the increasing accumulation of positional goods by the rich, in order to distinguish themselves from others. On the other hand, an individual's search for *status* as "unique" continues to need others to fully realise itself. Every privileged *status*, symbolised by the ownership of positional goods, also depends on the collective recognition of the prestige achieved. This recognition occurs, for example, through the feeling of exclusion suffered by those who aspired, without succeeding, to be "included" in the *koiné* of the super-rich. Even at the level of low-income classes, there is now a

[13] In the theory of imperfect competition, "positional" goods are defined as those particular goods that are offered in a number that cannot be increased to meet their demand. Positional goods therefore have a very high price because their limited accessibility makes them a symbol of social prestige.

feeling of exclusion. But the reasons are very different from the strong desire of the wealthy to feel "unique individuals". In the case of the weak classes, or those that are becoming such, the fear is of having to give up their social identity, or of being pushed back in terms of the standard of living that has been hard-won. One of the reasons for the sense of exclusion connected to economic discomfort is the proximity to the "last". The perception of cultural distance in terms of customs, religion, social norms of immigrants who have settled in the neighbourhood, is accompanied by the perception, widespread in large sections of the native populations, of being exposed to the danger of downward mobility due to competition from immigrants in work. The "excluded" from well-being seek, also through voting, to "exclude" in turn those who in history have never been part of their δῆμος if not from the country, at least from the benefits of Welfare.

This quick analysis clearly signals how poor economic performance reverberates on both concepts of mobility. The economic vulnerability that follows an economic recession represents not only a brake on *absolute* social mobility, the concept that concerns the aggregate of the population. *Absolute* mobility translates, for different individuals, into different "life events": that is, in social mobility upwards, or in the persistence over time of a given level of earnings, or in the descent below the poverty line. This has an important consequence. For individual people belonging to different social groups, each of these "life events" expresses the different value for him assumed by a phenomenon that concerns the aggregate of the population. In a capitalist economy, in order for the unfolding of the forms in which the evolution over time of *social mobility* is expressed not to heavily impact on *social cohesion*, there is no other collective "shield of protection" than public policies: from support for the poor to a good health system and good cultural and professional training through education;[14] to a labour market with good regulation, which even young people from "disadvantaged" families have easy access to; to the redistribution carried out by the welfare state to reduce income inequality.

[14] The category of common goods does not have in the economic literature a precise analytical formulation. The term refers to all those goods (from the quality of air, water, sea and food, to the safety of life in community) that society considers essential for its very existence, as they are the foundation of everyone's well-being. No person should risk being excluded from the enjoyment of such goods. They should therefore not be used as simple factors of production or final goods for the purpose of making a profit.

Social mobility is affected by the performance of the economy; to the point that an economic crisis affects not only *absolute* mobility but also *relative* mobility. Naturally, it is the mobility of most people to suffer—directly or indirectly—from an economic crisis. However, the condition of "economic vulnerability",[15] or the exposure of the individual to a worsening of their income and well-being condition, is different among individuals belonging to different social classes.

For the most "weak" classes, a simple fluctuation of GDP in the short term results in a blockage of social ascent of a much longer duration. People indeed have not only different sources of income and a different amount of salary per year, but also different economic means to react to a fall in income. During a crisis, for example, the rich possess significant financial and real estate wealth to draw upon, once it has been made somewhat liquid, to maintain their standard of living unchanged; the middle-low income classes usually possess it in a very small measure (in most cases, it is primarily the ownership of the house) and suffer a lowering of the quality of life; in the case of the *working-poor*, finally, in the probable absence of the *buffer stock* constituted by wealth, a dismissal or the decrease in earnings during a recession affects the standard of living in the medium-long term. At this point, in some countries, the "welfare state" intervenes to plug the "gaps" in the economic system based on individualism and the market economy.

In order for the externalities that are transmitted within the economy and society to be countered, however, particularly favourable conditions must be determined. This is the theme of the next paragraph.

[15] The main ways in which economic vulnerability manifests itself are as follows: a) divergent trajectories of earnings growth mean that the impact of a crisis can have divergent effects among social groups, due to the absence of "equality of conditions in the course of individual long-term income growth"; b) the "risk related to future income" consists instead in the occurrence of unforeseen events that generate economic insecurity and the impossibility of planning the future. The impact of the first type of vulnerability on mobility is interpretable as an interruption in the upward convergence of low incomes; that of the second concerns instead the divergence in the perception of uncertainty, which derives to individuals from their different degree of exposure to risk.

The *Trente Glorieuses*: The Expansion of GDP and the Welfare State

The empirical evidence that led to coining the definition of *Trente Glorieuses* for the post-war period of European history was the high growth rates and the expansion of social spending by welfare institutions. Their synergy has been named the "social multiplier" (Barth and Moene 2016). When absolute mobility driven by sustained economic growth set relative mobility in motion, social ascent tended to impact also outside the sphere of the economy. The strong growth of GDP allowed the "disadvantaged" classes to enjoy greater well-being and made social distances more tolerable. The political condition that allowed the impetuous economic growth to be directed towards the financing of the expansion of the welfare state was the hegemony[16] that the middle class managed to exercise over the low-income classes and the poor. An indication in this sense is given by a statistical indicator, the Palma Index. It shows that in advanced countries, in periods when the middle class increases its share of income redistribution, the share of redistribution of the poor also increases (and decreases, instead, when the share of the rich increases) (Cobham et al. 2015). This empirical evidence is fully compatible with the hypothesis that social democratic parties were successful in creating an alliance on non-ideological bases between low-income classes and the middle class (Przeworski 1980). The constellation of ideas that underpin the relations of production was changing. The aggregation of the interests of individual individuals in the progressive political and trade union movement took the form of the collective value of wealth creation. Even within the class division of society, the importance of work was recognised not just as a simple means of individual sustenance, but for its function, in combination with capital, of creating wealth for the community.

Economic growth was based on the *labour-augmenting* technologies of manufacturing productions. Together with a stronger articulation of the service sector, and a greater female participation in the labour market, the increase in employment and wages boosted demand (Eurofound 2017). From the ballot boxes emerged political majorities in government favourable to the use of the economic surplus in the construction of welfare

[16] According to Antonio Gramsci, hegemony is the ability of a social class to influence society by managing to impose in the political process its own "intellectual and moral direction" (Gramsci 1975, p. 2010).

institutions that reduced inequalities. Governments thus entrusted the welfare state with the task of making capitalism compatible with democracy.

During the *Trente Glorieuses*, the unequal distribution of resources between capital owners and workers was not an obstacle to cooperation for collective well-being. The strong expansion of industrial production and employment on the one hand increased the power of workers compared to the business system, on the other hand made the distributive conflict between profit and wage sustainable. Moreover, while the middle-low classes achieved a better quality of life, the middle-high class expanded its share of equity capital and public debt. Historical analysis also documents how during the *Trente Glorieuses* the increase in incomes, by allowing the increase in savings formation by the middle classes, led to a short period of deconcentration of the wealth (Milanović 2020).

The growth rates of the period were so substantial that they reflected in a significant increase in absolute *mobility*. This generated a harmonious progression of both social return—the benefit for society—and private return—the benefit for the company and for consumers. The impact of economic growth on individual income levels was also stimulated by the spread of collective bargaining in the private sector and the expansion of public employment. These structural changes also favoured a reshuffling of positions in the income distribution, primarily of relative *income mobility* upwards. A side effect of the rapid development of welfare programmes was that social conflict, which often associates with the phenomenon of relative *mobility*, was not fuelled. The substantial increase in welfare benefits indeed led to the perception of a strong rise in *status* and well-being for all social classes. In many nations, economic growth allowed middle-class parties to present themselves as the guarantors of development and well-being, thus encouraging the working classes to become independent from the influence of communist parties. The absolute *social mobility* and *relative* set in motion by productive growth not only served as proof of the advantages of collaboration between classes, but was seen, in the eyes of the working classes, as an important factor legitimising capitalism.[17]

[17] In countries culturally and geographically furthest from the ideological and military pressure of the Soviet Union, governments were nevertheless less influenced by the vote of the popular classes to anti-capitalist ideology parties. The construction of the welfare state was based on investment in public goods and it was not necessary to implement welfare programmes with a strong redistributive impact (Sant'Anna 2015).

The containment of wealth inequality and the reduction of income inequality had given substance to the "democratic class compromise" (Przeworski and Wallerstein 1982), the compatibility between capitalism and democracy. How fragile this "democratic compromise" was became apparent in the aftermath of the Kippur war of 1973–1974. The quadrupling of the price of oil sold by the Arab emirates to the West marked a watershed, as it triggered an inflationary process that compromised the delicate balance between democracy and capitalism that was painstakingly being achieved. On the level of ideas, the turning point was the unwillingness of the elites to accept the recognition of the social rights won by workers during the *Trente Glorieuses*. The granting to workers of a regulation of the labour market that would protect them from the erosion of the purchasing power of wages and from the risk of unemployment culminated in the solemn recognition of social rights. In 1988, in the European Union, the Delors Commission proposed the Community Charter of fundamental social rights of workers, later adopted by the European Council in 1989. In Italy, in 1970, the Workers' Statute was introduced. Many countries went beyond the boundaries of collective protections with the recognition of a series of fundamental human rights: gender equality, the legalisation first of divorce and then of abortion, the regularisation of immigrants etc. The Kippur war radically changed things. The difficulty encountered in passing on the narrowing of profit margins, through inflation, to the dynamics of real wages convinced companies to resolve the conflict around the distribution of income by using the power to change production choices and techniques productive.

Starting from the second half of the seventies, at the centre of politics and the economy of European countries, the blockage of investments and the shift to labour-saving production techniques inaugurated the strategy of weakening the working class through the increase in unemployment and restoring an income distribution favourable to profit. The role of work as a means of aggregation of the masses, established with the bargaining power won by unions during the post-war recovery, was put in crisis by stagflation, the reduction of real wages and by policies of deregulation of the labour market. With the transition to restrictive monetary and fiscal policies aimed at blocking the increase of the deficit and public debt, cuts to social spending compromised the alliance at the polls between the middle class and the poor, interrupting the redistribution strategy pursued by governments, finally plunging the nascent solidaristic democracy into crisis.

At the end of the twentieth century, the first doubts arose about the ability of capitalist economies to keep their promise as per the theory of incentives of orthodox economics, i.e. the increase in well-being for all those who commit themselves. From the new millennium, the fall in the wage share of income is no longer just caused by the weakening of bargaining power determined by the low labour content of production techniques and by the deregulation of the labour market. Primarily in the United States, but also in many European countries, it is the *superstar* low labour intensity companies, in which workers with intangible capital are concentrated, that are expanding production and profits.

Leading the new course of growth was the profound cultural change advancing on the wave of the spread of neoliberal thought. A report from the World Bank (1992) defined the governance of an economy as "the capacity and efficiency in the management of the public sector, accountability, the legal framework for development, and information and transparency. [...] Citizens must demand good governance" (ibid., p. 11). Under the guise of the governance, instead, the values and interests of the private sphere became hegemonic, to the detriment of the values and interests of the public sphere. The "economic-social balance" based on the alliance between middle class and the poor, of parallel expansion of GDP and social spending, therefore had a short duration. Perhaps it could not have gone differently: "Private ownership of productive resources limits the scope of the outcomes that can arise from the democratic process. The ruling class in government, whatever its *constituency* and its orientations, is bound in every capitalist system by the fact that crucial economic decisions, those that have an impact on employment and investment, are a private prerogative" (Przeworski 2016, p. 5).

The Impact of Neoliberalism on Inequalities and Social Ascension

Starting from the eighties, fearing that political democracy would turn into solidaristic democracy, the elites implemented a radical change in the "constellation of ideas" underlying public policies. Neoliberal thinking began to exert a strong influence on governments (Harvey 2005). The main guiding ideas were: a) the deregulation of the labour market aimed at lowering labour costs and the delegitimisation of direct redistribution aimed at reducing income inequality with the aim of concentrating Welfare in the *safety net* for the poor; b) the "trickle-down" approach, or policies aimed at stimulating economic growth by diverting public resources towards the private sector through the reduction of taxation on the rich; c) the austerity strategy, or the tightening of social spending, pursued by reducing the public deficit/GDP ratio and the principle of balancing the public budget as an ideological tool to impose the fastest possible cancellation of public debt. In line with the ordoliberal doctrine, the legal-economic ideology dominant in Germany, some countries of the European Union have indeed introduced with a constitutional amendment the balance as an objective of economic policy. This was a *unicum* in the history of public policies: the ideological totem of a specific theoretical approach to public intervention has been imposed on the entire community.

The current phase of capitalism has been defined as the "age of neoliberalism" (Stiglitz 2019). With the disappearance of the high rates of post-war GDP growth, the downsizing of absolute social mobility began to reflect in a slowdown of relative mobility. Post-modernity is the era of "individualisation" of the subject, in a process of emancipation that also cracks community ties (Beck and Beck-Gernsheim 2001). The affirmation of the individual as the cornerstone of the functioning of society, also favoured by the transition to the service economy, induced a profound cultural change. The function of work to represent the main road of reducing social distances came to an end.

An example is English society, which still today has a hierarchical structure within it. The *establishment* is made up of the elite, which maintains a strong cohesion, allowing little osmosis with the *middle class* and even less with the multiethnic society formed with the influx of immigrants from the former colonies. A cultural trait of British society, consolidated over the centuries, is the belief that hierarchy is an indispensable component of society. Therefore, both the identification of the British citizen with his or her class, whatever the level at which he or she is placed in the social scale, and the belief that individual commitment makes possible upward mobility within social stratification are strong. This second certainty is now fading. The association of the staticity of the English social structure with the economic decline that the United Kingdom is experiencing has been traced back to the progressive weakening of the "industrial spirit" in the country's culture (Wiener 1981). The sense of uncertainty that characterises today's self-representation of English society has been fuelled by political decay and the interruption of convergence with other advanced economies.[18] The economy of *Old Britannia* is in a condition of

[18] A measure of the median standard of life, the median family income available per person, has grown from 2000 to 2020 only from 24000 to 28000 pounds (at 2019 Ppp prices). The historical decline of the country is usually dated to the reduction in labour productivity in the

long-term stagnation of productivity, a condition that in the last three decades has been shared by Italy. In both countries, higher wage earnings, in line with productivity increases, are a very rare event. Wage dynamics are present only for the limited number of "high human capital" jobs; with the inevitable consequence of depressing young people's propensity to extend their education period.

International research institutes continue to regularly highlight how the origin of the *impasse* of social mobility of people is due to *both* unequal circumstances *and* unequal opportunities. In a statistical report based on data from the European Social Survey, a European research institute is very explicit in judging the influence of "circumstances" on people's future as decisive: "Since social background continues to have a profound effect on life chances, the European Union policymakers at national and regional level should recognise the importance of implementing measures aimed at promoting equality of opportunities for upward social mobility, so that everyone, regardless of social origin, has the opportunity to realise their potential" (Eurofound 2017, p. 2). The OECD has recently issued a clear verdict: "Today's inequalities in people's economic and social outcomes determine their access to education and good health opportunities and to the labour market, thus influencing their potential for social mobility" (OECD 2018a, p. 20). Estimates show that graduate parents have graduate children, while children of parents without a degree face significant obstacles in achieving an adequate level of professional training (ibid.). The "imperfect" functioning of capital and labour markets, which particularly penalises young people from "disadvantaged" families, weighs heavily on access to opportunities and the emergence of talents.

Orthodox theory has built its vision of the place the market occupies in society on the autonomous and mutually independent behaviour of individuals who perform the functions of organisers of productive factors and dependent workers. As already observed, this is a somewhat lacking conception of the economy. The representation of work is, for example, extremely poor: a commodity in search of a price. Its function as a tool for promoting collective well-being, in the combination of individual talents with capital, is essentially ignored. The post-war period consisted of

seventies. An empirical verification, based on the recent publication of a long-term database, documents that the slowdown in the growth of total factor productivity (Tfp) began 250 years ago. Following the Industrial Revolution, the Tfp growth path was lowered by recurring crises, starting from the exhaustion in the Edwardian period of the push that the "age of steam" exerted on the growth of GDP (Crafts and Mills 2020).

diverting resources to the construction of a social protection system, in exchange for freedom for companies to obtain large profit margins by slowing down wage dynamics. With the advent of neoliberalism, a "political exchange" was no longer necessary. The "socio-economic balance" has shifted towards full autonomy of the business system in making production and employment decisions.

In the name of the "compatibility" of worker protection rules with the competitiveness of the company in the market, the business system has exerted increasing political pressure on governments. The recommendation to launch reforms aimed at making the labour market "flexible" was argued with the need to increase economic efficiency. The pressure from entrepreneurs culminated in Europe in the introduction of new "rules of the game" by governments. The new "political exchange" consisted in the progressive abolition of legal protection of the job (the freedom for companies to dismiss: *Employment protection legislation*), in exchange for the guarantee of worker protection during the period of unemployment. The idea was propagated that replacing job protection with protection of the unemployed worker would remove the main obstacle to achieving full employment. However, worker protection has proved illusory, as the creation of permanent jobs has been declining. As all major international institutions, including the International Monetary Fund, have noted, "reforms that facilitate the dismissal of permanent workers have no statistically significant effects on employment on average" (IMF 2016, p. 115). Deregulation of the labour market, and the privatisation processes carried out in the 1990s, was followed by the abandonment of any prospect of industrial policy. The goal of achieving a balanced development process was completely delegated to the business system, which should take responsibility for creating "good jobs" (OECD 2018b).

With the introduction of a wide range of fixed-term employment contracts, the role of trade unions has been annihilated and the power asymmetry between companies and workers has increased. In the absence of the decisive factor for increasing employment—sustained economic growth—flexibility has not promoted employment but the reduction of labour costs.[19] Since in most European countries the rate of

[19] According to a study by the Bank of Italy, the deregulation reforms introduced in Italy in 2001 "contrary to the objectives set by the law had no effects on employment. [...] An increasing number of workers remained trapped in cycles of temporary and fragile low-paid occupations, with a greatly reduced probability of transition from temporary jobs to fixed-term jobs [...]. The main winners appear to be companies, as the cost of labour has fallen substantially, leading after the reform to an increase in profits. On the contrary, young

transformation of temporary work into permanent jobs has been low, the outcome of the reforms has been the expansion of involuntary part-time work and the "institutionalisation" of precarious work. The mediation of governments between business freedom and the impact of these changes in society has been completely absent. From the 1980s onwards, the wage share of income began to decline, wage inequality began to grow and welfare institutions were downsized.[20] The two epochal changes that took place between the end of the twentieth and the beginning of the twenty-first century were globalisation and the acceleration in the introduction of technical progress. Having almost completely eliminated worker protection during two epochal changes has meant that the social structure established during the process of expanding mass production has been disrupted.

The significant advantages that companies have received from globalisation find a limit in the disadvantage generated by the increasing uncertainty surrounding the rate of return on innovative investment, which usually materialises only in the medium to long term. This temporal asymmetry between innovative investment and profitability has incentivised companies to keep labour demand low, which has slowed the rise in GDP and penalised absolute mobility. Following the impact of globalisation and automation, in the sector of medium and low-skilled jobs, qualifications have led to a reduction in both job positions and remuneration (Rodrik and Sabel 2019).

Since the business system is aimed at short-term profit and not at the society's need for an increase in employment, "one of the fundamental problems of contemporary capitalism is its failure to produce an adequate number of 'good jobs'" (Rodrik and Stantcheva 2021). In shirking the task of creating jobs, the business system contributes to the multiplication of inequalities. For the most part, the job positions that are opened are not "good jobs", they are the precarious jobs of the *gig economy*, and piecework and "call" work. Behind the digital platforms that hire workers often hide employers at the head of large monopolies, who practise exploitation outside of any labour legislation. The concept of "good jobs" (Acemoglu 2001) is therefore a familiar term that is deeply at odds with reality. The

workers appear to be the main losers, as their wages have significantly reduced, resulting in an increase in the gap between young and old workers in the Italian labour market" (Daruich et al. 2023, p. 6).

[20] The theoretical analysis and statistical documentation of these phenomena can be found in Farina (2021, chaps. VII and IX).

opportunity to work well—and possibly to enrich oneself—now concerns the narrow "medium-high" portion of the supply of graduates and researchers able to occupy stable jobs because they have high productivity.

The impact of the introduction of technical progress on the labour market generates chain effects that reverberate within society. Without the workers being responsible, the condition of work is devalued and the wage of the *low-skilled* workers tends to fall to such a low level as to generate an increase in poverty (Frank 2011).

The last decades have placed austerity at the centre of government policies. Deregulation of the labour market has been accompanied by a downsizing of Welfare benefits and public educational and health structures. Governments have revoked part of the legal and monetary benefits introduced by the codification of social rights and have committed themselves to "freeing" the rich from the burden of progressive taxation. As Tony Atkinson prophetically expressed 25 years ago, "the retreat of the welfare state may be underway endogenously, as 'good' jobs, covered by unemployment benefits, are replaced by 'bad' ones, without coverage" (Atkinson 1999, p. 91). Short-term profit as a business objective has been accompanied by the expansion of market spaces with privatisations, private pension funds and the expansion of private provision in health and education. The troubled events of the European Monetary Union show how, following the austerity policies imposed by the European Commission, the manoeuvring space of national governments to protect workers and support "social inclusion" has been drastically reduced. While the expansive monetary policies of the ECB were aimed at cushioning the impact on incomes and jobs of the financial crises first and the Covid-19 pandemic later, the constraints placed by the various "pacts" on national fiscal manoeuvres, and sometimes even the market regulation of the Commission, have not allowed for effective employment policies.[21]

"Expansive austerity" is the catchy definition with which at the turn of the new millennium orthodox economists labelled the promise that by

[21] The internal economic balances of the countries are also strongly influenced by the "competition" to "downgrade" that takes place in the international economic scenario. Large multinational companies, in industrial production, in the banking and financial sector in the Tlc services, not only resort to the transfer of plants to low-wage countries, but practise the systematic violation of fundamental ethical norms—the ban on child labour, the renunciation of the practice of laundering dirty money—which should be non-negotiable, irrevocable or "universal".

cutting taxes and reducing public expenditures and economic recovery results. In recent decades, however, the promise has not been fulfilled. Austerity has proved to be recessive, as Keynes had said. The expansion of the space for private initiative in the market has only resulted in a strengthening of the command of companies over productive choices. As for "labour policies", the statistical reports of European governments—from the premier of the right-wing Italian government Meloni to the premier of the conservative English government Sunak—contain pieces of incomplete information, aimed at "inflating" the figures on employment. It is enough to remember that Eurostat classifies as "employed" those who have worked only one hour in the reference week, or those who are not paid employees but work in the family business, or are irregular workers without a contract; even those who are currently unable to work are declared "employable". Similar propaganda in the United Kingdom: there are no unemployed but the "temporarily out of work".

In the new millennium, the discrepancy between business command and democratic command has increased. The former has strengthened, the latter is losing ground.

The crisis of the political representation system means that each economic subject enters the market interaction completely detached from any form of political mediation.[22] In the market without constraints and without responsibility, where for the classes with little power in society the negative externalities multiply, the contradiction between large private benefits and scarce benefits for the community is more than ever striking.

Bibliography

Acemoglu, D. 2001 *Good Jobs versus Bad Jobs*, in «Journal of Labor Economics», XIX, 1, pp. 1–21.

Atkinson, A. B. 1999 The Economic Consequences of Rolling Back the Welfare State, *Mit Press, Cambridge.*

Barone, G. & Mocetti, S. 2021 Intergenerational Mobility in the Very Long Run: Florence 1427–2011 [Intergenerational Economic Mobility in the United States, 1940 to 2000], *in «Review of Economic Studies», LXXXVIII, 4, pp. 1863–91.*

[22] What happened in November 2022 is emblematic. Mark Zuckerberg, the entrepreneur who founded Facebook, called 2022 the "year of efficiency". Because, with a single stroke of the pen, he cut 11,000 jobs in his Meta, the seventh largest multinational in the world, or a full 13% of the total workforce, declaring that he had overestimated the company's growth potential.

Barth, E. & Moene, K. O. 2016 The Equality Multiplier: How Wage Compression and Welfare Empowerment Interact, *in «Journal of the European Economic Association», XIV, 5, pp. 1011–37.*

Beck, U. & Beck-Gernsheim, E. 2001 Individualization: Institutionalized Individualism and Its Social and Political Consequences, *Sage Publications, London.*

Berman, Y. 2022 *The Long-Run Evolution of Absolute Intergenerational Mobility*, in «American Economic Journal: Applied Economics», XIV, 3, pp. 61–83.

Canfora, L. 2004 La democrazia. Storia di un'ideologia, *Laterza, Roma-Bari.*

Cobham, A., Schlogl, L., Sumner, A. 2015 Inequality and the Tails: The Palma Proposition and Ratio Revisited, *Desa Working Paper n. 143.*

Crafts, N. & Mills, T. C. 2020 *Is the Uk Productivity Slowdown Unprecedented?*, in «National Institute Economic Review», 251.

Daruich, D., Di Addario, S., Saggio, R. 2023 The Effects of Partial Employment Protection Reforms: Evidence for Italy, *in «Review of Economic Studies», XC, 6, pp. 2880–942.*

DeLong, J. B. 2022 Slouching towards Utopia: An Economic History of the Twentieth Century, *Basic Books, London.*

Denzau, A. T. & North, D. C. 1994 Shared Mental Models: Ideologies and Institutions, *in «Kyklos», XLVII, 1, pp. 3–31.*

Eshaghnia, S., Heckman, J. J. Landersø, R., Qureshi, R. 2022 Intergenerational transmission of family influence, *Nber Working Paper 30412.*

Eurofound 2017 *Social Mobility in the EU*, Research Report, Luxembourg.

Farina, F. 2021 Lo Stato sociale. Storia, politica, economia, *Luiss University Press, Roma.*

Frank, R. H. 2011 The Darwin Economy: Liberty, Competition and the Common Good, *Princeton University Press, Princeton.*

Goldthorpe, J. H. 2013 Understanding – and Misunderstanding – Social Mobility in Britain: The Entry of Economists, the Confusion of Politicians and the Limits of Educational Policy, *in «Journal of Social Policy», XLII, 3, pp. 431–50.*

Gramsci, A. 1975 Quaderni dal carcere, *Einaudi, Torino.*

Greenfeld, L. 1992 *Nationalism: Five Roads to Modernity*, Harvard University Press, Cambridge.

Harvey, D. 2005 *A Brief History of Neoliberalism*, Oxford University Press, Oxford 2005.

Heinrich, J. 2020 The WEIRDest in the World, *Penguin Books, London 2020.*

Hobson, J. A. 1902 *Imperialism: A Study*, J. Pott&co, New York.

International Monetary Fund 2016 World Economic Outlook: Too Slow for Too Long, *aprile, Washington DC.*

Jäntti, M. & Jenkins, S. P. 2015 *Income Mobility*, in A. B. Atkinson & F. Bourguignon (eds), *Handbook of Income Distribution*, IIA-IIB, North-Holland, Amsterdam.

Jenkins, S. P. 2011 Changing Fortunes: Income Mobility and Poverty Dynamics in Britain, *Oxford University Press, Oxford.*

Macfarlane, A. 1978 The Origins of English Individualism: The Family Property and Social Transition, *Basil Blackwell, Oxford.*

Maddison, A. 2001 The World Economy: A Millennial Perspective, *Oecd Development Centre, Paris.*

Milanović, B. 2020 Capitalism, Alone: The Future of the System That Rules the World, *Harvard University Press, Cambridge 2019.*

Milanović, B. 2024 The Three Eras of Global Inequality, 1820–2020 with the Focus on the Past Thirty Years, *in «World Development», CLXXVII.*

Oecd 2018a A Broken Social Elevator? How to Promote Social Mobility, *Paris.*

Oecd 2018b Good Jobs for All in a Changing World of Work: The Oecd Jobs Strategy, *Oecd Publishing, Paris.*

Przeworski, A. 1980 Social Democracy as a Historical Phenomenon, *in «New Left Review», CXXII, pp. 27–58.*

Przeworski, A. 2009 *Self-Government in Our Times*, in «Annual Review of Political Science», XII, pp. 71–92.

Przeworski, A. 2016 *Democracy: A Never-Ending Quest*, in «Annual Review of Political Science», XIX, pp. 1–12.

Przeworski, A. & Wallerstein, M. 1982 The Structure of Class Conflict in Democratic Capitalist Societies, *in «American Political Science Review», LXXVI, 2, pp. 215–38.*

Reuter-Lorenz, P. A., Baynes, K., Mangun, G. R., Phelps, E. A. (eds) 2010 The Cognitive Neuroscience of Mind: A Tribute to Michael S. Gazzaniga, *Mit Press, Cambridge.*

Rodrik, D. & Sabel, C. 2019 *Building a Good Jobs Economy*, Working Paper, Harvard University.

Rodrik, D. & Stantcheva, S. 2021 *Fixing Capitalism's Good Jobs Problem*, in «Oxford Review of Economic Policy», XXXVII, 4, pp. 824–37.

Roy, R. K. & Denzau, A. T. 2020 Shared Mental Models: Insights and Perspectives on Ideologies and Institutions, *in «Kyklos», LXXIII, 3, pp. 323–40.*

Sant'Anna, A. A. 2015 A Spectre Has Haunted the West: Did Socialism Discipline Income Inequality?, *Mpra Paper n. 64756, University of Munich.*

Smith, V. L. 2008 Rationality in Economics. Constructivist and Ecological Forms, *Cambridge University Press, Cambridge.*

Sombart, W. 1967 *Der moderne Kapitalismus*, Duncker & Humblot, München-Leipzig 1916.

Stiglitz, J. E. 2019 The End of Neoliberalism and the Rebirth of History, *Project Syndacate, 4 novembre.*

Tanzini, L. & Tognetti, S. (eds) 2016 La mobilità sociale nel Medioevo italiano, *I*, Competenze, conoscenze e saperi tra professioni e ruoli sociali (secc. XII–XV), *Viella, Roma.*

Tocqueville, A. 1995 (1835–1840) La democrazia in America, *Rizzoli, Milano.*
Tomasello, M. 2005 Understanding and Sharing Intentions: The Origins of Cultural Cognition, *Cambridge University Press, Cambridge 2005.*
Wiener, M. J. 1981 English Culture and the Decline of the Industrial Spirit 1850–1980, *Cambridge University Press, Cambridge.*
Wilson, B. 2012 *Contra Private Fairness*, in «American Journal of Economics and Sociology», LXXI, 2, pp. 407–35.
World Bank 1992 Governance and Development, *Washington DC.*

CHAPTER 5

Social Dynamics: An Interpretative Scheme

Individual Freedom as Independence from Society

In the culture of the United States, the "model of the mind" of people is pervaded by the desire to feel fully autonomous in the social sphere. The systemic nature assumed by the interdependence between individuals does not in fact rise to the rank of interpretation of the functioning of society. It is likely that this intellectual attitude is the legacy of the rooting in society of the foundational category of social interaction that was dear to Thomas Jefferson: independence. In drafting the first draft of the United States Constitution, Jefferson wrote that "all men are created equal and independent". This last word, however, does not appear in the final text of the Constitution, which was approved while he was in France. The concept of independence is intended to have a reinforcing value of the right to freedom. The literature on social mobility is still largely inclined to assume—exactly as in the draft of the Constitution penned by Jefferson—that in their aspiration to social ascent all men are equally free and independent—that is, each on his own, without taking into account others. This questionable formulation of everyone's right to freedom serves to reject the idea that—as J. Stuart Mill well saw—everyone's freedom is inscribed within rules to prevent it from having negative consequences on others.

As the American philosopher John Dewey observed almost a century ago, "the Constitution sanctioned the birth of 'individualism', a theory

F. Farina, *The Rise of Inequality and the Fall of Social Mobility*, https://doi.org/10.1007/978-3-031-92843-7_5

that fixed individual people in isolation from any associative form [...]; the revolt against the old, limiting, associations was converted, on the intellectual plane, into the doctrine of independence from all associations [...]. The simplest way out was found in the return to the naked individual, in sweeping away all associations as foreign to his nature and his rights, unless they emanate from his voluntary choice" (Dewey 1927, pp. 87–8). Affirming the independence of each person legitimises personal interest as a prerogative of the individual to whose expression no limit should be placed. It is likely that an index of income inequality much higher in the United States than in most European countries dates back to the values of individualism that there, in the last two centuries, have settled in the characters of political and economic institutions. This has resulted in a "socio-economic equilibrium" characterised by deep gaps in the "life chances" between ethnic and social groups. The gaps arise before the market due to the heterogeneity of "circumstances" within the population, they consolidate with the inequality between incomes in the market, due to the deregulated labour market, and they persist after the operation of the market, due to the breadth—much less than in Europe—of the redistribution operated by the system of taxes and transfers and the absence of the equalising impact exercised by the public health and education systems (Blanchet et al. 2022).

Jefferson, with the addition of the word *independent* to the idea of equality between individuals, intended to affirm that freedom either has absolute value or it is not. Neoliberalism, in opposing in recent decades the liberal culture (the term used to define progressive political and economic thought), has restored in all its purity the vision of Jefferson's freedom. In the most dramatic months of the pandemic, however, Jefferson was contradicted by the federal government. The limitation of freedom was an indispensable measure to face the serious danger that systemic interdependence represents in case of a pandemic, both for the individual and for society as a whole. The population was forced to confront an idea that is largely alien to it: that freedom as independence, as absolute freedom of the individual, is contrary to public ethics.

Many layers of the population have not accepted a conception of freedom that is incomprehensible to them. To the point that during the protest demonstrations of 2020, against the lockdown introduced to curb the spread of the pandemic, a particularly revealing slogan was chanted: *You are being conditioned to view your liberty as selfish*. The protesters found it intolerable that rebelling against the limitation of individual freedom was "branded" as a form of "selfish" behaviour towards others. The protesters could not understand that—in other countries, in other cultures—the word freedom takes on a different meaning from the one to which they are accustomed. We will see how the political and cultural influence that the United States has exerted on the "old continent" in the post-war period has extended to the economic sphere with the spread also in continental Europe of the neoliberal ideology developed—in parallel with the United Kingdom—in the last 40 years.

The habit of considering freedom synonymous with independence ends up cutting off at the root the legitimacy of the theoretical paradigms that frame social interaction in a context not of "contract" between equal individuals, but of ideological opposition and social conflict. At the base of freedom as independence there is the idea of a "social contract" freely chosen, a peculiar idea of liberalism of which an excellent liberal like David Hume was not very convinced, defining it as a "fiction".[1] And indeed reality denies the society of "free and equal". For many individuals, "social immobility" is the product of power asymmetries that produce negative externalities in the market, which are added to the "disadvantaged circumstances" in which they were born and formed.

The Tension Between Freedom and Equality of "Life Chances"

The cultural values that have settled in the history of European countries are different from those of the United States. The conception of freedom has formed and settled in a social context on which—despite the passing of the centuries—the medieval hierarchical structure has continued to maintain a certain influence, starting—as seen in par. 1 of chap. III—from the transmission of wealth. In the consciousness of Europeans, the positive aspect of the legacy of the past is the humanism of Erasmus of

[1] Like Jeremy Bentham and J. Stuart Mill, David Hume did not attribute any logical coherence to the idea of such a social structure (whether "original" or not). In *Of the Original Contract*, the Scottish philosopher launched a corrosive criticism of the "social contract" theory propagated by the Whig party, the liberal party of England between the late seventeenth and mid- nineteenth centuries. He believed that the concept of "social contract" was a mere "fiction" (Hume 1971). By definition, consent to the social contract must be voluntary. Anyone who disagreed, should leave the community: but "can we seriously argue that a poor farmer or a craftsman have the free choice to leave their own country [...]?" (Hume 1985, p. 328).

Rotterdam, in particular the "common sense" of conceiving oneself as embedded in the social context. The originality of Michel Foucault's thought was to have introduced the idea of the social hetero-determination of the subject by institutions that are an expression of impersonal power. In *Surveiller et punir* (1975), he argued a strong thesis: in the eighteenth century those disciplinary institutions of society were conceived that served capitalism to make man's work functional to the Industrial Revolution. It is not, however, necessary to go to the extreme of identifying the organisation of the State with the indiscriminate power of disciplining social relations. It is enough to conceive individual identity as composed of a personal component and a component that links the subject to belonging to a social class. Pierre Bourdieu thus summarises: "We are born determined and we have a small chance of ending free" (Bourdieu 2010, p. 40).

In creating a "systemic interdependence" between people, social interaction ensures that each subject must claim the right to autonomy in a sense very different from absolute freedom, from independence from others. It can be said that for Europeans the precise sense of the concept of freedom consists in a coexistence based on the right not to suffer negative externalities when entering into relationship with others in the economy and society. It is precisely for this reason that the conception of freedom prevalent in Europe contemplates limits to the exercise of individual freedom. Up to the "exceptionality" of Germany, a country in whose culture—as was remembered in the Introduction—the idea is rooted that the identity of every *Mensch* (individual) is inscribed within the *Volk* (people) of which he is part. In continental Western Europe, the legislation concerning the regulation of the economy—in particular the labour market and the financial market—is a clear example. This does not mean, of course, that in the "age of rights" (Bobbio 1989) the legislation that regulates the spaces of freedom of the person in the private sphere goes beyond the objectives of limiting the inequalities that develop in the market.

It is the *status libertatis* not the *status civitatis*, the private sphere of the individual not the public one, to be—by nature—"independent". Long before the externalities linked to the asymmetry of power, in fact, people differ for the genetic factors and for the family differences that characterise them at birth. The nature does not distribute talents or parents equally. "The set of opportunities takes shape in the mother's womb. Of which parents one is a child, in which country they live, how rich they are, are conditions that make a big difference from the point of view of the opportunities for a person's well-being" (Ferreira and Walton 2006). It is difficult not to agree with this definition of life chances. Every day approximately 400,000 people are born. It is undeniable that people are unequal even before they see the light.

Let's assume again that the endowment of talents is equal for everyone. Certainly, it cannot be assumed that everyone will be able to benefit from them to the same extent. The chances of well-being and the prospects of social mobility that newborns will have during their future life depend on the care each one receives in the family, the quality of the socio-economic environment, the opportunities they have access to in the market and the quality of the country's welfare system. The "lottery of life" therefore does not end in the difference in talents, but also concerns the degree of development of the country of birth, gender, ethnicity, income and culture of the parents. To *nature* (the genetic heritage) is added *nurture* (the "care" in the first years of life) and then participation in society.

Let's go back to the historical roots. The acceleration of GDP growth towards the end of the eighteenth century coincided with the affirmation of Enlightenment thought. The authors of the *Encyclopédie* founded society on the individual as a rational and "universal" being. The emerging *political economy* adopted the image of a society of "free and equal" individuals, born from the consensus expressed by subjects when they enter into an ideal "social contract", and then participate in its implementation independently of each other. With the French and American revolutions, natural law migrated into legal positivism, natural rights were inserted into the Constitution to then be implemented with legislation in the organisation of society.

How could the division into classes and social conflict as a constitutive element of society coexist with the function of homogenising the "different" carried out by the Enlightenment category of *universalism*? The answer lies in the construction, at the beginning of the nineteenth century, of the constitutional state in the major advanced countries. The agenda of its tasks did not materialise in the drastic transition from serving the sovereign to serving the citizen, but at least it placed at the centre of state organisation the need to establish a smaller power gap between rulers and ruled. On the one hand, the state took on the task of guaranteeing the individual's security and respect for his property rights: in 1829, the United Kingdom was the first country to organise modern police on a professional basis. On the other hand, the progressive improvement in the quality of life allowed the ruling classes to use social mobility to soften social tensions, accustoming the "disadvantaged" classes to accept inequalities in the expectation of climbing the rungs of the social ladder. In fuelling this hope, the technological changes in productive activities that drove the expansion of GDP between the end of the eighteenth century and the beginning of the nineteenth were joined by the cultural changes produced by the endogenous push of social forces for the granting of political rights. Economic and cultural change was accompanied by the formation of a middle class whose composition grew with the expansion of urban professions and public administration. Of course, upheavals of this magnitude could only lead to the coagulation of claims and social resentments in crucial historical phases of political crisis (from the "revolutions" of 1848 to the Paris Commune). But to absolute mobility *absolute*, the "individual income growth" (Jenkins 2011), was only partly followed by mobility *relative*, in the form of a strong opposition of interests and values between social classes. Although the starting blocks in the race of life remained strongly misaligned, and different individuals and social groups enjoyed income increases of very different magnitude, the fact that everyone could participate in a certain social ascent also induced the least favoured by growth to psychological satisfaction, to derive satisfaction from the condition of equality of destiny, from being "in the race".

In the evolution of history, democratic coexistence prevailed over conflict between unequals. The category of *universalism* was strengthened in the power relations of representative democracy as a method of deliberation and as a political value capable of giving more substance to the idea of equality between people. The emerging liberalism made use of the idea of the universal individual. The liberal state, which was originally only an expression of the property classes, found in the civil rights of man affirmed by the Enlightenment the *medium* that allowed it to build an ideological bridge between a society marked by division into classes and the idea of the expanding market as a *morally-free zone*. The concept of democracy, which had remained obscured for centuries after its elaboration in the Greek world, regained a prominent place in the nineteenth century as the cornerstone of the "liberal revolution". The success of liberal thought derives from having presented—and installed in the "collective imaginary"—the market as the place where the homogenisation between individuals as offerers and demanders of goods bearing well-being is affirmed.

How has the analysis of social mobility related to *individualism*? The double rooting—in the individual and in society—of social mobility is connected with the different relationship that the two meanings of the concept—*absolute* and *relative*—have with income. The upward *absolute* mobility refers to the impact that on the standard of living of various subjects has the *joint venture* of GDP growth; the standard of living is affected by the speed with which individual earnings grow within the dynamics of the country's GDP. From the increase in absolute *mobility* both an "income effect" on consumption (the greater purchase of goods allowed by the higher earnings) and higher levels of well-being in fundamental dimensions such as health and education[2] are derived. Relative *mobility* instead tells of the individual aspiration to increase well-being and *status* in competition with other individuals and social groups. In the current phase of slow and discontinuous GDP growth, relative *mobility*—measured by the percentage of individuals (which in statistics is indicated as "objective probability") who from one period to another change position in the income ranking—is little supported by the growth of aggregate GDP. At this point it is possible to answer the question about the link between mobility and individualism: liberalism conceives the aspiration to social ascent—the competition between individuals aimed at climbing positions in the income and *status* scale—as a private matter. In liberal thought, social mobility is seen as a corollary of the exercise of individual freedom, it does not assume any other dimension than that of individual success. The rise in the income scale would be solely due to the commitment of the *homo faber*, even being associated—as seen in Chap. 3—with the category of merit. In this way, in the liberal conception of society, the interdependent nature of socio-economic relations within a community and the intrinsically conflictual character conferred on them by the asymmetry of power is ignored.

The Crisis of Democracy in Advanced Societies

Social mobility as a private matter must nevertheless be reconciled with participation in society. John Rawls, the most celebrated political philosopher of the twentieth century, seems to believe that the way can be no other than that suggested by Immanuel Kant: individuals with

[2] A database that harmonises longitudinal data from various countries allows the economic analysis of educational inequality to be combined with the frequency of diseases. The results again highlight a positive correlation between education and health: over a two-year period, unsurprisingly the impact of education on the deterioration, with age, of health is higher (and significant) in Western and Southern Europe and less strong (and not significant) in Northern Europe (Avendano et al. 2009).

different values and interests cooperate once they all accept the existence of the "moral law above us".[3] It is necessary for individualism to be combined with Kantian universalism, so that it is possible to define society as a "cooperative enterprise for mutual advantage" without social conflict playing any role. In Rawls' view, on the other hand, although it is true that individuals are unequal in wealth and income, capitalist society is not representable as the place where the determinants of "unjust inequality" take root. For a free society to also be just, it is sufficient that the principle of formal equality in access to opportunities, in the market (there must be no room for any kind of discrimination in participation in the labour market or in the conditions of supply and demand for goods and services) as well as in public offices. What a "just" society requires is "a fair system of cooperation between free and equal people" (ibid., p. 302). Moreover, Rawls is very clear in denouncing the "failures" produced by the roots in utilitarianism of the liberal conception of society. It is not admissible in his judgement, as the utilitarianism of the liberal-oriented economist John Harsanyi (1953, 1955) has no qualms about doing, that the well-being of the community is increased by bartering a bit of "utility" more for one individual with a bit of "utility" less for another, with the justification that this allows the maximisation of overall utility. According to Rawls, in fact, the expansion of GDP is the result of production as a *joint venture* of a cooperative type. The utilitarian calculation, in penalising the well-being of some subjects for the realisation of maximum aggregate well-being, does not respect the individual participants in the *joint venture* as it does not "take seriously the distinction between people" (Rawls 1982, p. 40).

Rawls' individualistic approach is however set in an overly idealised interpretation of society. The man of the interpretative scheme he elaborated is an example of the difference between what should be and what is. As David Hume stated in *A Treatise of Human Nature* (1739–1740), from an "ought" one cannot derive an "is". If it is good that individuals enter into reciprocal relations as "free and equal", as Rawls assumes in his "first principle of justice",[4] one cannot deduce that it is actually so, and

[3] According to Kant, it is the individual himself, as a rational subject, who freely chooses to submit to the command of the "moral law".

[4] In Rawls' *Theory of Justice*, the first principle states that "each person has an equal right to the most extensive scheme of equal basic liberties compatible with a similar scheme of liberties for others".

conclude that in pursuing their individual end people are in "equality of opportunities". Inequalities take shape even before participation in the market, at the different "starting blocks" in the race of life. This was written by Richard H. Tawney, socialist intellectual and economic historian, in his *Equality* (1931): "What is needed is not only an 'open road' but also an 'equal start'". In today's capitalist society, the goal of "equality of starting points", which would require a profound restructuring of the economic sphere, is increasingly less among the values to be admitted within the perimeter of public discourse. The silence on the absence in the structure of capitalist society of "equality of opportunities", primarily in education, is explained by the primacy gained by individualism understood as "freedom from constraints".

This vision of freedom is far from alien to the crisis that representative democracy is going through in the West. Its formal institutions often appear inadequate to address the structural issues that block social dynamics. In public discourse, it is rarely remembered how the percentage of votes obtained by the parties that form the governments of the countries of the European Union currently in office, with a few rare exceptions, is often far below 50%. This disaffection for politics, long present within American society, is accompanied by a dangerous ideological polarisation. Moreover, it is not far from the truth to assert—also in light of the high rate of voter abstention—that members of the community substantially participate in democratic life by giving their approval or disapproval to the outgoing government in each electoral round.

The crisis of democracy also lies in the lack of awareness—also widespread among the "disadvantaged" classes, attracted by the individualistic vision propagated by neoliberalism—of the asymmetry of power between social classes and its consequences on their well-being. Even in Europe, majorities of voters, accustomed to thinking that "alone is better", in fact vote against their own opportunities for improvement of well-being by inserting in the ballot a card with the symbol of parties that tend to downsize Welfare institutions (see Box 8.1). The same sovereignist parties have absorbed the neoliberal lesson and are against the rules of the labour market, and against public institutions in the production of goods of collective interest such as health and education and support for subjects with incomes below the poverty line. In the presence of an increasingly copious legislation on "equal opportunities", but in the desert of policies aimed at achieving "equality of starting points", work, health and education become goods to which to apply the logic of the market to make profits.

Freedom in Political Science and Economic Theory

The complex link between individual and society is often described in a not very pregnant way both by political science and by economic theory. In the standard model of orthodox economic theory, the Gee, decisions such as those relating to the desired level of human capital, the division between work time and free time, the commitment to be made in work, and so on, are completely reducible to the autonomous choices of individual subjects.

Almost a century and a half after the elaboration of this model, probably something more than the claim of individual freedom was needed to sweep under the carpet the asymmetry of power between social groups. Said and done. In order to propose a harmonious vision of the individual's relationship with self-realisation in society, neoliberal thought has raised the banner of merit. It is on this concept, discussed in Chap. 4, that the current interpretation of social mobility, in political science as in economics, hinges. The centrality assumed by merit is the other side of the emptying of meaning, of Thatcherian memory, that the concept of society has undergone. The metaphor of a social contract freely signed by subjects equal to each other is reflected in political science by the category of the *homo faber* and in economic theory by the category of the "representative individual" of all beings in the world. The protagonist of the Gee model makes meaningless, or at least inessential, the articulation of society into classes. In political science, the *pendant* of the "atomistic" vision of the individual of orthodox economics is the conception of the legal norm as a "general abstract case", in order to keep the law strictly distinct—placed above—with respect to the interests present in society. Hans Kelsen's (1934) "pure theory" of law is a formalistic defence of the separation between the political sphere and the economic sphere. The characteristic that unites the two versions—political-legal and economic—of the individual is that these, in both cases, are detached from the social context.

If freedom encounters no limits, man has the electrifying power to be the architect of his own destiny. *Ergo*, the merit of social ascent can only be entirely attributed to him. If it is enough to commit oneself, all income and *status* gaps will be overcome, the advantageous positions that others have easily acquired by birth do not count. It is still true that the opportunities to develop one's talents take shape within coordinates established by the legal and economic institutions of the country in which the individual achieves his human and professional formation. However, if these coordinates provide that companies make production and employment decisions in full autonomy, it is difficult to deny that the labour market is a space that escapes at the control of the rest of society.

Liberal thought, in rejecting the concept of social conflict on both the economic and political science fronts, sees in mobility *absolute*—in the "tide that lifts all boats"—the undisputed engine of social dynamics. This vision reflects very little reality. The mobility *relative* among individuals, the movement from one position to another on the income scale, gives immediate testimony of how social interaction inevitably encompasses social conflict. In the context of "systemic independence", the well-being of individuals is influenced by "externalities". They are often an expression of the power asymmetries that characterise the many relationships in which each individual finds himself. The Gee's estrangement from the economic theory of conflict between social classes is accompanied by the position of neutrality with respect to the power asymmetries of Hans Kelsen's "pure theory" of law, in which social conflict has no theoretical significance. Although the law of legal systems tries to ignore it, in capitalist society economic power uses the law: "Capital rules according to the law, and the reason is rooted in the fact that modern rights have emerged as private rights dependent on the State" (Pistor 2021, p. 212).

Contrary to the vision of *laissez-faire*, propagated in the mid-eighteenth century by liberals and physiocratic economists, the expansion of capitalism has never done without the collaboration of the State. In history, there are countless examples of cooperation between public power and private entities. In England of the seventeenth and eighteenth centuries, it was not the king's army but the English trading companies that subjected vast populations to the economic interests of the monarchy. At the end of the eighteenth century, a "libertarian" labour legislation greatly facilitated the expansion of the first industries, and public intervention also began in support of private enterprises. Since the Enlightenment denied the existence of a purpose of the community and invited men to abandon the teleology of the "kingdom of God", the relativism of values has been welcomed as the "compass" of ethical reasoning. A view of history more adherent to reality than that of many liberal texts traces the birth of the bourgeoisie not from the affirmation of natural law as the ideological substrate of a hypothetical "social contract" between free and equal, but from social conflict. The political institutions that baptised economic development were led by the bourgeois classes who ascended, in an also bloody contest, freeing themselves from the grip of absolute power and gradually replacing the aristocracy at the helm of society. The entrepreneurial bourgeoisie shapes the well-being of society based on the primacy of consumption, the satisfaction of which has been offered by companies in an increasingly varied choice of goods. The desire for happiness of men has been translated into the search for consumption, erected as the foundation of personal identity and of the *status* social (Bauman 2010).[5]

Neoliberalism, just as on the political science front it sinks the pluralism of opinions in the "social mind"—until today's homologation of the "*pensée unique*"—on the economic front it issues the verdict that there is no "polar star" to which society should aim, nor any "moral rule" for the distribution of income. Among "free and equal" subjects there are no opposed collective values, neither at the individual level, given the *autonomy* and the *separation* between the subjects of market, nor at the community level, given the "ethical relativism".

Just like in the standard model of orthodox economics, the concept of *social welfare* is not only rooted exclusively in the individual, but is also devoid of any connotation related to the community. The adjective *social* is not in fact referred to society as a whole, but to the overall result that arises from the independent behaviour of each individual. The success of liberal thought lies in having spread the conviction that the exercise of freedom—unlike its restrictions, those imposed by authoritarian regimes—does not fit into a collective purpose. The fact that until now freedom has not had such a framework—except for the parenthesis of the *Trente Glorieuses*—would be the historical proof that it cannot have it. The expedient with which neoliberalism has conquered the Western world is that of transferring into the sphere of the link between economy and society a key concept of Friedrich Nietzsche's thought. This is not the place to go into depth. Suffice it to say these verses by the Italian song-writer Francesco Guccini: "God is dead. I've seen people of my age go away along the roads that never lead to anything". In fact, it seems that in the age of ChatGpt the idea of freedom is still waiting to be brought into focus. In order for it to give us back the true image of society as composed of free men *but not* independent, the aperture of the camera lens must be much larger than that of both classical liberalism and neoliberalism.

On the political science front, the idea is still dominant that the multitudes of individuals who act in society, following their own idiosyncratic

[5] The happiness approach (*happiness*), based on the subjective perception that the subject has of their own multidimensional well-being, is outside the scope of this study.

purposes, generate the "spontaneous order" in the economic system. The implication is that individuals acting in the market have no need to be aware of the direction in which society is evolving. The concept of "spontaneous order" adopted by liberal thought is therefore in full coherence with the concepts of *autonomy* and *separation* between the subjects of the Gee model. In the liberal conception, freedom is primarily configured as "negative freedom" (Berlin 1989), freedom from any interference, the call to the duty to defend one's inalienable freedom from the imposition of an external authority such as the State, and to have "the courage to use one's own intellect without the guidance of another". As already mentioned, it was a liberal philosopher, John Stuart Mill (1859), who inscribed freedom within "systemic interdependence": "the freedom of each ends where the freedom of others begins". The limit to freedom that he saw in *On Liberty* is an example of foresight. What we have defined as "systemic interdependence" is the source of a series of externalities that take shape in the asymmetry of power between social classes. They compress freedom, more properly understood as *empowerment*, the freedom "to be and to do" to use the words of Amartya Sen.

Contrary to what methodological individualism claims, social mobility—or persistence—requires a conceptual apparatus that takes into account the complex interaction between individual and society. Individual action is set in a context of interdependence between people, mediated by the market and political and economic institutions. It is therefore difficult for the point of view of methodological individualism to be the right one when investigating the evolution of social structure. The attempt being made in this chapter is to build a bridge between the characteristics of social mobility and the *spillovers* that develop in market interaction regulated by the *governance* of the State. The problem, therefore, is that the evaluative criterion of the social sciences—methodological individualism—is not neutral. Having a "small" aperture, its camera focuses on only part of reality.

Social mobility, it has been said, is greatly facilitated by a continuous growth of a country's GDP. But with the increase in individual earnings, social conflict also sharpens and the phenomenon of *relative* mobility, competition along the rungs of the social ladder, gains weight. In the post-war period, the political management of a vigorous economic growth made it necessary to resort to policies aimed at "social inclusion". The more the expansion of well-being broadens the areas of life in which even "disadvantaged" individuals can plan their self-realisation, the more varied the placement of individuals on the scale of wealth and income, the more social conflict is fuelled. Once the democracy of the vote expresses itself in favour of social rights, and the laws passed by Parliaments give them legal recognition, the distribution of income between social classes changes.

As mentioned in Chap. 4, from the eighties onwards, the phenomenon of *relative* mobility has come up against the power asymmetry present in society. As mentioned, the business system successfully opposed the expansion of a demand for social rights that threatened their primacy. The restoration of business command in the market and the turn of governments towards austerity policy were the tools that neoliberal culture used to mitigate the conflicts that were triggered by the *relative* mobility of the rising social classes. Neoliberalism managed to stop the effective implementation of the social rights won by workers thanks to the political pressure of progressive movements. The march towards solidary democracy was blocked.

From Group Membership to Multidimensional Well-Being

The increasing interaction of people in various life spaces means that today's society is characterised by a high degree of complexity. The difficulty encountered in analysing it can be summarised as follows. In advanced countries, in demonstrations on employment and wages, a much higher percentage of older workers and pensioners take to the streets; there are few young people, who should be the most interested in the future fortunes of the country. The reason is well known. The social role of large organisations—parties, trade unions, the Church—which in the twentieth century aggregated people, influencing the economic outcome with their pressure on the government, has now been exhausted. The increased interdependence between people corresponds to the multiplication of life spaces for which they are responsible for the well-being outcome. Individuals today set up a much higher number of social interactions than in the past, in the market as well as telematically, achieving different results in various areas of life. The well-being of the individual has therefore taken on a more markedly multidimensional character. Overall well-being is the result of the "high" or "low" position that each individual occupies in each dimension.

This real anthropological change in the link between the individual and society leads to a differentiation between people that is much more marked than the class one that resulted from the simple measure of available wealth and income earned in the activity carried out. The process of articulating individual identity into a *multiple self* reduces the likelihood that a person will have a level of well-being equal to that of another in each of the various areas of life. This has a contradictory impact on personal identity. On the one hand, multidimensionality has the effect of fading the placement of each individual in the ranking of social *status*. The less clear the person's position at a certain step of the social ladder, the more an effect of homogenisation is generated in the person's self-perception as a "social being". On the other hand, it is the very plurality of the dimensions that make up personal identity that favours the perception of oneself as a *unicum*. The *multiple self* explains the explosion of narcissism, the need for as marked and unmistakable individualisation as possible. Think, among many examples, of the fashion for tattoos, the desire to show off in the role of the protagonist in a *TikTok* and so on.

This contradictory anthropological change has a precise impact on the person's connection with society. The multidimensional measurement of individual well-being has led to a downsizing of the role of income as an indicator of the person's *status*. With the severance of the close connection of personal identity with a quintile of distribution, the placement of an individual in a certain income category—that of the rich, the middle class and the poor[6]—tends to diminish. With income no longer in the foreground, the differentiation between individuals is much more articulated. But social interaction mediated by the compulsive pressure of mobile phone keys inevitably leads to new forms of homogenisation of individual identities. The *status* assigned to people by professional placement and earnings and the ideological glue that cemented their belonging to historical social groupings have given way to many niche groups. Individual identities are so fragmented within themselves that the multidimensional condition of an individual is hardly recognisable from the outside as a social class. The "acronyms" of the various groups (*influencers*, *tiktokers* etc.) designate the new styles on which personal identities are built. Each

[6] We usually distinguish between absolute poverty (the condition of destitution; not having—or having with great difficulty or intermittently—the primary resources for human sustenance) and relative poverty (having an income lower than 50% or 60% of the per capita income of a country).

belongs to—and is defined by—different "cultures" in which they "participate" in the same day. Nevertheless, the multidimensionality of personal identity does not attenuate the "singularity" of the individual, but on the contrary enhances it. This was intuitively understood by George Simmel. In *Social Differentiation*, the German sociologist writes: "the more the number [of social groups a person belongs to] grows, the more unlikely it is that other people have that same combination of groups and that the numerous circles intersect again at *one* point".

This is exactly what we are witnessing in today's world: the parcelisation of tasks in the automated factory and in services, as well as the spread of chats whose focus is increasingly disparate, accentuates the tendency of mass society towards the individualisation of multidimensional levels of well-being, with a consequent, even more marked, decay of class aggregates. The fragmentation of the person in the various combinations of multidimensional well-being primarily corresponds to the crumbling of the primacy in personal identity of the social group of belonging. The unfolding of existence in a plurality of different life spaces makes it more difficult to precisely place the individual within social stratification. Multidimensionality, in distributing people among a large number of different socio-economic positions, each corresponding to a certain dimension, has ended up diluting, to the point of cancellation, the symbolic places of class belonging. Work has lost its function of giving meaning to identity. Being employed, as a figure of a life path that is part of a "collective enterprise", is in serious crisis. To the point that in the outpost of Western civilisation, the United States, today we are witnessing the expanding phenomenon of resignations from dependent work. The subject's place within the social structure is now almost a personal choice, linked to the dimensions of well-being in which, like in a suit, the individual feels more comfortable. Émile Durkheim would certainly have defined a society composed of such people as suffering from anomie, from absence of norms. Pierre Bourdieu would be less worried, because there is something more fundamental: it is the "lottery" of birth that makes people "determined".

Individualism has so penetrated people's minds that they are less interested than before in understanding the meaning of their position in the income distribution. However, money continues to imprint the dominant mark in society. We are all less aware of belonging to a class, probably excluding the rich. But the stability of the capitalist system in which we live reminds us that income and wealth remain essential points of reference for people's "social identity"—the *status civitatis*. The human substance of the person continues to reside in the quality of life that is allowed by income. earned in the market, from the ability to promote one's own multidimensional well-being in important dimensions such as health and education (especially in the absence of the public system) and in the ability of the wealth that one may possess to counteract "economic vulnerability" in times of recession, and to supplement conditions of casual or precarious work.

Neoliberalism uses the end of ideologies to make—despite the diversity of the characteristic traits of the *multiple self*—the identity sets of people appear completely homologous. Although the *multiple self* are also very heterogeneous individuals in terms of income and wealth, modern technologies contribute to spreading over social stratification the veil of an imaginary equality, making people less recognisable under the profile of their power in society. The asymmetry of power, however, persists. The multidimensional nature assumed by individual well-being does not make us all "more free and more equal". The more we are interconnected, the more, at the same time, we differentiate among ourselves. But only as individuals. Beneath the surface of the articulation into multiple personal identities, in which professional placement is no longer dominant, the asymmetry of power between social groups remains. The social homogenisation in the *social media* compensates for the identity void generated by the end of aggregations on an ideological basis. For those who are not part of social groupings with power in society, the digital economy, in putting into communication on the network individual users with individual users, represents—for better or for worse—a factor of identity recovery. For those whose social reference is instead power—for example, for those who navigate among their shares of financial and real estate assets—the digital economy is a valuable aid. The wealth, the more it is hidden, the more it is protected.

The state of suffering of collective identity manifests itself today in the extreme forms of the search for identity. The spread of populism is proof of a disorientation. With the disappearance of the function of work as an unmistakable signal of the collective identity of the subject—of its *status civitatis*—the position of the individual in society has become more opaque. It is a fact that populist movements have accentuated their nationalist and anti-immigrant creed, often embracing an extreme right-wing ideology.[7] Many social strata, in perceiving themselves devoid of an identity that goes beyond that personal one, end up clinging to the sovereignist ideological identity. But populism is not the substance, it is only the most dangerous manifestation of the crisis of advanced societies. On the surface, there is the multiple individual. The substance lies in the asymmetry of power that characterises the current form of capitalism. It makes the social identity of the individual continue to depend significantly on the inequality of wealth and income. At the moment when neoliberalism has oriented the multidimensional man to the construction of the *multiple self* in the sign of individualism, the individual has suffered a loss of cultural identity. The multidimensional man is today a man who no longer knows his own *status civitatis.* The more individualism weakens the sharing of values and interests within and between groups, the more social cohesion suffers.

From the Social Function of Work to the Society of Interaction

The time we live in, it has been said, sees the evolution of the social structure blocked by the crisis of both forms of mobility. Absolute mobility slows down parallel to a process of slower economic growth and periods of crisis. The search by workers for stable and decently paid employment is frustrated. At the same time, relative mobility—due to the combined impact of slow GDP expansion and increasing income inequality—is stalling. Globalisation, labour market deregulation and technological progress have greatly reduced the power of trade unions. Competition in the market and society no longer concerns opposing groups but subjects separated from each other by working conditions and life areas that are very fragmented. Due to the fall of ideological beliefs that kept people tied to their social group, the social aggregation function that work played in the age of industrialisation has disappeared. The command of companies and finance over the growth process and the evolution of low-skilled occupations towards precarious jobs undermine the bargaining power of unions and bend the aspiration for social ascent of disadvantaged classes.

[7] The references to Nazism in some American political groups and in the European party scene are a sign of the need to take refuge in the most violent symbolism of collective identity, to identify oneself in being "against" an ethnicity.

In the "world of yesterday", the asymmetry of power was made evident and was rigidly established and regulated by the organisation of work in the factory. Each individual looked at society from the visual angle that belonging to their own group suggested: "A social world is a universe of assumptions, taken for granted by those who belong to it and invested with value by those who want to be part of it" (Bourdieu 2012, p. 410). The lifelong permanence in a condition of social subordination and the consequent staticity of the social structure have taken different forms. Unlike the market as a *morally-free zone*, where subjects "free and equal" among themselves independently realise their production and exchange plans, in the asymmetric social interactions of reality, the *cross-correlation* is enhanced. The complementarities that are established between the "negative externalities" multiply the opportunities and gains of some and penalise the opportunities and gains of others. It is now clear how there is a close link between the decreasing values of social mobility and the increasing values of Gini indices of income and wealth. The consolidation of power and gains in the hands of an elite progressively restricts access to opportunities for "disadvantaged" subjects, ultimately crystallising the division between social classes. Today, the asymmetry of power hides behind the multidimensionality of the individual's participation in society; it is no longer exclusively attributable to the laws of economics, to the direct command of capital in the sphere of production.

For people with few means, the extreme difficulty in leaving the lower rungs of the social ladder is due to the concentration of "negative externalities" in the multidimensional reality. There is a high objective probability—or, clear statistical evidence—that a "disadvantaged" subject in various areas of life is exposed to a plurality of "negative" outcomes due to the *spillovers* that propagate among the conditions of "disadvantage": for example, a "low" level not only in income, but also in health, education, housing context and so on. Since the complexity of advanced societies has articulated the condition of inequality on multiple dimensions of individual existence, in the rankings of various dimensions of well-being, the individual does not necessarily occupy the same position in income, health, education, employment and so on.

The powerful growth of European countries during the *Trente Glorieuses* leveraged the function of work as the foundation of the welfare society. Germany and Italy were examples of this, two countries in which manufacturing production was crucial in determining the course of the economy. The metalworkers' unions played a role in the long phase of economic growth. In those years, an embryo of solidary democracy took shape. The achievements obtained in wage negotiations in that key sector served as a viaticum for the claims of workers in other industrial sectors. The ability to coordinate claim actions with the economic policy objectives of governments allowed the economic expansion to be presented as a *joint venture* collective. Work in industry was a sure guarantee of a precise social placement; belonging to a social group was indeed defined by the work function covered.

The opportunity for the reaction against the political weight that work had assumed in the phase of *labour-augmenting* development was provided by automation. Already in the nineties, in the United States, the country leading the economic and political trends of the entire West, robotics began to change the balance of power in manufacturing industry; the weakening of workers' bargaining power allowed companies to return to a distribution of surplus favourable to profits. After the political choice of admitting China to the WTO, the preservation of economic dominance in the face of increasing competition in international markets was pursued by the Western leader country through globalisation and the use of ICT (*information and communications technology*).[8] The very idea of the existence of a strong link between work and personal identity has tended to fade in many low-income social strata. Although in all advanced countries the social structure tends to a progressive polarisation, and the number of poor people is increasing, on the surface society shows no signs of turbulence. It matters that in workplaces strong ideological positions do not coagulate, such as to lead in the polls to anti-capitalist voting majorities and to condition governments regarding market regulation and public policies. The mood of the square marks calm. Decades of neoliberalism have instilled in the culture of new generations an individualistic representation of their position in society that is in stark contrast with political aggregation and the resumption of social conflict.

Unlike what was theorised by the functionalist approach in vogue until the middle of the last century, income and *status* mobility is not today the consequence of a *function* that a young person is destined to perform as an adult in the social body. The reduction of the company size of

[8] "The enormous increase in imports from countries thousands of miles away and the complex global chains of supply determined by the transfer of jobs abroad to China or Mexico have been enabled by advances in communication technologies" (Acemoglu and Johnson 2023, p. 263).

manufacturing and the numerical decline of employees in manufacturing sectors, once defined as the workers aristocracy, are two phenomena that occurred, according to statistics, between 1970 and 2019. We have already mentioned the individualisation of employment contracts, the multiplication of precarious occupations of self-employed workers, the explosion in services of fixed-term contracts, or "discontinuous fixed" time, piecework (*target*) and "on call". Such fragmentation of work positions has not been compensated by the increase in permanent contracts in services and female participation in the labour market. The structural changes that have occurred in recent decades fall within the progressive abandonment of collective bargaining in favour of individual bargaining; with the consequence that unions, weakened by the disaffection of their members, they can no longer influence the conditions of workers. But all this happened concurrently with the change in the cultural paradigm. The crumbling of the individual's identification in a *status* social based on occupation and income—and the fragmentation of people's identity in the various combinations of well-being multidimensional—would not have been possible if work had preserved its function as a pivot of well-being both individual and collective.

The work does not only function as the "cement of society". It is still vivid the memory of the fundamental support of work to the vigorous post-war growth. Those who today look out onto the world of work were born in a completely different cultural context. It is therefore devoid of the perception of work as a collective function and is led to consider normal the condition of precariousness or the fragmentation of the work path. The worker self-perceives as a commodity in search of a job and a salary. The free market forces low-skilled workers to work more because this is the only way to ensure survival.

All this happens in the absence of a mobilization by unions, and of any effort of the social classes affected by the lack of social mobility to join and react. From collective experience, work has been reduced to individual responsibility. At the end of the nineteenth century, Chancellor Bismarck showed foresight in understanding how much collective defence from risks, guaranteed by the State to workers through social insurance, could represent a glue of the national community. Today, the threat of an antagonistic organisation of the masses no longer raises concern among the elites. With today's downsizing of the welfare state, not only is the mutuality of institutions defending against risks abolished, but it is charged to the worker the "adaptability to work". The "active" work policies—also called *welfare to work* or *workfare*—too often reduce to the request to the worker to take on the responsibility of being ready—whatever their "starting conditions" and the *skill* acquired—to keep up with the evolution of technical progress and labour demand. The problem is not in the request to the individual to take their own share of responsibility with the commitment in training and work. What is wrong is that the commitment to the unemployed worker in an "active competition for search for a job" does not correspond to any commitment of the class entrepreneurial to take on the responsibility of expanding jobs, nor of governments to give priority to public spending for labour policies (today increasingly penalised by austerity). The result is often "poor work", humiliating social discipline, the adaptation of society to what the market offers.

The problem is the context, often of strong discomfort, in which young people undertake their life project. The narrative of the "unemployed lying on the couch" is not only simplistic: it is a more or less conscious denial of the dignity of workers useful to hide the reality. The real question is why—according to statistics[9]—there are very few "poor and lazy" people, and instead many people who cannot be held responsible for their condition of "disadvantaged". A good part of the explanation for the reduced creation of jobs lies in the introduction of new automation technologies, which put at risk the expectation of social inclusion and social mobility of young people (Brynjolfsson and McAfee 2014; Frey and Osborne 2017). N. G. Mankiw, in the university text *Principles of Economics* most adopted in the world, denies the threat of what already in the thirties J. M. Keynes defined "technological unemployment": "History suggests, however, that most technological progress is instead of the type *labour-augmenting*" (Mankiw 2018, p. 367). In light of the historical statistics and data on the rapid process of automation in progress, this judgement finds only denials. It responds to the ideological need to apply to the condition of unemployed the neoliberal slogan of "individual responsibility".

Social dynamics should not be described today based on the concept of function, but based on the more neutral, and more indeterminate, concept of *interaction*, the meeting between individual subjects that takes place in the many interconnections of society. Unlike the *function*, which involves the commitment to perform a service for personal interest and for the purpose of common well-being, the *interaction* in society

[9]Consider the small number in Italy, compared to the total beneficiaries, of citizenship income payments that the judiciary has sanctioned for lack of requirements.

requires the individual to build a much weaker identity, and encourages him less to act in cooperative way. The transition from the collective dimension of the function to the individual one of the interaction has a repercussion in the political sphere. Those who were once citizens who exerted power through the organs of political representation are today often people who choose to participate in electoral appointments as they go to the market: that is, they go to the polls only insofar as, from time to time, they believe that the benefits offered by the various political proposals are able to meet their needs. As Zygmunt Bauman observed, we are today all inserted in a "global network of mutual dependence". Echoes him on the religious side, the preaching of Jorge Mario Bergoglio, always attentive to both the dignity of the individual and social cohesion, in the "conviction that everything in the world is intimately connected" (Bergoglio 2015, p. 11).

From the "Open Society" to the "Liquid Society"

In *The Open Society and Its Enemies* (1945), coinciding with the return of peace, Karl Popper defined as "open" the society in which the choices of individuals do not mature in a "magical or tribal or collectivist society". With "open society", Karl Popper meant the absence of obstacles in the market to social ascent, in the context of the rules of political democracy. In the first half of the twentieth century, on the other hand, not only was the income level very similar to that of parents but the job was passed down from father to son to an extent incomparably greater than today, whether it was self-employment, employment under an entrepreneur or in a public company. Intergenerational mobility was in fact very modest. In the following decades, with the opening of economies to free trade, and under the impulse of significant economic growth, the dynamics of the social structure would have greatly increased.

The reasons for such structural change must be framed in the virtuous intertwining, already highlighted, between income expansion and expansion of people's identity. In the post-war period, a cultural revolution took shape that was born as a strengthening of individual identity in the private sphere, with profound changes in the relationship between the sexes and between children and parents. The "age of rights" was the season that a little too optimistically was defined as a "'premonitory sign' (*signum prognosticum*) of the moral progress of humanity" (Bobbio 1989, p. 4). The movements born in the seventies, however, also carried forward a battle for the demolition of the boundary between political rights and social rights. The European left committed itself to directing the libertarian matrix of the cultural revolution from the "private" to the public sphere, towards forms of protest in production and wage claims that shortened the distance between social classes. For liberal thought, the rights of the individual should instead have been inscribed within the perimeter of the concept of the "open society". In the vision of Popper and his followers, the boundaries of this concept can be extended from the private sphere to include the expansion of "freedom of choice" in the markets for consumer goods and financial activities, but not also the sharing of entrepreneurial decisions. In other words, the "open society" gives space to the consumer in the market and to the voter in democratic life, but it cannot lead to the granting of rights to the worker in production, it must not cross the gates of companies.

Neoliberalism was born in the eighties to assert the supremacy of the market over society. One of the objectives was to stop the ongoing evolution towards a society of substantial democracy. Universalism, the concept on which the post-war welfare systems were built, had to be declined in a way consistent with an atomistic vision of the individual. People who find themselves in even very unequal conditions of income and wealth in many dimensions of well-being are not considered deserving of a specific treatment in Welfare. For this school of thought, it is not conceivable a judgement on whether income inequality is fair or not, as it is an "individual evil", caused primarily by lack of commitment.

The message is clear. From the "open society" we should expect the benefits of competition, not economic security. It doesn't matter that opportunities are greatly divergent between advantaged and disadvantaged people both in market competition and in risk protection. The conception of the functioning of the economy has thus returned—after the brief season of recognition of social rights in legislation—to the bed of the vision of liberal political science: which interprets society as the sum of individuals "free" from constraints, whose "equal freedom" finds expression in the formal sphere of law, not in the substantial sphere of the economy. The welfare state was originally entrusted with the mission of implementing social rights. The guiding criterion of the welfare state's programmes was universalism. The right to a dignified life and the protection of people from risky events are however in tension with the individualistic approach that is typical of the market. The holders of economic power have obtained from European governments that the compatibility of the welfare state with the individualistic functioning of the market be restored. Welfare systems thus began to retreat.[10] The neoliberalist line of thought established from the eighties onwards has propagated a version of individualism that has collided with the synergies between market and welfare institutions that many advanced countries had built in Europe in the 30 years 1945–1974. In many countries, the regime of progressive taxation has been gradually reformed in the direction of proportional taxation (*flat tax*); consistent with the idea that tax should not be levied in increasing proportion to each higher bracket of personal market income. The new stage of the process of individualisation has become the dismantling of collective institutions of "risk sharing", i.e. the welfare state. In order to prevent the welfare system from interfering with the flexibility of salary and job position, important protections for workers have been abolished, redistribution has been reduced. The adoption of the criterion of equal treatment of unequal people in merit goods has favoured the reduction of funding for health and public education, to make room for market forces.[11] In dimensions of well-being such as health and education, for example, protection from the greater risk that weighs on low-income individuals, who are often also at high risk of poor health and poor education, has been shifted onto the worker. People who are at different levels on the income scale also have different access to fundamental dimensions of well-being such as health and education, which are also fundamental factors for life expectancy.[12] The equalising function of unequal "starting points"

[10] The main tools of social equalisation were the following: increase in the minimum wage, defence of collective bargaining, prohibition of temporary and precarious contracts, decent unemployment benefits, active labour policies dedicated to the empowerment of young people with a poor socio-family background. Moreover, even in countries where they were conceived as a "package" of non-compressible programmes for the implementation of solidaristic democracy, institutions such as progressive taxation, income redistribution, the public system in education and health are in the process of retreating. Only in the current version, which does not provide for the respect of social rights, is Welfare considered compatible with the market economy.

[11] Consider, in Italy, the deficiencies in residential structures for the elderly, the restriction in healthcare of the eligibility criteria for in-kind services, and in public education the cuts to primary and secondary school institutions in small municipalities and the reduction of support teachers.

[12] In the annual report of the Inps presented to the Chamber of Deputies on 13 September 2023, it reads: "A former employee, with a marital income in the lowest bracket of the distribution, has a life expectancy at 67 years, almost 5 years lower than that of a former contributor to the Inpdai Fund, or the Pension Fund for executives".

performed by the state has been downsized, social spending has been "cut". In Europe, the decreasing funding is progressively narrowing Welfare to the objective of combating poverty (the minimum wage, in force in most countries, and unemployment benefits).

Welfare policies have thus been adapted to the market through a declination of universalism that shared with individualism a fundamental characteristic: the absence of distinction between people. The "generic individual" as a unit of analysis is today a common characteristic to both concepts, the market and the welfare state.

To understand how much the cultural climate established by neoliberalism has changed the world, here is a simple test. Consider this simple and clear concept expressed in a speech: "You don't take an individual who for years has been crippled by chains, free him, and bring him up to the starting line of a race, then tell him: 'you are free to compete with everyone else', and then you are also convinced that you have behaved in a fair way". Who said these words? It was not Mao Zedong. These words are taken from the inaugural speech of the academic year that in 1965 the President of the United States Lyndon B. Johnson, of Rooseveltian training, held at Howard University.[13] If I had written that those words were spoken by John Biden, would you have believed it? I think not. Not only Biden, but no other Democratic candidate for the presidency of the United States has ever uttered words similar to those for over half a century. The reason is simple: since 2 July 1964—the day Lyndon B. Johnson signed the *Civil Rights Act*, which prohibited "discrimination of race, skin colour, religion, gender and nation of origin"—no Democratic candidate for the presidency has ever won the majority of white voters' votes (Wilkerson 2020).

Neoliberalism has succeeded in transmitting to the economic sphere the rooting in individualism of people's beliefs and behaviours. The functioning of the economy has seen a strong push towards the reassertion of the company's command over labour and towards a downsizing of the welfare state aimed at individualising protection from risk: "everyone is

[13] A private university in Washington with a good ranking, historically attended by students of colour. This clarification doesn't change much. If the same speech were given today, in a completely different political and cultural climate, we would be struck by dismay. Just think how short-lived the indignation of Black Lives Matter was, a phenomenon that doesn't seem to have left lasting traces.

responsible for their own life; from destiny that it was, existence has become a task" (Beck 2000, p. 325).

Unlike the assumptions of so much of economic analysis, the evolution of society responds to social laws. In *The Misery of Philosophy* (1847), Marx wrote: "Economists have a peculiar way of proceeding [...]. By saying that the current relationships - the relationships of bourgeois production - are natural, economists mean that these are relationships within which wealth is created and productive forces are developed in accordance with the laws of nature. So these same relationships are natural laws independent of the influence of time. They are eternal laws that must always govern society. So there was history, but now there is no more. There was history because there were feudal institutions and because in these feudal institutions there were production relationships completely different from those of bourgeois society, which economists want to pass off as natural and therefore eternal".

The fact remains that capitalism manages, through crises, to regenerate and therefore to procrastinate. Let's look at its vanguard, American society. Today's version of the "natural law" as "eternal law" consists in the perception, very widespread in the population of the United States, of belonging to a single large middle class, despite statistical data showing social persistence or downward mobility. A reader who wants to investigate where the *genius loci* of the United States is hiding today has only the embarrassment of choice: the realism that pervades the works of writers—from Elizabeth Strout to Kent Haruf—wonderfully describes the alienating homogenisation of personal identities through cultural disorientation and the inner solitude of many existences. As much as political events testify to a strong polarisation of society, and literature describes us a not exciting way of being in the world, in the perception of the American middle class their own life is, all in all, satisfactory. Despite Marx, naturalism, with its eternal laws now imbued with minimalism, wins.

Economic factors alone could not have generated the upheaval that—following globalisation and technical progress—has affected the forms and institutions of social life. Piketty (2019) has linked the crisis of solidaristic democracy from the eighties, and the birth of populism, to the structural change caused by the progressive economic and cultural fracture between an intellectual elite and an entrepreneurial elite (the French economist defines them, respectively, *Brahmin left* and *merchant right*). The political dimension of the conflict was identified by him in the polarisation faults that in many advanced countries cross classes in the dimension not only of income but also of culture. Starting from the seventies and eighties, the vote for left-wing parties would gradually have concentrated in the portion of the electorate with a high degree of education: "the 'Brahmin' left is divided between those in favour of redistribution and those in favour of the market, and the 'merchant' right is divided between the nationalists-nativists and the supporters of the business world" (Gethin et al. 2022, pp. 848–9).

The discomfort of our days—not only of an economic and social type, but also of psychological origin—is explained by the impossibility, even for the worker with a secure job, to imagine their own social mobility based on the planning of their own life. Popper's idea of an "open society" does not seem to fit well with today's advanced societies. At most it can apply to the goods market, to the expansion of "freedom of choice" among a myriad of products on which the consumer can express their own preferences. The full autonomy, now regained by companies in the sphere of production after the turbulent seventies, is indeed also reducing the "degree of openness" of society.

The distance that in the globalised world has been created between the social function of work and the workers is visible in the decreasing ability of the market to guarantee the stability of jobs and therefore of the level of well-being achieved: "When there are large discrepancies between the social return - the benefit to society - and the private return - the benefit to a person or a company - markets, on their own, cannot do the work" (Stiglitz 2019, p. XXIII). In the nineteenth century, the gains guaranteed by the dizzying increase in hourly productivity allowed by technical progress were not directed to the benefit of the workers. Instead, as Marx argued in *Das Kapital*, "the economic paradox that the most powerful means of shortening working time was transformed into the most infallible means of transforming all the time of the worker's life and his family into working time available for the valorisation of capital". Gradually, Marx argues in the *Economic and Philosophical Manuscripts of 1844* (1932), workers lost the power to control, through the choice of work tools and their own *skills*, the productive activity, and underwent a process of "alienation". The discourse on alienation is taken by him to extreme conclusions in the *Grundrisse* (1857–1858) and in the *Unpublished sixth chapter* of *Capital* (Marx 1969): for "abstract labour" he means labour no longer as a quality of the person, but as the pure moment in which the work effort is delivered. Things seemed to improve in the twentieth century. The increases in productivity, under the pressure of trade unions, were to some extent used to reduce the length of the working day and to correct the less acceptable aspects of the condition of subordinate work. Today we are going back. Work is defined as "human capital" because the worker is identified with their skills. The essential productive contribution to capitalism is that concentrated in the knowledge that is utilised by workers with excellent training. Advanced sectors proceed to the selection of workers defined as "intangible capital", because they employ in the productive activity their—very high—immaterial skills. The final stage of this process of alienation is the introduction of automation techniques in progress. With the advent of researchers and workers carrying "intangible capital", the *skills* are definitively incorporated into robots, in which "flows the knowledge produced by science and technology" (Harvey 2020, p. 195). Things go differently in traditional sectors. For medium-skilled workers, working time and overtime increase. For low-skilled workers, the use of new labour-saving technologies leads to "exclusion" from factory production, almost always without the consultation of trade unions. They end up trapped in the unprotected occupations of the galaxy of *gig jobs* managed by information platforms. Likewise, the layoffs connected to the "relocations" of production plants, decided by multinational companies in complete autonomy from governments very timid in defending workers' rights, find no explanation either in their lack of commitment, or in the laws of supply and demand of the market. In summary, technical progress, the flow of knowledge made available by science, is "bent" to the achievement of the only goal of exploiting profit opportunities. It is difficult not to catch the echo of our time in these words of Marx: "The more capitalist production is developed in a country, the more variability is required in the labour force, the more the worker is indifferent to the particular content of his work, the more fluid and intense is the movement of capital from one sphere to another" (Marx 1969, p. 46).

Few today reflect on the lesson that, in *The Great Transformation*, Karl Polanyi simply stated: "the market is made for man, not man for the market". The denunciation of the limits of the market is a faint voice. The elites leading the economy continue to prioritise—in the words of Stiglitz—"the benefit for a person or a company", in the belief and expectation that society should adapt to the market and not, conversely, the market to serve society and the needs of people, once the redistribution of wealth makes it possible.

Popper's concept of "open society" has been revisited by Zygmunt Bauman (2006) using a definition—the "liquid society"—which proposes a critique of social reality updated to the new *Zeitgeist*, the spirit of the time of neoliberalism. The "liquid society" alludes to the insecurity suffered by an individual identity increasingly subject to the "externalities" it encounters in the market and in society. The dissolution of interests and values that found agreement in political parties and trade unions has placed people in a condition of isolation that could only lead to the explosion of individualism.

In the economy as in politics, neoliberalism has represented the transition from the expansion of individual opportunities in the "open society" to the fragile personal identity of the "liquid society". With the expansion of the sphere of individual autonomy in a context of declining relative mobility, the "open society" has transformed into a "liquid society" because it was not able to keep the promises of inclusion and social mobility. People with few resources in the economy and society—who have been offered few opportunities since childhood to strengthen their own freedom—must face conditions of increasing economic vulnerability and downward social mobility. In the "liquid society", also due to the decline of job continuity, the individual is more weakly defined by work.

Instead of solid job qualifications and stable occupations, we are witnessing the emergence of new worker figures from the vast world of social interaction. Identity construction has become hostage to the liquid character, and therefore inevitably changing, of socialisation. An intuition about the dynamics of "systemic interdependence" that are set in motion in modern societies is derived from everyday life. It is a fact that when we think about the community we no longer immediately associate this word with social interaction favoured by physical and geographical proximity. Rather, in our brain the association with all the individuals with whom we are interconnected telematically is triggered. In the virtual contiguity of the community, the formation of a common culture is influenced by the media. The container ends up counting as much as the content. The most widespread *devices* made available to the consumer by technical progress—voice assistants, traffic forecasts, automatic translations—are aimed at satisfying strictly individual needs.

Social stratification, which was previously easily definable in terms of economic factors such as income, and cultural factors like *status*, is today characterised by new forms of virtual aggregation promoted and regulated by *social media*. Social interaction entrusted to digital platforms offers users the possibility to imagine themselves as equal participants in a "flat field", rather than as subjects participating with different degrees of power in the "inclined field" of the market.[14]

The more the belonging of people to a precise professional and working position fades, the more the search for an identity that reflects the "uniqueness" of the person is strengthened. We are not far from the condition of the society prefigured by Simmel with the image—mentioned above—of the "numerous circles that hardly intersect", making it unlikely, as has been said, that many people share the same combination of group membership. The alternation for the individual, in various dimensions, of conditions of "advantage" and "disadvantage" means that today's aggregations are containers of individual-monads, bearers of a predominant dimension of life, from the "precarious" to the *influencer*. Social stratification by levels of occupation and income is no longer the *locus*—the conformation of a place—where the members of a community perform their specific task. Between those who play the role of entrepreneur and those who instead play the role of worker, the power gap has not changed. The cultural climate has changed. A situation of conflict like the closure (or relocation) of a company, being managed primarily by managers, little by the government, and even less by unions, mostly ends in the silent acceptance of defeat by the workers.

The "liquid society" is closely linked to the process of *commodification*: "Market principles and mechanisms have burst into areas of society where they were previously absent" (De Grauwe 2017, p. 8). With the return of *commodification*, the entry of market operators in place of public service has the effect of increasing inequalities. The expansion of the private sector's spaces has not only regarded, as mentioned, the traditional sectors of public Welfare: health, education, pension system. Many services that were predominantly the responsibility of families, and therefore remained in the sphere of private availability—adult leisure time, children's play, meal consumption, care services for the elderly and the disabled—have been transferred to market transactions. Consider the private offer in catering, personal care, services related to housing rental and so on. The most striking fact concerns the process of "marketisation" experienced by tourism, once managed in many countries by public agencies, which has now become the largest private sector in the world economy in terms of turnover. The tourism market is a typical manifestation of the link between

[14] In 2022, the percentage of the United States in the global market value of such platforms is 80%, that of China is 17% and of European countries only 2%.

mass consumption and individualism. The landing, or arrival, in *resorts* transforms once inaccessible natural paradises into places of easy appropriation. The escape from a not exciting life multiplies thanks to access to wonders in which to reflect with the *selfies* one's own narcissism. The "exotic travel" of travel packages is a further dimension that the "multiple individual" uses to define himself.

As argued in the Introduction, individualism contains a paradox little explored by public discourse. On the one hand, this concept places a strong emphasis on the uniqueness of each person, and therefore on the ineliminable differences that characterise identities. On the other hand, the granularity induced by the process of individualisation has been accompanied by a tendency to increase socio-economic interdependence. Within the network of social relations in the market and on the web, the individual is increasingly exposed to "externalities" on which *spillovers* it is not possible to exercise control. In the various dimensions of well-being, new inequalities are formed, which, however, do not fuel conflict within the social fabric, as they do not aggregate into organisations and therefore do not create new collective identities. The income and *status* of masses of workers employed in a multitude of sectors, professional categories and company jobs has been replaced by the individualisation of multidimensional well-being.[15] The functions determined by participation in the work framework in the company—for example, assembly line workers—have been replaced by the fragmentation of functions. The new job positions followed by the expansion of services consist of creative jobs, or self-representation, which in the CVs published on Facebook is called "works for himself". From a collective condition, work has become an individual experience. This shift of work from the foundation of the *res publica* to a simple individual condition is, however, the result of a change in cultural climate, of the ideological turn aimed at making credible, and therefore close to the truth, the reductionism adopted by economics textbooks to develop a rigorous analysis. It reads that the subject freely chooses between working time and free time, and then it is the market that determines the best possible combination between the supply and demand for work. In reality, as John M. Keynes well understood in establishing a logical precedence of the functioning of the goods market over that of labour, the

[15] It is now clear that social stratification no longer responds to criteria unambiguously related to income. Istat has started a project of multidimensional analysis a few years ago, with the aim of achieving a more precise identification of social groups.

market's allocative mechanism is subordinate to the investment and production decisions of companies. The worker's choice is often limited to the alternative between unemployment and "poor" or involuntary part-time work.

Populism and *Pensée Unique*: Mirror Ideologies

Max Weber wrote that "ideas are like railway switchmen, they direct an action guided by interest on one track or another" (Weber 1946, p. 280). It should be added that the comparison of ideas carrying interests, in order to be realised, needs a political space in which the process of composition of interests leading to the formation of a socio-economic balance can take place. We have given this political space the name of *res publica*. The current crisis of political democracy lies in the fact that this space has lost legitimacy. Populist thought and *pensée unique* are increasingly distant from imagining—and from promoting—a national community united by values and interests. The interpretation that populism gives of society is that of an undifferentiated mass of powerless individuals, called to face the power of the elites.

To a certain extent, populism is the result of the dissolution of large social aggregations, primarily democratic representation parties and trade unions. These organisations performed the function—essential in the social conflicts of a democratic regime—of provoking discussion of economic, cultural and social problems and initiating the elaboration of political proposals. Once the progressive cultural *humus* has run out, a part of the low-income classes has succumbed to the media indoctrination of the singers of individualism. It is well known that, primarily in the United States, where the income of the rich—the *top incomes*—understood as the income sometimes of the 10% or 1% richest of the population, has significantly increased in recent decades. Correspondingly, the rich also invest money in electoral campaigns, with the aim of shifting the vote of the weaker classes towards parties opposed to redistribution (Immervoll and Richardson 2011). Large corporations have accumulated substantial extra-profits: the 22 largest European ones made net profits of 172 billion in 2022, 66% more than the average profits of the 2018–2021 period (Oxfam 2023). Behind the large corporations are wealthy billionaires. Since 1% of the rich own 40% of the total financial assets, business owners and managers are able to exert a formidable action of *influence*, through the lobbies they finance, and through the information that is transmitted to the public opinion by the media they own. Another part of the low-income classes has instead developed a sense of social exclusion that has resulted in a political conception antagonistic to the system.

To the political conception of representative democracy, where parties are *pars pro toto*, populist movements replace the logic of the *pars pro parte*, the "power in the hands of the people" that opposes the elite (Urbinati 2020). The slogan "one dollar, one vote" instead of the democratic principle "one person, one vote", evokes the influence that the rich exert on the outcome of elections through substantial contributions to electoral campaigns.

In a constellation of ideas only apparently alternative, the *pensée unique* neoliberalism conceives the individual as solely responsible for his personal identity and sees a society without social classes, a set of "generic" individuals, detached from any field affiliation, as social conflict is absent. "A significant contribution to the rise of populist authoritarianism [...] was what appears to be its opposite - hyper-individualism" (Wolf 2023, p. 208). Once the search for being "unique" has become the constitutive figure of individuals, the door is open to homologation in the *pensée unique*, or to the drastic simplification of public discourse that coincides with the renunciation of the exercise of confrontation. Faced with the post-modern world, whose complexity ends up raising the bar of conscious deliberation higher, liberal thinkers choose to close their eyes. Public discourse is reduced to the primacy of the enterprise, guardian of efficiency and promoter of increasing well-being for all. The harmonious conception of the *trickle-down* does not call into question either classes or social conflict: growth will benefit everyone indiscriminately. Resources—once freed from the constraint of oppressive taxation, so as to remain concentrated in the hands of their owners—will be used by entrepreneurs and managers in the production of a *surplus* that will then be distributed among all participants in the production process. The process of homologation that cancels out the differences between individuals goes so far as to deprive the elaboration of different points of view of meaning. Neoliberals embrace the idea of the market as an *ethically-free zone*, the duty-free port of equality between subjects who offer work services and purchase goods and services bound only by their own preferences. In this way, neoliberalism has pursued the adaptation of society to the market, branding every critical position as populism. As has been clearly stated, in the neoliberal vision "the term 'populism' has become the ultimate weapon in the hands of objectively privileged social classes, a means to remove relevance from any critical evaluation of political visions and economic policy choices that they carry forward".

At the end of the last century, the best way to hide the asymmetry of power was to transform personal relationships, which are an expression of social conflict, into an aseptic market relationship. A neoclassical economist confessed between the lines: "An economic transaction is a solved political problem [...]. Economic theory has earned the title of queen of the social sciences by choosing as its field of investigation political problems that have already found a solution" (Lerner 1972, p. 259). The solution to the political problem has been given here the name of socio-economic equilibrium. The *pensée unique* neoliberalism has imposed its own socio-economic equilibrium, an equilibrium that occurs without the need for negotiation with workers' representation, so that one part makes economic decisions and the other accepts them. Tina (*there is no alternative*) is the deceptive simplification of the problems of the economy and society according to which the path indicated by the *pensée unique* is the only practicable one.

Weber's image of the "exchange manipulators" today, with neoliberalism, takes on the semblance of the narrative of individuals indiscriminately free from conditioning, despite their different socio-economic condition. Classical liberalism has always recognised the primacy of the pluralism of opinions. Neoliberalism has chosen the simplest solution of imposing the *pensée unique* in public discourse.

In many decades of the last two centuries (excluding the two world wars and periods of authoritarian regime in Europe) political democracy has worked because the ideologies of social classes confronted each other on the common ground of the *res publica*. Today, social classes are obscured, they seem not to exist. The "pluralistic" political space in which populist thought and "single" thought should confront each other no longer exists. The confrontation between opinions is increasingly polarised around these two visions, which are in reality two sides of the same coin. The process of convergence of ideas from which the composition of social conflict should emerge cannot therefore develop. If all the differences in culture and vision of the future have been flattened, so that social conflict has been expelled from democratic debate, what remains of politics?

Bibliography

Acemoglu, D. & Johnson, S. 2023 Power and Progress: Our Thousand-Year Struggle Over Technology and Prosperity, *Public Affairs, New York.*

Avendano, M., Hendrik, J., Mackenbach, J. 2009 Educational Level and Changes in Health across Europe: Longitudinal Results from SHARE, *in «Journal of European Social Policy», XIX, 4, pp. 301–16.*

Bauman, Z. 2006 *Liquid Life*, Polity Press, Cambridge 2005.

Bauman, Z. 2010 *Modernità e ambivalenza*, Bollati Boringhieri, Torino.

Beck, U. 2000 La società del rischio. Verso una seconda modernità, *Carocci, Roma.*

Bergoglio, J. M. 2015 *Laudato si'*, Libreria Editrice Vaticana, Roma.

Berlin, I. 1989 *Four Essays on Liberty*, Oxford University Press, Oxford 1969.

Blanchet, T., Chancel, L., Gethin, A. 2022 *Why Is Europe More Equal than the United States?*, in «American Economic Journal: Applied Economics», XIV, 4, pp. 480–518.

Bobbio, N. 1989 *L'età dei diritti*, Einaudi, Torino.

Bourdieu, P. 2010 *Le sociologue et l'historien* (conversation with R. Chartier), Agone, Paris.

Bourdieu, P. 2012 Capitale simbolico e classi sociali, *in «Polis», XXVI, 3, pp. 401–18.*

Brynjolfsson, E. & McAfee, A. 2014 The Second Machine Age: Work, Progress, and Prosperity in a Time of Brilliant Technologies, *Norton & Company, New York.*

De Grauwe, P. 2017 The Limits of the Market: The Pendulum Between Government and Market, *Oxford University Press, Oxford.*

Dewey, J. 1927 *The Public and Its Problems*, Alan Swellow Press, Denver.

Ferreira, F. H. G. & Walton, M. 2006 *Inequality of Opportunity and Economic Development*, Policy Research Working Paper Series 3816, World Bank.

Frey, C. B. & Osborne, M. A. 2017 The Future of Employment: How Susceptible Are Jobs to Computerisation?, *in «Technological Forecasting and Social Change», CXIV, pp. 254–80.*

Gethin, A., Martínez-Toledano, C., Piketty, T. 2022 Brahmin Left Versus Merchant Right: Changing Political Cleavages in 21 Western Democracies, 1948–2020, *in «Quarterly Journal of Economics», CXXXVII, 1, pp. 1–48.*

Harsanyi, J. C. 1953 Cardinal Utility in Welfare Economics and in Risk-taking, *in «Journal of Political Economy», LXI, pp. 434–5.*

Harsanyi, J. C. 1955 Cardinal Welfare, Individualistic Ethics and Interpersonal Comparison of Utility, *in «Journal of Political Economy», LXIII, pp. 309–21.*

Harvey, D. 2020 Anti-Capitalist Chronicles, *Pluto Press, London.*

Hume, D. 1971 *A Treatise of Human Nature* [1739–40], in *The Philosophical Works*, II, Scientia Verlag, Alen 1748.

Hume, D. 1985 *Essays. Moral, Political, and Literary*, (ed) E. F. Miller, Liberty Fund, Indianapolis.

Immervoll, H. & Richardson, L. 2011 Redistribution Policy and Inequality Reduction in Oecd Countries: What Has Changed in Two Decades?, *Iza Discussion Paper 6030.*

Jenkins, S. P. 2011 Changing Fortunes: Income Mobility and Poverty Dynamics in Britain, *Oxford University Press, Oxford.*

Lerner, A. 1972 The Economics and Politics of Consumer Sovereignty, *in «American Economic Review», LXII, 2, pp. 258–66.*

Mankiw, N. G. 2018 *Principles of Economics*, Cengage Learning, Boston.

Marx, K. 1969 Il Capitale. Libro I, capitolo VI inedito, *La Nuova Italia, Firenze.*

Oxfam 2023 Report 2023: Diseguaglianza. Il potere al servizio di pochi, *Oxfam Italia.*

Pistor, K. 2021 The Code of Capital: How the Law Creates Wealth and Inequality, *Princeton University Press, Princeton 2019.*

Rawls, J. 1982 *A Theory of Justice*, The Belknap Press of Harvard University Press, Cambridge 1971).

Stiglitz, J. E. 2019 The End of Neoliberalism and the Rebirth of History, *Project Syndacate, 4 novembre.*

Urbinati, N. 2020 Pochi contro molti. Il conflitto politico nel XXI secolo, *Laterza, Roma-Bari.*

Weber, M. 1946 *Essays in Sociology*, Oxford University Press, Oxford.

Wilkerson, I. 2020 Caste: The Origins of Our Discontents, *Random House, New York.*

Wolf, M. 2023 The Crisis of Democratic Capitalism, *Penguin Press, New York.*

CHAPTER 6

A Phenomenon Between Individual and Society

Competition in the Market and in Democracy: A False Equivalence

It is very plausible that social mobility is the locus of an antinomy, a contradiction between the market, whose space tends to overlap with that of society, and democracy whose founding core is the vote cast by the voter in the ballot box. Between interaction in the market and in society, and democratic power exercised in elections, the difference is not small. Joseph Schumpeter (1942) was however convinced of the opposite. He theorised that democratic competition between parties seeking the vote is the mirror image of the search for profit that takes place in the market between entrepreneurs, competing with each other to win the preference of consumers. In markets, voter-consumers "vote" by giving money in exchange for goods. His comparison between market and democracy fits into a harmonious conception of socio-economic dynamics. Based on the dual participation of subjects in the market (as entrepreneurs and as consumers) and in politics (as voters), the two methods of deliberation—the free market choice and the free vote—should according to Schumpeter be equated. At the time of his theoretical reflection, Schumpeter could not understand either that oligopolistic or monopolistic concentration is also the result of the selection between companies generated by their competition in the market, nor that the process of inclusion of the masses in political democracy would have known limits and distortions in the complex society of which he saw the beginnings.

F. Farina, *The Rise of Inequality and the Fall of Social Mobility*, https://doi.org/10.1007/978-3-031-92843-7_6

The idea of an equivalence between market and democracy does not take into account a stone guest, power. In the vision of liberal thought, among "free and equal" individuals united in the "social contract" there is an equality of power; or rather, power does not exist. Political democracy sees a majority of citizens delegate decisions to the government it expresses; but the government is held to the "accountability" of its actions. From the transparency of the government's actions should emerge the evaluation by the voters, which will manifest in the next electoral round with the confirmation or not of the governing team. The exercise of the democratic vote by citizens represents a sort of "veto right" limited to the institutions of political representation: "a majority has the power to send away the rulers it comes to detest" (Dunn 2006, p. 179). The equality between people in the "voting power" does not however correspond to their equal "economic power" in acting in the market. The choice between parties and programmes that voters express in electoral rounds does not project into the economic sphere, where power is exercised by companies and finance.

There is another equivalence worth talking about. When the institutions of democratic market economy countries are compared with those of authoritarian collectivist economy countries, the judgement that is unanimously formulated is clear: an exaltation of the former and a condemnation of the latter. What's wrong? Simple: the instrumental use that tends to be made of this judgement. Just observe how, in the dark times we are going through, information is bent to present the rot in the East as a stain remover for the rot in the West. Nothing new under the sky. *The Road to Serfdom* is the book written by Hayek in 1944 destined to become the manifesto of neoliberal thought. In reviewing it on the "Observer", George Orwell, a writer remembered for both memorable works and his civil commitment in favour of freedom and social democracy, reacted to the attempt of that book to divide the world into good and bad: "Professor Hayek does not see, or is not willing to admit, that for the great mass of people a return to free competition means a tyranny worse, because more irresponsible, than that of the State" (Orwell 1944). And so he continued: "The trouble with competitions is that someone wins them. Professor Hayek denies that free capitalism necessarily leads to monopoly, but in practice this is the point it reaches" (ibid.). The consequences of the tendency of perfect competition markets to result in oligopolies and monopolies has recently been rigorously demonstrated in the analysis of Mordecai Kurz (2023), who also identified the market power of large innovative companies as one of the main causes of the increase in inequalities. In many of his writings, Orwell denounced the inability of both systems—the market and the collectivist one—to effectively equalise the "starting points" among people and to solve the fundamental problem of the gaps in opportunities and well-being capacities that separate people from birth. The incisive considerations of Orwell's pages urge us to extend the criticism to the equivalence between market and democracy asserted by Schumpeter. The English writer attacked the capitalist system not in the name of a different order, but "from within", because in his opinion the "form of play" that it imposes on social parties is not sufficiently democratic. Orwell then pushes us to ask ourselves: why is democratic deliberation ineffective in overcoming the power gap that is at the basis of economic relations? A very crude definition of democracy was given by Adam Przeworski: "a system in which parties lose elections". The American political scientist intends to underline how citizens who vote in polling stations have the power—however limited—to freely elect their representatives in institutions. Within the company, however, things are different. The power of workers encounters an even more clear limit: the method of democratic deliberation is absent. The asymmetry of power between entrepreneur and workers is instead tangible: the work of workers in the workplace is subject to the discretionary decisions of managers, who are accountable for their actions only to their shareholders (also trying to take away their power, by assigning themselves *stock options*). The mechanism of coordination between individual actions based on market competition is therefore only formally impartial: behind the aseptic "playing field" levelled between "free and equal" subjects, hides the asymmetry of power. Unlike what the Austrian economist prophesied,[1] the capitalist system has evolved in the direction of widening the power distance between classes. The critical interpretation of neoliberalism proposed by Michel Foucault's theory of "governmentality"[2] tries to expose the strategy used. Foucault

[1] The capitalist development model centred on the figure of the entrepreneur-innovator was a happy insight of Schumpeter (1912). The prophecy elaborated 30 years later, of a progressive bureaucratisation of capitalist economic systems, has not been fulfilled (Id. 2002). This idea, matured in the decades of the Great Depression between the two world wars, has been denied in recent decades, characterised by processes of privatisation and liberalisations that have accompanied the deregulation of markets.

[2] Michel Foucault coined the term *gouvernmentalité*, merging *gouvernement* (government) and *rationalité* (rationality). In the political science of Europe both continental and Anglo-Saxon, the term summarises a point of view strongly critical of the organisation of power in the West. In the theoretical perspective of *gouvernmentalité*, the idea of "open society embodies the neoliberal goal of delimiting the set of "institutions, procedures, analyses [aimed at] structuring the field of possible action of others" (Foucault 1978, p. 28)".

reads in the method of negotiation the tool with which the capitalist power system has extended political deliberation by the "free and equal" to all areas of social life. The French philosopher interpreted neoliberalism as the state of affairs in which "the exercise of political power is completely modelled on the principles of the market economy" (Foucault 2008, p. 131). In the course of capitalist development, the asymmetry of power in which the conflict between social groups takes place and the continuous technological upheaval of economic activities that largely governs social reproduction multiply the conditions of inequality in the various spaces of people's well-being. To the *symmetry* of power between citizens in the expression of the vote corresponds an *asymmetry* of power in the economic sphere. Companies manage autonomously, with their own deliberations, the provision of physical capital and the introduction of innovations. Within society, moreover, the parents of the elite manage the educational chances of their children by financing their university studies, in order to ensure them the intangible capital (the most advanced skills and knowledge) and to procrastinate over time the social power of the family dynasty. The main inequality of power consists in the fact that in a capitalist market economy well-being is not made "contestable". The standard model of the economy conceals a simple truth: "although it is not the task of the market to resolve conflicts, individuals have conflicting interests on many issues" (Sen 1983, p. 78). Every market equilibrium is embedded in the social context, where interpersonal relationships are marked by the asymmetry of interests and power between social groups. The pursuit of profit can therefore easily lead to "a very divergent distribution of aggregate well-being among subjects" (ibid., p. 81), so that "equilibrium depends on the relative power of individuals" (ibid., p. 95).

Capitalism and Solidaristic Democracy

The first decades of the post-war period saw the birth in Europe of that alliance that had failed at the time of the French Revolution. In the Estates General of 1789, the Third Estate (the bourgeoisie and the wealthy peasants) won representation, but not the workers and the poor peasants. These two classes remained outside the constituent national assembly and were therefore called the "Fourth Estate". An alliance could have been formed between the peasants, who were calling for the abolition of the feudal rights over the lands, and the bourgeoisie, who were demanding constitutional reforms? Let's risk a counterfactual: *if* the Industrial Revolution of the late eighteenth century, instead of in England, had taken root in France, generating the take-off of industry, the alliance could have been realised. In a context of economic expansion, a nascent industrial bourgeoisie and the masses available for work in the factories would probably have been able to put the French economy and society on a different path from that of a strong opposition between classes, and the periodic recourse to a leader as the only possible bulwark against the explosion of conflict.

This counterfactual is intended as a parable: it underlines the importance of growth as a fundamental factor of social mobility. The "take-off" of growth at the beginning of the nineteenth century was also a catalyst for the widening of income gaps between social classes. One of the questions we ask ourselves about the precarious balance between democracy and capitalism is the following: "Is it thanks to growth, or to greater equality, that the continuous improvement of the material conditions of large sectors of the population leads to the coexistence of democracy and capitalism?" (Przeworski 2019, p. 24). Like Ralf Dahrendorf, Adam Przeworski sees democracy as "the method for managing conflicts". To the question he poses, this volume proposes to give the following answer: in order for capitalism, which is inherent in the asymmetry of power and social conflict, to be reconcilable with democracy, both a welfare state that reduces inequalities and a push for sustained GDP growth are needed.

In post-war Europe, the alliance between the Third and Fourth Estates lasted several decades because growth was accompanied by a decrease in income gaps between social classes. During the *Trente Glorieuses*, a majority vote in favour of income redistribution, and public policies of risk insurance, expressed governments that placed the "anointing" of equity on economic growth. The welfare state became in Europe the support for the precarious balance between democracy and capitalism: "the parties of the working class and the unions consented to capitalism, while the political parties of the bourgeoisie and the organisations of entrepreneurs accepted that a certain redistribution of income should be implemented" (ibid., p. 57). In the democratic systems of Western Europe, a "democratic class compromise" (Przeworski and Wallerstein 1982) took shape between the capitalist elite and the middle class allied with the poor. This "democratic class compromise" would have continued if the rich had been willing to tolerate higher taxation and the poor had been content to share with the middle class the redistribution of income (Benhabib and Przeworski 2006).

The expansion of the welfare state in Europe during the *Trente Glorieuses* has been defined as one of the "greatest results in the history of humanity and the quintessential achievement of civilised society" (Bauman 2007, p. 5). This judgement is correct. But it is not only for ethical reasons. The point is that inequalities, in the absence of the welfare state, can get out of control. This is the feeling one gets when watching the stories of "class struggle" told—with sober but sharp realism—in Ken Loach's movies. The role played by the welfare state is also fundamental today in limiting the loss of social cohesion that results from an unregulated market operation. It is only by making the operation of the market "sticky" that the economic mechanism is less exposed to the insecurity generated by high-income inequality and the social disasters that can result from full autonomy from companies. In this regard, a metaphor created by Schumpeter in support of market regulation is illuminating. When there is, "we drive cars at a speed greater than we would travel if cars did not have brakes". Welfare institutions have the task of producing these "brakes". It has also been noted that—in addition to labour market regulation and redistributive institutions—the state takes on the responsibility of realising the so-called common goods and merit goods, the essential services that the market is not normally able to make accessible to all.

To understand the importance of the regulation of the economy achieved by the welfare system, we can also think of a film shot in slow motion. In the absence of the welfare state, the dynamics of social stratification would become whirlwind, and the existence of society would be at risk. As Kenneth Arrow, Nobel laureate in economics in 1972, wrote, one cannot think of the market outside of the interdependence between people, and the norms that regulate their interaction: "the world of complete selfish interest of the *laissez-faire* model would not survive even ten minutes; its operation depends on an intricate network of mutual obligations even for companies and individuals competing with each other" (Arrow 2005, p. 477). Social mobility is an issue that is decided in an "open field" where the two main players are the market and the state. The synergy between the two institutions in resolving social conflict in a socio-economic equilibrium is indispensable if we want to prevent social mobility from turning downwards.

Margaret Thatcher did not think so. A strong libertarian ideology prevented her from acknowledging not only, understandably, the importance of solidaristic democracy, but even the equivalence between political deliberation and economic deliberation dear to Schumpeter. In the *Lecture* titled *What's Wrong with Politics?*, which she gave on 11 October 1968 at the Conservative Political Centre, she expressed herself as follows: "The way in which people can realise their own involvement and participation [in democratic life] is not by taking part in an ever-increasing number of government decisions, but by reducing the area of decisions within the government's competence". With these words, the future British Prime Minister was probably reflecting on the "French May", the street revolt that had broken out a few months earlier. Thatcher was also concerned about the pernicious tendency of the political space to heavily interfere with the economic space, even threatening its autonomy. Thatcherism was maturing, that is, the belief that to curb the demand for social rights, and the economic claims connected to them, the role of democratic prerogatives in public decisions should be limited. In clear terms: the freedom of citizens to express their legitimate needs is too broad and must be drastically compressed by weakening economic and social confrontation both inside and outside representative institutions. Across the Atlantic, this concept found an echo on 20 January 1981, in the first *State of the Union Address*, the inaugural speech of the newly elected President Ronald Reagan: "It is no accident that our current difficulties were born with the expansion of the role of government, and have developed in proportion to its intervention and its unnecessary and excessive intrusion into our lives".

Friedrich von Hayek had advanced this same vision of democracy by opposing "constructivist rationalism", or any evolution of institutions in the direction of recognising social rights. In *Law, Legislation and Liberty* (1973) the liberal philosopher and economist recommends preserving respect for property rights, and therefore the control of the capitalist over productive activity, particularly avoiding that too broad legislative power given to elected Parliaments leads institutions to redefine *ex nihilo* the rights of workers. It cannot be said that his lesson has been ignored. The foundations of liberal thought—freedom of opinion, the concept of tolerance, pluralism in the field of public ethics—have found increasing recognition in the sphere of individual private rights; much less in the sphere of confrontation and democratic deliberation on Welfare rights. The balance between the "three powers", which Montesquieu placed at the basis of the democratic regime, is increasingly threatened by the overflowing of executive power to the detriment of legislative power and often also of judicial power (this also happens in European countries, not only in the East). To this degeneration in the public sphere has been added the worsening of social interaction on the media, which jeopardises the correct use of information, and, in reflection, the aforementioned foundations of liberal thought.

It is a fact that the negative "externalities" caused by systemic interdependence expose people to the impact on well-being of events that transcend their responsibility. As has already been argued, the genesis lies both in globalisation and in the way in which technological progress is introduced. In the era of neoliberalism, this problem has been addressed by public powers in a disappointing way. Once liberal thought has succeeded in restoring full command of companies over the fate of the workforce, the "business risk" has been translated into the "individual responsibility" of the worker, in the form of acceptance of the precariousness of employment and working conditions (Hacker 2008). Similarly, neoliberal ideology has worked deeply in the sphere of political communication with the aim of pushing people towards "individual initiative" in insuring against risks, for example by accepting that fundamental dimensions of well-being such as health and education are entrusted to the market. It does not seem, however, that the market is invariably at the service of personal freedom. In order to influence people's choices, "surveillance" (Zuboff 2019) in the digital space is entrusted to private companies, to the point of violating their *privacy*. Similarly, in production, the motive of profit induces entrepreneurs to use artificial intelligence not only to study and guide consumer tastes, but to better monitor the behaviour of workers.[3]

Social Rights and Company Profits

From the post-war period until the end of the Second World War, social mobility proceeded with the brake on. After the dark decades of the authoritarian regimes of the governments that came to power between the two wars and the return of democracy in Western Europe (excluding Spain and Portugal), political representation in national parliaments took full democratic form, with the completion of the arrival at universal suffrage. In the words of Ralf Dahrendorf, after the end of the Second World War, "with Europe covered in ruins and the entry into the nuclear age [...] conditions were ripe for an orderly and democratic class struggle and for a unique economic miracle" (Dahrendorf 1989, p. 88). The wave of hope defeated fear and paved the way for economic and social change. It was not hindered by the fact that, after the peace of 1945, the Cold War had divided the world into two political blocs, military and economic. Although

[3] "Monitoring allows employers to cut wages and extract more work from workers. In this way, monitoring is configured as an activity of *rent-shifting*, or as a means to prevent the division of productivity gains and shift the rent away from workers, without productivity increasing" (Acemoglu and Johnson 2023, p. 322).

the ideological clash between NATO countries and those of the Warsaw Pact fuelled social conflict, within European countries, politics was moving in the direction of forms of cooperation both for GDP growth and for the distribution among social classes of increasing wealth (Farina 2021, par. 7.2).

European societies became aware of the value that "social inclusion" represented for a seamless evolution of economic recovery. In summary, the middle class assumed the role of representing the hinge—in the economy, politics and society—between the rich and the poor. Thus, from the fifties to the seventies, a "political exchange" took place (Boix 2003). By giving their consent to the programmes of strengthening the welfare institutions launched by the governments, companies were recognised the prerogative of slowing down the adjustment of wages to the dynamics of productivity in order to defend their competitiveness in foreign markets. On the other hand, social classes that for cultural roots—even beyond income-based membership—had been close to the conservative right, over the years adhered to the values affirmed by the progressive middle class, largely swelling the consensus for centre-left parties (Piketty 2018). The governments brought to power by the voting majorities that were formed in the polls launched public policies of labour market regulation and welfare institutions for income redistribution and risk insurance. A study conducted on data from the mid-seventies found a strong similarity between 12 advanced countries regarding the impact of welfare on social stratification (Erikson and Goldthorpe 1992).

The party coalitions that saw collaboration between the middle class, low-income classes and the poor led to the conviction—in political science—of the transformation of social democracy into a sort of cold fusion between liberalism and socialism. These two ideologies are, however, two alternative ways of organising the economy and society. They cannot be the subject of an alchemy experiment, the choice of the best of both, a *cherry-picking* of the ingredients to put in a crucible and transform into gold. And indeed, European socialdemocracies were not like that. The defeat of the progressive movement in Europe began with the idea that the problem was simply to distance oneself from the illiberal regimes of the "realised communism" countries, accept the primacy of "unfettered" freedom and dilute in the crucible a bit of socialism to derive a non-conservative version of liberalism. The advent of neoliberalism at the end of the twentieth century, in strengthening market forces, led the leaders and intellectuals of those parties to water down in their political programmes the theme of rebalancing power in society. The progressive European parties, which have reformed or were born in the last 40 years, have indeed grafted onto liberalism pieces of Catholic solidarity and the socialist thought tradition. The weakness of this operation emerged in the progressive incorporation of their policies into the "constellation of ideas" of neoliberalism.

Examples are not lacking. In the political reality of the nineties the "third way" took shape, the theoretical approach developed in the United States and the United Kingdom according to which social-democratic welfare should have given up prioritising equity and retreated towards the objectives of market efficiency. Its main intellectual creation, the "State of social investment" (Giddens 1998), contemplates the expansion of private enterprise spaces in a context of "inclusive" reformism. The features of such a political project have remained rather opaque. The labels that profusely invade the "market of politics" count little or nothing. In the last two centuries, the primacy of ideas has manifested elsewhere, in the translation of scientific discoveries by companies into productive strategies aimed at appropriating high profits at the expense of workers and in elaborating an ideological interpretation that presents them as progress towards the diffusion of well-being.[4] The "superstructure", as already mentioned, also counts in the introduction of technical progress.

Let's try to understand better by starting from afar. The value of human dignity, affirmed with the Renaissance, was progressively sacrificed for the higher good of the development of productive forces. Marx was so fascinated by it that he built on the primacy of the economic structure his theory of "historical materialism". Under this label, he indeed stated that when the productive forces of a certain stage of economic development come into conflict with the relations of production—"determined necessary relations independent of the will" of men—social conflict explodes and the capitalist production relationship ends up being subverted by revolution.

[4] "In medieval Europe, windmills, a better crop rotation and an increasing use of horses in agricultural work greatly increased productivity, but the improvement in the standard of living of the peasants was almost nil" (Acemoglu and Johnson 2023, p. 21). "During the early stages of the Industrial Revolution, as technology progressed, the wages should have risen. Instead, the real income of the majority stagnated. Working hours increased, but their conditions significantly deteriorated, with lower hourly wages while an increasing amount of work was extracted from English workers" (ibid., p. 179).

In the last century, the idea of a mode of production based on the appropriation by capitalists of the surplus produced by workers, which therefore sees the economic structure in a preeminent position compared to the superstructure, has proven to be fallacious. If it were correct, the validity of every theoretical system, of every "cultural superstructure", would be confined to the only period of "material history" (everything that distinguishes itself from the immateriality of culture) in which it was conceived (Mannheim 1928). The engine of history is ideas. The very introduction of technical progress, the propellant of the productive structure, is not imprinted on the materialism of the productive forces but is guided by the strategic vision of entrepreneurs, driven by the motive of profit. Following political instability and during the economic crisis of the 1970s, the elite in charge of businesses feared that a change in income distribution in favour of workers could be followed by a shift in power relations. A question on which neither political science nor economic theory have yet shed sufficient light is why the reaction of businesses has not been opposed, in recent decades, by social groups that politically position themselves on the left, particularly in voting behaviour. The majority of the electorate, in expressing their preference for parties opposed to income redistribution at the polls, votes against their own economic interest. It can indeed be demonstrated that there is—in principle—a majority within the electorate that would benefit from redistribution carried out by welfare institutions (Box 6.1 and Box 8.1).[5] As it is very likely that they have a positive balance between benefits (high) and taxes (low), the poor and low or medium-skilled workers of the middle class (who usually make up the majority of voters) should express a vote in favour of parties proposing redistributive policies at the polls. The majority vote, however, increasingly goes to right-wing parties, whose ideology is usually opposed to income redistribution policies. Once increasingly large strata of workers—showing hostility towards taxation and distrust of the state's management of their money through public spending—have embraced individualistic ideology, the weight of dominant ideas has thus ended up prevailing over the economic interest of their social groups.

[5] An econometric verification conducted on the statistical data of advanced countries shows that the correlation between the height of median income compared to average income and the extent of redistribution (the difference between the Gini income inequality index before and after redistribution) is negative: the poorer the median voter is relative to the average voter, the wider the income redistribution (Farina 2021, paras. 8.3 and 8.4).

Box 6.1 Should low-income people vote in favour of the welfare state?
This question, in addition to the obvious intuitive answer, has also had an axiomatic answer with the Median Voter Theorem (Mvt). This theory was born with the models of Romer (1975) and Roberts (1977); its elaboration is due to Meltzer and Richard (1981). The kernel (the method of estimating income distribution) tells us that the ordering of income levels, from the poorest to the richest subject, has as its main characteristic the same shape in all nations of the world: a large "hump" on the left side of the graph. The reason is that the subjects that appear on the vertical axis of the graph on the left are in number (they have a frequency) greater at low-income levels that appear on the horizontal axis "at the beginning" of the distribution. In descriptive terms, the explanation of the interest of low-income voters in redistribution is this. Distinguishing median income (that of the subject who occupies the central position in the distribution) from average income (the ratio between GDP and population), one can notice a consequence of the presence of the "hump": most people—the poor and those who, finding themselves in the middle of the distribution, receive median income—receive an income lower than the average income. This peculiarity of the kernel is at the origin of the Mvt. In summary, the theorem says that—in front of the ballot boxes, from their own self-interested point of view—those who receive the average income are "neutral" with respect to the redistribution programmes presented by the parties (approximately, the benefits of Welfare correspond to the taxation they suffer), while all subjects from the poorest to those who receive the average income—i.e. the majority of people—have everything to gain from the welfare state. It should be noted that the voter with the median income of the entire distribution not only has to his left 50% of the electorate (the poor or low-income voters interested like him in redistribution) but in addition, to his right in the distribution, he has those who earn more than him but less than the voter with average income i.e. the "neutral" voter.

The conditions for the Mvt to be able to predict the electoral result can be summarised as follows: (1) *Electoral preferences with a single*

(*continued*)

Box 6.1 (continued)

"peak" (*single-peakedness*). More simply, the voter's behaviour is assumed to be rational. It is assumed that each subject has a monotonically decreasing preference order, in the sense that they rank the preferred electoral programme first, and then, decreasingly, those less and less preferred. Assuming that political preferences reflect traditional ideological orientations, we imagine that programmatic platforms linked to three different positions on public policies are presented: proceeding from the right of the party alignment towards the centre and then towards the left, the hypothesis is that the preferred electoral programme provides, respectively, a low, medium and high level of social spending. Being rational, the monotonicity of preferences implies that the ideologically right-oriented voter prefers the centre's social spending policy to that of the left, while the centre voter has a preference that differs from the social spending policy of both the right and the left. In light of this condition, as long as voters' political preferences reflect traditional ideological orientations (right, centre, left) it is not permissible, for example, from the point of view of rational choice, a preference primarily directed at the left-wing programme or the right-wing programme, placing the centre programme last. (2) *Monothematicity*. The presence in each party's programme of a single theme, and not a plurality of objectives to be achieved. Clearly, this requirement is not reflected in reality. However, the political ideology to which parties refer, which usually unifies the thematic plurality and allows voters to save on information costs, or to "vote based on experience, and not on specific issues", does downplay the relevance of the thematic plurality of electoral programmes. (3) *Unanimity*. A limitation as serious as it is unavoidable of the Mvt is that its axiomatic structure requires all voters to go to the polls. Although it is natural that there is a certain gap between theory and reality, the participation in the vote of the majority of those entitled is an essential requirement of democracy. A turnout at the polls around 70–80% is considered the minimum acceptable for the democratic representativeness of the election result.

The Market Is Not a Morally-Free Zone

After this quick *excursus* into history, let's return to today. The power that comes from private property makes the market an institution far from representing an ethically neutral ground. Schumpeter's parallel between democracy and the market stops at the gates of the company. Here the equality between "free and equal" subjects loses its formal guise. "Private property of productive resources limits the breadth of outcomes that can arise from the democratic process. The ruling class in government, whatever its electorate and its orientations, is bound in every capitalist system by the fact that crucial economic decisions, those that have an impact on employment and investment, are a private prerogative" (Przeworski 2016, p. 5). The accumulation of capital in the hands of shareholders and the management of the company on their behalf by managers translates into the asymmetry of command over the use of resources. Stakeholders,[6] or those who in various ways have interests in the company—from workers to consumers—are excluded from its management. In the Report illustrating the "Global Social Mobility Index 2020" it reads: "One conclusion emerges strongly: economies that follow a model of stakeholder capitalism occupy a better position in the index than those that favour shareholder capitalism or state capitalism" (World Economic Forum 2020, p. 12).

According to orthodox theory, this view would not correspond to truth. The rights to productive choices would indeed be entirely legitimately assigned to those who on behalf of shareholders make the most responsible decision in the company, that of investing in production. However, this is a circular argument: instead of admitting that the representatives of property "decide because they have command", it is asserted that "they command because they decide". That those who carry out the most important actions in producing wealth should be precisely those who carry their own interests—i.e. the owners of the majority of capital rights, or their representatives—is an *a priori* assumption. It's like saying: since the market promotes equality among all individuals by homogenising them in the role of consumers, the system of companies has the task of managing productive activity to create well-being for all. The "privatisation" of productive choices contradicts this function. The command of

[6] Economic theory defines with this term the community of individuals and groups (customers, employees, unions) involved in the company's activity and in the results achieved by it not only in terms of profit but also of the more general objectives of collective well-being.

those who lead companies—whether it is a single entrepreneur, the corporate structure based on the "hard core" of the major shareholders, or an investment fund that controls the majority share package—in implementing the innovation and production strategies that are developed by researchers and managers—unfolds a series of externality effects. Many, fundamental, company decisions aimed at reducing production costs end up, directly or indirectly, penalising labour.

Technological progress is not neutral. In the judgement of "progressive" economists, its use is influenced by ideas: "how we use knowledge and science depends on the vision - the way in which human beings understand how to turn knowledge into techniques and methods aimed at solving specific problems [...]. The visions of powerful people have a disproportionate impact on what we do with production tools and on the direction of innovation" (Acemoglu and Johnson 2023, p. 24). The introduction of technological progress is aimed at obtaining higher profits in the shortest possible time, considering the impact on the labour factor a residual issue. As observed by the institution that monitors the development of advanced countries, "prioritising efficiency objectives may have undermined the resilience of societies by neglecting equity and sustainability objectives" (Oecd 2020, p. 3).

The location of plants in a country—or their transfer to another—is based on the choice of the most favourable tax regime, without the workers who are consequently laid off having any power to oppose the decision of the Board of Directors to close the company. In many company choices, the asymmetry of power also benefits from the "information asymmetry" it boasts over workers: the jobs to be opened or cancelled are decisions that the company makes solely based on its own information and its own autonomous expectation of the economic cycle.

The current development model then multiplies the negative externalities caused by polluting energy sources, which are the major culprits of environmental destruction. The motive of maximum short-term profit is in stark conflict with a long-term strategy of environmental defence—the common good par excellence—through policies aimed at combating its increasing deterioration and ensuring sustainable development (Giovannini 2018). However, in public discourse, it is still accepted as a "law of nature" that companies are insensitive to environmental problems. The threat of dismissal of all employees by a polluting company, when invited to adapt the production process to environmental standards, is well known to everyone.

In summary, in decisions aimed at increasing profits on capital, the interests of those who do not own shares (or own a very small share), the workers, are affected. As political philosopher Elizabeth Anderson wrote, "workers effectively cede all their rights to their employers, except those guaranteed to them by law, for the duration of the employment relationship. The authority of employers over workers, outside of collective bargaining and a few other contexts [...], is indiscriminate, arbitrary and unaccountable, like a notification, a process, an appeal" (Anderson 2017, pp. 53–4). In glossing over the power asymmetry, neoclassical economists turn their attention to the labour market as a context of coordination between subjects characterised by its impartiality. There would be an equivalence between the contractual relationship within the company and the transactions that take place in this market: "The company has no power, no authority, no disciplinary action, that minimally differs from the elementary market bargaining between two people" (Alchian and Demsetz 1972, p. 777). In other words, to deny that there is a power asymmetry in the company, orthodox economists focus on the functioning of the free market, and advance the idea of an equivalence between the entrepreneur's freedom to dismiss and the worker's freedom to leave the company. The description of the market as a *morally-free zone* thus rests on extending to workers those same laws of competition to which every entrepreneur must submit. This "subordinate condition" to the market would put capital on the same level as labour. In the equilibrium position of the Gee model negotiations (the reference is therefore to the hypothetical world of perfect competition), each dismissal of a worker by the entrepreneur would correspond to the instantaneous hiring of the dismissed worker in a new job. This implausible result obviously recalls the unrealistic assumptions of *autonomy* and *separation* between the subjects of the Gee model.

But there's more. To refute the re-proposition of the market as a *morally-free zone* are the conditions of "imperfect competition" in which almost all real markets find themselves. To the prerogative of *price-maker* companies to regulate the *distribution* of surplus to their advantage—through "market power", the setting of a price that contains a *mark-up*, an extra compared to the cost of production—many companies add another power, exercised in the sphere of *production*. Monopsony is an illuminating example of how the "control" of the territory in which production takes place is one of the factors that determine the decline in the share of labour income (Brooks et al. 2021). This form of market is a typical case of "market failure" caused by a company behaviour that creates a negative externality from which it is difficult for workers to escape. In monopsony, as observed in the Introduction, the power of a company that concentrates labour demand is not effectively countered by the competition mechanism, because the entry of other companies encounters almost insurmountable obstacles. When there is only one company demanding labour in an area, not only does that company have the power to set the level of employment of the present workforce, but workers are forced to accept the wage that is offered to them. Rarely, in fact, can they bear the material and human cost of moving to another area, or—to put it in the words of orthodox economists—the "freedom of the worker to leave the company". The wage level is therefore lower than what would be determined in the ideal world of perfect competition (Naidu and Posner 2022). The labour policies adopted by the governments of many European countries consider the power asymmetry between company and worker as an objective fact. The economic policy debate that has been dragging on in Italy for decades is indicative. On the one hand, based on the Italian "economic dualism", particularly the territorial gap in the cost of living, there is a call for a return to the "wage cages" that in the fifties set lower wage tables in the South. On the other hand, unemployment support legislation requires an unemployed person in the South to accept—under penalty of losing the subsidy—the job offered by the employment agency, even if the job is far from their residence. Yet, it is clear that the transfer costs are much higher than the modest benefit, living in the South, of a lower inflation rate compared to the North.

Economic theory, in focusing attention on the functioning of the market, overlooks the impact that the power gap between business and workers has on social stratification. The English sociologist John H. Goldthorpe has levelled the accusation against orthodox economics of concealing the decline in occupational mobility caused by the strategies adopted by businesses.[7] In pointing out the labour crisis as the primary cause of low social mobility, Goldthorpe hits the nail on the head. The autonomy of the entrepreneur, when it does not find a limit in the relationship with the unions, represents in his opinion a pure exercise of power. To understand this criticism, it is enough to remember the "incentive theory". The manager's difficulty in monitoring the worker's activity leads to the presumption of ***moral hazard*** of the worker, an expression with which neoclassical

[7] For his empirical investigations, Goldthorpe used the Isco-88 scheme, reduced to eight occupational classes (Erikson and Goldthorpe 1992).

economics indicates the failure to comply with the contractual obligation to work commitment.[8] The "incentive theory", and the presumption implicit in it of the provision of a productive contribution from the worker lower than the remuneration he receives, is often brought up by supporters of meritocracy, who see work commitment as the main driver of social mobility. In short, workers are *a priori* attributed the rational self-interested behaviour of being "shirkers".

The reality is different. Firstly, under the cloak of the "incentive theory" hides the power asymmetry. Economic theory calls "contractual incompleteness" the impossibility of foreseeing and regulating in the employment contract all possible future contingencies. Work commitment is therefore a purely political issue, subject to the power gap between business and worker. In underlining, rightly, that productivity must be guaranteed, the orthodox theory ignores the fact that the worker has a strong disincentive to practice the behaviour of "moral hazard". The condition of weakness of dependent work indeed derives from a contractual relationship based on the command of the entrepreneur. The "incentive theory" does not give weight to the fact that the company is entirely autonomous in choosing the type of contract and the salary that are offered to a worker.

Secondly, the thesis that social spending (in particular, various forms of basic income) has a disincentive effect on work is constantly touted. This thesis can be refuted with a few figures: it is precisely in the Nordic countries where the highest social spending is (in Sweden, it is equal to 15,000 euros per capita; in Denmark, to 18,000 euros per capita) that participation in the labour market (the sum of the employed and people looking for work) reaches the highest levels (89% in Sweden and 85% in Denmark). In Italy, on the other hand, with a social spending per capita less than 10,000 euros, participation in the labour market is only 73%.

The autonomy of managers is not limited to the decision on the profit strategies of the company. Since the profitability of the investment often

[8] The employment contract is by its nature an "incomplete contract", an agreement exposed to disputes that may arise due to an eventuality that has not been foreseen. It is impossible to precisely include in the contract all the unknown future contingencies that could influence the worker's behaviour or the entrepreneur's expectations about his productivity. An attempt to solve the problem was made in the second half of the twentieth century. The "efficiency wage theory" argues that the entrepreneur, by paying a higher than average wage for each level of *skill*, would be able to select the most efficient workforce, thereby achieving the desired level of productivity in the company.

matures in the long term, entrepreneurs and managers have the incentive to realise profits in the short term also for the purpose of offering shareholders the benefit of a higher stock market value of the shares owned and thus favour their own reappointment by the next Board of Directors. The legal right to exercise the command of the company on behalf of the shareholders should be opposed by the right to a stable job and a growth in wages in line with productivity dynamics. As mentioned above, the workers' right to have their interests recognised on the same footing as those in command of the company does not find adequate recognition in legislation. "The State has established the constitution of workplace governance: it is a form of private government" (Anderson 2017, p. 54). With the ideological primacy it has won, neoliberalism seems to have made less credible the sociologists' point of view that "capitalism can be taught how to behave" (Therborn 2013, p. 171).

It should be remembered that the "incentive theory" contains a principle of "distributive justice". It states that to induce a certain behaviour it is necessary to offer an adequate economic stimulus. The incentive system currently adopted by capitalist economies, however, goes in the opposite direction: instead of guaranteeing a stable job with a decent salary, it discourages commitment with precarious work contracts and with indecent remunerations.[9] In a country like Italy, where precarious work has exceeded the figure of 3 million workers (Istat survey, June 2023), the public debate on the minimum wage is not focused on the right of the person to a dignified life. The "minimum wage" is instead put in competition with a principle of solidaristic democracy such as the "collective bargaining". Either one or the other. The setting of wages is thus placed, at low levels of qualification, in competition with the higher levels; if not even belittled to a mere numerical issue, one euro more or one euro less.

Moreover, the 2008 Nobel laureate in economics Paul Krugman, in a 1997 article in the magazine "Slate" titled *In Praise of Cheap Labour*, before moving to the progressive field in the new millennium, argued that the Anti-globalisation movements did not want to understand that "bad jobs at bad wages are better than no jobs at all". A good way to argue the "Tina vision", *there is no alternative.*

[9] The "fixed discontinuous" employment contract was introduced in Spain to circumvent the legislation on permanent contracts. The "intermittent" work according to the company's convenience charges the public unemployment subsidy for periods of inactivity, without increasing the statistical unemployment rate.

Inherited Wealth and the Emergence of Talent

The famous thought of Louis D. Brandeis, a judge of the Supreme Court of the United States from 1916 to 1939 and a fervent supporter of solidaristic democracy, remains: "We must make our choice. We may have democracy, or we may have wealth concentrated in the hands of a few, but we cannot have both". About a century later, in the United States, wealth inequality has increased and the "rate of democracy" (of which voting participation is an important indicator) has decreased. In 2022, the Federal Reserve (the Central Bank) certifies that the richest 1% owns 53.8% of the wealth in stocks and investment funds.

The problem, although not in these proportions, concerns all advanced countries. As soon as the issue of wealth redistribution is raised in public discourse, governments tend to cover it with a veil of silence. The reasons are two: (1) if there really is a link—as Schumpeter believed—between market competition among companies and competition among parties in political elections, this link must be found in *short-termism*: the race, by all means, more or less lawful, to the "last profit" of companies and the "last vote" of parties. Two inappropriate behaviours, because of which the economy and democracy lose out. The fragility of political balances, today aggravated by strong fluctuations of voters from one side to the other of the political spectrum, suggests to the ruling classes of advanced countries to profess moderation. Given the close link between economic stability and political stability, a redistribution of wealth, even of a relatively modest size, is judged destabilising, due to the repercussions it would generate in the economy; (2) if income inequality is "fair", that is, it is not caused by unfair circumstances, it must be judged fully legitimate even if it is continuously fuelled by the unequal distribution of wealth (which in turn fuels). In other words, it is forgotten that wealth is usually inherited and it is argued that income inequality is solely the result of "merit", a real *pass-partout* concept (as seen in Chap. 3). The discourse on income distribution is in fact inseparable from that on wealth distribution. Possessing and not possessing wealth (or possessing a very low share of it) opens a fracture within society that is reflected primarily in the availability of opportunities—high or low—to earn in the market.

The inviolability of property—despite the strong concentration of wealth—is much more difficult to justify than income inequality: it is practically impossible to do so. It has even been proposed—through the elaboration of the *Limitarianism*—that a maximum limit be set on the accumulation of wealth (Robeyns 2023). The transmission of the stock of wealth plays a decisive role in the passage from one generation to the next. First: even in the hypothesis where the *absolute* flows of income do not change, the rich parents' inheritance to their children can affect the *relative* mobility. In fact, in the case where the amount of wealth transmitted is very large, the reshuffling of positions in the income scale often leads to greater income inequality (Palomino et al. 2022). Second: are we sure that we climb the wealth ranking—that we become "magnates"—only by practising frugality and saving? Even in the hypothesis where wealth has been acquired more with work than by the mere presence of the hereditary right, there is no reasonable defence of the inviolability of individual wealth. The more the share of financial capital (in shares, in public debt) and real estate increases in total income compared to that of labour, the more capital income increases. Since share ownership is predominantly in the hands of the rich, the increase in financial returns increases interpersonal income inequality. In the absence of policies aimed at reducing the concentration of capital, financial and real estate wealth in the hands of the shareholders of large *corporations* and large family dynasties does nothing but grow; not only because capital incomes are largely reinvested, but also following the tendency of governments to reduce taxes on capital ownership and inheritance (Boserup et al. 2016; Elinder et al. 2018; Nolan et al. 2022). The concentration of wealth is largely the consequence of the transmission through inheritance of the right of ownership over resources from one generation to the next. Today, there is no way to bring out in public discourse a simple truth: as Kaushik Basu, chief economist of the World Bank between 2012 and 2016, wrote, "one thing is the right of ownership over what you have earned, another is the right of ownership over what someone else has earned" (Basu 2011, p. 200).

Social mobility is at the junction between income growth (from which *absolute*) and the interpersonal distribution of income from work and capital (the reshuffling of income positions along the social scale, from which relative mobility derives). When *all* members of a community rise *to the same extent* on the income scale compared to the level reached by their parents, the community records greater absolute intergenerational mobility, while relative mobility may not increase. If, in fact, *all* children end up as adults reaching nothing more than the *same level* of income as their parents, by definition absolute intergenerational mobility has not increased. However, this does not mean that there cannot have been a reshuffling of income positions from one generation to the next. Relative mobility could also have increased. Let's give a somewhat unrealistic but clear example.

What could have caused a change in income positions on the social scale, when the GDP growth rate from one generation to the next was zero? The answer is simple: considering the long-term fall in the wage share of income, an entire social group, the employees, could rise, or plummet, along the scale. A relative downward mobility can also be triggered by a decrease in the total income of those who only earn income from work; or it can result from the fact that owners of financial and real estate capital, as their capital increases (for example, by receiving an inheritance), record an increase in capital income.

In recent decades, policy choices regarding capital taxation have favoured the concentration of wealth and therefore against intergenerational mobility. The children of the rich, in acquiring more wealth, have a larger capital to make profitable, they invest it, and increase the income gap compared to other young people. Although the City is the most important financial centre in Europe, in the UK it is primarily the real estate owned by the elite that is the component of wealth that—in being passed down from generation to generation—ends up widening the amount of wealth and the level of income from the rest of the population (Gregg and Kanabar 2022). A study on wealth data from France, Germany, the UK, Ireland, Italy, Spain and the United States has recently documented how the internal dynamics of social stratification, which is largely constituted by the phenomenon of social persistence and often also downward mobility, is also the consequence of national legislations that do little to affect the consistency of inheritances and donations *inter vivos* of families (Palomino et al. 2022).

The *trickle-down* vision contains a defence of the concentration of wealth. The narrative disseminated by many governments wants austerity to strengthen growth. The expectation is that wage flexibility and welfare cuts will stimulate an economic recovery, thus giving a boost to absolute mobility. The promise that putting more resources in the hands of innovative companies will make well-being "trickle down" to all layers of society would then become a reality. The dynamics within social stratification would become more fluid, promoting relative mobility and the convergence of "starting points". However, it does not seem that the emergence of talents is today less hindered than usual by class membership. By crossing patent data with tax data from more than a million inventors, Bell et al. (2019a, 2019b) show that the chances of becoming inventors are closely dependent on the characteristics of young people at birth: those belonging to families at the top of the income distribution (1%) have a probability of becoming inventors ten times higher than young people belonging to medium-low income families.

This gap, since it persists even after controlling for their respective responses to cognitive tests from childhood, is largely attributable to "circumstances", primarily family background and the degree of technological advancement of the area of residence. The failure to enable all young people to express their talents is evident in England. "The education system reflects the hierarchical class culture from which it originates [...]. Boys from lower social classes or with less educated parents who score high on cognitive tests are less likely to achieve the same educational levels as boys of equal ability from higher social classes or with more educated parents" (Major and Machin 2019, p. 185). A political scientist has clarified that there is also a social cost of exclusion. It was Jon Elster (1989) who defined the "cement of society" as the social norms that in the societies of advanced countries prevent the limits of individual rationality —and the heterogeneity of beliefs and preferences that accentuate the distance between the behaviours of subjects—from breaking up social order.

In summary, it is only when the socio-economic environment is particularly fertile for a technological innovation that creates employment, that the talents of young people have a greater chance of becoming effective *ability* to succeed in life. Regarding the suitability of the "cut" in taxes on higher incomes to stimulate the emergence and affirmation of new inventors, the judgement of the study by Bell et al. is clear: there is no correlation. Certainly, it can be added, the greatest growth in well-being is achieved when the talents of all young people are put to good use. In the vision of the *trickle-down* advocated by neoliberals, there is instead the idea that in channelling resources into the hands of investor-innovators neither the circumstances in which they were formed as young people, nor the inheritance they received, should be relevant. Everything that comes *before the* market does not matter; just as the accumulation of wealth through inheritance. The culture of capitalism claims its exclusive foundation in entrepreneurial risk. However, it is not at all taken for granted that talents are concentrated in the generation of children who have been able to receive more parental care and in whose bank accounts (or in the shares of investment funds held by the family) inheritance law has poured substantial assets.[10]

[10] The contribution of inheritance to wealth inequality in France, Germany, the United Kingdom and the United States ranges between 26% and 36%, percentages that are reduced to a range between 9% and 17% if the influence of family background is eliminated.

The right not to have inheritance taxed is also argued with a questionable justification: wealthy families must have the opportunity to test their young people with the use of the inheritance received in investing in their own education and in the family business. Public discourse, however, is silent on an issue of far greater relevance to social mobility: how to identify talents among all citizens and not just among the rich? Between inheritance rights and the opportunity for all young people to bring out their own talents there is an obvious contradiction. As mentioned in the Introduction, wealth taxation is the right tool. It is necessary to find the political will to do it. The transmission of inheritance from parents to children has an increasing impact on inequality of opportunity, as it benefits to a much larger extent the rich (Palomino et al. 2022). As will be explored in Chap. 11, the long-term support in major capitalist countries to the link between education and wealth of the "dynasties" of elite families is primarily the inheritance legacy. Figure 6.1 shows the correlation for 2014 in the United States between access to tertiary education for young people between 19 and 21 years old and the income percentile of their parents. The distribution of parents' incomes, from the poorest to the richest,

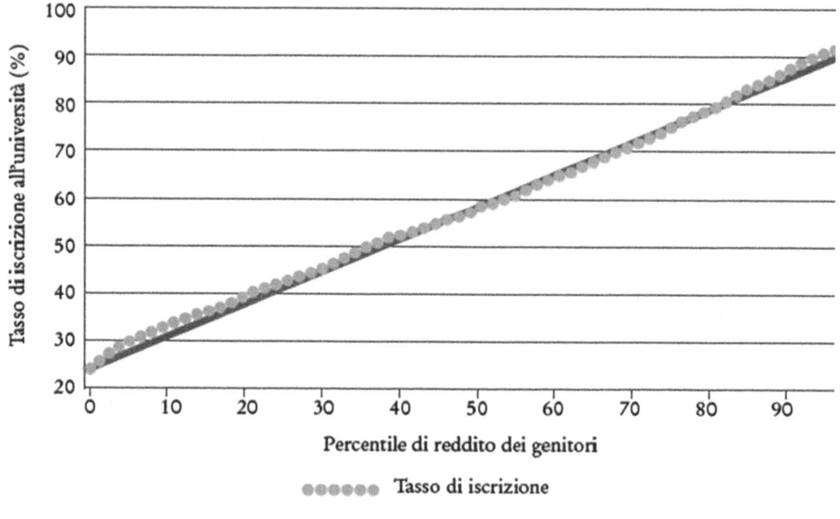

Fig. 6.1 University enrolment rate and parents' income percentile (United States, 2014). (Source: Piketty (2020). Translation: University enrolment rate (%), Parents' income percentile, Enrolment rate)

corresponds—almost exactly—to the percentage of children enrolled in university. One cannot help but be shocked by the linearity of the correlation: "enrolments come from the poorest 10% of families barely in the measure of 30% and from the richest 10% of the population by as much as 90%" (Piketty 2018, p. 35).

There is another issue regarding which an ideological interpretation of reality serves to obscure the class structure of society. The problems that accumulate around public debt are not easy to understand. Making them even more opaque is the manipulation hidden under the guise of seemingly informative information. A typical example is the concept of the "burden of public debt weighing on the shoulders of every newborn": a fraudulent way of communicating, aimed at eliciting an emotional reaction in order to impose an interpretation that is a distillation of ideology.

Point 1. The public debt that according to quite a few orthodox economists "weighs on the shoulders" of newborns of the new generation is nothing more (net of the share of securities held by foreign entities) than the wealth in public debt securities owned by the parents that will be inherited and will end up "in the pockets" of the newborn children once they become adults. If this fact of reality is not enough to understand the difference between "burden" and owned wealth, one can cite a witness who fears no contradiction: Herbert Hoover, president of the United States from 1929 to 1933, observed: "new generations are blessed, because they will inherit the public debt". To clarify the reassuring sense of this statement, let's give the word to a leading figure in the international monetary establishment. Vítor Constâncio, who was vice president of the ECB from 2010 to 2018 (only one year difference from Mario Draghi's presidency: 2011–2019), unmasked in a *tweet* from his account the *fake news* of public debt as a burden borne by the young: "In the future, when the monetary amount of maturing securities is returned, some members of the future generation will pay - in case it is necessary to renew part of the public debt - a certain amount of taxes, while other members of that same generation, in exchange for the securities in their possession that have matured, will receive money. There is no burden on the future generation". It doesn't seem like a difficult reasoning to understand and not even to disseminate, but today's media information continues to propagate the reasoning exactly opposite to that of Constâncio. Difficult, at this point, to deny the existence of the *pensée unique*.

Point 2. The real problem of a country's public debt is its sustainability, which must be evaluated in relation to the growth of GDP with which it will have to be repaid. The way in which we reason about the *public debt/GDP* ratio is often misleading. Although this indicator is far from irrelevant to the issue of social mobility, its link with intergenerational equity—not only in the media, but also in the scientific literature—is little explored. Let's try to explain. The ones who collect the value of public securities at maturity, after inheriting them, are the children of those in whose hands the financial wealth of the parents has ended up. We must therefore disaggregate. The most popular disaggregation is not, however, the one that would be expected, the one that has to do with economic inequality. It is the more aseptic one, between the aggregate of fathers and the aggregate of children. This is the intergenerational equity that is continually evoked by the media. It is denounced that the State distributes too much pension income to parents, forgetting that to the children—the coming generation—it will be up to repay the public debt public. However, we have already seen that this is financial wealth that the children have inherited. Moreover, if we consider these children all together, without dividing them among the social classes to which they belong, we are assuming that the ownership of the debt securities is distributed equally in the population.

It has already been noted that financial wealth is strongly concentrated in the hands of the rich. And it is known that the inherited legacy that goes to the children is far greater in rich families than in those of the middle class and the poor.[11] It is therefore surprising that with regard to public debt a (debatable) unfair treatment between the aggregates of fathers and children is denounced, but no question of intergenerational equity is raised about the substantial inherited legacy received by the subset of children who have had the fortune to have rich parents, and from the little or no inheritance received by the subset of children of poor parents. The young people who inherit the public debt and the young people who with their earnings pay the taxes that serve to extinguish it are two aggregates of distinct people. For some young people—the richest, being those without financial wealth excluded from the game of the intergenerational legacy—a possible increase in taxation intended to finance the expenditure

[11] According to the latest "Survey of Household Finances" by the Bank of Italy, published in 2018, while the poorest 30% of families owned only 1% of the existing wealth in the country in 2016, a full 75% was held by the 30% of the wealthiest families (if from this 30% the 10% of the wealthiest families is separated, the percentage is 44%; if the 3% of super-wealthy families is separated, the percentage drops slightly: 34%).

for interest on the country's public debt will be far less than the money they received as repayment of the loan to the owners of the maturing debt.

Public debt is a game with a neutral distributive outcome only when the old and the new generation are computed as aggregates of indistinct people, and social classes disappear. It is therefore necessary to go beyond the comparison between the aggregate of parents and the aggregate of children. As long as the new generation is reasoned in terms of a single aggregate of people, even the issue of intergenerational equity between classes ends up being ignored. When in fact we go to disaggregate between those who inherit the securities, and cash in their nominal value at the time of maturity, and those who do not inherit them, being nevertheless called to contribute with taxes to the extinction of the public debt of their own country, it emerges on surface that the "playing field" is tilted on one side.

Bibliography

Acemoglu, D. & Johnson, S. 2023 Power and Progress: Our Thousand-Year Struggle Over Technology and Prosperity, *Public Affairs, New York.*

Alchian, A. & Demsetz, H. 1972 Production, Information Costs, and Economic Organization, *in «American Economic Review», LXII, 5, pp. 777–95.*

Anderson, E. S. 2017 Private Government: How Employers Rule Our Lives (and Why We don't Talk about it), *Princeton University Press, Princeton.*

Arrow, K. J. 2005 *A Cautious Case for Socialism*, lecture given at Columbia University in the *Terzo Lionel Trilling Seminar* in the academic year 1977–78, in «Economics in Practice», II, 1, pp. 472–80.

Basu, K. 2011 Beyond the Invisible Hand: Groundwork for a New Economics, *Princeton University Press, Princeton.*

Bauman, Z. 2007 Welfare assediato. Sono forse io il custode di mio fratello?, *in* Homo Consumens. Lo sciame inquieto dei consumatori e la miseria degli esclusi, *Erickson, Gardolo.*

Bell, A. et al. 2019a Do Tax Cuts Produce more Einsteins? The Impacts of Financial Incentives VerSus Exposure to Innovation on the Supply of Inventors, *Joseph Schumpeter Lecture, Eea Annual Congress 2017, in «Journal of the European Economic Association», XVII, 3, pp. 651–77.*

Bell, A. et al. 2019b Who Becomes an Inventor in America? The Importance of Exposure to Innovation, *in «Quarterly Journal of Economics», CXXXIV, 2, pp. 647–713.*

Benhabib, J. & Przeworski, A. 2006 The Political Economy of Redistribution under Democracy, *in «Economic Theory», XXIX, pp. 271–90.*

Boix, C. 2003 *Democracy and Redistribution*, Cambridge University Press, Cambridge.

Boserup, S., Kopczuk, W., Kreiner, C. 2016 Wealth Inequality: Evidence from the Role of Bequests in Shaping Wealth Inequality, *in «American Economic Review», CVI, 5, pp. 656–61.*

Brooks, W. J., Kaboski, J. P., Li, W. A., Qian, W. 2021 Exploitation of Labor? Classical Monopsony Power and Labor's Share, *in «Journal of Development Economics», CL, maggio.*

Dahrendorf, R. 1989 The Modern Social Conflict: An Essay on the Politics of Liberty, *Weidenfeld and Nicolson, London 1988.*

Dunn, J. 2006 Setting the People Free: The Story of Democracy, *Atlantic Books, London 2005).*

Elinder, M., Erixson, O., Waldenström, D. 2018 Inheritance and Wealth Inequality: Evidence from Population Registers, *in «Journal of Public Economics», CLXV, pp. 17–30.*

Erikson, R. & Goldthorpe, J. H. 1992 The Constant Flux: A Study of Class Mobility in Industrial Societies, *Clarendon Press, Oxford.*

Farina, F. 2021 Lo Stato sociale. Storia, politica, economia, *Luiss University Press, Roma.*

Foucault, M. 1978 La governamentalità, *in «Aut-aut», CLXVII–CLXVIII.*

Foucault, M. 2008 The Birth of Biopolitics: Lectures at the Collège de France, 1978–1979, *Palgrave Macmillan, Basingstoke.*

Giddens, A. 1998 The Third Way: The Renewal of Social Democracy, *Polity Press, Cambridge.*

Giovannini, E. 2018 *L'utopia sostenibile*, Laterza, Roma-Bari.

Gregg, P. & Kanabar, R. 2022 Intergenerational Wealth Transmission and Mobility in Great Britain: What Components of Wealth Matter?, *Iser Working Paper Series 2022–02, Institute for Social and Economic Research.*

Hacker, J. S. 2008 The Great Risk Shift: The New Economic Insecurity and the Decline of the American Dream, *in «Oxford University Press», Oxford.*

Kurz, M. 2023 The Market Power of Technology: Understanding the Second Gilded Age, *Columbia University Press, New York.*

Major, E. L. & Machin, S. 2019 *Social Mobility*, Centre for Economic Performance, London School of Economics.

Mannheim, K. 1928 *Das Problem der Generationen*, in «Kölner Vierteljahreshefte für Soziologie», 7.

Meltzer, A. H. & Richard, S. F. 1981 *A Rational Theory of the Size of Government*, in «Journal of Political Economy», LXXXIX, 5, pp. 914–92.

Naidu, S. & Posner, E. A. 2022 *Labor Monopsony and the Limits of the Law*, in «Journal of Human Resources», LVII, S, S284–323.

Nolan, B., Palomino, G. C., Van Kerm, P., Morelli, S. 2022 The Wealth of Families: The Intergenerational Transmission of Wealth in Britain in Comparative Perspective, *in «Economic Letters», XLIII, 2, pp. 179–99.*

Oecd 2020 Beyond Growth. Towards a New Economic Approach, *Paris.*

Orwell, G. 1944 A Review of The Road to Serfdom by F. A. Hayek, *in «The Observer», 9 aprile.*

Palomino, J. C., Marrero, G. A., Nolan, B., Rodríguez, J. G. 2022 Wealth Inequality, Intergenerational Transfers, and Family Background, *in «Oxford Economic Papers», LXXIV, 3, pp. 643–70.*

Piketty, T. 2018 Brahmin Left vs Merchant Right: Rising Inequality & the Changing Structure of Political Conflict: Evidence from France, Britain and the Us, 1948–2017, *Wid.world Working Paper Series n. 7.*

Piketty, T. 2020 *Capital et idéologie*, Éditions du Seuil, Paris 2019.

Przeworski, A. 2016 *Democracy: A Never-Ending Quest*, in «Annual Review of Political Science», XIX, pp. 1–12.

Przeworski, A. 2019 *Crisis of Democracy*, Cambridge University Press, Cambridge.

Przeworski, A. & Wallerstein, M. 1982 The Structure of Class Conflict in Democratic Capitalist Societies, *in «American Political Science Review», LXXVI, 2, pp. 215–38.*

Roberts, K. W. S. 1977 *Voting over Income Tax Schedules*, in «Journal of Public Economics», VIII, 3, pp. 329–40.

Robeyns, I. 2023 Limitarianism: The Case against Extreme Wealth, *Astra House, London.*

Romer, T. 1975 Individual Welfare, Majority Voting and the Properties of a Linear Income Tax, *in «Journal of Public Economics», VII, pp. 163–88.*

Schumpeter, J. A. 2002 *Socialism, and Democracy*, Harper & Bros, New York 1942.

Sen, A. K. 1983 *The Profit Motive*, in «Lloyds Bank Review», pp. 1–20.

Therborn, G. 2013 The Killing Fields of Inequality, *Polity Press, Cambridge.*

World Economic Forum 2020 The Global Social Mobility Report 2020: Equality, Opportunity and a New Economic Imperative.

Zuboff, S. 2019 The Age for Surveillance Capitalism: The Fight for a Human Future at the New Frontier of Power, *Profile Books, L.*

PART II

The Crisis of Social Dynamics

CHAPTER 7

Inequality of Opportunity and Intergenerational Mobility

Individual Aspirations and Socio-economic Context

Charles Dickens is considered the founder of the social novel. A writer with liberal sentiments, he was very concerned about the damage that the extreme form of capitalism of his time was causing in people's lives. He never stopped nurturing the hope that English society could over time become a safer and more liveable place, free from conflicts and poverty. After a first version, Dickens decided to rewrite the ending of *Great Expectations*—the coming-of-age novel of a poor boy, Philip Pirrip, known as Pip—precisely because he did not want to give up a narrative that suggested the protagonist's arrival at a satisfying social condition. The traditional way of representing social mobility reflects Dickens' point of view well: social ascent as an escape from poverty, and as self-realisation by a young person. However, in the current historical phase, the manifestations of social mobility seem to have little in common with the image that the history of the last centuries has handed down to us.

It is difficult to see the economic growth of our days, continually exposed to adverse winds in the markets and international finance, and today overwhelmed by wars, as a process of continuous diffusion of income and well-being for all (absolute *mobility*), in which social advancement is also facilitated by the reshuffling of income positions (relative *mobility*). Today's phenomena of social mobility are dystopian. It seems that the norm is becoming social persistence; if not the regression of

F. Farina, *The Rise of Inequality and the Fall of Social Mobility*,
https://doi.org/10.1007/978-3-031-92843-7_7

income and *status* of significant strata of the social body. The increase in the Gini index of income inequality that has occurred in recent decades has been accompanied in many countries by polarisation between high and low incomes. According to a study by the Economic Policy Institute in Washington, the wealthiest 10% of US families will own 76% of the wealth in 2023. In the "high" portion of the distribution, the elastic of earnings of the richest among the rich (the 0.01% compared to the 1%) has tended to stretch towards stratospheric levels. Fig. 7.1 testifies to the great economic success achieved in recent decades by the *top incomes* in the advanced countries of the West. Almost half of the "people of the rich" is today concentrated in the population of Western Europe, North America and Oceania (Wenao).

For the set of Wenao countries, the individual with the median income (who, as will be remembered, stands exactly in the middle of the income distribution from the poorest to the richest) is a person who on a planetary level appears really very rich; in the overall global distribution, they indeed appear at the 90th percentile (in particular, the income of the median individual in the United States is at the 93rd). On the opposite side, in the portion of the poor and low-income classes, frequencies have increased due to the crisis that has hit the weakest strata of the middle classes of the Wenao countries. "The United States was the first to create the middle-class society, but Europe was never too far behind and in the post-war

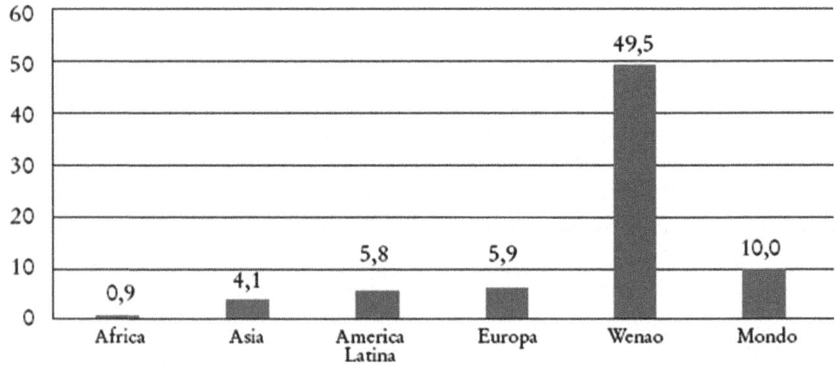

Fig. 7.1 Percentage of population in each geographical area belonging, in the income distribution, to the decile of top incomes. (Source: Milanović 2023. Translation: Africa, Asia, Latin America, Europe, Wenao, World)

period has overtaken the United States in creating opportunities for its own citizens" (Stiglitz 2019, p. 5). Things have changed, the middle class in the West has today become the epicentre of polarisation.

In the North of the world, a profound socio-economic upheaval is indeed underway, which marks a break from the second half of the twentieth century. Social mobility is no longer the opportunity for social redemption idealised by Dickens. The upward progress of the income of the poor has suffered a significant slowdown. A step forward in understanding the link that connects social mobility to income dynamics is Fig. 7.2: the graph shows the number of generations that must succeed each other so that the income of the young person whose family belongs to the poorest 10% of the population "rises" towards the average income of the country. In the graph, we observe histograms of lesser and greater height. The "distance" from the average income of their own country that the poor family will have to bridge for the average of the advanced countries (OECD) oscillates between four and five generations. This means

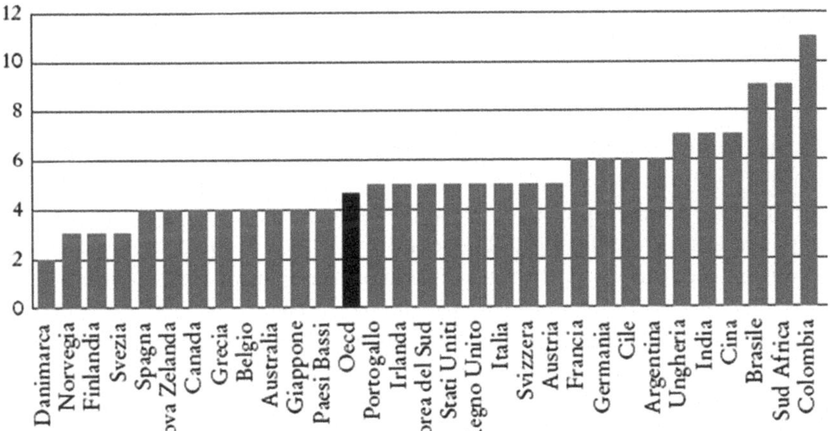

Fig. 7.2 Number of generations needed for those born in low-income families to reach the average income of their own country. (Source: Oecd 2018. Translation: Denmark, Norway, Finland, Sweden, Spain, New Zealand, Canada, Greece, Belgium, Australia, Giappone, Netherland, Oecd, Portugal, Ireland, South Korea, United States, United Kingdom, Italy, Switzerland, Austria, France, Germany, Chile, Argentina, Hungary, India, China, Brazil, South Africa, Colombia)

that, for four generations (starting from this decade), poor parents cannot expect that their children will enjoy social redemption. This number naturally changes over time, depending on the dynamics of the per capita GDP of the country of origin, and the macroeconomic instability that often permeates the path of growth. What is certain is that for the children and grandchildren of today's "disadvantaged" families, the future will be less uncertain the more they are supported by the political and economic institutions present in society (Occorsio and Scarpetta 2022).

The "circumstances"—the factors of different origin for which one is not responsible, but which substantially influence life choices from childhood—are so heterogeneous among people as to compromise the solidity of the interpretative schemes built on aggregate data. Being different the living conditions in which people are formed, typically between one young person and another the "starting blocks" of the race of life are misaligned. Let's look at Fig. 7.3. The objective probability[1] that a young person will be part of the income elite as an adult (defined as the 25% of rich people present in a nation) is related to his socio-economic background (having a poor or rich father).

One aspect that the graph immediately highlights is that the percentages of persistence of children at the income level of the family of origin are quite high. Not surprisingly, such percentages are higher for the *top incomes* than for the *low incomes*. For young people with a rich father (the fourth income quartile consisting of the 25% of people with the highest earnings), staying as an adult in that same group has a probability of occurring approximately equal to 40%, and reaches 50% in the United States, Germany and Luxembourg. The children whose fathers belong to the section with the lowest earnings of the workforce appear as adults for 42% in the section of poor workers (the first quartile). The turnover in top positions is very limited: in most advanced countries, the rise of young people with a poor father to the group of *top incomes* has a probability not greater than 20%. To what extent does the socio-economic and institutional context of various countries impact personal performance? It's unlikely that contexts don't matter. If one individual's earnings are roughly half of another's, it's improbable that this is due to the latter's greater work commitment. Take two countries at opposite ends of the spectrum

[1] By objective probability we mean the data obtained from the reality of the probability of a certain event. For example, the frequency of a certain income level or the number of subjects in a population who receive that income.

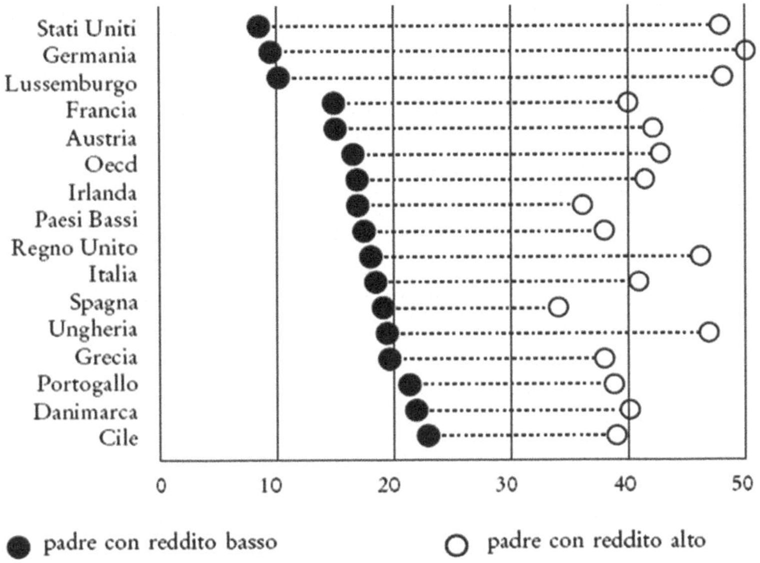

Fig. 7.3 Percentage of children, respectively with a father with low income and with a father with high income, who as adults are placed in the richest 25% of the population. (Source: Oecd (2018). Translation: United States, Germany, Luxembourg, France, Austria, Oecd, Ireland, Netherland, United Kingdom, Italy, Spain, Hungary, Greece, Portugal, Denmark, Chile, Low-income father (black), High-income father (white))

for public social cohesion intervention. The significant divergence of children's destinies from their fathers' conditions in the United States compared to Denmark is striking. In the group of countries appearing in Fig. 7.3, children with poor fathers have, respectively in the two countries, the highest and lowest persistence in the lowest income quartile and the least and greatest probability of rising to the rich's income quartile.

Naturally, both the family's income and the environment in which the young people are placed matter. In *The Buddenbrooks*, Thomas Mann (1901) described the slow but inexorable decline, lasting four generations, of a family from the great merchant bourgeoisie of Lubeck. He outlined both the genetic transmission and the evolution of the economic *status*. In young Hanno, the former suffers from poor health and the latter from the weakening of the "animal spirits", the entrepreneurial vigour of the dynasty. Today, for large family dynasties, things seem to be going even better than at the beginning of the development of industry and commerce. For wealthy families, the socio-economic environment is undoubtedly particularly fertile, for the young people of the "dynasties" of the rich the future prospects are more than favourable. A mystery that we will have to delve into and clarify, considering that economic growth has become increasingly slow and discontinuous.

Even more surprising is another result. Take Denmark and Chile. Denmark is a country with a social democratic political tradition, whose governments have managed in the past to preserve low-income inequality by dedicating themselves to the construction of the welfare state. Chile, a country that lived under an extreme right-wing authoritarian regime from 1973 to 1990, is still characterised today by the very high-income inequality produced under the dictatorship. How is it possible that, as seen in Fig. 7.3, the two countries have almost equal social mobility? It is unthinkable that the life paths of these young people are impervious to the different socio-economic context. It is more likely that this empirical evidence exposes the ambiguous nature of social mobility from a political perspective. The income result of young Danes and Chileans in the labour market deviates from that of their parents much more than elsewhere not so much (or not only) due to a different disposition to commit themselves to training and work, but because of the many channels through which the social and institutional context influences individual destinies, impacting to a greater or lesser extent on the dynamics of the social structure.

The institutional context is decisive. Income and *status* positions are mainly reshuffled through two welfare policies: (a) labour market institutions, which if particularly weak increase income polarisation: in the years following Pinochet's coup, in Chile the working week went to 45 hours; the deregulation of the labour market boosted the transition of part of the middle class towards the elite of the rich, while the lower-middle income classes plummeted towards the quintile of the poor; (b) redistributive policies implemented by the most developed welfare systems: at the end of the twentieth century, in social democratic Denmark the aspiration for social redemption of the weak classes, supported by welfare, was successful. The fact that the two countries have high social mobility thus finds a simple explanation. As argued elsewhere in the book, if Denmark was committed to building solidarity democracy, Pinochet's Chile was dedicated to the creation of economic institutions aimed on the one hand at raising the incomes of the elite that supported the regime and on the other at putting obstacles in the way of promoting the welfare of workers, potential opponents of the regime.

Public policies aimed at strengthening welfare institutions—those present *in the market* (unemployment benefits, minimum wage, citizenship income and so on) and those that operate *after the market* (the mechanism of taxes and income redistributive transfers)—help to reduce the handicap of disadvantaged young people both for unfavourable circumstances and for scarce market opportunities. The difference between the two countries lies in the choice of the social class that public policies intend to favour. The trend of relative social mobility must therefore be evaluated using a disaggregated analysis for social classes. It is thus discovered that methodological individualism, the analytical perspective that hypothesises the autonomy of individual behaviour from the collective context, is not the right perspective to frame the phenomenon of social mobility. Based on the political orientation of governments, young people's commitment to realising their life project is either stimulated or hindered. "Disadvantaged" people often tend to correct their expectations downwards for fear of social exclusion.[2] In this way, they risk transmitting to their work and their earnings the tendency towards exclusion that is rooted in every unequal society. This consideration, seemingly obvious, unfurls a series of issues into which we will delve further later. Even before the Welfare *in the* market and *after the* market, social mobility depends on public policies *before the* market.[3] These are the most complicated to implement, those that attack the "circumstances" of disadvantage, "liberating" the talents of disadvantaged young people.

The Driving Factors of Mobility: Sustained Growth and Low Inequality

Among social phenomena, it is now clear, mobility is one of the most difficult to focus on. It consists of two distinct aspects, one of an individual nature—the impact of GDP growth on the mobility *absolute* of each

[2] "A malnourished, undernourished, homeless and sick person can still be happy if they have learned to have realistic desires and find pleasure in small mercies" (Sen 1985, p. 21).

[3] "It is not only primary and secondary school and advanced education, but the social inequalities that precede them, that determine whether people from low-income families, peripheral residential areas, or 'excluded' minorities, can improve their social circumstances" (Marginson 2016, p. 421).

individual—and another that pertains to interaction within the community—the mobility *relative*. What is the profound meaning of this dual nature?

Raj Chetty, a Harvard economist of Indian origin, is a convinced supporter of the possibility and necessity of "developing tools capable of approximating scientific experiments to obtain reliable answers to specific policy problems [...] to transform the economy into a discipline firmly based on facts" (Chetty 2013). It's easy to agree: the so-called "weak thought"—if you will, the "bounded rationality"—is today such also because we are overwhelmed by an avalanche of information (true or only presumed such) in which the facts that count no longer emerge on their own. We interpret with the help of Chetty the trend of social mobility by putting growth in relation to income inequality. In Fig. 7.4, a percentile of parents after another, the probabilities of children earning more than their parents are indicated based on two types of calculation. The graph shows the traces (for the years 1940 and 1980) of the income mobility of children compared with the earnings of parents (measured in percentiles) both in relation to growth, respectively in 1940 and 1980 (continuous line), and in relation to a combination of growth and income distribution (dashed line). In such combinations, the *economic growth* of one year, on which the mobility *absolute* depends, is combined with the (unequal) *income distribution* of the other year, which is in fact an indicator of mobility *relative*, or of the reshuffling of income positions of subjects within the overall distribution. The analysis of Chetty's team concerns the issue of social mobility in the United States (Chetty et al. 2017). Although the traces present in the graph are constructed from longitudinal data[4] of that single population, the results of the survey can be attributed a sufficient validity for all advanced countries. It is also because they usually precede the transformation of the markets of other advanced countries that the economic events of the country that has been leading the evolution of the capitalist economy for over a century are of great interest.

The first result, the one that is obtained with the calculation that only takes into account the growth of income 1940 and 1980, is simple and clear. The position in the graph of the two continuous traces documents how American society has become much more static in 1980 (trace below) compared to the dynamism it showed in 1940 (trace above). On average

[4] Longitudinal data collect information related to the evolution of an individual (or other unit of analysis) over time.

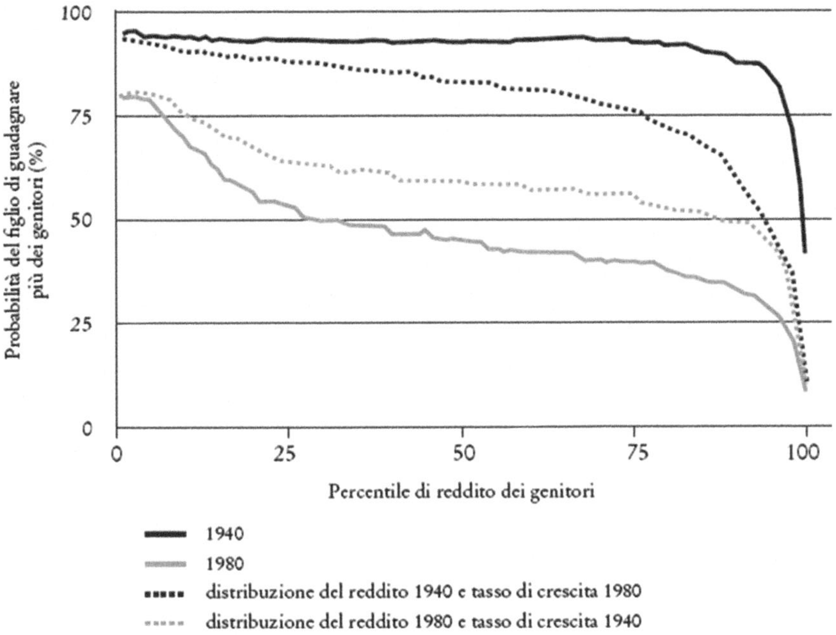

Fig. 7.4 Conditions for high absolute mobility: sustained growth and low levels of inequality. (Source: Chetty et al. (2017). Translation: Son's probability of earning a higher-than-father's income (%), 1940, 1980, Income distribution 1940 and income growth rate 1980, Income distribution 1940 and income growth rate 1980)

of the population, the authors inform us in the text, the percentage of young people who have achieved as adults an income higher than that of their parents reached 90% in 1940, while in 1980 it fell to 50%. But their counterfactual analysis disaggregated by income levels of the family suggests two very significant reflections. Intergenerational mobility is significantly higher—*in all percentiles*—in the socio-economic context of 1940 compared to the socio-economic context of 1980. However, while in 1940 the probability of mobility of young people compared to parents (vertical axis) remained consistently high for all percentiles of income of parents except among the richest, in 1980 there is a drop in mobility from the first to the hundredth income percentile (horizontal axis).

The second result is perhaps even more interesting. The graph shows how intergenerational mobility changes if the data of income growth of one of the two years is associated with the data of income inequality of the other year. History, it is true, is not made with ifs. However, this study is proof of how useful it is the use of a "counterfactual". Asking *what would have happened if...* is a fruitful tool of investigation to understand the link between growth and social context. The study asks: how would intergenerational mobility have gone if the phase of growth (of 1940 or 1980) in relation to which it is calculated had occurred under the socio-economic conditions (the income distribution of 1980 or 1940) of the other year? The authors calculate the percentage increase in income compared to their parents that young Americans would have achieved based on the *growth* of the GDP of 1940 in combination with the *distribution* of income of 1980; and the percentage increase in income compared to their parents that young Americans would have achieved based on the *growth* of the GDP of 1980 in combination with the *distribution* of income of 1940.

From one calculation to the other, the phenomenon of intergenerational income mobility changes appearance. In the outlined trajectory, the dynamics of intergenerational income is greater (appears above the continuous one) in the first combination, while it is less (appears below the continuous one) in the second combination. What message can we take from this empirical analysis? Does high growth matter more than high inequality? Or, conversely, does low growth matter more than low inequality? As observed in the graph, compared to the trajectory of a given year (1940 or 1980), intergenerational mobility is higher for all percentiles when high *growth* (1940) is accompanied by high *inequality* (1980) and lower for all percentiles when low *growth* (1980) is accompanied by low *inequality* (1940). The answer is therefore that for intergenerational mobility, high growth matters more, even if it is accompanied by high inequality. In other words, it is the higher growth rate (1940), in stimulating absolute *mobility*, that favours—despite being associated with a higher income inequality (1980)—intergenerational mobility.

In addition to these two important results, the study by Chetty et al. also helps to understand the different trends of intergenerational mobility in the percentiles of high incomes and those of low incomes. If we look at the graph at the trajectories of the counterfactual *1940 growth-1980 distribution* (where intergenerational mobility is higher compared to the calculation referring to the *tout court* 1980 mobility of the dashed trajectory), the conclusion to be drawn is that "high" growth increases intergenerational mobility in society, but in combination with a "high" income inequality in the percentiles of the poor, upward mobility drops significantly. In the case of the counterfactual *1980 growth - 1940 distribution*, where intergenerational mobility is lower compared to the trajectory of the *tout court* 1940 mobility, mobility drops more slowly in the percentiles of the poor compared to the continuous trajectory. The empirical evidence that emerges from the disaggregation by social classes is probably explained by the less disadvantaged income conditions of the poor in correspondence with the (less unequal) income distribution of 1940, despite its combination with the low growth of 1980 producing lower values of intergenerational mobility for all percentiles. It can be hypothesised that, at the advent of the neoliberal ideology adverse to the welfare state, the robust economic growth that took place in the fifties and sixties continued to generate expectations of greater *relative* mobility in the future. The perception of "good times" for the future may have made it easier (because less feared, at least by the middle class) to erase the goal of equity in public policies. These results are important, because they are in line with the study by Voitchovsky (2005) that we will examine in Par. 2 of Chap. 12. From that analysis, exactly as in the study by Chetty et al., it emerges that the "low" portion of the income distribution particularly benefits from sustained growth in the presence of limited inequality. On the contrary, young people from low-income families see their aspirations for social ascent penalised by "high" inequality.

This analysis is also very useful to clarify a dilemma present in all public policies: "should priority be given to the fight against poverty, or to the fight against inequality?" It can be argued: it is certainly true that growth "does good to the poor" (Dollar and Kraay 2002), as well as to other social groups, but income inequality can have a negative impact on their mobility, such as to weaken the positive effect exerted on them by the expansion of GDP. The thesis that "growth is good for the poor" must then be completed with this clarification, which also deserves quotation marks: "but for the poor to benefit, both good growth and a not too unequal income distribution are needed". The considerations to be made are therefore two. First, "disadvantaged" circumstances at birth (a low level of income of parents) not only weigh negatively on the success in life *of all young people* if the growth rate is low, but the impact on "disadvantaged" young people is greater if inequality is high. Second, in the combination *growth 1980-distribution 1940* Intergenerational mobility is much lower in the percentiles of parents with medium-high incomes than in the other combination: that is, the persistence of young rich people in their income position is greater in the other combination (*growth 1940-distribution 1980*)—that is, in the presence of the most unequal distribution of 1980, as expected. These two results of the counterfactual analysis when the 1980 distribution is involved—the loss of mobility of young poor people and the "persistence" of young rich people (who therefore remain rich)—are an indication of an evolution of the US economy that is not conducive to what was once called "social justice".

Access to Opportunities and Well-Being of New Generations

The introduction of technical progress was conceived by Schumpeter (1912) as "creative destruction", the process of overcoming the "stationary equilibrium" driven by the entrepreneur-innovator. More than a century ago, when the peoples of the North of the world were far from prosperity, the emphasis placed by the Austrian economist on the benefits of the innovative capabilities of large companies was more than justified. Certainly, as economic historian Deirdre McCloskey (2019) argues, the virtue of capitalism has been to create new ideas, to find "better ways of doing things", which requires much experimentation and a process of learning through "trial and error". Researchers, and managers on behalf of shareholders, are constantly engaged in transforming the knowledge developed in research laboratories into product and process innovations. However, ruthless competition drives large companies to accumulate profits immediately after the introduction of innovation, because the competitive advantage could soon disappear.

What are, considering this scenario, the long-term prospects of growth? An excessively high levy on company profits would represent a disincentive to the risk associated with innovative activity, and would slow down economic growth, ultimately depriving the entire community of well-being. While lower taxation would allow companies to have higher profit expectations, encouraging them to increase innovative investments. As already mentioned, orthodox economics proposes the theory of *trickle-down*. The higher rate of investment incentivised by tax cuts would set in motion synergies between companies' innovation activity and GDP dynamics. The initial earnings increases that would benefit the rich would then "trickle down", in the hopes of orthodox economists, towards the middle and bottom of the income distribution. The hypothesis of a close causal link between low taxes and high innovative investments would therefore advise prioritising economic growth driven by technological progress, and then compensating *ex post* with specific *ad hoc* support programmes the "losers", the workers laid off, for example due to automation (Aghion and Durlauf 2014). The goal of putting the economy on a path of long-term economic growth, in order to promote absolute social mobility *absolute*, is subject to a pre-condition: the stimulus of an increase in total factor productivity (Tfp).[5] Such a stimulus seems to be lacking (Gordon 2018). The evidence of Fig. 7.5 is clear. The slowdown in the increase in hourly

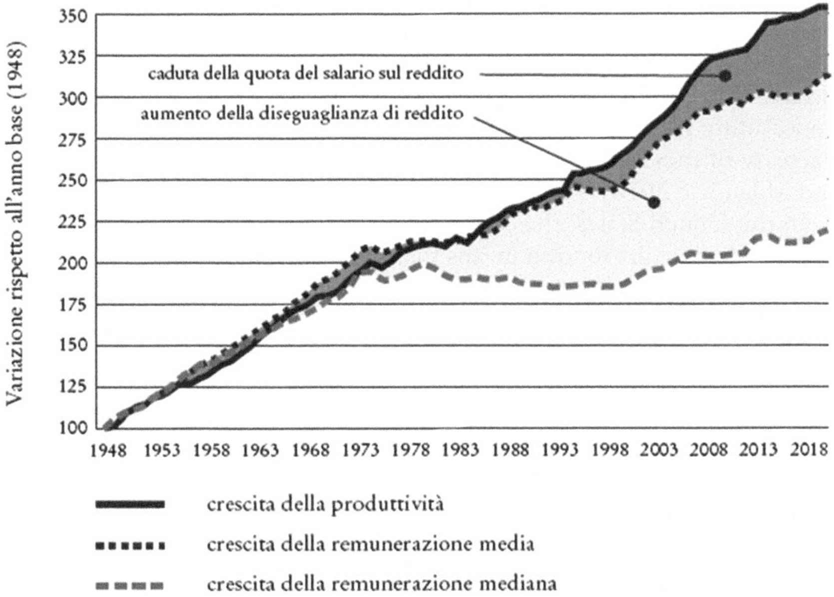

Fig. 7.5 United States: productivity growth and slower growth of average wage and median wage. (Source: Van Reenen (2020). Translation: Variation with respect to base year (1984), Falling labour share (dark grey area), Rising income inequality (light gray area), Productivity growth, Mean pay growth, Median pay growth)

[5] "Total factor productivity" is considered the measure of economic efficiency, as it is the part that remains of a country's GDP, once the amounts related to the contribution of the productive factors labour and capital have been subtracted from this value.

productivity in the United States took place in the new century. On the other hand, the growth paths of median and average wages had already started to no longer keep pace with that of productivity from the late seventies.

The "compensation" policy suggested by Aghion has the limitation of conceiving the social cost of job loss as a temporary phenomenon. A simple positive shock on growth is not enough to boost job creation. Due to the tendency to replace *low-skilled* and *middle-skilled* workers with *high-skilled* ones, the former see their wages and their jobs reduced. The longer the opportunities for re-employment are delayed, the more the *skills* of unemployed workers become obsolete. The relative social mobility *relative* of families with scarce economic resources and little human capital thus tends towards the lower positions in the income scale. The positive effects on growth, linked to the acceleration by the capital owners of innovative investment projects induced by lower tax collection, are opposed by the downward slide of opportunities for young people with "unfavourable circumstances". In the long term, the failure to reduce inequality of opportunity generates depressive effects on growth due to the low productivity of these workers (Marrero and Rodriguez 2013; van der Weide and Milanović 2018).

In the United States, the combination of the Tfp deadlock and a more uneven income distribution means that the distribution of growth among various social groups tends to diverge. The impact on absolute social mobility of GDP growth is uneven across the various sections of the income distribution (Chetty et al. 2018). In principle, a 1% income increase in the top 10% of the population is associated with a reduction in social mobility of about 5%; while with the same income increase in the section of the poorest subjects, social mobility increases by 12%. The most significant data is the tendency of the rich towards "social persistence". The children of parents belonging to the highest quintile of the income distribution, at the beginning of the new millennium, have a 36.5% chance of remaining there, against a 10.9% chance of moving to the lowest one. For the children of parents belonging to the lowest quintile, the probabilities are 33.7% and 7.5% respectively. Statistics also say that "for those who start from the bottom of the income ladder there is a worrying tendency towards poor upward mobility over a period of 5 to 10 years" (Isaacs 2016, p. 2). In the literature, the empirical evidence agrees: for the social group of the poor, there is a much higher percentage of persistence of intergenerational poverty conditions and low mobility towards the highest deciles (Jenkins and Van Kerm 2006). Finally, it turns out that in families at the centre of the income distribution, intergenerational social mobility has become sticky. The middle class, the social group that in the first decades after the Second World War had enjoyed the greatest intergenerational mobility, is losing positions in the income distribution. The tendency of technological progress to erase jobs typically occupied by members of the middle class is pushing down the social mobility of its weakest layers. For the children of middle-class parents, social mobility stagnates: these young people have almost equal chances of ending up in any of the various quintiles (Chetty et al. 2014a, 2014b). When the income inequality index of the aggregate of families increases from one generation to the next, for many young people from low-income families, opportunities for well-being also decrease at a multidimensional level. In the United States, life expectancy has recently fallen for three years in a row, something that has not happened in any advanced country since 1918 (Deaton and Case 2021).

The Great Gatsby Curve

In the novel *The Great Gatsby*, Francis Scott Fitzgerald describes the dazzling climb to "high society" and the tragic end of the protagonist. His life, from humble origins to social ascent, exposes the dark side of the "American dream". In the graph known as the *Great Gatsby Curve* (Ggc) (Corak 2013), the Gini index of income inequality appears on the horizontal axis and the "intergenerational elasticity of earnings" (Iee) on the vertical axis. The Iee indicator is the inverse of intergenerational earnings mobility: the closer the value of the Iee is to *zero*, the more the children's earnings are "independent" of the earnings achieved by the parents (*social mobility*); and the closer it is to *one*, the more the children's earnings are linked to (or "depend on") those of the parents (*social persistence*). In other words, in the comparison between how much the child earns as an adult and how much the parents earn, the value *one* signals the absence of intergenerational mobility, while the value *zero* signals complete intergenerational mobility. The *cross-country* correlation described by the *Great Gatsby Curve* is positive: as income inequality *increases*, intergenerational social mobility *increases*, the complement to *one* of the Iee. The hypothesis is that high income inequality tends to inhibit the ability of individuals to move from one income position to another on average. Indeed, it is the countries where income inequality is lower—which are also those whose welfare system better addresses the problem of unequal opportunities within social stratification—that have the highest intergenerational social mobility in Corak's (2013) graph.

Corak's idea is simple: the *deus ex machina* that explains the correlation of income inequality with the Iee is the inequality of opportunity. However, the econometric strategy he used is not so powerful as to deliver such an ambitious result. Although the estimate does not claim to interpret a simple correlation as a causal link, the inequality of opportunity remains a hypothetical and rather generic *trait d'union*.

Corak's graph is usually presented with this caption: "In countries with less inequality of opportunity and income, social mobility is greater". The role of the *link* between the Iee and the Gini index played by inequality of opportunity is, however, only a hypothesis, albeit a very plausible one, of Corak's study. In the estimate, the variable *inequality of opportunity* is absent. This is quite significant. Both the Gini index of income inequality and the Iee that measures the income gap between children and parents are indicators that do not distinguish, respectively, between the gain that follows commitment and access to opportunities that instead depends on "circumstances" and market imperfections. It is also difficult for income mobility from one generation to the next—a fact recorded at the level of individual subjects—to be explained by income inequality which is an aggregate measure. The interpretative framework therefore suffers from the fact that inequality of opportunity is configured as a "hidden variable" (Box 7.1). Moreover, the two explanatory variables—the Iee and the Gini index—are not only statistically associated but also mathematically dependent on each other (Berman 2017). This makes it difficult to believe that they can "bridge" between individual level and aggregate level, in order to arrive at a correct comparison between countries through the correlation of the income inequality index with the comparison between the earnings of children and the earnings achieved by parents in the most productive period of their life.

Box 7.1 Intergenerational mobility and income and opportunity inequality

Miles Corak entrusts the explanation of intergenerational mobility (measured by the Iee) to the income inequality of parents, interpreted as the indicator of children's access to opportunities. The study is conducted by estimating the following equation in logarithms: $\ln Y_{child} = \alpha + \beta \ln Y_{parents} + \varepsilon i$, where Y is income (adjusted for age and measurement error), β is the elasticity of children's income with respect to parents' income and εi is the statistical error. The elasticity (β) measures persistence, and its complement to one measures mobility: $1 - \beta$ indeed represents the percentage of children who can expect to rise to a higher income position than their parents.

Many problems, both statistical and non-statistical, of this interpretative framework have been indicated in the literature. First, if in the generation of young people, when they become adults, inequality is increasing, this variation can affect the correlation between parents' income and children's income, also complicating the comparison between countries with different trends in income distribution. Among other things, the model used (regression to the mean with Ols) underestimates the differences in the two tails of the distribution (Marrero et al. 2022). Second, many advanced countries have recorded, in recent decades, both an increase in education and an increase in incomes linked to the spread of "good jobs" (Bouchard St-Amant et al. 2020). Such changes, being both linked to the dependent variable and the independent one, could complicate the interpretation of the correlation between the Gini index and intergenerational mobility: the value of the slope of the interpolant of the Ggc could be a spurious result, due to an endogeneity problem. Third, the series of econometric verification are not treated appropriately in the estimation of the model. In the measurement of the Gini index presented in Corak (2013) it happens that the cohorts of young people end up overlapping those of their parents, so it is difficult to establish whether it is the inequality present in the generation of parents in the fullness of their working career or that of

(*continued*)

Box 7.1 (continued)
the generation of young people (Song 2022) that is correlated with the Iee. In other words, the temporal distance between the working life of children and that of parents is collapsed, with the result of compromising the verification of an intergenerational dependence in the degree of inequality of opportunity between the two cohorts. If the income inequality between the adulthood of parents and that of children increases, the Gini index could vary solely as a result of a "composition effect", due to a greater (or smaller) proportion of subjects present in a certain percentile of income. The correlation with the mobility indicator, the Iee, would vary in this case for reasons not associated with the diversity of opportunities, thus distorting the comparison between countries.

Beyond the analytical issues, what is of interest here is the reliability of the Iee and the Gini index as a measure of intergenerational mobility. The Iee is a deficient indicator, because it completely flattens the impact of income inequality, for children as for parents, on income mobility, without taking into account the other dimensions of well-being.[6]

It is also not easy to identify how intergenerational mobility can be traced back to what is perhaps the main "opportunity creator", education. In fact, for the same Gini index between two countries, the level of the Iee in one country may be higher (low mobility) due to insufficient spread of public education, or due to a larger share of "unfair" inequality, due for example to a strong concentration of wealth that increases the "inequality of opportunities" between social groups in education. These are very different situations: in the first case the problem is that of inadequate state support for the educational opportunities of the *aggregate* of young

[6] The heterogeneity of income between subjects belonging to different social groups is determined, for example, also by health and education opportunities, which are different between rich and poor; especially when health and educational services, instead of being offered by the public sector as meritorious goods, are offered by market operators. Richard Wilkinson and Kate Pickett (2009) have estimated a correlation from which it appears that the interpersonal inequality of health and education conditions of the population is greater in countries with high income inequality.

people, in the second case of scarce educational opportunities for the group of "disadvantaged" young people.

The disaggregated analysis by social classes of the impact of "inequality of opportunity" on social mobility in various countries is one of the most important tasks that the economy should undertake. A goal that economic research should aim for—once appropriately disaggregated data are available—is to move to an analysis that compares the mobility of young people from various social classes compared to their parents based on the "advantage" or the "disadvantage" in the various economic and cultural dimensions of well-being. The most appropriate strategy is to build indicators of inequality of opportunity (the variable that in the correlation of Corak's Great Gatsby curve remains implicit). In a broad comparative study, conducted in many countries (Brunori et al. 2013), an index based on "circumstances" (place of birth, family of origin, parents' background, etc.) that expands the measurement of the condition of "advantage" or "disadvantage" of opportunity compared to the sole income dimension.[7] As observed in the graph of Fig. 7.6, based on data from Brunori et al. 2013, income inequality and opportunity inequality tend to manifest together: the best performances are obtained in the cluster of European countries (low values for both variables, starting from the Nordic countries; followed, with progressively higher values, by continental Europe, Southern Europe and Eastern Europe) and Australia; finally, the clusters (with greater variability within them) of countries in North and Central America, Asia, Latin America and Africa.

Another promising step in the direction of analysing intergenerational mobility in terms of multidimensional is the empirical research of Hufe and Peichl (2018), carried out using the Eu-Silc survey database (*Eu Statistics on Income and Living Conditions*) of 2011 (see Fig. 7.7).

The graph in Fig. 7.7 shows a sufficiently robust *cross-country* correlation: on the vertical axis appears the Gini index of interpersonal income inequality; on the horizontal axis the analysis carried out by the authors instead moves away from the mobility of income between generations of the Great Gatsby curve, because a multidimensional variable is introduced, which considers alongside income a series of non-income factors.[8] The

[7] Specifically, the Human Opportunity Index is used, which measures young people's access to basic services, adjusted for differences determined by circumstances.

[8] The functioning of the market and the type of political and economic institutions shape a multidimensional environment, determined by both economic and extra-economic factors.

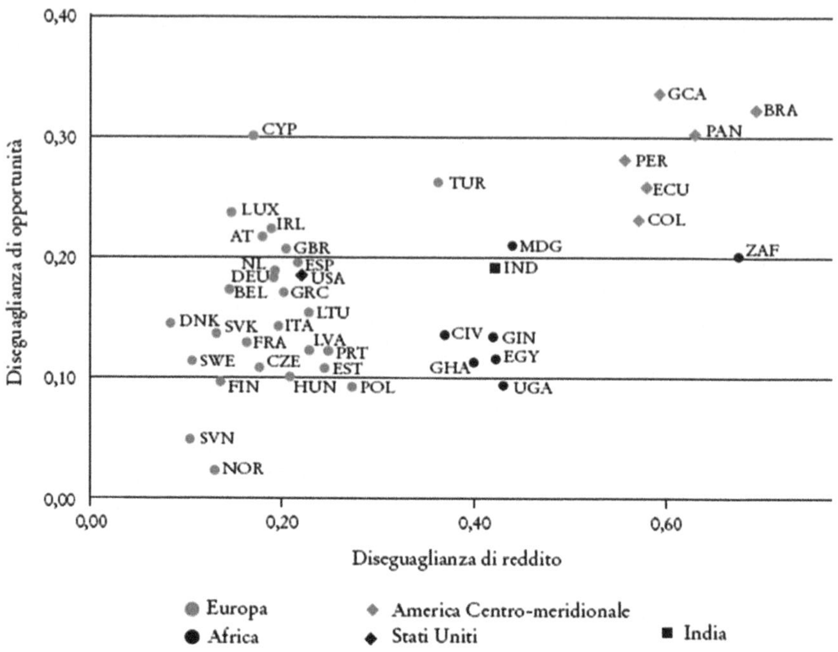

Fig. 7.6 Inequality of opportunity and income inequality. (Source: Brunori et al. (2013). Translation: Inequality of opportunity, Income inequality, Europe, Central-South America, Africa, United States, India)

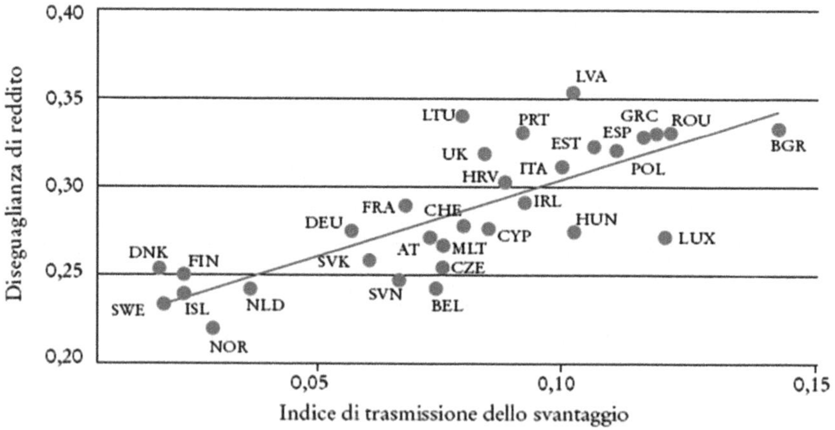

Fig. 7.7 Income inequality and "Disadvantage Transmission Index". (Source: Hufe and Peichl (2018). Translation: Income inequality, Disadvantage transmission index)

reductionist approach of considering income as the only determinant of the degree of "independence" of the position in society that children achieve compared to that of their parents is thus overcome: a composite index is constructed of the living conditions of the population aged 25 to 59 for 31 European countries, in which people are divided into various "types" of different socio-economic types through the processing of four alternative pairs of personal characteristics.[9]

The strategy consists in exploiting the multidimensional nature of well-being to analyse the different opportunities that the context of life makes available to people in acquiring the *capabilities* necessary to realise themselves. The *capabilities* depend on the income position of parents and their culture, from the care that parents have dedicated to their education, and from the socio-economic environment in which they were formed. The opportunities of individual people are measured by calculating their individual deviation from the average value of the category of belonging. The deviation represents the "advantage" or the "disadvantage" of each of them in the various dimensions of well-being. Following Roemer and Trannoy (2016), the inequality from well-being of individuals belonging to a "type" is determined based on factors for which they predominantly cannot be held responsible. This results in an "index of transmission of disadvantage" (Itd). In the graph, on the horizontal axis, the complement to one of such measure expresses the multidimensional nature of "non-equity in access" to well-being.

Let's give two possible examples of the mix of circumstances that go beyond individual responsibility. (1) A combination of "types" for which formal access to opportunities is not realised: a native *low-skilled* worker, due to his insufficient level of professional training, risks a strong vulnerability in the face of the evolution of technical progress towards automation. (2) An access to opportunities that is not followed by the acquisition of *capabilities*: a *high-skilled* migrant worker—let's say—from Sudan, who has been granted citizenship but is delayed a fundamental right to social

Consider, for example, how a good cultural background of the parents can counterbalance a low family income; or the "macroeconomic vulnerability", which in the event of a severe macroeconomic shock consists both in the standard of living close to poverty connected to a very low salary and the risk of becoming unemployed due to an insufficient level of *skill*.

[9] The four variations of personal characteristics are: belonging to the group of women or men, immigrants or natives, having parents who are less or more educated; being workers with high, medium or low *skills*. This leads to the number of 36 ($2 \times 2 \times 3 \times 3 = 36$) sets of combinations of "types" that isolate the heterogeneous "circumstances".

protection such as access to the NHS, in case he suffers from poor health risks falling into a condition of multidimensional deprivation. That the economic vulnerability of young natives is not adequately contested and that immigrants are discriminated against in the recognition of the right to Welfare are obstacles to the *empowerment*, in the first case, due to insufficient *capabilities*, in the second due to the absence of the recognition of the right to enjoy equal opportunities.

The estimate presented in Fig. 7.7 can be considered as an attempt to "endogenise" the inequality of opportunities, considering the "Index of transmission of disadvantage" a sort of multidimensional proxy of social immobility. Given the complexity of the issues involved in such a comparison between countries, the substitution of the Iee with the Itd allows only an impressionistic evaluation of how income inequality is correlated—through the mediation of this indicator of inequality of opportunities—with social mobility. The graph indicates that the more you proceed towards higher values of "multidimensional immobility", the greater is the income inequality. The results assign to the group of Nordic nations the palm of virtuous countries, for the social cohesion testified by a "low" income inequality, and for access to opportunities, measured by the Its.

The "social immobility" of Neet

There is a habit to designate young people *neither in employment nor in education and training* with the sterile acronym of Neet. As we know, the incentive to commit to earning an income plays an important role in human nature. Too often, however, the analyses of orthodox economists forget the long-term consequences of what happens *before the* market, the role of circumstances in people's destiny. The most direct statistical estimate of the importance of circumstances lies in identifying how early inequalities in education arise among young people. Through the verification of the understanding of a text, of mathematics and of the sciences, the Pisa indicator measures cognitive ability at the age of fifteen. At that age, in fact, the young person has not yet proven his commitment and developed his disposition to work, so in the valorisation of the genetic heritage the influence of the family and the social context is still dominant.[10] The statistical evidence released by the Oecd is very eloquent on the fact that

[10] The *Programme for International Student Assessment* (Pisa) is the Oecd project that studies the educational process of young people.

in many "rich" countries educational deficiencies affect young people with disadvantaged family and social conditions to a much greater extent (Oecd 2019a). The unequal circumstances that separate "disadvantaged" young people from "advantaged" young people have a heavy influence in blocking access to opportunities and therefore the emergence of talents. But this area of study is neglected by mainstream research. It is as if everything that is before entering the world of work, not concerning the market, should not be the concern of economics. For its part, sociology often proceeds by induction. Starting from the percentages contained in statistical surveys, interpretative categories are constructed in a descriptive and often purely nominalistic way, without investigating within the class structure of society.

The social immobility of young Neets therefore puts both disciplines to a hard test. This is not surprising, as the phenomenon is a failure that originates in the dual nature of mobility, which is both individual and social. The separation of Neets from the world of education and work—and therefore also from social life—is a case of social exclusion that arises within the structure of society and that has its presuppositions in the circumstances in which young people grow up, primarily in a disadvantaged family condition. This phenomenon is then typical of areas of economic deprivation, with high unemployment or a high rate of crime, from the outskirts of large cities (think of social distress in Paris and Marseille) to areas of old industrialisation where mining and steel companies have been dismantled (for example, in Germany), to regions where the State is almost absent (for example, some regions of Southern Italy). In these contexts, young people receive little encouragement to commit and lose the motivation to train and to find work. A young person may not be aware of his own talents—and try to bring them out—simply because the low level of human and social capital of the socio-family environment paves the way for the fall of individual aspirations. The abandonment of the path of education is often a decision taken perhaps in a completely rational way, but it cannot always be said to be a decision taken in a truly autonomous way.

Neets are a group that is not born "excluded" but becomes so. They are the young people who are left out of the progression of life after a part of those who seemed to encounter a difficulty in integrating into society has been "promoted" to a condition that has protected them from discomfort. These young people with problems have been more fortunate than others, either because they have a family behind them with the right social relations, thanks to which they have managed to have any job, or

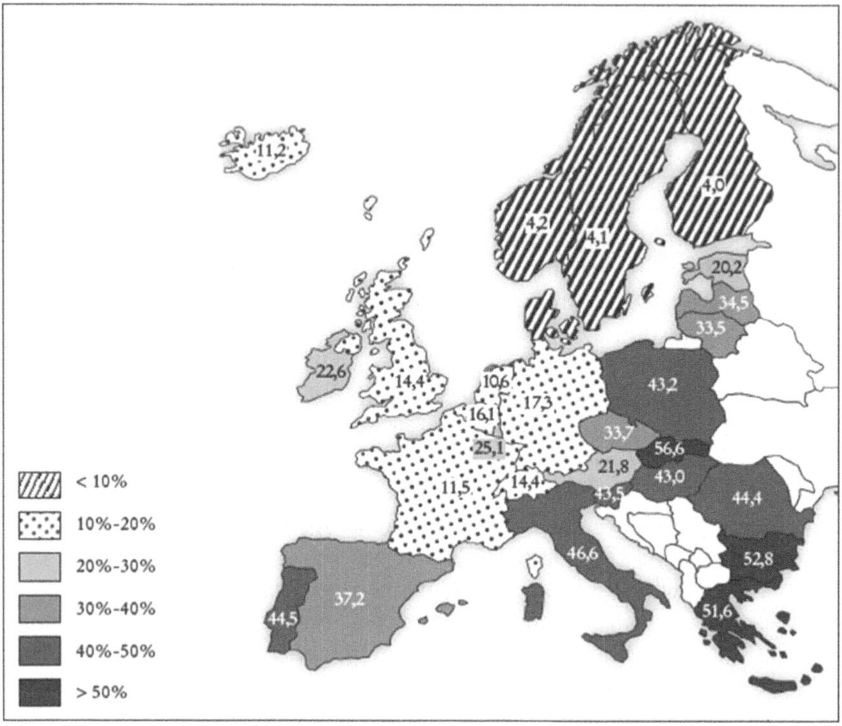

Fig. 7.8 Percentage of young people (25–34 years old) living with their parents. (Source: Eurostat, Office for National Statistics (United Kingdom))

because their parents have a cultural background to allow them not to succumb to depression and thus induce them to continue their educational path. Neets constitute a good percentage of young people aged 25 to 34 who still live with their family (Fig. 7.8). This category of young people often represents a sort of an atypical indicator of "social immobility", because it arises due to the poverty of the "social capital" of the area of residence, which has the effect of exacerbating depression and impoverishing the existence of young Neets, leading them to surrender in the face of difficulties.

A condition very similar to that of the Neets is also widespread in the lowest portion of the employed workforce, the precarious workers who are often *working poor* living in their parents' home. As was easy to expect, with the beginning of the new millennium, "for young people without tertiary education on average in Oecd countries, the probability of not being neither in education nor employed has increased, and so has the probability of being, if employed, in a low-skilled job" (Oecd 2019b, p. 65).[11] Sometimes it is the poor parents who oppose a psychological resistance to investing in their children's education. Or it often happens that the economic condition of the family pushes a young person to decide to interrupt early their educational path to look for a "little job". Those who do not have sufficient education, and decide to take on a temporary job, in fact give up the aspiration to social mobility, as they preclude the possibility of building, by continuing their studies, a satisfying life project. The difficult match *mismatch* between demand and supply is one of the main problems of the labour market. The phenomenon of youth unemployment is often interpreted as an effect of *overeducation*, the outcome of an excessive investment in education by some young people. An alternative interpretation is that the crisis of the link between market and society is reflected both in the demand and supply of labour. On the one hand, in a phase of low long-term growth, mass schooling may not reflect in a virtuous match between the characteristics of the demand for labour from companies and the programmes of secondary school and university courses. On the other hand, the labour supply of an increasing percentage of young people suffers from the shortcomings of the school in alleviating the cultural discomfort inherited from the "disadvantaged" family and social context. An important policy for combating the phenomenon of Neets is apprenticeship. This training opportunity is aimed at initiating young people into the labour market. The training programmes *vocational education and training* (Vet) should take care of professional insertion in industry and services through the teaching of *skills* related to digitalisation and automation.[12] This strategy to overcome the problems of young people who suffer from "disadvantaged" circumstances due to the family environment or the socio-economic

[11] Italy is among the top places in Europe, with 25% of young people between the ages of 15 and 34 who do not study, do not work, do not train. According to Eurostat data in 2022, they were 19% (1.6 million) between the ages of 15 and 29, compared to a European average of 11.7%.

[12] The main policy tool available to European Union countries is the *Youth Guarantee* project, which aims to better align training with labour demand also through apprenticeship and *vocational training* reforms.

context usually does not achieve satisfactory results: "among young people who have followed a *vocational* programme, rather than the general programmes of secondary school or non-university post-secondary, the Neet rates are higher" (Oecd 2023, p. 60).

Bibliography

Aghion, P. & Durlauf, S. N. (a cura di) 2014 Handbook of Economic Growth, *Elsevier, Amsterdam.*

Berman, Y. 2017 Understanding the Mechanical Relationship between Inequality and Intergenerational Mobility, *mimeo.*

Bouchard St-Amant, P.-A., Marceau, N., Garon, J-D. 2020 Uncovering Gatsby Curves, *Research Square.*

Brunori, P., Ferreira, F. H. G., Peragine, V. 2013 Inequality of Opportunity, Income Inequality, and Economic Mobility: Some International Comparisons, *in Paus 2013.*

Chetty, R. 2013 *Yes, Economics Is a Science*, in «New York Times», 13 ottobre.

Chetty, R. et al. 2014a Is the United States still a Land of Opportunity? Recent Trends in Intergenerational Mobility, *in «American Economic Review», CIV, 5, pp. 141–7.*

Chetty, R. et al. 2014b Where Is the Land of Opportunity? The Geography of Intergenerational Mobility in the United States, *in «Quarterly Journal of Economics», CXXIX, 4, pp. 1553–623.*

Chetty, R. et al. 2017 The Fading American Dream: Trends in Absolute Income Mobility since 1940, *in «Science», CCCLVI, 6336, pp. 398–406.*

Chetty, R. et al. 2018 The Opportunity Atlas: Mapping the Childhood Roots of Social Mobility, *Nber Working Paper 25147.*

Corak, M. 2013 Income Inequality, Equality of Opportunity and Intergenerational Mobility, *in «Journal of Economic Perspectives», XXVII, 3, pp. 79–102.*

Deaton, A. & Case, A. 2021 Deaths of Despair and the Future of Capitalism, *Princeton University Press, Princeton 2021.*

Dollar, D. & Kraay, A. 2002 *Growth Is Good for the Poor*, in «Journal of Economic Growth», VII, 3, pp. 195–225.

Gordon, R. J. 2018 Why Has Economic Growth Slowed When Innovation Appears to be Accelerating?, *Nber Working Paper n. 24554.*

Hufe, P. & Peichl, A. 2018 Inequality and Unfairness in Europe, *Cesifo Forum, XIX, 2, pp. 26–34.*

Isaacs, J. B. 2016 International Comparisons of Economic Mobility, *Brookings Institution, Washington DC.*

Jenkins, S. P. & Van Kerm, P. 2006 Trends in Income Inequality, Pro-poor Income Growth, and Income Mobility, *Oxford Economic Papers, LVIII, 3, pp. 531–48.*

Marginson, S. 2016 Global Stratification in Higher Education, *in S. Slaughter & B. Taylor (ed)*, Higher Education, Stratification and Workforce Development: Competitive Advantage in Europe, the Us and Canada, *Springer International Publishing, Switzerland.*

Marrero, G. A. & Rodríguez, J. G. 2013 *Inequality of Opportunity and Growth*, in «Journal of Development Economics», CIV, C, pp. 107–22.

Marrero, G. A., Palomino, G. C., Sicilia, G. 2022 Inequality of Opportunity in Educational Achievement in Western Europe: Contributors and Channels, *Ecineq Working Paper Series n. 612.*

McCloskey, D. 2019 Why Liberalism Works: How True Liberal Values Produce a Freer, More Equal, Prosperous World for All, *Yale University Press, Yale.*

Milanović, B. 2023 Visions of Inequality: From the French Revolution to the End of the Cold War, *Harvard University Press, Cambridge.*

Oecd 2018 A Broken Social Elevator? How to Promote Social Mobility, *Paris.*

Oecd 2019a Pisa 2018, *VI,* Are Students Ready to Thrive in an Interconnected World?, *Paris.*

Oecd 2019b Employment Outlook 2019: The Future of Work, *Paris.*

Oecd 2023 Education at a Glance, *Paris.*

Occorsio, E. & Scarpetta, S. 2022 Un mondo diviso. Come l'Occidente ha perso crescita e coesione sociale, *Laterza, Roma-Bari.*

Roemer, J. E. & Trannoy, A. 2016 *Equality of Opportunity: Theory and Measurement*, in «Journal of Economic Literature», LIV, 4, pp. 1288–332.

Schumpeter, J. (1912). The theory of economic development, Harvard University Press, Cambridge MA.

Sen, A. K. 1985 Commodities and Capabilities, *North-Holland, Amsterdam.*

Song, L. 2022 Examining the Relationship Between Intergenerational Upward Mobility and Inequality: Evidence from Panel Data, *in «Social Indicators Research», XVI, 1, pp. 1–27.*

Stiglitz, J. E. 2019 The End of Neoliberalism and the Rebirth of History, *Project Syndacate, 4 novembre.*

Van der Weide, R. & Milanović, B. 2018 Inequality Is Bad for Growth of the Poor (but Not for That of the Rich), *in «World Bank Economic Review», XXXII, 3, pp. 507–30.*

Van Reenen, J. 2020 Innovation Policies to Boost Productivity, *The Hamilton Project, CentrePiece.*

Voitchovsky, S. 2005 Does the Profile of Income Inequality Matter for Economic Growth? Distinguishing between the Effects of Inequality in Different Parts of the Income Distribution, *in «Journal of Economic Growth», X, 3, pp. 273–96.*

Wilkinson, R. & Pickett, K. 2009 The Spirit Level: Why Greater Equality Makes Societies Stronger, *Bloomsbury Press, New York.*

CHAPTER 8

Welfare Institutions and the Dynamics of Social Structure

The Multidimensionality of Inequality and Poverty

Since transactions of goods and services take place in currency, economic factors have a heavy weight in influencing social dynamics. In a famous quip, Groucho Marx observed that "in life there are many things more important than money, but to buy them you need to have bucks". Said in a more sober way, the level of income is "a fundamental means to important ends" (Anand and Sen 2000, p. 100). However, each person's identity is an archipelago composed of many selves. In his great poetic composition *Leaves of Grass*, the American poet Walt Whitman, with the famous line "I am large, I contain multitudes", wanted to translate his existential journey into verse. He considered the contradictions and complementarities that accompany the individual's participation, through income, in a plurality of life spaces. It is certainly no coincidence that Whitman placed the construction of the individual's identity in a relationship of continuity with nature and with the feeling of life that unites all men. The "multiple self" (Elster 1985) is the reflection of the social interaction in which the individual constructs his own well-being. On the one hand, income is the pre-condition for mobility; on the other hand, it is the socio-economic factors at work in society that diversify the opportunities for social mobility among people.

Amartya Sen (2000) has emphasised how well-being depends—in addition to income—on socio-cultural factors: "The income levels of the

F. Farina, *The Rise of Inequality and the Fall of Social Mobility*,
https://doi.org/10.1007/978-3-031-92843-7_8

population are important, because each level coincides with a certain possibility of purchasing goods and services and enjoying the corresponding standard of living. However, it often happens that the level of income is not an adequate indicator of important aspects such as the freedom to live a long life, the ability to avoid preventable diseases, the possibility of finding decent employment or living in a peaceful community free from crime" (Id. 2001, p. 74). This multiplicity of the dimensions of well-being also explains why people who achieve a similar economic result, and whose perception is that they belong to the same social class, have different opinions on "social justice" and on the *status* that society recognises them (Piketty 1995).

The Oecd invites us to reflect: "Economics and economic policy must correctly understand the sociality of human life [...]. People do not maximise individual utility as in the myth told by economic theory: they have multidimensional preferences and ethical values formed in social contexts and cultural" (OECD 2020, p. 30). This leads to two important implications. At an individual level, the *spillovers* that transmit an impulse from one dimension to another can accentuate inequality among people due to "circumstances" in the transition from market opportunities to the achievement of actual *capabilities* through the emergence of talents. At the collective level, "systemic interdependence" generates *spillovers* that transmit—and sometimes multiply, due to power asymmetry—inequality among people from one area of life to another. The concentration in the hands of the elites of the condition of "multidimensional advantage" (in income, health, education, housing, to name only the main dimensions) tilts the structure and dynamics of society in their favour. The impact of a crisis on individual multidimensional well-being must indeed be evaluated in light of both income distribution and wealth distribution (Renahy et al. 2018). Economic vulnerability is the typical example of the causal link between an individual's level of wealth and income. The decline in income during an economic crisis makes the risk of a fall in multidimensional well-being a much more serious event for the poor and low-income classes than it is for the rich (Foster and Sen 1997).

The rich have a wealth to draw on in case of economic shock. Wealth, as mentioned, is indeed a sort of *buffer stock*, a reserve of economic resources that can be made liquid in case of need. A low-income person, on the other hand, during a crisis that lowers—even if only temporarily—their earnings, perceives uncertainty about the future as severely penalising. Not having accumulated equity capital, their economic vulnerability is very high and is only partially mitigated by possible home ownership. There is therefore an explanation for the "tendency of people to prefer a steady flow of income, or a steadily growing flow, to one that oscillates continuously" (Shorrocks 1978, p. 392).

Let's then broaden our view from the economic analysis of social mobility to the multidimensional consideration of well-being. This will allow us to distance ourselves from an approach based solely on the aggregate sizes of the economy, where it seems that individuals are all equal, before, during and after their participation in the market. Let's imagine dividing a population of 100 individuals into five groups of equal size (20 subjects). Statistics call them quintiles. We arrange these groups in ascending order of income (the average income of the quintile) and name them as follows: the poor, the low-middle income subjects, the middle class, the high-middle income subjects, the rich. The income categories into which we have divided individuals are only a first approximation. The multidimensional analysis suggests—and empirical evidence confirms it—that inequality must be declined based on the multiple characteristics of the person. The heterogeneity among individuals must indeed be completed by the multiple articulation of identity, by the result of each individual in all dimensions (in addition to income, health, education, housing, environment and so on) involved in their social interaction. Amartya Sen conceived his theory of *capabilities* starting from the mutual influence between the various dimensions of well-being. It is through the amalgamation between income and other dimensions that the individuals acquire their *capabilities*. The intensity of poverty, for example, is not determined by the simple level of income, but by the overall deprivation that a person suffers: "handicaps such as age, or disability, or illness, reduce the ability to earn an income. But they also make it more difficult to convert income into capabilities, since an elderly person, or a person with more disabilities or with very serious illnesses needs more income [...] to achieve the functions (even when such achievement is perfectly possible)". A good condition of health and education allows to achieve greater skills and a better ability in work, which usually corresponds to a high income; likewise, conversely, a high level of income favours good health and good education. From the variety of components that form the multiple identity of the individual, an obvious, but very important, consequence follows. It is not at all said that the various rankings in which individuals are ordered, that of income and those of other dimensions, coincide. An equal income does not necessarily correspond to an equal level of well-being of people in other areas of life. "The size of the real inequalities of opportunity that people have to face cannot be immediately deduced from the extent of income inequality, since what people can or cannot do or obtain does not depend only on incomes but also on the variety of physical and social characteristics that influence our lives and make us what we are" (Id. 1992, p. 28). It can happen that people with an equal level of income find themselves in conditions of "advantage" or "disadvantage" multidimensional of different width.

Individuals are heterogeneous among themselves. The first factors that contribute to determining the multiple identity of people are gender and ethnicity. It is primarily for such personal characteristics that remuneration often varies even among workers who have equal *skills* and exert an equal work effort (Brunori et al. 2013). Subsequently, the phenomenon of *cross-correlation*, the mutual influence that develops between the various dimensions of individual well-being, contributes to the overall well-being outcome. This latter should be interpreted as a series of externalities that develop, between one dimension and another, as a result of the individual's participation in social interaction. The link between the various areas of life brings changes to the multidimensional well-being indicator due to *spillover* effects—of positive or negative sign—which are of different magnitude, in various life spaces, for different people. The statistical analysis conducted on the data from the *surveys* on people's multidimensional well-being clearly highlights the degree of complementarity that exists between the level of income and the other main dimensions: moving backwards from the last to the first income quintile (i.e., proceeding from the quintile of the rich to that of the poor) normally lower values are also found in the other two main dimensions of well-being, the degree of health and the level of education (Farina 2021, par. 10.11). The complementarity between these dimensions is strengthened if other factors that are associated with a fairly high income are taken into account: a satisfying job, a correct lifestyle, a balanced psychological condition favoured by a good level of education and so on. Therefore, the *cross-correlation* is an important reason to start from the analysis of income distribution, but without this dimension exhausting the analysis of multidimensional well-being (Renahy et al. 2018). The "disadvantaged" subjects with a low level of income (and wealth) tend to transmit their "economic disadvantage" from one dimension to another. "Inequality can be accentuated due to the association of income inequality and heterogeneous positions of" advantage "in converting income into *capabilities*. These two factors together have the effect of intensifying the problem of inequality in terms of opportunities and freedoms" (Sen 1993, p. 536). An empirical research, conducted on the data of the population of the European Union, shows that people who are part of the same group—who have earned an equal income in the market—often achieve different levels of overall well-being (Fusco et al. 2010).

The hypothesis of *cross-correlation*, of mutual influence between dimensions, with the effect of strengthening their impact on overall well-being, is also supported by calculations conducted on the Eu-Silc database. The results relating to the three main indicators of the well-being of people at high risk of socio-economic hardship (risk of poverty, living in a family whose members are unemployed, suffering from material deprivation) show that as many as two thirds of the subjects are "disadvantaged" in more than one dimension (Atkinson et al. 2010, p. 217). These three indicators, although certainly definable as socio-economic, have a strong relationship with income. However, due to the *cross-correlation* of income with the different dimensions, income-based membership in one of the social classes—the rich, the middle class and the poor—is transmitted to varying degrees from one dimension of well-being to another.

The extent to which the different characteristics of people, in the various dimensions of well-being, contribute to differentiating their overall well-being levels also depends on political and economic institutions. In countries where the welfare system is reduced and income redistribution is of limited extent, low-income classes also record low levels of health and education in a greater proportion than in countries with strong welfare institutions. Having to buy health and educational services in the market, a point reduction in income has a much greater impact on a poor person's levels of health and education. The higher the public offer in health and education compared to the market offer, the wider—due to the positive externalities that its use generates on the weaker classes—will be the "equalising" impact on their multidimensional well-being. Not having to buy such goods in the market from private schools and universities, and private hospitals, people can allocate the saved income to increase their level of well-being in all other dimensions.

The Role of Welfare in Economic Resilience

A comparison between the United States and Germany suggests that the different degree of resilience to economic vulnerability of advanced economies is attributable to welfare institutions. The two main sources of "economic vulnerability" —the amplitude and duration of cyclical fluctuations and uncertainty about future income flows (Jenkins 2011)—have a negative impact in particular on the upward mobility of "disadvantaged" subjects. Between 1984 and 1993, the expansion of GDP—on which absolute social mobility depends—was greater in the United States than in West Germany. In the nineties, the judgement that was given in the same Federal Republic of Germany on the economic growth was relentless: a "laggard economy", also burdened by the support to be given to businesses and the population of the East after reunification (Sinn 2003). How come German society subsequently demonstrated a resilience to "economic vulnerability" greater than that of the United States, despite the gap in "individual income mobility", or a lower growth rate in Germany compared to that of the United States? Jenkins and Van Kerm (2006) investigated the economic performance of the two countries during the eighties and nineties. Dividing the income distribution into sections, what were the changes? Both the United States and the western German Länder experienced in those two decades economic growth capable of reducing poverty. The increase in individual incomes in the group of the poor, approaching those of the middle class, favoured social ascent. In the groups of the middle and lower-middle income classes, however, earnings fell. So what was the overall impact of the income growth of these groups on social mobility? A paradox arose: from the reduction of poverty sprang an increase in the Gini index of income inequality. The paradox has an easy explanation. The rise in income that allowed many poor people to leave the first quintile, and move to the second or third, was of lesser magnitude than the re-ranking of income downwards of layers of the middle and lower-middle income classes that slipped to lower levels. Therefore, in both countries, due to the decline in income of individuals who until then had belonged to the third or second quintile and now descended towards the first, the outcome of the so-called pro-poor effect of growth was an increase in inequality. From the second half of the nineties, the events of the two countries diverged. In Germany, the re-ranking downwards ended, so the increase in income inequality stopped. Moreover, individuals with middle-low income who had fallen among the poor rose to higher income levels. On the contrary, the resumption of GDP growth saw in the United States part of the "new" poor remain "trapped" in the lowest section of the distribution. Given the persistence at a low level of the wages of unskilled workers, the phenomenon of the working poor lowered the level of average income of the first two deciles. The initial re-ranking of the poor upwards was therefore followed by the return below the poverty threshold of Americans who—thanks to the absolute mobility favoured by growth—had initially experienced relative upward mobility, escaping from poverty. Therefore, considering the entire period, income inequality remained essentially unchanged in Germany, while it steadily increased in the United States. Why, unlike what happened in Germany, despite the good performance of GDP, did the sliding towards low levels of the earnings of the poor and the middle-lower classes become long-term in the United States? The explanation seems to be found in the greater support that Welfare gives to German workers. In other words, the welfare state mitigated the impact of the "economic vulnerability" suffered particularly by the weaker classes, blocking their social mobility downwards. The welfare state, it was said in Chap. 6 citing Schumpeter, provides the brakes that allow for safe running. As shown by the persistence at higher levels of income of the poor who rose to the second decile, and the return to previous income levels by the middle-lower classes, the "economic vulnerability" of the weaker social strata was better countered in Germany. Despite the growth rates being on average lower than those of the United States, the weaker classes showed greater resilience. In the United States, as welfare benefits are not high, for the poor and for middle-low income individuals, the "resilience" to a shock was much lower than in Germany. A characteristic of the American labour market is the fluidity that accompanies its deregulated operation. Workers continue to rise or fall each year in the income scale in much greater numbers than in Germany. Relative mobility, the reshuffling in income positions, is therefore very pronounced. Individuals who at the initial year of an economic crisis are included in the bottom 25% of the income distribution remain in that position in a smaller percentage in the United States than in Germany. Simplifying, in the absence of labour market regulation, within that 25%, the working poor become unemployed, or the unemployed become working poor. What does the paradox of pro-poor growth leading to an increase in income inequality teach us? It is a signal that the methodological perspective of economic analysis needs to be changed. The study of social mobility should not be approached by looking only at the aggregate data of GDP growth, or absolute mobility. Social mobility has a lot to do with relative mobility because it depends on how GDP growth is distributed among social classes. Moreover, income to take into consideration is what is available, that is, the measure of income after the operation of Welfare institutions. Despite the deregulation of the labour market in the early nineties favouring an increase in income inequality in Germany, the characteristics of German Welfare, particularly the orientation of social insurance towards the socialisation of risks, favour in the long term a certain stickiness of subjects even at the centre of the income distribution in their positions of multidimensional well-being. In other words: if, in addition to helping the poor, the welfare state intervenes in the dynamics of GDP to prevent the middle class from becoming impoverished, it is better.

To recap. After the reshuffling of income positions in the short and medium term during a crisis, in Germany there is a return to income inequality—and to the social structure—prevailing *ex ante*. Once the reshuffling effect—the relative mobility in the deciles of the middle class and the poor—has subsided, economic growth resumes driving *absolute* mobility. We can therefore add a further postscript to our critical assessment of the thesis of Dollar and Kraay (2002). (1) Certainly, growth "does good to the poor". (2) Income inequality, however, can extinguish the social mobility of the weaker classes. (3) However, if a robust welfare system intervenes, the poor will probably be able to overcome the economic vulnerability to which income inequality has exposed them.

The arrival in continental Europe of the long wave of neoliberalism, of whose policies the two great Anglo-Saxon nations have been the *front-runners*, has changed things. Another study shows that in the last two decades the German welfare state has abdicated its "equalising" function. Income inequality has been increasing in Germany not only *in* the market, due to temporary contracts, but also in the measure of the Gini index *ex post* in relation to market functioning, i.e. even after the correction made by redistributive welfare (Bönke et al. 2015). It is not only individual income growth, the progression over time from a person's first salary to earnings in mature age, that has shown a slowdown. The cohorts of German workers who have succeeded each other around the turn of the new millennium have not increased their earnings uniformly from the beginning to the end of their working life. Only the *baby-boomers* born after the end of the Second World War have experienced an increasing income trend, while for those born in the early sixties, belonging to families at the bottom of the income distribution, a decline in opportunities has begun.

The gap between the incomes of members of the working classes and those of the owners of capital has progressively increased. The empirical verification of Bönke et al. (2015) should be read in the light of Jenkins' concepts. The study indeed documents that the "positional income mobility" upwards has been scarce also because within social stratification the problem of "economic vulnerability" has emerged: the more frequent fluctuations of GDP have led to a very discontinuous income trend for the most "weak" subjects. For these workers, even for different circumstances, such as the professional qualification they have been able to achieve, the "equal conditions in the course of individual income growth" have not materialised.

Looking at the dispersion of earnings from the point of view of individual income paths over time—that is, looking at the intra-personal indicator from which "positional income mobility" derives—is undoubtedly an enlightening method for understanding the evolution of individual well-being. Contrary to Milton Friedman's belief, however, this intrapersonal measure makes the analysis of how interpersonal income inequality has evolved anything but irrelevant. Personal income variation paths often differ over time, as they involve the distribution among social classes of GDP growth. As already observed, a negative macroeconomic shock, or a negative trend in absolute mobility, has a different outcome on the relative mobility of subjects belonging to different social groups. The impact of the shock on "positional income mobility" is different for two subjects who are in two different job positions—for example, a *high-skilled* job and another *low-skilled*. In the overall distribution among social classes of GDP growth, in fact, the income drop that workers suffer following the shock is of very different magnitude. Unlike what happened with late twentieth-century welfare, once a *low-skilled* worker's income has fallen below his or her path, the income drop often tends to persist over time. If the "conditions in the course of individual income growth" are not equal among social groups, the "risk relative to future income" is also different. The different trend of "individual income growth"—absolute mobility—however, does not only influence *relative* mobility between one entire generation and the next. A different placement among workers in the *skill* scale reverberates—through the level of income and family well-being—on the opportunities of the new generation. The intergenerational mobility "disaggregated" of workers *low-skilled* is significantly weakened.

The research by Bönke et al. (2015) shows that a large intensity shock affects the relative "disaggregated" mobility of the two fundamental classes of the economic structure differently. The income gap between members of the working classes and the owners of capital has indeed widened. The message regarding the resilience of a country to a shock is that simply combating poverty is not enough to protect the weak classes from "social exclusion". The transfer of knowledge into profit-oriented technologies is taking place, after the advent of automation, in a context of corporate structure that is quite different in Germany and the United States. Germany of the last decades has experienced the partial dismantling of the defence of workers in the market, and of redistribution after the market. Despite this, a *corporate governance* inspired by German culture aimed at preserving the stability of the social structure has allowed the defence of employment levels within the factory. "In the automotive industry, the number of workers has grown between 2000 and 2018. [...] This increase was accompanied by the increase in the share of" blue collars "and specialised work tasks [...]. In the United States, where automotive production has followed a similar trajectory to that of Germany, employment has decreased by about 25%, without an increase in professional qualification" (Acemoglu and Johnson 2023, p. 286).

Corporate systems "are able to counteract the increase in earnings instability associated with active labour market policies through the degree of unionisation of the workforce, the regulation of the product market and the tax wedge" (Sologon and O'Donoghue 2014). A fundamental contribution to the sustainability of the German corporate model is also given by public policies. A pillar of the German vision of the welfare state is the implementation of risk protection based on the principle of "actuarial fairness": that is, the contribution to the functioning of welfare institutions should be as close as possible to the probabilistic exposure to risk of individuals, so as not to generate income redistribution (for example, regarding public health, from high-income and low-risk individuals to those with low income and high risk). The legal apparatus on which German welfare is based is also inspired by respect for intergenerational equity, "the balance of contributions and benefits linked to welfare for each preceding and succeeding cohort" (Hinrichs 1993, p. 23).

In the "New York Times" of 13 September 1970, Milton Friedman wrote that "there is one and only one social responsibility of business, to use its resources in activities aimed at increasing profits". The dominant neoliberal thought has embraced his vision: it is necessary to give free rein to companies, avoiding state interference in market rules and limiting welfare to a "safety net" for the poor. The reality of the deregulated economy of the United States is instead that assistance to the *worst-off* with the aim of reducing poverty not only does not produce a decrease in income inequality but does not even stably reduce poverty (Rohde et al. 2020). When we disaggregate the evolution of income inequality by social groups, the evolution of individual incomes also appears differently from the vision of the neo-liberistic economist.

Milton Friedman believed that for two people whose *patterns* of intertemporal income present an equal "present value" (the value of income regardless of when it was received), the *intra-personal* income flows can only be similar (see *supra*, Chap. 2, par. 4). Friedman's idea is that there will be a convergence upwards of the intertemporal income paths of two subjects. This idea does not hold once—instead of examining the evolution of aggregate GDP—we evaluate how the different exposure to economic vulnerability clearly separates the income paths between social classes. The divergence of the paths of the two fundamental classes is also reflected in heterogeneity of intergenerational income mobility. Compared to the beginning of their working career, German workers have indeed had an 85% higher probability than their fathers of experiencing an increase in intra-personal income inequality, a departure from the linear trend of the earnings path that in the percentage between 20% and 40% is explained by the increase in periods of unemployment. The slowdown in the progression over time of individual incomes (from the first to the last salary) has then reverberated from one generation to another, with greater persistence of children in their parents' income positions. The study by Bönke et al. (2015) thus arrives at a result opposite to Friedman's thesis: the statistical data regarding the intra-personal and the inter-personal inequality are both necessary in order evaluate social mobility. Workers have not increased their earnings uniformly from the beginning to the end of their working life (absolute mobility); nor do they seem to have experienced in significant numbers an "upward positional mobility" (relative mobility). The message of the empirical evidence is clear. In the absence of welfare policies, reducing poverty increases inequality and blocks social mobility. The two objectives of fighting poverty and fighting inequality are inseparable.

In conclusion. The propellant that drives social mobility is economic growth; but social mobility is strongly impacted by inequalities on one hand and the welfare state on the other. The next step in the study of social mobility through disaggregated analysis for social classes involves expanding the processing of individual results from income level alone to results in other dimensions. The "disadvantage transmission index" constructed by Hufe and Peichl (2018) encompasses conditions of discomfort in multiple dimensions that add to low income in limiting opportunities.

This indicator of equity conditions in access to opportunities is a good measure of "unfair inequality", as it represents a multidimensional estimate of the penalty suffered by members of "disadvantaged" social classes in their aspiration to upward social mobility.

Reduction of Poverty and Increase in Income Inequality

Natura non facit saltus. Sustained growth is good for *social mobility*, but if it is accompanied by high income inequality, a minority benefits. If, as has happened in advanced countries in recent decades, dispersion in the last quintile increases upwards, by definition it is the mobility *relative* of the super-rich that increases. If then, as is also happening, the middle classes suffer a contraction of jobs and earnings, the phenomenon of polarisation arises. On the other hand, since *social cohesion* depends on balanced economic growth among social classes, the increase in income inequality causes its weakening. Families at the bottom of the income distribution suffer and the consequent worsening of the well-being of disadvantaged young people has the effect of slowing down intergenerational *relative* mobility upwards. What indications can be drawn regarding the dilemma "fight against poverty or against income inequality"? What should be the priority objective of the welfare system?

Between income growth and the well-being of the poor there is an important *medium*—an inescapable linking factor: inequality of opportunity. We have defined it as the "hidden variable" of the Great Gatsby curve. Alongside income growth, a more equitable distribution among all members of the community favours the decline in inequality of opportunities, which in turn paves the way for growth. Recent IMF research finds a positive correlation in advanced countries between low income inequality and greater GDP dynamics. It hypothesises that economic growth is favoured by the lesser inequality of opportunity that accompanies a not too unequal distribution (Dabla-Norris et al. 2015). It can also be added that intergenerational social mobility is reduced by income inequality to a greater extent in the portion of the distribution occupied by the poor than in that of the rich. The reason is immediately intuitive. "Disadvantaged" young people need both robust GDP growth and an interpersonal income distribution in which their families' incomes can approach middle-class income levels, in order to have more opportunities.

That opportunities are the crux of the matter should not surprise. Low inequality of opportunity is indeed at the convergence between individual success in earnings—the individualistic aspect of mobility—and the equal ability for all to exploit their talents—the collective aspect of mobility. A recent study by García and Heckman (2022) shows the importance of directing public support towards disadvantaged families. *Bolsa Familia*, the world's largest public policy for the inclusion of disadvantaged families, is more than a hint, it is proof of the thesis supported in this volume: the goal of achieving a society in which collective well-being and social cohesion are promoted must have as its first stage a plan of direct funding to reduce the handicap that "disadvantaged" young people suffer due to the unfortunate circumstances in which their parents find themselves. In progressive Brazil of the first decade of the millennium, this economic support programme (conditional on assigning parents the responsibility of respecting the obligation of attendance of their children), managed to reduce income inequality by a significant measure between 16% and 21% (Soares 2012).

In recent decades, the attention of the governments of advanced countries has shifted from the objective of reducing income inequality—which by definition involves individuals belonging to all social classes—to that of reducing the number of poor people and the intensity of poverty (the distance of the standard of living of the poor from the poverty threshold). As argued above, the vaguely populist title of Dollar and Kraay's (2002) work—"the Growth is good for the poor"—this is only partially true. For an inequality indicator based on the income gap between the middle class and the poor—the interdecile ratio (50/10), the fraction between the average income of the middle class decile and the average income of the poor decile—to start falling, the income growth of the poor must be faster than that of the middle classes. The comparison between the United States and Germany has highlighted how the evolution of the two social groups is strongly intertwined. A welfare system more oriented towards combating "disadvantageous circumstances", in facilitating income growth in the poor decile, should put a brake on the tendency of growth to expose the middle class to economic vulnerability, with the result of increasing income inequality.

This approach, which aims to combine the fight against poverty and the containment of inequality, is now at risk of becoming obsolete. Complicating the national and international socio-economic picture has been the recent acceleration of migratory flows, the long wave of globalisation. Many thousands of dispossessed people continually flee from wars, persecutions and lands undergoing desertification, seeking refuge in rich countries. The exodus from inhospitable countries finds the peoples of the

West—including those of the Nordic countries, where social norms of solidarity have long been rooted—completely unprepared for the "inclusion" of people foreign to their own community. The arrival of migrants has generated a feeling of distrust towards all "social inclusion" policies. An increasingly large portion of European public opinion opposes migrants—and imposes on governments—the policy of "social exclusion", in order to defend their own share of welfare. The inhabitants of advanced countries lack solidarity for the "stranger" because they themselves have now lost the ability to perceive the emancipatory value of feeling part of a common destiny (Bauman 2016). On the level of civil coexistence between human beings, it should make no difference to belong to a country at an "advanced" level of development, or to a country afflicted by misery. As has been observed, the loss of identity is indeed affecting societies of every ethnicity and culture: "Is not planetary exile perhaps an effect of globalisation that has affected everyone?" (Id. 2010, p. 259). The concept of emigration must be handled with care, because it is something much more complex than simple territorial mobility. The exodus from their own country of thousands of patriots, after the repression of the revolution of 1830, is remembered in the history of Poland as the "Great Emigration": "The homeland became for them the country from which they *have come*" (italics in the text) (Baczko 1981, p. 897). If upon their arrival the ports were open and they were welcomed, the migrants coming from the countries of the southern Mediterranean coasts, Saharan Africa or the Middle East would utter the same words of hybridisation of their own culture with that of the arrival countries.

The complexity that *heterogeneity* of people and *interdependence* among people create within the social structure—from diversity in working conditions to inequalities—suggests that focusing only on economic growth as the sole driver of social mobility is simply wrong. Growth helps "disadvantaged" people climb income positions only if the greater gain is combined with the opportunity to achieve good results also in other dimensions of well-being. It is far from certain that absolute mobility leads to a reduction in relative poverty. The "rising tide", the increase in income in which the level of all boats rises, is not enough. There are many conditions for a process of convergence of the poor towards the average income within the income distribution to be established.

In addition to growth, it is necessary that the social interaction of the poor is not hindered by the negative effects that often derive from a strong interdependence between the dimensions of well-being. As already observed, the poor suffer from the negative impact of high income inequality on their performance *before* the market and *in* the market, and from access to welfare benefits *after* the market. The thesis that "growth is good for the poor" (Dollar and Kraay 2002) is often disproved. The phenomenon of the *working poor*, born in the United States, and now widespread also in Europe, is not a product of low growth but of a long-term increase in inequality induced by the absence of corrections to the functioning of the market. The governments of advanced countries are however adopting the theory of *trickle-down*, the idea that social mobility is identifiable with the ability of growth to allow the "exit from poverty". It would be enough to leave the market free to function. Neoliberalism has succeeded in getting the message across that as soon as wage moderation by workers and the liberation of capitalists from progressive taxation will allow growth to strengthen, well-being will increase "trickling down" from the rich to the middle class, to the poor.

This idea is like the snake that eats its tail. The "trickle-down" does not occur by giving more space to market forces and shrinking the Welfare State, as the market and the Welfare State are complementary institutions. Pairing the Welfare State with market forces lowers the "degree of risk" of economic activity, and therefore plays a fundamental role in facilitating the restoration of social mobility (Sinn 1995, 1996). Lowering wages and downsizing the Welfare State are not favourable conditions for long-term economic growth. On the contrary, they are policies that stifle growth, because they generate an increase in income inequality linked to the lowering of wages for less skilled workers. The dominance of neoliberalism in the media has ensured that in public discourse what was common sense up to forty years ago has been erased: the close dependence of upward social mobility on the reduction of wealth and income inequality. The common belief is that we live in a world of "free and equal" where social ascent is a realistic ambition for everyone. Perhaps there is an explanation for the fact that merit is so fashionable today. A megaphone is needed to announce that the equalisation ensured in many dimensions by Welfare institutions hinders the individual's desire to stand out. As the neoliberal information of the whole advanced world states, "the Welfare State is not the solution but the problem". "Merit" is the euphemistic term used in an attempt to convince the "disadvantaged" that their level of well-being depends exclusively on their will. They must therefore take responsibility for it (Box 8.1).

Box 8.1 Why do low-income people today vote against the Welfare State?

In Box 6.1, it was explained using the Mvt why low-income people should vote in favour of the Welfare State. This analysis of voting orientation was empirically confirmed in advanced countries, up to about the nineties, in the majority vote in favour of income redistribution at the opening of the polls. A fall in the median voter's income compared to the average income generated a wider majority vote in favour of redistribution. As explained in Box 6.1, for the majority of the population (and therefore, approximately, of the electorate), i.e. for those with incomes between the poorest and the median income voter, the balance between Welfare benefits and taxes was positive. The political pressure expressed at the polls led to more substantial Welfare programmes and therefore Welfare benefits of a greater amount than the taxes paid. What is the reason for the disappearance at the polls of the "rational choice" in favour of the expansion of Welfare? Statistical data show that voters who would benefit from a wide redistribution are still a majority. Is the downsizing of the Welfare State then attributable to cultural factors? What is certain, as we will now see, is that the axioms of the Mvt are no longer valid today, they no longer reflect reality. Referring to what was said in Box 6.1, let's try to understand why the evolution of social reality has moved voting behaviour away from the assumptions on which the Mvt is based.

(1) *Single-peakedness.* The characteristic of *single-peakedness* of voting expression has fallen. Voters' behaviour no longer reflects a monotonically decreasing preference order guided by ideological affiliation: voting to the left, centre and right no longer corresponds to the preference for an electoral programme that proposes, respectively, a large, medium or small Welfare State. The voter seems to violate this *continuum* in the ordering of preferences on which the Mvt is based. The trend, typically reflected by the "constellation of ideas" of populist movements, is to prefer the extremes and place first and second (or vice versa) the vote in favour of the political proposal of the left or the right, usually placing the centre of the political spectrum last (which is often identified with a political class that has built a system of power, and sometimes also of corruption, to stay in power permanently). (2) *Monothematicity.* The electorate

(*continued*)

Box 8.1 (continued)
does not vote today in accordance with the condition of monothematicity of the political offer. The space of voting preference is multidimensional; and the glue of ideology that allowed it to be considered one-dimensional is greatly downsized in the new political framework. Populist movements, in particular, submit to voters political programmes within which themes and positions belonging to even opposing ideological areas coexist. Populists are for example against austerity, as a factor of propagation of inequalities (a left-wing position), but often at the same time they are against the freedom of movement of people (established, within the European Union, by the Schengen Treaty), as they are against enacting a legislation that guarantees the reception of migrants (a right-wing position). On the other hand, the political demand formulated with the ballot deposited in the ballot box is multidimensional because the vote is expressed by a subject *multiple self*. The vote reflects not only the income level of the voter but also his values. In recent decades, a series of "fault lines" have opened up in the cultural values of the parties representing the middle class. As has been observed, "globalisation and the expansion of education have given rise to new dimensions of inequality and conflict" (Piketty 2018, p. 57). As stated in the text (Chap. 5, par. 5), the majority of left-wing voters are no longer the poor and the middle class as much as the educated middle and upper classes (Piketty calls them the "Brahmins"). (3) *Unanimity*. Voter turnout is not very high in the United States and now also in European countries. The disillusionment in the prospects of improving one's economic condition, especially among the poor, has decade by decade increased the disaffection towards the right to vote, to the point of questioning the democratic representativeness of legislative assemblies and governments. Abstention produces the serious effect of distorting the outcome of the vote: the non-vote does not distribute normally (it does not reduce in the same proportion the votes of all parties) but is more present among low-income voters, who were traditionally oriented to vote left.

In the text, the analysis of sovereignty and the *pensée unique* (Chap. 5, par. 6) tries to explain the deep cultural change reflected by the vote against the welfare state.

Governments have been deprived of much of their ability to influence economic events. The most politically significant decisions are now made by powers—large companies, international finance and in Europe possibly supra-national institutions—that have nothing to do with the democratic process that takes place in national political institutions. The underlying invitation to today's public discourse is to nurture trust in the *pensée unique*, to share the narrative that is proposed by the media controlled by the ruling classes on each issue. Hence, the *pro-rich bias*, the favourable prejudice enjoyed by the opinions of the rich and powerful. Herbert Marcuse (1964), a supporter in 1968 of the movements that associated the expansion of individual freedom with the recognition of civil and social rights, described the tendency of capitalist society towards totalitarianism with the image of a "one-dimensional universe of thought" that deprives of legitimacy any opinion not placeable within the ideology of conservation.

The political class is today weakly legitimated by the democratic vote. In most Western countries, the representatives of the groups that compete in institutions are brought to power by the preferences expressed in the polls by a fluctuating electorate and almost halved by abstentionism. Political institutions, which once were the seats of democratic representation of political parties, are teeming with small and large interest groups and do not prove capable of formulating a coherent collective choice.

The crisis of democracy cannot surprise. More than sixty years ago, a leading American political scientist questioned the resilience of democracy by asking the following question: "in a political system where virtually every adult can vote, but where information, wealth, social position, proximity to administrators and other things are distributed unevenly, who actually governs?" (Dahl 1961, p. 45). The *impasse* of social mobility reflects a society in which the right to work and to a decent income proves fictitious. One of the reasons is that governments formed by political parties are almost powerless in the face of the independence now gained by companies from any form of governance of market economies. The social discomfort suffered by the poor and the weakest classes extends to involve the middle class. The space in which the free choice of the individual who does not belong to the elite, who does not enjoy power in the market and in society, is made up of rights that struggle to translate into opportunities.

Until the eighties, the "social body" was held together by the adherence of various social groups—although they were among themselves opposed—to a common goal: development, and with it well-being. The main glues were the function performed in the economy and the place of their members within social stratification.

With the advent of neoliberalism, the characteristics of social mobility have progressively changed. As mentioned, the closing of the phase of powerful growth of the thirty years 1945–1974 opened fractures in the social fabric.

With the reduction of union pressure on companies, the competition in the negotiation on working conditions and on wages has seen a decrease in social conflict. The command of entrepreneurs has thus stiffened and workers have shown a substantial acceptance of the dependence of wages on the orientation of technological progress, and therefore also of the decreasing remuneration of low-*skill* workers and the lesser protection of job security. In the voting competition in Europe, the alternation between governments formed by parties or coalitions of centre-right and centre-left has been weakened by the constraints imposed by globalisation (and the European Union) on national policies. It is difficult to escape the impression that there is a cause and effect relationship between the hegemony acquired by business and finance in the advanced world and the narrowing of the powers of intervention of national political institutions in economic affairs. The ground of political conflict has been transferred from the national level to the European one. The European Commission is constantly seeking an *appeasement* with the powers, hardly contestable, of multinationals and international finance. Instead of the traditional confrontation at the national level between monetarist policies favourable to capital and Keynesian policies favourable to labour, we now have the transition to the *pensée unique* of austerity as the only economic policy of global capitalism. National governments, engaged in the search for compatibility of national economic objectives with the choices of the European supranational institutions, are forced into continuous negotiation amongst themselves. In turn, these supranational European institutions are obliged to reach an agreement with the higher level of economic—and consequently political—decision-making: the global capitalism of multinationals and finance. In this scenario, where low and discontinuous growth hampers absolute social mobility, social conflict has been subdued and as a result, relative social mobility has also suffered a slowdown.

Bibliography

Acemoglu, D. & Johnson, S. 2023 Power and Progress: Our Thousand-Year Struggle Over Technology and Prosperity, *Public Affairs, New York.*

Anand, S. & Sen, A. K. 2000 *The Income Component of the Human Development Index*, in «Journal of Human Development», I, 1, pp. 83–106.

Atkinson, A. B., Marlier, E., Monatigne, F., Reinstadler, A. 2010 Income Poverty and Income Inequality, *in Atkinson - Marlier 2010.*

Baczko, B. 1981 *Utopia*, in *Encyclopedia*, Einaudi, Torino, XIV, *ad vocem.*

Bauman, Z. 2010 *Modernità e ambivalenza*, Bollati Boringhieri, Torino.

Bauman, Z. 2016 *Strangers at Our Door*, John Wiley et Sons, Hoboken 2016.

Bönke, T., Giesecke, M., Lüthen, H. 2015 The Dynamics of Earnings in Germany: Evidence from Social Security Records, *Diw Berlin, Discussion Papers n. 1514.*

Brunori, P., Ferreira, F. H. G., Peragine, V. 2013 Inequality of Opportunity, Income Inequality, and Economic Mobility: Some International Comparisons, *in Paus 2013.*

Dabla-Norris, E. et al. 2015 Cause and Consequences of Income Inequality: A Global Perspective, *Imf, Staff Discussion Note 13.*

Dahl, R. A. 1961 Who Governs? Democracy and Power in an American City, *Yale University Press, New Haven.*

Dollar, D. & Kraay, A. 2002 *Growth Is Good for the Poor*, in «Journal of Economic Growth», VII, 3, pp. 195–225.

Elster, J. 1985 *The Multiple Self*, Cambridge University Press, Cambridge.

Farina, F. 2021 Lo Stato sociale. Storia, politica, economia, *Luiss University Press, Roma.*

Foster, J. E. & Sen, A. K. 1997 On Economic Inequality after a Quarter Century, *in Sen 1997.*

Fusco, A., Guio, A.-C., Marlier, E. 2010 Characterising the Income Poor and the Materially Deprived in European Countries, *in Atkinson - Marlier 2010.*

García, J. L. & Heckman, J. J. 2022 Parenting Promotes Social Mobility Within and Across Generations, *Nber Working Paper n. 30610.*

Hinrichs, K. 1993 Public Pensions and Demographic Change: Generational Equity in the United States and Germany, *University of Bremen Zes Arbeitpapier n. 16/93.*

Hufe, P. & Peichl, A. 2018 Inequality and Unfairness in Europe, *Cesifo Forum, XIX, 2, pp. 26–34.*

Jenkins, S. P. 2011 Changing Fortunes: Income Mobility and Poverty Dynamics in Britain, *Oxford University Press, Oxford.*

Jenkins, S. P. & Van Kerm, P. 2006 Trends in Income Inequality, Pro-poor Income Growth, and Income Mobility, *Oxford Economic Papers, LVIII, 3, pp. 531–48.*

Oecd 2020 Beyond Growth. Towards a New Economic Approach, *Paris.*

Piketty, T. 1995 *Social Mobility and Redistributive Politics*, in «Quarterly Journal of Economics», CX, 3, pp. 551–84.

Piketty, T. 2018 Brahmin Left vs Merchant Right: Rising Inequality & the Changing Structure of Political Conflict: Evidence from France, Britain and the Us, 1948–2017, *Wid.world Working Paper Series n. 7.*

Renahy, E. et al. 2018 Connections between Unemployment Insurance, Poverty and Health: A Systematic Review, *in «European Journal of Public Health», XXVIII, 2, pp. 269–75.*

Rohde, N. et al. 2020 Welfare-Based Income Insecurity in the US and Germany: Evidence from Harmonized Panel Data, *in «Journal of Economic Behavior and Organization», CLXXVI, pp. 226–43.*

Sen, A. K. 1992 *Inequality Reexamined*, Clarendon Press, Oxford.

Sen, A. K. 1993 Markets and Freedoms: Achievements and Limitations of the Market Mechanism in Promoting Individual Freedoms, *in «Oxford Economic Papers», XLV, 4, pp. 519–41.*

Sen, A. K. 2000 *Merit and Justice*, in Arrow, Bowles, Durlauf.

Sen, A. K. 2001 *Development as Freedom*, Oxford University Press, Oxford 1999.

Shorrocks, A. F. 1978 *Income Inequality and Income Mobility*, in «Journal of Economic Theory», XIX, pp. 376–93.

Sinn, H.-W. 1995 *A Theory of the Welfare State*, in «Scandinavian Journal of Economics», XCVII, 4, pp. 495–526.

Sinn, H.-W. 1996 *Social Insurance, Incentives, and Risk Taking*, in «International Tax and Public Finance», III, 3, pp. 259–80.

Sinn, H.-W. 2003 Can Germany Be Saved? The Malaise of the World's First Welfare State, *Mit Press, Cambridge.*

Soares, S. S. D. 2012 *Bolsa Famìlia, Its Design, Its Impacts and Possibilities for the Future*, International Policy Centre for Inclusive Growth, Working Paper n. 89.

Sologon, D. M. & O'Donoghue, C. 2014 Shaping Earnings Insecurity: Labour Market Policy and Institutional Factors, *in «Review of Income and Wealth», LX, pp. S205–S232.*

CHAPTER 9

Global Social Mobility

The Expanding Global Middle Class

Globalisation is the new canon, the paradigm that has become the interpretative framework of the world. The absolute and relative mobility that is activated in various advanced countries must be examined in the light of global inequality. It is the glaring wealth gaps, which have widened with globalisation in Africa, Asia and Latin America, that, along with the ethnic conflicts and wars that have multiplied in the new century, drive population mobility towards the geographical areas where the rich countries are. The graph in Fig. 9.1, drawn up by Branko Milanović (2024), is very eloquent in indicating in which direction it is how mobility has evolved on the planet for various social groups and what new characteristics social stratification is taking on at a global level. The graph shows on the horizontal axis the values of income (in logarithmic scale) and on the vertical axis the values of frequency (the number of people who are located at each level of income).

In the social stratification of the planet, the modal value[1] of global GDP—the income level with the highest frequency in the world population—has changed. Over the course of globalisation—in the transition

[1] The modal value (or mode) of a distribution is the term that has the highest frequency. In Fig. 9.1, the mode was approximately equal to 600 dollars per year (in real terms, PPP) in 1988 and has risen to about 3000 dollars in 2018.

F. Farina, *The Rise of Inequality and the Fall of Social Mobility*,
https://doi.org/10.1007/978-3-031-92843-7_9

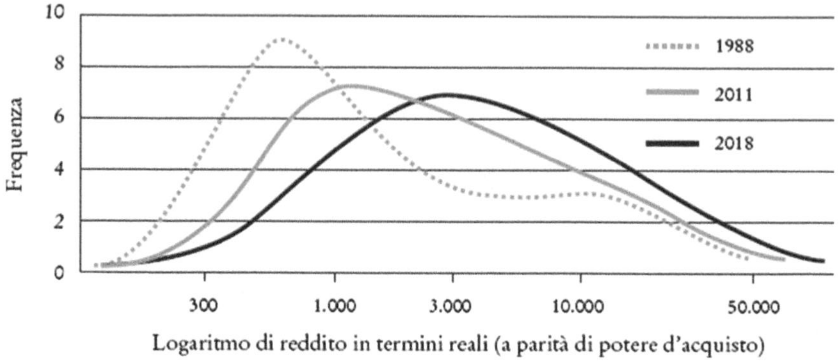

Fig. 9.1 Global income distribution (1988, 2011, 2018). (Source: Milanović (2024). Translation: Frequency, Log of income in real terms (PPP))

from the survey from the year 1988 to 2011, and then to 2018—the distribution has progressively modified, the values at the centre of the distribution have become increasingly higher. The consequence is noteworthy: the social group that today gathers in absolute terms the largest number of people in the world population is no longer represented by the poor, but by what can be defined as the "global middle class".

Following the strong increase in individual incomes generated by the economic growth of emerging countries, the nationalities of people belonging to the various levels of the global income distribution have changed. The frequencies in the central portion of the global distribution are today occupied by people who testify to the arrival of well-being of the peoples of the East. On the other hand, the poor of the rich countries, who previously at a planetary level belonged to the privileged world of the well-off, today no longer belong to it, as they no longer appear in the high-income percentiles of the global distribution.

The socio-cultural features of the "global middle class" are also very different from those that in the twentieth century shaped the development of the societies of the United States and European nations. Indeed, the national traits of the middle class have greatly faded: defining the well-being of the "global middle class", its unifying character at a global level, are the consumer goods of the new digital technologies.

The path that appears three times in succession in the graph resembles a wave. The apex, the summit of the wave, is the mode, a term that—as has been said—designates the most numerous portion in the world population. Raising the wave is the high number of frequencies (vertical axis), the high number of people who have that given income. Over the course of 30 years, the level of income (horizontal axis), around which the wave swells each time, has become increasingly higher: from about 600 in 2008, it went to 1200 in 2011, and to about 3000 in 2018. The increase in people with average income—the "global middle class"—was mainly contributed by the growth rates of emerging countries, which have been much higher over the past decades compared to those of advanced countries. The fact that the apex of the global distribution tends to shift to the right over time, mainly testifies of the remarkable rise in the earnings of the social strata of the Asian peoples who have moved from poor to middle class.

Today, swelling the central section of the global income distribution is mainly the middle classes of China (Box 9.1) and, immediately after, India. The exceptional growth performance of China in recent decades, driven by the peculiar model of "authoritarian capitalism" (Milanović 2023) of the country, has greatly accelerated social mobility, especially in the section of the most dynamic middle class; that of the new large urban conglomerates, engaged in the development and productive use of the most advanced technologies. In the 20-year period 2000–2019, the share of emerging and developing countries in global GDP grew from 21% to 41% (China did the lion's share, with 66% of the increase). Correspondingly, the share of advanced countries[2] has decreased.

Box 9.1 Social mobility in an authoritarian regime: China

The recent history of China testifies to the role of both cultural and economic factors in the dynamics of social structure. The economic growth objectives that the ruling elite establishes are indeed an expression of the ideological orientation of the group of leaders of the Chinese Communist Party who succeed in power. After the Communist Revolution led by Zedong in 1949, the fifties saw the

(*continued*)

[2] Between 1980 and 2016, the "citizens of the world" with a low-to-middle income, with an income increase of 75%, have climbed the ranking of the global income distribution moving from the 15th to the 45th percentile, while the global middle-to-high income class, with an income increase of 50%, has moved from the 60th to the 95th percentile.

Box 9.1 (continued)

failure of the "great leap forward" towards greater well-being promised to a population afflicted by great poverty. In the decade 1966–76, China was then shaken by the serious turbulence of the Cultural Revolution. Mao Zedong's attempt to consolidate his power by mobilising some younger social groups, allowed them to reposition themselves upwards in the social scale. Absolute social mobility upwards intertwined—and clashed—with the competition for relative mobility. The attempt to impose with violence the goal of faster growth, by restraining values and interests consolidated in traditional culture could only be destined to fail. These years of hard ideological confrontation and physical clash plunged the country into a state of serious frustration. The crisis of the economy and the harsh divisions within society were no longer sustainable. With the arrival in power of Deng Xiaoping in the eighties, the revolutionary ideology was abandoned. From his economic reforms sprang, in the system of companies, the progressive contraction of the share of resources of public property (state-owned enterprises have gone from 70% of 1975 to 30% of 2015). The country's entry into the WTO in 2001 has indeed had the effect of giving a strong boost to the development of the private sector. In the "Middle Kingdom", there has been a strong acceleration of GDP growth, and therefore an increase in social mobility *absolute*. "China forty years ago was a developing communist country. Paradoxically, communism has enabled colonies and backward societies to abolish feudalism and build capitalism endogenously" (Milanović 2019, p. 75). From Deng Xiaoping to the current president Xi Jinping, the market opening pursued by the party has contributed to the achievement of the goal of a significant increase in income and the well-being of the population; but it has also involved the abandonment of the goal of equality, both between city and countryside, and within the large metropolises. Even today, although at more "Western" rates, income growth continues to affect all percentiles of the distribution. However, income increases are very uneven. As always, and everywhere, the family is the institution that most affects the life course of young people. Archive data and current census data show that young

(*continued*)

Box 9.1 (continued)

people whose grandparents—about 40 years ago, during the Cultural Revolution—belonged to the elite have accumulated 11 years more of education, and earn 16% more than young people whose grandparents did not belong to the elite (Alesina et al. 2020). In other words, social mobility *relative* was not sufficient to shuffle income positions within the cohort of grandchildren of the elite that was in power during the revolutionary period between 1966 and 1976. In a country like China, where the communist revolution should have directed the economic structure towards egalitarianism, income inequality has accelerated in recent decades. The mobility *relative* of income and territorial mobility from the countryside to the cities are social phenomena in which the ideological orientation of the political leadership and the autonomous economic choices of private entrepreneurs encounter difficulties in finding reconciliation. The decrease in the poor population present in rural areas is indeed achieved through careful regulation—through the system of permits *jouko* and the increase in hiring of workers in the city—of the flows of territorial mobility towards metropolitan areas.

In focusing attention on the tendency of economic growth to accentuate inequalities, Piketty has deeply investigated the role of the cultural values of advanced Western countries, especially the cultural division between Brahmins and merchants within the middle class (Gethin et al. 2022, pp. 848–9). In its own way, China seems to reproduce in the East this socio-political scheme avoiding the confrontation between social groups that develops in advanced Western countries. The new political elite, strongly open to the world, that leads the country has given priority to the cultural and ideological value of the emancipation of the masses from poverty, giving a lot of space to private entrepreneurs. According to the World Bank, the poverty rate of the Chinese population has decreased from 53% in 1981 to 8% in 2001. A stunning result, considering that according to the Caritas 2023 Report on *Poverty and social exclusion in Italy*, almost one in ten Italians is considered poor. At the same time, the new entrepreneurial and financial class has been left free to operate and enrich themselves. This has resulted in the bursting of a speculative

(*continued*)

Box 9.1 (continued)

bubble in the real estate sector, as happens in the Western world. The powerful socio-economic change towards greater prosperity and adherence to the values of individual success have not coincided with equal social mobility for all. The question that only future history can answer is whether the primacy of ideology, in particular the party's persistent reference to equality as the primary goal of communist society, will be more resistant than the individualistic spirit instilled by the turn towards Western values. The question is this: will the authoritarianism that characterises the political regime be able to preserve the social cohesion put at risk by the gaps in wealth and living standards that have opened within the population?

Such countries are today characterised by upward mobility within the elite of the rich, by the "social persistence" of some social strata with medium income, and by downward social mobility of the low-skilled classes.

Let's compare the social stratification of China (urban population) and Italy, as it has evolved from 1988 to 2018. Figure 9.2 puts the position in the percentile of global per capita income of the two populations on the vertical axis, in correlation with the corresponding value in the disaggregation by deciles on the horizontal axis. In the 30-year period 1988–2018, all social classes of the Chinese population living in urban areas have improved their position in the world ranking (the dark grey trace is higher, in a nearly uniform way, than the light grey trace). The graph shows how there is, for each decile of Chinese GDP, an increase (as a percentile of global per capita income) of approximately 20 points. In Italy, on the other hand, a growth process that in the 30-year period has been not only slow and discontinuous, but also very unequal among the various social classes, has made it so that—in the global distribution of per capita income—the deciles of the poor and low-to-middle income classes have recorded a significant deterioration; only from the subjects of the fourth decile has the position of Italians in the per capita income ranking of the world population improved (the dark grey line surpasses the light grey line).

In the world, inequality *between* the richest and poorest countries has decreased (there are fewer poor and more middle class), while inequality *within* countries has increased (there is less middle class and sometimes

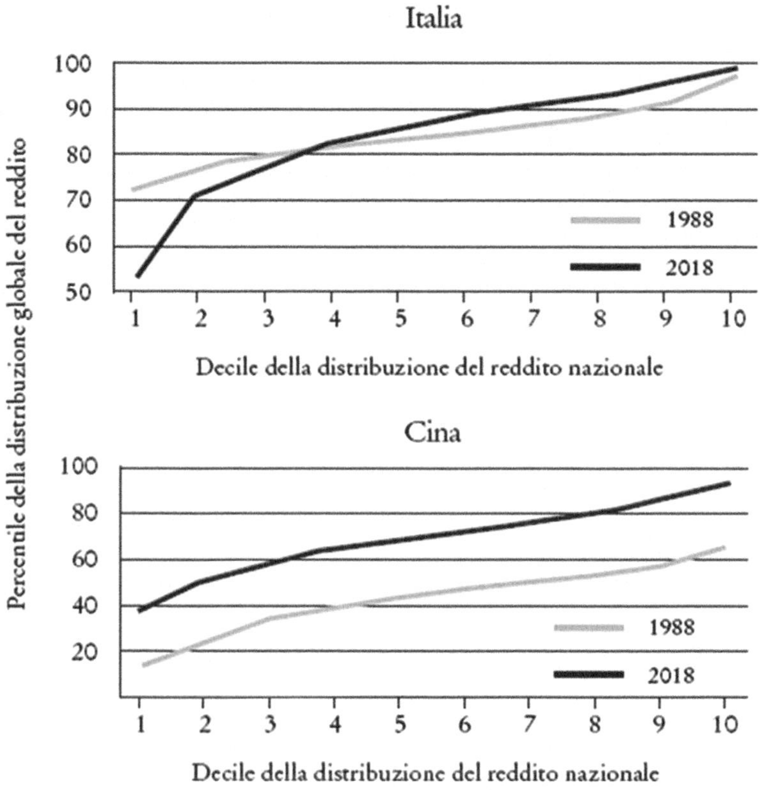

Fig. 9.2 Position of Italy and China (urban population) by income deciles in the global income distribution. (Source: Milanović (2023). Translation: Percentile of the global income distribution, Italy, Decile of the income distribution, China, Decile of the income distribution)

more poor) (Milanović 2023).[3] The advanced countries of the West continue to hold the bulk (approximately 90%) of the world's highest

[3] The interpretative framework that has been proposed is in line with the concept of "conditional convergence" developed by growth theory. The idea is not to focus on the vague concept of a continuous, general, increase in income at a planetary level. The convergence between nations is no longer conceived in terms of the "catching-up" of poor countries, of "absolute convergence" towards the richer countries. The analysis of convergence must instead take into account the heterogeneity between countries, their unequal availability of capital and the very varied quality of political and economic institutions. Showing a tendency to converge are groups of countries with similar economic and institutional characteristics.

incomes—the largest global share of *top incomes*—although the presence of wealthy Chinese in this category is significantly increasing.

Globalisation has had very different effects on social mobility in the various geo-economic areas of the planet. The South of the world has seen mainly absolute mobility increase. In the North of the world, however, the impact has particularly affected relative mobility: in the manufacturing industry sectors—i.e., those where automation has spread the most—the income and status of less skilled and more exposed workers have been penalised due to the competition of emerging and developing countries in global markets, leading to a decrease in wages. In the future, the growth of India's GDP could "fuel" global social mobility by increasing the planet's middle class. This remains a big unknown. Will the hoped-for economic development of the African continent also contribute to the expansion of the planet's middle class? Or will the migratory wave pouring into Europe prove unstoppable precisely because of its failed "economic take-off", and a consequent increasing share—compared to flows from the Middle East and Central Asia—of migrants from a band of nations in severe political and social crisis, and often devastated by endemic civil wars, ranging from north-western Africa to north-eastern Africa?

Trans-Continental Mobility: Migratory Flows

As the distribution of the world's population among different geographical areas changes, migratory flows to the North of the world are profoundly altering the social stratification of advanced countries. Trans-continental mobility overlays the phenomenon of relative mobility with that of absolute mobility because it grafts the destinies of immigrants—as well as within the income scale of the social structure—into the growth process of the host countries. Especially in a phase of not exciting economic growth, the peoples of rich countries are not at all prepared to deal with the request for hospitality coming from the dispossessed of the South of the world. The socio-cultural categories elaborated by Robert D. Putnam (1993), a scholar situated on the ridge between economic history and political science, help us understand how complicated the process of cultural opening to the "inclusion" of immigrants is. He developed his vision of "social capital" drawing inspiration from the spread of "networks of norms and civic commitment" in the communities of medieval Central-northern Italy. The problem lies in the two possible ways of manifesting social capital. The *bonding* form is the ability of people to establish cooperation and trust ties within their community, which has been structured in history mainly through custom. The *bridging* form of social capital, on the other hand, sees groups of different ethnicity and culture communicating with each other, and is therefore more demanding: it requires a cultural attitude of an "inclusive" type, aimed at welcoming individuals foreign to one's culture.

In Europe, the electoral consensus of sovereignist and far-right movements and parties is continually growing. One of the factors at the origin of the phenomenon is undoubtedly the emotional reaction of citizens to the perception—progressively spread in society—of the extent of the socio-economic upheavals implied by the migratory phenomenon. Economic theory, not recognising the existence of a precise link between the migratory phenomenon and social mobility, struggles to develop the policy proposals indispensable for the inclusion of immigrants. The much higher level of development of the host countries means that immigrants are hired in activities and jobs with a wage level that, although often low, is much higher than that of the country of origin (Borjas 2015).[4] The lower the levels of education and health of immigrants, the higher the cost of immigration for the Welfare system of the country in which they ask to be welcomed (Ruhs 2013). However, some argue that the positive externality represented by the long-term support that future generations of immigrants should guarantee to the GDP will prevail over the costs of immigration. Young immigrants would also contribute to the demographic recovery, so as to reverse the curve of declining birth rates, and to the sustainability of a pension system whose funding is in distress due to low birth rates and working careers characterised by discontinuity and low wages. Others are worried about tensions between natives and immigrants, linked to the fear, on the part of the workers, *low-skilled* natives, that their wages, as well as jobs, might be reduced as an effect of the arrival of foreign workers. A study on the perception of the phenomenon in the populations of advanced countries has identified in the redistributive consequences of migrants' aspiration to well-being, a more important alarm than that linked to differences in social norms and cultural distances compared to the native population (Alesina et al. 2023). The European sovereignist parties push voters to believe that to maintain their current levels

[4] On the other hand, one cannot ignore the fact that the integration of immigrants is in conflict with the long-term economic growth of developing countries. Emigration causes the loss of human capital by poor countries (Collier 2013, 2018).

of Welfare benefits it is essential to slow down immigrants' access to rights (*entitlements*) (a significant example, being a country once of solid social democratic tradition, is that of Denmark: to qualify for a pension, you must now have obtained Danish citizenship, and have resided in the country for at least ten years). An increasing percentage of citizens today seem convinced that the only way—albeit more drastic—to solve the *trade-off* between their own interests and those of immigrants is the blocking of their access to rights, abolishing the principle of the "universal" eligibility of people for social rights.

From experimental economics research, conducted in a wide range of countries, it appears that the degree of cooperation and the attitude to have trust in others as a lubricant of socio-economic interaction are however higher *within* nations than *between* nations (Gächter et al. 2010). Migration flows towards rich countries make the spread of trust in socio-economic relations within advanced nations very problematic. Today, within nations, immigrants face strong discomfort with the national δῆμος. The less institutions and ruling classes are oriented to promote and accompany "inclusion", the less feelings of trust and cooperation—which need the proximity of interests and cultural values to spread—involve also immigrants.

The visible border between the United States and Mexico; the invisible wall represented by a natural border, the Mediterranean Sea; the highly guarded borders of Eastern European countries, which block the path of the most tormented peoples of the Middle East do not stop what is—in all respects—an attempt at social ascent. The fact that the transfer of people from one nation to another is all the more intense the closer the poor peoples are to the rich peoples explains why the determination of migrants, despite the serious risks they run, is not destined to decrease. What economic theory reads reductively as a simple globalisation of the supply of labour services is actually an exodus of people trying to escape death, or who are in search of a better quality of life.

In antiquity, the uncertainty that accompanied the encounter with the stranger was translated into the linguistic ambiguity enclosed in welcoming him a bit as a guest (*hospes*) and a bit as enemy (*hostis*). Nothing has changed since then. Centuries of ethnocentric culture have made the populations of the West to have internalised the *habitus* of thinking about interaction with other peoples in a self-referential way. It is a fact that in the countries of arrival, migration flows shake social balances. With his usual acumen, regarding the willingness to be solidary, Zygmunt Bauman (1993, p. 42) observed: "moral sensitivity must be excessive to be sufficient".

"Social capital" and Immigration

We all know that every newborn in an advanced world country, especially if European, enjoys a significantly higher probability of having a good life than those born in a poor country. It has been defined the "citizenship premium" (Milanović 2016). This fortunate condition does not only concern the opportunities that he will find in the market, but also the advantage—primarily in Europe—of enjoying protection from risks that the welfare state guarantees. It is precisely the fear of losing the benefits that the "lottery of life"—with the gift of a "citizenship premium"—has assured them to induce the rich peoples—often precisely the people belonging to the lower income classes—to see the influx of immigrants as a threat to their well-being and their lifestyle.

In a time before today's transcontinental migrations, Amartya Sen (2002) denounced the contradiction inherent in the principle of universalism embodied by Welfare. The welfare state is not usually "open" to migrants. In almost all advanced countries the Welfare model is "closed" to other ethnicities, because it is designed to promote the well-being of people historically belonging to the *δῆμος* national. Cultural identity is an ambivalent concept: "it can at the same time be positive for intra-community relations and negative as it generates or supports the tendency to exclude others; this tendency includes violent actions and" anti-immigrant "feelings, as can be observed in some regions of impeccable community solidarity" (Id. 2004, p. 341). The welfare state has a national matrix that opposes the universal value of solidarity with the destitute, the persecuted, the forgotten. Welfare rights, as much as they play a propulsive role in promoting social mobility within nations, are experienced as a national "common good". Since the *ethos* of the indigenous populations is ideologically alien to the promotion of the "inclusion" of migrants, transcontinental mobility is hindered.

A definition of "social capital" emphasises the individual's rootedness in the society to which they belong: "the sum of resources, material or otherwise, that each individual or social group obtains thanks to participation in a network of interpersonal relationships based on principles of reciprocity and mutual recognition" (Bourdieu 1980, p. 119). The decay of these principles, which we are witnessing, depends on the prevalence of the collective sentiment against immigrants over the inclination to solidarity that is present in every human being. On the other hand, in groups of migrants moving towards North America and the countries of the

European Union, there is—more or less consciously—resentment for the injustices suffered, if not a spirit of repressed revenge. This feeling is sometimes motivated by the awareness of the exploitation of their resources in the post-colonial era (exploitation that still continues today, with the race to grab rare, and therefore precious, mineral resources) (Berman et al. 2023). In the nineteenth and twentieth centuries, a per capita income gap formed between the colonial countries and their colonies, which prevented the latter from enjoying the welfare benefits that the great powers obtained thanks to technical progress (the classic example is the deindustrialisation of India caused by the policy pursued by the United Kingdom in its colony).

Bauman was right: in order to be satisfied, the aspiration of migrants to be welcomed should rely on a formidable disposition to solidarity from the populations of the countries where they arrive. The opposite happens. That the political dominance exercised by the "rich" countries at a global level is reflected in a defence of privilege, also achieved through the exploitation of colonies, is demonstrated by the refusal to give space to the demands for a less inequitable distribution of economic power at an international level. At least indirect evidence of this cultural closure is the fact that the expansion over the years, on the wave of globalisation, of the migratory phenomenon has coincided with the progressive undermining—carried out by the hegemonic power—of the role of the UN. This international organisation, in which the peoples of the South of the world represent the majority, would by its nature be responsible for the *governance* of this epochal phenomenon. Behind the "walls" opposed to the arrival of immigrants—made of reinforced concrete or metaphorical—there is the deception of sovereignist governments that blame the arrival of migrants on "human flesh traffickers". What is actually behind the departure of the boats is the will to emigrate of hundreds of thousands of people. And hunger is its primary determinant.[5] The hypocrisy of the political class of many countries will not be enough to curb a historical process that needs to be well regulated. It is also written in the "Financial

[5] According to the FAO (ourworldindata.org), at a global level the minimum cost for a healthy meal is 3.54 dollars per day. In many African countries from which migrants come, almost the entire population does not have the means to afford this diet (Nigeria: 93.5%; Congo: 91.5%; Niger: 92%; Central African Republic: 94.6%). These figures are enough to explain why thousands of people risk (and often lose) their lives at sea.

Times": "the crucial question about immigration is *how* to regulate it, not *whether* to regulate it or not" (Wolf 2023).

The scope of recognition of citizenship rights for migrants has a perimeter that today varies from country to country. In establishing rights elaborated with reference to the cultural belonging of citizens to their own ἔθνος, national legislations very rarely refer to a δῆμος inclusive of immigrants. If we consider the advantages of an increase in the workforce in a historical phase of falling birth rates, and the contribution to the public budget of the tax revenue from immigrant workers, the problem is not of cultural homogeneity, but mainly of political choice on the extent to which to grant access to opportunities for well-being. Being influenced by emotion, our ideological beliefs "certainly have a genetic component" (Van Bavel and Pacher 2021, p. 97). But it is also true that knowledge learned "rationally" has a weight in the search for a social identity. For example, we are often "exposed to misinformation" (ibid., p. 276). The problem is the manipulation of the public opinion by the sovereign parties. In fact, the weakest social strata have nothing but etc., where concern about competition from migrants (both in the labour market and in welfare benefits) is concentrated, have nothing but to gain from a far-sighted redistributive policy, could make its way into public discourse. The margins for a redistribution of income that reverses the trend towards downsizing the welfare state, and overcomes the opposition between indigenous citizens and migrants, exist. It would favour the social mobility of both indigenous people and migrants. The constraint of economic resources can be overcome even in countries that have a high public debt/GDP ratio. It has been shown that large fortunes can be tapped into without necessarily resulting in serious problems for macroeconomic equilibrium (Atkinson 1997, 2015). Instead of demonstrating it with a model, here is a simple calculation. A hypothetical plan for the redistribution of his own wealth magnanimously decided by Elon Musk—the richest man in the world (237 billion dollars, according to "Forbes")—would be enough to make two million poor families in the United States middle class (Fagereng et al. 2022).[6]

[6]The conventional classification wants the middle class to be made up of families whose disposable income is between 75% and 200% of the median disposable income of each country: the social class of the rich therefore includes families above 200% and the social class of the poor those below 75%. This method of measurement allows to maintain a distance between the statistical lower limit of the middle class (75%) and the relative poverty threshold (for example, reference is made to a family income of about 50% lower than the average income).

In the United Kingdom, governments have demonstrated a very pragmatic approach in the implementation of welcoming policies, particularly in the granting of citizenship. Despite having to face, in recent decades, ethnic crises that have resulted in street riots, the United Kingdom has managed to preserve the *status quo* of coexistence and mutual tolerance among different groups of different cultures. The story is different in France. The country's ruling class has never abandoned the traditional "monocultural" approach. The "universalistic" idea of citizenship—born with the Enlightenment and the French Revolution—has been interpreted in the vision of cultural integration of immigrants. The French strategy of encouraging their adherence to the country's values is rendered ineffective by a blatant contradiction. The Enlightenment conception of the "universal" equality of all residents in a country in terms of civil and political rights—regardless of ethnic affiliation—is easy to formally implement. But the formal recognition of equality in rights becomes problematic in everyday life when it comes to rights related to people's private sphere. In fact, the "Enlightenment universalism" is not extended in France to include everyone's freedom to publicly express their cultural and religious identity. The right to wear the veil in schools and universities is not recognised in France. To the weakness of this schizophrenic approach to "cultural inclusion" is added the condition of severe inequality of opportunity—and of life domains—of immigrants. A growing divergence of income and well-being separates from the native young people the children of the first generations of immigrants from the ex-colonies. The socio-economic deprivation of the latter is exacerbated by the existential condition of people "segregated" in the *banlieu*, while their parents are forced to commute to work in the city centres.

The concept of *bridging* social capital is key to understanding how deeply immigration is impacting the shared values of the people of wealthy countries. Political democracy shows all its impotence in the face of issues involving the distribution of income and well-being. The tendency of the people of advanced countries is to turn a blind eye and express in the ballot box their rejection of the idea of welcoming. A political scientist has stated that democracy "is a form of government adapted [...] to the current needs of the order of selfishness [...] which imposes precise limits on equality" (Dunn 2006, p. 186). The attitude of rejection expressed in many countries by the majority vote in the ballot box, contrary to any serious proposal aimed at addressing the migration problem, is a signal not to be ignored. This attitude is indeed explained once it is admitted that the "walls" that stop migrants have been erected primarily *inside* people. It is well known that the concept of *bridging* was interpreted—by all the countries that dedicated themselves to colonial expansion—in the forms of oppression and slavery. Moreover, as already mentioned, the predatory posture of rich countries towards poor countries—in the West as in the East—is expressed today in the hoarding, through agreements with developing countries, of the minerals required by new technologies.

The consequence of the "stalemate" of "inclusion" policies is a more pronounced stickiness of social stratification. In the United States, social mobility is blocked by a society culture still influenced today by concepts such as hierarchy and racial purity. In her book *Caste: The Origins of Our Discontents*, in which she draws a parallel between the caste system of India[7] and latent racism in American society, Isabel Wilkerson (2020) writes: "Caste is insidious, and therefore powerful, because it is not associated with contempt, it is not necessarily referred to the person [...]; it is a social order that has existed for so long that it appears as the natural order of things" (p. 64). A thought that finds a precise correspondence in empirical research. An experimental economics study (Cox et al. 2020) conducted in India among the inhabitants of the villages of West Bengal shows that the lack of trust and cooperation in the population cannot be explained by the discrimination carried out by the members of the upper classes towards the members of the lower classes: while the former show among themselves a certain capacity for cooperation and willingness to reciprocity, the latter do not show a sufficient propensity to cooperate among themselves. The reasoned judgement in the study is that they seem to have internalised the negative cultural prejudice that connotes their identity, namely belonging to a low caste. Adaptation—or resignation—is an emotional reaction to socio-economic discomfort also common among the fragile people of advanced countries. The *impasse* of social mobility makes people passive, keeps them locked in their respective grouping. In Wilkerson's words, "caste is the state of mind that keeps everyone prisoner".

[7] In Indian culture and society, the upper castes are made up of Brahmins (priests, intellectuals, and Vedic teachers) and Kshatriyas (administrators and warriors); the third caste is made up of Vaishya (merchants and traders), the fourth by Shudras (workers and servants). The Dalits (the "oppressed") are outside the caste system. The Constitution of the Indian Union now prohibits discrimination of Dalits, who were defined as "untouchables" because engaged in work activities considered impure.

Bibliography

Alesina, A., Miano, A., Stantcheva, S. 2020 *The Polarization of Reality*, in «American Economic Review, Papers and Proceedings», CX, pp. 324–8.

Alesina, A., Miano, A., Stantcheva, S. 2023 *Immigration and Redistribution*, in «Review of Economic Studies», XC, 1, pp. 1–39.

Atkinson, A. B. 1997 Bringing Income Distribution in From the Cold, *in «Economic Journal», CVII, 441, pp. 297–321.*

Atkinson, A. B. 2015 *Inequality. What Can Be Done?*, Harvard Economic Press, Cambridge 2015).

Berman, N., Couttenier, M., Girard, V. 2023 *Mineral Resources and the Salience of Ethnic Identities*, Aix-Marseille School of Economics, Working Paper n. 2232.

Borjas, G. J. 2015 *Immigration and Globalization. A Review Essay*, in «Journal of Economic Literature», LIII, 4, pp. 961–74.

Bourdieu, P. 1980 Questions de sociologie*, Minuit, Paris.*

Collier, P. 2013 Exodus: Immigration and Multiculturalism in the 21st Century, *Oxford University Press, Oxford.*

Collier, P. 2018 The Future of Capitalism: Facing the New Anxieties, *Allen Lane, London.*

Cox, J. C., Sadiraj, V., Sen, U. 2020 Cultural Identities and Resolution of Social Dilemmas, *in «Economic Inquiry», LVIII, 1, pp. 49–66.*

Dunn, J. 2006 Setting the People Free: The Story of Democracy*, Atlantic Books, London 2005).*

Fagereng, A., Guiso, L., Pistaferri, L. 2022 Assortative Mating and Wealth Inequality*, Cepr Discussion Paper 17148.*

Gächter, S., Herrmann, B., Thoeni, C. 2010 *Culture and Cooperation*, The Centre for Decision Research and Experimental Economics, School of Economics, University of Nottingham, Discussion Papers n. 9.

Gethin, A., Martínez-Toledano, C., Piketty, T. 2022 Brahmin Left Versus Merchant Right: Changing Political Cleavages in 21 Western Democracies, 1948–2020*, in «Quarterly Journal of Economics», CXXXVII, 1, pp. 1–48.*

Milanović, B. 2015 Global Inequality of Opportunity: How Much of Our Income Is Determined by Where We Live?, in «Review of Economics and Statistics», XCVII, 2, pp. 452–60.

Milanović, B. 2016 Global Inequality: A New Approach for the Age of Globalization, *Harvard University Press, Cambridge 2016.*

Milanović, B. 2019 Capitalism, Alone: The Future of the System That Rules the World, *Harvard University Press, Cambridge.*

Milanović, B. 2023 Visions of Inequality: From the French Revolution to the End of the Cold War*, Harvard University Press, Cambridge.*

Milanović, B. 2024 The Three Eras of Global Inequality, 1820–2020 with the Focus on the Past Thirty Years, *in «World Development», CLXXVII.*

Putnam, R. D. 1993 Making Democracy Work: Civic Traditions in Modern Italy, *Princeton University Press, Princeton.*

Ruhs, M. 2013 The Price of Rights: Regulating International Labor Migration, *Princeton University Press, Princeton.*

Sen, A. K. 2004 *Elements of a Theory of Human Rights*, in «Philosophy & Public Affairs», XXXII, 4, pp. 315–429.

Van Bavel, J. & Pacher, D. J. 2021 *The Power of Us*, Headline Publishing Group, London.

Wilkerson, I. 2020 Caste: The Origins of Our Discontents, *Random House, New York.*

Wolf, M. 2023 The Dangers of Magical Thinking on Health Policy, *in «Financial Times», 23 gennaio.*

PART III

Why It Happened

CHAPTER 10

Technical Progress: Occupational and Wage Mobility

Power Asymmetry and New Technologies

In *Prometheus Bound*, Aeschylus takes the side of the hero who defied Zeus and gave fire to human beings. It is undeniable that scientific progress is one of the greatest achievements of man. Scientists, the creators of new knowledge, bear his name: "he who thinks first". New knowledge is transformed by companies into innovations introduced in production. These autonomous decisions have a very wide impact. Although it influences deeply the evolution of society, and also has effects not immediately knowable on the environment, the application of technical progress does not typically pass the scrutiny of any public ethics. Dante's verses come to mind: "Truly often things appear/ that give false matter for doubt/ for the true reasons that are hidden" (*Purgatory*, XXII).[1]

In his volume *The Great Transformation* (1944), Karl Polanyi, economist and anthropologist, defined the Industrial Revolution the historical event that changed the world. A few years before him, many philosophers had spoken of the subordination of nature and man to technology. Polanyi was clear that the transformations brought about by the development of technologies in economic systems should not be interpreted as a natural process. The *téchne*, the ability of technologies to transform the way of

[1] "Indeed, we often see things which, because their true causes remain hidden, offer false argument of doubt".

F. Farina, *The Rise of Inequality and the Fall of Social Mobility*,
https://doi.org/10.1007/978-3-031-92843-7_10

combining physical and human resources, is not neutral because it finds expression in the form of the capitalist mode of production. The key to the success of companies lies in the efficient combination of technologies with the skills of workers. It is on the full autonomous use of the flow of scientific knowledge by companies that we need to question. At the beginning of the millennium, the free economic initiative symbolised by the birth of new innovative companies signalled a change in progress. The capitalist spirit has come to be identified with the launch of start-ups, where the projective capacity of young people with knowledge in search of economic success has been combined with financial support and the spin-offs of the "military-industrial complex".

The fact is that the growth of technological innovation, productivity and GDP on the one hand exalts the power of private ownership of technology (one aspect of innovation is its dependence on accumulated experience, being *path dependent*), on the other hand it finds a growing impulse in *venture capital* (Schumpeter's most significant contribution to economic theory is his understanding of the fundamental role of credit that finances the innovator). The birth of innovative sectors of new technologies has largely been realised thanks to the investment of capital in the application of scientific knowledge in new directions by start-ups. The dimensional expansion of these new companies in advanced sectors was then accompanied by the financial support of institutional investors (investment funds, but also the Pentagon, NASA, etc.).

Contrary to what Schumpeter thought, however, companies in the market usually also have the ability to defend the extra-profits they obtain. In addition to patents, companies on the "technological frontier" can deploy a series of strategies to exercise market control and make themselves immune from the erosion of extra-profits by competitors. Schumpeter sensed the contradiction between the company's need to reward innovation and the equally important need for public action aimed at preventing the innovative company from turning extra-profits into rent.

Schumpeter was among the few economists to sense that capitalism is not at risk of perishing due to the irruption of an exogenous factor (for the winning challenge launched by a movement bearer of a new socio-economic order, for example socialism), but rather for a decay of endogenous origin. He warned, well in advance of the times, of the danger that entrepreneurs with great market power give rise to a plutocracy, that degeneration of the original "bourgeois spirit" praised by Sombart (1916) that in these years is taking hold through corruption and the practice of "capture", the alliance of companies with the demagogues of the political class.[2]

As Mordecai Kurz argued in his *The Market Power of Technology: Understanding the Second Gilded Age* (2023), new technologies, by favouring the concentration of production in the largest, most productive companies, also end up increasing the market power of companies that introduce innovations. Market power is indeed a very powerful weapon. So much so, according to Kurz, that it represents one of the most significant causes of the increase in income and wealth inequality.

Another of the major scholars of technical progress observes how in socio-economic contexts in which knowledge is of great importance—industrial automation, health services, energy—the distortions produced by innovations are the cause of a lowering of collective well-being (Acemoglu 2023).

In continuously transforming production techniques, companies also transform social relations. The latest developments in technology tell us this. Digital companies (Google, Facebook, etc.) exploit the enormous amount of data they have for profit, without having to fear too much the power of regulation or taxation of state institutions. The artificial intelligence called ChatGpt is an advanced natural language processing tool.[3] Its application, not only in production but also in the processing of knowledge, represents a threat of technological unemployment in many fields. The leap in quality of AI compared to the autonomy that had already been conquered by the big digital companies is the complexity that makes it difficult to control by public regulation. As is known, within advanced economies, the introduction of technical progress has proceeded in recent decades under the sign of deregulation of national production systems. This has resulted in a greater ability of companies to resist the erosion of extra-profits by competitors theorised by Schumpeter. The decline of public powers in the face of the power of companies represents an important accelerator—as Kurz (2023) explains—of the increase in income and

[2] "The modern joint-stock company, while being a product of the capitalist process, socialises the bourgeois mentality; continuously reduces the field of action of the bourgeois motive; not only that, but it tends to undermine its foundations" (Schumpeter 1942, p. 162).

[3] Using learning algorithms through information processing, ChatGpt competes with human thought, constructing a response to each question received. Today a subset of artificial intelligence (AI), the *Machine learning* (Ml), is concerned with creating systems that learn or improve performance based on the data they use (G. Roncaglia 2023).

wealth inequality. The globalisation of markets has taken place in the interest of the profit of a few, forgetting that most people live on wages and salaries. The market is part of society, not the other way around. As has been authoritatively denounced, "the link between globalisation, technology and financialisation have weakened the ties between the economy and society" (Kelly and Snower 2021, p. 853). On the other hand, *hyperglobalisation* could not but rekindle conflicts on the international stage, where competition between companies in the most innovative sectors is intertwined with competition between the great powers, putting a brake on globalisation.[4]

What is the most appropriate model of capitalism for social mobility? The answer is simple: an economic system in which companies, in introducing innovations, act in the interest of society, create stable jobs with a decent wage, the "good jobs" (Rodrik and Stantcheva 2021). Instead, it happens that "recent technological change has been distorted towards automation, with insufficient attention to the creation of new tasks in which work can be productively employed" (Acemoglu and Restrepo 2020, p. 25). This judgement makes it clear that an important factor of social mobility is occupational mobility within the production system. In the United States, in 1913, applying the systemic logic of Taylorism, Henry Ford introduced the assembly line in car manufacturing. In the Fordist model of production, occupational mobility coincided with the increase of workers in the large industry of the most dynamic sectors. The productions leading economic growth drove the increase in demand for mass consumer goods: the workers in the industry were the consumers of the goods they themselves produced. To this virtuous endogenous process of increasing welfare, J. M. Keynes gave the name "income multiplier".

In the post-Fordist model, established concurrently with the end of a long phase of employment and income growth, occupational mobility has ceased to be an expression of work as a driving factor of economic expansion, and the function of work as a tool of social inclusion has progressively been lost: "In fact, globalisation and automation have been synergistic, both driven by the same desire to cut labour costs and lay off

[4] For example, American innovation start-ups, which become large companies, try to take away from Chinese state companies the control of markets of minerals today considered precious because indispensable for the ecological and digital transition. Emblematic of the revival of political initiative is the United States' attempt to establish its own political hegemony over the patent network that binds the advanced component companies of the United States, China and Taiwan.

workers" (Acemoglu and Johnson 2023, p. 263). Individual commitment in training and work is no longer sufficient to drive income and *status* dynamics. With the exhaustion of its function of social redemption, relative social mobility ends up losing its raison d'être as support for identity—primarily, for *status civitatis*—ending up coinciding with individual competition for success.

The increase in profits, sometimes of great magnitude in a very short period of time, as well as the shortening of job positions reflect the full autonomy in which companies make production decisions. Although occupational mobility continues to be a significant event for the career prospects of individual workers, it has fallen into a much more rugged GDP growth path; it is therefore part of a socio-economic environment that sees the worker subject to greater economic vulnerability.

The economy of Robinson Crusoe is not only the happy offspring of Robert Louis Stevenson's imagination but also the simplistic stylisation contained in the models of orthodox economics. The conceptual framework of neoclassical theory does not in fact foresee social interaction. Market conditions characterised by "externalities" would consist of episodic phenomena of suspension of the validity of the assumptions of perfect competition, or in "market failures" in efficiently coordinating individual actions. Such phenomena are described as the consequence of exceptional situations, which can sometimes modify the level of individual welfare, but which do not have a substantial influence either on the market structure or on the dynamics of the social structure. And yet today the opposite happens: "A deregulated economy, despite being subject to a continuous process of technical change, cannot be a competitive economy, because the market power generated by technology is permanent, and technological competition does not remove it" (Kurz 2023, p. 402).[5] Orthodox theory is essentially silent on the role that companies play in creating externalities: since in the Gee model companies are *price-takers* (prices are determined in the market equilibrium), it is excluded *a priori* that they can create externalities in making their own decisions. On the contrary, as mentioned, in introducing innovation the company acquires the competitive advantage of increasing its own market power, not only by building barriers to entry aimed at preventing the entry into the market of

[5] The extra-profits guarantee the company the financial advantage of acquiring control of companies that agree to submit to a leading company, preferring to avoid having to innovate by designing superior technology.

possible competitors, but also through the practice of defending with the patent its own interest in prolonging the achievement of extra-profits. A company that introduces an innovation also has the advantage of the *first mover*, i.e. of using reputation to delegate to joint ventures with small start-ups part of the research commitment, and then using the private information it has acquired—the new knowledge—to strengthen its own market power, applying selling prices higher than costs and lowering wages.

In "progressive" economic thought, there is no shortage of critical voices to the individualistic approach of economic analysis: "Since the moment that the theoretical core of standard economics considers rational agents with stable, consistent and autonomous preferences that are not at all influenced by the social context, social determinants of decision-making are neglected" (Hoff and Stiglitz 2016, pp. 3 and 7). Today's neoliberal view merely re-proposes the imaginary reality of autonomous subjects separated from each other outlined by the Gee model. Its approach ignores the mutual externalities that bind people in the market and in society; it underestimates how the introduction of technical progress and the investment and production choices of companies are part of the general process of social reproduction (Bosworth et al. 2016). The judgement of Tony Atkinson, an economist as rigorous as he is alien to ideological inclinations, is damning: "The goal of a high rate of return, or a short-term horizon, can inhibit entrepreneurs from hiring new workers. Companies may not invest in job creation" (Atkinson 1998, p. 10).

From the complete autonomy of large companies in the introduction of technical progress, and from their decisions regarding jobs and wages offered, two important externalities arise: the impact, on workers with *different skills*, of the type of occupation and tasks required. Acemoglu and Johnson (2023) provide abundant evidence that technical progress is not neutral, because it is always the reflection of a political decision: "there is nothing automatic about the way new technologies bring widespread prosperity. Whether this happens or not is an economic, social and political choice" (ibid., p. 13). The distribution of surplus is strongly conditioned not only by the market power of companies (the level to which it is possible to raise the selling price) but above all by the unbalanced balance of power between managers and workers' unions: the choice of the most modern production techniques has the effect of compressing the level of labour cost. "When the tasks performed by robots and algorithms increase [...], average productivity increases, but the marginal productivity of the worker is reduced by automation" (ibid., p. 17). The loss of productive efficiency of tasks performed by ***middle-skilled*** workers following the use of AI represents a threat to the survival of many job positions and a disincentive for companies to create new ones. It follows that the ongoing technological evolution "could result in applications of the emerging generative artificial intelligence that are even more destructive on a social level" (ibid., p. 316). The autonomy of the company in its productive choices has an important implication also with regard to the positive image of the link between technical progress and economic growth, an association commonly understood (at least until the birth of the ecological question) as a safe and valuable driver of well-being and progress for all humanity. The dynamic version of the standard model of economics also predicts a harmonious extension of economic development towards poor countries, by virtue of the attraction on the investments of companies in rich countries exercised by low wages. This reassuring vision has long been denied by the tendency of companies in advanced countries that have located themselves in developing countries to adopt the same labour-saving production techniques as plants in advanced countries. The loss of the productive function of work due to AI represents a direct threat to occupational mobility not only in the advanced world but also for developing countries.[6]

One consequence of the power of large companies on the world stage is their influence on trends in international trade. The promise that the inclusion of less developed economies in the "global value chains" would have led those countries to increase occupational mobility—and to reduce, through the transfer of technological knowledge, the distance with the advanced world—risks being unfulfilled. The involvement in the economic expansion of the North of the world, obtained by the South of the world with globalisation, could send a misleading message about transcontinental mobility: that of an easy integration of developing countries into the global world, the perfect antidote to migratory flows. While it is true that income inequality between rich and poor countries has decreased, the improvement in well-being has not reached all social strata.

[6]The production stages outsourced by companies from advanced countries are those where the lowest-skilled workforce is employed. In the emerging or developing countries where they settle, outsourcing creates an excess of demand for skilled labour, which leads, as in advanced countries, to a polarisation of wage levels between high- and low-level *skill* workers. As happens in the Heckscher-Ohlin international trade model (Farina 2021, box 11.1), there is a correlation between a "high" high-skilled *labour* /low-skilled *labour* ratio and "high" wage inequality *high-skilled / low-skilled* .

As usual, disaggregation is needed. The phenomenon to focus on is that trade between the nations of the world develops more *within* the same sector rather than *between* productive sectors. This has an impact within the social structure of countries. In intra-sectoral trade, companies in less developed countries are in direct competition with companies in developed nations in the same productive sector; in the exchange of products of the same type, however, they appear at a different level of quality. Only companies in advanced economies are able to specialise in the highest range of each good. Intra-sectoral trade therefore has the effect of making the distribution of wealth more unequal among social classes in poor countries. If Italy specialises in luxury shoes, and China in flip-flops, the lowering of the price produced by more intense competition in global markets primarily benefits the rich in rich countries.

The analyses conducted by the OECD (2018a, 2018b, 2018c, 2019b) highlight how in advanced countries, technological progress no longer promises to distribute to the community the benefit of greater well-being. The declining power of workers is documented in Fig. 10.1 by the simultaneous occurrence of two trends: the decrease in the wage share of income and the increase in wage inequality. The evolution of job mobility is now in the direction of "social exclusion". Since the strongest command of companies has occurred in close competition with international finance, the time horizon has also shortened: the goal of profitability in production has aligned with the *short-termism* typical of speculative finance. The introduction of technological progress is thus reflected in working conditions as a case of "negative externality", suffered by the weaker part of the production relationship. "The leap forward towards economic and technological rationality does not inevitably also imply a leap forward towards democratic and meritocratic rationality. For a very simple reason: technology, like the market, knows neither limit nor morality" (Piketty 2014, p. 359). The primacy of advanced sectors, in whose productive activity the knowledge acquired by a small proportion of workers is fundamental, while in traditional sectors a growing proportion of unskilled workers is employed in low-productivity tasks, fits into the process of progressive devaluation of work, a real "social disaffiliation" (Castel 1995).[7]

[7] *The Great Resignation* is the trend spreading among the new generations in the United States—and which is rapidly spreading to Europe with a boom in resignations—to leave their own company. The factors are numerous: the demotivation that accompanies an uninterest-

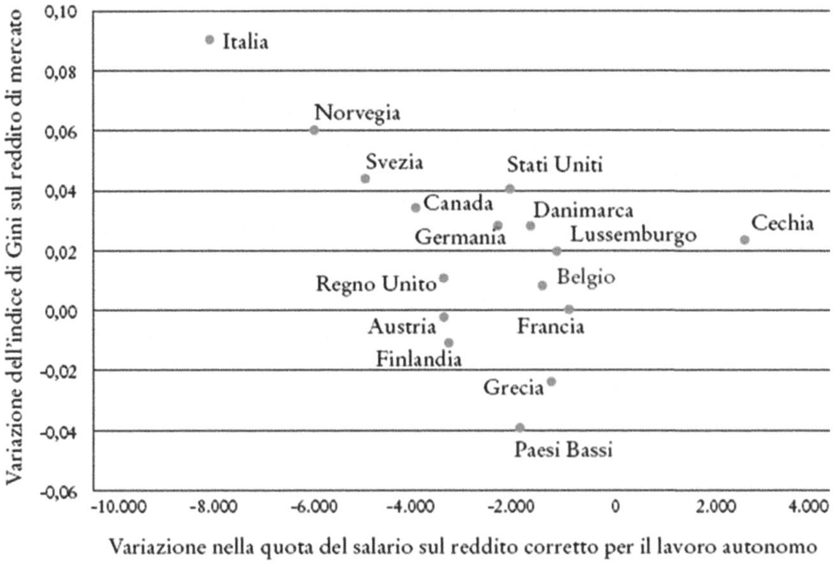

Fig. 10.1 Wage share of income and wage inequality (% changes, 2000s). (Source: Oecd, income distribution database, Ocs Stan, Klms. Translation: Italy, Norway, Switzerland, United States, Canada, Germany, Denmark, Czech Republic, Luxembourg, UK, Belgium, France, Austria, Finland, Greece, Netherlands, Variation of the Gini Index (market income), Labour share (adjusted for autonomous labour))

On the other hand, there is a lack of a balancing action of companies' choices by public policies. Managers and owners of capital, in autonomously controlling the knowledge produced by innovation, and in employing new technologies in production, encounter no restrictions, they are often one step ahead of the possibilities of regulation by political institutions. A weak and poorly applied anti-trust regulation has given free rein to corporations in exploiting market power.[8] The organs of political representation, among whose tasks is to regulate the use of innovations based on the choices of the community, are increasingly less the place of a democratic deliberation committed to imposing on companies the "rules

ing job that does not strengthen identity, the workload overload that generates psychological stress and so on.

[8] See par. 5.3.2 and 11.3 in Farina 2021.

of the game". Citizen-voters are today very reluctant to embody public ethics. Faced with the tendency of entrepreneurs and financial operators to favour short-term profit, governments with very fragile voting majorities, which often vary from one electoral deadline to another, are far from even perceiving the relevance of the long-term public goal of spreading well-being in all strata of society.

Professional Skills and Job Mobility

In the eighties, in large US companies, job mobility towards high-skilled jobs led to the formation of a "wage premium" in favour of *high-skilled* workers. According to the *Skill-Biased Technical Change* (Sbtc) model, technical change consisted of new productive technologies that made it necessary to replace *middle-skilled* and *low-skilled* workers with *high-skilled* ones. The introduction of the flow of inventions within companies revealed the medium-high *skills* acquired through education and vocational training to be central. The growing wage inequality, revealed by empirical surveys among groups of workers with different levels of *skill*, accounted for the widening educational distance within the workforce. The increase in professional qualification induced by the expectation of a higher income was the main driver of *relative* mobility, it gave the impetus to overtake income positions within social stratification. When the share of employed people in the total workforce is disaggregated among workers, respectively, with high, medium and low *skill* (Fig. 10.2), a picture of wage variation by *skill* level is obtained. In almost all countries, *middle-skilled* workers have been penalised. In that phase of technological evolution, workers were selected—and a "wage premium" was assigned to them—directly based on education and professional qualification. From the process of shifting labour demand towards a higher level of qualification, the phenomenon of the hollowing out of the share of *middle-skilled* workers, whose decrease in the twenty-year period 1995–2015 has been called "polarisation" based on the level of *skills* (Fig. 10.2). "The share of occupations *middle-skilled* has decreased while the share of occupations *high-skilled* and *low-skilled* has increased [...]. In almost all countries, this has resulted in an overall shift in employment towards *high-skilled* jobs" (Oecd 2019b, p. 64).

Today, the most appropriate interpretation of the link between technology, professional qualification and wage no longer seems to be this. Technological advancement and occupational and remuneration mobility

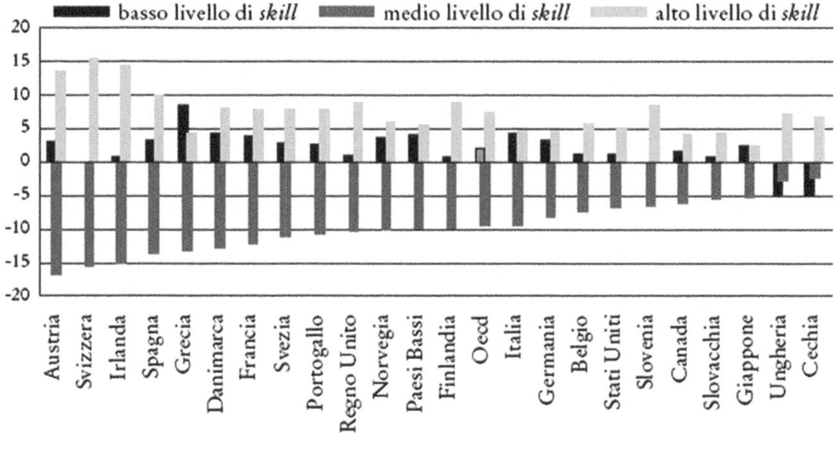

Fig. 10.2 Change in employment by level of professional qualification (1995–2015). (Source: Oecd Employment Outlook, 2019. Translation: Low-skilled, middle-skilled, high-skilled, Austria, Switzerland, Ireland, Spain, Greece, Denmark, France, Sweden, Portugal, UK, Norway, Netherlands, Finland, Oecd, Italy, Germany, Belgium, United States, Slovenia, Canada, Slovakia, Japan, Hungary, Czech Republic)

depend on the ability of workers with high skills in information technologies to perform the tasks required in productive activity. A clue is given by the analysis developed by Robert Gordon (2018). After the exceptional performance of the years between 1996 and 2004, due to the revolution of the *Information Communication Technologies* (Ict), from 2004 onwards US growth would have returned to the long-term path of the twenty-year period 1975–1995. The lower rate of growth in per capita income is associated by Gordon with the slower growth of total factor productivity (Tfp).[9] Why does the introduction of technological progress no longer represent the central factor in the causal link that goes from the flow of young graduates to the degree of knowledge required at the workplace? The American economist interprets the Ict revolution as a shock of temporary increase in Tfp (Gordon and Sayed 2020). The decreased dynamics of Tfp, which is linked to lower GDP growth rates, is the clue that in the

[9] The unsatisfactory growth performance of advanced economies in recent decades has led some economists to hypothesise that Western advanced economies are reaching their stage of "mature development", in which high-yield investments become rarer (Summers 2015).

productive fabric the ***diffusion*** of existing innovations is prevailing, rather than a flow of new ***inventions*** (Galor and Tsiddon 1997). Microelectronics provides a significant data point in this regard. The number of transistors contained in a computer chip has grown exponentially, doubling every two years, but the number of researchers required is eighteen times greater than in the early seventies (Bloom et al. 2020). Today, there is less creation of new ideas and more development, application ability, of new ideas.

The phase of technological evolution in which we find ourselves does not select workers and does not assign them a "wage premium" directly on the basis of the level of education and professional qualification, but allows "a wider range of substitution possibilities between groups of workers with equal *skills*. Therefore, the allocation of *skills* to tasks is endogenised. Technological changes do not increase the wages of all workers, with the significant consequence that a favourable change for one type of worker can reduce the wage of another group of workers [...]. A new machine can directly replace work tasks that were performed by workers belonging to different levels of *skill*. [...] This type of technological change [...] makes it more likely that negative effects on the real wages of the group that is directly replaced by the machine will occur" (Acemoglu and Autor 2011, p. 1158).

In the current trend of technological advancement of companies, occupational mobility—the "transition" from one occupation to another—therefore has a weaker link than in the past with the level of education. In the strategy of introducing innovations, the company puts first the productive organisation of the company according to the type of tasks required by the technological innovation to be introduced. Subordinately, the selection of workers takes place based on the level of education that the worker must possess to occupy the work position connected to the task. Moreover, "such tasks are clearly defined for the vast majority of workers, but require a degree of coordination, foresight and physical flexibility that are not easily automatable" (ibid., p. 1157).

It is the organisational strategies of large companies (often determined by their placement within global value chains) that guide the attraction of workers with higher skills. As Mordecai Kurz (2023) observes, each innovation generates two types of knowledge: purely technological, which can be transformed into a patent, and another that emerges during the use of the new technology and has to do with the productive organisation that is associated with the new technique. The model that is being affirmed is called "task-based technical change" (Tbtc) (Autor and Dorn 2013).

Figure 10.3 shows how the evolution of the use of the workforce towards the Tbtc model has been articulated in relation to the competence of workers in the tasks required by technology. The share of employees with non-routine high-competence (*cognitive*) tasks has progressively grown from the eighties to the nineties and the two thousands; that with routine tasks has undergone a strong downsizing especially in the last period, when that with non-routine tasks (the employees, in particular, in low-qualification services) has experienced a certain recovery. It also often happens that in becoming a leader in a certain market a company *superstar* increase its share of the overall sector surplus through the hierarchical organisation of a conglomerate of companies.[10] The divergence between innovative and traditional companies is accompanied by a "polarisation" of workers *middle-skilled* belonging to both the high and low portion of professional qualification.[11] Both in companies that have accelerated the use of ICT and in those that have increased R&D sectors, those who have particularly lost their jobs are the middle-skilled workers *middle-skilled* of non-manual routine tasks (Michaels et al. 2014).

The most innovative companies close to the "technological frontier", in accelerating the process of automation of production processes, select workers who best adapt to the evolution of non-routine tasks *non-routine*, paying them, for the same level of education and *skill*, higher wages than those of workers who performed routine tasks *routine*. On the other hand, in the more static companies from a technological point of view, "the increasing penetration of information technology and robotics has eroded job positions with traditionally middle-skill routine tasks" (Criscuolo et al. 2021, p. 203). In recession phases, moreover, it happens that the

[10] "When the company breaks down into a network in which a leading company sets prices in order to increase its own share of the common turnover, at the expense of weaker companies and their employees […], it is impossible to determine to what extent a higher labour productivity return is due to the efficiency of the workers or to the entrepreneur's greater ability to claim his own share of the value produced" (Appelbaum 2017, p. 521).

[11] Katz and Krueger (2018) have documented in a *survey* how much the structure of occupations in the United States has changed between 1995 and 2015. Routine manual tasks performed by *low-skilled* workers (assembly lines) and non-manual (clerical) have seen a decrease in labour demand (given their substitutability with ICT); non-routine non-manual tasks (researcher, manager, professional) have recorded an increase (given their high complementarity with ICT); those non-routine manual tasks (cleaning, security, driving transport, etc.) covered by *middle-skilled* (given their neutrality with respect to ICT) show no change; the number of contractors (*contractors*), online intermediaries, contract employees, call centre employees, freelance workers has expanded.

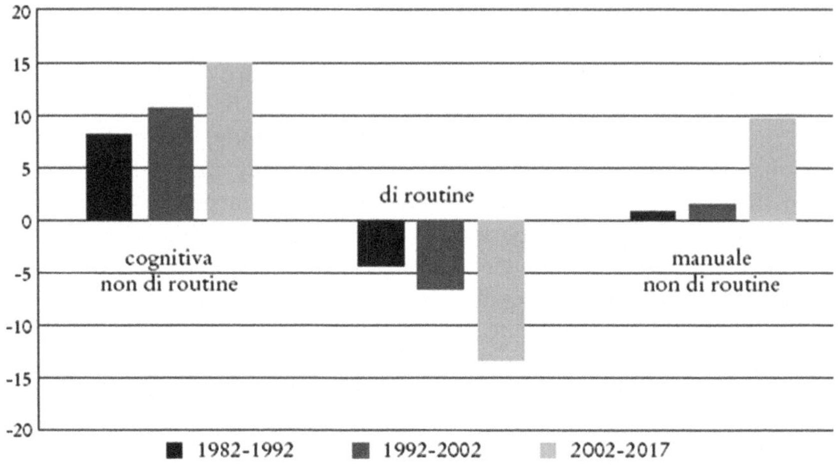

Fig. 10.3 Percentage change in the share of employed by job (United States, 1982–2017). (Source: Elaboration in Jaimovich and Siu 2020, on Labor Force Statistics (Current Population Survey), United States. Translation: Non-routine cognitive, routine, non-routine manual)

reallocation of dismissed workers with low qualifications and routine tasks fails, with the consequence that unemployment increases (Faia and Shabalina 2023).

The spread of information technologies is closely linked to *digital capital*, the form of intangible capital that is most concentrated in the small group of the most innovative companies, the *superstar* companies. Since digital language is understandable by machines, automated processes replicate routine tasks. In a context where middle-skilled jobs are decreasing, occupational mobility is activated by the ability to adapt to the flexibility required by tasks related to the use of *digital capital*.[12] The complementarity of the workforce with high computer skills with investments in organisational innovation allows large companies—through the use of patents and a network of externalities within the *corporation*—to enjoy

[12] The term *digital capital* refers to tangible goods—software, servers, routers, online platforms, etc.—but today mainly to the creation of digitised systems by highly skilled researchers, the so-called "intangible capital".

significant economies of scale.[13] In the Tbtc model, it is the profit motivation, more than technical progress, the rule of the roost.

Innovation guarantees the company that introduces it a market power that consists not only—as mentioned—in the freedom to set the monopolist price. The most important market power derives from the innovator controlling resources that competitors do not have, and therefore from the freedom to plan its own expansion and consolidate the advantage of enjoying extra-monopolistic profits. The innovative company often ends up discouraging potential competitors from entering the market. Instead of the entry of new companies, we witness the prudent strategy adopted by potential competitors who do not want to face the risk of failing to supplant the *incumbents*: being bought by the monopolist. According to the vivid definition of an entrepreneur, "competition is for losers" (Thiel 2014, p. 1).

The result is the acceleration of the process of capital concentration. With the increase in the turnover share of the most innovative sectors, the number of competitors decreases and the market power of a limited number of large companies increases. "High mark-up companies, as they become larger, consolidate their market leader position and market concentration grows" (Akcigit et al. 2021, p. 11). The motto "the winner takes the most" fits well with multinational ICT companies: being able to replicate products at almost zero marginal cost, they gain a huge advantage from having low production costs and a very limited number of employees compared to turnover. Another saying, "winner take all politics" (Hacker and Pierson 2010), is then the sign of the prominent role assumed by large *corporation* at the level of a country's institutions. By pressuring (*lobbying*) the political class, leading companies obtain deregulation reforms of the economy and the enactment of legislative measures that guarantee them the appropriation of rents through the formation of

[13] The key to understanding the current phase of technological progress would therefore lie in a simple empirical evidence: "Between 2000 and 2014 both in Europe and the United States there was a significant increase in industrial concentration" (OECD 2019b, p. 68). The process of productive concentration has made the market structure evolve towards an increasing divergence between advanced and traditional companies. The companies in the upper portion of the Tfp distribution have improved their ability to combine the *digital capital* with *skilled* workers, while traditional companies that have not made investments in new technologies are precluded from the organisational advancements that allow them to enjoy economies of scale and positive externalities. The introduction of intangible digital technologies therefore tends to enlarge the efficiency gap in resource use within the company system.

"entry barriers" that "make it more difficult for smaller companies to grow and enter the market for new ones" (Autor et al. 2020, p. 669). Nothing unusual. Adam Smith described it in *The Wealth of Nations*: "The clamour of our merchants and manufacturers has forced the hand of the legislator, to support their absurd and oppressive monopolies" (Smith 1776, p. 640). For the top managers of the company, gaining a small competitive advantage over the *corporation* being competitors is often enough to guarantee the company the far majority share of the turnover obtainable from a certain product or service. This advantage translates for top managers into their upward social mobility. In the United States, the richest 1% of the population has almost doubled its income from 11% to 20% in the last thirty years. Only with the excess demand for labour that occurred during the post-Covid economic recovery, wage inequality has reversed the trend: the data show a slight wage compression (Autor et al. 2023).

Concentration of Companies and Wage Polarisation

The wage structure follows the change in the market structure towards sectoral concentration centred on large *corporations*. Wage levels, while being connected to the level of *skills* that workers acquire through their education and professional training path, are predominantly determined by the tasks of the various job positions offered by large advanced companies.

The most convincing proof of the evolution from Sbtc to Tbtc is a fact emerged in empirical checks. The "wage polarisation" no longer takes place *within* companies *between* groups of workers ordered by level of education, i.e. *between* the three groups of secondary school graduates, graduates and PhD graduates. The "wage polarisation" manifests itself today both *between* advanced and traditional companies, and *within each educational group*. The divergence of workers' remuneration—more or less qualified—required by the tasks envisaged by the technology adopted by the company is indeed intertwined with that determined by the divergence between innovative and non-innovative companies. The wage dispersion *within* educational levels is indeed accentuated for the different needs of large companies that attract workers with more intangible capital and small- and medium-sized companies with a lower degree of innovation (Autor et al. 2020). The workers' bargaining power on the distribution of the surplus—and the wage premium they obtain—is therefore greater the more it is linked to the intangible capital necessary for the performance of tasks in a superstar company.[14] The following fact is more than a clue: most of the dispersion between the salaries at the beginning of the millennium occurred *between* young employed graduates, while the dispersion changed in a smaller proportion within the group of young non-graduate workers.

This interpretation is supported by a research conducted on 13 Oecd countries in the period 1995–2017: "Differences in the average wage between companies - which amounts to half of the total inequality - are mainly explained by differences in wage premiums (the part of the wage that depends exclusively on the characteristics of the companies), rather than in the composition of the employed workforce" (Criscuolo et al. 2021, p. 2). The evolution of the productive structure towards concentration is connected to the composition effect represented by the shift of excellent graduates towards high-innovation *superstar* companies.[15] The diversity of remuneration turns out to be the norm at the highest levels of professional competence, because it is also present within the group of young excellent workers (Corak 2016). In summary, wage inequality increases *between* companies, due to the concentration in large *superstar* companies of workers with higher skills; and it increases at the same time *within* educational groups in relation to the task for which a worker has the appropriate intangible capital.[16]

The divergence between the two groups of companies also reverberates on the income shares of the two productive factors. The greater

[14] "Half of the increase in wage inequality between firms explains half of the overall inequality [...]; and it is due to two-thirds (65%) to the wage premium, for one third (35%) to the sorting (*sorting*) of workers" (Criscuolo et al. 2020, p. 7). "Employment has increased in high-skill jobs, such as human resources management and IT support" (OECD 2020, p. 203). This confirms the dependence of remuneration both on professional qualification and on the link between skills and *digital capital* typical of the organisation of the most advanced companies.

[15] "Since information technologies represent the most direct way to replace workers with routine tasks, employment becomes polarised, with a faster growth of jobs at the top and bottom of the skill distribution" (OECD 2018a, p. 25).

[16] "The dispersion of the 'wage premium' is wider in countries with greater productivity dispersion, suggesting that it is at least partly due to productivity dispersion" (Criscuolo et al. 2021, pp. 10–1).

complementarity with capital (whose price has been reduced following globalisation) of high-skilled workers also means that the distribution of income shifts in favour of the share of earnings appropriated by ***high-skilled*** workers (Karabarbounis 2023). The trend towards different remuneration at the same level of education is indeed a sign that in large advanced companies the intangible capital required by tasks is very selected, which is also reflected in wage levels: "the sectors with the highest concentration rate show the most significant falls in the [wage] share, a phenomenon that primarily takes place *between* companies rather than *within* companies" (Autor et al. 2020, p. 664). The consequences on the losing part of the workforce are all too visible. The wages of medium-low skilled workers are penalised much more than would be justified by their level of education.

The wage polarisation is also influenced by the market form. Companies that enjoy a monopsonistic position in the territory collude with each other, especially in traditional sectors, with the aim of lowering the wage below the productivity of the workers. This strategy is favoured by the high cost of transferring to another area, often unsustainable for workers with scarce skills and low wages: "The lowering is systematically wider in countries and sectors where mobility is more limited, where low-productivity companies can afford to pay wages below productivity without a significant portion of workers leaving their jobs" (Criscuolo et al. 2021, p. 2). "Any impediment that raises the transaction costs of workers - for example, the cost of transport [...] - increases the bargaining power of the employer" (Howell and Kalleberg 2019, p. 38).[17] The productive reorganisation induced by sectoral concentration contributes to the "devaluation" of low-skilled work: "the reallocation of workers between companies [...] occurs to a greater extent in sectors where there is the greatest increase in market concentration [...] the reallocation of production between companies also plays a role, with shifts towards companies with low (and declining) wage shares" (Autor et al. 2020, p. 668). It is therefore not surprising if statistical data indicate that, in the manufacturing industry of advanced countries, the recovery of employment after crises (the financial crisis of 2008, the pandemic of 2020–22) tends to focus on the creation of high-skilled jobs.

[17] After the expansion of low-wage jobs, workers have experienced very limited mobility out of low pay; the Great Recession has caused a further deterioration of their wage condition (Howell and Kalleberg 2019, p. 14).

Technological Change and the Dynamics of Social Classes

The technological transformation of professions and the impact on the occupational structure of globalisation have changed social stratification. Accentuating the mobility of top incomes towards the top of the income distribution is the push that the power of CEOs in negotiating emoluments receives from the position of dominance reached in the market by their own company. This does not authorise the belief that a considerable remuneration signals considerable merit. The drastic technological reduction of the marginal cost of ICT products has weakened the link between remuneration and productivity in two respects: 1) companies have increased their market power, especially in the United States. The higher mark-up on costs has created inflation, with the effect of reducing real wages; 2) in large companies, the increased discretion of CEOs in strategic decisions affects the distribution of surplus, with the effect of increasing the share of capital in income. Indeed, the greater their command over production and employment, the more they grow—in addition to earnings—also the stock options of the company's top managers (Philippon 2019). In the last 40 years, CEO emoluments have gone from 20 times to 300 times the income of the median worker. "The net wealth of the 10 richest billionaires has more than doubled (+119%) [...] since the beginning of the pandemic, exceeding the aggregate value of 1500 billion dollars, which is over 6 times the stock of net wealth of the poorest 40% [...] of adult citizens worldwide" (Oxfam 2021, p. 5). While the increase in earnings is reflected in increases in wealth for managers, wage polarisation penalises the middle classes. The consequences of the command of the top of large companies on middle-skilled workers are analysed in a book entitled *The Paradox of Profit*: "Market forces [...] are penalising not only the poor, but also the middle class and small entrepreneurs. The capitalism of large corporations leads to the failure of the economic prospects of most families, where offspring do worse than parents [...]. Technological innovation has a natural tendency to accumulate wealth in a few hands" (Eeckhout 2021, p. 276).

The strengthening of the power of business executives within social stratification is one of the causes of the accentuation recorded by the distances between the incomes of social groups. There is a substantial risk that "a seventh of all middle-class families and a fifth of those close to low incomes will slide down into the poorest 20% within four years. There are clear signs that this risk has increased in the last two decades. [...] For

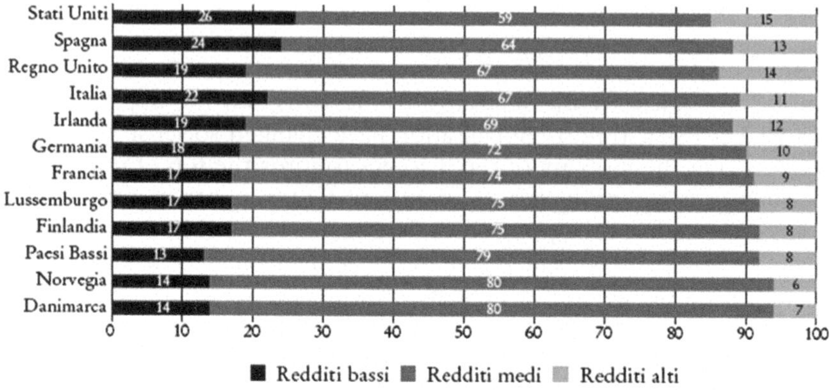

Fig. 10.4 Share of income on total: poor, middle class, rich (2010). (Source: Pew Research Center, Washington DC. Translation: US, Spain, UK, Italy, Ireland, Germany, France, Luxembourg, Finland, Netherlands, Norway, Denmark, low-income, middle-income, high-income)

those close to the lowest incomes and for part of the poorest 40% of the income distribution, the risk of falling even further down in life has increased. [...] Middle-class families closer to wealthier families have a lower risk of falling to a low income or into poverty. These are the signals that the middle class is fragmenting" (OECD 2018b, p. 16).

Around 1980, at the age of twenty 70% of baby boomers were middle class, today only 60% of millennials are. In 25 out of 35 OECD countries, those earning an annual income of 23,000 dollars fall into the middle class. This is not a figure that guarantees a very comfortable life. The aggregate income of all the belonging to the middle class, which was four times that of the top incomes (people with an income double the median income), today it has reduced to less than triple (Oecd 2019a).

Also due to the low rate of redistribution of the American social state, social mobility is decreasing and poverty is increasing, especially in families whose working-age members are not employed (Kenworthy and Smeeding 2013). As Fig. 10.4 documents, the United States stands out among the major advanced economies for the greatest impact of economic inequalities on the dynamics of social classes.[18]

[18] "Countries with a very unequal distribution of human capital, such as the United States, or many emerging countries, have lower rates of intergenerational mobility than countries in which fewer individuals appear at the tails of the distribution" (Becker et al. 2018, p. 3).

Social stratification is characterised, compared to European countries, by the larger size of the classes at the two extremes, and by a share of middle-class income that is reducing mainly due to the changes we have seen occur in labour demand following the transition to Tbtc.

The parallel trend between the polarisation of the skills required of workers and wage polarisation, as well as to factors endogenous to the market structure of the productive sector—the divergence between large innovative companies and traditional companies—is probably also linked to the "financialisation" of economies. Figure 10.5 shows the "overtaking", which occurred in the early nineties, of the share of credit in financial circulation compared to that related to productive activities. This structural change could have influenced wage polarisation. Firstly, in fact, workers carrying intangible capital are present in large numbers in the finance sector. Secondly, the economic culture that is imparted to students of the countless university and post-university finance courses scattered around the world has no connection with welfare economics, whose II Theorem is concerned with combining the objective of efficiency with

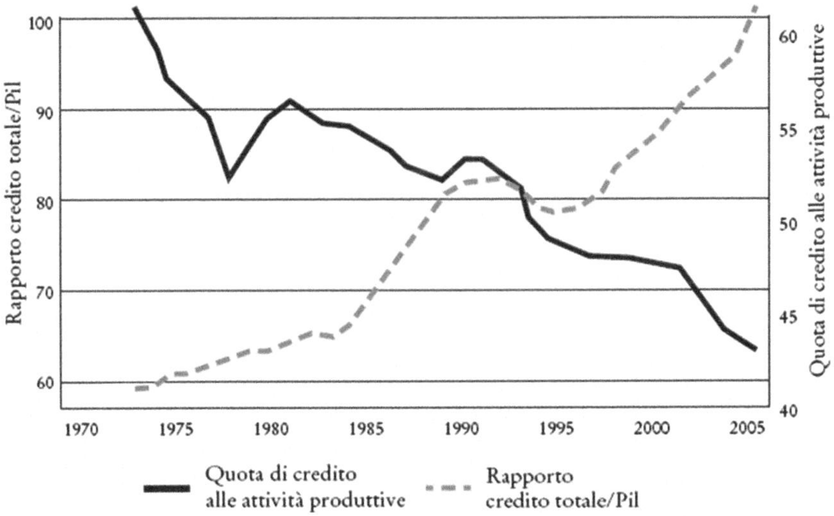

Fig. 10.5 Financialisation of the economic system. (Source: Bezemer et al. 2018. Translation: Share of bank credit to production, Total amount of bank credit / GDP ratio)

that of equity. As numerous as they are, and difficult to investigate, more than one transmission channel that the rapid process of 'financialisation' has activared in advanced countries lead to the growth of income inequality.

The trend towards polarisation and its effects on social mobility are also increasing in Europe, due to a variety of factors: job insecurity; the dissolution of institutions that with their role of aggregation protected the worker; and, more recently, the fading of the role of the social state as a system of protection from macroeconomic risk factors (a fall in income) and microeconomic (a low level of health or education). Economic vulnerability has been partly contained, on both sides of the Atlantic, by the role of *buffer stock* played by wealth. The trend towards lowering the qualification of traditionally occupied job positions, and therefore to receive a lower share of income, may have induced the more affluent middle class to dispose of part of the property—both equity and real estate—owned, in order not to give up the standard of consumption reached and the *status* social acquired. On the other hand, the impoverishment of the lower band of the middle class swells the number of *working poor*, as evidenced by the large share of income of subjects belonging to the deciles of the poor.

Regarding the disappearance of the social function of work, and the social irrelevance that follows from the fall in the income level of the weakest people, this consideration is enlightening: "The poor have always been present in all known societies, but today's poor are in worse conditions than those of the past, perhaps because, for the first time in history, they have no social function to perform" (Bauman and Tesler 2002, p. 70).

Bibliography

Acemoglu, D. 2023 Distorted Innovation: Does the Market Get the Direction of Technology Right?, *in «American Economic Journal, Papers and Proceedings», CXIII, pp. 1–28.*

Acemoglu, D. & Autor, D. 2011 Skills, Tasks and Technologies: Implications for Employment and Earnings, *in Ashenfelter - Card 2011, pp. 1043–171.*

Acemoglu, D. & Johnson, S. 2023 Power and Progress: Our Thousand-Year Struggle Over Technology and Prosperity, *Public Affairs, New York.*

Acemoglu, D. & Restrepo, P. 2020 The Wrong Kind of Ia? Artificial Intelligence and the Future of Labour Demand, *in «Cambridge Journal of Regions, Economy, and Society», XIII, 1, pp. 25–35.*

Akcigit, U. et al. 2021 Rising Corporate Market Power: Emerging Policy Issues, *Imf Staff Discussion Note n. 1.*

Appelbaum, E. 2017 *Domestic Outsourcing, Rent Seeking, and Increasing Inequality*, in «Review of Radical Political Economics», XLIX, 4, pp. 513–28.

Atkinson, A. B. 1998 *Social Exclusion, Poverty and Unemployment*, in A. B. Atkinson & J. Hills (eds), *Exclusion, Employment and Opportunity*, London School of Economics, Centre for Analysis of Social Exclusion, n. 4.

Autor, D. H. & Dorn, D. 2013 The Growth of Low-skilled Service Jobs and the Polarization of the Us Labor Market, *in «American Economic Review», CIII, 5, pp. 1553–97.*

Autor, D., Dorn, D., Katz, L., Patterson, C., Van Reenen, J. 2020 The Fall of the Labor Share and the Rise of Superstar Firms, *in «Quarterly Journal of Economics», CXXXV, 2, pp. 645–709.*

Autor, D., Dube, A., McGrew, A. 2023 The Unexpected Compression: Competition at Work in the Low Wage Labor Market, *Nber Working Paper n. 31010.*

Bauman, Z. & Tesler, K. 2002 Società, etica, politica. Conversazioni con Zygmunt Bauman, *Raffaello Cortina, Milano.*

Becker, G., Kominers, S. D., Murphy, K. M. Spenkuch, J. L. 2018 *A Theory of Intergenerational Mobility*, in «Journal of Political Economy», CXXVI, S1, pp. 7–25.

Bezemer, D., Ryan-Collins, J., van Lerven, F., Zhang, L. 2018 Credit Where It's Due. A Historical, Theoretical and Empirical Review of Credit Guidance Policies in the 20th Century, *Ucl Institute for Innovation and Public Purpose, Working Paper n. 11.*

Bloom, N., Jones, C. I., Van Reenen, J., Webb, M. 2020 *Are Ideas Getting Harder to Find?*, in «American Economic Review», CX, 4, pp. 1104–44.

Bosworth, S. J., Singer, T., Snower, D. J. 2016 *Cooperation, Motivation and Social Balance*, in «Journal of Economic Behavior & Organization», CXXVI, pp. 72–94.

Castel, R. 1995 Les Métamorphoses de la question sociale. Une chronique du salariat, *Fayard, Paris.*

Corak, M. 2016 Economic Theory and Practical Lessons for Measuring Equality of Opportunities, *Oecd Statistics Working Paper n. 2.*

Criscuolo, C. et al. 2020 Workforce Composition, Productivity and Pay: The Role of Firms in Wage Inequality, *Oecd Social, Employment and Migration Working Paper n. 241.*

Criscuolo, C. et al. 2021 The Firm-level Link between Productivity Dispersion and Wage Inequality: A Symptom of Low Job Mobility?, *Oecd Economics Department Working Paper n. 1656.*

Eeckhout, J. 2021 The Profit Paradox: How Thriving Firms Threaten the Future of Work, *Princeton University Press, Princeton.*

Faia, E. & Shabalina, E. 2023 Distributional Consequences of Technology Shocks through Labour Reallocation, *Cepr Discussion Paper n. 18546.*

Farina, F. 2021 Lo Stato sociale. Storia, politica, economia, *Luiss University Press, Roma.*

Galor, O. & Tsiddon, D. 1997 Technological Progress, Mobility, and Economic Growth, *in «American Economic Review», LXXXVII, 3, pp. 363–82.*

Gordon, R. J. 2018 Why Has Economic Growth Slowed When Innovation Appears to be Accelerating?, *Nber Working Paper n. 24554.*

Gordon, R. J. & Sayed, H. 2020 Transatlantic Technologies: The Role of ICT on the Evolution of U.S. and European Productivity Growth, *in «International Productivity Monitor», XXXVIII, pp. 50–80.*

Hacker, J. S. & Pierson, P. 2010 Winner-Take-All Politics and Political Science, *in «Politics and Society», XXXVIII, 2, pp. 266–82.*

Hoff, K. & Stiglitz, J. E. 2016 Striving for Balance in Economics: Towards a Theory of the Social Determination of Behavior, *in «Journal of Economic Behavior & Organization», CXXVI, IssuePB, pp. 25–57.*

Howell, D. R. & Kalleberg, A. L. 2019 *Declining Job Quality in the United States: Explanations and Evidence*, in «The Russell Sage Foundation, Journal of the Social Sciences», V, 4, pp. 1–53.

Jaimovich, N. & Siu, H. E. 2020 *Job Polarization and Jobless Recoveries*, in «Review of Economics and Statistics», CII, 1, pp. 129–47.

Karabarbounis, L. 2023 Perspectives on the Labor Share, *Nber Working Paper n. 31854.*

Katz, L. F. & Krueger, A. B. 2018 The Rise and Nature of Alternative Work Arrangements in the United States, 1995–2015, *in «Ilr Review», LXXII, 2, pp. 382–416.*

Kelly, C. & Snower, D. J. 2021 *Capitalism Recoupled*, in «Oxford Review of Economic Policy», XXXVII, 4, pp. 851–63.

Kenworthy, L. & Smeeding, T. 2013 *Growing Inequalities and Their Impacts in the United States*, Gini Country Report, Aias (Amsterdam Institute for Advanced Labour Studies).

Kurz, M. 2023 The Market Power of Technology: Understanding the Second Gilded Age, *Columbia University Press, New York.*

Michaels, G., Natrai, A., Van Reenen, J. 2014 Has Ict Polarized Skill Demand? Evidence from Eleven Countries over 25 Years, *in «Review of Economics and Statistics», XCVI, 1, pp. 60–77.*

Oecd 2018a A Broken Social Elevator? How to Promote Social Mobility, *Paris.*

Oecd 2018b The Future of Social Protection. What Works for Non-standard Workers?, *Paris.*

Oecd 2018c Good Jobs for All in a Changing World of Work: The Oecd Jobs Strategy, *Oecd Publishing, Paris.*

Oecd 2019a Under Pressure: The Squeezed Middle Class, *Paris.*

Oecd 2019b Employment Outlook 2019: The Future of Work, *Paris.*

Oecd 2020 Beyond Growth. Towards a New Economic Approach, *Paris.*

Oxfam 2021 Inequality Report.

Philippon, T. 2019 The Great Reversal: How America Gave Up on Free Markets, *Harvard University Press, Cambridge.*

Piketty, T. 2014 *Le capital au XXIe siècle*, Éditions du Seuil, Paris 2013.

Rodrik, D. & Stantcheva, S. 2021 Economic Inequality and Insecurity: Policies for an Inclusive Economy, *in Blanchard - Tirole 2021.*

Roncaglia, G. 2023 L'architetto e l'oracolo. Forme digitali del sapere da Wikipedia a ChatGpt, *Laterza, Roma-Bari.*

Schumpeter, J. A. 1942, Socialism, and Democracy, Harper & Bros, New York 1942.

Smith, A. 1776 An Inquiry into the Nature and Causes of the Wealth of Nations, Methuen, London.

Sombart, W. 1916 Der moderne Kapitalismus, Duncker & Humblot, München-Leipzig.

Summers, L. H. 2015 *Demand Side Secular Stagnation*, in «American Economic Review: Papers & Proceedings», CV, 5, pp. 60–5.

Thiel, P. 2014 *Competition Is for Losers*, in «Wall Street Journal», C1, 13 settembre.

CHAPTER 11

Mobility in Education: Economic Incentive or Family Resources?

"The School, Central Organ of Democracy"[1]

History, reflected Zygmunt Bauman, helps to understand why "the world has come to be what it is" (Bauman and Tesler 2002, p. 43). In saying that history shows us the evolutionary path the world has taken, Bauman was right. However, it is not always the case that a well-formulated goal leads to the desired outcome. In the most developed countries of eighteenth-century Europe, the historical story of education began under the best auspices. The Enlightenment Revolution, which exalted the rational disposition of the individual, also highlighted how the educational process of each person fits into a collective dimension. Being a basic aspect of the life of every community, education for life and profession should no longer be reserved for the offspring of the nobility and imparted by tutors. In the First French Republic, the Enlightenment conviction that cultural formation should underpin the identity of all citizens, and that the State should take responsibility for it, received legal recognition. It was in 1792 that the French mathematician Jean-Antoine Caritat de Condorcet drafted and presented to the French legislative assembly the *Report on Public Education*.

[1] Quote taken from a speech of 11 February 1950 by Piero Calamandrei, one of the founders of the Italian Partito d'Azione and one of the drafters of the Constitution of the Italian Republic.

F. Farina, *The Rise of Inequality and the Fall of Social Mobility*,
https://doi.org/10.1007/978-3-031-92843-7_11

This Report was the first project of "universal" education conceived in Europe. And it was also the second comprehensive public policy to develop, after the programmes to assist the poor.[2] In agrarian society, it is known, literacy played a marginal role. With industrialisation and urbanisation—in the "old continent" and in the United States—it was primarily the public sector that was tasked with raising the level of education of the population, adapting it to the needs of a more dynamic and more articulated society (Gellner 1983). At the dawn of mass society, the ruling classes became aware that the construction of a system of cultural and professional education not only helps the integration of individuals into society, making possible their rise in income and *status*, but also increases the quality of social interaction and collective well-being. In the most advanced European countries (and more slowly in the United States, due to racial segregation)[3] a national compulsory education system began to be organised. Education, which at the beginning of the nineteenth century had spread very unevenly among social classes, improved with the standardisation of school programmes across the national territory, and the introduction of ethical codes for teachers and students.

The institutions responsible for collective welfare were consolidated in the late nineteenth century, when the first redistributive and insurance policies of the welfare state were organised. In his main work, *The Great Transformation* (1944), Karl Polanyi focused attention on a coincidence: social protection institutions had arisen concurrently with the affirmation of the capitalist economy. In his view, nothing else could have happened. The capitalist mode of production, in the absence of welfare institutions, would have proved unsustainable: "it could not have lasted long without annihilating the human and natural substance of society" (Polanyi 1974, p. 3).[4] That this achievement was not without ambiguity soon became clear. At the turn of the nineteenth and twentieth centuries, what has been called "the entry of the masses into history" began to show cracks: the ruling classes were becoming fearful that the right to vote would act as a

[2] Public assistance to the poor had taken its first steps in England in 1601, with the *Old Poor Laws* introduced by Queen Elizabeth I; with the enactment of the *New Poor Laws* in 1834, it moved from parish management to that of the central state.

[3] Compulsory public education was extended to all school-age children and in all states with the *Education Act* of 1870. Previously, it was only present in the New England states, where the black population was almost entirely absent.

[4] As will be remembered (*supra*, chap. V, par. 2), Ken Arrow used very similar words about the "world of laissez-faire".

catalyst for the subversion of the subordinate classes: "the elites imposed mass education on their populations to serve their own interests, which were put at risk by democracy" (Alesina et al. 2021, p. 8). On the other hand, there was a logic behind the fact that the spread of voting democracy and the spread of the right to education went hand in hand. If the right to vote, a political weapon hard-won by the middle class and then by the poor, had not been added to access to public education, the concession of this welfare institution would have had a hard life. The scant favour that the expansion of education enjoyed among an elite fearful of losing power would indeed have slowed down the process of its "democratisation" (Acemoglu and Robinson 2000).

The organisation of compulsory public schooling contributed greatly to generating in the population, from school age, both rational and emotional attachment to a collective cultural identity (Gellner 1983). Faced with this epochal change, the ruling classes remained uncertain for a long time, wavering between the choice to expand public education and the fear that raising the cultural level of the population would backfire. In those same decades, moreover, the era of military and colonial powers in conflict for primacy on the international scene was opening. The educational objective pursued by governments then took a more precise direction, that of cementing the national spirit around the interests of the dominant social groups. Public education was thus directed at instilling in the people the pride of being part of the same culture as its most glorious figures, the *pantheon* of the nation, and at the same time supporting its military power (Hobsbawm 1990).

Despite the ambiguities of power, after two world wars, the combination of income growth and education consolidated. From the massive empirical verification coordinated by two World Bank economists, a "universal" fact emerges: intergenerational social mobility manifests itself jointly in the dimensions of income and education in all countries and in all stages of their development. "A higher level of GDP is associated with higher educational mobility" (Narayan et al. 2018, p. 21). This judgement admits a dual causal link. The increase in GDP can favour the advancement of society towards greater autonomy of young people in cultural and professional training compared to the opportunities their parents had. At the same time, the increase in GDP and the absolute mobility of young people depend, among other things, on the level of education reached by the population.

The Market Incentive for Social Mobility: "The more you learn, the more you earn"

The United States is the nation that has most convincingly focused on "quality" university education to support growth. At the end of the nineteenth century, the acceleration of industrial production increased the demand for graduates with technical and scientific training. The strongest universities in training, those defined as "research", had a great development, taking over from the colleges. By the middle of the twentieth century, 80–90% of young people in the United States completed secondary education, compared to 20–30% of young people in Germany, France and Japan (Piketty 2018). In the 1920s, in the Nobel Prize rankings, US universities surpassed in number of "graduate" teachers those of the major European countries (MacLeod and Urquiola 2021). According to the Barro-Lee Educational Attainment Dataset, the United States holds the record for the fastest increase in the population with a university education in the last century (Barro and Lee 2013). The pre-eminence that education had throughout the twentieth century in driving the economic growth of that country (Goldin and Katz 2008) contributes to making the epithet of "American century" more than deserved.

The percentage of the population with university education, the indicator of *absolute educational mobility*, reached such high levels at the end of the twentieth century as to push up both the training certificates required by companies and the emoluments offered to graduates. Education has become the driving force of individual economic success. Income inequality is largely attributable to the wage gap due to different degrees of education of professional qualification. One fact for all: only 1.3% of American workers who stopped at the *high school* diploma and only 17.2% of those with a university degree earn more today than a typical professional with a *high school* diploma (Markovits 2019). According to the *surveys* conducted by the US Bureau of Labor Statistics, in 2015 in a location in the state of Indiana, a full 60% of job vacancies required a *bachelor degree* (three-year degree), a master's or a Ph.D. The median monthly earnings offered were respectable: 4500, 5300, 6800 dollars, respectively. A *topos* of American society is the slogan "learning equals earning".[5]

[5] Motto attributed to Warren Buffett, wealthy entrepreneur and American philanthropist.

Economic research has followed this slogan. A few decades ago, Gary Becker, Nobel laureate in economics 1992, investigated, together with Nigel Tomes, inter-generational social mobility in the United States. The two economists pointed to equality of educational opportunities as the essential pre-condition for the advent of the "open society". Becker and Tomes took into account the heterogeneity among people facing a credit market that is by definition "imperfect": horizontal equity, equal treatment for all credit applicants, is not respected. In the absence of strong public support for access to education, which is typical of a model where education provision is predominantly private, those who are unable to provide the necessary *collateral* are excluded from financing. Poor young people thus do not have the means to finance the expense of acquiring an adequate education. Becker and Tomes seemed to recognise the asymmetry between rich families and poor families in terms of their children's education: "It is known that boys receive endowments of capital determined by the reputation and social connections of their families, from learning *skills*, from life goals and other family assets acquired through belonging to the family culture" (Becker and Tomes 1979, p. 158). However, the heterogeneity of young people's "circumstances" was removed by them. It is true that the empirical verification of their model was conducted by Becker and Tomes both *with* and *without* the assumption of "perfect" markets. Only in the conclusions did heterogeneity end up not assuming relevance. The assumption that the prospects for social mobility were high even in the "model with imperfect markets", i.e. in the presence of the "liquidity constraint" for poor families, performed the magic.

The "liquidity constraint" that penalises poor families was exorcised with these embarrassing words: "Intergenerational mobility of earnings depends not only on the inheritability of wealth, but also on the willingness of poor families to self-finance the investment in their own children" (Becker and Tomes 1986, p. 291). The two economists advanced the prediction that the *question social* of low mobility of "disadvantaged" young people in access to education would have been cancelled out in a few decades: "the relationship between permanent income of fathers and sons is no larger than 0.40, so all the advantages or disadvantages of ancestors will disappear in only three generations [...]. In 'open societies' parents influence very little the earnings of children and grandchildren" (*ibid.*, p. 286). In the nation-symbol of Popper's "open society", the expectation of a strong intergenerational income mobility guaranteed by the spread of education has been denied by reality. Fig. 7.2 shows that normally a poor American family needs five generations for a child to aspire to reach the average income of the country. The last thirty years have seen an increase up to 0.54 in the persistence of children's incomes at the level of those of their parents. The trend towards "social immobility"—from the bottom up—of American society has a dual explanation: in the presence of a predominantly private educational system, a very unequal distribution of income and wealth has been followed by the widening of the gap in educational opportunities; and, conversely, the widening of opportunities for social ascent has been followed by an increase in inequalities.

How is the impact of education on earnings and social mobility expressed in intergenerational terms? The conclusion reached by two well-known economists, Galor and Tsiddon, is this: "The interaction of technological progress with the two components of individual earnings - the human capital of parents and the skills acquired by children - presides over the evolutionary paths of intergenerational mobility of earnings, the speed of technological progress and economic growth" (Galor and Tsiddon 1997, p. 375). However, there is a difference. In the phases of *primary technological innovations*, economic growth, and therefore mobility, would depend directly on the skills expressed by children in creating new products and production methods at the end of their training process. These are indeed the phases in which talents, or the capacities of excellence, are in the foreground demonstrated by the young of the new generation. In the phases of *technology diffusion* within the productive fabric, the main determinant of intergenerational mobility is instead found in the human capital of parents, transmitted to children through genetic and cultural means. Here, the family's push to prolong the educational journey of their children as much as possible is paramount. It is easy to understand that in this second type of technical progress, the asymmetry of social power is dominant. While the children of the elite are advantaged in achieving an excellent education, young people coming from "disadvantaged" families struggle to have access to bank credit for education. Many of them are excluded from education, especially tertiary education.

Orthodox economics identifies the "rate of return of education" (the increase in earnings associated with a longer period of education) as the "guiding star" of the educational journey of young people. The higher the expected return from education, the greater their investment in the education market should be. In this view of young people's education, the logic of methodological individualism on which economic theory is based is expressed to the highest degree. According to Becker, the formation of human capital and the autonomy of earnings from parents that children manage to achieve are explained by the individual investment of young people: "instead of assuming that wage differences reflect the good or bad occupations of workers, the human capital approach asserts that earnings primarily measure how much they have invested in *skills* and knowledge" (Becker 2011, p. XIII). But who are, more precisely, the people to whom the pronoun "they" refers?

The president of the United States Ronald Reagan, in presenting the 1988 federal budget, had no doubts about the group he was addressing with the appellation "they". He stated that "students are the main beneficiaries of their investment in university education. It would therefore be reasonable to expect that they - and not the taxpayers - should bear most of the costs of such investment". In referring the pronoun "they" to the *aggregate* of students, Reagan changed the cards on the table a bit. Especially in a country where the public sector is not of such size as to be able to play a propulsive role in education, because private institutions dominate the provision of education, it is the family that assumes a leading role. For a long time, credit was given to the individualistic approach to education: a high return on education on the one hand would push young people to prolong their studies, on the other hand, it would represent one of the main determinants of intergenerational income mobility. But reality is different: which young people are more likely to obtain a high human capital, or what their social origin is, is well explained in Solon (2004). The real "guiding star" of the educational journey of young people—especially Americans—is the economic position of the parents. American students "advantaged", even when they receive a C grade at university (given in that educational system to the "non-deserving"), go on—and often even a lot—in life. The condition is that they come, indeed, from a high-ranking family. Here is the confession of a student "advantaged" but not talented. In the speech he gave at Yale University in 2001, accepting the degree *honoris causa*, 33 years after graduating from the same university, then US President, George W. Bush said: "To those of you who received honours, awards, and distinction, I say, well done. And to the C students, I say, you too can be president of the United States" (Ballarino et al. 2014). A joke that is actually a confession. It is proof of how an educational system based on the initiative—and interest—of private individuals can end up rewarding wealth rather than merit.

Let's then delve into how much the incentive of "expected individual earnings" counts in advanced countries in allowing a young person to rise in income compared to the income achieved by their parents. Fig. 11.1 presents the correlation of "expected individual earnings" with two different indicators: intergenerational earnings mobility for 2008 (Fig. 11.1a) and multidimensional intergenerational mobility for 2018 (Fig. 11.1b).[6] The chart at the top relates on the horizontal axis the "private rate of return on education",[7] and on the vertical axis the values of the intergenerational income mobility indicator, which has previously been measured with the Iee, its complement to one.

Fig. 11.1a tells us that for the average of advanced countries the increase in earnings, to which the theory of market incentives assigns the task of encouraging young people to extend their period of education, is not a good "predictor" of the rise in income position. The message of the *cross-country* the graph at the top shows that for the set of countries, intergenerational mobility is hardly linked to the "reward" received by extending the period of education, the "rate of return" expected from obtaining a more advanced degree.[8] The heterogeneity among countries of the correlation between the independent variable (horizontal axis) and the dependent variable (vertical axis) is very high. The "reward", sometimes high, for the extension of education by children often results in a "climb" to income positions higher than those of their parents in really minimal proportions. The denial of the orthodox economic theory of the incentive to education is clamorous. Considering intergenerational mobility in the multidimensional terms of Table 1.1, the graph at the bottom (Fig. 11.1b) allows only an indicative comparison with the graph at the top (on the vertical axis, between the two mobility indicators the comparison is

[6] Multidimensional data are those estimated by the World Economic Forum (the synthetic index calculated for 2018, as seen in the Introduction), which includes a wide range of indicators of multidimensional well-being.

[7] The data on the rate of return of tertiary education are two different measures, presented in the annual publication of the OECD, *Education at a Glance*, of the increase in earnings obtained with the prolongation of studies. In the top graph the measure is defined as "private internal rate of return" (OECD 2008) and in the bottom one as "net financial return" (OECD 2021).

[8] The correlation would have been better if the observed values had been closer to the estimated ones, i.e. to the interpolating line drawn in the graph. The Iee data of many countries is well above the interpolating line. This indicates that their "elasticity" value—and therefore the persistence of children at the income level of their parents—is higher than for the sample average.

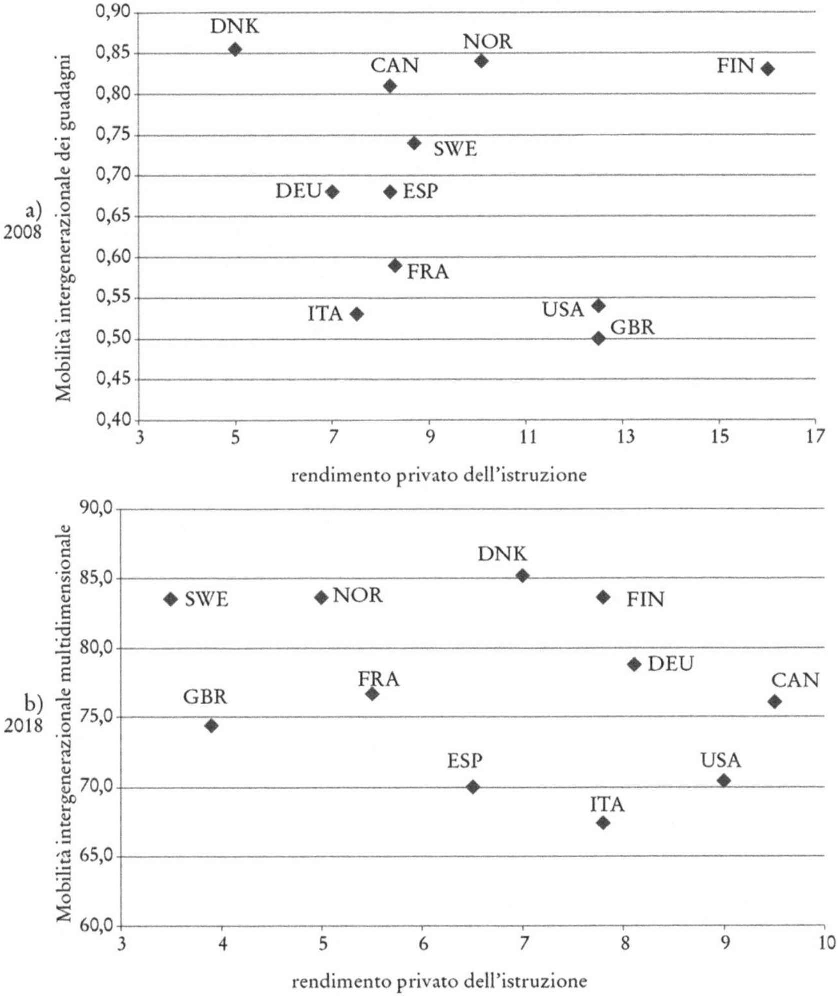

Fig. 11.1 Private return on education and social mobility. Translation: a) Intergenerational earnings mobility, private return on education, b) Multidimensional earnings mobility, private return on education. (Note: The values of the private return on education are calculated as the increase in earnings (difference between a job after obtaining a university degree compared to a job after high school graduation), net of taxes and individual private costs for university fees and for giving up paid activities. The values of multidimensional intergenerational mobility are derived from Table 1.1. Source: Author's own elaboration on Oecd data and Economic World Forum)

obviously of an ordinal type). The most important information obtained from Fig. 11.1 can be summarised as follows: between 2008 and 2018, the economic incentive continues to be a modest "predictor" of social mobility (in many countries the private return of education is reduced). Intergenerational mobility, in general, does not seem to have changed much. In the graph at the bottom, the addition to income, in the calculation of mobility, of the other main dimensions of well-being only reaffirms the low impact of the economic incentive on intergenerational mobility. In many countries, however, the addition in the indicator of non-income variables seems to improve the dynamics of the social structure, probably due to the impulse exerted by the welfare state through public provision in education and health; while in 2008 the United States, the United Kingdom and Italy shared high values of "immobility" social, in 2018 the "social immobility" is confirmed for the United States, increases in Italy and decreases in the United Kingdom (a country in which, however, the return of education has been greatly reduced); the performance of the Nordic countries is even more detached from that of the other countries in 2018. While in 2008 the values of the return of education were very heterogeneous, in 2018 these values have condensed, so the impact of the "rate of return" on asking for more education has become more similar; Germany catches up with France in the rate of return of education; in Spain this rate continues to be slightly better than in Italy, a country which, however, approaches for a decreasing social mobility, moving away, compared to 2008, from the data of Germany.

The data of the two major Anglo-Saxon countries—the United States and the United Kingdom—is particularly surprising. In these education systems based on the market supply of education, with a clear predominance of private universities and secondary education institutes, it is indeed expected that the "private return of education" guaranteed by the market will play a predominant role in social mobility. In the econometric estimate, however, the return is found to be very high and the "social mobility" very low. This result is a warning bell for these countries. The empirical evidence available for the United States, in Fig. 11.2, shows that the decreasing trend of intergenerational income mobility has been in constant decline since the cohort born in 1940. To understand more, let's ask ourselves what role the destination of GDP to public spending for education plays in promoting the educational mobility of children compared to parents.

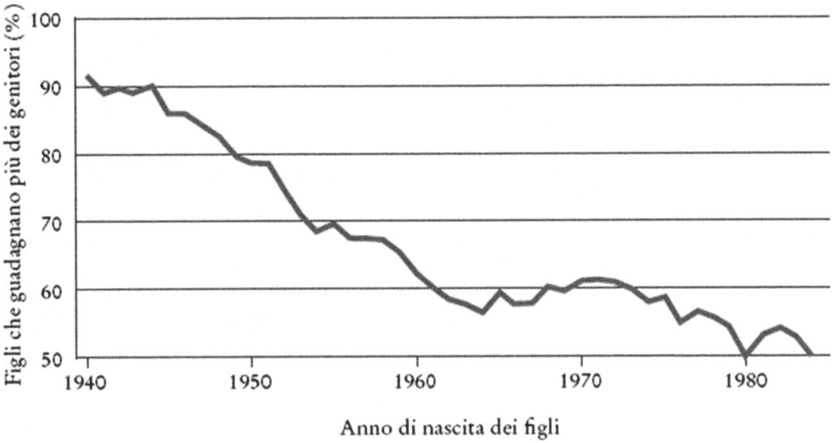

Fig. 11.2 Intergenerational income mobility in the United States by year of birth of children (1940–1985). (Source: Chetty et al. 2017a. Translation: Sons with income higher than their parents (%), Year of birth of sons)

As documented in Fig. 6.1, although education has supported, much more than in Europe, the expansion of GDP, and therefore the social mobility *absolute* of the population, in the United States the gap between rich and poor families in access to tertiary education for young people between 19 and 21 years has enormously increased at the turn of the new millennium.

The forecast of a continuation over time of the "intergenerational immobility" suggested by this empirical evidence is confirmed by observing the histograms in Fig. 11.3: the spending of rich parents for the education of their children has progressively distanced—between 1972–1973 and 2005–2006—from that of poor parents.

That the goal of families is the social mobility of their children and that the probability of their educational success should be increased by aiming at the best universities is then demonstrated, already for the final decades of the twentieth century, by Fig. 11.4. There is a growing dynamic in the correlation between the income position of parents and the position in the quality ranking of the universities attended by their children, with the inclination to the exponential form already around the medium-low levels of income. In summary, from the empirical evidence of Figs. 11.2, 11.3 and 11.4 one belief emerges: when assessing the impact of economic

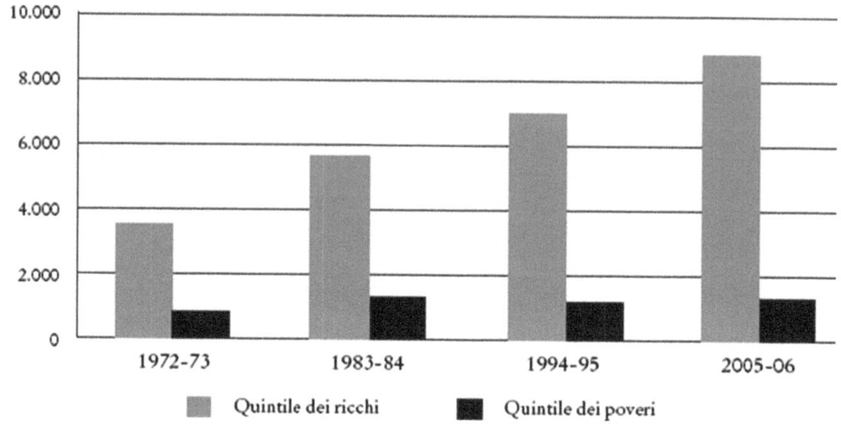

Fig. 11.3 Expenditure of social groups (last and first quintile of income distribution) for children's education (in US dollars, 1972–2006). (Source: elaboration in Duncan - Mundane 2011, on data from the Bureau of Labor Statistics, United States. Translation: Rich quintile, Poor quintile)

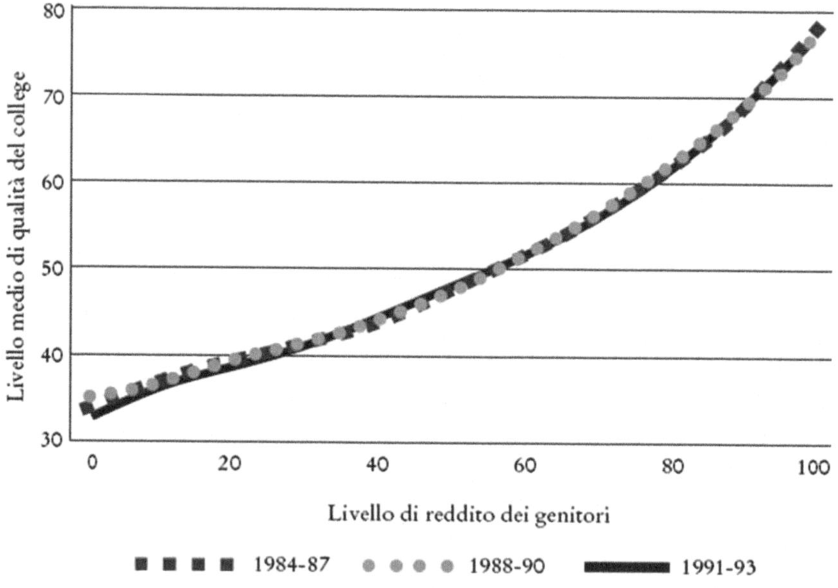

Fig. 11.4 Quality of college and attendance of young people in the United States by parents' income level. (Source: Chetty et al. 2014a. Translation: Average quality of the college, Parents' income level)

factors on intergenerational mobility, the prolongation of education by young people does not depend so much on the expectation of a higher income, but primarily on the income and wealth resources of their parents.

Intergenerational Mobility in Education and Income

The graph of Fig. 11.5 shows, for each country, on the horizontal axis the expenditure on education out of the total public expenditure in 1995 and on the vertical axis the index of intergenerational educational mobility in the following period. The focus on socio-economic development usually leads governments to care about raising the human capital of the population. Even within the group of Oecd countries, however, there are significant differences. The empirical evidence that appears in the graph also shows a high heterogeneity in the "universalistic commitment to education", or the data of public educational expenditure in relation to GDP *among* countries. This corresponds to a result in terms of intergenerational educational mobility that is equally heterogeneous. The overall picture reflects a certain proportionality between "state expenditure" and "return" in terms of intergenerational educational mobility.

We can say that the indicator on the vertical axis reveals, for the "richer" countries, the success in keeping pace with their overall development, both technological and social welfare? It does not seem so. The

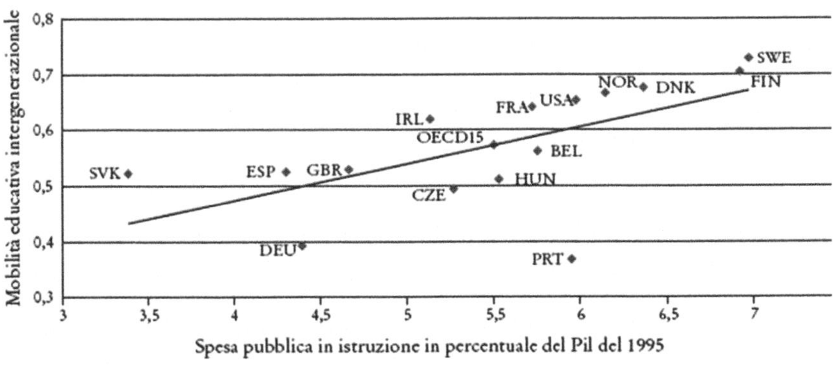

Fig. 11.5 Intergenerational educational mobility and public spending/ GDP. (Source: Oecd 2018. Translation: Intergenerational mobility in education, Public expenditures in education as a percentage of 1995 GDP)

cross-country analysis of the graph reveals a certain heterogeneity. It has just been said that in two of the major "rich" countries intergenerational mobility presents a not particularly high value; also the share of public expenditure for education out of the total GDP is not particularly high. Among the "rich" countries, those that succeed in promoting intergenerational educational mobility—through a public expenditure for education in relation to GDP ranging from 6.2% to 7%, compared to an average value equal to 5.5% of GDP for 15 Oecd countries—are mainly the Nordic countries (the analysis conducted by Chevalier 2019 on the microdata of the European Social Survey confirms this message).

An interpretative problem arises. It should be "physiological" that in a country with a "high" level of economic development there is a "high" intergenerational educational mobility. What the graph shows is a proportionality between an indicator for the population as *aggregate*—intergenerational educational mobility—and the *public education expenditure on GDP*, which is a *subset* of the aggregate expenditure for education in relation to GDP. One can then ask: how much does private expenditure in education contribute to the increase of upward intergenerational educational mobility? The estimate only allows to formulate a hypothesis. In light of the modest educational mobility values of many rich countries present in Fig. 11.5, and considering that private expenditure for education tends to increase the inequality of opportunity between rich and poor, it would seem that it does not contribute enough. Moreover, among the "rich" countries, it is the Nordic countries that register the best performance of intergenerational mobility despite the "private incentive" to education represented by the "rate of return" not being particularly high. It is clear, therefore, that many of the difficulties that advanced countries encounter in promoting social mobility alongside social cohesion are embedded in the education system.

This doubt about the "private incentive" inevitably generates another one about public commitment. Since educational mobility is a concept closely linked to the raising of the level of training and professional qualification of the population towards a level generally more adequate to the needs of development, one must ask how effective the economic "effort" of a government for education is—*within* the country—in guaranteeing "educational inclusion", or the upward convergence of the level of education of the "disadvantaged" classes. We must therefore ask ourselves: is the "universalistic" commitment of the public sector sufficient to promote intergenerational educational mobility? In other words, can we say that the ratios *public expenditure for education/GDP* "push" educational mobility between generations in *all* social classes? A clue that leads to a negative answer to this question is the correlation between the family's position in the income ranking and the children's access to university, the trend of which seems to predict a future society divided into castes: to each higher level in the independent variable corresponds a higher level, of almost equal amplitude, in the dependent variable.

Gary Solon, one of the major promoters of studies on mobility educational, over twenty years ago warned: "The intergenerational elasticity of earnings [...] inversely depends on the *progressiveness* of government investment in the human capital of young people" (Solon 2002, p. 65). The italics in the text allow us to apply to "educational inclusion" the criterion of "unequal treatment of the unequal": public sector investment will remain inadequate in promoting upward educational mobility if it is not designed based on "solidaristic universalism", or aimed at supporting the social rise of "disadvantaged" young people. When we disaggregate the impact of social spending on education on intergenerational educational mobility by social classes, we discover its dependence on income distribution. Graphs 1, 18, 19 and 20 are a strong indication that the intergenerational mobility of young people is severely hindered by the impact of parents' economic conditions on their life chances. The trend of the "hidden variable"—the inequality of opportunity—is decisive in intergenerational mobility both in education and in income. In an unequal world, "universalism *tout court* " is not enough. The more progressive public spending on education is, the higher the percentage of "disadvantaged" young people who manage to study longer than their parents did, and to climb higher on the income scale compared to their low earnings. Public educational spending in relation to GDP must not only be "high", but must also be "differentiated". Although the heterogeneity of tax treatment is provided for both in the progressive taxation regime (with the variability of tax rates based on income), and by legislation on the right to different welfare benefits (in case of specific personal situations), equalising public policy programmes should be more extensive and better structured. For example, as we will see in Chap. 12, in the case of merit goods the criterion of "progressiveness" is not adopted; on the contrary, given the tendency of the rich to *opting-out* of social insurances, the trend is towards regressivity.

Theoretical models on the intergenerational transmission of *status* socio-economic do not manage to untangle the complex relationship of complementarity that binds the human capital background of parents with the investment in the human capital of children (Solon 2013). OECD statistics confirm that among the most important non-income determinants of children's "circumstances" is the level of education of parents.[9] And based on its estimates, the World Bank comes to this peremptory conclusion: "the educational success of children depends on the educational success of parents" (Van der Weide et al. 2021, p. 30). If the *social spending/GDP* ratio of education does not prove capable of giving a powerful boost to intergenerational educational mobility, it is because—within the aggregate of young people of the new generation—"disadvantaged" young people encounter serious difficulties in overcoming the "inequality of circumstances" in which they have become adults. Since the level of education of parents is usually proportional to their economic resources, the "combined effect" of the level of both education and income of parents is the main determinant of intergenerational educational mobility. The degree of market imperfection also counts: the credit market enhances the impact of "circumstances" on the educational mobility of young people.

How valid is the hypothesis that the low income mobility between generations highlighted by Fig. 11.1 can be explained—rather than by the expected earnings of young people as an incentive to prolong studies—by intergenerational educational mobility ***disaggregated by social classes***?

To understand intergenerational mobility, the "missing link" of aggregate analyses is precisely the unequal access to opportunities, which

[9] To the result of high (or low) social mobility, the culture of parents probably contributes in the same measure as the father's income. Compare two differences: the wage difference between a young with a diploma whose father is a graduate, and a young person with a diploma whose father is only a diploma holder; and the salary difference after the two young graduates have both achieved a degree. We must ask ourselves whether the first difference is wider than the second. The aim is to establish whether the higher level of education (the degree) achieved by the father is an indicator—or not—of the son's salary level. If the micro-data shows that having had a graduate father has given an advantage to the first young person (as a graduate he gets a higher salary than the second), we have a clue that in determining a child's salary, the father's level of education also counts. In fact, for the son whose father is only a diploma holder, the incentive represented by the "rate of return" of higher education (the increase in salary after obtaining a degree) is not sufficient to "bridge the gap" from the son whose father is a graduate. The intergenerational income mobility that is expected from the increase in education is therefore increased by the "cultural push" that the young person receives in the family. A non-income variable, the father's level of education, seems to be an important determinant of the son's mobility.

is particularly evident in the two major Anglo-Saxon countries. "The signs of equality of opportunity are very weak in the United States and completely absent in the United Kingdom" (Dardanoni et al. 2006, p. 59). The glaring contradiction found in these two countries—characterised by a private supply of education and very "fluid" markets—between a high "rate of return" and low intergenerational mobility of education could find a plausible explanation precisely in the inequality of educational opportunities within the population. The tendency towards income polarisation present in the two Anglo-Saxon countries depends on the strong heterogeneity of their social structure. Ethnic groups are many and have different characteristics from each other: "The United States and the United Kingdom have high-income groups of small size and low-income groups of larger size. The distribution *between* groups of different size is more unequal than in countries like Germany, Japan, Sweden. At the same time, the distances *within* the groups are greater in these latter countries. The first factor tends to decrease polarisation, while the second tends to increase it" (Esteban et al. 2007, p. 13). As expected, from Esteban's research it turns out that in the United States and the United Kingdom polarisation takes place mainly *between groups*. Furthermore, due to ethnic fragmentation particularly varied, in the United States the dispersion *within groups* is very variable from group to group.[10]

Even on an evidential basis (in the absence of data on educational mobility *disaggregated by social classes*), the verdict is unescapable. In the two major Anglo-Saxon countries, young people belonging to families at the top of the social scale easily obtain both the desired education and highly remunerative occupations; while young people belonging to families at the bottom of the social scale cannot afford the high fees of the educational system and consequently, do not have access to high earnings.

[10] The degree of polarisation of a distribution is the algebraic sum of two dispersion indicators: 1) inequality within groups and 2) inequality between groups. The polarisation index of a country increases as a function of the following factors: a) if the Gini index increases between the groups into which society is divided (i.e. if the income distance increases between subjects below the median and subjects above the median); b) if the Gini index within groups decreases (i.e. if subjects above and below the median have incomes closer to each other); c) if the *top incomes* are further from the average income. Greater (lesser) inequality within a group increases (reduces) the total inequality of the population, but reduces (increases) polarisation.

Empirical analyses on inequality of education and income confirm that in both these countries there is the greatest educational gap between young people belonging to poor families compared to young people from wealthy families (Schuetz et al. 2008).

Education and Social Mobility in Anglo-Saxon Countries

In the Great Gatsby curve (chap. VI, par. 4) presented by Miles Corak (2013), the research objective is identified in estimating the correlation between the income level of children and that of parents in relation to the income distribution of various countries. The analysis conducted based on the curve identifies an inverse relationship between the income inequality of a country and a particular type of mobility *relative*, that which starts from the ambition of young people to overtake their parents in the level of earnings. Although it does not claim to establish a causal link, the negative correlation that Corak (2013) establishes between the index of income inequality and intergenerational income mobility, in addition to some econometric problems (see Box 7.1), has the methodological limit of proposing as a link that connects the two variables—as a key to reading—a very broad concept, the "inequality of opportunity", in which a huge number of socio-economic factors are included.

Let's then take a different path. As the Stiglitz, Sen, Fitoussi Report (2009) has extensively documented, aggregate GDP is not a reliable guide for understanding social phenomena. One aspect of the criticism developed in the Report concerns the heterogeneity of the condition of social classes in the different dimensions of well-being. Looking at the aggregate data of income mobility from one generation to another obscures what the disaggregated data would be able to highlight. The most accredited hypothesis is of "low intergenerational mobility at both extremes of the income distribution, together with a mobility of the middle class" (Becker et al. 2018, p. 8). In short, the rich seem to present a high persistence in the percentiles at the top of the income distribution, the middle class a mobility that is partly upwards and partly downwards, and the poor the lowest mobility towards the higher percentiles. At this point, it is necessary to investigate how a particular factor of opportunity—the unequal access to education—intertwines with the income distribution. The reason is simple: the more the social stratification of a population tends to be polarised—that is, there are many subjects with a lot, and many also subjects with little, income—also the distribution of human capital will end up being polarised, and intergenerational educational mobility will be affected.

As seen in Fig. 11.1, even when market incentives should rule, the high expected gain from a high level of education does not act as a driver to social mobility.

The continuous decrease, cohort after cohort, from those born in 1940 to those born in 1980, of intergenerational social mobility—so evident in Fig. 11.2—certainly testifies to the difficulty that American society encounters in transforming a growth of GDP based on the market into a growth of income and well-being for all. This decrease is better understood if we look inside both the income distribution of parents and the educational paths of young people. In short, we need to disaggregate. A research conducted on US graduates, whose results are summarised in Fig. 11.6, allows to disaggregate the intergenerational income mobility in terms of social classes, or to connect the quintile of children's earnings as adults (vertical axis) with the quintile of parents' earnings (horizontal axis), based on whether or not a university degree has been obtained (histograms).

Let's try to reason in disaggregated terms for social classes. Does the high income inequality have anything to do with the divergence between social classes in educational opportunities? Observing in Fig. 11.6 the data of intergenerational mobility of young graduates in the United States it seems so. The graph is generated by two pieces of information: a) the income of parents, divided into five quintiles on the horizontal axis; b) the lack of access (histogram on the left) or access (histogram on the right) of children to the title of a college education. For those born to parents of the first quintile, that of the poor, if a college degree is not achieved, there is a 47% chance of remaining there as an adult; if, on the other hand, it is achieved, the probability drops to 10%. The social rise of the children of the poor then records a probability of rising to the second and third quintile which is collectively 63% if they achieve a degree, and 42% if they do not. The probability of young poor people jumping to the quintile of the rich is naturally very low: 3% without a degree and 10% with a degree. If, on the other hand, one is born to parents of the last quintile, that of the rich, there is a 25% chance of staying there without a degree, and 51% with a degree. Finally, the sum of the probabilities of falling from the quintile of the rich to the third and fourth quintile is almost equal (respectively

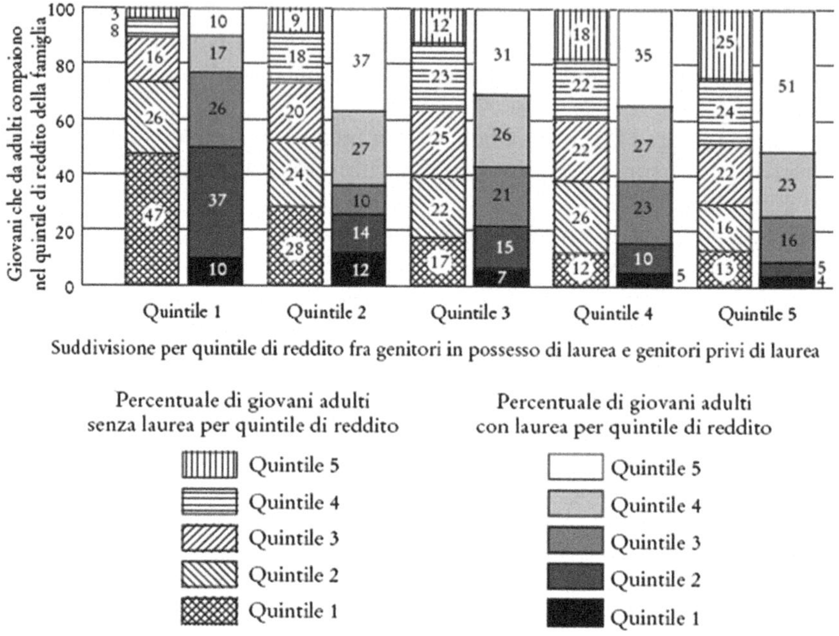

Fig. 11.6 Income mobility of young people without and with a university degree (% per quintile of parents' income: United States 2021). (Note: Income adjustment based on family size. Source: Pew Research Center, Washington DC, 2021. Translation: Youngs sharing the same quintile of their household when adults, Breakdown by income quintile (left histogram: graduate parents; right histogram: ungraduated parents), Share of ungraduated youngs when adults, Share of graduate youngs when adults)

38% and 39%); while the probability of the rich ending up among the poor is very similar to that of the poor becoming rich: in the two cases, respectively, 4% and 13%. These percentages seem to indicate that the factors of "social descent" from the elite of the rich to the middle-income classes should not be identified in education. On the fate of those born to middle-class parents, the importance of education seems to be more marked. Young people from third quintile families have a decent chance (57%) of rising to the two higher income positions (the last two quintiles) if they achieve a degree (without a degree, the probability drops to 35%); but also non-negligible probabilities of descending into the first two quintiles, equal to 39% without a degree and 22% with a degree.

Being deprived of the emancipatory value of education, for "disadvantaged" young people the opportunities for social ascent remain scarce. Their future continues to be weighed down by their family of origin and the social context in which they grew up. On the other hand, tertiary education and therefore also the incentive of a higher income do not seem to be able to represent a sufficient stimulus to entrust their expectations of social ascent to study. The histograms of the graph show that young people from the quintile of the poor reach the same percentage (26%) of middle-low income (second quintile) if they are not graduates, and middle income (third quintile) if they are graduates. An offer of university education which is not followed by a confirmation of its promises once you enter the job market can only discourage the demand for education. The upward income mobility of young people belonging to low-income families—once they become adults—is lower than that of young people belonging to middle or high-income families. It is a result—not only reliable, but also rigorous—that allows us to hypothesise an explanation of the low intergenerational mobility that is recorded in the United States. It is plausible that the poor impact on social mobility from generation to generation—in the presence of a high "rate of return" of education—can be traced back to an attraction of investment in tertiary education that is weaker the more disadvantaged the family is. Comparing the columns of income mobility as adults between graduate and non-graduate young people, the percentages indicate not only that the low income of parents is an obstacle to an increase in income of their children, but also that this obstacle becomes much greater if they have not attended university.

In conclusion, the peculiarity of the American case is that the high rate of return of education does not seem to be a market incentive capable of counteracting the obstacle to intergenerational income mobility represented by the inequality of educational opportunities of "disadvantaged" young people. Empirical research conducted in the United States agrees in assigning to the family (and its structure: couple of parents or single, working condition, etc.) an important role in the formation of human capital, especially in local communities where social capital is degraded, and therefore the percentage of young people who drop out of school is high (Coleman and Hoffer 1987; Coleman 1988). In light of this consideration, across the Atlantic the slogan that gives its name to par. 2 of this chapter (*the more you learn, the more you earn*) should be modified in the more realistic: "if you *wanted* to earn more, your parents *should* earn more, and you *should* be more educated".

We have seen how much the defence, pursued with financial support to their children, of the class interest of the family dynasties of the rich counts in the demand for education of young people.

In addition to the genetic transmission of intelligence, the parents of the elite employ their resources in favour of the new generation, before transmitting to them a material inheritance made of real estate and capital. Public funding for universities, on the other hand, does not meet the demand for education from other social classes. In the United States, "in tertiary education, despite the significant increase in enrolments between 2000 and 2009, spending on education has not kept pace; spending per student has therefore decreased" (OECD 2012, p. 217). Being low the share of public education offer, the gaps in educational opportunities between social groups widen, with consequent accentuation of the persistence of income and *status*.

In the model of Becker et al. (2018), built on the basis of US data, the main result is the persistence of the rich at the top of the education and income pyramid. The condition of advantage that their children enjoy in making the most of their own talents makes it so that the complementarity between income and wealth on one hand, and the intergenerational transmission of talents on the other, exerts a multiplicative effect on the divergence of income and wealth among the classes of society (Houmark et al. 2020).

The longitudinal studies of Chetty et al. (2014a, 2014b, 2017a, 2017b), in showing a decline in the United States of intergenerational mobility in terms of income, suggest that the correlation of this mobility indicator with the increase in income inequality probably configures a causal link that goes from the slowdown in GDP growth to the loss of positions in the income ranking of new generations compared to the positions occupied by their parents, which is more pronounced the weaker the social class of belonging (relative downward mobility). A study of occupational status mobility, which consists of assessing the position of children compared to fathers in the ranking of occupations, finds that, from the seventies onwards, the prospect of improving one's occupational position in the ranking has run out. As the decades have passed, intergenerational mobility "seems to resist major short-term social transformations [...]. In other words, the changes that have occurred in society have probably changed the overall opportunities to move up and down, but not the chances of relative mobility" (Song et al. 2020, p. 255). The evolution of aggregate GDP, therefore, seems to limit the opportunities for absolute mobility; at the disaggregated level of social groups and individuals, however, relative mobility continues to change the distribution of chances for income and status improvement.

The slowdown in absolute mobility is reflected in the trend of relative mobility as a function of the level of education. The market no longer rewards the degree obtained at college to the extent that it did in the cohorts of those born in the forties. However, it appears that between 1989 and 2016 the median values of the "premium" of income and wealth for heads of households with a diploma compared to heads of households without a diploma continue to be positive. However, when disaggregation is carried out, differences emerge: "from the comparison between families similar in ethnicity, decade of birth, number of members, it turns out that the variability of the 'premiums' on income and wealth is very high […]. Among those born in the eighties, the 'premium' on the wealth of families with a diploma and that on the wealth of families with a post-university degree are statistically indistinguishable from zero for all groups, except for white families with a diploma" (Emmons et al. 2019, p. 301). The increase in remuneration conferred by university education has therefore taken on a strong class matrix based on skin colour.

Public policies like that of decades ago of school buses, which took poor students to attend schools located in the residential neighbourhoods of the rich, in order to stimulate ethnic equality in opportunities, were not successful. In the United States, the result was indeed to unsettle the rich. The raising of school fees in quality private institutions increased the "skimming", the census-based selection of students (Doepke et al. 2019). The private provision of education thus became a "positional good" reserved for the children of the rich. The research project promoted by Raj Chetty, Nathaniel Hendren and John Friedman of Harvard University, the Opportunity Policy Insights, calls for multidimensionality as a foundational character of policies for social mobility, in the same way as we have seen in relation to inequality. We will see if it will be able to more effectively address the presumed trade-off according to which diversity would constitute an obstacle to the spirit of community.

The multi-ethnic nature of American society is well suited to a disaggregation between three social groups, identified through skin colour (white, black, brown). A study that applies statistical decomposition techniques of the overall income distribution to microdata collected on a monthly basis has made it possible to identify income growth performance on an ethnic basis (Blanchet et al. 2022). The study revealed that the fall in income of the coloured population and the Hispanic population was much greater and of longer duration in the Great Recession of 2008 than during the Covid-19 pandemic; moreover, in the first crisis, the recovery of the level preceding its outbreak by the black population was slower than the recovery of white income; while in the second crisis, the fall in income was of similar magnitude for whites and blacks, and less marked in the Hispanic population. Macroeconomic income support policies aimed at stabilising the economy would gain in effectiveness if they were differentiated based on the actual loss of income of each ethnic group. Similarly, income redistribution policies implemented by Welfare institutions would gain in equity if they took into account the fact that the gap between ethnic groups is wider in terms of capital income than in terms of labour income; in particular, the gap of blacks is greater in capital income than in wealth, since the latter is held in much greater proportion in assets—real estate and pension funds—with a lower return compared to equity capital.

On the other hand, the "protection" of elite parents is not only manifested in favouring the acceptance of their children's enrolment applications by top universities through donations. In having or not having the opportunity to access tertiary education—which should pave the way for the acquisition of the *ability*—social class matters (in addition to wealth and income, the social network of parents often manages to secure a profitable occupation for their children: chap. II, par. 4). A high price for education (a high tuition fee at a private university) very often does not only select the most gifted students, but also those with little desire to study—such as George W. Bush—belonging to wealthy families. These young people, whose parents through the *charities* are often generous with funding to universities, see their applications accepted and are often also recipients of the generous offer of particularly easy study courses (Brunello and Rocco 2008). In the public discourse at the end of the last century, the aphorism "it's not what you know; it's who you know" was in vogue; it naturally indicated the superior importance, in finding a job, of social relations compared to skills. The need to study more does not then seem to be so essential. The slogan "the more you learn, the more you earn" should perhaps be revised again: "the more your parents earn, the further you go in your studies".

A recent study shows how the values instilled in children by parents change according to social class: while wealthy parents who expect successful managerial careers from their children—and who possess the substantial economic resources and social influence necessary to favour them—are careful in instilling in them the value of independence, the virtue of entrepreneurial spirit, low-income families impart the value of obedience, to avoid their children finding themselves in difficult situations at work (Acemoglu 2022).

The interpretative picture becomes clearer when we proceed to the disaggregation not only by cohorts but also by social classes. The *baby boomers*, in recent decades, have experienced in the United States, compared to previous generations, a strong increase in wealth accumulated through greater savings made in the second half of their working life cycle, favoured by the boom in the prices of financial assets and real estate in the eighties. A portion of this wealth was transferred, around retirement age, to the "upper" portion of the *millennials*, the middle classes with the greatest economic success. Along with an increase in wealth inequality, there has been an intertwining between the distribution of wealth among the most recent generations and between social classes, because the increase in wealth has remained the prerogative of the top 10% of the owning class (Bauluz and Meyer 2024). The picture that emerges from the statistics seems to lead to the following consideration, as paradoxical as it is alarming: the more the social bases of economic growth are narrowed—the concentration in the classes of the *top incomes* of both high-salary workers employed in large companies and graduates with excellent skills from the major universities—the darker the prospects for social mobility appear.

In the collective imagination of the white population of the United States, social stratification is dominated by the presence of a large middle class. The perception is that the United States is the country where the reshuffling of income positions predominantly takes place within the middle class. In reality, the United States is characterised today by social persistence. The unsatisfactory degree of social mobility that the country suffers from is a phenomenon that is set in motion within the communities of the various states (Chetty et al. 2022). The significant differences in income and quality of life between the ethnically based social groups present in the population determine a degree of social mobility that varies considerably from one state to another. The heterogeneity of social mobility between social classes and ethnic groups depends on the multidimensionality of inequality, and the *cross-correlation* that accompanies it. In fact, "variability is strongly correlated with five factors: residential segregation, income inequality, the quality of schools, social capital and family structure" (Chetty et al. 2014b, p. 1580) (Box 11.1).

Box 11.1 The geography of social mobility opportunities in the United States

In the United States of the early nineteenth century, mobility was incentivised by the availability of land to exploit due to the absence of property rights on it. During the formidable economic expansion that took place from the mid-nineteenth century to 1980, the country changed skin. The rapid increase in industrial production led to the collapse of the persistence of sons in the same occupation as their fathers: the rate of intergenerational "immobility" declined from about 40% for the cohort born in 1830 to 25% of the cohort born in 1980. The trend is now reversed: from the cohort born in 1940 onwards, the occupational mobility downwards of sons compared to fathers has increased from 17% to about 32%. The dynamics of social structure is a phenomenon that also depends on the social reshuffling induced by the movement of population between the various states. In the country of the "frontier", territorial mobility has represented a traditional propulsive factor of social mobility. Social mobility has been "aided" by territorial mobility. In the United States, the distances between the economic areas formed by a set of states intertwine with income distances. Social stratification at the state level appears today more blocked than in the regions of the countries of the European Union: the areas of the country with greater social mobility have lower values than the more "immobile" regions of Norway and Sweden (Bratberg et al. 2017). Social persistence has reached high levels in recent decades, when the *millennials*—the children of the *baby boomers*—have struggled to find work and consequently have shown a low probability of upward mobility (Song et al. 2020). Today it happens that "low-income families tend to live in areas that offer few opportunities for upward social mobility" (Bergman et al. 2023). In an era where both income and employment expansion is conditioned by automation, the territorial mobility of the US population consists mainly of emigration from low-income areas to those with higher per capita income. A sign of this is that in recent decades upward social mobility has decreased in the Southern states and has instead grown in the Western and Northeastern states. Transfers depend on the greater economic dynamism of some areas compared to those showing signs of decline.

(*continued*)

Box 11.1 (continued)

Those states that, due to an increasing availability of jobs, become the destination of internal migration usually also see the birth of better quality schools and more dynamic social networks, two essential factors to accelerate socio-economic development (Connor and Storper 2020).

Familiarity with the public development programs of Latin American countries taught Albert Hirschman not to forget the cultural roots of the areas from which one emigrates. In other words, the market cannot be left to guide decisions on territorial mobility. In his analysis of the ambiguity and risks inherent in the choice of *exit*—the "exit" from one's own *humus* cultural—he expressed "a preference for the approach of the "collective push", rather than the model of social mobility represented by the 'flight' or the '*melting pot*'" (Hirschman 1970, p. 111). The German economist emphasised that "the promoters of the redemption of regions lagging far behind within a nation assign a minor role to emigration, considering it not a contribution to the 'lifting' of the region but an unfortunate haemorrhage of its best talents" (*ibid.*).

A public strategy for development planning, to which Hirschman alludes, is not completely foreign to the history of the American Federation. The spirit of the New Deal was embodied by the Tennessee Valley Authority, the federal agency created in 1933 with the aim of reviving the economy of the state in the aftermath of the Great Depression. However, American culture is now firmly oriented towards the pursuit of short-term market success, and does not attribute value to the negative effects of territorial mobility in the long term. This is documented by an original empirical research (Chetty et al. 2014b). In this study, income social mobility appears to depend on the alternation of various economic areas in the role of pioneer of the development of technological innovation sectors. Seen from the perspective of territorial mobility, the social rise of the children of native "immigrants" in a region is favoured by the combination of technological knowledge development and private investment. As Silicon Valley teaches, the acceleration of the development of innovative sectors is accompanied by both the increase in

(*continued*)

Box 11.1 (continued)
jobs in start-up companies that attract graduates and researchers from excellent universities and the concentration of wage increases in the high band of professional skills. The start-ups that survive the "natural selection" and expand are the signal that in technologically advanced areas social mobility largely concerns the group of successful entrepreneurs and researchers rewarded for their high propensity to risk. The divergence between the various states based on the concentration of innovative companies and the growth rate of GDP induces the divergence of their earnings compared to those of other social strata. The territorial dimension of US economic development therefore testifies to both the phenomenon of income mobility and that of inequality.

The context of high income inequality and low social mobility that has for many decades united the United States and the United Kingdom is the legacy of an individualistic culture, which was only put on hold from the mid-thirties to the mid-seventies, respectively, by Roosevelt's New Deal and the welfare state promoted by Lord Beveridge. The change in cultural climate that occurred in the United States is well summarised in this passage by sociologist Richard Sennett: "When the Great Depression began in the thirties, only one American worker in a hundred was insured against unemployment, less than one in eight had a pension plan, less than one in twenty had health care; very few English workers had the means to have access to hospitals, and practically no one attended university" (Sennett 2003, p. 167). The programs of the Rooseveltian New Deal, together with the productive effort organised by the state during the Second World War, were the engine that in the first decades of the post-war period supported the growth of the middle class and social mobility in the United States.

The redistributive policies and expansion of common goods such as health and education, elaborated in the Beveridge Report and implemented in the United Kingdom, deviated from those across the ocean. Beveridge's policies had as their primary objective not the formation of a "large middle class" but rather the alleviation of poverty, in the tradition of the *Poor Laws*, in order to protect the lifestyle of the *middle class* from the potentially harmful consequences of social unrest. The idea of a single, large, social class is quite foreign to the English, accustomed to the image of their country as a place of mutual tolerance between social groups: on one hand, that of the English of many generations, on the other, that formed on ethnic bases, following the flow of immigrants from various continents, placed at different levels of income and *status*.

On the balance between tolerance and class prejudice there are however different ideas. In 1941, in *The Lion and the Unicorn*, George Orwell judged the United Kingdom "the nation under the sun most oppressed by classism" (Orwell 1941, p. 53). The history of the English education system is another piece of the limit of universalism *tout court*. In fact, the liberal vision of the equal right of the rich and the poor to enrol in an educational institution ends up acting as a screen and support for the persistence of a culture favourable to the division of society into castes. The privileged classes seem on the other hand unwilling to accept the principle of "inclusive education" and entrust its implementation to the public education system: "the hereditary flaw that weighs on the British education system is the fact of having an organisation based on class divisions" (Tawney 1952, p. 154). "Private education for the rich is more institutionalised in the United Kingdom than in the United States" (*ibid.*, p. 82). A comparative study conducted in the United Kingdom on data from the decade 2005–2015 reveals, unsurprisingly, "that students belonging to the *upper class* are much less averse to student debt than students of the *lower class*" (Callender and Mason 2017, p. 33). The "educational immobility", the strong correlation in the lower quintiles between the level of education achieved by fathers and the level achieved by sons, proves the failure of education in the objective of shortening the social distances of the United Kingdom. The static nature of social stratification seems indeed to have been influenced by the role played by the middle class in the low educational mobility that the country suffers from (Box 11.2).

Box 11.2 The English middle class and low educational social mobility

Based on an estimate conducted on family earnings and income taxation, income inequality in the United Kingdom is perhaps higher than the high level that was reached on the eve of the Second World War (Atkinson and Jenkins 2020). Social mobility began on the wave of change in the occupational structure determined by the process of industrialisation of the nineteenth and twentieth centuries. After the extension of the vote on a census basis enacted by the

(*continued*)

Box 11.2 (continued)

Reform Bill of 1884–1885, the "universalism" of male and female suffrage was achieved in 1928. These advances in civil society favoured the raising of schooling but not the transition from the school for the elite to the "school of equals". In the post-war period, the "golden age" of sustained growth and the intellectual influence of the Labour welfare programme, the English middle class was united and leaned more towards the weak classes than towards the elite. However, public education failed to undermine the dominance of the elite in society. Despite having given impetus to the Beveridgean welfare state, English governments did not commit enough to promoting the evolution towards an organic system of social rights.

The increase in the average duration of the training period for young English people has not corresponded to a decrease in educational inequality (Blanden and Machin 2004; Blanden and Macmillan 2014). With the defeat of Labour and the advent of Margaret Thatcher, the ideological conflict took precedence over cultural belonging to the middle class. A good part of the middle groups joined the owning classes in defending interests, consistently voting for the conservatives. The problem of the high level of social persistence (a high value of the Iee) lies in the intertwining of education policies and distribution of power between social classes. The cultural upliftment of the population has traditionally had to contend with the resistance opposed by the elite to a downsizing of their own social power and their privileges. At the beginning of the eighties, as we have seen happen to the other main dimensions of well-being throughout Europe, a brake was put on the policy of "inclusive education": "from 1977 to 1984 English university students achieved the highest financial support ever [...] and had access to the social insurance system [...]. During the eighties these began to be cut [...]. From 1990, the *grants* for study maintenance were frozen and were progressively replaced by subsidised bank loans for all students" (Blanden et al. 2003, p. 7).

In promoting social dynamics, particularly in influencing parents' preferences regarding the type of school to send their children to, the organisation of education has mainly dedicated itself to protecting the chances of young people belonging to the middle class. Basil

(*continued*)

Box 11.2 (continued)

Bernstein has even argued that in the United Kingdom "the history of the education system is the history of the middle class" (Power and Whitty 2002, p. 595). The judgement on the impact of the education system on social cohesion is harsh. The English middle class is accused of having contributed, in collusion with the elite, to accentuate the inefficiency of the education system: "although the *upper* and the *middle class* have benefited from an education system that was built to serve their interests, these classes have also been to some extent damaged by the unacceptable functioning of an unfair system that emphasises division and hierarchy at the expense of sharing and everything that different groups have in common in society" (Reay 2017, p. 131). The vast majority of English sociologists see in the country's education system the mirror of the failure of the project of an "inclusive" society, primarily with regard to access to education. The English education system is accused of having tolerated the *status* privileged of schools for the elite, accentuating the division of society into "stagnant compartments" (Ferguson and Savage 2020). Empirical evidence shows how high educational inequality has contributed to keeping social mobility low (Blanden et al. 2022).

One of the causes of the rise in the Gini index of income inequality is precisely educational inequality within the population, which in turn stems from the greater availability of income of the rich in financing the education of their children. In turn, the class division in the level of education, in differentiating opportunities within social stratification, contributes to the persistence of high income inequality: "in the United Kingdom [...] there is a certain persistence at the top of the ranking and a wide mobility at the bottom of the income ranking" (Oecd 2018, p. 80). The static nature of the high portion of the English social structure is also the result of a strong concentration of property ownership in the elites of society. Since the 1970s, in the cohorts of adults who were children of parents who in turn did not own their own home, the percentage of homeowners has remained very low (Blanden and Machin 2017).

The rigidity of the class hierarchy is revealed by a simple intergenerational comparison: "More than half of the children born in 1975 achieved by the age of 30 earnings equal to or higher than those of their parents. However, this result was only achieved by a third of the children born in 1985. The dream of doing just a little better, let alone climbing the social ladder, is fading" (Major and Machin 2019, pp. 2–3). These percentages, already worrying for the aggregate of each cohort, are even more so once disaggregated based on social origin. It is likely, therefore, that the low average value of social mobility, indicated by the persistence of the Iee at high levels, depends on the narrow bases of access to an advanced education title that gives access to high earnings. The tragedy of social persistence is not exhausted in a question of social justice, but strikes at the heart of individualist culture. The market society, in forgetting equity, also forgets efficiency, for the "waste of talents" of young people belonging to disadvantaged classes. Major and Machin advance the hypothesis that greater social mobility *relative* could renew the ruling elites, replacing the closed culture of the already wealthy social class with the greater openness of the "disadvantaged" classes: "Cognitive diversity, like ethnic and gender diversity, improves the decision-making process in the business world" (*ibid.*, p. 171).

The disaggregation by social groups with different backgrounds documents that it is the "advantaged" young people who achieve in much higher percentages a high level of education already at 11 years old, have access to the best universities, achieve the most advanced degrees and undertake the most exclusive professions with the highest remuneration. This does not happen to the "disadvantaged" on an equal footing. "Young people from poor families rarely manage to achieve tertiary and post-university education degrees" (Crawford et al. 2016, p. 571). This *impasse* in the ability of the education system to increase educational mobility is suggesting to governments to alleviate the problem of persistent gaps in both education and earnings among young people belonging to different social classes, increasing the chances of finding employment for "disadvantaged" students who will not go to university. "Vocational education and training (Vet) programmes are an essential part of a country's education system as they offer an alternative to academic training" (Oecd 2023, p. 21); "on average, in Oecd countries, 44% of secondary school students are enrolled in programmes that combine school and work" (*ibid.*, p. 22). On the other hand, not everything depends on the education one can boast. "In post-university education, achieving an academic qualification - even from an institution of excellence - is not a passport for equal access to prestigious professions and the highest earnings" (Oecd 2018, p. 16). What determines the asymmetry of power in society is not only the existing educational opportunity gap between classes. The "glass ceiling" of income rise (chap. II, par. 4) is still thick for women: "although a higher level of education achieved reduces gender differences in the employment rate, the Gender wage gap does not vary much between educational levels" (OECD 2023, p. 95). In the search for employment and the outcome achieved in the labour market, social networks and barriers to entry into professions, which block upward relative mobility, are not insignificant. Having in mind the rigidity of his country's class structure, John Goldthorpe (2013) emphasised how the influence of the socio-family context greatly contributes to the rigidity of the social structure at a multidimensional level.

Sociologist Basil Bernstein (1970), in observing that "the battle [is] between preference for a selective school or for the universalism of the public school", stated that the battle for equal educational opportunity cannot be won because "education cannot counterbalance society's problems" (*ibid.*, pp. 601–2). More recently, Goldthorpe (2013) also warned against considering the education system, particularly the phenomenon of mass schooling, as a tool capable of promoting a less classist society. The post-war governments' attempts to describe the country as a "meritocracy", where anyone willing to work hard would climb the social ladder, have not been successful: "Britain has remained a society where birth counts more than commitment" (Todd 2015, p. 153).

Considering the spread of automation at the beginning of the new millennium, things are unlikely to improve for low-skilled classes. There is a very negative fact: 21% of men and 25% of women between the ages of 30 and 50 have experienced downward social mobility in recent years (Social Commission Mobility 2020). Occupational mobility sees stable proportions of dependent workforce with *generic skills* in productive activities and the phenomenon of father-to-son transmission of work activity in self-employment and professions. The modest reshuffling of individual income positions therefore tends to leave the stratification into three social groups unaffected. The high value that the English show in an experimental study to attribute to mobility probably reflects a feeling of deprivation of the lower-middle classes and the poor in the face of the substantial staticity of the social structure (Amiel et al. 2015). In the United Kingdom, educational mobility and income mobility end up coinciding: both are blocked.

To summarise. The reason why in the United States the "rate of return" is an unreliable indicator of intergenerational income mobility seems to be the polarisation between wealthy families—which favour a social mobility *relative* that tends to be restricted to the young elite—and the rest of the population. In the United Kingdom, the class division of society is equally decisive, but the causes of the "failure" of educational mobility are different. In the society of our cousins across the Atlantic, the game of excellent education has been won by the *top incomes*. As a result, the rich, by providing their children with resources and ensuring them the best educational opportunities, manage to extend upward income inequality, in the sense that from educational polarisation has sprung for the rich of the latest generations a growing distance, within the group of *top incomes*, between those who are part of the 0.01% and those of the 1%. In the United Kingdom, it was the middle class that lost the game of excellent education. The loss of weight of this social class, also indicated by the shift to the right of its political preferences with an increasing percentage of voters in favour of the conservatives, is symbolised by the inability to reform the education system in a democratic way in Parliament.

In the American population, there is a belief, not supported by the data of reality, that in achieving economic success, merit counts more than luck (chap. II, par. 1): "whatever the reality, Americans believe that the path to success has nothing to do with good luck, but with hard work and ambition" (Bradbury et al. 2015, p. 2). A simple explanation of the discrepancy between survey findings and reality is the habit of drawing conclusions based on aggregate data. If the data is disaggregated, as the authors of the study do, it is observed that "disadvantaged" children are "left behind". This same empirical research documents how—also due to the private sector's organisation of the health and education systems—inequality of opportunity between rich and poor *before the market* is much more pronounced in the United States than in the United Kingdom, Canada and Australia. These distances do not then decrease much *in the market* (because labour market regulation is almost non-existent) and *after the market* (due to the low redistributive impact of Welfare). It is also a shared thesis that the concentration of wealth and income at the top of the social ladder has ended up weakening the well-being of the middle class (Frank 2013).

It is essential to delve into the class structure of society, disaggregate the Iee values, the overall data of intergenerational income mobility from the estimate of the "Great Gatsby". It is understood that generating income dynamics between generations is not only the "rate of return", the market incentive that acts as I trail the question of education. Within each cohort of young people, the inequality between levels of earnings is closely intertwined with the inequality of income and education between the parents of the "advantaged" young people and the parents of the "disadvantaged" young people. In intergenerational social mobility, the primary factor is represented by the family background, both in terms of income and culture. This empirical evidence struggles to be accepted and become common knowledge. The OECD, in a research study not many years ago—equating private education with public education—has spoken in favour of the right of private institutions to receive resources from the State: "In some [countries] the share of private funding of institutions for tertiary education is high enough to challenge the view that education is primarily a state responsibility. In fact, this view has been gradually replaced by the idea that the costs and responsibilities for university education should be shared between those who directly benefit from it and society as a whole (families, businesses and governments), on the basis that it also distributes both public and private returns" (OECD 2008, p. 14). In emphasising that the benefits of education are not only the prerogative of individuals but also of society as a whole, the OECD seems to forget that the problem lies in unequal access. This is highlighted by the fact that in advanced countries, parallel to the expansion of private educational provision, the amount of public resources allocated to support "disadvantaged" students for university education is decreasing. However, the horizon in which the desire for education of young people is inscribed cannot be understood unless the individual aspiration is placed in the context of the opportunities that stratification into classes determines in society. In the previous chapters, we have spoken of the concern that advanced countries are sliding towards a caste society. We are returning to Jeremy Bentham, a very straightforward moral philosopher: "The link between wealth and power is very tight [...], they are, respectively, a tool for producing the other" (Bentham 1983, p. 48). Bentham was also the first philosopher of modernity to deny that the concept of society has real substance: "the community is a fictitious body [...] the interest of the community is nothing but the sum of the interests of the many members who constitute it" (Id. 2013, p. 12). If the castes were to return, Margaret Thatcher, in uttering her famous phrase,[11] would have hit the mark! In 2019, almost a third of the total expenditure for tertiary education in OECD countries came from the private sector (OECD 2022). Private universities attract the best teachers by offering them generous salaries, thus managing to set very high fees. As has been observed, "the students with a privileged background monopolise the educational resources of the world's most prestigious universities" (Marginson 2016, p. 30). Even the procedures for recruiting teachers and admitting students are often distorted. The more the selection mechanisms are linked not to the market but to the power of the parents' money, the more tertiary education ends up representing a positional good. Insofar as it also has the effect of reducing the opportunities for access to university for young people with a poor family background, the economic and status power of elite families represents a limiting factor of relative educational mobility (Torche 2011).

A World Apart: The Nordic Countries

There is therefore a methodological problem. Economists prefer aggregate analysis. Macroeconomic analyses underestimate the need to disaggregate the link between education and growth by social classes. The predominantly private organisation of education provision in Anglo-Saxon countries results in low relative mobility of education for young people belonging to the weaker classes. In Europe, the expectation of relative educational mobility for young people belonging to "disadvantaged" families does not find as high a barrier as in the United States, where to afford a university and post-university education that gives access to the most remunerative and prestigious job positions you need to have rich parents. The heterogeneity between families connected to the division into classes of society is a factor that often makes educational outcomes very divergent between "advantaged" and "disadvantaged" young people. At the beginning of the Introduction, the reader was warned of the deception that can hide in the aggregate data of the social mobility index of Table 1.1. From being a country in a good position in the ranking, hasty conclusions should not be drawn. The fact is that this caveat does not apply to the Nordic countries. Not only do they all appear at the top. But, even more importantly, the aggregate data does not hide a greatly skewed reality

[11] In the course of a 1987 interview, Margaret Thatcher stated: "There is no such thing as society. There are individual men and women, and there are families".

between social classes in the rise to higher income positions. A good rate of reshuffling of income positions among individuals, a good relative mobility within the social stratification, in fact, combines in those countries with tolerable income inequality indices. As mentioned, the problem of the Nordic countries lies in the emotional and cultural distance towards immigrants, which translates at the polls into support for often xenophobic-oriented parties.

If it is true that education is a fundamental factor for social inclusion, it is not surprising that the Nordic countries occupy the top spots in the ranking of Table 1.1 of social mobility. Among these, despite a high and very similar degree of social mobility (as Fig. 11.1 informed us), there is a considerable variability of the "private return rate of education". The strong dispersion in Fig. 11.1 of the values of the return rate of education of the Nordic countries suggests that the presence of high intergenerational income mobility—the low value of the Iee that unites them—has nothing to do with market incentive; and that the expectation of economic success—measured by the "return rate" incentive—is not the most relevant factor among the determinants of the demand for children's education. A study conducted on a sample of Swedish families (Gärtner et al. 2023) documents how important the cultural education of parents is in transmitting to children a positive approach to facing life: these parents, the more affluent and educated they are, and even if they think that good luck plays a role far from secondary in self-realisation, push their children to believe that their future depends only on their commitment. The high social mobility present in these countries is therefore not the result of an efficient functioning of the market in generously rewarding an excellent educational path. It is rather the proof that the dynamics of the social structure can respond to causes other than the pure market incentive represented by individual earnings. How else would you explain a level of children's earnings that remains in the Nordic countries at the level of parents only in the percentage between 10% and 20%, or that the income of a young person is on average almost independent of that of parents belonging to the previous generation?

The low income inequality with which high intergenerational income mobility correlates is a sign of low inequality of opportunity. The thesis that sees public education at the origin of the reduction of the distance of opportunity between young people from different social classes in the Nordic countries finds support in empirical works that place it among the main factors at the origin of low income inequality (Björklund and Jäntti

2009). Let's focus on Sweden, the country with the best performance of intergenerational mobility both in income and education. The reform of the Swedish educational system, enacted in 1940, served to encourage students from families with a poorly educated father (as well as a low income) to continue their studies until the completion of secondary school. In a school system where as many as 98% of students enrol in secondary school, young people with a "disadvantaged" family and social context have thus benefited from conditions to make the most of their talent much more favourable than in most advanced countries. The driving factor of social mobility in Sweden has been the low level of educational inequality. Public spending on education in relation to GDP (in Fig. 11.5, the highest value among all OECD countries) seems to have given a significant boost: the impact of public education on multidimensional well-being seems to have been greater than that exerted by the level of income (Mackenbach et al. 1997).

Is this a fact that contradicts what has been said about the need for a "solidaristic universalism" orientation in education? A point in favour of the "universalistic" orientation of public education policies? Not exactly. What makes the impact of the social structure of the Nordic countries on education different, primarily compared to the two major Anglo-Saxon countries, is being those—at least until the problem of immigration arose—"inclusive societies" in the full sense of the word. The low inequality of opportunity between social classes—favoured both by low income inequality and by efficient Welfare institutions—has constituted the ideal socio-economic environment for the aspiration to social ascent of the less favoured young people to succeed, thus giving impetus to intergenerational income mobility. The success of the Nordic countries in equalising access to education is therefore not immediately attributable to the universalistic direction of public education policies. What made the society of the Nordic countries dynamic from the point of view of repositioning along the income scale—relative mobility—are the characteristics of the social structure, that is, the context of reducing inequalities in which the public education system is immersed. In these nations, the dynamics within social stratification have not been centred on the simple market mechanism. Market and society do not communicate only through money. The incentive of earnings is not the main stimulus of the demand for education. The cultural humus of social norms oriented towards social solidarity has settled in the construction of Welfare institutions aimed at reducing the gap that divides young people of different social origin in acquiring the capabilities to realise their own life project.[12]

As argued elsewhere in the book, the persistence of collective values over time is always at risk. The last two decades have seen conservative or right-wing governments, inspired by the neoliberal vision of "individual responsibility", come to power in Nordic countries. This cultural orientation reflects the idea of a contrast between personal freedom (*status libertatis*) and participation in the community (*status civitatis*).[13] The neoliberal culture induced by globalisation has found full acceptance in government programmes, so that the individualistic spirit has been able to make inroads in the field of education. The split between the individual and society is also expressed in the exclusion from the public sphere of expectations of social advancement from any source, whether native or immigrant. Just as the trend towards *commodification* of education—the organisation of educational services based on supply and demand in the market—gives the individual control over their own life path, so too the right to receive welfare benefits is now being "discriminated" in favour of national taxpayers who have contributed more to the financing of social state institutions over the years.

In conclusion. Public spending on education is an example of "universalistic" public investment that fails the egalitarian objective that the "culture of rights" established during the *Trente Glorieuses* had promised. The weak point of public education policies in advanced countries lies in the underestimation of the fact that their universalistic approach—in the absence of precise *targeting* in favour of young people from low-income families—ends up reproducing inequality of opportunity between social classes. The wealth, both financial and genetic, is profitably inherited by the children of the rich. For "disadvantaged" young people, on the other

[12] The empirical verification coordinated by Narayan et al. (2018) allows us to take a step forward in the discussion. It clarifies how in the initial phase of development, when a population is emerging from conditions of extreme poverty, the disparity of educational opportunities between advantaged and disadvantaged subjects has not yet fully manifested in the market. This means that economic growth does not immediately suffer from the "inequality of circumstances". Things become more complicated in the mature phase of economic development; the one in which the advanced countries we are studying are now found. The distance between life spheres has consolidated. In social groups that due to scarce economic and cultural resources see access to advanced education as well as to the most sought-after job positions precluded, there is a low relative intergenerational income mobility.

[13] The *urbs* was the physical place and the *civitas* was its moral place of community life.

hand, financial wealth is non-existent and the possibility of capitalising on their genetic wealth is strongly conditioned by the "inequality of circumstances" and the "market failure" in guaranteeing equal access to opportunities. The family background and social context that make young people very different from each other are not affected. The consequence is that the universalistic approach to education makes the rise to a higher social position from one generation to the next—the ability for intergenerational educational mobility—very heterogeneous among social classes.

Social Classes and Equality in Education: The Limits of "Universalism"

Education, which is at the root of the issue of people's social advancement, is a decisive factor in the formation of "social capital" (Coleman 1990)[14] in every country. The OECD explains the increase in education by giving absolute priority to the individual: "Higher levels of education usually translate into better job opportunities and higher earnings. The possibility of obtaining a higher and growing income over time [...] represents for individuals a significant incentive to pursue education and vocational training" (OECD 2021, p. 83). The main research institute of advanced countries naturally knows very well that young people are not all on an equal footing when it comes to access to education. A few pages later, however, the OECD merely proposes an individualistic approach to education: it is explained that acquiring university education is an important "individual responsibility" of young people: "Adults who complete tertiary education obtain a 'return' in their working life because they are more likely to be hired and to earn more than without a degree" (*ibid.*, p. 99). This presentation of the issue of education is flattened on the neoliberal vision of the "market society", of the extension of the market value system to society. Who are the "adults" to whom the OECD refers in the opening of the quotation? It is not given to know. Anyway, they are too few. It was much braver, in calling the "adults" by their name, the *Dr. Johnson's Dictionary of the English Language* published in 1755, which defined "the liberal individual: 'the non-miserable'; the non 'low-born'". This conception of man, halved between the *mean* and the *gentleman*, was well rooted in the culture of sixteenth-century society. John Locke (1968),

[14] The line of studies on "social capital" deals with the basic social norms—primarily, trust and reciprocity—that underpin the interpersonal relationships that take place in society.

who will be considered in the following centuries the father of liberalism, "wrote his Treatise on education with the children of the *gentlemen* in mind, the moral ἦθος he promoted was aristocratic" (Rosenblatt 2018, p. 23).

Today we are a little further ahead in addressing the complexity of the education problem. But in the analytical framework that underlies public education policies, awareness is often lacking. On the other hand, there are many difficulties that social science research faces. The Canadian economist Miles Corak (2013) had the merit of focusing empirical verification on the inequality of opportunity as a brake that blocks social mobility. The main fallout from such inequality is precisely on the demand for education. As seen in Fig. 11.1, in countries with a predominantly private supply of education, where therefore education is expensive even at secondary school level, the "private rate of return on education" is equally high. High the price of the input (*university education*), high the price of the output (*high qualification job*). However, the impact on intergenerational income mobility of extending the training period is modest at best.

Clearly, an aggregate analysis of the demand for education for the purpose of social climbing can only fail. In driving the rise in the income scale, the "private rate of return on education" counts only for the minority of young people who can afford the high cost of university and post-university education. The *gentlemen*, as John Locke would have said. In summary, the market is important for achieving the aspiration to success in life, but the decisive mediation between aspirations and achievements goes through the structure of society, which is characterised by the asymmetry of power. In reducing the functioning of society to that of the market, the neoliberal vision ignores the problem of the social context in which young people are trained. As explained in Box 7.1, in the correlation elaborated by Corak, we move directly from the Gini index of income inequality, an expression of power asymmetry, to the increase in the difficulties that children encounter in social climbing the lower the income of their parents. Having skipped the link between income mobility and educational mobility, his analysis of intergenerational mobility is incomplete. We do not have econometric estimates that make explicit the variable *inequality of opportunity* and its impact on the acquisition of capacity by "disadvantaged" young people.

The universalism implicit in the strategy of mass schooling is considered an inviolable principle because it asserts the right of all participants in the "social contract" to the same educational treatment. Despite a differentiation based on income being provided both in the progressive taxation regime, with the variability of rates, and by legislation on the right to different welfare benefits in case of specific personal situations, in the case of merit goods this criterion is not adopted. However, if access to education is not declined by public policies according to the logic of "differentiated treatment"—that is, taking into account the different needs of different social groups in all dimensions of well-being—this principle does not lead to "educational inclusion", but ends up reproducing the existing social stratification. Philosopher Bernard Williams hypothesised that a supporter of the English private education system, probably coming from the elite, would feel no shame in stating that "characteristics related to wealth" justify selective access to quality higher education for the children of the rich (Williams 2005, p. 133). After primary school, in fact, few young people who do not belong to the elite pass the selection and enrol in a "grammar school", so the majority of students enter a "secondary modern school". In English culture, moreover, the concept of social cohesion has never made a breakthrough. Not even Labour governments have ever thought that the compactness of the hierarchical pyramid of society should be affected by the introduction of a unified middle school system, as happened in Italy with the 1963 reform. The reality tells us that elitism has been, and remains, a serious limitation of the English educational system. It is documented that the abolition of the dual training system—a class system that early separated the fate of students from poor families from that of students from wealthy families—has contributed in Italy to intergenerational income mobility (Marzadro and Schizzerotto 2011). However, we must note that in 2023, with the reform of technical and professional institutes, a simplistic conception of the education-work link aimed at providing "human capital" to companies began in Italy the restoration, the return to educational hierarchy.

The "universalistic" approach of public education policies has not given the hoped-for results. The raising of the school obligation implemented in Europe during the *Trente Glorieuses* (we recall the most important reforms: France 1952; United Kingdom 1947 and 1979; Italy 1963 and 2007) was not a success as a policy of "inclusion". Attendance of a uniform path for all and the educational obligation for a longer period can hardly improve the level of education and income of "disadvantaged" families in the same way as "advantaged" families can benefit. An econometric verification, to evaluate who benefited more from mass education, used a rather singular indicator: the performance gap between the child who, at the age of 10, had many books at home and the child who did not have any (Brunello et al. 2012). This confirms the importance of the cultural and income level of parents in the intergenerational transmission of well-being.

Reasoning in aggregate terms would be easier in the ideal world of "perfect" markets: there should not be a substantial difference among young people who have a high income level and a substantial wealth, and young people who have to resort to credit to finance their investment in education (the only difference is in the interest to be paid). However, reality is not made up of "perfect" markets. As mentioned above, the credit market is "imperfect": banks do not offer equal treatment to all credit applicants. The uncertainty associated with the time between the loan and its repayment is transferred to the "customers", for fear of their poor solvency. Young people who cannot provide guarantees are denied the university loan and must give up educating themselves.

In advanced countries, inequality in access to education is one of the most serious problems because the "imperfection" of the credit market hinders the emergence of talents. However, we should not delude ourselves that we all agree on the need to distinguish between favoured and disadvantaged social classes in access to education. On the contrary, many agree with Ronald Reagan's vision. In the vision of the "free and equal" society, there is no room for "circumstances", and there is also no attention to the "imperfection" of the credit market. Instead of these two facts, an opinion is substituted: the firm belief that the acquisition of human capital—simply because it has to do with the individual propensity to invest in education—should fall within the sphere of "individual responsibility". And, as often happens, the simplicity of an opinion easily acquires the authority of a fact.

There is no doubt that greater human capital formation in new generations, particularly in the United States, generates a more efficient interaction between advanced skills and frontier technologies (Acemoglu and Autor 2012). However, making intergenerational social mobility depend solely on the positive impact on economic growth of the spread of education in the population means underestimating the heterogeneity in access to education among social classes. In the previous chapter, we highlighted what this implies in the introduction of technological innovations by companies: the narrowing of highly knowledgeable workers and their concentration in superstar companies. However, if the opportunities for excellent job positions are concentrated in the high end of professional training, the link between excellent training and a high level of income and wealth inevitably increases. In the United States, the main determinant of the demand for education is found in the economic resources of families. The probability of attending an Ivy League college is 77 times greater for young people from families in the top 1% of the income distribution than for young people in the income quintile of the poor (Chetty et al. 2017b).

The Ivy League is effectively the university system of the elite, since two-thirds of its students come from the richest 20% of the population. "This astonishing inequality in admission is partly due to inherited legacies and donor appreciation (the back door), but also to the advantages that propel young people from wealthy families through the main door" (Sandel 2020, p. 11). Access to educational opportunities is denied not only to the poor but also to increasingly large strata of the middle class. The fact that the most renowned American universities, considered the "cathedrals of educational merit", make a mockery of the so-called "meritocratic principle" cannot but cast a shadow on the credibility of the principle itself. The United Kingdom has followed in the footsteps of its American cousins. The fact that the young people who go to Cambridge (and, to a lesser extent, Oxford and the University of London) are predominantly students from private secondary schools, and that the children of the elite of managers and professionals are overrepresented among graduates, makes the "long arm" of the family's influence clearly visible (Bukodi et al. 2023, p. 558). Continental Europe is far from immune to the distortion that class privilege introduces into access to excellent education. Despite the fact that public university education is essentially free, the role of the family ends up reinforcing inequality of opportunity. Just consider that the children of the French elite, who make up no more than 23% of the population in their age group, represent as much as 92% of the students at the highly selective École Polytechnique.

The powerful growth of the Trente Glorieuses, accompanied by a decrease in inequalities, could not guarantee an evolution towards equal opportunities in education. However, a Latinist had the problem very clear. Concetto Marchesi, in a report for the works of the Italian Constituent Assembly of 1947, wrote: "the democracies of almost the whole world have made the right equal, but have left only the less the possibility to exercise it". In fact, the criterion of "universalism" adopted by many democracies promised, right at the beginning of the Trente Glorieuses, the real enjoyment of social rights by all. But universalism tout court, by putting rich and poor on the same level, confuses the "impartiality" towards all of public policies with egalitarianism.

In today's advanced societies, which are very little inclusive beyond proclamations, the goal of social inclusion can hardly be entrusted to the market. By its nature, the free market does not have the tools to address the "inequality of circumstances". Market opportunities open up to young people only *after* the training period. The OECD has observed that market solutions to the problem of social inclusion are "often very expensive and ineffective in improving educational outcomes" (OECD 2018, p. 263). The private provision of education, which should be the main factor of inclusion, is not oriented towards solving the problem of "disadvantaged" circumstances. Usually, as we have seen, even public educational structures do not address the problem.

One way to develop public policies that tackle the issue of power asymmetry in education is perhaps to use a multidimensional approach. The methodological novelty contained in Chetty et al. 2022 is the suggestion to address social mobility with policies that are conducted by developing intervention tools capable of intervening in the process of forming individual identity, in order to improve the *abilities* of people. It has indeed been shown that the effectiveness of policies depends on the interaction between parental care, *peer effects* in schools and social environment (Doepke et al. 2020; Agostinelli et al. 2022). Statistical data show that children who grow up in areas where young people with low *status* socio-economic maintain relationships of knowledge and friendship with a large number of young people with higher *status* socio-economic have higher rates of upward mobility. As the example of the positive impact of *peer effects* on disadvantaged young people shows, the attendance during the formative period of people from another class, from another social context, is important: their influence changes the goals, desires, behaviours of the "disadvantaged".

The perception of reality, the "model of the mind" shared by people, is modified and enriched by interclass relationships that only a public collective choice approach can design. In longitudinal studies conducted by Raj Chetty, interactions between rich and poor young people turn out to be—unlike what has been so far common belief among social scientists—a better "predictor" of social mobility than factors such as the availability of "good jobs". To implement broad-spectrum policies, aimed at the multidimensional well-being of "disadvantaged" young people, the role of the Welfare system remains central. The evidence that appears in Fig. 11.1 is contradictory. In the graph, the United States and the United Kingdom present on the horizontal axis very high values of "educational return".

The remunerations that young people obtain are linked to the degree achieved by purchasing the educational services offered: the higher the degree, the higher the earnings. The labour market seems to react efficiently to the expectation of rewarding educational excellence. A clue, this is, that not only the socio-economic environment but also incentives work as an incentive to the demand for education. It's a pity that this can only happen for a few.

The scenario indeed changes when we look at the vertical axis of Fig. 11.1a.[15] A good expected return from investment in education (horizontal axis) does not correspond to a high intergenerational income mobility (vertical axis). The aggregate data is that young people who enter the labour market today have the same probability as young people born in the seventies of climbing higher in the income ranking than the level reached by their parents (Chetty et al. 2014a). It seems that the slogan *learning equals earnings* does not find—precisely in capitalist countries where its truthfulness should be more manifest—a great response in terms of intergenerational mobility. The value that appears on the vertical axis shows that the correlation is not particularly robust. A high rate of return on education therefore coexists with very limited intergenerational income mobility. Precisely in the two nations where faith in the "perfect" functioning of markets is one with faith in meritocracy, a high "return on education" does not correlate with earnings of the young "independent" from those of parents, or higher.

The Iee is high in both countries, signalling a strong social persistence: children have on average a hefty 50% chance objective of not exceeding the income level reached by their parents. The more excellent the degree of education achieved by a young person, the more one would expect that the "wage premium" that the market recognises him is such as to allow him to rise to a position of income higher than that of his own parents. The two nations that at the beginning of the twentieth century exchanged the baton of the leading economic system of capitalist development show values of intergenerational income mobility really disappointing in comparison with the expected earnings that stimulate the demand for

[15] On the other hand, it should be noted that in the United States the rate of return on university education, after having significantly increased from 1980 to 2000 by 6.5 logarithmic points (college) and by 10.9 (post college), between 2000 and 2017 has seen a much smaller increase.

education. Why is it that in the United States and the United Kingdom the "rate of return" of education is high but society is very little "mobile"?[16]

Ours are times of paradoxes. On *TikTok* young influencers have no qualms about stepping up to the pulpit and giving lessons of life to adults. It is the same young people who use educational services but—as is obvious and right—they do not pay either the taxes that finance public education, nor the fees of private school and university. The real protagonists of the demand for education, especially in systems with a predominantly private supply of education, are in fact the parents (and grandparents), to the extent that they invest in the education of their children (and grandchildren).[17] The smaller the public supply of education, the more the (wealthy) family is in tune with the "market society".

In the United States, the dynastic interest, through the promotion of family prestige, and the interest in increasing the financial power of the family are aimed at ensuring a high degree of education for the new generation. And society is organised to give young "advantaged" people an adequate reward for their commitment to training.[18] The investment of parents in their children's education is all the greater not only the higher the "private rate of return on education" but especially the greater their financial wealth (which the aggregate analysis of intergenerational mobility prevents from seeing). For young people who do not have wealthy families behind them, the risk of "educational exclusion" is high.[19] The economic literature is beginning to take note of reality. In the multi-

[16] It should be clarified that, compared to the decade to which the graph data refers, in the United Kingdom the economic incentive to demand for education is declining. Despite the space occupied by the private educational system, compared to the public one, remains very large in both countries, the rate of return on education in the United Kingdom has dropped to about a third of that in the United States (Oecd 2021, p. 98).

[17] At the beginning of the twentieth century, the inequality among young Americans in achieving a university degree had decreased. However, the value of this indicator of educational inequality began to rise again from the cohort of those born in the 1960s (Bernardi et al. 2018).

[18] The family (and its structure: couple of parents or single, working condition, etc.) plays an important role in the formation of human capital. The role of the family is particularly relevant in local communities where the capital the social fabric is degraded, and therefore the percentage of young people who drop out of school is high (Coleman and Hoffer 1987; Coleman 1988).

[19] The affirmative action regarding access to education seems to have fallen into disgrace in the United States. In June 2023, the Supreme Court declared President Biden's plan to reduce debt (a discount of up to $20,000) illegitimate, which burdens tens of millions of students, almost always from "disadvantaged" families in terms of income and ethnicity.

authored article in which Gary Becker appears as the first author (published years after his death), the "private rate of return" on education is not the incentive to which children respond: it is presented as the main factor that drives parents to finance their children's professional training (Becker et al. 2018).

Since it is the parents who face the cost of their children's education based on their incomes (in the expectation that children educational outcomes also depend on their own level of education), the aggregate data on education spending says little about the spread of knowledge in the population. In choosing to invest "in *skills* and knowledge", the pronoun "their" used by Reagan should be referred to the fortunate subset of students whose parents can afford to pay for their children's university education. In conclusion, the real slogan should then be: "The richer your parents are, the more you can educate yourself".

Unequal Opportunities for Education and the Emergence of Talents

In the United States, the incentive of earnings represented by the high "rate of return on education" is not a signal of high intergenerational social mobility. Contributing to keeping the value of the correlation low is income inequality. Paradoxically, public universities, in keeping tuition fees close to more moderate amounts than private ones, play the role of improving the correlation. Despite the dominance of private supply in Anglo-Saxon educational systems, in accordance with the principle of universalism, the rich are beneficiaries of public spending on education to the same extent as the poor. In the face of this equal formal treatment, once private spending on education is also considered, the young elite end up getting an "unequal treatment" to their advantage. In fact, the public financial support for education that they enjoy is "additional" to the financing of their education by their parents. This results in a singular outcome. Social mobility of the population, instead of increasing, stalls: "when a substantial mobility of individuals occurs within the boundaries of classes, but not between them, even modern societies are in fact built on social classes" (Becker et al. 2018, p. 20). Frederick Hayek did not believe this was a problem. In *The Constitution of Liberty* (1960), he wrote: "If the defence of freedom implies that everyone is treated the same, it is not because it postulates actual equality among men; [it] insists on the fact that individual differences provide no reason for diversity of treatment and, indeed, rejects those differences in treatment that would in fact be necessary to ensure an equal position of individuals in social life [...] because this would involve a further and discriminatory coercion" (Hayek 1960, p. 184).

A theoretical framework of the issue, of great clarity and mirror to that of Hayek, is due to the philosopher and jurist Ronald Dworkin: "what impartiality seems to require is not that everyone receives equal treatment, but rather that everyone is treated as an equal" (Dworkin 1977, p. 227). If we believe that there is a "right to social mobility", the real ethical problem is not in achieving equality (whatever its content), but in avoiding that the differences of which Hayek speaks violate the right of all to be considered equal. The English political philosopher Derek Parfit has deduced that to maximise social welfare it is necessary to introduce the criterion of giving "priority to those who are behind", or a deviation from the deceptive universalistic criterion according to which "we are all equal". In public policies, greater value should be attributed to the welfare of the individual with the lowest income. The Prioritarianism asserts that "those who are more 'disadvantaged' should count more in redistribution" (Parfit 2000, p. 101).

In public finance, the progressivity of taxation corresponds to the progressivity of welfare benefits. The redistribution of income from the rich to the poor through monetary transfers is supplemented by the implicit redistribution in the operation of public health systems.[20] In public education, the approach is to promote equal access for all. Specifically, in the public funding of university education, with universalism *tout court*, any orientation towards equalisation between social classes is excluded. It is necessary to adopt the principle of "solidaristic universalism", or differentiated among social groups, giving priority to supporting the education of "disadvantaged" families, as this is the phase of people's lives in which the "inequality of circumstances" most "bites".

"Differentiated universalism" consists in shaping public policies towards "unequal treatment", the only conception of universalism capable of

[20]The lower contribution of low-income classes to the financing of the National Health System (NHS), due to the progressivity of tax rates, corresponds to their greater use of public health. On a probabilistic basis, the net balance between contribution to the operation of public health and use of health services is therefore positive for the poor and negative for the rich.

guaranteeing true impartiality. If individuals unequal in "circumstances"—*in primis*, wealth, income and the culture of their parents—receive unequal treatment with the aim of making them less unequal, the "disadvantage" from which they are variously penalised in the different dimensions of well-being should decrease.

The implementation of the principle of "differentiated universalism" requires public planning that makes use of a large amount of information. Rigorous recent research based on microdata confirms that, in the dimension of education, the low level of income and education of parents and the "imperfections" of the market have a strong impact on the level of education achieved by children and on their future income. The method for achieving "differentiated universalism" must necessarily make use of a comparative evaluation between the sets of opportunities of people (Farina et al. 2004). The *big data* now available, and artificial intelligence technologies, are an unexpected opportunity; but, at the same time, their use contains a great threat. On the one hand, the wide availability of microdata could provide the opportunity for a revival of solidaristic universalism. The design of public policies oriented towards "unequal treatment" in the education of "unequal" subjects—with the aim of promoting the equalisation of educational opportunities among young people belonging to families with different income and *status* positions—is no longer a utopia. On the other hand, like any new knowledge, the use of this new direction of technical progress is anything but neutral. It is far from unlikely that as a result of its development the power gap between social groups will end up increasing. In the production of generative artificial intelligence, particularly the construction of Gpu microprocessors,[21] there are all the prerequisites for the processing and dissemination of information to be distorted, and even to be directed towards manipulation and surveillance (Zuboff 2019). A few considerations are enough to understand how uneven the contest is—in a "playing field" already significantly tilted—for the affirmation of "solidaristic universalism" and democratic information.

The efficient use of generative AI is measured in the number of elementary operations (for example additions) that can be performed in a certain

[21] Generative artificial intelligence, the specific type of artificial intelligence capable of generating text, images, videos, music, etc., depends on the production of microprocessors. The graphics processing unit (Gpu), the graphics processing unit (or graphics processor), is an electronic circuit designed to accelerate the creation of images through so-called floating point operations (Flop).

time. Since the speed of Gpu processors is decisive, the evolution of this technology depends on having substantial economic resources available for their development. The major problems are: a) the competition to secure leadership in the graphics microprocessor sector;[22] b) the competition between artificial intelligence companies to attract the best computer scientists. Generative AI is today the field in which the non-neutrality of the production and use of technological innovations is most evident. Between the private sector and the public sector—and what are, in principle, their respective objectives, profit and the common good—the fight is uneven. To the extreme difficulty that the governments of advanced countries are encountering in regulating AI is added the clear advantage of the private sector over public companies and public universities in financing research and in the production of microprocessors. The problem is one of political and social choice. If the "constellation of ideas" is that of "solidaristic universalism", using the *big data*, it would be possible to greatly improve, through the "personalisation" of the intervention, the convergence of the educational performance of young people belonging to different social classes. For example, by constructing for each individual a multidimensional profile on the "differentiated treatment" necessary to enable them to overcome their deficiencies in training. The difficulty naturally does not escape economic research: "Levelling the background circumstances, reducing the direct effect of circumstances on educational performance, requires a long-term intervention that can take generations to be effective" (Marrero et al. 2022, p. 26).

What is the causal sequence that goes from potential talents to *capabilities* deployed in the socio-economic reality? We have argued that the functioning of the market does not guarantee equal opportunities for all, and that educational policies—even when inspired by universalism—do not have equalising outcomes, but often support the strategies of elites opposed to social "inclusion". The emergence of talents is linked to overcoming disadvantaged economic conditions due to "circumstances", the factor that most hinders equality in educational opportunities. Circumstances impact on the opportunities to earn an income also by influencing other important dimensions such as health, education and

[22] The American company Nvidia is the world leader in the production of microprocessors. Today there is a fierce competition between the United States, capable of building the most powerful microprocessors, and China, whose production of components US companies, particularly Nvidia, depend on.

vocational training. The poor results achieved by public education support programmes in the fight against inequalities expose the limits of universalism.

Economic research does not overlook the enormous benefits of a solidaristic universalism. Since "it is likely that the waste of human potential occurs at the bottom of the income distribution, policies favourable to greater relative mobility can promote a model of growth more oriented towards inclusion" (Van der Weide et al. 2021, p. 29).[23] The econometric estimates conducted in the first systematic study on the impact of circumstances on educational opportunities are eloquent: "In almost all countries, the most important contribution to opportunity inequality comes from the cultural environment of the family and, among all other factors [...], the most relevant is the number of books in the family" (Marrero et al. 2022, p. 16).[24]

Further refutation of the idea that the "rate of return" of education is the predominant determinant of the propensity to educate, there is another cultural factor in the demand for education: the interest of parents in the future of the family dynasty seems to count more than the incentive

[23] The inequality of opportunity can be expressed in terms of income mobility. The indicator of absolute inequality of opportunity is the number of subjects who register an income deviation from the average income of their group (for example, a lower income, attributable to unfair circumstances and not to a lack of commitment at work). The relative inequality of opportunity is instead the impact of such a deviation on the total overall income inequality. Furthermore, absolute intergenerational educational mobility is measured by the percentage of children who exceed the level of education (instead of income) of their parents; and relative intergenerational educational mobility is measured by the degree to which the socioeconomic success of children is independent of the level of education (instead of income) of their parents.

[24] Italy, for example, is a case of stagnation of social mobility that is particularly difficult to solve. The absence of a large number of medium-large companies that exert a growing demand for qualified work, stimulating young people to commit to training, is accompanied by the absence of an education policy, highlighted by the scarcity of resources available to public education, since governments continue to reduce its funding. These two factors depress the incentive for young people to train: only 20% of Italians between the ages of 25 and 34 have a degree compared to an OECD average of 30%. "Currently, Italy is trapped in a low-skills equilibrium, a low level of generalised skills: a situation in which the poor supply of skills is accompanied by weak demand from companies" (OECD 2017, p. 2). Among the seven most advanced countries (G7), Italy is the only one with a smaller share of workers with tertiary education employed in routine tasks (tasks that require following a set of defined rules) compared to non-routine workers (tasks that require more complex activities, such as problem solving).

of expected earnings by the children. “Firstly, the ability of more advantaged parents to always use their superior resources to promote their children’s education and thus preserve their position of advantage; secondly, students with a more advantaged background who do not achieve good results can still receive family resources that protect them from any serious problem of downgrading” (Goldthorpe 2013, p. 21). Faced with these considerations, it is hard not to recall the “unjust inequality”. This concept is very close to the concept of inequality of opportunity. It encompasses both the diversity of circumstances between advantaged and disadvantaged young people, and a functioning of the market in which the former have more opportunities to exploit educational opportunities and thus translate talents into *abilities*. Therefore, educational inequality accentuates both the wage inequality of the present generation and the social mobility of the future generation (Blanden et al. 2022). Despite statistical evidence clearly indicating the link between educational gaps among young people and the heterogeneity of the economic outcome they achieve as adults, the public education policies of advanced countries continue to be dictated by aggregate objectives, not taking into account the fact that class membership significantly affects the level of education and the level of income at which the individual is placed. When the opportunities that determine individual behaviours are not observable, one must resort to the “counterfactual” method: how would things have gone *if there had been no disparity in initial circumstances, and if the market had guaranteed equal opportunities to all*, so that the talents of all could emerge?

The *Great Gasby Curve* (Ggc) in education is the statistical tool that links income levels with levels of educational mobility of children compared to the level achieved by parents. In the Ggc relating to advanced countries, there is a significant correlation between indicators of income inequality among parents and those of educational mobility among young people. However, another statistical indicator, the scores obtained by young people in school tests (*test score*), seems to contradict this result. The correlation of educational inequality from one generation to another with the *test score* is very low. How to explain this asymmetry between *input* and *output* of education? Why does the advantage of opportunities that rich parents provide for their children not translate into a corresponding excellence in their result compared to that of young people from “disadvantaged” families? Part of the answer is this: the significant educational gap between rich and poor parents is filled to a greater extent by the children of poor families, who "rise", for example, from a diploma to a degree, while it is less likely that the child of the rich "rises" from a BA degree to a doctorate. In slightly more precise terms, there would be a divergence between the high "productivity" of the "disadvantaged" parents' investment in their children's education, starting from the low levels of education of the parents, and the rapidly decreasing "productivity" of the investment of elite and middle-high class families (Blanden et al. 2022). Confirmation comes from the United States. Studying disaggregated data, in the face of the increasing investment of wealthier parents in their children's education, there has been a stability of educational outcomes in recent decades (Hanushek et al. 2022). This is an indication that it is in potential contradiction—in terms of results—with the effectiveness attributed to the *influence* exercised in various ways by parents on schools and universities with the aim of facilitating the educational path of their children (Gregg et al. 2015).

The gap—in job stability as well as in earnings—between the high skills of the elite workers in technologically advanced sectors and the de-skilled and precarious jobs in services related to new technologies (digital platforms) reflects the widening of educational opportunities between social classes. In other words, there is a lack of "inclusion" of a wider range of young people in the educational process of raising *abilities*. The Ggc education is an example of how the aggregate analysis of socio-economic indicators says very little. Not only because it hides the very different "educational starting points" between rich and poor families. But also because the educational opportunities that are lacking for "disadvantaged" young people, if made available to them, would have a much greater impact—in terms of basic education, skills acquisition, income and well-being—than those same resources have for the children of the elite.

Another aspect of the limits of any analysis of society based on aggregate data comes to light if one reflects on the "shortsightedness" that the standard model of the economy—designed for individuals separated from each other—introduces into economic reasoning. The externalities, both negative and positive, that are connected to social interaction are completely ignored. The centrality of public policies of "solidaristic universalism", i.e. aimed at rebalancing educational opportunities between social classes, is also grasped by reflecting on the enormous positive externalities for the community. From solidaristic universalism would benefit not only the *relative* mobility of less fortunate people compared to more fortunate ones, but also the factor at the origin of *absolute* mobility, the rate of GDP growth. Public policies that use *big data* can indeed today serve the community more effectively, resulting in higher levels of both well-being and social cohesion (Chetty 2021).

Bibliography

Acemoglu, D. 2022 Obedience in the Labour Market and Social Mobility: A Socioeconomic Approach, *in «Economica», LXXXIX, S1, pp. 2–37.*

Acemoglu, D. & Autor, D. 2012 What Does Human Capital Do? A Review of Goldin and Katz's the Race between Education and Technology, *in «Journal of Economic Literature», L, 2, pp. 426–63.*

Acemoglu, D. & Robinson, J. A. 2000 Why Did the West Extend the Franchise? Democracy, Inequality, and Growth in Historical Perspective, *in «Quarterly Journal of Economics», CXV, 4, pp. 1167–99.*

Agostinelli, F, Doepke, M., Sorrenti, G., Zilibotti, F. 2022 When the Great Equalizer Shuts Down: Schools, Peers, and Parents in Pandemic Times, *in «Journal of Public Economics», CCVI, pp. 1045–74.*

Alesina, A., Giuliano, P., Reich, B. 2021 *Nation-Building and Education*, in «Economic Journal», CXXXI, 638, pp. 2273–303.

Amiel, Y., Bernasconi, M., Cowell, F., Dardanoni, V. 2015 *Do We Value Mobility?*, in «Social Choice and Welfare», XLIV, 2, pp. 231–55.

Atkinson, A. B. & Jenkins, S. P. 2020 A Different Perspective on the Evolution of UK Income Inequality, *in «Review of Income and Wealth», LXVI, 2, pp. 253–66.*

Ballarino, G., Barone, C., Panichella, N. 2014 Social Background and Education in Occupational Attainment in 20th Century Italy, *Eui Working Papers, Fiesole.*

Barro, R. & Lee, J.-W. 2013 *A New Data Set of Educational Attainment in the World, 1950–2010, in «Journal of Development Economics», CIV, pp. 184–98.*

Bauluz, L. & Meyer, T. 2024 *The Wealth of Generations*, World Inequality Lab, Working Paper n. 4.

Bauman, Z. & Tesler, K. 2002 Società, etica, politica. Conversazioni con Zygmunt Bauman, *Raffaello Cortina, Milano.*

Becker, G. S. 2011 Reflections on the Economics of Education, *in Hanushek, Machin, Wößmann 2011.*

Becker, G. S. & Tomes, N. 1979 An Equilibrium Theory of the Distribution of Income and Intergenerational Mobility, *in «Journal of Political Economy», LXXXVII, 6, pp. 1153–89.*

Becker, G. S. & Tomes, N. 1986 *Human Capital and the Rise and Fall of Families*, in «Journal of Labor Economics», IV, 2, pp. S1–S39.

Becker, G., Kominers, S. D., Murphy, K. M. Spenkuch, J. L. 2018 *A Theory of Intergenerational Mobility*, in «Journal of Political Economy», CXXVI, S1, pp. 7–25.

Bentham, J. 1983 *The Collected Works of Jeremy Bentham*, a cura di F. Rosen e J. H. Burns, I, Clarendon Press, Oxford.

Bergman, P. et al. 2023 Creating Moves to Opportunity: Experimental Evidence on Barriers to Neighborhood Choice*, Nber Working Paper n. 26164.*

Bernardi, F., Hertelb, F. R., Yastrebovac, G. 2018 A U-turn in Inequality in College Attainment by Parental Education in the Us?*, in «Research in Social Stratification and Mobility», LVIII, pp. 33–43.*

Bernstein, B. 1970 *Education Cannot Compensate for Society*, in C. Stoneman et al. (eds), *Education for Democracy*, Penguin Education Special, London.

Björklund, A. & Jäntti, M. 2009 Intergenerational Income Mobility and the Role of Family Background*, in Salverda et al. 2009.*

Blanchet, T., Saez, E., Zucman, G. 2022 *Real-Time Inequality*, Nber Working Paper n. 30229.

Blanden, J. & Machin, S. 2004 Educational Inequality and the Expansion of UK Higher Education*, in «Scottish Journal of Political Economy», LI, 2, pp. 230–49.*

Blanden, J. & Machin, S. 2017 *Home Ownership and Social Mobility*, Cep Discussion Papers dp1466, Centre for Economic Performance, Lse.

Blanden, J. & Macmillan, L. 2014 *Education and Intergenerational Mobility: Help or Hindrance?*, Case Papers n. 179, Centre for Analysis of Social Exclusion, Lse.

Blanden, J., Gregg, P., Machin, S. 2003 *Changes in Educational Inequality*, Centre for Market and Public Organisation n. 79, University of Bristol.

Blanden, J., Doepke, M., Stuhler, J. 2022 *Educational Inequality*, Nber Working Paper n. 29979.

Bradbury, B., Corak, M., Waldfogel, J., Washbrook, E. 2015 *Too Many Children Left Behind*, Russell Sage Foundation, New York.

Bratberg, E. et al. 2017 A Comparison of Intergenerational Mobility Curves in Germany, Norway, Sweden, and the Us*, in «Scandinavian Journal of Economics», CXIX, 1, pp. 72–101.*

Brunello, G. & Rocco, L. 2008 Educational Standards in Private and Public Schools*, in «Economic Journal», CXVIII, 533, pp. 1866–87.*

Brunello, G., Weber, G., Weiss, C. T. 2012 Books are Forever: Early Life Conditions, Education and Lifetime Earnings in Europe*, in «Economic Journal», CXXVII, pp. 271–96.*

Bukodi, E., Goldthorpe, J. H., Steinberg, J. 2023 Continuing Complexity: The University Careers of a Scientific Elite in Relation to Their Class Origins and Schooling*, in «British Journal of Sociology», LXXIV, pp. 547–65.*

Callender, C. & Mason, G. 2017 Does Student Loan Debt Deter Higher Education Participation? New Evidence from England, *in «Annals of American Political and Social Science», DCLXXI, 1, pp. 20–48.*

Chetty, R. 2021 Improving Equality of Opportunity: New Insights from Big Data, *in «Contemporary Economic Policy», XXXIX, 1, pp. 7–41.*

Chetty, R. et al. 2014a Is the United States still a Land of Opportunity? Recent Trends in Intergenerational Mobility, *in «American Economic Review», CIV, 5, pp. 141–7.*

Chetty, R. et al. 2014b Where Is the Land of Opportunity? The Geography of Intergenerational Mobility in the United States, *in «Quarterly Journal of Economics», CXXIX, 4, pp. 1553–623.*

Chetty, R. et al. 2017a The Fading American Dream: Trends in Absolute Income Mobility since 1940, *in «Science», CCCLVI, 6336, pp. 398–406.*

Chetty, R. et al. 2017b Mobility Report Cards: The Role of Colleges in Intergenerational Mobility, *Nber Working Papers 23618.*

Chetty, R. et al. 2022 Social Capital II: Determinants of Economic Connectedness, *in «Nature», DCVIII, 7921, pp. 122–34.*

Chevalier, T. 2019 Political Trust, Young People and Institutions in Europe. A Multilevel Analysis, *in «International Journal of Social Welfare», XXVIII, 4, pp. 418–30.*

Coleman, J. S. 1988 Social Capital in the Creation of Human Capital, *in «American Journal of Sociology», supplemento* Social Capital in the Creation of Human Capital, Sociological and Economic Approaches to the Analysis of Social Structure, *XCIV, pp. S95–S120.*

Coleman, J. S. 1990 *Foundations of Social Theory*, Harvard University Press, Cambridge.

Coleman, J. S. & Hoffer, T. B. 1987 Public and Private Schools: The Impact of Communities, *Basic Books, New York.*

Connor, D. S. & Storper, M. 2020 The Changing Geography of Social Mobility in the United States, *in «Pnas, CXVII, 48.*

Corak, M. 2013 Income Inequality, Equality of Opportunity and Intergenerational Mobility, *in «Journal of Economic Perspectives», XXVII, 3, pp. 79–102.*

Crawford, C. et al. 2016 Higher Education, Career Opportunities, and Intergenerational Inequality, *in «Oxford Review of Economic Policy», XXXII, 4, pp. 553–75.*

Dardanoni, V., Fields, G. S., Roemer, J. E., Sanchez Puerta, M. L. 2006 How Demanding Should Equality of Opportunity Be, and How Much Have We Achieved?, *in S. Morgan, D. Grusky, G. S. Fields (eds),* Mobility and Inequality: Frontiers of Research from Sociology and Economics, *Stanford University Press, Stanford.*

Doepke, M., Sorrenti, G., Zilibotti, F. 2019 *The Economics of Parenting*, in «Annual Review of Economics», XI, 1, pp. 55–84.

Doepke, M., Agostinelli, F., Sorrenti, G., Zilibotti, F. 2020 It Takes a Village: The Economics of Parenting with Neighborhood and Peer Effects, *Cepr Discussion Paper n. 14637.*

Dworkin, R. 1977 *Taking Rights Seriously*, Harvard University Press, Cambridge.

Emmons, W. R., Kent, A. H., Ricketts, L. R. 2019 Is College Still Worth It? The New Calculus of Falling Returns, *in «Federal Reserve of St. Louis Review», CI, 4, pp. 297–329.*

Esteban, J., Gradín, C., Ray, D. 2007 An Extension of a Measure of Polarization, with an Application to the Income Distribution of Five Oecd Countries, *in «Journal of Economic Inequality», V, 1, pp. 1–19.*

Farina, F., Peluso, E., Savaglio, E. 2004 *Ranking Opportunity Sets in the Space of Functionings*, in «Journal of Economic Inequality», II, 2, pp. 105–16.

Ferguson, D. & Savage, M. 2020 Controversial Exams Algorithm to Set 97% of Gcse Results, *in «The Guardian», 15 agosto.*

Frank, R. H. 2013 Falling Behind. How Rising Inequality Harms the Middle Class, *University of California Press, Berkeley.*

Galor, O. & Tsiddon, D. 1997 Technological Progress, Mobility, and Economic Growth, *in «American Economic Review», LXXXVII, 3, pp. 363–82.*

Gärtner, M., Mollerstrom, J., Seim, D. 2023 Intergenerational Transmission of Luck versus Effort Beliefs, *in «Economic Letters», CCXXXII, pp. 88–109.*

Gellner, E. 1983 *Nations and nationalism*, Cornell University Press, Ithaca.

Goldin, C. & Katz, L. F. 2008 *The Race between Education and Technology*, Belknap Press of Harvard University Press, Cambridge.

Goldthorpe, J. H. 2013 Understanding – and Misunderstanding – Social Mobility in Britain: The Entry of Economists, the Confusion of Politicians and the Limits of Educational Policy, *in «Journal of Social Policy», XLII, 3, pp. 431–50.*

Gregg, P., Macmillan, L., Vittori, C. 2015 Nonlinear Estimation of Lifetime Intergenerational Economic Mobility and the Role of Education, *DoQSS Working Paper n. 3, Quantitative Social Science Ucl Social Research Institute.*

Hanushek, E. A. et al. 2022 The Intergenerational Transmission of Cognitive Skills: An Investigation of the Causal Impact of Families on Student Outcomes, *Working Paper n. 9, University of Konstanz.*

Hayek, F.A. 1960 The Constitution of Liberty, Routledge & Kegan Paul, London.

Hirschman, 1970 Exit, Voice, and Loyalty: Responses to the Decline of Firms, Organizations, and States, Harvard University Press, Cambridge.

Hobsbawm, E. 1990 Nations and Nationalism since 1780: Programme, Myth, Reality, *Cambridge Univeristy Press, Cambridge.*

Houmark, M. A., Ronda, V., Rosholm, M. 2020 The Nurture of Nature and the Nature of Nurture: How Genes and Investments Interact in the Formation of Skills, *Iza Discussion Paper n. 13780.*

Locke, J. 1968 (1693) Some Thoughts Concerning Education, *in J. L. Axtell (a cura di),* The Educational Writings of John Locke, *Cambridge University Press, Cambridge.*

Mackenbach, J. P. et al. 1997 Socioeconomic Inequalities in Morbidity and Mortality in Western Europe. The Eu Working Group on Socioeconomic Inequalities in Health, *in «Lancet», n. 349 (9066), pp. 1655–9.*

MacLeod, W. B. & Urquiola, M. 2021 Why Does the Us Have the Best Research Universities? Incentives, Resources, and Virtuous Circles, *in «Journal of Economic Perspectives», XXXV, 1, pp. 185–206.*

Major, E. L. & Machin, S. 2019 *Social Mobility*, Centre for Economic Performance, London School of Economics.

Marginson, S. 2016 Global Stratification in Higher Education, *in S. Slaughter* & *B. Taylor (ed)*, Higher Education, Stratification and Workforce Development: Competitive Advantage in Europe, the Us and Canada, *Springer International Publishing, Switzerland.*

Markovits, D. 2019 The Meritocracy Trap: How America's Foundational Myth Feeds Inequality, Dismantles the Middle Class, and Devours the Elite, *Penguin Press, New York.*

Marrero, G. A., Palomino, G. C., Sicilia, G. 2022 Inequality of Opportunity in Educational Achievement in Western Europe: Contributors and Channels, *Ecineq Working Paper Series n. 612.*

Marzadro, S. & Schizzerotto, A. 2011 Le prospettive di mobilità sociale dei giovani italiani nel corso del XX secolo, *in Schizzerotto, Trivellato, Sartor 2011.*

Narayan, A. et al. 2018 Fair Progress? Economic Mobility across Generations around the World, *World Bank, Washington DC.*

Oecd 2008 Education at a Glance 2008, *Paris.*

Oecd 2012 Education at a Glance 2012, *Paris.*

Oecd 2017 Strategia per le competenze dell'Ocse. Italia. Sintesi del Rapporto, *Paris.*

Oecd 2018 A Broken Social Elevator? How to Promote Social Mobility, *Paris.*

Oecd 2021 Better Life Index, *Paris.*

Oecd 2022 Education at a Glance, *Paris.*

Oecd 2023 Education at a Glance, *Paris.*

Orwell, G. 1941 The Lion and the Unicorn, Secker & Warburg, London.

Parfit, D. 2000 *Equality or Priority?*, in M. Clayton & A. Williams (ed), *The Ideal of Equality*, Palgrave Macmillan, Basingstoke.

Piketty, T. 2018 Brahmin Left vs Merchant Right: Rising Inequality & the Changing Structure of Political Conflict: Evidence from France, Britain and the Us, 1948–2017, Wid.world Working Paper Series n. 7.

Polanyi, K. 1974 The Great Transformation, *Farrar & Rinehart, New York 1944.*

Power, S. & Whitty, G. 2002 *Bernstein and the Middle Class*, «British Journal of Sociology of Education», XXIII, 4, pp. 595–606.

Reay, D. 2017 Miseducation. Inequality, education, and working classes, *Policy Press, Bristol.*

Rosenblatt, H. 2018 The Lost History of Liberalism, from Ancient Rome to the Twenty-First Century, *Princeton University Press, Princeton.*
Sandel, M. J. 2020 The Tyranny of Merit. What's Become of the Common Good?, *Penguin Books, London.*
Schuetz, G., Ursprung, H., Woessmann, L. 2008 Education Policy and Equality of Opportunity, *in «Kyklos», LXI, pp. 279–308.*
Sennett, R. 2003 Respect. The Formation of Character in a World of Inequality, Allen Lane, London.
Social Commission Mobility 2020 Research Report. Technical Annex: Quantitative Analysis of Downward Mobility, *London.*
Solon, G. 2002 Cross-Country Differences in Intergenerational Earnings Mobility, *in «Journal of Economic Perspectives», XVI, 3, pp. 59–66.*
Solon, G. 2004 A Model of Intergenerational Mobility Variation over Time and Place, *in M. Corak (ed),* Generational Income Mobility in North America and Europe, *Cambridge University Press, Cambridge.*
Solon, G. 2013 Theoretical Models of Inequality Transmission across Multiple Generations, *Nber Working Paper n. 18790.*
Song, X., Massey, C. G., Rolf, K. A., Xie, Y. 2020 Long-term Decline in Intergenerational Mobility in the United States since the 1850s, *Proceedings of the National Academy of Science Usa, CXVII, pp. 251–8.*
Tawney, R. H. 1952 (1931) *Equality*, Halley Stewart Lectures, G. Allen & Unwin, London.
Todd, S. 2015 The People: The Rise and Fall of the Working Class, 1910–2010, *John Murray, London.*
Torche, F. 2011 Is a College Degree still the Great Equalizer? Intergenerational Mobility across Levels of Schooling in the United States, *in «American Journal of Sociology», CXVII, 3, pp. 763–807.*
Van der Weide, R. et al. 2021 *Intergenerational Mobility around the World*, World Bank Policy Research Working Paper n. 9707, Washington DC.
Williams, B. 2005 In the Beginning Was Uke Deed: Realism and Moralism in Political Argument, Princeton University Press, Princeton.
Zuboff, S. 2019 The Age for Surveillance Capitalism: The Fight for a Human Future at the New Frontier of Power, *Profile Books, L.*

CHAPTER 12

The Education Market and the Talents of Young People

The "adaptation" of Education to the Market

"A poor school is always the sign of a poor democracy" (Scotellaro 1951). It is also for this reason that Nelson Mandela's famous phrase, "education is the most powerful weapon you can use to change the world", is considered the torch of hope for the redemption of democracy. The more social mobility is rigid, the more Mandela's phrase gains significance. Education, as mentioned at the beginning of the previous chapter, owes its nature as a merit good to the peculiar characteristic of raising both individual and collective well-being. In addition to the increase in an individual's education, there are the multiple benefits that the community obtains by virtue of the "positive externality" represented by the greater diffusion of knowledge in the population that the public education system ensures.

The advanced world seems to be going in the opposite direction today. The public education system is in crisis. It is incapable of achieving its objectives because it has fallen into the "market society". It is weakened by the joint attack to which it is exposed due to the decline in public budget funding and the increasing educational offer from private secondary school and university institutions. Education as a "merit good" was born in the Enlightenment of the eighteenth century and expanded in the nineteenth century parallel to the expansion of the middle class. It was then a pillar of the welfare state promoted by the progressive party coalitions that

F. Farina, *The Rise of Inequality and the Fall of Social Mobility*,
https://doi.org/10.1007/978-3-031-92843-7_12

came to power in post-war Europe. In the era of the "market society", the phenomenon of polarisation could be the death knell of the hope of founding on the expansion of cultural education the *empowerment* of young people penalised by conditions of "disadvantage" in the main dimensions of well-being. With the shrinking, in the income scale, of the *status* and the well-being of the middle class—in which the upper portion is approaching the rich, and the lower one the poor—nothing but emphasises the inequality of educational opportunity.

An indispensable requirement of "a fully human life" is to have access to education. Article 34 of the Italian Constitution introduces a principle, which is closely linked to the concept of democracy set out in the Introduction: "School is open to all. Lower education, imparted for at least eight years, is compulsory and free. The capable and meritorious, even if without means, have the right to reach the highest degree of studies". Note: in affirming this right, the Italian Constitution does not say "*the* capable and *the* meritorious", but encloses the holders of the right in a single category. It intends to draw attention to the fact that in society there are too many "capable and meritorious" young people, but without the means to realise themselves.

Education has a great impact on relative *mobility* precisely because it touches the nerve centre of the unequal distribution among social groups of the chances of success in life. A high degree of *commodification* of the offer of education carries the risk of "educational exclusion" of young "disadvantaged" people. In tying the educational demand of young people to income level, the organisation of the private sector's educational offer disregards the circumstances in which these young people grow up. The educational opportunities to which low-income classes have access depend on the set of Welfare institutions.[1] The fact is that in many advanced countries the State, as also happens in the case of health, forgets to finance public policies to the extent necessary for the effective enjoyment of constitutional rights by "disadvantaged" subjects. The theoretical

[1] Among public education policies, not only student residence for "out of town" university students should be considered, but also the complementarity between residential housing and *peer effects* in education. The improvement of the quality of housing in less prestigious residential areas could convince the middle class to live in neighbourhoods where there is a strong presence of ethnic groups with medium-low income, "without educational efficiency being detrimentally affected, but rather realising gains in both efficiency and equity" (Causa and Johansson 2010, p. 37).

elaboration of Ken Arrow (1971), Nobel laureate in Economics 1972, on the limits of the standard model of economics proves that the market economy is not a *morally free zone*. Arrow argues that the two constraints for the "optimal education policy"[2] from the point of view of efficiency are far from promoting equity in access to education. It follows that the private organisation of education is unsuitable for promoting the social mobility of "disadvantaged" young people.

Today we are witnessing the downsizing of the welfare state. The process of European integration is the most typical case of "asymmetry" in *governance* economic: policies that promote efficiency through the reduction of labour costs and the expansion of precarious work have been strengthened, while those of social protection have been downsized. In most of the countries of the European Union, the process of globalisation has taken away from governments much of their sovereignty. On the one hand, states are obliged to reduce tax rates on profits to avoid the relocation of multinational companies to countries with lower labour costs. On the other hand, the rich increasingly behave like cosmopolitans. The more they obtain a reduction in their tax burden with institutional reforms such as the replacement of progressive taxation with the *flat tax*, and the more they do *opting-out* from the public welfare system by migrating to private health insurance and private education, the more their contribution to public spending and therefore the total amount of funding available for public health and education systems decreases. The negative externality that weighs on all other citizens is enormous. Institutional changes such as the reduction of the public offer and the transition to the market have significant consequences for social mobility. Not having sufficient income to face the expenses for education and health, in losing the services offered by the public sector due to the progressive decline in social spending funding, "disadvantaged" groups suffer a severe fall in their multidimensional well-being.

[2] One of the many significant scientific contributions that Arrow gave to economic theory are the two constraints that preside over the organisation of an education system. The elasticity of individual utility to the demand for education depends on the "participation constraint" (the university institution, whether public or private, must offer conditions that allow those who demand education to obtain a utility at least equal to that of the alternative institution) and the "incentive compatibility constraint" (it is typical of the private institution a scheme of incentives in which the quality and high price of education push the student to provide a level of effort adequate to the gains expected from education).

While the choice of the ruling classes to appease the power of which multinationals and the rich enjoy leads to the downsizing of *governance* macroeconomic and the welfare state, economic research is producing a large amount of empirical work that gives *policy* indications in the opposite direction. The results unequivocally indicate how progressive taxation and welfare benefits aid mobility and social cohesion. A study on education in the European Union shows that inequality of opportunity decreases as university education becomes more accessible to population strata that suffer from an "opportunity disadvantage" due to a high percentage of negative "circumstances" (Palomino et al. 2019). In Europe, "the aspect that most contributes to inequality of opportunity is constituted by differences in the family cultural environment [...], followed by the occupation of the parents" (Marrero et al. 2022, p. 25). "Equalisation" policies of opportunities, for example in education, insofar as they increase intergenerational mobility, favour both equity and growth (Marrero and Rodríguez 2013). A growth process driven by a technical progress focused on the skills of the workers *high-skilled* "tends to benefit disproportionately the owners of capital and the high-skilled workers to the detriment of low-skilled workers (Cerra et al. 2021, p. 38). Its weak point lies in underestimating the propulsive impact of reducing opportunity inequality on growth: "equality of opportunity does not oppose economic growth: expanding access to health, education, justice, social protection, finance can simultaneously stimulate growth and inclusion" (ibid., p. 40).

Based on a very large database of microdata collected for 26 European countries, another study finds that the main channel of inequality generation is the type of occupation that the education diploma gives access to (Palomino et al. 2018). Moreover, using a method that allows for a more accurate estimation of the tails of the distribution, this study shows that children from middle-high income families have less persistence at the level of parents' income than the children of the poor (the lower the income, the higher the negative correlation between income inequality and social mobility). Reinforcing the relevance of public intervention on mobility is also the data of "institutional diversity". A comparison between the United States and Canada (Corak et al. 2011) showed that in the former country the deregulated labour market and less "progressive" public policies are factors that add to the family context in determining low social mobility between generations.

Educational Opportunities and Economic Growth

The link between social mobility and growth is very strong. It has been observed that sustained growth is associated with a phase of social conflict quietness and a greater dynamic within the social structure. The counterfactual verification conducted in the study by Chetty et al. (2017) (discussed in Chap. 7) suggests that a strong persistence of the rich at the top of the income scale and a low upward mobility of the poor are the outcome of a period in which less robust economic growth is associated with higher income inequality. In the transition to adulthood, the cohorts of those born in the eighties encountered conditions of low growth and high inequality. The channels through which high or low inequality contributes to growth, however, remain unclear.

An econometric estimate (Voitchovsky 2005) evaluates the impact of the Gini index on growth by separating the effect of an increase in inequality at high income levels from that at low income levels: an increased divergence in the former has a positive effect on growth, while in the latter it has a negative effect. The logic that gives rise to this result is that an upward leap in the earnings of the richest among the rich has a positive effect on growth, because it encourages the owners of equity capital to invest; while a greater inequality at the bottom of the distribution—that is, a divergence of incomes downwards within the group of the poor—has a potentially negative impact on growth. The disaggregation by social classes greatly aids the understanding of the link between income distribution and *relative* mobility. The strong slowdown that occurs in the reshuffling of positions in the income scale can be read in the light of Voitchovsky's analysis. When income inequality increases, both in the high section and in the low section of the distribution, the tendency towards social persistence is accentuated. Indeed, from the impulse to invest the higher earnings of the rich will derive that increase in their resources that will allow their children to remain among the *top incomes*. While the worsening of the disadvantageous condition of young people belonging to low-income families penalises their aspiration to social ascent.

What has changed in the last forty years to cause the serious *impasse* in which social mobility finds itself? A clue lies in the evolution of capitalist economies towards *homoploutia*, or towards a social context in which people enrich themselves both with the return on capital and with more skilled work. "The rich both in terms of property and *skill* (human capital) end up creating a *upper class* well protected from unfavourable macroeconomic developments in work (unemployment), or in capital (stock market value decline) because they obtain from the other factor sufficient resources to rely on" (Berman and Milanović 2020, p. 2). The authors therefore argue that the acceleration experienced by the concentration of capital in the hands of the rich has exerted a strong upward push in interpersonal income inequality. It is not just a clue that the amount of surplus reached to low-income classes has reduced, negatively affecting the access of young "disadvantaged" people to opportunities, with the result of blocking their social ascent. It is also the clue of a new factor blocking social mobility: alongside capital returns, in the earnings of the rich there is a growing presence of increasingly higher labour incomes. These substantial incomes go to finance the expenditure for the education of their children.

In calling into question the limits of aggregate analysis, this clue is linked to that of econometric works that reveal a low correlation of aggregate GDP growth with the increase in human capital formation.[3] In fact, by disaggregating the chances that young people have based on their different circumstances, the gaps in educational opportunities are captured. In the United States, it has been found that the mandatory standardised tests[4] that measure the degree of mathematical knowledge of students, particularly in *high school*, reflect with alarming precision "the fact that students are inserted into an intricate environmental system, consisting of many interconnected levels that include families, school, *peer groups* and local community" (Maroun and Tienken 2024, p. 8). The *capabilities* of students are heavily affected by the absence of "social capital, and its being fruitful, like other forms of capital, in enabling the achievement of otherwise unattainable objectives" (ibid., p. 9). An empirical study of disaggregated assessment of income distribution, conducted on a US longitudinal database, reiterates the negative effects that in the growth process can be determined on the well-being of the weakest subjects. Inequality of opportunity due to socio-economic factors beyond the control of the individual reduces economic growth (Marrero and Rodríguez 2013). For example, an insufficient rate of tertiary education in the population causes both

[3] Orthodox theory makes economic growth depend on the professional training that follows the incentive to acquire human capital. The different opportunities for access to education among young people belonging to different social classes help to explain why econometric estimates do not find a good correlation of the growth rate of aggregate GDP with the increase in human capital of the population (Croci Angelini and Farina 2007).

[4] These tests are largely equivalent to the national Invalsi tests that take place in Italy to monitor knowledge of Italian, mathematics, English, sciences.

unfair and slower economic growth, because it deprives a country of the "externality" represented by a high level of human capital. As in the study by Voitchovsky (2005), in the "low" portion of income distribution, occupied by low-income classes and the poor, it is a *lesser* inequality that favours growth. From an intergenerational perspective, when young people from less favoured classes acquire the skills to climb income positions through a strong commitment in education and work effort, to the absolute mobility driven by growth is added relative mobility. It has already been observed that relative mobility does not coincide with individual competition. Only apparently, therefore, the overcoming of opportunity inequality is seen as a phenomenon confined to the decision-making sphere of the individual. When socio-economic conditions are such as to seriously risk the emergence of the talents of young "disadvantaged" people, the growth of social well-being produced by a high level of human capital in the country comes to be lost (Frank 2005). Offering the talents of all young people the opportunity to flourish not only increases individual well-being, but in accelerating growth has the effect of improving the prospects for well-being of the entire country.

Education and Human Capital

In countries where the organisation of education is entrusted mainly to the public sector, the universalistic principle of equal access to educational services for all applies. A series of studies conducted on microdata from the United States, Germany and Italy on intergenerational transmission of income and education, and on aggregate data on income and education inequality, concludes that the best strategy to increase the educational performance of the "disadvantaged" would be to increase public investment in university education (Checchi 2005). The majority of economists trust in the causal link that goes from human capital to growth, in the belief that it is the accumulation of human capital the decisive factor both for long-term economic expansion and for social mobility. In other words, in the public organisation of education, the universalistic criterion would serve both the objectives of efficiency and equity.

The analysis developed in this book suggests instead that the "universalistic" approach to education is not the right strategy. The universalistic approach to public education of current public policies consists in a distribution of Welfare benefits to the rich and poor without distinction. However, public funding is configured for young rich people not in terms substitutive but complementary to private funding assured by the family. This means that the equality of opportunity between social classes—as the objective of public support for the education of young people—ends up further favouring the upward mobility of the rich.

The "universalistic" criterion to which public education responds does not therefore have a direct equalising effect with regard to the "inequality of circumstances" and the "imperfection" of the credit market, which is expressed in the lack of loans for education to disadvantaged young people, putting their access to university education at risk. "There is clear evidence that poorer children with high performance at the age of 11 have a much lower probability - in comparison with children from rich families - of continuing their studies and achieving good results in secondary school" (Crawford et al. 2016).

In tertiary education, as shown by the fact that among university students the percentage of rich young people is far higher than that of poor young people, the universalistic criterion does not dent the advantageous position of the young elite; while poor young people have a lower chance of playing their chances of social ascent by accessing university education. Empirical checks indeed document that "subsidising university has probably a regressive impact [on income distribution], subsidising primary education has probably a progressive impact" (De Fraja 2004, p. 25). The fight against educational poverty should start at nursery school and end with the achievement of a degree. Paradoxically, with the increase in public spending on education, the principle of universalism has weakened the redistributive solidarity of educational opportunities towards "disadvantaged" students: "the strong expansion of university education has disproportionately benefited people who are relatively richer in terms of family background" (Callender 2016, p. 141). This judgement reaffirms the thesis of Blanden and Machin (2004). These authors have documented, through a longitudinal empirical analysis,[5] that the creation in the UK of a larger university system has brought the benefit of an increase in human capital mainly among young people from rich families, without improving the level of education of young people from low-income and poorly educated families.

[5] A longitudinal statistical analysis measures the evolution over time of one or more characteristics of an individual or a family, through periodic interviews.

In countries with high *commodification* of education, moreover, the system of market incentives—in short, the expected gain from higher education—obviously discriminates even more against young people from low-income families. The expansion of the educational offer of private institutions and private universities ends up accentuating the gap in educational opportunities between disadvantaged and non-disadvantaged young people. In this way, society risks increasing, rather than reducing, inequality among young people in the process of acquiring *skills*. In the institutes of excellence where only students advantaged by the cultural and financial background of their parents manage to enter, the *peer effects*, the virtuous effects of imitation and collaboration between "peers", which increase the performance of less prepared students, are lost. For "disadvantaged" young people, the problem of the emergence of talents, which as mentioned are not unobservable, and their transformation into *skills* is far from solvable by appealing to "individual responsibility". The failure to unfold the benefits of "diversity in abilities" connected to *peer effects* ends up having negative consequences on the efficiency, as well as on the equity, of the educational system (MacLeod and Urquiola 2012). Public education of a universalistic nature thus risks increasing, rather than decreasing, the inequality among young people in the *skills* acquired. The less the benefit that "diversity in abilities" brings to the level of education of the young population is exploited, the more the acquisition of *skills* for the whole of students is reduced.

It is of course true that "heterogeneity in various countries in the role of the family, the state and the market can induce different relationships between inequality and mobility" (Bloome 2014, p. 28). However, like what happens with insurance companies and private sector companies operating in health care, the private organisation of education does not take into account—by its nature, being profit-oriented—the "social cost" associated with the damage to well-being caused by a population with an insufficient average level of education.[6] As we will now see, in the education reform programmes born in the Anglo-Saxon cultural environment,

[6] An econometric estimate uses a composite indicator of cognitive abilities (from comprehension skills to abilities in mathematics and sciences) as an explanatory factor of the long-term increase (1960–2000) of GDP per capita. Within the considerable increase in the average education of the population of 50 countries, it should be noted the enormous educational effort made by Asian nations that has exerted a great push on economic growth (Hanushek et al. 2022).

great benefits for the education of young people are attributed to the systems of *tracking* (the early selection of the most deserving students) and vouchers to be used at public or private institutions, in order to create a mixed, public and private, educational offer.

The "social cost" of *Tracking*

In many advanced countries, especially those whose educational system is predominantly private, the organisational model resorts to the method of early selection (*tracking*) of students with better academic performance. This strategy consists in creating classes composed only of students—in most cases they are the ones "advantaged" by the family context—who have already demonstrated their abilities in primary school. The introduction of *tracking* (also defined as *early streaming*) is justified by the "peer effects".[7] The idea is that the teacher can deliver better quality teaching to a class with a high concentration of the most capable students engaged in common learning. By assigning students to homogeneous classes in terms of basic preparation, it would prevent students who are struggling with learning from slowing down the learning of students "advantaged" by their family background or who appear, prematurely, more gifted.

Is it right to adopt the strategy of *tracking*, that is, to start, after primary school, the selection by differentiating the *curricula* and forcing students to be channelled into a specific educational path in order to maximise efficiency? There are few doubts in answering negatively. The OECD has long ago stigmatised the fact that "early streaming of students based on their abilities seems to considerably reduce mobility between generations" (D'Addio 2007, p. 7). It is hard to understand how organisational methods that reward privileged conditions are adopted in a key sector in combating inequality of "circumstances". The higher the percentage of students entering a vocational path, the greater the cost in terms of equity—in all dimensions, material and non-material, of well-being—caused by "educational segregation" (Epple and Romano 2003). This is

[7] "The aspect that in all countries contributes most to equality of opportunity is the family cultural environment (mainly measured by the number of books in the house), followed by the occupation of the parents. The importance of school characteristics in inequality of opportunity in terms of educational outcomes (Dore) is mainly linked to the *peer effects* (the average socio-economic level of students in a school); this effect is significant in countries with the highest Dore values (Central Europe, Italy, Greece and the United Kingdom)" (Marrero et al. 2022, p. 25).

all the more true if, from the earliest childhood, free access to nursery school is a solution to that crucial factor of divergence between people's sets of opportunities represented by insufficient cultural, economic and social resources of the family (Björklund and Salvanes 2011).

Selecting students with a better *curriculum* already in the early stages of the training process, in order to impart them a *syllabus* more advanced than that of the traditional organisation in classes formed on an equal basis, is a method that ends up increasing the distance between young people's life spheres. Since talents are not observable *a priori*, an early dropout from education by young people from low-income families can cause their talents to remain hidden. Yet, after the disastrous results of the Pisa tests in 2023, which signal a continuous deterioration in young people's skills, in many European countries, to reverse the trend of educational decline, they think of resorting to *tracking* (in France, the formation of classes divided into three groups of students, with initial placement tests, has been adopted). The goal seems to be to defend the privilege of students with a high family background, not to eliminate it. "Disadvantaged" students are deprived of the opportunity to enjoy positive *peer effects* consisting of exposure to the influence of students "advantaged" by family and social background. The obvious result is to enhance persistence rather than social mobility. The *peer effects* also have a strong complementarity with a "circumstance" of the social context, namely the "neighbourhood effects", social interactions closely linked to residence, which affect well-being (Oreopoulos 2007). This complementarity is typical of the United States (Durlauf 2004). When the prevailing behaviours in the environment frequented by a boy are virtuous, the "neighbourhood effects" are of great help for the formation of "disadvantaged" young people (Durlauf and Ioannides 2010).[8] Therefore, the *tracking* accentuates inequality in educational opportunities and strengthens the impact of family background on young people's earning prospects (Brunello and Checchi 2007). Together with the "imperfection" of the credit market (Loury 1981; Id. 2002), the *tracking* is a tool that penalises the upward social mobility of "disadvantaged" young people (Ferreira and Gignoux 2014). Moreover, in the United States, rich students who enjoy *peer effects*

[8]A study conducted in the United States on more than 7 million people concluded that the *neighbourhood effects* have a significant influence on intergenerational mobility, both educational (the college enrolment rate) and income (the future earnings of young people) (Chetty and Hendren 2018).

in private schools do not always achieve better educational results than public school students (De Fraja 2002).

The perverse causality link long established in the United States between family wealth and privileged access of rich young people to university education is a serious cause of "educational immobility". The United States is the advanced country that today has the greatest "educational segregation". Not only can poor young people not afford the high fees of universities (not only those of excellence), but the "skimming" of the most capable does not necessarily lead to the selection of the best talents, these gifts being *a priori* unknown. The ones who carry out the *cream-skimming* are also the *rating* agencies, whose preference for private universities influences the demand for enrolment: the greater the university's reputation, the greater the self-selection of students who can afford to pay a usually very high fee (Cook and Frank 1993).[9] The "unequal treatment" in young people's access to university with limited means is the consequence of excessively high university fees. A student who has had to take out a bank loan due to the limited number of scholarships upon graduation has accumulated a debt to repay of up to 300,000 dollars. The poor student, assuming the loan was granted, could not afford the risk of repayment. This is likely another reason to forgo university enrolment.

The line of research pursued by Ray Chetty is generating a leap in understanding the professional outcomes of university students. The main problem lies in the rooting in the social context of the divergence in educational performance. The empirical research conducted by Chetty et al. (2023) shows that in American society, leadership positions are occupied by graduates of the most selective universities (those of the *Ivy League*, plus Stanford, Duke, MIT, Chicago) in a proportion of the total that is overwhelmingly dominant. The big banks recruit their financial experts from these universities: 75% of the managers hired come from the top 10 *law schools*. The innovative result to which the research arrives is that it is not just about the advantages that the children of *top incomes*, as mentioned earlier, have in enrolling at the best universities. As the estimates conducted by the authors on granular data indicate, the vast majority of

[9] Access to the best universities is effectively denied to young people from low-income families. In the United States, the annual tuition fee declared by the top ten universities today fluctuates between 34,000 and 42,000 dollars. The increase in fees, equivalent to about 600% from the eighties to today, has increased both ethnic separation and income inequality among the student population: the student population is 80% white in elite universities; in others, 75% of young people belonging to ethnic minorities study.

the minority of graduate children of *top incomes* have obtained a degree (or a doctorate) of the highest quality simply because they proved to be better, from the moment they passed the entrance tests with greater success. Alongside money, parental care counts. The entire educational journey of these young people has benefited from the commitment made by parents to ensure them—from nursery school, to time spent reading together, to curricular and extracurricular activities—a cultural and professional education that enables them to express their talents to the fullest.

However, the issue of the heterogeneous degree of access among social groups to quality university education remains central. Neither the goal of equity nor that of efficiency is served if the relative educational mobility *upwards* of many young people—who could be "talented but disadvantaged"—is prejudiced by a family background that predestines them to be penalised by *tracking*.

"Freedom of choice": The Formal Neutrality of the Voucher

In Friedman's (1967) conception of freedom, "freedom of choice" in education plays a prominent role. Families should be left with the power to decide autonomously the educational service deemed most appropriate for their children's education: all children have a right to a "voucher" —in Anglo-Saxon slang, "a backpack full of money"—and parents make their choice. In addition to expanding freedom of choice in education, the use of "vouchers" allows individual preferences to be respected through "competition by comparison": in the face of the demand for education, public and private institutions are put on an equal footing.[10] Moreover, empirical research shows that distributing education vouchers to families, even if it does not have an impact on students' education, can stimulate public institutions to be more efficient (Epple et al. 2017).

On the use of the voucher tool, opinion is strongly divided. Some emphasise that this tool promotes both efficiency, as it stimulates competition among providers to attract students, and equity, as it would eliminate the advantage of the rich in choosing private education, so that access to educational opportunities would be "levelled". Others argue that this tool

[10] Since the amount of the voucher for enrolment in both types of institutions is usually equal to the average cost that, for the provision of the service, weighs on the public system, equality of conditions should stimulate the efficiency of both the public and private offer.

does not erase, but rather obscures, the discrimination between advantaged and disadvantaged students. The equality of schools in the face of the voucher system takes away from public school the social function of planning the education of young people according to quality standards programmed for all students, providing the appropriate additional services if they come from poor families. On the contrary, in adopting the strategy of *cream skimming*, private educational institutions put the interest of society in educating a future generation where everyone can achieve an adequate level of education (Newbery and Stiglitz 1984) in the background. On the other hand, the "freedom of choice" between public and private education is quite restricted, if it exists at all, for low-income families, who often find themselves unable to pay exorbitant school fees.[11]

Box 12.1 Vouchers and educational inequality in the United States
In the United States, intergenerational social mobility is influenced by a socio-cultural context made more challenging by the many fault lines that cross it: ethnic segregation, the wide dispersion in the quality of schools, the enormous variation in crime rates from one housing block to another, the atypicality, compared to countries of the old continent, of housing segregation, with the poor in the city centre and the rich in the residential suburbs[a]. The formation of student classes, even in public schools, based on the sharing of certain characteristics—ethnicity, income and parental education, primarily—ends up promoting social exclusion, rather than inclusion. Educational inequality is not solely attributable to income and wealth. Ethnic segregation is an additional factor (Chetty et al. 2018). The tendency of high-income families to pursue "educational separation" is well documented. In the United States, between 1972 and 2007, the richest 20% of families increased their spending on their children's education by almost 300% compared to an increase of less than 50% for the poorest 20% of families (Duncan and Murnane 2011). Private spending on education by wealthier families is a multiplier

(*continued*)

[11] The asymmetry between private and public education in the pursuit of economic efficiency is similar to that existing in the Anglo-Saxon model of the "quasi-market" in health, the "mixed" organisation of health services (Farina 2021, par. 13.6).

Box 12.1 (continued)

of inequalities. An example of the complementarity between dimensions as a cause of worsening multidimensional inequality is the addition of educational segregation to housing segregation, a phenomenon that has seen a significant acceleration since the 1980s (Epple and Romano 1998). The high price of housing triggers social discrimination mechanisms that lead to the expulsion of poor families from entire neighbourhoods, creating a concentration in a territorial area of particularly wealthy families. A wealthy residential neighbourhood in turn generates *spillover* of imitation and attraction of new high-income residents, which in turn fuels the supply in the area of high-end and high-priced private services (typical examples are garages, restaurants, gyms). It is the same phenomenon of territorial segregation that transforms certain goods and services in the area into positional goods. These goods, which precisely because of their limited availability lend themselves to guaranteeing a privileged social *status* (exclusive schools, quality apartments, pleasant nature, wellness centres and so on), end up being concentrated in areas well separated from others (the boundary is often marked by the presence of private security agents).

In an initial phase, the voucher policy tended to favour white middle-upper class families, who used the allocation of a fixed amount of money to abandon public institutions and enrol their children in elite private schools. This created a dual system, as private institutions proliferated attracted by the prospect of meeting the increased demand for private enrolment from families abandoning public school. The ethnic issue was exacerbated with the introduction of the voucher system. In a society model like the American one, where residence also determines children's school enrolment, low-income families of colour cannot afford to live in the "high" neighbourhoods where the public school is of better quality. The strategy of promoting ethnic integration and *peer effects* to equalise opportunities among young people from different social classes has not, however, been definitively defeated.

It is indeed true that the voucher tool, in promoting freedom of choice in education, has set in motion a process of territorial mobility within low-income areas. This "school mobility" certainly does

(*continued*)

Box 12.1 (continued)
not improve ethnic integration, but in some cases seems to contribute to reducing segregation. This financial support indeed allows poor families access to a good private school. Unless *tracking* is practised, poor students can benefit from the positive *peer effects* associated with proximity to wealthier students. Moreover, the "freedom of choice" allowed by the voucher system is appreciated by the rich who are "risk averse" to their children's failure. Empirical evidence shows that many parents of students who appear to be less talented are induced to prefer residence in a low-income area, for fear that in a school in a high-income area their children will end up in the lower educational track (De Fraja and Martinez-Mora 2014).

[a] *Moving to Opportunity* is a project launched by the federal government of the United States. The aim is to improve the quality of those local socio-economic environments where particularly degraded living conditions are present. Efforts are mainly focused on raising the chances of adult well-being for young people, starting from childhood living conditions.

The pursuit of profit, on the other hand, induces private schools to organise an educational offer aimed at satisfying the particular demands of wealthy families and the multiplication of the offer to be favoured when parents make their "free choice".[12] Private institutions, for example, place their offer in a relationship of complementarity with the tool of *peer effects*; in the case they are located in the most exclusive neighbourhoods, the complementarity extends to *neighbourhood effects*. The selection of applications for enrolment at a private university also takes into account the economic condition of the student with the aim of targeting the "creaming off" of students who have been facilitated by their family in the educational journey of primary and secondary school. The voucher tool, far from putting public and private education on the same level, exposes the

[12] In acknowledging the diversity of opportunities among young people, caused by the "inequality of circumstances", it has been proposed to equalise educational chances among different social classes, making the voucher system "progressive" through a subsidy to students with a disadvantaged background (Zingales 2012).

public offer, which has the obligation to guarantee universal access to learning, to the risk of being penalised compared to the private offer. In fact, therefore, this tool does not respect the principle of market coordination neutrality towards its operators. The "freedom of choice" of families between public and private school corresponds to a competitive advantage in favour of private education institutions (Box 12.2).

Box 12.2 Public schools and private schools in Sweden and Denmark

In the twentieth century, Sweden had earned a considerable reputation for the pursuit of equity in public policies. Faced with the swelling of the migratory wave, the country's governments have progressively lightened their virtuous social norms baggage. The traditional spirit of solidarity now stops at the border of the national community, excluding from many welfare institutions the immigrant communities. The principle of "freedom of choice" which inspires the legislation imposes in the educational system the horizontal equity—the "equal treatment"—between public and private. The Swedish private schools therefore have a right to support equivalent to the financing of public institutions. Education is the place where the perverse implications of the principle are most evident. Municipalities have the legal responsibility to provide children with access to education in a place close to their residential home. Profit-making schools however do not have such an obligation and prefer to settle in the city centres. Moreover, municipalities do not have the power to refuse students; while private schools have the ability to put students on a waiting list. Since the major costs in schools, represented by teachers and classrooms to be equipped, are more or less fixed, the maximum profit comes from maximising the number of students per teacher and per classroom. Private schools, pursuing the goal of maximising the funding ensured by the vouchers received, thus form classrooms with many students; the height of the fees is not then a problem, because their concentration in the historic centres protects them from a reduction in applications. On the contrary, the public administration (the municipalities), having the obligation of the fair distribution of schools on the territory, especially in areas where the demand for private education is high, ends up managing

(*continued*)

Box 12.2 (continued)

schools in whose classrooms there is a smaller number of students, with the consequence that the average cost per student is higher than in private education. On the other hand, public schools must by law guarantee the educational obligation and set the standard for funding. This triggers a vicious circle. Public schools lose students, and therefore funding, in favour of profit-making schools. Since the cost per student of public schools consequently increases, the standard cost also increases for private schools, which see the amount of funding provided by the public administration grow, and thus have the possibility of becoming even more attractive. It is therefore not difficult to understand why formal equality between public and private offer produces educational segregation and the lowering of the quality of teaching in public institutions. More generally, the downsizing of Welfare in the last two decades, according to data from the Luxembourg Income Study (Lis), has meant that Sweden's Gini index of income inequality, which had fallen to 0.23 in 1980, has reached 0.31.

The case of the Danish educational system is just as significant as the Swedish one precisely because of the presence of both problems, that of equity and that of efficiency. Statistical data indicate that the percentage of students attending private schools has greatly increased (Heckman and Landersø 2017). Also in this country, the choice of native parents has increasingly turned towards private schools, both to preserve their children from cultural hybridisation with the children of immigrants and for the better educational offer. It is easy to understand what the consequences are on social mobility: the "freedom of choice" allows the rich to enrol their children in public institutions in very low percentages, so that the classrooms of public schools are predominantly attended by the children of immigrants. Since the greater incidence of "non-equity" in access to opportunities is usually hidden in the low income portion of the distribution, in public institutions the *peer effects* can only develop among the children of immigrants and the most "disadvantaged" native parents. The link between Welfare and ethnic educational inequality is very

(*continued*)

Box 12.1 (continued)
evident in Denmark. In the twentieth century, the role of the welfare state was particularly important for the goal of equal opportunities in education. School reforms were successful in significantly increasing social mobility—in the cohorts of those born in the years forty and sixty—of students penalised by a disadvantaged family background. The expansion of private university education has instead favoured young people with an advantaged family background from the cohorts born from the seventies onwards, so that upward social mobility has slowed down (Karlson and Landersø 2021).

For an Affirmative Action *in Education*

The inadequacy of the principle of individualism *tout court* has been repeatedly emphasised. The criterion of equal treatment for all is a blunt weapon when the problem is to try to remedy the two factors—the "inequality of circumstances" and the "imperfections of the market"—that typically harm "disadvantaged" young people in acquiring *skills*. An illuminating example is the provision of public competition for services and monetary support for university education ("packages" that primarily include scholarships and a place in a residence). The criteria for awarding scholarships and residence are only on paper aimed at ensuring that the most talented are at the top of the winners' list. A support provision programme should indeed seek out the talented even among students whose talent has more difficulty emerging.

The allocation of support is the typical "failure" encountered by equal—universalistic—access to scholarships and residence. The talented "disadvantaged" end up in the ranking, probably through no fault of their own, behind the "advantaged" simply because they have not had the opportunity to signal their talents in order to access university and acquire *skills* of excellence. The non-observability *a priori* of the different talent of the candidates means that not all young people capable of acquiring their own *skills* can be identified. This problem hinders a distribution of scholarships that is truly fair. It is possible that there are many students who are not particularly talented but who—enjoying a privileged position due to their economic and cultural "advantage" background—end up occupying positions in the ranking of scholarship and residence winners despite being less good than other talented young people whose talents will therefore remain unexpressed. Directing universalism towards the emergence of the talents of all young people is the virtuous way of understanding *peer effects*. By supporting the emergence of the potential of "talented but disadvantaged" students—in addition to achieving actual respect for efficiency in the use of public resources for education—the community would achieve significant gains in both efficiency and equity.[13]

How to establish the ranking in the allocation? The simple criterion adopted on the basis of universalism is that the scholarship should go to whoever arrives before another because—based on the score and the number of scholarships available—"deserves" more than those who are not above the line that excludes the "less good". To circumvent the risk of "social immobility" of disadvantaged young people, political scientist Michael Sandel (2020) has proposed establishing a minimum threshold of education achieved for the admission of a certain number of students to university, and then covering the remaining places by lottery. This proposal has the drawback of emphasising, rather than countering, the role of luck in personal destinies and therefore of fuelling the feeling of being excluded from society by a whim of fate.[14] A policy of university education *for all*, such as to truly level the "playing field", finds in the *affirmative action* of the allocation of the "package" of university support the most appropriate tool.

Since talents do not fully manifest themselves until the period of university and post-university education, the chances of acquiring *skills* by young people with talents—but not yet observable—can be equated to the chances of "advantaged" young people in accessing tertiary education opportunities through a "quota of advantage" (a reserve of 60%) in the allocation of support to students. Fig. 12.1 shows how the causes of the lesser or greater degree of intergenerational educational mobility need to

[13] An econometric research conducted on data from the *European Value Survey* shows a positive correlation between "generativity" (the combination of creativity and care for the *well-being* of others) and *well-being* subjective (Becchetti and Conzo 2021).

[14] An example of educational discrimination is that caused by the Covid-19 pandemic, an event that has accentuated inequality in access to education due to the prolonged closure of schools. Students with a "disadvantaged" family background often did not have support from their parents or adequate online connections. Since learning is a cumulative process, the educational loss they have suffered is destined to be prolonged in the long term, with negative effects on their opportunities for social mobility (Agostinelli et al. 2022).

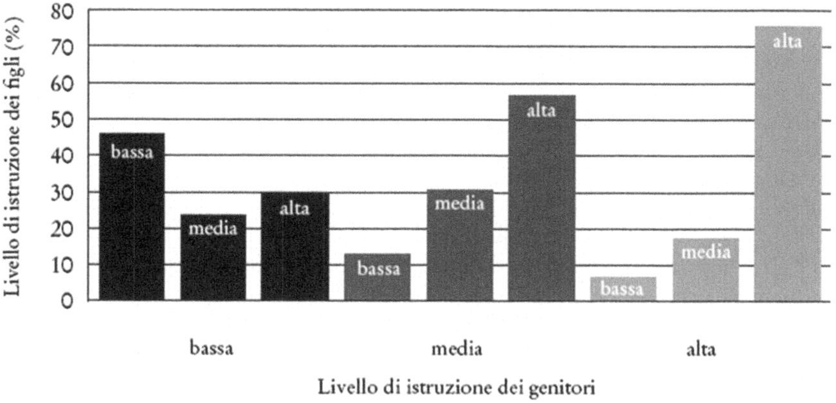

Fig. 12.1 Educational mobility of children, as a percentage of parents' education (Spain, 2019). (Source: elaboration in Salazar 2019 with data from the Survey on living conditions in Spain. Note: Low education: middle school diploma or lower. Medium education: high school diploma. High education: university degree. Translation: Sons' educational level (%), low, medium, high, Parents' educational level (%))

be deepened by disaggregating the generation of parents by levels of education. Its histograms do not only replicate the information contained in Figs. 11.2, 11.3, 11.4 and 11.6, that is, the great advantage of having rich or well-off parents. Fig. 12.1 suggests that the educational mobility of young people, their arrival at levels of education higher than those of their parents, it is not—as one might expect—linearly dependent on the distribution of the parents' level of education—low, medium, high. In the histograms relating to low-income families, there is indeed a clue that stimulates a disaggregated search for educational opportunities, allowing the development of more appropriate education policies to bring out the talents of all. The fact that only in the case of young people belonging to "disadvantaged" families for education (low educational level of parents) the probability of achieving a "high" education is greater than the probability of achieving a "medium" education could be the sign of the decisive role that—if adequately supported by public policies—is played by both talent and the psychological drive for social affirmation. An *affirmative action* in university education—in creating a preferential lane for the extension of the education of disadvantaged young people—is the best antidote to protect us from the return to the caste society.

Bibliography

Agostinelli, F, Doepke, M., Sorrenti, G., Zilibotti, F. 2022 When the Great Equalizer Shuts Down: Schools, Peers, and Parents in Pandemic Times, *in «Journal of Public Economics», CCVI, pp. 1045–74.*

Arrow, K. J. 1971 Essays in the Theory of Risk-Bearing, *North-Holland, Amsterdam.*

Becchetti, L. & Conzo, G. 2021 Resilience, Social Capital, Active Citizenship and Subjective Wellbeing: the Contribution of Generativity, *Research Paper n. 522, Ceis, Università Tor Vergata, Roma.*

Berman, Y. & Milanović, B. 2020 Homoploutia: Top Labor and Capital Incomes in the United States, 1950–2020, *Lis Working paper n. 806.*

Björklund, A. & Salvanes, K. G. 2011 Education and Family Background: Mechanisms and Policies, *in Hanushek, Machin, Wößmann 2011.*

Blanden, J. & Machin, S. 2004 Educational Inequality and the Expansion of UK Higher Education, *in «Scottish Journal of Political Economy», LI, 2, pp. 230–49.*

Bloome, D. 2014 Income Inequality and Intergenerational Income Mobility in the United States, *Harvard University Department of Sociology-Harvard Kennedy School.*

Brunello, G. & Checchi, D. 2007 Does School Tracking Affect Equality of Opportunity? New International Evidence [«Educational opportunities and the role of institutions»], *in «Economic Policy», XXII, 52, pp. 782–861.*

Callender, C. 2016 Cost-sharing and Student Support, *in Scott et al. 2016.*

Causa, O. & Johansson, A. 2010 Intergenerational Social Mobility in Oecd Countries, *in «Oecd Economic Studies», 1, pp. 1–44.*

Cerra, V., Lama, R., Loayza, N. 2021 Links between Growth, Inequality, and Poverty: A Survey, *Imf Working Paper n. 68.*

Checchi, D. 2005 The Economics of Education: Human Capital, Family Background and Inequality, *Cambridge University Press, Cambridge.*

Chetty, R. & Hendren, N. 2018 The Impacts of Neighborhoods on Intergenerational Mobility I: Childhood Exposure Effects, *in «Quarterly Journal of Economics», CXXXIII, 3, pp. 1107–62.*

Chetty, R., Deming, D. J., Friedman, J. N. 2023 Diversifying Society's Leaders? The Determinants and Causal Effects of Admission to Highly Selective Private Colleges, *Nber Working Paper n. 31492.*

Chetty, R. et al. 2017 The Fading American Dream: Trends in Absolute Income Mobility since 1940, *in «Science», CCCLVI, 6336, pp. 398–406.*

Chetty, R. et al. 2018 The Opportunity Atlas: Mapping the Childhood Roots of Social Mobility, *Nber Working Paper 25147.*

Cook, P. J. & Frank, R. H. 1993 The Growing Concentration of Top Students at Elite Schools, *in Clotfelter - Rothschild 1993.*

Corak, M., Curtis, L., Phipps, S. 2011 Economic Mobility, Family Background, and the Well-being of Children in the United States and Canada, *in Smeeding et al. 2011, pp. 73–108.*

Crawford, C. et al. 2016 Higher Education, Career Opportunities, and Intergenerational Inequality, *in «Oxford Review of Economic Policy», XXXII, 4, pp. 553–75.*

Croci Angelini, E. & Farina, F. 2007 Macroeconomia dell'Unione europea, *Carocci, Roma.*

D'Addio, A. C. 2007 Intergenerational Transmission of Disadvantage: Mobility or Immobility across Generations? A Review of the Evidence for Oecd Countries, *Oecd Social, Employment and Migration Working Paper n. 7.*

De Fraja, G. 2002 *The Design of Optimal Education Policies*, in «Review of Economic Studies», LXIX, 2, pp. 437–66.

De Fraja, G. 2004 *Education and Redistribution*, in «Rivista di Politica Economica», XCIV, 3, pp. 3–44.

De Fraja, G. & Martinez-Mora, F. 2014 *The Desegregating Effect of School Tracking*, in «Journal of Urban Economics», LXXX, C, pp. 164–77.

Duncan, G. J. & Murnane, R. J. 2011 Introduction: The American Dream, Then and Now, *in Idd. (eds),* Whither Opportunity? Rising Inequality, Schools, and Children's Life Chances, *Russell Sage, New York.*

Durlauf, S. N. 2004 *Neighbourhood Effects*, in J. V. Henderson & J.-F. Thisse (a cura di), *Handbook of Urban and Regional Economics*, Elsevier Science, Amsterdam, IV, pp. 2173–242.

Durlauf, S. N. & Ioannides, Y. M. 2010 *Social Interactions*, in «Annual Review of Economics», II, 1, pp. 451–78.

Epple, D. & Romano, R. E. 1998 Competition between Private and Public Schools, Vouchers, and Peer-Group Effects, *in «American Economic Review», LXXXVIII, 1, pp. 33–62.*

Epple, D. & Romano, R. E. 2003 Neighborhood Schools, Choice, and the Distribution of Educational Benefits, *in Nber 2003, pp. 227–86.*

Epple, D., Romano, R. E., Urquiola, M. 2017 *School Vouchers: A Survey of the Economics Literature*, in «Journal of Economic Literature», LV, 2, pp. 441–92.

Farina, F. 2021 Lo Stato sociale. Storia, politica, economia, *Luiss University Press, Roma.*

Ferreira, F. H. G. & Gignoux, J. 2014 The Measurement of Educational Inequality: Achievement and Opportunity, *in «World Bank Economic Review», XXVIII, pp. 210–46.*

Frank, R. H. 2005 Positional Externalities Cause Large and Preventable Welfare Losses, *in «American Economic Review», XCV, 2, pp. 137–41.*

Friedman, M. 1967 *Efficienza economica e libertà*, Vallecchi, Firenze (ed. or. *Capitalism and Freedom*, Chicago University Press, Chicago 1962).

Hanushek, E. A. et al. 2022 The Intergenerational Transmission of Cognitive Skills: An Investigation of the Causal Impact of Families on Student Outcomes, *Working Paper n. 9, University of Konstanz.*

Heckman, J. & Landersø, R. J. 2017 The Scandinavian Fantasy: Sources of Intergenerational Mobility in Denmark and the Us, *in «Scandinavian Journal of Economics», CXIX, 1, pp. 178–230.*

Karlson, K. B. & Landersø, R. 2021 The Making and Unmaking of Opportunity: Educational Mobility in 20th Century-Denmark, *Iza Discussion Paper n. 14135.*

Loury, G. C. 1981 Intergenerational Transfers and the Distribution of Earnings, *in «Econometrica», XLIX, 4, pp. 843–67.*

Loury, G. C. 2002 *The Anatomy of Racial Inequality*, Harvard University Press, Cambridge.

MacLeod, W. B. & Urquiola, M. 2012 Anti-Lemons: School Reputation, Relative Diversity, and Educational Quality, *Iza Discussion Paper 6805.*

Maroun, J. & Tienken, C. H. 2024 The Pernicious Predictability of State-Mandated Tests of Academic Achievement in the United States, *in «Education Sciences», XIV, 2, pp. 1–29.*

Marrero, G. A. & Rodríguez, J. G. 2013 *Inequality of Opportunity and Growth*, in «Journal of Development Economics», CIV, C, pp. 107–22.

Marrero, G. A., Palomino, G. C., Sicilia, G. 2022 Inequality of Opportunity in Educational Achievement in Western Europe: Contributors and Channels, *Ecineq Working Paper Series n. 612.*

Newbery, D. M. & Stiglitz, J. E. 1984 *Pareto Inferior Trade*, in «Review of Economic Studies», LI, 1, pp. 1–12.

Oreopoulos, P. 2007 Do Dropouts Drop Out Too Soon? Wealth, Health and Happiness from Compulsory Schooling, *in «Journal of Public Economics», XCI, 11–12, pp. 2213–29.*

Palomino, J. C., Marrero, G. A., Rodríguez, J. G. 2018 One Size Doesn't Fit All: A Quantile Analysis of Intergenerational Income Mobility in the U.S. (1980–2010), *in «Journal of Economic Inequality», XVI, 3, pp. 347–67.*

Palomino, J. C., Marrero, G. A., Rodríguez, J. G. 2019 *Channels of Inequality of Opportunity: The Role of Education and Occupation in Europe*, in «Social Indicators Research: An International and Interdisciplinary Journal for Quality-of-Life Measurement», CXLIII, 3, pp. 1045–74.

Sandel, M. J. 2020 The Tyranny of Merit. What's Become of the Common Good?, *Penguin Books, London.*

Scotellaro, R. 1951 Le riviste di cultura e il nostro tempo, *in «Il Nuovo Corriere», 26 agosto.*

Voitchovsky, S. 2005 Does the Profile of Income Inequality Matter for Economic Growth? Distinguishing between the Effects of Inequality in Different Parts of the Income Distribution, *in «Journal of Economic Growth», X, 3, pp. 273–96.*

Zingales, L. 2012 A Capitalism for the People: Recapturing the Lost Genius of American Prosperity, *Basic Books, New York.*

CHAPTER 13

Conclusions

Is it an inescapable characteristic of capitalism to give rise to a social structure where classes remain rigidly separate? The first three decades of the post-war period refute this judgement. In the model of economy and society that saw its beginnings in those years, a powerful growth not only allowed all classes to improve their level of well-being. This was not the only change. Absolute mobility was accompanied by relative mobility. Although all classes enjoyed the increase in earnings, the extent to which each enjoyed the increase in GDP was different, which gave impetus to the reshuffling of people among different income and status positions. The increase in well-being primarily had the effect of boosting the individual component of identity, the *status libertatis*. But the other component, the *status civitatis*, was also enhanced, because the dignity of work in the joint venture of production increased. By the end of the sixties, in most Western European countries, wage dynamics accelerated, linking to that of productivity. The working class was able to obtain the "just reward" theorised by Aristotle for the first time. During the seventies, the conquest of social rights by workers fuelled social conflict. While workers were gaining the dignity of work, the resulting income redistribution began to pose a threat to socio-economic balance. It challenged the power asymmetry between social groups. At the beginning of the eighties, in the large companies that were protagonists in the global markets, in the major banking and financial institutions, and in the political class of advanced countries, the belief

F. Farina, *The Rise of Inequality and the Fall of Social Mobility*,
https://doi.org/10.1007/978-3-031-92843-7_13

spread that the "shape of the game" of capitalism, being based on the full command of companies over income distribution, could not withstand further shocks.

Neoliberalism is the cultural turn that in the following decades gave concrete form to the principles affirmed in 1947 by the Mont Pelerin Society (*supra*, chap. I, par. 4). The various "belongings" that define people's identities—the family context and the social context shaped by political and economic institutions (Acemoglu and Robinson 2012, 2019)—make the paths that people find themselves on very different from each other. This interpretative scheme is foreign to the neoliberal school of thought. This ideological movement arose in defence of the freedom of the enterprise in production and employment choices and as a bulwark of the economic and social culture of the elites in power in advanced countries. In the decades that followed the *Trente Glorieuses*, social conflict was subdued. A backward journey began with respect to the social rights won with the help of robust growth and under the impetus of voting for progressive political coalitions. Neoliberalism managed to tune society to the values of individualism. As economic historian David Harvey wrote, "neoliberalism attributes to market exchange the value of an ethic in itself" (Harvey 2005, p. 3). With privatisations, liberalisations, market deregulation reforms and the downsizing of the welfare state, the business system regained its autonomy in directing the evolution of the economic system. Large companies and owners of large capital, in pursuing the goal of generating profits in a condition of "unfettered freedom" in the management of production and innovative investments, impose negative externalities on workers. In this way, the equal right to freedom of other members of the community is compressed: "if the power of *corporations* steals your personal freedom", then the promises of neoliberalism amount to nothing (ibid., p. 79). Work no longer represents the "cement of society", it has returned to being a simple private activity, a condition belonging to the individual sphere. This ideological revolution carried out by neoliberalism is precisely reflected in the way work is considered in the policies of national and supra-national institutions. The worker who does not work but has not been dismissed is excluded from the calculation of the unemployment rate, because he falls within the estimate of the employment rate. According to the rules of Eurostat, those who are on redundancy fund, although not participating in the employed workforce, despite the fact that at the end of such a regime they may be dismissed, are classified as "employed". The deep reason is that neoliberal ideology considers the condition of the worker as circumscribed to the individual, without regard to the fact that in reality he is not taking part in the *joint venture* of production. With the introduction of the logic of profit even in sectors once aimed at collective interest (health, education, pensions), society has been incorporated into the perimeter of the economy. To put it in words of just under a century ago, but which today appear prophetic, we have "social relations dropped into the economy, instead of an economy dropped into social relations" (Polanyi 1974, p. 57). The rebalancing of power in favour of businesses brought about by neoliberalism has been accompanied by a downward slide in the long-term GDP growth rate. Social mobility, a phenomenon balanced between individual and society, could not fail to be affected by the change of scene. Individual social ascent, particularly the access of young people from "disadvantaged" families to the citadel of well-being, cannot do without a collective context at whose centre is sustained economic growth. In the last forty years, social mobility has therefore been greatly affected by the lack of GDP expansion. In the asymmetry of power of the "form of the game" of capitalism, with each expansion of the market space, competition for social ascent strengthens the stronger social classes. With the closing of the season of labour-intensive technologies in the seventies, the distribution of wealth has ended up playing an increasingly decisive role in the market with the "financialisation" of economies: "the financial sector wastes both human and real resources. It is largely a machine for extracting rent" (Wolf 2023, p. 153). For their part, companies, in introducing technical progress, have prioritised the realisation of short-term profit. Globalisation has on the other hand marked the transition of individual behaviours to "spaces of action that are constructed in cosmopolitan terms" (Beck 2016, p. 11). Following the process of concentration in multinational companies, the power of economic elites has greatly increased, while the power of governments is weakening. The narrowing of economic objectives to which the forces of globalisation force national institutions makes the relationship with democracy of the ruling political class more difficult. The traditional imbalance in the power relationship between rulers and ruled is accentuated by the weight that wealth has in the "capture" of resources (the media and the *media* in general) through which democratic consensus is formed. The governed have the perception of a creeping engulfment of the prerogatives of their representatives by global economic powers and supranational institutions. This depresses voting participation. Representative institutions, which should constitute the guarantee of democracy as shared power, are in serious distress. Orthodox theory conceives of technical progress as an exogenous flow of innovations that shifts the production function of the economy upwards. In today's capitalist system, the connection of technical progress to productive expansion is far from this neutral conception of *téchne*. The introduction of innovations is in fact framed in the competition that takes place within the business system. According to Schumpeter (1912), being a successful "competitive company" means having the ability to introduce innovative investments. On the other hand, he hypothesised that the pre-eminent position of innovative companies was destined to run out over time. Things have evolved in a different way. In the new century, as we have seen, the great enterprise that is located on the technological frontier relies on intangible capital and new roles related to automation and the digital economy. The reshuffling among companies on the "technological frontier" seems to be a less frequent event. While the process of "creative destruction" imagined by Schumpeter starts from the attack launched by a new innovative company on a company present in the market (*incumbent*), innovations are largely made by companies already present in the market (Garcia-Macia et al. 2019).

The conception of innovation as a strategy of creation and of increasing market power by companies assigns a leading role to the ability of researchers and managers in designing the evolutionary growth of the innovative company, with the aim of consolidating their position of preeminence. Since profits are not the result of atomistic behaviour in a perfect competition market, but the fruit of market power actively pursued by the company, not only the contribution that technical progress gives to social welfare is diverted by the company to its own advantage, but income and wealth inequality increases as the *management* has the opportunity to orient the functional distribution of income in favour of the capital share at the expense of that of labour (Kurz 2023). What benefit of new jobs do technological innovations manage to bring? It is a question far from the ethical horizon of companies. The design of new goods and new services is not aimed at creating a labour demand adequate to the labour supply; it responds to the private logic of maximising the return on shares held by shareholders. Large companies, to which an increasing share of production is headed, attract mainly *high-skilled* workers, selected on the skills of excellence required by the tasks provided by new technologies. It follows that wage inequality predominantly does not occur *between* companies but *within* companies: "the largest share of wage dispersion in the twenty-first century comes from increasing wage inequality among graduates" (Autor et al. 2020, p. 348).

The consequences within the social structure are clearly visible. To the slowdown of absolute social mobility *absolute* has corresponded a relative social mobility *relative* focused on the growth of jobs and remuneration of the narrow group of workers of the most competitive companies. Not only is the economic process increasingly less oriented towards raising the income and well-being of the poor towards the levels of the middle class, but sectors of workforce *middle-skilled* with degrees not in demand by the market have regressed towards low-skilled and low-paid job positions. When they are not employed by companies in traditional sectors with constant technology, middle-class workers performing *routine* tasks risk exiting the regular labour market; if they want to avoid unemployment or early retirement they must find refuge in precarious occupations of low-skilled services linked to digital platforms. The "social persistence" of the *working poor* at the quality levels of life granted by precarious work and job positions in the underground, where the majority of immigrants are employed, is no longer the exception but the norm of the labour market.

Contrary to what is stated in the most used economic theory textbooks in universities around the world, in advanced societies the demand for education of young people does not reflect the behaviour expected by the "theory of incentives". The very modest values of the correlation between the incentive of earnings and the impulse that prolonging education gives to intergenerational social mobility are a message to reflect on. The role of inequality of opportunity in intergenerational mobility, fundamental *trait d'union* in estimating the Great Gatsby curve (*supra*, chap. VI, par. 4) in Corak's analysis (2013) remains at the level of intuition.

The discussion on how to promote equality of opportunity is only at the beginning. In fact, it is not public policies that are dealing with it more. In the demand for education, the economic resources of the family to which the student belongs count more than the economic incentive of a high rate of return on education. The phenomenon of "social immobility" from one generation to the next reveals that the "premium" of a high income recognised to young people who have committed to a long period of training finds little correspondence, in most advanced countries, at the level of intergenerational income mobility. The prevalence of private education supply and the fluidity of the labour market should guarantee an easy connection between the market incentive of a high income and the educational demand of young people. On the contrary, as we have seen, precisely in the major free market countries—United States and United Kingdom—the upward intergenerational income mobility is limited at the aggregate level, it takes place mainly within the group of "rich" (i *top incomes*). Intergenerational mobility is instead high in all Nordic countries. The educational demand of young people does not respond, however, to the "theory of incentives": the "rate of return of education" is concentrated around not very high levels. In this socio-cultural area, where it was the welfare state that shaped the market and not vice versa, opportunities are created that are not too unequal in their ability to give rise to relative income mobility of children compared to their parents, extended to all social classes.

In light of the current state of affairs, so far from the hopes that were born during the *Trente Glorieuses*, economic democracy appears as *the road not taken* by the traveller of Robert Frost's verses. The spread of education is the first, fundamental, factor of growth of democracy as shared power. The obstacles to access to a high level of education for "disadvantaged" young people continue to be very strong. In the major advanced countries, the "elite of excellence in education" still coincides with the "money elite". The equivalent of the goal of the nobles of the eighteenth century to secure a male heir to whom to transmit their own noble title is today represented by the goal of rich parents to transmit the opportunity for high earnings to their children, through a substantial investment of money in excellent education at elite universities. In recent decades, while the culture of neoliberalism pursued the subjugation of society to the market, the training of young people who do not belong to the families of the elite and the high-qualification middle class has lost value in the eyes of the ruling classes. The very idea of a public strategy to raise the average education and professional qualification of the population has been abandoned. This is demonstrated by the reduction in funding for public education and the policy of "freedom of choice" within a menu of fragmented educational paths, which seem for the most part to correspond to a demand for low-skilled work in constant technology companies and in "poor" services. The declining interest of the ruling classes in a society in which all young people are equipped with adequate cultural training is reflected in the retreat of the welfare state in the education sector. The ideal that sees in an efficient and fair public education system the prerequisite for young people's participation in the market as well as in democracy is gradually losing followers. The "equality of starting points"—from public nurseries to an organisation of university education based on residence and scholarships for "disadvantaged" students—would be a goal of primary importance, equally for the well-being of individuals and for the well-being of the community. As intuitively illustrated by the images in Fig. 13.1, this goal is not today guaranteed. It is not guaranteed by the market: in the design on the left, in the absence of the equalising mechanisms of the welfare state, the income earned in the free market is of very different height among social classes, does not allow non-privileged young people to sufficiently raise their own "view of the world". And it is not even with the support of the universalistic Welfare of advanced countries: in the design in the centre, the welfare state modifies the result of the market just enough for the middle class and insufficiently for the poor. In other words, equal treatment of the "unequal" can reduce inequality of opportunity, but does not impact enough on the problem of *empowerment*, or on the need to guarantee all young people the skills to realise their own life project by making the most of their talents. In the design on the right, progressive taxation and differentiated treatment of benefits manage to equalise access to opportunities, and therefore to put everyone on an equal footing in making the most of the abilities inherent in the natural talents that individuals are endowed with at birth. A model of society oriented towards solidaristic universalism ensures that young people with a "disadvantaged" background, in order to afford to get to a degree or doctorate and bring out their talents, receive unequal differentiated welfare treatment.

Once the engine of economic growth has jammed, the asymmetry of power between social classes has been amplified by the concentration of educational opportunities and social mobility increasingly higher up the

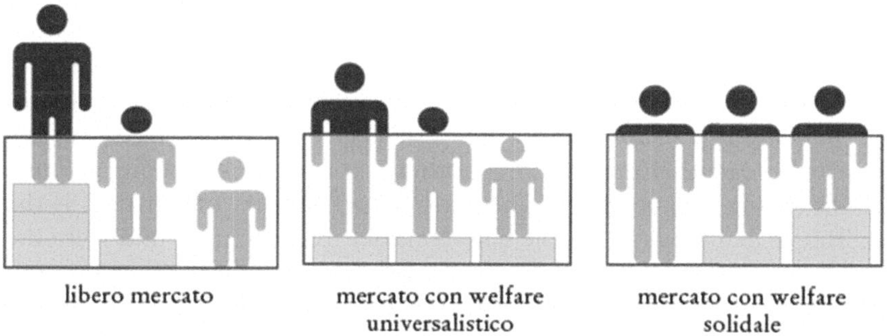

Fig. 13.1 Institutions and the "worldview". (Source: Author's elaboration. Translation: Free Market, Market + Universalistic Welfare, Market + Solidaristic Welfare)

income scale: education has become—together with technological progress—the most relevant factor of multiplication of inequalities. At the origin of the crisis of social mobility of "disadvantaged" young people is the crisis of the idea of cultural education as *humus* that makes the life of a community fertile. In the twentieth century, if in Europe there could exist the utopia—from Simon Weil to Adriano Olivetti—of linking culture to the factory, it was also because there were ruling classes that saw in education the support to the social function of work, as a factor of promotion of growth and well-being. Today, the political class finds it easier to perpetuate itself in power by favouring the cultural homogenisation of the popular classes in the values of modernity, rather than in the promotion of critical spirit. The space of cultural education has shrunk to that of the selection of excellent workers, whose skills allow companies to transform scientific inventions into technological innovations for the service of profit.

The consequence is that a large proportion of young people, deprived of a solid cultural and professional education, find a guide to life no longer in education but in the individualistic culture spread by the media and by the *social* networks. From the turn given by neoliberalism towards the primacy of individualistic identity, the substantial erasure from the constellation of young people's ideas of the *status civitatis*, or the collective dimension of identity, was born. Moreover, young people see in individualism—which allows everyone to define themselves as "unique"—the cultural attitude most suited to feeling all equal. Young people from "disadvantaged" social classes—whose income is low and whose education is inadequate—have no other choice but to find satisfaction in individualism. This lifestyle is the refuge in which they hide—primarily, more or less consciously, from themselves—their subordinate condition. Giacomo Leopardi, in his *Operette morali*, abandoned the idea of pessimism, as Rousseau had done before him, founded in history. At the beginning of the *Dialogue of Tristan and a friend* it reads: "The human race [...] will never believe neither that it knows nothing, nor that it is nothing, nor that it has nothing to hope for". The "cosmic pessimism" of our days is the nihilism of many young people who consider freedom unbound from the shackles of culture, a "skin freedom", pure expression of their uncontaminated nature. At this point, what interest can voting have in their eyes?

It has been authoritatively observed: "Now that we have had experience of what has happened, can we perhaps be surprised that trust in the elites has collapsed? [...] The simultaneous dissolution of trust in neoliberalism and democracy is not a mere coincidence or a simple correlation.

Neoliberalism has undermined democracy for forty years" (Stiglitz 2019). It is a fact that an anthropological storm has hit the latest generations. Today the perception that one's work activity is part of a context of common contribution to the goal of social well-being has faded. Entry into the world of work, or the main social dimension of the individual, has become more complicated the more one has been born into a "disadvantaged" family. The "collective imaginary" of neoliberalist culture is that of the individual defined by the forms that the *status libertatis* of people takes under the influence of new technologies. Social interaction develops through the use of computer and telematic tools that imprint in the mind the image of hyperconnected individuals who nevertheless remain in mutual isolation. Each individual is in continuous interaction with other individuals on the planet through the internet, but can carry out market operations while remaining separate from others. Autonomy, from no longer being limited by physical space, extends to the severing of community ties; for some, up to the condition of *cosmopolitans*, the *happy few* richest, who have freed themselves from the conditioning of the state organisation in which they were born. It is increasingly difficult to make rosy predictions about the anthropological future of the young people of tomorrow, when the great minds at the head of artificial intelligence companies are able to collect an extraordinary amount of information about us, to predict what we think, and to manipulate our consciences. In his lawsuit against OpenAI, the non-profit research laboratory on artificial intelligence that has converted to profit breaking the pact with the one who had founded and financed it, Elon Musk, the champion of meritocracy, has gone so far as to claim that "Gpt-4 reasons better than the average of human beings".

Typical of the vision of the student as an individual in formation, but detached from the social context, are the educational policies promoted by the culture of American society, long in vogue also in Europe. The tendency of companies to a more intense selection of workers who guarantee high productivity in the tasks required by new technologies seems to merge with the tendency to concentrate the commitment of the educational system in the training of the most promising students, through the use of *tracking*, and in the competition between public and private in the provision of education through vouchers. The tool of *tracking* is aimed at "protecting" the "early" students from the *peer effects*, in particular from the disadvantage that could derive from them from the sharing of the same educational path with students whose learning difficulties—potential, since talents are not normally observable during childhood—could instead be exclusively due to the socio-family environment. The tool of the vouchers, which combines public education with the market offer of educational services by private secondary and university institutes, is the typical example of a shortsighted approach to public education policies. The greater space given to the market in the educational system creates a further divergence between the educational opportunities of advantaged young people and those of disadvantaged young people.

Educational social mobility has become a class issue. As it has been pointedly observed, "what is conventionally called merit is in fact an ideological concept, constructed to 'clean up' an allocation of advantage that is fundamentally unfair" (Markovits 2019, p. 268). The heart of the problem is indeed upstream of the educational issue, it lies in the asymmetry of power between social groups, on which rights fail to impact: "Legal systems [...] establish that everyone is equal before the law, and yet the law often ends up nevertheless favouring someone at the expense of others" (Pistor 2021, p. 209). The rebalancing of power in society is only possible with the *affirmative action* in the field of education, a real commitment to the *empowerment* of disadvantaged young people through a much more significant financial investment than that of the *Next Generation Eu* in the field of technological and environmental transformation.

However, the neoliberal worldview does not take into account the consideration that the best way to accelerate the growth of collective well-being is to prioritise the emergence of the talents of young people who have scarce economic and social opportunities to equip themselves with the necessary training to put them to good use. The selection of workers carried out by large innovative companies follows the selection of students that results from the class structure of society. The business system rewards young people with excellent knowledge who have enjoyed the economic resources to better position themselves in the groove of adapting the educational path to the laws of the market. As for the others, there is "a growing disaffection towards the economic system, which weakens social cohesion and discredits politics" (Narayan et al. 2018, p. 20). On the seriousness of this trend, the statistical data do not lie. Two researchers from the OECD have identified a *trade-off*—a contradiction—between policies to stimulate businesses for economic growth and the absence of policies aimed at equalising opportunities among young people, essential support for intergenerational social mobility (Causa and Johansson 2010).

The statistical data therefore leave no doubt about the crisis of social mobility. In light of the evidence on the downward evolution of the wage share of income and the upward trend of wage inequality, the OECD has found that mobility, from the nineties onwards, is not on the rise but on the decline: "in no country does high inequality combine with high social mobility" (OECD 2018, p. 35). Today's public discourse ignores the simple truth of the dependence of mobility on growth in conditions of low inequality. "Insufficient relative mobility is not only deeply unfair, as it perpetuates intergenerational inequality, but it is also harmful to economic growth and represents a loss of human potential that makes inefficient the allocation of resources [...] and hinders absolute mobility towards upwards" (Narayan et al. 2018, p. 2).

To appreciate this judgement, consider an objective fact, which escapes any ideological distortion: from statistical surveys it emerges that those born in the eighties are the first generation in peacetime history that now—in significant percentages—achieves a level of well-being that is lower than that of their parents. The neoliberal ideal, the vision according to which from the availability of entrepreneurs of large economic resources comes the *trickle-down*, the spread of well-being from rich investors to wider social strata, is therefore disappointed. The decreasing number of subjects who are located in the central section of the income distribution is a reflection of the drop in both jobs and the wages of *middle-skilled* workers. Workers who come out "losers" from the introduction of automation and AI in production processes are expelled from work through no fault of their own and suffer a fall in well-being that affects the chances of their children's realisation. The causal link goes from income inequality to inequality of opportunity much more than vice versa. The *impasse* of long-term social mobility in advanced countries depends on the fact that the *inequality of wealth and income* in each generation translates into an *inequality of opportunity* in the next generation.

The most likely most relevant conclusion of this study is far from the progressive opinion, which has in the universalism of public policies its flag. The empirical analyses of Voitchovsky and the research team of Chetty give a clear message about the complex interactions between growth, inequality and poverty, and their impact on the goal of social mobility. Putting together their results lead to the conclusion that the fight against poverty cannot be separated from the reduction of inequality. The problem of social equalisation worsens when the relative mobility *relative* of the poor is penalised by an absolute mobility *absolute* slowed down by slow and discontinuous growth like that of recent decades, and seriously hindered by conditions of high inequality. Universalism *tout court*, in putting rich and poor on the same level, interprets the "impartiality" of public policies as the guarantee of equal access for all to opportunities.

The public policies of the governments of advanced economies, progressive or conservative, are often ineffective because they are too prone to the neoliberal vision; they tend to limit themselves to non-organic measures to combat poverty, without considering the close connection existing between inequality and poverty. The analyses carried out in this book suggest that in a phase of unsatisfactory growth, where social mobility cannot count on its *absolute* dimension, universalism *tout court* is not the most appropriate principle of social justice. The absence of appropriate public policies leaves the field open to the tendency, fuelled by market forces, towards income polarisation. The risk is that the relative upward mobility of disadvantaged young people is blocked, and that the most vulnerable middle classes fall below the poverty line. This would extinguish any hope of social cohesion.

Capitalism is distinguished by its chameleon-like ability to regenerate. The last two centuries are not only those of its triumph in Western societies, but also those in which its ability to balance private objectives with the fragile stability of a complex and articulated social structure has unfolded. The idea that capitalism has the virtue of reforming itself—even, and especially, through crises—is not new. Karl Marx was aware of this, rebelling against the claim of his contemporary economists to read in this the inevitability of a law of nature. The advent of neoliberalism, in determining the turn towards the conception of individualism as absolute freedom, represents the attempt to reshape society according to a naturalistic vision—of estrangement from the social context—of the laws of the market.

The estrangement from the social context, which represents the epitome of the Gee model, has its political philosophy counterpart in the theory of the social contract between "free and equal". Social differentiation, born with the division of labour, laid the foundations for the pronounced "individualisation" typical of our times. It is a fact that the "social mind" of recent generations has been reshaped by the disappearance of the social dimension of work. The perception that one's work activity fits into a context of common contribution to the objective of social well-being has faded in the individual. Neoliberalism is the ideology that—in erasing the experience of the Trente Glorieuses—has removed from public discourse the reality of social conflict as the engine of history, to propagate the fiction of the social contract between "free and equal". On the other hand, as Karl Mannheim observed in 1928 in *Das Problem der Generationen,* one cannot ignore the fact that "events and experiences of the past are important only if they actually exist in the present" (Mannheim 1974, p. 344). Only a cultural regeneration, capable of making the new generations aware of the lessons of history, will be able to reverse the course of history.

John Stuart Mill was a man of his time. A time when it did not seem that the class division of society had a connection with the developments of technology in the world of production. The liberal political philosopher believed that production fell within the realm of natural laws, so a "principle of social justice" should only be implemented at the time of income distribution. It has been argued, however, that the inequity of the limitation of freedom caused by negative externalities—generated by some to the detriment of others—is also recognisable in the sphere of production decisions. Almost a century ago, Karl Polanyi hoped that the "market society", of which he had glimpsed the beginnings, could only be a parenthesis. Today we find ourselves noting that "the prosperity of the economy has become detached from the prosperity of society" (Kelly and Snower 2021, p. 852).

An indirect signal of the increased influence of companies on society is the loss of incisiveness of the welfare state. The regained centrality of the market has negatively reflected on the support of the unemployed, on the collective bargaining that protected the wages of low-skilled workers, on the defence of jobs from relocations decided by multinational corporations.[1] The expansion of market spaces is not only evidenced by tracking policies and vouchers. The return to the cultural primacy of commodification has replaced the social protection of Welfare with "individual responsibility". With the advent of the "society of individuals", Condorcet's ideal of giving a "collective dimension" to the education system also seems to be fading. In an increasing number of countries, to defend oneself from the risks of not having had a good education and of not enjoying good health, one must now turn to the market. However, companies that provide health and educational services respond to the motive of profit,

[1] In January 2024, the workers of the Swedish Tesla plant asked the American car company that If Metal, the metalworkers' union, negotiate a collective contract. Faced with Tesla's refusal to give up individual bargaining, the Swedish workers declared a strike. Unlike similar cases that have occurred in Europe, it is Solidarity that has been triggered among Nordic workers. The dockworkers of Denmark, Norway and Finland have decided to block Tesla vehicles destined for Sweden.

together with intermediaries such as insurance companies discriminate against subjects at higher risk of illness. A great economist completely immune from ideological fury like Ken Arrow wrote: "the laissez-faire solution for medicine is intolerable" (Arrow 1963, p. 967). "Intolerable" is also a good adjective for the creeping replacement of public education with private education.

The link between individual education and what we have defined as the "collective dimension" of education affirmed by Condorcet should consist in conceiving the dignity of the individual in an educational path that is not interrupted by disadvantaged circumstances and in extending to disadvantaged young people the opportunity to let their talents flourish. On the contrary, in all advanced countries, there is a widening gap between the classes in the chances of parents to bring out the talents of their children through the acquisition of adequate skills. In obedience to the ideology of adapting society to the market, in countries where the education system is based on private companies, education is conceived as a commodity to be Selling and buying, not as a good to which everyone should have access. Just as the top managers of the most advanced companies choose technologies that narrow the selection of their workforce to workers with high skills for tasks related to *digital capital*, education in excellent schools and universities is a prerogative that exclusively benefits young people from wealthy families.

This book has raised a methodological issue: economic analysis must stop privileging the study of the aggregate, and deal with what happens within the social stratification in terms of inequality between social classes in circumstances, opportunities and abilities that young people manage to acquire. The pedagogy of individualism has given increasing space to meritocracy in public debate. In the individualistic approach to well-being proposed by neoliberalism, however, the social dimension of "deserving" is not included. If we want to redeem the concept of merit from the lack of clarity, and from the little insight with which it is daily promoted, we need to go beyond the neoliberal narrative. The reference of merit to the individual whose talent emerges with the acquisition of education in the market makes it a crippled concept. Personal identity has both a biological matrix and a cultural matrix. And it is necessary that the institutions of society are committed to creating equal access for all—compensating with unequal treatment the inequality of starting points and opportunities—to the achievement of abilities. In this way, the biological matrix of identity will be able to unfold in the emergence of the talents of each individual.

The most aware wing of the community of economists today denounces how the road taken by "shareholder capitalism" from the eighties onwards is without an outlet. The increasing fragmentation of advanced societies can be stemmed only with the increase in well-being that comes from both access for all to a "good education" and from the creation of "good jobs": "it is necessary to shift attention from the world of business and shareholders to that of stakeholders and, in addition to this, look at social value" (Kelly and Snower 2021, p. 29).

The market is a formidable mechanism for increasing the number of goods available to people; but it is also an imperfect mechanism, due to its tendency to fuel inequalities, after they have been generated by socio-family circumstances. If this tendency is not corrected, it favours the social injustice of not allowing all young people to test their talents. Only a change in the "form of play" of capitalism—a different *corporate governance*—can trigger a more virtuous mechanism, in which the market and the State are complementary institutions.

The *affirmative action* in education should therefore be accompanied by an *affirmative action* in *corporate governance*. The current "form of play" of capitalism is based on a strong asymmetry in the distribution of power between entrepreneurs and workers, which does not help social mobility. We need a *corporate governance* in which the representatives of the workers manage to overcome the informational asymmetry that they typically have compared to management. Once in a position to evaluate on an equal information basis the current and expected performance of the company, the unions can more effectively defend the interests of the workers—the main stakeholders—in sharing with the shareholders the power of the company's productive choices. For the purpose of a resumption of social mobility, the main objective of the representatives of the workers should be to commit the Board of Directors to link the introduction of innovations to the creation of jobs. In this perspective, the representation of workers in the Board of Directors has boosted in Germany the use of Welfare institutions such as apprenticeship to train young workers in the use of new technologies and has slowed their transition among the unemployed caused by automation through the relocation with new tasks of *middle-skilled* workers within the same company (Battisti et al. 2023). In some countries, "co-determination" systems have mitigated social distances: "The presence of workers in management has limited wage inequality and has in particular put a brake on the dizzying growth of executive remuneration recorded in many countries". In 1941, in the "Ventotene

Manifesto" Altiero Spinelli and Ernesto Rossi wrote: "economic forces must not dominate men, but be subjected to them, guided, controlled in the most rational way, so that the great masses are not victims of them". These words have now been forgotten by the political class of the countries of the European Union. In abandoning the ideals of economic democracy to submit to the conception of society advocated by orthodox economics, Europe is reducing itself—to say it with Chancellor Metternich—to a mere "geographical expression". Solidaristic democracy will be able to resume the path interrupted more than forty years ago when in European countries voting majorities will be formed in support of a reform of the *corporate governance*.

In 1989, the American political scientist Francis Fukuyama saw in the fall of the Berlin Wall the completion of a centuries-old journey towards the "end of history". The political choice of the United States in 2001 to "open" to China's entry into the WTO led many to believe in a world unified in prosperity under the banner of the global economy. Economic integration, in accommodating the loss of power of the great national states, was supposed to strengthen economic incentives, allowing individuals less subordinate to political power constraints to increase their own well-being (Alesina and Spolaore 2003). But the rise of the United States to the only planetary power was not followed by the *pax americana* predicted by Fukuyama. Economic globalisation has provided the most favourable context for China's "authoritarian capitalism", which has positioned itself in competition as a political, military and economic power with the United States. In the Western world, with the return of the division of the world into opposing blocks, it is not national governments that count. The task of managing political command over the course of market economies is now the Atlantic Alliance. The idea has taken hold that to overcome the problem of the absence of hegemony in the world economy it is necessary to intervene in globalisation *manu militari*. Even the fiscal rules of the European Union—for decades presented as the precipitate of good economic theory from virtuous principles—are bent to the needs of war: the new Stability Pact establishes that member countries, to obtain a more flexible evaluation of their budgets, must launch an increase in military spending.

A further factor compressing social mobility—both *absolute* and *relative*—in the European Union today is the crisis in Germany. After having staked everything on *hyper-globalisation*, the "limitless globalisation", the largest industrial power in Europe finds itself with three knots that come to a head: dependence on China for exports, dependence on Russia for energy resources, dependence on the United States for security. The uncertain fate of Germany is a further boulder falling on the narrow path of social mobility of the weaker classes of European countries.

The economic policies of many governments of advanced countries have long been intertwined—in the name of growth and the well-being of all—with the private interests of the holders of economic and financial power. It is not from the political class but from the top of Goldman Sachs, one of the largest investment banks in the world, heavily involved in the subprime crisis of 2008 and saved by the Treasury Department with a generous financing of the *Troubled Asset Relief Program*, that the Secretary of State often comes in the United States since the nineties. Similarly, Mario Draghi, governor of the European Central Bank from 2011 to 2019, and prime minister of the Italian Republic between 2021 and 2022, was appointed in 2002 *vice chairman* and *managing director* of Goldman Sachs (and a member of the Executive Committee from 2004 to 2005). These are indications that the democracies of advanced countries are not in good health. Two political visions are confronted today, which share an insidious simplification of social reality. Populism and *pensée unique* both make the common mistake of believing that the articulation of society into classes does not exist. The former, in compacting all of society in opposition to the elite, denies it by hypothesis; the latter believes that in the post-modern world it has now been overcome in the classless society regulated by the market. Both visions deny the *res publica* as the place of social conflict between classes.

In a 1956 dialogue inspired by the dialectical method, two authoritative philosophers of the last century defined late capitalism as "a type of false classless society, consisting in appearing as the perfect classless society, while in reality it is its exact opposite" (Adorno and Horkheimer 2011, p. 33). Populism asserts that society generically understood is in conflict with the elite; neoliberalism proposes the fiction of the individualistic society of the "free and equal". The reality is instead that of a society evolving towards the return to the hierarchy of medieval castes, and of an economy conditioned by geopolitics that tends to ask for financial support from States.

The current socio-economic equilibrium is made fragile by having lost the support of a constant expansion of GDP, which this book has presented as the "green fuel" of social compromise. In the phase of robust post-war growth, the classes with few resources managed to negotiate their share of the surplus. The "polar star" of neoliberalism today is the "market society". The asymmetry of power has increased because the elite of entrepreneurs, no longer having the certainty—given the modest prospects of growth—of a satisfactory share of the *surplus*, imposes its decisions *a priori*, so that the equilibrium is achieved without a coordination with the workers. Populism and *pensée unique* neoliberalism are both symptoms of the disease that is weakening democracy. This disease is the increase to its own advantage, pursued in recent decades by the elite, of the asymmetry of power in the market and in society. A proof, almost "the smoking gun", are these few data that can be read in the OECD statistics for 2021: the three major advanced countries with the highest Gini index of income inequality are the United States (0.4), the United Kingdom (0.35) and Italy (0.34); trust in the government is only 31% in the United States, at 39% in the UK and 35% in Italy. If the growth of inequalities and the "crisis of democracy" are increasingly intertwined, how can we be surprised if upward social mobility has stalled? The reductive conception of individualism as a pure need for individual affirmation has conceived the aspiration to social mobility as a severance of the bond with the feeling of participation in a collective enterprise. The identity of the person has been reduced to the sole *status libertatis* and delivered to the ideology of "individual will" in market decisions—those related to professional training, commitment to work—and to "individual responsibility" in decisions on health and education—goods about which externalities ensure that personal well-being is beyond the control of the individual. The feeling of being forced to give up the expectation of upward social mobility can be compared to the *tunnel effect*, the disappointment of facing one's own line of cars stuck in traffic in a tunnel (Hirschman and Rotschild 1973). When the functioning of markets increases inequality to levels that find no legitimacy in any law of economics, "tolerance for inequality" runs out. The political events of the last fifteen years testify to the outlet in the vote, with the success of populist and sovereignist movements, of the economic discomfort of the popular classes.

Bronisłav Bazcko wrote that "utopias are advanced as solutions to be applied, *hic et nunc*, in order to respond to the crisis that afflicts society" (Baczko 1981, p. 889). Today's utopia is individualism, the dazzling ideological promise that power groups use to hide the increase in the asymmetry of power they have imprinted on the organisation of society.

We are facing a vicious circle: motivating the vote of voters is a "model of the mind" increasingly exposed to the flattery of individualism. Under an individualistic "model of the mind", in a democratic regime, the ruling class is obliged to follow the demand of the electorate. Income and wealth taxes are therefore progressively reduced, with the consequence that public resources—instead of increasing greatly, to regenerate both the natural and social environment—decrease. Those who suffer most are the conditions of the weakest classes, who are also the most penalised by "modernisations": think of the workers in the steel and automobile industries, exposed to costly and not easy technological reconversions of production, to farmers squeezed between the alignment of prices imposed by the global market and the quality standards of food; to the futureless workers of the *gig economy*. In democratic capitalism systems, consensus is made fragile by the paradox of rights that belong to individual individuals, and of aggregations of people united not by the ideological sharing of interests and values, but by the socially divergent impact of globalisation and technical progress.

The trick to hide the disappearance of social mobility is the utopia of living in a classless society, where everyone belongs to a single "universe". Friedrich Hayek wrote in 1974, in polemic with the Great Society, the project of "social inclusion" conceived by President L. B. Johnson in 1964: "the common interests of those whose position is touched by the same circumstances will produce common ideas [...] and provide a motive for common action [...]. Ensuring an income or a particular position to its members creates an obstacle to integration into the Great Society" (Hayek 1973, p. 347). That from "common ideas" (*common prior*) common beliefs arise (*common beliefs*), and therefore a "common action" (cooperation?), is a convenient simplification—or an intellectual naivety—that the best economists of the "game theory" have shown to be completely false. It happened that the ruling classes of the West did not aim at the "unified universe" of the "classless society", but at the hegemony of entrepreneurs and financial operators in the functioning of the capitalist system. Blocking "social inclusion" was not the indispensable "unequal treatment" in favour of the "disadvantaged" but, on the contrary, a growing "asymmetry of power" in favour of the "advantaged". This has resulted in an insufficient growth rate and the betrayal of merit and welfare gains that many young people could have achieved if they had had the opportunity to demonstrate their talents.

However, history cannot be ignored. It teaches us that the law that moves the world is not the illusion of the *homo faber* but the struggle for power that always sees a contrast between social groups each convinced—even if engaged in cultural projects distant from each other, if not divergent—of pursuing a common goal. The forms of social conflict are of infinite multiplicity, because they depend on the context in which the opposition takes place. In Florence in 1478, the Pazzi family conspired to overthrow the economic and political power of the Medici. In the last two centuries, the *campesinos* in search of a more dignified life have given rise to many revolts in Latin America. Today, in the advanced world, the conflict for power in society is more muffled. The "form of the game" of capitalism recalls the reflection of the poet: "Depth must be hidden. Where? On the surface" (Von Hofmannsthal 1922). The asymmetry of power is the surface of the "form of the game" of the capitalism where the depth of its problem is hidden, a social basis for economic decision-making that is too narrow.

The era we find ourselves living in is one where the reasons for conflict are hidden, to better be countered. The depth of the hidden problem of capitalism—its too narrow social base—however, now forcefully emerges on the surface. The block of social mobility showcases the betrayal of merit that many young people would have achieved if they had had the opportunity to demonstrate their talents. The "form of the game" of capitalism is manifested in the negative "externalities" it generates in the economy and in society: the technical progress introduced by companies that takes centrality away from work and makes low-skilled workers superfluous; the private education system, which pushes the new generations of the elite to the top of economic power, destined to prolong the concentration of wealth in the hands of the "dynasties of the rich". The limits of today's "form of the game" of capitalism are revealed and laid bare by its most manifest consequence: the crisis of political democracy, the absence of effective *governance* of social reality. The asymmetry of power is no longer countered by the exercise of democratic power of the vote in support of a fairer future. Discouragement for "immobility" or social regression along with poor education have become a powerful factor in distancing from the democracy of the vote and from participation in civil society. In the United States, in the 2016 presidential elections, the percentage of the poor (average annual income of the decile: 5000 dollars) who went to the polls was only 48%, that of the rich 85% (Akee et al. 2018). As abstentionism increases, scarce economic resources intertwine with poor education: "The Resource Model of Voting predicts that possessing resources uniformly increases voting participation; but the results suggest that a voting model more closely aligned with existing human capital models may be more accurate" (ibid., p. 32). Once the cloaked garments of scientific language are put on, these words suggest that the inability of the universalistic organisation of education to bridge the gap suffered by the "disadvantaged" classes has now reached the polling stations. The "progressive" ideal of formal equality of "universal" access—equal for all—to public education ignores the fact that equal treatment of unequal people cannot certainly solve the problem of giving everyone the opportunity to "deserve". Universalism, in summary, represents the union between the liberal idea of individual rights and the socialist idea of social justice. As argued, in order to realise the principle inherent in them of the "equal right", it would be necessary for the design of Welfare institutions to be based on the "unequal treatment" of the different. The reality is that "universalism" does not give young "disadvantaged" people of the new generations the *empowerment* they would need to acquire—on the same level as young "advantaged" people—the abilities "to be and to do", exploiting their own talents. The dormant state of social conflict is primarily attributable to the fact that the majority of people do not possess today the knowledge, or simply the information, that would be necessary to have to choose—and to vote—for a fairer future. Populism, moreover, is expressed in the renunciation of voting, therefore to choose. The advanced societies of the West are gradually abandoning democracy to entrust themselves to the plutocracies that are at the top of their countries.

Today the asymmetry of power between social classes is accepted because the individualistic cultural message that one is rich because one has "deserved" has been accepted. The future of advanced countries could see the tragic return to castes, with some graft "from below" of young people selected by the rich, in the logic of the "co-optation of the most capable" hoped for by Vilfredo Pareto. To prevent the crisis of social mobility from leading to a "caste society", the commitment of a community truly committed to the well-being of future generations should be to offer all social classes a dignified formation of the person based on fundamental needs: the right of children to care, to prevent inequalities from forming just after birth; the guarantee to all of the opportunity of a long formative period: not only equal formal rights, but equal effective chances, to save young people from the risk of being "excluded". In this way, it would become possible for university education to lead to the emergence of the talents of all young people, whether they belong to "advantaged" or "disadvantaged" families. Today in society there is a lack of those forces of aggregation of values and interests that carry forward the objective of a fairer society in favouring the individual aspirations of social ascent, and more convinced in directing the talents of all towards shared well-being. This book has documented how the problem that hinders the affirmation of this solidaristic vision is of cultural origin. As John Dewey argued, education is the most direct way to revitalise democracy: on a psychological level, it has the task of promoting the development of critical thinking in people; on a sociological level it teaches the individual to be part of the society.

The expansion of inequalities and the acceleration of environmental deterioration are both expressions of the spread of externalities that weigh on the workforce. Externalities that have assumed a global dimension as a consequence of globalisation, that has projected all peoples into "systemic interdependence".

In studying capitalism, which thrives on the ability to exploit—and continually recreate—"the disparities of the unequal world of men", a great historian wrote: "in fact, the true fate of capitalism has always been played out on the terrain of social hierarchies" (Braudel 2010, p. 67).

In the market, the realm of individualism, universalism is now advancing. The main common goods subjected to the market—social cohesion within states that is compromised by inequalities, and the environment, the degradation of which we all now feel—are at high risk. Both are crises caused by the pursuit of short-term profit. The link between social injustice and environmental degradation is evoked by the new slogan of the environmental movement: *Climate Justice Now*. Ethical conceptions fail to solve the problems that arise in the society of the context of systemic interdependence: inducing men to cooperate and the social classes in which they are aggregated to social cohesion. Regarding the environment, where the problem concerns the relationship between man and nature, so that men are a single aggregate opposed to nature, the problem arises in terms of *the tragedy of the commons*. In the absence of the Kantian ideal of a world community, men could avoid ruining the planet only if each one renounced creating externalities on others, to adopt the moral behaviour *other-regarding*. The expansion of inequalities and the acceleration of environmental deterioration are both expressions of the spread of externalities that weigh on the workforce, which from the national perimeter have ended up assuming a global dimension with the move towards systemic interdependence. "The tragedy of the commons" arises because the members of a community, acting independently of each other, use resources in a self-interested way instead of sharing costs and benefits. The increase in inequalities and the environmental crisis are phenomena concerning the population as an aggregate. The first, however, is backed by a privatised management of economic resources within nations. The second leads to the estimation of the values of carbon dioxide production, sea temperatures, etc., which concern the aggregate of the population. This creates a contrast between those who respect nature and those who want to use it for profit. As argued in a recent study in "Science", "economic inequality and climate inequality are intimately linked, both between countries and within them; rich nations and individuals appropriate fossil resources to a far greater extent than other nations and individuals, but rarely pay the social cost of coal energy, often on the assumption that they can protect themselves from the adverse consequences of its use" (Pande 2023, p. 15).

Ultimately, inequalities and environmental crisis are increasingly linked planetary issues, whose *governance* is now only possible by involving the supranational level (Stern and Stiglitz 2023). The absence in the world of an international *governance* exposes the entire human community to increasingly serious welfare losses. An ethically unacceptable aspect of the intertwining of inequalities and environmental crisis is that the poorer half of the world's population—4 billion people who live mainly in sub-Saharan Africa, in the hottest areas of the planet destined in the very near future to become uninhabitable—produces only 20% of total emissions.

It has been said that social mobility is the litmus test of the health of a socio-economic system. The *Trente Glorieuses* were the historical moment when it seemed that various "rules of the game" were maturing in order to correct the power asymmetry of capitalism. The birth of the social role of work and the acceleration of social mobility gave the idea of a cultural break, a leap forward into a new era of the world. It even seemed that the denigrators of the idea of progress were wrong.

But the "circular time" then took over again. Today's world reflects the verses that open T. S. Eliot's *First Quartet*: "Present time and past time/ are perhaps present in future time,/ future time is contained in past time". In the present time, growth benefits the social mobility of a few. The social mobility of others has stopped, and the future threatens to be that of castes, where each generation tends to reproduce the characteristics, cultural and material, of the previous one. The development of the future must then return to the past, when the idea of development was synonymous with progress. This betrayed word contained individualism, but it meant as the *empowerment* of all young people who start behind at the starting blocks of life.

This book is a critique of the existing. The messages elaborated in it are these. 1) Methodological individualism is not a useful key to reading for the analysis of society. The "form of the game" of capitalism, the power asymmetry between shareholder and stakeholder, deprives the vision of a social contract between "free and equal" of its significance. 2) In the era of "systemic interdependence", the groups in power determine externalities in the market that are transmitted within society in forms that deepen welfare distances. Relative social mobility is not a phenomenon circumscribed to the need for individual affirmation, but it is only understandable using the category of social conflict. The degree of social mobility of the community cannot be measured with the tool of aggregate GDP, but must be based on a disaggregated analysis of the different chances of well-being of the various social classes. 3) In confronting the issue of the *impasse* of social mobility, a progressive policy cannot be based on the category of universalism *tout court*. The social rise of young "disadvantaged" people will only regain strength if it is supported by the commitment to address the problem of self-realisation of people who have—due to the disadvantage determined by circumstances and opportunities—scarce *capabilities* for a good life. The right path is not in the simple approach of social inclusion in the "market society", but in confronting the problem of power asymmetry by investing in *affirmative action* projects. In the era of automation and AI, the introduction of technical progress in productive activity must be reoriented towards job creation. In the era of individual autonomy in the interconnected world, education cannot be left to market forces. If this were to happen, the spread of ChatGpt would create a society in which intellectual processing would be fragmented in content and dangerously flattened in cultural homogenisation. The public education system needs to be rethought in ways and forms that are up to the colossal question of how culture will shape the future structure and dynamics of society.

The pursuit and exercise of power take shape—in people and in states—on the slippery ridge between individualism and solidarity, between selfish interest and collaboration for the pursuit of collective well-being. In order for solidarity and collective well-being to prevail, we must focus on the *status civitatis* of people. People's nature is often univocally oriented towards the *status libertatis*, the identity closest to human nature. If it is true that the engine of history is culture, then culture must become the "productive factor" of the *status civitatis*. The *Weltanschaung* that guide the application of scientific knowledge in productive strategies cannot be elaborated only by a part of society. For young people who are at a disadvantage at the starting blocks of life, power can only be given by culture. The contribution of economic policy is indispensable. The most effective one is called the education system.

The great inequalities today do not only depend on the capital inherited, but above all on the considerable opportunities for education enjoyed by the children of rich families, who receive stratospheric earnings for the excellent skills with which they create and apply new technologies. In the same direction of the privileged access of the young elite to the benefits of innovation, goes the work of nature. The most recent research on the human genome is bringing to light the preeminent role played over the centuries in genetic transmission by members of the elite. Having the rich more chances to reproduce, thanks to the superior level of health and the longer life expectancy, the "success" of their genes is assured: "since they tend to mate with each other, the link between inequality and biology will gain more strength in the future [...]. It is likely that inequality will erase ethnic differences between social classes with *status* high. In a globalised world, ethnic identity will be relegated to social classes with *status* lower" (Lalueza-Fox 2022, p. 135).

In the chapters of the book, the *impasse* that social mobility has encountered in advanced countries due to the choices made by companies and governments has been highlighted. Its title may appear perhaps overstated. However, at stake is the distribution of the chances of a sustainable future among people who start from increasingly unequal circumstances and opportunities. The alternative is this: give disadvantaged groups the dignity of equal chances, or let neoliberal ideology end up trapping them in the caste society. In a world whose key is limitless individualism, the choice of this second path, now dominant, is destined to increase individual fragilities. It is certainly possible that the current *impasse* is only temporary. However, if the "rules of the game" of capitalism are not corrected, our tomorrow could see the disappearance of social mobility. "Time is running out" is the slogan coined by environmental movements to draw attention to the deterioration of the environment that looms over humanity. "Time is running out" is also good for saying that our "polar star" must be the care of cultural education for all. Education must not be abandoned, if we do not want to witness the sunset of the hope of a more dynamic and cohesive society.

Bibliography

Acemoglu and Robinson, 2012 Why Nations Fail: The Origins of Power, Prosperity and Poverty, Profile Books, London.

Acemoglu and Robinson, 2019 The Narrow Corridor. States, Societies, and the Fate of Liberty, Penguin Press, New York.

Adorno, T. W. & Horkheimer, M. 2011 Towards a New Manifesto, *Verso, New York.*

Akee, R. et al. 2018 Family Income and the Intergenerational Transmission of Voting Behavior: Evidence from an Income Intervention, *Nber Working Paper n. 24770.*

Alesina, A. & Spolaore, E. 2003 *The Size of Nations*, Mit Press, Cambridge.

Arrow, K. J. 1963 Uncertainty and the Welfare Economics of Medical Care, *in «American Economic Review», LIII, 5, pp. 941–73.*

Autor, D., Goldin, C., Katz, L. F. 2020 *Extending the Race between Education and Technology*, in «American Economic Review, Papers and Proceedings», CX, pp. 347–51.

Baczko, B. 1981 *Utopia*, in *Encyclopedia*, Einaudi, Torino, XIV, *ad vocem.*

Battisti, M., Dustmann, C., Schönberg, U. 2023 *Technological and Organizational Change and the Careers of Workers*, in «Journal of the European Economic Association», XXI, 4, pp. 1551–94.

Beck U. 2016 The Metamorphosis of the World, Polity Press, Cambridge.

Braudel, F. 2010 La dinamica del capitalismo*, il Mulino, Bologna.*

Causa, O. & Johansson, A. 2010 Intergenerational Social Mobility in Oecd Countries, *in «Oecd Economic Studies», 1, pp. 1–44.*

Corak, M. 2013 Income Inequality, Equality of Opportunity and Intergenerational Mobility, *in «Journal of Economic Perspectives», XXVII, 3, pp. 79–102.*

Garcia-Macia, D., Heich, C.-T., Klenov, P. J. 2019 *«How Destructive is Innnovation?»*, in «Econometrica», LXXXVII, pp. 1507–41.

Harvey, D. 2005 *A Brief History of Neoliberalism*, Oxford University Press, Oxford 2005.

Hayek, F.A. 1973 Law, Legislation and Liberty: A New Statement of the Liberal Principles of Justice and Political Economy, University of Chicago Press, Chicago.

Hirschman, A.O. and Rotschild, M. 1973 The Changing Tolerance for Income Inequality in the Course of Economic Development, in «Quarterly Journal of Economics», LXXXVII, pp. 544–66.

Kelly, C. & Snower, D. J. 2021 *Capitalism Recoupled*, in «Oxford Review of Economic Policy», XXXVII, 4, pp. 851–63.

Kurz, M. 2023 The Market Power of Technology: Understanding the Second Gilded Age*, Columbia University Press, New York.*

Lalueza-Fox, C. 2022 Inequality: A Genetic History*, Mit Press, Cambridge.*

Mannheim, K. 1974 Essays on the Sociology of Knowledge, *Routledge, London 1952.*

Markovits, D. 2019 The Meritocracy Trap: How America's Foundational Myth Feeds Inequality, Dismantles the Middle Class, and Devours the Elite, *Penguin Press, New York.*

Narayan, A. et al. 2018 Fair Progress? Economic Mobility across Generations around the World, *World Bank, Washington DC.*

Oecd 2018 A Broken Social Elevator? How to Promote Social Mobility, *Paris.*

Pande, R. 2023 The Climate Crisis Is a Crisis of Inequality, *in «Science», CCCLXXXI, 6661.*

Pistor, K. 2021 The Code of Capital: How the Law Creates Wealth and Inequality, *Princeton University Press, Princeton 2019.*

Polanyi, K. 1974 The Great Transformation, *Farrar & Rinehart, New York 1944.*

Stern, N. & Stiglitz, J. E. 2023 *Climate Change and Growth*, in «Industrial and Corporate Change», XXXII, pp. 277–303.

Stiglitz, J. E. 2019 The End of Neoliberalism and the Rebirth of History, *Project Syndacate, 4 novembre.*

von Hofmannsthal H. 1922, Buch der Freunde, Leipzig, Insel.

Wolf, M. 2023 The Crisis of Democratic Capitalism, *Penguin Press, New York.*

Bibliography

Aaberge, R. et al. 2002 Income Inequality and Income Mobility in the Scandinavian Countries Compared to the United States, *in «Review of Income and Wealth», XLVIII, 4, pp. 443–69.*

Abravanel, R. 2021 Aristocrazia 2.0. Una nuova élite per salvare l'Italia, *Solferino, Milano.*

Acemoglu, D. 2001 *Good Jobs versus Bad Jobs*, in «Journal of Labor Economics», XIX, 1, pp. 1–21.

Acemoglu, D. 2022 Obedience in the Labour Market and Social Mobility: A Socioeconomic Approach, *in «Economica», LXXXIX, S1, pp. 2–37.*

Acemoglu, D. 2023 Distorted Innovation: Does the Market Get the Direction of Technology Right?, *in «American Economic Journal, Papers and Proceedings», CXIII, pp. 1–28.*

Acemoglu, D. & Autor, D. 2011 Skills, Tasks and Technologies: Implications for Employment and Earnings, *in Ashenfelter - Card 2011, pp. 1043–171.*

Acemoglu, D. & Autor, D. 2012 What Does Human Capital Do? A Review of Goldin and Katz's the Race between Education and Technology, *in «Journal of Economic Literature», L, 2, pp. 426–63.*

Acemoglu, D. & Johnson, S. 2023 Power and Progress: Our Thousand-Year Struggle Over Technology and Prosperity, *Public Affairs, New York.*

Acemoglu, D. & Restrepo, P. 2018 The Race between Man and Machine: Implications of Technology for Growth, Factor Shares, and Employment, *in «American Economic Review», CVIII, 6, pp. 1488–542.*

F. Farina, *The Rise of Inequality and the Fall of Social Mobility*, https://doi.org/10.1007/978-3-031-92843-7

Acemoglu, D. & Restrepo, P. 2020 The Wrong Kind of Ia? Artificial Intelligence and the Future of Labour Demand, *in «Cambridge Journal of Regions, Economy, and Society», XIII, 1, pp. 25–35.*

Acemoglu, D. & Robinson, J. A. 2000 Why Did the West Extend the Franchise? Democracy, Inequality, and Growth in Historical Perspective, *in «Quarterly Journal of Economics», CXV, 4, pp. 1167–99.*

Acemoglu, D. & Robinson, J. A. 2006 Economic Origins of Dictatorship and Democracy, *Cambridge University Press, Cambridge.*

Acemoglu, D. & Robinson, J. A. 2013 Why Nations Fail: The Origins of Power, Prosperity and Poverty, *Profile Books, London 2012.*

Acemoglu, D. & Robinson, J. A. 2020 The Narrow Corridor. States, Societies, and the Fate of Liberty, *Penguin Press, New York 2019.*

Acemoglu, D., Egorov, G., Sonin, K. 2018 Social Mobility and Stability of Democracy: Reevaluating De Tocqueville, *in «Quarterly Journal of Economics», CXXXIII, 2, pp. 1041–105.*

Acemoglu and Robinson, 2012 Why Nations Fail: The Origins of Power, Prosperity and Poverty, Profile Books, London.

Acemoglu and Robinson, 2019 The Narrow Corridor. States, Societies, and the Fate of Liberty, Penguin Press, New York.

Adorno, T. W. 1942 Reflections on Class Theory, *in Adorno 2003.*

Adorno, T. W. 2003 Can One Live After Auschwitz? A Philosophical Reader, *Stanford University Press, Stanford.*

Adorno, T. W. & Horkheimer, M. 2011 Towards a New Manifesto, *Verso, New York.*

Aghion, P. & Durlauf, S. N. (a cura di) 2014 Handbook of Economic Growth, *Elsevier, Amsterdam.*

Aghion, P., Antonin, C., Bunel, S. 2021 The Power of Creative Destruction: Economic Upheaval and the Wealth of Nations, *Belknap Press of Harvard University, Cambridge 2021.*

Agostinelli, F, Doepke, M., Sorrenti, G., Zilibotti, F. 2022 When the Great Equalizer Shuts Down: Schools, Peers, and Parents in Pandemic Times, *in «Journal of Public Economics», CCVI, pp. 1045–74.*

Akcigit, U. et al. 2021 Rising Corporate Market Power: Emerging Policy Issues, *Imf Staff Discussion Note n. 1.*

Akee, R. et al. 2018 Family Income and the Intergenerational Transmission of Voting Behavior: Evidence from an Income Intervention, *Nber Working Paper n. 24770.*

Alchian, A. & Demsetz, H. 1972 Production, Information Costs, and Economic Organization, *in «American Economic Review», LXII, 5, pp. 777–95.*

Alesina, A. & Spolaore, E. 2003 *The Size of Nations*, Mit Press, Cambridge.

Alesina, A. & Glaeser, E. R. 2004 Fighting Poverty in the US and Europe: A World of Differences, *Oxford University Press, New York.*

Alesina, A. & Angeletos, G.-M. 2005 *Fairness and Redistribution: Us versus Europe*, in eAmerican Economic Review», XCV, 4, pp. 960–98.

Alesina, A., Stantcheva, S., Teso, E. 2018 Intergenerational Mobility and Preferences for Redistribution, *in «American Economic Review», CVIII, 2, pp. 521–54.*

Alesina, A., Miano, A., Stantcheva, S. 2020a *The Polarization of Reality*, in «American Economic Review, Papers and Proceedings», CX, pp. 324–8.

Alesina, A., Seror, M., Yang, D., You, Y., Zeng, W. 2020b *Persistence through Revolutions*, Bristol Economics Discussion Paper n. 20/722, University of Bristol.

Alesina, A., Giuliano, P., Reich, B. 2021 *Nation-Building and Education*, in «Economic Journal», CXXXI, 638, pp. 2273–303.

Alesina, A., Miano, A., Stantcheva, S. 2023 *Immigration and Redistribution*, in «Review of Economic Studies», XC, 1, pp. 1–39.

Almås, I., Cappelen, A. W., Tungodden, B. 2020 Cutthroat Capitalism versus Cuddly Socialism: Are Americans More Meritocratic and Efficiency-Seeking than Scandinavians?, *in «Journal of Political Economy», CXXVIII, 5, pp. 1753–88.*

Alvaredo, F., Garbinti, B., Piketty, T. 2017 On the Share of Inheritance in Aggregate Wealth: Europe and the USA, 1900–2010, *in «Economica», LXXXIV, 334, pp. 239–60.*

Amiel, Y., Bernasconi, M., Cowell, F., Dardanoni, V. 2015 *Do We Value Mobility?*, in «Social Choice and Welfare», XLIV, 2, pp. 231–55.

Anand, S. & Sen, A. K. 2000 *The Income Component of the Human Development Index*, in «Journal of Human Development», I, 1, pp. 83–106.

Anderson, E. S. 2017 Private Government: How Employers Rule Our Lives (and Why We don't Talk about it), *Princeton University Press, Princeton.*

Andre, P. 2022 *Shallow Meritocracy*, University of Bonn, Discussion Paper n. 318.

Antonietti, R., Farina, F., Fontini, F. 2016 A Rational Explanation for the Redistribution Paradox. Theory and Empirical Evidence, *in «Scottish Journal of Political Economy», LXIII, 5, pp. 539–55.*

Appadurai, A. 2004 The Capacity to Aspire: Culture and the Terms of Recognition, *in V. Rao & M. Walton (eds.),* Culture and Public Action, *World Bank, pp. 59–84.*

Appelbaum, E. 2017 *Domestic Outsourcing, Rent Seeking, and Increasing Inequality*, in «Review of Radical Political Economics», XLIX, 4, pp. 513–28.

Arbatlı, C. E., Ashraf, Q. H., Galor, O., Klemp, M. 2020 *Diversity and Conflict*, in «Econometrica», LXXXVIII, 2, pp. 727–97.

Arendt, H. 2009 *The Life of the Mind*, Harcourt Brace Jovanovich, New York 1978.

Arrow, K. J. 1963 Uncertainty and the Welfare Economics of Medical Care, *in «American Economic Review», LIII, 5, pp. 941–73.*

Arrow, K. J. 1971 Essays in the Theory of Risk-Bearing, *North-Holland, Amsterdam.*

Arrow, K. J. 1973 *Higher Education as a Filter*, in «Journal of Public Economics», II, 3, pp. 193–216.

Arrow, K. J. 2005 *A Cautious Case for Socialism*, lecture given at Columbia University in the *Terzo Lionel Trilling Seminar* in the academic year 1977–78, in «Economics in Practice», II, 1, pp. 472–80.

Arrow, K. J., Bowles, S., Durlauf, S. N. (a cura di) 2000 *Meritocracy and Economic Inequality*, Princeton University Press, Princeton.

Ashenfelter, O. & Card, D. (a cura di) 2011 Handbook of Labor Economics, *Elsevier, Amsterdam.*

Ashok, V., Kuziemko, I., Washington, E. 2015 Preferences for Redistribution in an Era of Rising Inequality: Some New Stylized Facts and Tentative Explanations, *in «Brookings Papers on Economic Activity», XXXIV, pp. 367–405.*

Atkinson, A. B. 1997 Bringing Income Distribution in From the Cold, *in «Economic Journal», CVII, 441, pp. 297–321.*

Atkinson, A. B. 1998 *Social Exclusion, Poverty and Unemployment*, in A. B. Atkinson & J. Hills (eds), *Exclusion, Employment and Opportunity*, London School of Economics, Centre for Analysis of Social Exclusion, n. 4.

Atkinson, A. B. 1999 The Economic Consequences of Rolling Back the Welfare State, *Mit Press, Cambridge.*

Atkinson, A. B. 2015 *Inequality. What Can Be Done?*, Harvard Economic Press, Cambridge 2015).

Atkinson, A. B. & Brandolini A. 2013 On the Identification of the Middle Class, *in Gornick - Jäntti 2013.*

Atkinson, A. B. & Marlier, E. (a cura di) 2010 Income and Living Conditions in Europe, *Eurostat, Luxembourg.*

Atkinson, A. B. & Jenkins, S. P. 2020 A Different Perspective on the Evolution of UK Income Inequality, *in «Review of Income and Wealth», LXVI, 2, pp. 253–66.*

Atkinson, A. B. & Søgaard J. E. 2016 *The Long Run History of Income Inequality in Denmark*, in «Scandinavian Journal of Economics», CXVIII, 2, pp. 264–91.

Atkinson, A. B., Marlier, E., Monatigne, F., Reinstadler, A. 2010 Income Poverty and Income Inequality, *in Atkinson - Marlier 2010.*

Attanasi, G. & Nagel, R. 2008 A Survey of Psychological Games: Theoretical Findings and Experimental Evidence, *in Innocenti - Sbriglia 2008.*

Autor, D. 2019 *Work of the Past, Work of the Future*, in «American Economic Review, Papers and Proceedings», CIX, pp. 1–32.

Autor, D. H. & Dorn, D. 2013 The Growth of Low-skilled Service Jobs and the Polarization of the Us Labor Market, *in «American Economic Review», CIII, 5, pp. 1553–97.*

Autor, D., Goldin, C., Katz, L. F. 2020a *Extending the Race between Education and Technology*, in «American Economic Review, Papers and Proceedings», CX, pp. 347–51.

Autor, D., Dorn, D., Katz, L., Patterson, C., Van Reenen, J. 2020b The Fall of the Labor Share and the Rise of Superstar Firms, *in «Quarterly Journal of Economics», CXXXV, 2, pp. 645–709.*

Autor, D., Dube, A., McGrew, A. 2023 The Unexpected Compression: Competition at Work in the Low Wage Labor Market, *Nber Working Paper n. 31010.*

Avendano, M., Hendrik, J., Mackenbach, J. 2009 Educational Level and Changes in Health across Europe: Longitudinal Results from SHARE, *in «Journal of European Social Policy», XIX, 4, pp. 301–16.*

Baczko, B. 1979 Lumières de l'utopie, *Payot, Paris 1978.*

Baczko, B. 1981 *Utopia*, in *Encyclopedia*, Einaudi, Torino, XIV, *ad vocem.*

Balboni, C. A., Bandiera, O. R., Ghatak, M., Heil, A. 2021 *Why Do People Stay Poor?*, Nber Working Paper n. 29340.

Ballarino, G. & Bernardi, F. (a cura di) 2016 Education, Occupation and Social Origin: A Comparative Analysis of the Transmission of Socio-Economic Inequalities, *Edward Elgar, Cheltenham.*

Ballarino, G., Barone, C., Panichella, N. 2014 Social Background and Education in Occupational Attainment in 20th Century Italy, *Eui Working Papers, Fiesole.*

Bao, R., De Loecker, J., Eeckhout, J. 2022 Are Managers Paid for Market Power?, *Cepr Discussion Paper 17182.*

Barkow, J. H., Cosmides, L., Tooby, J. (a cura di) 1992 The Adapted Mind: Evolutionary Psychology and the Generation of Culture, *Oxford University Press, New York.*

Barone, G. & Mocetti, S. 2021 Intergenerational Mobility in the Very Long Run: Florence 1427–2011 [Intergenerational Economic Mobility in the United States, 1940 to 2000], *in «Review of Economic Studies», LXXXVIII, 4, pp. 1863–91.*

Barro, R. 2013 *Education and Economic Growth*, in «Annals of Economics and Finance», XIV, 2, pp. 301–28.

Barro, R. & Lee, J.-W. 2013 *A New Data Set of Educational Attainment in the World, 1950–2010, in «Journal of Development Economics», CIV, pp. 184–98.*

Barros, R. 2012 *From Lifelong Education to Lifelong Learning*, in «European Journal for Research on the Education and Learning of Adults», III, 2, pp. 119–34.

Barth, E. & Moene, K. O. 2016 The Equality Multiplier: How Wage Compression and Welfare Empowerment Interact, *in «Journal of the European Economic Association», XIV, 5, pp. 1011–37.*

Basu, K. 2011 Beyond the Invisible Hand: Groundwork for a New Economics, *Princeton University Press, Princeton.*

Battisti, M., Dustmann, C., Schönberg, U. 2023 *Technological and Organizational Change and the Careers of Workers*, in «Journal of the European Economic Association», XXI, 4, pp. 1551–94.

Bauluz, L. & Meyer, T. 2024 *The Wealth of Generations*, World Inequality Lab, Working Paper n. 4.

Bauman, Z. 1996 *Post-Modern Ethics*, Blackwell, Oxford 1993.

Bauman, Z. 2006 *Liquid Life*, Polity Press, Cambridge 2005.

Bauman, Z. 2007 Welfare assediato. Sono forse io il custode di mio fratello?, *in* Homo Consumens. Lo sciame inquieto dei consumatori e la miseria degli esclusi, *Erickson, Gardolo.*

Bauman, Z. 2010a Does Ethics Have a Chance in a World of Consumers?, *Harvard University Press, Cambridge 1982.*

Bauman, Z. 2010b *Modernità e ambivalenza*, Bollati Boringhieri, Torino.

Bauman, Z. 2016 *Strangers at Our Door*, John Wiley et Sons, Hoboken 2016.

Bauman, Z. & Tesler, K. 2002 Società, etica, politica. Conversazioni con Zygmunt Bauman, *Raffaello Cortina, Milano.*

Becchetti, L. & Conzo, G. 2021 Resilience, Social Capital, Active Citizenship and Subjective Wellbeing: the Contribution of Generativity, *Research Paper n. 522, Ceis, Università Tor Vergata, Roma.*

Beck, U. 2000 La società del rischio. Verso una seconda modernità, *Carocci, Roma.*

Beck U. 2016 The Metamorphosis of the World, Polity Press, Cambridge.

Beck, U. 2017 *The Metamorphosis of the World*, Polity Press, Cambridge 2016.

Beck, U. & Beck-Gernsheim, E. 2001 Individualization: Institutionalized Individualism and Its Social and Political Consequences, *Sage Publications, London.*

Becker, G. S. 2011 Reflections on the Economics of Education, *in Hanushek, Machin, Wößmann 2011.*

Becker, G. S. & Tomes, N. 1979 An Equilibrium Theory of the Distribution of Income and Intergenerational Mobility, *in «Journal of Political Economy», LXXXVII, 6, pp. 1153–89.*

Becker, G. S. & Tomes, N. 1986 *Human Capital and the Rise and Fall of Families*, in «Journal of Labor Economics», IV, 2, pp. S1–S39.

Becker, G., Kominers, S. D., Murphy, K. M. Spenkuch, J. L. 2018 *A Theory of Intergenerational Mobility*, in «Journal of Political Economy», CXXVI, S1, pp. 7–25.

Beckfield, J. 2020 Rising Inequality Is Not Balanced by Intergenerational Mobility, *in «Pnas», CXVII, 1.*

Bell, A. et al. 2019a Do Tax Cuts Produce more Einsteins? The Impacts of Financial Incentives VerSus Exposure to Innovation on the Supply of Inventors, *Joseph Schumpeter Lecture, Eea Annual Congress 2017, in «Journal of the European Economic Association», XVII, 3, pp. 651–77.*

Bell, A. et al. 2019b Who Becomes an Inventor in America? The Importance of Exposure to Innovation, *in «Quarterly Journal of Economics», CXXXIV, 2, pp. 647–713.*

Bell, B., Pedemonte, S., Van Reenen, J. 2021 Ceo Pay and the Rise of Relative Performance Contracts: A Question of Governance?, *in «Journal of the European Economic Association», XIX, 5, pp. 2513–42*

Benabou, R. & Ok, A. 2001 Social Mobility and the Demand for Redistribution: The Poum Hypothesis, *in «Quarterly Journal of Economics», CXVI, 2, pp. 447–87.*

Bendix, R. & Lipset, S. M. 1975 Social Mobility in Industrial Society, *University of California Press, Berkeley 1959.*

Benhabib, J. & Przeworski, A. 2006 The Political Economy of Redistribution under Democracy, *in «Economic Theory», XXIX, pp. 271–90.*

Benhabib, J., Bisin, J., Jackson, M. (eds) 2016 *Handbook of Social Economics*, IA, North-Holland, Netherlands.

Bentham, J. 1983 *The Collected Works of Jeremy Bentham*, a cura di F. Rosen e J. H. Burns, I, Clarendon Press, Oxford.

Bentham, J. 2013 Introduzione ai princìpi della morale e della legislazione, *Utet, Torino.*

Bergman, P. et al. 2023 Creating Moves to Opportunity: Experimental Evidence on Barriers to Neighborhood Choice, *Nber Working Paper n. 26164.*

Bergoglio, J. M. 2015 *Laudato si'*, Libreria Editrice Vaticana, Roma.

Bergoglio, J. M. 2020 *Fratelli tutti*, Libreria Editrice Vaticana, Roma.

Berlin, I. 1989 *Four Essays on Liberty*, Oxford University Press, Oxford 1969.

Berlin, I. & Sen, A. K. 1990 *La dimensione etica nelle società contemporanee*, Edizioni della Fondazione Giovanni Agnelli, Torino.

Berman, Y. 2017 Understanding the Mechanical Relationship between Inequality and Intergenerational Mobility, *mimeo.*

Berman, Y. 2022 *The Long-Run Evolution of Absolute Intergenerational Mobility*, in «American Economic Journal: Applied Economics», XIV, 3, pp. 61–83.

Berman, Y. & Milanović, B. 2020 Homoploutia: Top Labor and Capital Incomes in the United States, 1950–2020, *Lis Working paper n. 806.*

Berman, N., Couttenier, M., Girard, V. 2023 *Mineral Resources and the Salience of Ethnic Identities*, Aix-Marseille School of Economics, Working Paper n. 2232.

Bernardi, F. 2009 Globalizzazione, individualizzazione e morte delle classi sociali: uno studio empirico su 18 paesi europei, *in «Polis», 2, pp. 195–220.*

Bernardi, F., Hertelb, F. R., Yastrebovac, G. 2018 A U-turn in Inequality in College Attainment by Parental Education in the Us?, *in «Research in Social Stratification and Mobility», LVIII, pp. 33–43.*

Bernasconi, M. & Profeta, P. 2012 Public Education and Redistribution When Talents Are Mismatched, *in «European Economic Review», LVI, 1, pp. 84–96.*

Bernstein, B. 1970 *Education Cannot Compensate for Society*, in C. Stoneman et al. (eds), *Education for Democracy*, Penguin Education Special, London.

Betti, G. & Lemmi, A. (eds) 2008 Advances in Income Inequality and Concentration Measures, *Routledge, London.*

Beveridge, W. 1948 Full Employment in a Free Society, *Allen - Unwin, London 1944.*

Bezemer, D., Ryan-Collins, J., van Lerven, F., Zhang, L. 2018 Credit Where It's Due. A Historical, Theoretical and Empirical Review of Credit Guidance Policies in the 20th Century, *Ucl Institute for Innovation and Public Purpose, Working Paper n. 11.*

Bigot, G. 2010 La responsabilità dell'amministrazione in Francia. Storia e teoria, *in «Scienza & Politica», XLII, pp. 21–37.*

Bishop, J. A. & Salas, R. (a cura di) 2012 Inequality, Mobility and Segregation: Essays in Honor of Jacques Silber, *in «Research on Economic Inequality», XX.*

Bishop, J. A., Rodriguez, J. G., Zeager, L. A. 2019 A Multifaceted Approach to Earnings Mobility Comparisons, *Society for the Study of Economic Inequality, Paris.*

Björklund, A. & Jäntti, M. 1997 Intergenerational Income Mobility in Sweden Compared to the United States, *in «American Economic Review», LXXXVII, 5, pp. 1009–18.*

Björklund, A. & Jäntti, M. 2009 Intergenerational Income Mobility and the Role of Family Background, *in Salverda et al. 2009.*

Björklund, A. & Salvanes, K. G. 2011 Education and Family Background: Mechanisms and Policies, *in Hanushek, Machin, Wößmann 2011.*

Björklund, A., Jäntti, M., Roemer, J. 2012a Equality of Opportunity and the Distribution of Long-Run Income in Sweden, *in «Social Choice and Welfare», XXXIX, 2, pp. 675–96.*

Björklund, A., Roine, J., Waldenström, D. 2012b Intergenerational Top Income Mobility in Sweden: Capitalist Dynasties in the Land of Equal Opportunity?, *in «Journal of Public Economics», XCLVI, 5, pp. 474–84.*

Black, S. E. & Devereux, P. J. 2011 Recent Developments in Intergenerational Mobility, *in Ashenfelter - Card 2011, pp. 1487–541.*

Blanchard, O & Tirole J. 2021 Major Future Economic Challenges, *France Stratégie, Paris.*

Blanchet, T., Chancel, L., Gethin, A. 2022a *Why Is Europe More Equal than the United States?*, in «American Economic Journal: Applied Economics», XIV, 4, pp. 480–518.

Blanchet, T., Saez, E., Zucman, G. 2022b *Real-Time Inequality*, Nber Working Paper n. 30229.

Blanden, J. & Machin, S. 2004 Educational Inequality and the Expansion of UK Higher Education, *in «Scottish Journal of Political Economy», LI, 2, pp. 230–49.*

Blanden, J. & Machin, S. 2017 *Home Ownership and Social Mobility*, Cep Discussion Papers dp1466, Centre for Economic Performance, Lse.

Blanden, J. & Macmillan, L. 2014 *Education and Intergenerational Mobility: Help or Hindrance?*, Case Papers n. 179, Centre for Analysis of Social Exclusion, Lse.

Blanden, J., Gregg, P., Machin, S. 2003 *Changes in Educational Inequality*, Centre for Market and Public Organisation n. 79, University of Bristol.

Blanden, J., Doepke, M., Stuhler, J. 2022 *Educational Inequality*, Nber Working Paper n. 29979.

Blau, P. & Duncan, O. D. 1967 The American Occupational Structure, *John Wiley & Sons, New York.*

Bloom, N., Jones, C. I., Van Reenen, J., Webb, M. 2020 *Are Ideas Getting Harder to Find?*, in «American Economic Review», CX, 4, pp. 1104–44.

Bloome, D. 2014 Income Inequality and Intergenerational Income Mobility in the United States, *Harvard University Department of Sociology-Harvard Kennedy School.*

Bobbio, N. 1989 *L'età dei diritti*, Einaudi, Torino.

Boix, C. 2003 *Democracy and Redistribution*, Cambridge University Press, Cambridge.

Bönke, T., Giesecke, M., Lüthen, H. 2015 The Dynamics of Earnings in Germany: Evidence from Social Security Records, *Diw Berlin, Discussion Papers n. 1514.*

Borjas, G. J. 2015 *Immigration and Globalization. A Review Essay*, in «Journal of Economic Literature», LIII, 4, pp. 961–74.

Bosco, A. & Guderzo, M. (a cura di) 2016 The Euro and the Struggle for the Creation of a New Global Currency, *Florence University Press, Florence.*

Boserup, S., Kopczuk, W., Kreiner, C. 2016 Wealth Inequality: Evidence from the Role of Bequests in Shaping Wealth Inequality, *in «American Economic Review», CVI, 5, pp. 656–61.*

Bosworth, S. & Snower, D. J. 2021 Technological Advance, Social Fragmentation and Welfare, *Cepr Discussion Paper n. 15665.*

Bosworth, S. J., Singer, T., Snower, D. J. 2016 *Cooperation, Motivation and Social Balance*, in «Journal of Economic Behavior & Organization», CXXVI, pp. 72–94.

Bouchard St-Amant, P.-A., Marceau, N., Garon, J-D. 2020 Uncovering Gatsby Curves, *Research Square.*

Bouchet-Valat, M., Peugny, C., Vallet, L. A. 2016 Inequality of Educational Returns in France. Some Evidence of Change in the Relative Importance of the Effect of Education and Social Background on Occupational Careers, *alshs-01395565.*

Bourdieu, P. 1974 The School as a Conservative Force: Scholastic and Cultural Inequalities, *in Eggertsson 1974.*

Bourdieu, P. 1980 Questions de sociologie, *Minuit, Paris.*

Bourdieu, P. 1981 La représentation politique. Éléments pour une théorie du champ politique, *in «Actes de la Recherche en Sciences Sociales», XXXVI–XXXVII, pp. 3–24.*

Bourdieu, P. 1984 Distinction: A social critique of the judgement of taste, *Harvard University Press, Cambridge.*

Bourdieu, P. 2010 *Le sociologue et l'historien* (conversation with R. Chartier), Agone, Paris.

Bourdieu, P. 2012 Capitale simbolico e classi sociali, *in «Polis», XXVI, 3, pp. 401–18.*

Bourdieu, P. & Passeron, J.-C. 1972 *La reproduction. Eléments pour une théorie du système d'enseignement, Minuit, Paris 1970.*

Bovenberg, L., Hansen, M. I., Sørensen, P. B. 2012 Efficient Redistribution of Lifetime Income through Welfare Accounts, *in «Fiscal Studies», XXXIII, 1, pp. 1–37.*

Bowles, S. 1972 *Schooling and Inequality from Generation to Generation*, in «Journal of Political Economy», LXXX, 3, pp. S219–S251.

Bowles, S. & Gintis, H. 1976 Schooling in Capitalist America: Educational Reform and the Contradictions of Economic Life, *Basic Books, New York.*

Bowles, S., Durlauf, S. N., Hoff, K. (a cura di) 2006 *Poverty Traps*, Princeton University Press, Princeton.

Bradbury, B., Corak, M., Waldfogel, J., Washbrook, E. 2015 *Too Many Children Left Behind*, Russell Sage Foundation, New York.

Brancaccio, E., Giammetti, R., Lopreite, M., Puliga, M. 2018 Centralization of Capital and Financial Crisis: A Global Network Analysis of Corporate Control, *in «Structural Change and Economic Dynamics», pp. 94–104.*

Brandolini, A., Rosolia, A., & Torrini, R. 2012 The EU-wide Earnings Distribution, *in Bishop - Salas 2012.*

Bratberg, E. et al. 2017 A Comparison of Intergenerational Mobility Curves in Germany, Norway, Sweden, and the Us, *in «Scandinavian Journal of Economics», CXIX, 1, pp. 72–101.*

Braudel, F. 2010 La dinamica del capitalismo, *il Mulino, Bologna.*

Breen, R. & Jonsson, J. O. 2007 Explaining Change in Social Fluidity: Educational Equalization and Educational Expansion in Twentieth-Century Sweden, *in «American Journal of Sociology», CXII, 6, pp. 1775–810.*

Brooks, W. J., Kaboski, J. P., Li, W. A., Qian, W. 2021 Exploitation of Labor? Classical Monopsony Power and Labor's Share, *in «Journal of Development Economics», CL, maggio.*

Brown, P. & James, D. 2020 Educational Expansion, Poverty Reduction and Social Mobility: Reframing the Debate, *in «Journal of Educational Research», C, pp. 1–9.*

Brunello, G. & Checchi, D. 2007 Does School Tracking Affect Equality of Opportunity? New International Evidence [«Educational opportunities and the role of institutions»], *in «Economic Policy», XXII, 52, pp. 782–861.*

Brunello, G. & Rocco, L. 2008 Educational Standards in Private and Public Schools, *in «Economic Journal», CXVIII, 533, pp. 1866–87.*

Brunello, G., Weber, G., Weiss, C. T. 2012 Books are Forever: Early Life Conditions, Education and Lifetime Earnings in Europe, *in «Economic Journal», CXXVII, pp. 271–96.*

Brunori, P., Ferreira, F. H. G., Peragine, V. 2013 Inequality of Opportunity, Income Inequality, and Economic Mobility: Some International Comparisons, *in Paus 2013.*

Brynjolfsson, E. & McAfee, A. 2014 The Second Machine Age: Work, Progress, and Prosperity in a Time of Brilliant Technologies, *Norton & Company, New York.*

Bukodi, E. & Goldthorpe, J. H. 2019 Social Mobility and Education in Britain: Research, Politics and Policy, *Cambridge University Press, Cambridge.*

Bukodi, E., Goldthorpe, J. H., Steinberg, J. 2023 Continuing Complexity: The University Careers of a Scientific Elite in Relation to Their Class Origins and Schooling, *in «British Journal of Sociology», LXXIV, pp. 547–65.*

Caldarelli, G. 2022 *Senza eguali*, Egea, Milano.

Callender, C. 2016 Cost-sharing and Student Support, *in Scott et al. 2016.*

Callender, C. & Mason, G. 2017 Does Student Loan Debt Deter Higher Education Participation? New Evidence from England, *in «Annals of American Political and Social Science», DCLXXI, 1, pp. 20–48.*

Canfora, L. 2004 La democrazia. Storia di un'ideologia, *Laterza, Roma-Bari.*

Cappelen, A. W., Moene, K. O., Skjelbred, S. E., Tungodden, B. 2017 *The Merit Primacy Effect*, Working Papers 2017-047, Human Capital and Economic Opportunity Working Group.

Cappelen, A., Mollerstrom, J., Bjørn-Atle Reme, B.-A., Tungodden, B. 2022 A Meritocratic Origin of Egalitarian Behaviour («Income Inequality and Income Mobility in the Scandinavian Countries Compared to the United States»), *in «Economic Journal», CXXXII, 646, pp. 2101–17.*

Castel, R. 1995 Les Métamorphoses de la question sociale. Une chronique du salariat, *Fayard, Paris.*

Caucutt, E. M. & Lochner, L. 2020 Early and Late Human Capital Investments, Borrowing Constraints, and the Family, *in «Journal of Political Economy», CXXVIII, 3, pp. 1065–147.*

Causa, O. & Johansson, A. 2010 Intergenerational Social Mobility in Oecd Countries, *in «Oecd Economic Studies», 1, pp. 1–44.*

Cerra, V., Lama, R., Loayza, N. 2021 Links between Growth, Inequality, and Poverty: A Survey, *Imf Working Paper n. 68.*

Charness, G., Masclet, D., Villeval, M. C. 2014 *The Dark Side of Competition for Status*, in «Management Science», LX, 1, pp. 38–55.

Checchi, D. 2005 The Economics of Education: Human Capital, Family Background and Inequality, *Cambridge University Press, Cambridge.*

Chetty, R. 2013 *Yes, Economics Is a Science*, in «New York Times», 13 ottobre.

Chetty, R. 2021 Improving Equality of Opportunity: New Insights from Big Data, *in «Contemporary Economic Policy», XXXIX, 1, pp. 7–41.*

Chetty, R. & Hendren, N. 2018 The Impacts of Neighborhoods on Intergenerational Mobility I: Childhood Exposure Effects, *in «Quarterly Journal of Economics», CXXXIII, 3, pp. 1107–62.*

Chetty, R., Deming, D. J., Friedman, J. N. 2023 Diversifying Society's Leaders? The Determinants and Causal Effects of Admission to Highly Selective Private Colleges, *Nber Working Paper n. 31492.*

Chetty, R. et al. 2014a Is the United States still a Land of Opportunity? Recent Trends in Intergenerational Mobility, *in «American Economic Review», CIV, 5, pp. 141–7.*

Chetty, R. et al. 2014b Where Is the Land of Opportunity? The Geography of Intergenerational Mobility in the United States, *in «Quarterly Journal of Economics», CXXIX, 4, pp. 1553–623.*

Chetty, R. et al. 2017a The Fading American Dream: Trends in Absolute Income Mobility since 1940, *in «Science», CCCLVI, 6336, pp. 398–406.*

Chetty, R. et al. 2017b Mobility Report Cards: The Role of Colleges in Intergenerational Mobility, *Nber Working Papers 23618.*

Chetty, R. et al. 2018 The Opportunity Atlas: Mapping the Childhood Roots of Social Mobility, *Nber Working Paper 25147.*

Chetty, R., Hendren, N., Jones, M. J., Porter, S. R. 2020 Race and Economic Opportunity in the United States: An Intergenerational Perspective, *in «Quarterly Journal of Economics», CXXXV, 2, pp. 711–83.*

Chetty, R. et al. 2022a Social Capital I: Measurement and Associations with Economic Mobility, *in «Nature», DCVIII, 7921, pp. 108–21.*

Chetty, R. et al. 2022b Social Capital II: Determinants of Economic Connectedness, *in «Nature», DCVIII, 7921, pp. 122–34.*

Chevalier, T. 2019 Political Trust, Young People and Institutions in Europe. A Multilevel Analysis, *in «International Journal of Social Welfare», XXVIII, 4, pp. 418–30.*

Cholli, N. A. & Durlauf, S. N. 2022 *Intergenerational Mobility*, Nber Working Paper n. 29760.

Clotfelter, C. T. & Rothschild, M. (a cura di) 1993 Studies of Supply and Demand in Higher Education, *University of Chicago Press, Chicago.*

Cobham, A., Schlogl, L., Sumner, A. 2015 Inequality and the Tails: The Palma Proposition and Ratio Revisited, *Desa Working Paper n. 143.*

Cohen, G. A. 1989 *Equality of What? On Welfare, Goods and Capabilities*, in «Recherches économiques de Louvain», LVI, 3/4, pp. 357–82.

Coleman, J. S. 1988 Social Capital in the Creation of Human Capital, *in «American Journal of Sociology», supplemento* Social Capital in the Creation of Human Capital, Sociological and Economic Approaches to the Analysis of Social Structure, *XCIV, pp. S95–S120.*

Coleman, J. S. 1990 *Foundations of Social Theory*, Harvard University Press, Cambridge.

Coleman, J. S. & Hoffer, T. B. 1987 Public and Private Schools: The Impact of Communities, *Basic Books, New York.*

Collet, M. & Pénicaud, E. 2019 La mobilité sociale des femmes et des hommes: évolutions de 1977 à 2015 in France, *«Portrait Social», Insee.*

Collier, P. 2013 Exodus: Immigration and Multiculturalism in the 21st Century, *Oxford University Press, Oxford.*

Collier, P. 2018 The Future of Capitalism: Facing the New Anxieties, *Allen Lane, London.*

Connor, D. S. & Storper, M. 2020 The Changing Geography of Social Mobility in the United States, *in «Pnas, CXVII, 48.*

Cook, P. J. & Frank, R. H. 1993 The Growing Concentration of Top Students at Elite Schools, *in Clotfelter - Rothschild 1993.*

Corak, M. (ed) 2004 Generational Income Mobility in North America and Europe, *Cambridge University Press, Cambridge.*

Corak, M. 2006 Do Poor Children Become Poor Adults? Lessons from a Cross Country Comparison of Generational Earnings Mobility, *in «Research on Economic Inequality», XIII, 1, pp. 143–88.*

Corak, M. 2013 Income Inequality, Equality of Opportunity and Intergenerational Mobility, *in «Journal of Economic Perspectives», XXVII, 3, pp. 79–102.*

Corak, M. 2016 Economic Theory and Practical Lessons for Measuring Equality of Opportunities, *Oecd Statistics Working Paper n. 2.*

Corak, M. 2020 Intergenerational Mobility: What Do We Care about? What Should We Care about?, *in «Australian Economic Review», LIII, 2, pp. 230–40.*

Corak, M., Curtis, L., Phipps, S. 2011 Economic Mobility, Family Background, and the Well-being of Children in the United States and Canada, *in Smeeding et al. 2011, pp. 73–108.*

Corak, M., Lindquist, M., Mazumder, B. 2014 A Comparison of Upward and Downward Intergenerational Mobility in Canada, Sweden and the United States, *Working Paper Series 5/2014, Stockholm University, Swedish Institute for Social Research.*

Cox, J. C., Sadiraj, V., Sen, U. 2020 Cultural Identities and Resolution of Social Dilemmas, *in «Economic Inquiry», LVIII, 1, pp. 49–66.*

Crafts, N. & Mills, T. C. 2020 *Is the Uk Productivity Slowdown Unprecedented?*, in «National Institute Economic Review», 251.

Crawford, C. et al. 2016 Higher Education, Career Opportunities, and Intergenerational Inequality, *in «Oxford Review of Economic Policy», XXXII, 4, pp. 553–75.*

Criscuolo, C. et al. 2020 Workforce Composition, Productivity and Pay: The Role of Firms in Wage Inequality, *Oecd Social, Employment and Migration Working Paper n. 241.*

Criscuolo, C. et al. 2021 The Firm-level Link between Productivity Dispersion and Wage Inequality: A Symptom of Low Job Mobility?, *Oecd Economics Department Working Paper n. 1656.*

Croci Angelini, E. & Farina, F. 2006 The Size of Redistribution in Oecd Countries: Does It Influence Wage Inequality?, *in Farina - Savaglio 2006.*

Croci Angelini, E. & Farina, F. 2007 Macroeconomia dell'Unione europea, *Carocci, Roma.*

Croci Angelini, E. & Farina, F. 2008 Technological Choices under Institutional Constraints: Measuring the Impact of Earnings Dispersion, *in Betti - Lemmi 2008.*

Croci Angelini, E. & Farina, F. 2016 Integration without Convergence in the European Currency Area, *in Bosco - Guederzo 2016.*

Crompton, R. 1999 Class and Stratification. An Introduction to Current Debates, *Polity Press, Cambridge 1998.*

Cunha, F. & J. J. Heckman 2007 *The Technology of Skill Formation*, in «American Economic Review», XCVII, 2, pp. 31–47.

Cunha, F. & Heckman, J. J. 2009 *The Economics and Psychology of Inequality and Human Development*, in «Journal of European Economic Association», VII, 2–3, pp. 320–64.

Cunha, F., Heckman, J. J., Schennach, S. M. 2010 Estimating the Technology of Cognitive and Noncognitive Skill Formation, *in «Econometrica», LXXVIII, 3, pp. 883–931.*

Dabla-Norris, E. et al. 2015 Cause and Consequences of Income Inequality: A Global Perspective, *Imf, Staff Discussion Note 13.*

D'Addio, A. C. 2007 Intergenerational Transmission of Disadvantage: Mobility or Immobility across Generations? A Review of the Evidence for Oecd Countries, *Oecd Social, Employment and Migration Working Paper n. 7.*

Dahl, R. A. 1957 *The Concept of Power*, in «Behavioral Science», II, 3, pp. 201–15.

Dahl, R. A. 1961 Who Governs? Democracy and Power in an American City, *Yale University Press, New Haven.*

Dahrendorf, R. 1963 Soziale Klassen und Klassenkonflikt in der industriellen Gesellschaft, *Enke, Stuttgart 1957; (ed. am.* Class and Class Conflict in Industrial Society, *Stanford University Press, Stanford 1959).*

Dahrendorf, R. 1989 The Modern Social Conflict: An Essay on the Politics of Liberty, *Weidenfeld and Nicolson, London 1988.*

Dallinger, U. 2010 Support for Redistribution. What Explains Cross-National Differences?, *in «Journal of European Social Policy», XX, 4, pp. 333–49.*

Dardanoni, V., Fields, G. S., Roemer, J. E., Sanchez Puerta, M. L. 2006 How Demanding Should Equality of Opportunity Be, and How Much Have We Achieved?, *in S. Morgan, D. Grusky, G. S. Fields (eds),* Mobility and Inequality: Frontiers of Research from Sociology and Economics, *Stanford University Press, Stanford.*

Daruich, D. & Kozlowski, J. 2020 Explaining Intergenerational Mobility: The Role of Fertility and Family Transfers, *in «Review of Economic Dynamics», XXXVI, pp. 220–45.*

Daruich, D., Di Addario, S., Saggio, R. 2023 The Effects of Partial Employment Protection Reforms: Evidence for Italy, *in «Review of Economic Studies», XC, 6, pp. 2880–942.*

Deaton, A. 2021 Ora paghi chi ha guadagnato, *in «Nuova Atlantide», 3.*

Deaton, A. & Case, A. 2021 Deaths of Despair and the Future of Capitalism, *Princeton University Press, Princeton 2021.*

Decancq, K. 2023 Cumulative Deprivation: Identification and Aggregation, *in Wagle 2023.*

de Cervantes, M. 1974 Don Chisciotte della Mancia, *Mondadori, Milano.*

De Fraja, G. 2002 *The Design of Optimal Education Policies*, in «Review of Economic Studies», LXIX, 2, pp. 437–66.

De Fraja, G. 2004 *Education and Redistribution*, in «Rivista di Politica Economica», XCIV, 3, pp. 3–44.

De Fraja, G. & Martinez-Mora, F. 2014 *The Desegregating Effect of School Tracking*, in «Journal of Urban Economics», LXXX, C, pp. 164–77.

De Grauwe, P. 2017 The Limits of the Market: The Pendulum Between Government and Market, *Oxford University Press, Oxford.*

De Loecker, J., Eeckhout, J., Unger, G. 2020 The Rise of Market Power and the Macroeconomic Implications, *in «Quarterly Journal of Economics», CXXXV, 2, pp. 561–644.*

DeLong, J. B. 2022 Slouching towards Utopia: An Economic History of the Twentieth Century, *Basic Books, London.*

Deneulin, S. & Shahani, L. 2009 An Introduction to the Human Development and Capability Approach, Freedom and Agency, *Earthscan, London.*

Denzau, A. T. & North, D. C. 1994 Shared Mental Models: Ideologies and Institutions, *in «Kyklos», XLVII, 1, pp. 3–31.*

De Ruggiero, G. 1925 Storia del liberalismo europeo, *Laterza, Bari.*

De Smedt, M., Giovannini, E., Radermacher, W. J. 2019 *Measuring Sustainability*, in Stiglitz, Fitoussi, Durand 2019.

Dewey, J. 1927 *The Public and Its Problems*, Alan Swellow Press, Denver.

DiPrete, T. A. 2020 The Impact of Inequality on Intergenerational Mobility, *in «Annual Review of Sociology», XLVI, pp. 379–98.*

Doerr, S., Drechsel, T., Lee, D. 2022 Income Inequality and Job Creation, *Cepr Discussion Papers n. 17342.*

Dollar, D. & Kraay, A. 2002 *Growth Is Good for the Poor*, in «Journal of Economic Growth», VII, 3, pp. 195–225.

Doepke, M., Sorrenti, G., Zilibotti, F. 2019 *The Economics of Parenting*, in «Annual Review of Economics», XI, 1, pp. 55–84.

Doepke, M., Agostinelli, F., Sorrenti, G., Zilibotti, F. 2020 It Takes a Village: The Economics of Parenting with Neighborhood and Peer Effects, *Cepr Discussion Paper n. 14637.*

Downs, A. 1988 An Economic Theory of Democracy, *New York 1957.*

Duncan, G. J. & Murnane, R. J. 2011 Introduction: The American Dream, Then and Now, *in Idd. (eds),* Whither Opportunity? Rising Inequality, Schools, and Children's Life Chances, *Russell Sage, New York.*

Dunn, J. 2006 Setting the People Free: The Story of Democracy, *Atlantic Books, London 2005).*

Durkheim, E. 1963 (1895) Le regole del metodo sociologico. Sociologia e filosofia, *Edizioni di Comunità, Milano.*

Durkheim, E. 1969 (1928) Le Socialisme. Sa définition. Ses débuts. La doctrine saint-simonienne, *Les Retz, Paris.*

Durkheim, É. 2016 *Du la division du travail social*, Presses Universitaires de France, Paris 1893.

Durlauf, S. N. 1996 *A Theory of Persistent Income Inequality*, in «Journal of Economic Growth», I, 1, pp. 75–93.

Durlauf, S. N. 2002 Groups Social Influences and Inequality: A Membership Theory Perspective on Poverty Traps, *Wisconsin Madison-Social Systems Working Paper n. 18.*

Durlauf, S. N. 2004 *Neighbourhood Effects*, in J. V. Henderson & J.-F. Thisse (a cura di), *Handbook of Urban and Regional Economics*, Elsevier Science, Amsterdam, IV, pp. 2173–242.

Durlauf, S. N. & Ioannides, Y. M. 2010 *Social Interactions*, in «Annual Review of Economics», II, 1, pp. 451–78.

Durlauf, S. N., Kourtellos, A., Ming Tan, C. 2022 *The Great Gatsby Curve*, in «Annual Review of Economics», XIV, 1, pp. 571–603.

Dworkin, R. 1977 *Taking Rights Seriously*, Harvard University Press, Cambridge.

Dworkin, R. 1981 *What Is Equality? Part 2: Equality of Resources*, in «Philosophy and Public Affairs», X, pp. 283–345.

Eagleman, D. E. 2012 Incognito: The Secret Life of the Brain, *Pantheon Books, New York 2011.*

Eagleman, D. E. 2021 Livewired, *Penguin Random House, New York 2020.*

Eeckhout, J. 2021 The Profit Paradox: How Thriving Firms Threaten the Future of Work, *Princeton University Press, Princeton.*

Eggertsson, G. B. (a cura di) 1974 Contemporary Research in Sociology of Education, *Methuen, London.*

Egidi, M. 2023 The Internal Fragility of Representative Democracy: Was Schumpeter Right?, *in «Journal of Evolutionary Economics», XXXIII, 3, pp. 645–70.*

Elango, S., García, J. L., Heckman, J. J., Hojman, A. 2016 Early Childhood Education, *in Moffitt 2016.*

Elias, N. 1978 *What Is Sociology?*, Hutchinson & Co., London.

Elias, N. 1990 Die Gesellschaft der Individuen, *1987; ed. ingl.* The Society of Individuals, *Continuum, London-New York 1991.*

Elinder, M., Erixson, O., Waldenström, D. 2018 Inheritance and Wealth Inequality: Evidence from Population Registers, *in «Journal of Public Economics», CLXV, pp. 17–30.*

Elster, J. 1985 *The Multiple Self*, Cambridge University Press, Cambridge.

Elster, J. 1995 The Cement of Society: A Study of Social Order, *Cambridge University Press, Cambridge 1989.*

Emmons, W. R., Kent, A. H., Ricketts, L. R. 2019 Is College Still Worth It? The New Calculus of Falling Returns, *in «Federal Reserve of St. Louis Review», CI, 4, pp. 297–329.*

Epple, D. & Romano, R. E. 1998 Competition between Private and Public Schools, Vouchers, and Peer-Group Effects, *in «American Economic Review», LXXXVIII, 1, pp. 33–62.*

Epple, D. & Romano, R. E. 2003 Neighborhood Schools, Choice, and the Distribution of Educational Benefits, *in Nber 2003, pp. 227–86.*

Epple, D., Romano, R. E., Urquiola, M. 2017 *School Vouchers: A Survey of the Economics Literature*, in «Journal of Economic Literature», LV, 2, pp. 441–92.

Erikson, R. & Goldthorpe, J. H. 1992 The Constant Flux: A Study of Class Mobility in Industrial Societies, *Clarendon Press, Oxford.*

Erikson, R., Goldthorpe, J. H, Portocarero, L. 1979 Intergenerational Class Mobility in Three Western European Societies: England, France and Sweden, *in «British Journal of Sociology», XXX, 4, pp. 415–41.*

Ernaux, A. 2014 *La Place*, Gallimard, Paris 1983.

Ernaux, A. 2015 *Les Années*, Gallimard, Paris 2008.

Eshaghnia, S., Heckman, J. J. Landersø, R., Qureshi, R. 2022 Intergenerational transmission of family influence, *Nber Working Paper 30412.*

Esping-Andersen, G. 1990 *The Three Worlds of Welfare Capitalism*, Princeton University Press, Princeton.

Esping-Andersen, G. 2015 *Welfare Regimes and Social Stratification*, in «Journal of European Social Policy», XXV, 1, pp. 124–34.

Esping-Andersen, G. & Cimentada, J. 2018 Ability and Mobility: The Relative Influence of Skills and Social Origin on Social Mobility, *in «Social Science Research», LXXV, pp. 13–31.*

Esposito, P. & Scicchitano, S. 2020 Educational Mismatches, Technological Change and Unemployment: Evidence from Secondary and Tertiary Educated Workers, *Global Labor Organization (Glo), Discussion Paper, n. 465.*

Esteban, J., Gradín, C., Ray, D. 2007 An Extension of a Measure of Polarization, with an Application to the Income Distribution of Five Oecd Countries, *in «Journal of Economic Inequality», V, 1, pp. 1–19.*

Eucken, W. 1939 Die Grundlagen der Nationalökonomie, *G. Fischer, Jena.*

Eurofound 2017 *Social Mobility in the EU*, Research Report, Luxembourg.

Eurofound 2023 *Unaffordable and Inadequate Housing in Europe*, Publications Office of the European Union, Luxembourg.

Fagereng, A., Guiso, L., Pistaferri, L. 2022 Assortative Mating and Wealth Inequality, *Cepr Discussion Paper 17148.*

Faia, E. & Shabalina, E. 2023 Distributional Consequences of Technology Shocks through Labour Reallocation, *Cepr Discussion Paper n. 18546.*

Falk, A. et al. 2021 Socioeconomic Status and Inequalities in Children's Iq and Economic Preferences, *in «Journal of Political Economy», CXXIX, 9, pp. 2504–45.*

Farina, F. 2021 Lo Stato sociale. Storia, politica, economia, *Luiss University Press, Roma.*

Farina, F. & Savaglio, E. (a cura di) 2006 Inequality and Economic Integration, *Routledge, London.*

Farina, F., Ottone, S., Ponzano, F. 2019 On the Collective Choice among Models of Social Protection: An Experimental Study, *in «Games», XLI, 10, pp. 1–17.*

Farina, F., Peluso, E., Savaglio, E. 2001 *Inequality of Opportunity in Income and Functionings*, Quaderni del Dipartimento di Economia politica, Unversità di Siena, n. 333.

Farina, F., Peluso, E., Savaglio, E. 2004 *Ranking Opportunity Sets in the Space of Functionings*, in «Journal of Economic Inequality», II, 2, pp. 105–16.

Feinstein, L. 2003 Inequality in the Early Cognitive Development of British Children in the 1970 Cohort, *in «Economica», LXX, pp. 73–97.*

Feldman, M. W., Otto, S. P., Christiansen, F. B. 2000 *Genes, Culture, and Inequality*, in Arrow, Bowles, Durlauf 2000.

Ferguson, D. & Savage, M. 2020 Controversial Exams Algorithm to Set 97% of Gcse Results, *in «The Guardian», 15 agosto.*

Ferreira, F. H. G. 2023 *Is There a «New Consensus» on Inequality?*, Lse International Inequalities Institute, Working Paper n. 101.

Ferreira, F. H. G. & Gignoux, J. 2014 The Measurement of Educational Inequality: Achievement and Opportunity, *in «World Bank Economic Review», XXVIII, pp. 210–46.*

Ferreira, F. H. G. & Walton, M. 2006 *Inequality of Opportunity and Economic Development*, Policy Research Working Paper Series 3816, World Bank.

Fields, G. S. 2010 Does Income Mobility Equalize Longer Term Incomes? New Measures of an Old Concept, *in «Journal of Economic Inequality», VIII, 4, pp. 409–27.*

Fields, G. S. 2019 *Concepts of Social Mobility*, Wider Working Paper n. 106.

Fitoussi, J.-P. & Saraceno, F. 2013 European Economic Governance: The Berlin-Washington Consensus, *in «Cambridge Journal of Economics», XXXVII, 3, pp. 479–96.*

Fleurbaey, M. 2008 Fairness, Responsibility, and Welfare, *Oxford University Press, Oxford.*

Foster, J. E. & Sen, A. K. 1997 On Economic Inequality after a Quarter Century, *in Sen 1997.*

Foucault, M. 1976 Surveiller et punir: Naissance de la prison, *Gallimard, Paris 1975.*

Foucault, M. 1978 La governamentalità, *in «Aut-aut», CLXVII–CLXVIII.*

Foucault, M. 2008 The Birth of Biopolitics: Lectures at the Collège de France, 1978–1979, *Palgrave Macmillan, Basingstoke.*

Frank, R. H. 2005 Positional Externalities Cause Large and Preventable Welfare Losses, *in «American Economic Review», XCV, 2, pp. 137–41.*

Frank, R. H. 2011 The Darwin Economy: Liberty, Competition and the Common Good, *Princeton University Press, Princeton.*

Frank, R. H. 2013 Falling Behind. How Rising Inequality Harms the Middle Class, *University of California Press, Berkeley.*

Franzini, M. & Messori, M. (eds) 1991 Impresa, istituzioni e informazione. Letture di microeconomia non tradizionale, *Clueb, Bologna.*

Franzini, M., Patriarca, F., Raitano, M. 2020 Market Competition and Parental Background Wage Premium: The Role of Human and Relational Capital, *in «Journal of Economic Inequality», XVIII, 3, pp. 291–397.*

Frey, C. B. & Osborne, M. A. 2017 The Future of Employment: How Susceptible Are Jobs to Computerisation?, *in «Technological Forecasting and Social Change», CXIV, pp. 254–80.*

Friedman, M. 1967 *Efficienza economica e libertà*, Vallecchi, Firenze (ed. or. *Capitalism and Freedom*, Chicago University Press, Chicago 1962).

Friedman, S. & Laurison, D. 2016 The Class Pay Gap in Higher Professional and Managerial Occupations, *in «American Sociological Review», LXXXI, 4, pp. 668–95.*

Friedman, M. & Savage, L. J. 1948 *The Utility Analysis of Choices Involving Risk*, in «Journal of Political Economy», LVI, 4, pp. 279–304.

Furman, J. & Orszag, P. 2018 A Firm-Level Perspective on the Role of Rents in the Rise in Inequality, *in Guzman 2018.*

Fusco, A., Guio, A.-C., Marlier, E. 2010 Characterising the Income Poor and the Materially Deprived in European Countries, *in Atkinson - Marlier 2010.*

Gächter, S., Herrmann, B., Thoeni, C. 2010 *Culture and Cooperation*, The Centre for Decision Research and Experimental Economics, School of Economics, University of Nottingham, Discussion Papers n. 9.

Gallegati, M. 2021 Il mercato rende liberi e altre bugie del neoliberismo, *Luiss University Press, Roma.*

Galor, O. & Tsiddon, D. 1997 Technological Progress, Mobility, and Economic Growth, *in «American Economic Review», LXXXVII, 3, pp. 363–82.*

García, J. L. & Heckman, J. J. 2022 Parenting Promotes Social Mobility Within and Across Generations, *Nber Working Paper n. 30610.*

Garcia-Macia, D., Heich, C.-T., Klenov, P. J. 2019 *«How Destructive is Innnovation?»*, in «Econometrica», LXXXVII, pp. 1507–41.

Gärtner, M., Mollerstrom, J., Seim, D. 2023 Intergenerational Transmission of Luck versus Effort Beliefs, *in «Economic Letters», CCXXXII, pp. 88–109.*

Gazzaniga, M. S. 1989 Il cervello sociale. Alla scoperta dei circuiti della mente, *Giunti, Firenze (ed. or.* The Social Brain: Discovering the Networks of the Mind, *Basic Books, New York 1985).*

Gazzaniga, M. S. 2009 Human. Quel che ci rende unici, *Raffaello Cortina, Milano (ed. or.* Human: The Science Behind What Makes Us Unique, *Dana Press, Washington DC 2008).*

Gellner, E. 1983 *Nations and nationalism*, Cornell University Press, Ithaca.

Gethin, A., Martínez-Toledano, C., Piketty, T. 2022 Brahmin Left Versus Merchant Right: Changing Political Cleavages in 21 Western Democracies, 1948–2020, *in «Quarterly Journal of Economics», CXXXVII, 1, pp. 1–48.*

Giddens, A. 1975 The Class Structure of the Advanced Societies, *Barnes & Noble, New York 1973.*

Giddens, A. 1998 The Third Way: The Renewal of Social Democracy, *Polity Press, Cambridge.*

Giddens, A. 2001 Sociology: Introductory Readings, *Polity Press, Cambridge.*

Gilens, M. & Page, B. J. 2014 Testing Theories of American Politics: Elites, Interest Groups, and Average Citizens, *in «Perspectives on Politics», 18 settembre, pp. 564–8.*

Giovannini, E. 2018 *L'utopia sostenibile*, Laterza, Roma-Bari.

Glaeser, E. L., Ponzetto, G., Shleifer, A. 2007 *Why Does Democracy Need Education?*, in «Journal of Economic Growth», XII, pp. 77–99.

Goldin, C. 1990 Understanding the Gender Gap: An Economic History of American Women, *Oxford University Press, New York.*

Goldin, C. & Katz, L. F. 2008 *The Race between Education and Technology*, Belknap Press of Harvard University Press, Cambridge.

Goldin, C. & Katz, L. F. 2011 Putting the «Co» in Education: Timing, Reasons, and Consequences of College Coeducation from 1835 to the Present, *in «Journal of Human Capital», V, 4, pp. 377–417.*

Goldthorpe, J. H. 2007 On Sociology: Volume Two: Illustration and Retrospect, *Stanford University Press, Stanford.*

Goldthorpe, J. H. 2013 Understanding – and Misunderstanding – Social Mobility in Britain: The Entry of Economists, the Confusion of Politicians and the Limits of Educational Policy, *in «Journal of Social Policy», XLII, 3, pp. 431–50.*

Goldthorpe, J. H. & Jackson, M. 2012 La meritocrazia dell'istruzione e i suoi ostacoli, *in «Stato e Mercato», XXXI, 1.*

Goldthorpe, J. H. & McKnight, A. 2006 The Economic Basis of Social Class, *in Morgan, Grusky, Fields 2006.*

Goldthorpe J. H., Llewellin, C., Payne, C. 1987 Social Mobility and Class Structure in Modern Britain, *Clarendon Press, Oxford.*

Gordon, R. J. 2018 Why Has Economic Growth Slowed When Innovation Appears to be Accelerating?, *Nber Working Paper n. 24554.*

Gordon, R. J. & Sayed, H. 2020 Transatlantic Technologies: The Role of ICT on the Evolution of U.S. and European Productivity Growth, *in «International Productivity Monitor», XXXVIII, pp. 50–80.*

Gornick, J. C. & Jäntti, M. (a cura di) 2013 Income Inequality. Economic Disparities and the Middle Class in Affluent Countries, *Stanford University Press, Stanford.*

Gramsci, A. 1975 Quaderni dal carcere, *Einaudi, Torino.*

Grawe, N. D 2004 Intergenerational Mobility for Whom? The Experience of High-and Low-earning Sons in International Perspective, *in Corak 2004.*

Gregg, P. & Kanabar, R. 2022 Intergenerational Wealth Transmission and Mobility in Great Britain: What Components of Wealth Matter?, *Iser Working Paper Series 2022–02, Institute for Social and Economic Research.*

Gregg, P., Macmillan, L., Vittori, C. 2015 Nonlinear Estimation of Lifetime Intergenerational Economic Mobility and the Role of Education, *DoQSS Working Paper n. 3, Quantitative Social Science Ucl Social Research Institute.*

Greif, A. 2006 Institutions and the Path to the Modern Economy: Lessons from Medieval Trade, *Cambridge University Press, Cambridge.*

Greif, A., Milgrom, P., Weingast, B. R. 1994 Coordination, Commitment, and Enforcement: The Case of the Merchant Guild, *in «Journal of Political Economy», CII, 8, pp. 745–76.*

Greenfeld, L. 1992 *Nationalism: Five Roads to Modernity*, Harvard University Press, Cambridge.

Grimalda, G., Farina, F., Conte, A., Schmidt, U. 2022 Why Do Preferences for Redistribution Differ across Countries? An Experimental Analysis, Kiel Working Papers, 2230.

Gurevič, A. J. 1983 Le categorie della cultura medievale, *Einaudi, Torino.*

Guzman, M. 2018 Toward a Just Society: Joseph Stiglitz and 21 Century Economics, *Columbia University Press, New York.*

Gylfason, T. 2016 Efficiency, Fairness, and Social Cohesion in Europe and the United States: Incomes, Hours of Work, and Equality with an Afterthought on Iceland, *Cesifo Working Paper Series n. 6025.*

Hacker, J. S. 2008 The Great Risk Shift: The New Economic Insecurity and the Decline of the American Dream, *in «Oxford University Press», Oxford.*

Hacker, J. S. & Pierson, P. 2010 Winner-Take-All Politics and Political Science, *in «Politics and Society», XXXVIII, 2, pp. 266–82.*

Hahn, F. 1980 *General Equilibrium Theory*, in «The Public Interest», Special Issue, *The Crisis in Economic Theory*, pp. 123–38.

Hanushek, E. A., Machin, S., Wößmann, L. (eds) 2011 Handbook of the Economics of Education, *IV, North Holland, Amsterdam.*

Hanushek, E. A. et al. 2022 The Intergenerational Transmission of Cognitive Skills: An Investigation of the Causal Impact of Families on Student Outcomes, *Working Paper n. 9, University of Konstanz.*

Harsanyi, J. C. 1953 Cardinal Utility in Welfare Economics and in Risk-taking, *in «Journal of Political Economy», LXI, pp. 434–5.*

Harsanyi, J. C. 1955 Cardinal Welfare, Individualistic Ethics and Interpersonal Comparison of Utility, *in «Journal of Political Economy», LXIII, pp. 309–21.*

Hart, C. S. 2016 *How Do Aspirations Matter?*, in «Journal of Human Development and Capabilities», XVII, 3, pp. 324–41.

Hart, O. & Zingales, L. 2017 *Companies Should Maximize Shareholder Welfare Not Market Value*, in «Journal of Law, Finance, and Accounting», II, 2, pp. 247–75.

Harvey, D. 2005 *A Brief History of Neoliberalism*, Oxford University Press, Oxford 2005.

Harvey, D. 2020 Anti-Capitalist Chronicles, *Pluto Press, London.*

Hassler, J., Rodríguez Mora, J. V., Zeira, J. 2007 *Inequality and mobility*, in «Journal of Economic Growth», XII, 3, pp. 235–59.

Hayek, F. A. 1948 *Individualism and Economic Order*, Chicago University Press, Chicago.

Hayek, F. A. 1960 The Constitution of Liberty, Routledge & Kegan Paul, London.

Hayek, F. A. 1973 Law, Legislation and Liberty: A New Statement of the Liberal Principles of Justice and Political Economy, University of Chicago Press, Chicago.

Hayek, F. A. 1989 Law, Legislation and Liberty: A New Statement of the Liberal Principles of Justice and Political Economy, *University of Chicago Press, Chicago 1973.*

Hayek, F. A. 1990a The Sensory Order: An inquiry into the Foundations of Theoretical Psychology, *Routledge and Kegan Paul, London 1952.*

Hayek, F. A. 1990b Individualismo. Quello vero e quello falso, *Rubbettino, Soveria Mannelli.*

Hayek, F. A. 1995 *The Road to Serfdom*, Routledge, London 1944.

Hayek, F. A. 2002 (1968) *Competition as a Discovery Procedure*, in «The Quarterly Journal of Austrian Economics», V, 3, pp. 9–23.

Hayek, F. A. 2011 *The Constitution of Liberty*, Routledge & Kegan Paul, London 1960.

Heckman, J. & Landersø, R. J. 2017 The Scandinavian Fantasy: Sources of Intergenerational Mobility in Denmark and the Us, *in «Scandinavian Journal of Economics», CXIX, 1, pp. 178–230.*

Heckman, J. & Landersø, R. 2022 Lessons for Americans from Denmark about Inequality and Social Mobility, *in «Labour Economics», LXXVII, C.*

Heckman, J. J. & Mosso, S. 2014 The Economics of Human Development and Social Mobility, *in «Annual Review of Economics», VI, 1, pp. 689–733.*

Hegel, G. W. F. 1999 Lineamenti di filosofia del diritto, *Laterza, Bari-Roma.*

Heinrich, J. 2020 The WEIRDest in the World, *Penguin Books, London 2020.*

Herrnstein, R. J. & Murray, C. 1994 The Bell Curve: Intelligence and Class Structure in American Life, *Free Press, New York.*

Herzog, L. 2024 Citizen Knowledge, Markets, Experts, and the Infrastructure of Democracy, *Oxford University Press, Oxford.*

Hills, J., Ditch, J., Glennerster, H. (eds) 1994 Beveridge and Social Security, *Clarendon Press, Oxford.*

Hinrichs, K. 1993 Public Pensions and Demographic Change: Generational Equity in the United States and Germany, *University of Bremen Zes Arbeitpapier n. 16/93.*

Hirschman, 1970 Exit, Voice, and Loyalty: Responses to the Decline of Firms, Organizations, and States, Harvard University Press, Cambridge.

Hirschman, A. O. 1982 Exit, Voice, and Loyalty: Responses to the Decline of Firms, Organizations, and States, *Harvard University Press, Cambridge 1970.*

Hirschman, A. O. and Rotschild, M. 1973 The Changing Tolerance for Income Inequality in the Course of Economic Development, in «Quarterly Journal of Economics», LXXXVII, pp. 544–66.

Hobbes, T. 1976 (1651) *Leviatano*, La Nuova Italia, Firenze.

Hobsbawm, E. 1990 Nations and Nationalism since 1780: Programme, Myth, Reality, *Cambridge Univeristy Press, Cambridge.*

Hobson, J. A. 1902 *Imperialism: A Study*, J. Pott&co, New York.

Hoff, K. & Stiglitz, J. E. 2016 Striving for Balance in Economics: Towards a Theory of the Social Determination of Behavior, *in «Journal of Economic Behavior & Organization», CXXVI, IssuePB, pp. 25–57.*

Hörisch, H. 2007 Is the Veil of Ignorance only a Concept about Risk? An Experiment, *Munich Discussion Paper n. 4.*

Houmark, M. A., Ronda, V., Rosholm, M. 2020 The Nurture of Nature and the Nature of Nurture: How Genes and Investments Interact in the Formation of Skills, *Iza Discussion Paper n. 13780.*

Hout, M. & Diprete, T. A. 2004 What We Have Learned: RC28's Contributions to Knowledge About Social Stratification, *Working paper, University of California, Berkeley.*

Howard, G & Weinstein, R. 2022 «Workhorses of Opportunity»: Regional Universities Increase Local Social Mobility, *Iza Discussion Paper n. 15622.*

Howell, D. R. & Kalleberg, A. L. 2019 *Declining Job Quality in the United States: Explanations and Evidence*, in «The Russell Sage Foundation, Journal of the Social Sciences», V, 4, pp. 1–53.

Hufe, P. & Peichl, A. 2018 Inequality and Unfairness in Europe, *Cesifo Forum, XIX, 2, pp. 26–34.*

Hugo, V. 1981 *I miserabili*, Garzanti, Milano.

Hume, D. 1777 An Enquiry Concerning the Principles of Morals, *A. Millar, London.*

Hume, D. 1971 *A Treatise of Human Nature* [1739–40], in *The Philosophical Works*, II, Scientia Verlag, Alen 1748.

Hume, D. 1985 *Essays. Moral, Political, and Literary*, (ed) E. F. Miller, Liberty Fund, Indianapolis.

Iacono, R. & Palagi, E. 2022 Still the Lands of Equality? Heterogeneity of Income Composition in the Nordics, 1975–2016, *in «The B.E. Journal of Economic Analysis & Policy», XXII, 2, pp. 221–68.*

Immervoll, H. & Richardson, L. 2011 Redistribution Policy and Inequality Reduction in Oecd Countries: What Has Changed in Two Decades?, *Iza Discussion Paper 6030.*

Innocenti, A. & Sbriglia, P. 2008 Games, Rationality and Behaviour: Essays in Behavioural Game Theory and Experiments, *Palgrave Macmillan, Houndmills, Basingstoke.*

International Monetary Fund 2016 World Economic Outlook: Too Slow for Too Long, *aprile, Washington DC.*

Isaacs, J. B. 2016 International Comparisons of Economic Mobility, *Brookings Institution, Washington DC.*

Istat 2018 Rapporto annuale 2017. La situazione del Paese, *Istat, Roma.*

Jacobs, M. & Mazzucato, M. (eds) 2017 Rethinking Capitalism, Economics and Policy for a Sustainable and Inclusive Growth, *Wiley-Blackwell, London 2016.*

Jaimovich, N. & Siu, H. E. 2020 *Job Polarization and Jobless Recoveries*, in «Review of Economics and Statistics», CII, 1, pp. 129–47.

Janeway, W. H. 2023 The Political Economy of Technology, *«Project Syndicate», 25 August.*

Jäntti, M. & Jenkins, S. P. 2015 *Income Mobility*, in A. B. Atkinson & F. Bourguignon (eds), *Handbook of Income Distribution*, IIA-IIB, North-Holland, Amsterdam.

Jäntti, M. et al. 2007 American Exceptionalism in a New Light: A Comparison of Intergenerational Earnings Mobility in the Nordic Countries, the United Kingdom and the United States, *Warwick Economics Research Paper Series n. 781.*

Jencks, C. & Tach, L. 2006 Would Equal Opportunity Mean More Equality?, *in Morgan, Grusky, Fields 2006.*

Jenkins, S. P. 2011 Changing Fortunes: Income Mobility and Poverty Dynamics in Britain, *Oxford University Press, Oxford.*

Jenkins, S. P. & Van Kerm, P. 2006 Trends in Income Inequality, Pro-poor Income Growth, and Income Mobility, *Oxford Economic Papers, LVIII, 3, pp. 531–48.*

Jensen, M. C. & Meckling, W. H. 1976 Teoria dello studio. Comportamento manageriale, agenzia Costi e struttura della proprietà, *in «Journal of Financial Economics», III, 4, pp. 305–60.*

Judt, T. 2007 *Postwar. A History of Europe since 1945*, Vintage, London 2005.

Karabarbounis, L. 2023 Perspectives on the Labor Share, *Nber Working Paper n. 31854.*

Karlson, K. B. & Landersø, R. 2021 The Making and Unmaking of Opportunity: Educational Mobility in 20th Century-Denmark, *Iza Discussion Paper n. 14135.*

Katz, L. F. & Krueger, A. B. 2018 The Rise and Nature of Alternative Work Arrangements in the United States, 1995–2015, *in «Ilr Review», LXXII, 2, pp. 382–416.*

Kelly, C. & Snower, D. J. 2021 *Capitalism Recoupled*, in «Oxford Review of Economic Policy», XXXVII, 4, pp. 851–63.

Kelsen, H. 1967 Reine Rechtslehre. Einleitung in die rechtswissenschaftliche Problematik, *Wien 1934.*

Kenworthy, L. & Smeeding, T. 2013 *Growing Inequalities and Their Impacts in the United States*, Gini Country Report, Aias (Amsterdam Institute for Advanced Labour Studies).

Keynes, J. M. 1968a A Short View of Russia, *in* Essays in Persuasion, *Macmillan, London 1931.*

Keynes, J. M. 1968b *Essays on Persuasion*, Macmillan, London 1931.

Keynes, J. M. 2001 *National Self-Sufficiency*, in «The Yale Review», XXII, 1933, 4, pp. 755–69.

Keynes, J. M. 2010 (1925) *Sono un liberale?*, Adelphi, Milano.

Kosut, M. 2006 Professorial Capital: Blue-Collar Reflections on Class, Culture, and the Academy, *in «Cultural Studies <=> Critical Methodologies», VI.*

Kpmg - Bridge Group 2022 Social Mobility Progression Report 2022: Mind the gap, *diecember.*

Kuhn, P. & Lozano, F. 2006 Understanding Trends in Long Work Hours Among U.S. Men, 1979–2002, *in «Journal of Labor Economics», XXVI, 2, pp. 311–43.*

Kurz, M. 2023 The Market Power of Technology: Understanding the Second Gilded Age, *Columbia University Press, New York.*

Kuziemko, I., J Shen, Pan, J., Washington, E. 2018 The Mommy Effect: Do Women Anticipate the Employment Effects of Motherhood?, *Nber Working Paper n. 24740.*

Kweon, H. et al. 2022 Human Brain Anatomy Reflects Separable Genetic and Environmental Components of Socioeconomic Status, *in «Science Advances», VIII, 18 maggio.*

Lalueza-Fox, C. 2022 Inequality: A Genetic History, *Mit Press, Cambridge.*

Landes, D. S. 2003 The Wealth and Poverty of Nations: Why Some Are So Rich and Some So Poor, *W. W. Norton & Company, New York 1999.*

Lee, D., Doerr, S., Drechsel, T. 2022 *Income Inequality and Job Creation*, Federal Reserve Bank of New York Staff Reports, n. 1021.

Lefranc, A., Pistolesi, N., Trannoy, A. 2009 Equality of Opportunity and Luck: Definitions and Testable Conditions, with an Application to Income in France, *in «Journal of Public Economics», XCIII, 11–12, pp. 1189–207.*

Lerner, A. 1972 The Economics and Politics of Consumer Sovereignty, *in «American Economic Review», LXII, 2, pp. 258–66.*

Lerner, M. J. 1980 The Belief in a Just World: A Fundamental Delusion, *Plenum Press, New York.*

Locke, J. 1968 (1693) Some Thoughts Concerning Education, *in J. L. Axtell (a cura di),* The Educational Writings of John Locke, *Cambridge University Press, Cambridge.*

Loury, G. C. 1981 Intergenerational Transfers and the Distribution of Earnings, *in «Econometrica», XLIX, 4, pp. 843–67.*

Loury, G. C. 2002 *The Anatomy of Racial Inequality*, Harvard University Press, Cambridge.

Luhmann, N. 1973 Theorie der Gesellschaft oder Sozialtechnologie, *1971.*

Lukes, S. 1974 Power: A Radical View, *Macmillan, London.*

Macfarlane, A. 1978 The Origins of English Individualism: The Family Property and Social Transition, *Basil Blackwell, Oxford.*

Machin, L. E. & Machin, S. 2018 Social Mobility: And Its Enemies, *Pelikan Books, London.*

Mackenbach, J. P. et al. 1997 Socioeconomic Inequalities in Morbidity and Mortality in Western Europe. The Eu Working Group on Socioeconomic Inequalities in Health, *in «Lancet», n. 349 (9066), pp. 1655–9.*

MacLeod, W. B. & Urquiola, M. 2012 Anti-Lemons: School Reputation, Relative Diversity, and Educational Quality, *Iza Discussion Paper 6805.*

MacLeod, W. B. & Urquiola, M. 2021 Why Does the Us Have the Best Research Universities? Incentives, Resources, and Virtuous Circles, *in «Journal of Economic Perspectives», XXXV, 1, pp. 185–206.*

Macpherson, C. B. 1990 The Rise and Fall of Economic Justice and Other Essays, *Oxford University Press, Oxford 1985.*

Maddison, A. 2001 The World Economy: A Millennial Perspective, *Oecd Development Centre, Paris.*

Major, E. L. & Machin, S. 2019 *Social Mobility*, Centre for Economic Performance, London School of Economics.

Mankiw, N. G. 2018 *Principles of Economics*, Cengage Learning, Boston.

Mannheim, K. 1928 *Das Problem der Generationen*, in «Kölner Vierteljahreshefte für Soziologie», 7.

Mannheim, K. 1974 Essays on the Sociology of Knowledge, *Routledge, London 1952.*

Mannheim, K. 1999 *Ideologie Und Utopie*, Verlag Vittorio Klosterman, Berlin 1929.

Marcuse, H. 1967 One-Dimensional Man: Studies in the Ideology of Advanced Industrial Society, *Beacon Press, Boston 1964.*

Marginson, S. 2016 Global Stratification in Higher Education, *in S. Slaughter* & *B. Taylor (ed),* Higher Education, Stratification and Workforce Development: Competitive Advantage in Europe, the Us and Canada, *Springer International Publishing, Switzerland.*

Markovits, D. 2019 The Meritocracy Trap: How America's Foundational Myth Feeds Inequality, Dismantles the Middle Class, and Devours the Elite, *Penguin Press, New York.*

Maroun, J. & Tienken, C. H. 2024 The Pernicious Predictability of State-Mandated Tests of Academic Achievement in the United States, *in «Education Sciences», XIV, 2, pp. 1–29.*

Marrero, G. A. & Rodríguez, J. G. 2013 *Inequality of Opportunity and Growth*, in «Journal of Development Economics», CIV, C, pp. 107–22.

Marrero, G. A., Palomino, G. C., Sicilia, G. 2022 Inequality of Opportunity in Educational Achievement in Western Europe: Contributors and Channels, *Ecineq Working Paper Series n. 612.*

Marshall, T. H. 1950 Citizenship and Social Class, and Other Essays, *Cambridge University Press, Cambridge.*

Marx, K. (1943), Zur Kritik der Hegelschen Rechtsphilosophie.

Marx, K. 1968a *Il capitale*, I e III, Editori Riuniti, Roma (ed. or. 1867).

Marx, K. 1968b Ökonomisch-philosophische Manuskripte aus dem Jahre 1844, *1932.*

Marx, K. 1968–1970 Grundrisse der Kritik der politischen Ökonomie, *1857–58.*

Marx, K. 1969 Il Capitale. Libro I, capitolo VI inedito, *La Nuova Italia, Firenze.*

Marx, K. 1971 Das Elend der Philosophie. Antwort auf Proudhons "Philosophie des Elends", *Druck und Verlag voon J. H. W. Dietz, Stuttgart 1847.*

Marx, K. 1983 Zur Kritik der Hegelschen Rechtsphilosophie, *1843.*

Marx, K. & Engels, F. 1972 *Opere*, V, *1845–1846*, Editori Riuniti, Roma.

Marzadro, S. & Schizzerotto, A. 2011 Le prospettive di mobilità sociale dei giovani italiani nel corso del XX secolo, *in Schizzerotto, Trivellato, Sartor 2011.*

McCloskey, D. 2019 Why Liberalism Works: How True Liberal Values Produce a Freer, More Equal, Prosperous World for All, *Yale University Press, Yale.*

Meltzer, A. H. & Richard, S. F. 1981 *A Rational Theory of the Size of Government*, in «Journal of Political Economy», LXXXIX, 5, pp. 914–92.

Michaels, G., Natrai, A., Van Reenen, J. 2014 Has Ict Polarized Skill Demand? Evidence from Eleven Countries over 25 Years, *in «Review of Economics and Statistics», XCVI, 1, pp. 60–77.*

Mijs, J. J. B. 2019 The Paradox of Inequality: Income Inequality and Belief in Meritocracy Go Hand in Hand, *in «Socio-Economic Review», XXXIX, pp. 1–39.*

Milanović, B. 2015 Global Inequality of Opportunity: How Much of Our Income Is Determined by Where We Live?, in «Review of Economics and Statistics», XCVII, 2, pp. 452–60.

Milanović, B. 2016 Global Inequality: A New Approach for the Age of Globalization, *Harvard University Press, Cambridge 2016.*

Milanović, B. 2017 Global Inequality: A New Approach for the Age of Globalization, *Harvard University Press, Cambridge 2016.*

Milanović, B. 2019 Capitalism, Alone: The Future of the System That Rules the World, *Harvard University Press, Cambridge.*

Milanović, B. 2020 Capitalism, Alone: The Future of the System That Rules the World, *Harvard University Press, Cambridge 2019.*

Milanović, B. 2023 Visions of Inequality: From the French Revolution to the End of the Cold War, *Harvard University Press, Cambridge.*

Milanović, B. 2024 The Three Eras of Global Inequality, 1820–2020 with the Focus on the Past Thirty Years, *in «World Development», CLXXVII.*

Mill, J. S. 1981 *Utilitarianism*, Oxford University Press, Oxford 1861.

Mill J. S. 1991 *On Liberty*, Walter Scott Publishing Co., London 1859.

Miller, D. 1995 *On Nationality*, Oxford University Press, Oxford.

Mocetti, S. 2007 *Intergenerational Earnings Mobility in Italy*, in «The B.E. Journal of Economic Analysis & Policy», VII, 2.

Moffitt, R. A. (a cura di) 2016 Economics of Means-Tested Transfer Programs in the United States, *II, University of Chicago Press, Chicago.*

Moretti, F. 1999 The Way of the World: The Bildungsroman in European Culture, *Verso, London 1987.*

Morgan, S. L. 2006 Past Themes and Future Prospects for Research on Social and Economic Mobility, *in Morgan et al. 2006.*

Morgan, S. L., Grusky, D. B., Fields, G. S. (eds) 2006 Mobility and Inequality: Frontiers of Research in Sociology and Economics, *Stanford University Press, Stanford.*

Morin, E. 2017 La sfida della complessità, *Le Lettere, Firenze.*

Mosca, G. 1896 Elementi di scienza politica, *Fratelli Bocca, Torino.*

Munshi, K. & Rosenzweig, M. 2006 Traditional Institutions Meet the Modern World: Caste, Gender, and Schooling Choice in a Globalizing Economy, *in «American Economic Review», XCIV, 4, pp. 1225–52.*

Musgrave, R. A. 1959 The Theory of Public Finance, *McGraw Hill, New York.*

Naidu, S. & Posner, E. A. 2022 *Labor Monopsony and the Limits of the Law*, in «Journal of Human Resources», LVII, S, S284–323.

Narayan, A. et al. 2018 Fair Progress? Economic Mobility across Generations around the World, *World Bank, Washington DC.*

Nber 2003 The Economics of School Choice, *Cambridge (Mass.).*

Nedergaard, P. 2013 The Influence of Ordoliberalism in European Integration Processes: A Framework for Ideational Influence with Competition Policy and the Economic and Monetary Policy as Examples, *Mpra Paper n. 52331.*

Newbery, D. M. & Stiglitz, J. E. 1984 *Pareto Inferior Trade*, in «Review of Economic Studies», LI, 1, pp. 1–12.

Nolan, B., Palomino, G. C., Van Kerm, P., Morelli, S. 2022 The Wealth of Families: The Intergenerational Transmission of Wealth in Britain in Comparative Perspective, *in «Economic Letters», XLIII, 2, pp. 179–99.*

Oecd 2008a Growing Unequal? Income Distribution and Poverty in Oecd Countries, *Paris.*

Oecd 2008b Education at a Glance 2008, *Paris.*

Oecd 2011 Divided We Stand: Why Inequality Keeps Rising, *Paris.*

Oecd 2012 Education at a Glance 2012, *Paris.*

Oecd 2017a Strategia per le competenze dell'Ocse. Italia. Sintesi del Rapporto, *Paris.*

Oecd 2017b How Technology and Globalisation Are Transforming the Labour Market, *in Oecd,* Employment Outlook 2017.

Oecd 2018a A Broken Social Elevator? How to Promote Social Mobility, *Paris.*

Oecd 2018b The Future of Social Protection. What Works for Non-standard Workers?, *Paris.*

Oecd 2018c Good Jobs for All in a Changing World of Work: The Oecd Jobs Strategy, *Oecd Publishing, Paris.*

Oecd 2019a Pisa 2018, *VI,* Are Students Ready to Thrive in an Interconnected World?, *Paris.*

Oecd 2019b Under Pressure: The Squeezed Middle Class, *Paris.*

Oecd 2019c Employment Outlook 2019: The Future of Work, *Paris.*

Oecd 2020 Beyond Growth. Towards a New Economic Approach, *Paris.*

Oecd 2021 Better Life Index, *Paris.*

Oecd 2022 Education at a Glance, *Paris.*

Oecd 2023a Education at a Glance, *Paris.*

Oecd 2023b Employment Outlook 2023: Artificial Intelligence and the Labour Market, *Paris.*

Ogeda, P., Ornelas, E., Soares, R. 2024 *Labor Unions and the Electoral Consequences of Trade Liberalization*, in «Journal of the European Economic Association», in press.

Oreopoulos, P. 2003 The Long Run Consequences of Growing up in a Poor Neighbourhood, *in «Quarterly Journal of Economics», CXVIII, 4, pp. 1533–75.*

Oreopoulos, P. 2007 Do Dropouts Drop Out Too Soon? Wealth, Health and Happiness from Compulsory Schooling, *in «Journal of Public Economics», XCI, 11–12, pp. 2213–29.*

Orwell, G. 1941 The Lion and the Unicorn, Secker & Warburg, London.

Orwell, G. 1944 A Review of The Road to Serfdom by F. A. Hayek, *in «The Observer», 9 aprile.*

Orwell, G. 1960 *The Road to Wigan Pier*, Harcourt Brace, London 1937.

Orwell, G. 2007 *The Lion and the Unicorn*, Secker & Warburg, London 1941.

Occorsio, E. & Scarpetta, S. 2022 Un mondo diviso. Come l'Occidente ha perso crescita e coesione sociale, *Laterza, Roma-Bari.*

Ostry, J. D., Berg, A., Tsangarides, G. D. 2014 Redistribution, Inequality, and Growth, *Imf Staff Discussion Note n. 2.*

Ostry, J. D., Loungani, P., Furceri, D. 2016 *Neoliberalism: Oversold?*, in «Finance and Development», pp. 38–41.

Oxfam 2021 Inequality Report.

Oxfam 2022 Annual Report 2021–22: The Future is Equal, *Oxfam Italia.*

Oxfam 2023 Report 2023: Diseguaglianza. Il potere al servizio di pochi, *Oxfam Italia.*

Palomino, J. C., Marrero, G. A., Rodríguez, J. G. 2018 One Size Doesn't Fit All: A Quantile Analysis of Intergenerational Income Mobility in the U.S. (1980–2010), *in «Journal of Economic Inequality», XVI, 3, pp. 347–67.*

Palomino, J. C., Marrero, G. A., Rodríguez, J. G. 2019 *Channels of Inequality of Opportunity: The Role of Education and Occupation in Europe*, in «Social Indicators Research: An International and Interdisciplinary Journal for Quality-of-Life Measurement», CXLIII, 3, pp. 1045–74.

Palomino, J. C., Marrero, G. A., Nolan, B., Rodríguez, J. G. 2022 Wealth Inequality, Intergenerational Transfers, and Family Background, *in «Oxford Economic Papers», LXXIV, 3, pp. 643–70.*

Pande, R. 2023 The Climate Crisis Is a Crisis of Inequality, *in «Science», CCCLXXXI, 6661.*

Pareto, V. 1919 *Manuale di economia politica*, Società Editrice Libraria, Milano.

Pareto, V. 1964 *Trattato di sociologia generale*, Edizioni di Comunità, Milano (ed. or. Barbera, Firenze 1916).

Parfit, D. 2000 *Equality or Priority?*, in M. Clayton & A. Williams (ed), *The Ideal of Equality*, Palgrave Macmillan, Basingstoke.

Parolin, Z. 2019 The Effect of Benefit Underreporting on Estimates of Poverty in the United States, *in «Social Indicators Research», CXLIV, pp. 869–98.*

Parsons, T. 1962 Structure of Social Action, *McGraw-Hill, New York 1937.*

Parsons, T. 1965 *The Social System*, Free Press, Glencoe 1951.

Paus, E. (a cura di) 2013 *Getting Development Right*, Palgrave Macmillan, New York.

Peugny, C. 2019 The Decline in Middle-skilled Employment in 12 European Countries: New Evidence for Job Polarization, *in «Research and Politics», 6, pp. 1–7.*

Philippon, T. 2019 The Great Reversal: How America Gave Up on Free Markets, *Harvard University Press, Cambridge.*

Pickett, K. E. & Wilkinson, R. G. 2015 The Ethical and Policy Implications of Research on Income Inequality and Child Well-Being, *in «Pediatrics», CXXXV, Suppl. 2, pp. 839–47.*

Piketty, T. 1995 *Social Mobility and Redistributive Politics*, in «Quarterly Journal of Economics», CX, 3, pp. 551–84.

Piketty, T. 2014 *Le capital au XXIe siècle*, Éditions du Seuil, Paris 2013.

Piketty, T. 2015 Putting Distribution Back at the Center of Economics: Reflections on Capital in the Twenty-First Century, *in «Journal of Economic Perspectives», XXIX, 1, pp. 67–88.*

Piketty, T. 2018 Brahmin Left vs Merchant Right: Rising Inequality & the Changing Structure of Political Conflict: Evidence from France, Britain and the Us, 1948–2017, *Wid.world Working Paper Series n. 7.*

Piketty, T. 2020 *Capital et idéologie*, Éditions du Seuil, Paris 2019.

Piketty, T. 2021 Une brève histoire de l'égalité, *Seuil, Paris 2021.*

Piketty, T., Saez, E., Zucman, G. 2018 Distributional National Accounts: Methods and Estimates for the United States, *in «Quarterly Journal of Economics», CXXXIII, 2, pp. 553–609.*

Pistor, K. 2021 The Code of Capital: How the Law Creates Wealth and Inequality, *Princeton University Press, Princeton 2019.*

Polanyi, K. 1974 The Great Transformation, *Farrar & Rinehart, New York 1944.*

Popper, K. 1970 The Open Society and Its Enemies, *Routledge, London 1945.*

Power, S. & Whitty, G. 2002 *Bernstein and the Middle Class*, «British Journal of Sociology of Education», XXIII, 4, pp. 595–606.

Prescott, E. C. 2004 Why Do Americans Work so Much More than Europeans, *in «Quarterly Review», XXVIII, pp. 2–13.*

Przeworski, A. 1980 Social Democracy as a Historical Phenomenon, *in «New Left Review», CXXII, pp. 27–58.*

Przeworski, A. 2009 *Self-Government in Our Times*, in «Annual Review of Political Science», XII, pp. 71–92.

Przeworski, A. 2016 *Democracy: A Never-Ending Quest*, in «Annual Review of Political Science», XIX, pp. 1–12.

Przeworski, A. 2019 *Crisis of Democracy*, Cambridge University Press, Cambridge.

Przeworski, A. & Wallerstein, M. 1982 The Structure of Class Conflict in Democratic Capitalist Societies, *in «American Political Science Review», LXXVI, 2, pp. 215–38.*

Putnam, R. D. 1993 Making Democracy Work: Civic Traditions in Modern Italy, *Princeton University Press, Princeton.*

Raitano, M. & Vona, F. 2016 Assessing Students' Equality of Opportunity in Oecd Countries: The Role of National- and School-Level Policies, *in «Applied Economics», XLVIII, 33, pp. 3148–63.*

Ravallion, M. 2019 Global Inequality When Unequal Countries Create Unequal People, *in «European Economic Review», CXI, C, pp. 85–97.*

Rawls, J. 1982 *A Theory of Justice*, The Belknap Press of Harvard University Press, Cambridge 1971).

Rawls, J. 1985 *Justice as Fairness: Political not Metaphysical*, in «Philosophy & Public Affairs», XIV, 3, pp. 223–51.

Ray, D. 2006 *Aspirations, Poverty and Economic Change*, in A. Banerjee, R. Benabou, D. Mookherjee (eds), *Understanding Poverty*, Oxford University Press, New York.

Reay, D. 2017 Miseducation. Inequality, education, and working classes, *Policy Press, Bristol.*

Renahy, E. et al. 2018 Connections between Unemployment Insurance, Poverty and Health: A Systematic Review, *in «European Journal of Public Health», XXVIII, 2, pp. 269–75.*

Reuter-Lorenz, P. A., Baynes, K., Mangun, G. R., Phelps, E. A. (eds) 2010 The Cognitive Neuroscience of Mind: A Tribute to Michael S. Gazzaniga, *Mit Press, Cambridge.*

Richerson, P. J. & Boyd, R. 2005 Not by Genes Alone: How Culture Transformed Human Evolution, *University of Chicago Press, Chicago.*

Roberts, K. W. S. 1977 *Voting over Income Tax Schedules*, in «Journal of Public Economics», VIII, 3, pp. 329–40.

Robeyns, I. 2011 *The Capability Approach*, Stanford Encyclopedia of Philosophy, Stanford.

Robeyns, I. 2023 Limitarianism: The Case against Extreme Wealth, *Astra House, London.*

Rodrik, D. & Sabel, C. 2019 *Building a Good Jobs Economy*, Working Paper, Harvard University.

Rodrik, D. & Stantcheva, S. 2021a *Fixing Capitalism's Good Jobs Problem*, in «Oxford Review of Economic Policy», XXXVII, 4, pp. 824–37.

Rodrik, D. & Stantcheva, S. 2021b Economic Inequality and Insecurity: Policies for an Inclusive Economy, *in Blanchard - Tirole 2021.*

Roemer, J. E. 1996 *Theories of Distributive Justice*, Harvard University Press, Cambridge.

Roemer, J. E. 1998 *Equality of Opportunity*, Harvard University Press, Cambridge.

Roemer, J. E. 2008 Equality of Opportunity, *in S. N. Durlauf & L. E. Blume (eds),* The New Palgrave Dictionary of Economics, *Basingstoke.*

Roemer, J. E. & Trannoy, A. 2016 *Equality of Opportunity: Theory and Measurement*, in «Journal of Economic Literature», LIV, 4, pp. 1288–332.

Roemer, J. E. et al. 2003 To What Extent Do Fiscal Regimes Equalize Opportunities for Income Acquisition among Citizens?, *in «Journal of Public Economics», LXXXVII, pp. 539–65.*

Rohde, N. et al. 2020 Welfare-Based Income Insecurity in the US and Germany: Evidence from Harmonized Panel Data, *in «Journal of Economic Behavior and Organization», CLXXVI, pp. 226–43.*

Romer, T. 1975 Individual Welfare, Majority Voting and the Properties of a Linear Income Tax, *in «Journal of Public Economics», VII, pp. 163–88.*

Roncaglia, A. 2023a Il potere. Una prospettiva riformista, *Laterza, Roma-Bari.*

Roncaglia, G. 2023b L'architetto e l'oracolo. Forme digitali del sapere da Wikipedia a ChatGpt, *Laterza, Roma-Bari.*

Rosenblatt, H. 2018 The Lost History of Liberalism, from Ancient Rome to the Twenty-First Century, *Princeton University Press, Princeton.*

Rothschild, M. & Stiglitz, J. E. 1976 Equilibrium in Competitive Insurance Markets: An Essay on the Economics of Imperfect Information, *in «Quarterly Journal of Economics», XC, 4, pp. 629–49.*

Rousseau, J.-J. 1969 (1762) Il contratto sociale, *Einaudi, Torino.*

Roy, R. K. & Denzau, A. T. 2020 Shared Mental Models: Insights and Perspectives on Ideologies and Institutions, *in «Kyklos», LXXIII, 3, pp. 323–40.*

Ruhs, M. 2013 The Price of Rights: Regulating International Labor Migration, *Princeton University Press, Princeton.*

Runciman, W. G. 1966 Relative Deprivation and Social Justice, *Routledge and Kegan Paul, London.*

Rustagi, D. 2022 *Historical Self Governance and Norms of Cooperation*, Working Paper, University of Nottingham, Nottingham.

Saez, E. & Zucman, G. 2019 The Triumph of Injustice: How the Rich Dodge Taxes and How to Make them Pay, *W.W. Norton, New York.*

Salverda, W., Nolan, B., Smeeding, T. (eds) 2009 *Handbook of Economic Inequality*, Oxford University Press, Oxford.

Sant'Anna, A. A. 2015 A Spectre Has Haunted the West: Did Socialism Discipline Income Inequality?, *Mpra Paper n. 64756, University of Munich.*

Samuelson, P. A. 1947 *Foundations of Economic Analysis*, Harvard University Press, Cambridge.

Sandel, M. J. 2020 The Tyranny of Merit. What's Become of the Common Good?, *Penguin Books, London.*

Santambrogio, M. 2021 Il complotto contro il merito, *Laterza, Roma-Bari.*

Scheve, K. & Stasavage, D. 2016 Taxing the Rich: A History of Fiscal Fairness in the United States and Europe, *Princeton University Press, Princeton.*

Schizzerotto, A., Trivellato, U., Sartor, U. (eds) 2011 Generazioni disuguali Le condizioni di vita dei giovani di oggi e di ieri: un confronto, *il Mulino, Bologna.*

Schuetz, G., Ursprung, H., Woessmann, L. 2008 Education Policy and Equality of Opportunity, *in «Kyklos», LXI, pp. 279–308.*

Schumpeter, J. (1912). The theory of economic development, Harvard University Press, Cambridge MA.

Schumpeter J. A. 1942, Socialism, and Democracy, Harper & Bros, New York 1942.

Schumpeter, J. A. 1977 Theorie der wirtschaftlichen Entwicklung, *Duncker & Humblot, Berlin 1912.*

Schumpeter, J. A. 2002 *Socialism, and Democracy*, Harper & Bros, New York 1942.

Scotellaro, R. 1951 Le riviste di cultura e il nostro tempo, *in «Il Nuovo Corriere», 26 agosto.*

Scott, P., Gallacher, J., Parry, G. (eds) 2016 New Languages and Landscapes of Higher Education, *Oxford University Press, Oxford.*

Sen, A. K. 1983 *The Profit Motive*, in «Lloyds Bank Review», pp. 1–20.

Sen, A. K. 1985a *Goals, Commitment, and Identity*, in «Journal of Law, Economics, and Organization», I, 2, pp. 341–63.

Sen, A. K. 1985b Commodities and Capabilities, *North-Holland, Amsterdam.*

Sen, A. K. 1990 La libertà individuale come impegno sociale, *in Berlin - Sen 1990.*

Sen, A. K. 1992 *Inequality Reexamined*, Clarendon Press, Oxford.

Sen, A. K. 1993 Markets and Freedoms: Achievements and Limitations of the Market Mechanism in Promoting Individual Freedoms, *in «Oxford Economic Papers», XLV, 4, pp. 519–41.*

Sen, A. K. 1997 *On Economic Inequality*, ed. accresciuta con un testo integrativo di J. E. Foster e A. K. Sen, Clarendon Press, Oxford.

Sen, A. K. 2000 *Merit and Justice*, in Arrow, Bowles, Durlauf.

Sen, A. K. 2001 *Development as Freedom*, Oxford University Press, Oxford 1999.

Sen, A. K. 2004 *Elements of a Theory of Human Rights*, in «Philosophy & Public Affairs», XXXII, 4, pp. 315–429.

Sen, A. K. 2005 *Rationality and Freedom*, Harvard University Press, Cambridge 2002.

Sen, A. K. 2009 *The Idea of Justice*, Allen Lane-Harvard University Press, Cambridge.

Sennett, R. 2003 Respect. The Formation of Character in a World of Inequality, Allen Lane, London.

Shorrocks, A. F. 1978 *Income Inequality and Income Mobility*, in «Journal of Economic Theory», XIX, pp. 376–93.

Siedentop, L. 2016 Inventing the Individual: The Origins of Western Liberalism, *Allen Lane, London 2014.*

Simmel, G. 1982 *Über sociale Differenzierung*, Duncker & Humblot, Leipzig 1890.

Simmel, G. 2019 *Zur Psychologie des Geldes*, Verlag von Dunker & Humblet, Leipzig 1900.

Sinn, H.-W. 1995 *A Theory of the Welfare State*, in «Scandinavian Journal of Economics», XCVII, 4, pp. 495–526.

Sinn, H.-W. 1996 *Social Insurance, Incentives, and Risk Taking*, in «International Tax and Public Finance», III, 3, pp. 259–80.

Sinn, H.-W. 2003 Can Germany Be Saved? The Malaise of the World's First Welfare State, *Mit Press, Cambridge.*

Smallenbroek, O., Hertel, F., Barone, C. 2022 Measuring Class Hierarchies in Postindustrial Societies: A Criterion and Construct Validation of Egp and Esec Across 31 Countries, *in «Sociological Methods & Research», LI, pp. 1–41.*

Smeeding, T., Jäntti, M., Erickson, R. (eds) 2011 Persistence, Privilege and Parenting: The Comparative Study of Intergenerational Mobility, *Russell Sage Foundation, New York.*

Smith, A. 1973 An Inquiry into the Nature and Causes of the Wealth of Nations, *Methuen, London 1776.*

Smith, A. 1776 An Inquiry into the Nature and Causes of the Wealth of Nations, Methuen, London.

Smith, A. 1991 *Theory of Moral Sentiments*, a cura di A. Millar, A. Kincaid, J. Bell, Strand, Edinburgh 1759.

Smith, V. L. 2008 Rationality in Economics. Constructivist and Ecological Forms, *Cambridge University Press, Cambridge.*

Snower, D. J. & Bosworth, S. J. 2016 *Identity-Driven Cooperation versus Competition*, in «American Economic Review», CVI, 5, pp. 420–4.

Snower, D. J. & Bosworth, S. J. 2021 Economic, Social and Political Fragmentation: Linking Knowledge-biased Growth, Identity, Populism and Protectionism, *in «European Journal of Political Economy», LXVII.*

Snower, D. J. & Wilson, D. S. 2022 Rethinking the Theoretical Foundation of Economics I: The Multilevel Paradigm, *in «Econjournal», 30.*

Soares, S. S. D. 2012 *Bolsa Famìlia, Its Design, Its Impacts and Possibilities for the Future*, International Policy Centre for Inclusive Growth, Working Paper n. 89.

Social Commission Mobility 2020 Research Report. Technical Annex: Quantitative Analysis of Downward Mobility, *London.*

Sologon, D. M. & O'Donoghue, C. 2014 Shaping Earnings Insecurity: Labour Market Policy and Institutional Factors, *in «Review of Income and Wealth», LX, pp. S205–S232.*

Solon, G. 2002 Cross-Country Differences in Intergenerational Earnings Mobility, *in «Journal of Economic Perspectives», XVI, 3, pp. 59–66.*

Solon, G. 2004 A Model of Intergenerational Mobility Variation over Time and Place, *in M. Corak (ed),* Generational Income Mobility in North America and Europe, *Cambridge University Press, Cambridge.*

Solon, G. 2013 Theoretical Models of Inequality Transmission across Multiple Generations, *Nber Working Paper n. 18790.*

Sombart, W. 1916 Der moderne Kapitalismus, Duncker & Humblot, München-Leipzig.

Sombart, W. 1967 *Der moderne Kapitalismus*, Duncker & Humblot, München-Leipzig 1916.

Song, L. 2022 Examining the Relationship Between Intergenerational Upward Mobility and Inequality: Evidence from Panel Data, *in «Social Indicators Research», XVI, 1, pp. 1–27.*

Song, X., Massey, C. G., Rolf, K. A., Xie, Y. 2020 Long-term Decline in Intergenerational Mobility in the United States since the 1850s, *Proceedings of the National Academy of Science Usa, CXVII, pp. 251–8.*

Sorokin, P. 1965 *Social Mobility*, Harper & Brothers, New York 1927.

Soysal, Y. & Strange, D. 1989 Construction of the First Massive Education Systems in 19th Century Europe, *in «Sociology of Education», LXII, 4, pp. 277–88.*

Spence, M. 1973 *Job Market Signalling*, in «Quarterly Journal of Economics», LXXXVII, 3, pp. 355–74.

Stern, N. & Stiglitz, J. E. 2023 *Climate Change and Growth*, in «Industrial and Corporate Change», XXXII, pp. 277–303.

Stiglitz, J. E. 1975 The Theory of «Screening» Education, and the Distribution of Income, *in «American Economic Review», LXV, 3, pp. 283–300.*

Stiglitz, J. E. 2013 Selected Works of Joseph E. Stiglitz, *II*, Information and Capital Markets, *Oxford University Press, Oxford.*

Stiglitz, J. E. 2017 *The Coming Great Transformation*, in «Journal of Policy Modeling», XXXIX, 4, pp. 1–14.

Stiglitz, J. E. 2019 The End of Neoliberalism and the Rebirth of History, *Project Syndacate, 4 novembre.*

Stiglitz, J. E. 2020 People, Power, and Profits: Progressive Capitalism for an Age of Discontent, *Norton & Company, New York 2019.*

Stiglitz, J. E., Fitoussi, J.-P., Durand, M. (a cura di) 2019 Measuring What Counts: The Global Movement for Well-Being, *The New Press, New York.*

Stiglitz, J. E., Sen, A. K., Fitoussi, J. P. 2009 Gdp Beyond Gdp: What is Actually There?, *New Press, New York.*

Summers, L. H. 2015 *Demand Side Secular Stagnation*, in «American Economic Review: Papers & Proceedings», CV, 5, pp. 60–5.

Swedberg, R. 1994 *Economics and Sociology*, Princeton University Press, Princeton 1990).

Tanzini, L. & Tognetti, S. (eds) 2016 La mobilità sociale nel Medioevo italiano, *I*, Competenze, conoscenze e saperi tra professioni e ruoli sociali (secc. XII–XV), *Viella, Roma.*

Tawney, R. H. 1952 (1931) *Equality*, Halley Stewart Lectures, G. Allen & Unwin, London.

Tertilt, M., Doepke, M., Hannusch, A., Montenbruck, L. 2022 *The Economics of Woman's Rights The Mary Paley and Alfred Marshall Lecture*, Discussion Paper Series N. 372, University of Bonn-University of Mannheim.

Tester, K. 2005 Il pensiero di Zygmunt Bauman, *Erickson, Trento.*

Therborn, G. 2013 The Killing Fields of Inequality, *Polity Press, Cambridge.*

Thiel, P. 2014 *Competition Is for Losers*, in «Wall Street Journal», C1, 13 settembre.

Tilly, C. 1992 Conflitto sociale, *in* Enciclopedia delle scienze sociali, *Treccani, Roma,* ad vocem.

Tocqueville, A. 1995 (1835–1840) La democrazia in America, *Rizzoli, Milano.*

Todd, S. 2015 The People: The Rise and Fall of the Working Class, 1910–2010, *John Murray, London.*

Tomasello, M. 2005 Understanding and Sharing Intentions: The Origins of Cultural Cognition, *Cambridge University Press, Cambridge 2005.*

Tomasello, M. 2016 *A Natural History of Human Morality*, Harvard University Press, Cambridge 2016.

Tönnies, F. 1963 *Gemeinschaft und Gesellschaft*, Fues, Leipzig 1887.

Tooby, J. & Cosmides, L. 1992 The Psychological Foundations of Culture, *in Barkow, Cosmides, Tooby 1992.*

Torche, F. 2011 Is a College Degree still the Great Equalizer? Intergenerational Mobility across Levels of Schooling in the United States, *in «American Journal of Sociology», CXVII, 3, pp. 763–807.*

Torche, F. 2015 Intergenerational Mobility and Equality of Opportunity, *in «European Journal of Sociology», LVI, pp. 343–71.*

Touraine, A. 1970 La société post-industrielle. Naissance d'une société, *Denoël, Paris 1969.*

Touraine, A. 1975 *Production de la société,* Editions du Seuil, Paris 1973.

Touraine, A. 2008 Un nouveau paradigme. Pour comprendre le monde d'aujourd'hui, *Fayard, Paris 2005.*

Urbinati, N. 2020 Pochi contro molti. Il conflitto politico nel XXI secolo, *Laterza, Roma-Bari.*

Van Bavel, B. 2016 The Invisible Hand? How Market Economies Have Emerged and Declined since AD 500, *Oxford University Press, Oxford.*

Van Bavel, J. & Pacher, D. J. 2021 *The Power of Us*, Headline Publishing Group, London.

Van der Weide, R. & Milanović, B. 2018 Inequality Is Bad for Growth of the Poor (but Not for That of the Rich), *in «World Bank Economic Review», XXXII, 3, pp. 507–30.*

Van der Weide, R. et al. 2021 *Intergenerational Mobility around the World*, World Bank Policy Research Working Paper n. 9707, Washington DC.

Van der Weide, R. et al. 2024 Intergenerational Mobility Around the World: A New Database, *in «Journal of Development Economics», CLVI.*

Van Lange, A. M. & Balliet, D. 2015 *Interdependence Theory*, in M. Mikulincer, P. R. Shaver, J. A. Simpson, J. F. Dovidio (eds), *American Psychological Association Handbook of Personality and Social Psychology*, III, American Psychological Association, Washington DC.

Van Reenen, J. 2020 Innovation Policies to Boost Productivity, *The Hamilton Project, CentrePiece.*

Voitchovsky, S. 2005 Does the Profile of Income Inequality Matter for Economic Growth? Distinguishing between the Effects of Inequality in Different Parts of the Income Distribution, *in «Journal of Economic Growth», X, 3, pp. 273–96.*

von Hofmannsthal H. 1922, Buch der Freunde, Leipzig, Insel.

von Hofmannsthal, H. 1963 *Buch der Freunde*, 1922.

Wagle, U. R. (ed) 2023 Research Handbook on Poverty and Inequality, *Edward Elgar, London.*

Walzer, M. 2023 The Struggle for a Decent Politics. On «Liberal» as an Adjective, *Yale University Press, New Haven 2023.*

Weber, M. 1946 *Essays in Sociology*, Oxford University Press, Oxford.

Weber, M. 1970 Die Protestantische Ethik und der Geist des Kapitalismus, *1905.*

Weber, M. 1973 Politik als Beruf, Wissenschaft als Beruf, *Matthes & Seitz, Berlin 1917.*

Weber, M. 1974a Gesammelte Aufsätze zur Wissenschaftslehre, *J.C.B. Mohr, Tübingen 1922.*

Weber, M. 1974b *Wirtschaft und Gesellschaft*, Mohr, Tübingen 1922.

Wiener, M. J. 1981 English Culture and the Decline of the Industrial Spirit 1850–1980, *Cambridge University Press, Cambridge.*

Wier, L. & Erasmus, H. 2023 The Dominant Role of Large Firms in Profit Shifting, *in «Imf Economic Review», LXXI, 3, pp. 791–816.*

Wier, L. & Zucman, G. 2022 Global Profit Shifting, 1975–2019, *Wider Working Paper n. 121.*

Wilkerson, I. 2020 Caste: The Origins of Our Discontents, *Random House, New York.*

Wilkinson, R. & Pickett, K. 2009 The Spirit Level: Why Greater Equality Makes Societies Stronger, *Bloomsbury Press, New York.*

Williams, B. 2005 In the Beginning Was Uke Deed: Realism and Moralism in Political Argument, Princeton University Press, Princeton.

Wilson, B. 2012 *Contra Private Fairness*, in «American Journal of Economics and Sociology», LXXI, 2, pp. 407–35.

Wolf, M. 2023a The Crisis of Democratic Capitalism, *Penguin Press, New York.*

Wolf, M. 2023b The Dangers of Magical Thinking on Health Policy, *in «Financial Times», 23 gennaio.*

Wooldridge, A. 2021 The Aristocracy of Talent: How Meritocracy Made the Modern World, *Allan Lane, London.*

World Bank 1992 Governance and Development, *Washington DC.*

World Economic Forum 2020 The Global Social Mobility Report 2020: Equality, Opportunity and a New Economic Imperative.

Yonzan, N. 2020 Assortative Mating and Labor Income Inequality: Evidence from Fifty Years of Coupling in the U.S., *Stone Center Working Paper n. 15.*

Young, M. 1958 The Rise of the Meritocracy (1870–2033), *Thames & Hudson, London.*

Zingales, L. 2012 A Capitalism for the People: Recapturing the Lost Genius of American Prosperity, *Basic Books, New York.*

Zingales, L. 2017 *Towards a Political Theory of the Firm*, in «Journal of Economic Perspectives», XXXI, 3, pp. 113–30.

Zuboff, S. 2019 The Age for Surveillance Capitalism: The Fight for a Human Future at the New Frontier of Power, *Profile Books, L.*

Index[1]

A

Absolute mobility, 104, 119–128, 134

Access to opportunities, 222–227, 231–233

The "adaptation" of education to the market, 367–370

Asymmetry of power, 46–47, 49

B

Birth cohorts, 7

C

Capitalism, 180, 182–186, 192, 197, 201

The 'cement of society,' 161

Classic liberalism, 8–10, 23

Company profits, 186–191

Competition in democracy, 179–182

Competition in the market, 179–182, 198

Concentration of companies, 296–298

D

Democracy, 107–109, 111, 112n3, 113–119, 128–130

"Differentiated universalism," 355, 356

The dynamics of social classes, 299–302

E

Education and human capital, 373–376

Educational opportunities and economic growth, 371–373

Education and social mobility in Anglo-Saxon countries, 324–342

The emergence of talents, 349, 354–361

Equality of life chances, 143–147

The expanding global middle class, 255

Externalities, 12–20, 24, 26

[1] Note: Page numbers followed by 'n' refer to notes.

F. Farina, *The Rise of Inequality and the Fall of Social Mobility*,
https://doi.org/10.1007/978-3-031-92843-7

F

The fiction of the social contract between "free and equal," 403
For an affirmative action in corporate governance, 405
For an affirmative action in education, 385–387
"Freedom of choice": the formal neutrality of the voucher, 379–385

G

The Great Gatsby Curve, 225–232

H

Heterogeneity of people, 252

I

Immigration, 271–275
Income and opportunity inequality, 227–228
Increasing income inequality, 265
Individual aspirations, 211–217, 233
Individual freedom, 141–144, 147, 150
"In no country does high inequality combine with high social mobility," 401
Interdependence among people, 252
Intergenerational mobility, 211–236
Intergenerational mobility in education and income, 319–324

L

Liberal thought, 50–57
The limits of "universalism," 335, 346–354, 358
The link between inequalities and the environmental crisis, 413
Liquid society, 163–173
Low inequality, 217–222

M

The market incentive for social mobility, 310–318
Mass society, 106–112
Merit, 59–91
Methodological Individualism, 8–10, 27
Migratory flows, 251
The 'model of mind,' 113–119, 121, 122
Morally-free zone, 192–197
The multidimensionality of inequality and poverty, 239–243
Multidimensional well-being, 152n5, 154–158, 172

N

Nature, 67, 71n10, 74, 79, 83, 84, 87, 90
The neoliberal society, 25–26
Nurture, 87

O

Occupational mobility, 281–302
Open society, 163–173
Opportunities for education, 35

P

Pensée unique, 152, 173–175
Populism, 157, 158, 167, 173–175
Principles of justice, 70–77
Public schools and private schools, 383–385

R

The "rate of return of education," 312, 316, 327
Reduction of poverty, 265
Relative mobility, 104, 118–128, 131
Res publica, 102, 114–119, 117n6

S

"The school, central organ of democracy," 307–361
Social capital, 268, 269, 271–275
Social classes, 41–46, 49
Social conflict, 10–22, 24, 29–31, 33
The "social cost" of tracking, 376–379
The social function of work, 158–163, 168
The "social immobility" of Neet, 232–236
Social inclusion, 108–111, 117, 135
Social mind, 87
Social mobility, 1, 4–9, 16, 18, 22, 25, 27, 28, 30, 31, 33–35
Social persistence, 97–101
Social rights, 185–191
A "society of individuals," 403
Social stratification, 290, 299, 301
Socio-economic context, 211–217, 219, 235–236
Solidarity democracy, 182–186, 197, 198
Sustained growth, 217–222
Systemic interdependence, 10–22, 26

T

Talents, 1, 4–8, 27–29, 32, 32n19, 33, 35
Technological change, 284, 292, 299–302
Technological progress, 19
The "tragedy of the commons," 16
The Trente Glorieuses, 118, 119, 127–130

U

Unequal opportunities for education, 354–361
Utilitarianism, 18

W

Wage mobility, 281–302
Wage polarization, 296–299, 301
Welfare State, 125–130, 135
Well-being of new generations, 222–225
Work ethic, 59–64

The manufacturer's authorised representative in the EU is Springer Nature Customer Service Centre GmbH, Europaplatz 3, 69115 Heidelberg, Germany. If you have any concerns regarding our products, please contact ProductSafety@springernature.com

Printed and bound by CPI Group (UK) Ltd, Croydon, CR0 4YY

01/10/2026

02225953-0015